Nicholas Rhea is the pen-name of Peter N. Walker, formerly an inspector with the North Yorkshire Police and the creator of the *Constable* series of books from which the Yorkshire TV series *Heartbeat* has been derived. In the three *Constable* books in this volume, *Constable Across the Moors*, *Constable Around the Village* and *Constable on the Hill*, Nicholas Rhea tells of some of the colourful incidents and eccentric Yorkshire characters encountered by a country constable, stories which have provided the basis for the adventures of PC Nick Rowan, played by Nick Berry, in the TV series. Peter N. Walker is also the author of *Portrait of the North York Moors* and, married with four children, lives in Ampleforth in North Yorkshire.

Also by Nicholas Rhea

Heartbeat: Constable Among the Heather
and Other Tales
of a Yorkshire Village Bobby
Constable on the Prowl
Constable in the Dale
Constable by the Sea
Constable Along the Lane
Constable Through the Meadow

Portrait of the North York Moors

Heartbeat: Constable Across the Moors

and Other Tales of a Yorkshire Village Bobby

Nicholas Rhea

HEADLINE

First published in this edition in 1993
by HEADLINE BOOK PUBLISHING PLC

10 9 8 7 6

ISBN 0 7472 4125 2

Printed and bound in Great Britain by
HarperCollins Manufacturing, Glasgow

HEADLINE BOOK PUBLISHING PLC
Headline House
79 Great Titchfield Street
London W1P 7FN

CONTENTS

Constable
on
the Hill

One

The police house at Aidensfield in North Yorkshire occupies what is probably the most beautiful site in the country. High on an escarpment overlooking Ryedale, it surveys two valleys, one to the back and the other to the front, with its own finger of land neatly dividing them. It is a detached house, built of local yellow stone, and boasts a garage, an office and extensive views to the south, east and north, with moderate views to the west. It stands alone on its hill top, a sentinel for all to note and there is nothing around it save green grass, deciduous trees and oceans of fresh moorland air laced with the multifarious scents of rural England.

Looking north from the rear bedroom window, one sees the three white radomes of Fylingdales Ballistic Missile Early Warning Station, like a clutch of duck eggs sitting among the heather, the gorgeous autumn purple of those distant moors, and the lush greenery of Ryedale with its host of tiny communities. To the east stands the tiny Minster of Thackerston and beyond that, the coast; on a clear day, it is possible to imagine the North Sea off Scarborough but distance and blue hazes can confuse the eye and baffle the brain. Is that blue really the sea or is it just a blue haze? It doesn't matter – it is attractive and therefore worthy of interest.

To the south is a smaller valley with a farm seemingly at one's feet, for it lies just over the fringe of trees at the foot of the garden. Beyond are the wooded hills lined with rows of regimented larch and spruce trees. Down on the flat valley floor are more small communities of farms and people. To the west, the view is not so extensive, for the policeman's hill continues to rise, taking its metalled road to the heights of the Hambleton Hills and then to Sutton Bank with its high-flying gliders. From that supreme vantage point, one can look across the vast vale of York, described by Chevalier Bunsen as "the most beautiful and romantic vale in the world, the Vale of Normandy excepted". The lower Yorkshire Dales lead skywards towards the Pennines which form a fitting and rugged backcloth to this land of castles and abbeys, rivers and roads, villages and heights.

This piece of England, called Romantic Ryedale by its inhabitants, is famous to those people as "God's own country". They worship the place. It contains everything for the country-lover: wildlife in all its forms, centuries of stirring history, folklore and legends, fascinating people, a local dialect, and a landscape comprising some of the most panoramic and impressive views in the whole of England. My police house commands one of those views.

It was to this area, therefore, that I came one summer day. It must be said that I had not come from choice, for I had been posted to Aidensfield as its new village policeman. With my wife Mary and my family of three tiny children, I had driven from our old home and arrived an hour or so ahead of the removal van with its meagre load of our sparse belongings.

After only five years of marriage and with five mouths to feed, we had very little furniture, but a lack of possessions was a great comfort to a policeman in a county police force. My liability to be posted to far-flung locations meant I did not buy objects like fitted carpets or expensive curtains. Instead, all county policemen acquired functional furnishings like tables which folded into corners, chairs which were easily portable, beds which were not four-posters and small square carpets that would sit anywhere and be complementary to almost any wallpaper.

On that removal day, we had packed a picnic and I reckoned we would arrive at our new house around lunchtime; we decided to picnic there. Over the final miles, I drove through Maddleskirk with its impressive Benedictine abbey, then found myself in Aidensfield. This is a beautiful village, built snugly into a steep hillside so that no northern wind can chill its homes. The southern sun warms them all and the spring daffodils bloom three weeks ahead of those in less congenial climes, like my hill top. I passed through Aidensfield very slowly, looking at the squat parish church, the ultra-modern Catholic church, the friendly pub, the garage and the village shop, all within a hundred yards of one another. One or two people pottered along that peaceful street, and I wondered if they realised that the battered old Hillman cruising suspiciously slowly contained their new bobby.

Once up the steep hill at the distant end of Aidensfield, I turned right and there, standing magnificently on its own hill-top site, was that lovely police house. It was ten minutes to one, and the children were as excited as a three-year-old, a two-year-old and a one-year-old could be.

I steered the gallant old vehicle through the open gate of the police house and halted on the concrete drive. The house was empty, of course, the previous occupants having been moved out that same morning. Happily, the day was fine and dry, but many is the time policemen have moved house during rain or snow, to suffer the indignity of wet-footed removal men tramping all over clean floors. We were very fortunate to have such a lovely day in June.

The key, I had previously been told, would be concealed in the garage, under a half-full tin of paint. I found it, and from the attached label, saw it was for the front door. By now, the children were pottering about the spacious lawn, exploring their new territory with a curiosity that could lead to problems, but Mary decided to leave them there, took the key and together we approached our front entrance.

We were surprised to find a cabbage in a string bag hanging from the door knob. Mary looked at me for guidance and I looked at the cabbage. It seemed a good solid cabbage, but there was no note and no indication of its *raison d'être*. Initially, I suspected some form of skullduggery, and therefore decided to examine the other doors before taking further action. Was it full of sneezing powder or water? Was it a plastic one? I advised Mary to keep well away from the object and made my way to the back door, leading into the kitchen. It was located in a passage, access to which was through an outer door next to the garage. This was not locked, so I opened it, turned towards the kitchen and found a brace of wood pigeons hanging from that door knob. Then, on the office door, was a monster of a hare. As we would say in Yorkshire dialect, it was a "greeat awd ram-cat of a heeare".

I knew of the age-old custom of giving presents to country policemen, but here was I, on my very first day at Aidensfield, with presents all around me, and not a single hint as to their origins. Having discovered the fur and feather, I accepted the cabbage for what it was – a useful gift. It was a lovely welcome. I unlocked the door and with due solemnity, carried Mary across the threshold and the children followed, shouting and running about the entrance hall and ground-floor rooms in sheer exuberance. They'd have to stop that caper when the van arrived.

To the right of the entrance hall was the door into my office; the office had a door leading into the garden but that was seldom used. Most of the callers came to the front door of the house. The office had a counter across the middle with shelves beneath it and in the centre was an official looking desk and telephone.

The house was in a state of complete cleanliness, thanks to the outgoing couple and we could move straight in. On the left immediately inside the door was the staircase and already two of the youngsters were scrambling noisily up the bare wooden steps. Jane was too young to attempt such feats so she accompanied Mary and me as we examined the house. The dining-room had a plain-looking electric fire and a window looking south; next to it was the lounge with a fireplace for coal blazes, and a window looking south. Those views were glorious, taking in an entire valley with conifers beyond, scattered farms below and the distant wolds of the East Riding of Yorkshire.

The kitchen was unbelievably tiny and there was an ancient coke boiler in one corner with a pantry beneath the stairs. The kitchen door led out into the back passage near the garage, where I'd found the pigeons. Upstairs, were two reasonable bedrooms, with windows looking south, plus a smaller one with windows looking north, and a bathroom – with windows looking north.

A big garden with soft fruit, vegetables and flowers sloped away from the house on its southern aspect, just beyond the lawn underneath the lounge and dining-room windows. There would be about one-third of an acre of garden, much of it allowed to go to waste but about a quarter of which had been cultivated. Our June arrival meant we gained from the work of others – sometimes, you won, sometimes you lost! An attractive rockery edged the lawn at the front, but the lawn extended completely around the house which meant the children could gallop around and around in ever-decreasing circles. It was a marvellous way to tire them for bed and to occupy them as the men unloaded our belongings.

We enjoyed our picnic on the lawn, sitting on the shorn grass and gazing south across my new beat. I could see farmers working in the fields, cars moving in the distance with sun glinting from their glass, trees swaying in a gentle breeze and rooks soaring high above in the clear sky. There were the summer sounds of an unseen tractor, the constant hum of bees at work nearby and the voice of a skylark on high. We sat there for about an hour, thoroughly enjoying those precious moments of peace.

I was reminded of the words of William Shenstone who wrote:

> Devoid of hate, devoid of strife,
> Devoid of all that poisons life.

Then the removal men arrived.

It was evident that they had sampled some of the local ale *en route* for they arrived at our house in a benevolent mood, albeit determined to be unpacked and away before five that afternoon. Because the road ran directly past my front gate, the driver, a squat man with two or three days growth of beard, decided he would reverse his vehicle into my gateway. This would enable our furniture to be emptied onto the concrete forecourt of the garage, and thus make it easier to carry indoors. I thought it a sound idea and moved my car into the garage beside my official motor-cycle. So far, so good. We decided that the carpets must be first into the house because once they were in position, the removal men would place the larger items wherever we decided.

The driver, whose name I never knew, began to manoeuvre his huge vehicle backwards towards my gate. It was a narrow

gate, even for the passage of a family car, and was most
definitely not designed for the antics of reversing pantech-
nicons. The driver, however, seemed very confident that he
could squeeze its bulk through the gap, while his mate, the
thinnest man I've ever seen, leapt out and began to shout
directions. By darting backwards and forwards, he encouraged the lumbering lorry to inch its way towards my gate
posts. I issued the inevitable warnings, but the lorry hit both
gateposts, as I knew it must; it did so in spite of the driver's
confidence, and in spite of the mate's incomprehensible
shouts. My yells were ignored.

It didn't stop there. It came on. The rear wheels crunched
across the remains of the posts and smashed the fallen gates
into matchwood. Only when the rear was some twelve feet
into my garden, did the driver stop.

"That's better," he said, leaping from his cab. "Now we
can get cracking."

"Look there!" I shouted, pointing to the mangled gates and
their accessories. "Smashed . . . the sergeant will play hell
with me . . . I'm new here."

"Forget it, son," said the driver. "We've moved every
bobby into this house since it was built, and we always smash
the gates down. It's t'only way to get in. And it gets you a set
o' new gates every three years or so. Good logic that – the
insurance will see to it. Good thing, insurance."

"The insurance will see you all right," said the thin one,
and with no more ado, they got to work. They worked most
efficiently, unloading our meagre, battered belongings and
positioning them in the house under Mary's instructions. She
brewed the inevitable cups of tea and they dropped the
inevitable mirror and crockery, excusing themselves by saying, "The insurance will see you all right."

Somehow, a key to the wardrobe was lost, which the
insurance would see to, and one of the bedroom windows got
cracked, while they were manoeuvring a dressing-table into
position. The insurance would see to that, I was told. They
unloaded the larger items more quickly than we could determine their position so when a backlog occurred, they stopped
and drank tea. That was when we made decisions about the
location of our furnishings which would prevail until we left

this house with the assistance of another furniture wagon and its insurers.

Sometimes the lanky one, whose name I learned was Sid, would stop and admire a recently acquired piece of furniture. For example, after unloading our radiogram, the pair of them placed it on the ground, walked around it and Sid said, "You've come on since last time, eh?"

This pair had apparently moved us into our previous house, four years earlier, and now took an opportunity to comment upon the proliferation of children and the acquisition of new furniture and other belongings. During one of our many breaks for tea, and with the children getting in the way, I asked Sid how he'd remembered us from all the other policemen he'd moved around the North Riding.

"That bloody piano," he motioned with his head towards the wagon. My piano was still aboard.

I laughed at the memory. The piano was gigantic with a solid iron frame. It was a Broadwood and therefore a useful instrument. It had been a twenty-first birthday present to me, having belonged to my grandparents. Because we could not accommodate it in our very first home at Strensford, it had remained at my grandparents' home until we made our first move to more suitable premises. It had been impossible to get it into the Strensford police house because of winding steps and narrow passages. Upon our move from there, we had arranged for a local garage to store the piano overnight on the eve of our transfer; we would collect it the following morning. We did that. The ivory-toothed monster demanded every skill known to those strong men, but after much panting and heaving, they got it aboard their removal van, shut the tail-board and off we went. Upon our arrival at North-allerton, the piano was first off the lorry. The men placed it on the footpath outside that suburban house, and its wheels promptly sank into the macadam which surfaced the path. It sank the full depth of those small metal wheels; retrieval was messy and tricky and its marks remained for many years as a monument to our presence there. Getting it into that house had been a further problem; it sat outside in the rain until the very last minute, when finally, after much cursing and de-bating, we managed to inch it inside.

Having got it inside that house, we breathed a sigh of relief – and then remembered we'd left Mary's bicycle at Strensford, outside the garage which had kindly stored the piano. We'd placed it there while we lifted the piano aboard, and had forgotten all about it. I rang a friend at the police station and he took the cycle into protective custody until we could collect it. We never did collect it – perhaps it's still there, in the cell passage?

For those reasons, therefore, the piano lingered in the memories of these removal men. Now that Sid had mentioned it, I began to wonder if we would get it into this house. The entrance hall was very narrow and short, and that instrument demanded lots of space and massive strength. The strength was there in those sinewy bodies, but space? I could always keep it in the garage.

The piano was taken off the lorry and left on the garage forecourt until everything else was inside the house. The children did their best, losing things, carrying things, getting in the way and falling into and over everything. By four-thirty, the van was empty the house was full and we had a cup of tea. Only the piano remained.

Using a little trolley, they steered it towards the front door and Sid measured up the prospects with his eyes.

"Nay," he said. "It'll not go in."

"It'll have to," I said in what must have been a pleading tone. "It can't stay on the lawn."

"It'll mean taking it to bits." He leaned on the lid. "Piece by piece, with screwdrivers. It'll be a long job, and it'll never be right again. Bad to tune are pianos that have been taken to bits."

"But overtime for you, eh?" I smiled.

"Aye, happen," he grinned.

But his mate wasn't interested in overtime. "We can do it if that front door comes off," he said. "Take t'front off t'piano, an' all. It'll sidle round that banister end, and go in."

"You and your bloody piano," Sid growled at me. "Why do you have to cart a thing that size around with you?"

"I can't live without it," I told him. "It's part of my life!"

"You bloody pianists are all alike – kinky. Why don't you play summat like a flute?"

I didn't tell him that I couldn't play a note. I daren't tell him, not now. I'd always wanted to play a piano, ever since I was a small boy, but somehow never found the time, even if I had found the instrument. I had learned the violin and the recorder, but had always hankered after the piano. I had therefore asked for this one as my twenty-first birthday present because it belonged to the family and because it might otherwise be sold. All those years after moving into Aidensfield, I still have the piano and it continues to cause problems whenever we move house. And I still cannot play it.

By removing the front door and by sheer brute strength and skill, those men got it inside the house and somehow reached the lounge.

"It's not damaged," they said, proudly.

"It's a good job it isn't!" I said, "It would have been a big insurance job."

"That's it, then," Sid announced. "All in. Report the gateposts to your sergeant and write to my firm about the breakages. Insurance jobs, all of them."

I gave them a tip, said farewell until next time and watched them take the lorry away from the house. I was left with two broken gates and three children who couldn't wait to get onto the road. Until now, the lorry's front end had effectively blocked this exit, but I managed to stand up the gates by propping them against old packing cases, then Mary and I set about the massive task of putting the house straight.

We were allowed one day off duty before a removal, a day for the removal and one day off duty afterwards. That's all – after that, it was work as normal. By half-past-five, the children were beyond themselves with fatigue and hunger, so Mary made us a meal. We bathed them and plonked them into their beds, thankful that they, at least, were no longer a liability.

Then we turned our attention to the packing cases and began the long task of finding somewhere to put everything. We turned in just after midnight, completely exhausted and the children woke us next morning at six. We struggled, aching, from our beds and began another long day's work. The tasks seemed without end, but several villagers telephoned during the day, just to welcome us. I had no idea who they were. All of them said, "Welcome," and all said, "We'll be meeting you soon." It helped us through that tiring day. No one acknowledged leaving the cabbage, the pigeons or the hare, but already I began to feel at home. It did not take too long to make the house habitable, and besides, county policemen of those times never unpacked everything, in case they were soon on the move.

Like those men, I maintained a useful collection of empty and half-full tea-chests which I lodged in garages and attics. Sometimes, we received only one week's notice of a removal to a new station, sometimes less, therefore we remained ready for instant exit. Happily, things have changed but at that time, I decided to position my tea-chests in the office.

The phone rang during the late afternoon of that first day, and a voice said,

"Rhea?"

"Yes?" I answered.

"Sergeant Blaketon here. I'm your section sergeant. I'm at Ashfordly. You're on at nine in the morning. Spend the first hour in your own office, finding things. Check the inventory. Then get the bike out and come down here. Be here before half-past-ten. Right?"

"Yes, Sergeant," I heard myself say, and the phone died.

He didn't ask if I could ride the official motor-cycle and I didn't know either, so I went into the garage to examine it. There was plenty of room for my car and the bike. It was a Francis Barnett two-stroke with a windscreen at the front and a radio on the back. A tall, flexible aerial protruded from the rear, like an upright tail, and the speaker was fixed to the handlebars, just above the tank. The entire machine was black and very clean, so I sat astride. I shook it and found it was full of petrol, kicked the starter and it burst immediately into life in the confines of the garage. I chugged outside, did a shaky tour of the lawn much to the amusement of my family and returned it to its place in the garage. I had ridden a motor-cycle as a teenager but had rapidly decided on a car after Mary and I ploughed through a hedge on our old machine. That incident put me off work for eight weeks.

But now I must ride again. On a summer's day, it would be very pleasant and I was looking forward to it. My gear was in the office, including a crash helmet of the correct size. Water-proof leggings and several coats completed the outfit, all sent along ahead of me by our efficient Clothing Department. I wondered how it would feel to ride a motor-cycle in police uniform. There's a certain difference between roaring along on one's own machine at the age of nineteen and steering a police motor-cycle about its legitimate business. I would soon know that difference.

At seven the following morning, the children earned their keep by waking us, and I dressed and shaved. I put on a smart uniform and breakfasted, then went into my little office well before eight-thirty. I searched the drawers of the desk and found a mileage book for the motor-cycle. This had to be completed after every journey and after every filling of the petrol tank. I found the inventory for the house and office, checked it and found everything there. Also in the office were files of offence reports, the work of my predecessor, files full of circulars bearing details of unsolved local and national crimes, and masses of other papers. There were leaflets about warble fly, anthrax and foul pest, about firearms and vehicle accidents, about Colorado beetles and police dances. And there was the Beat Report.

This was a most useful compilation, for it was an encyclo-paedia of information appertaining to that beat. It provided me with the names of people like doctors, vets, RSPCA officials, Water Board officials, Gas Board and electrical wizards. It told me who to trust and who to watch; it named local villains and ne'er-do-wells; it had phone numbers of important institutions like the garages and pubs, and it listed churches, schools, experts on sundry things and a whole host of other useful material.

As I browsed through its pages, the phone rang.

"P.C. Rhea," I answered, somewhat nervously, for this could be my first job, my first piece of live duty.

"It's Alwyn Foxton down at Ashfordly," came the voice. "Pleased to make your acquaintance. You're coming in, Serge tells me, to have a look around this office?"

"Yes, about half-ten."

"There's a lot of messages for you," he said. "Routine stuff – stolen vehicles, wanted and missing persons, housebreakings and larcenies. That sort of thing. Nothing urgent."

"I'll pick it up when I get in, eh?"

"Fine. See you then."

And he rang off.

From this point, I knew I was doing real police work. After spending the past four years in an office, working with filing systems, accounts and housing problems, it was refreshing and exciting to return to real police work. Out here on one's own, there was no knowing what lay around the corner, no idea what was going to happen during the next day, next hour or even next minute. I was on duty twenty-four hours a day, although I worked a basic eight hours per day. That did not prevent me from being knocked out of bed at any time to deal with anything, even on my official day off. But that kind of life has its compensations, like freedom to patrol the beat as one wishes, freedom to mix with the people of the area and freedom to make one's own decisions, plus the thrill of finding cabbages on door knobs.

By ten o'clock, I had found my way around the office and had discovered the whereabouts of everything I needed. I found the switch for the heater, the key for the office door and the piece of chalk that every policeman carried in those days. It was used to mark the position of car wheels on the road surface when dealing with traffic accidents; it meant the cars could be moved before measurements were taken and so avoid congestion. I popped the chalk into my pocket, found a roll-up ruler too, had a cup of coffee and sallied forth into Ashfordly, four miles away.

I drove very steadily, the Francis Barnett wobbling alarmingly from time to time, and I forgot to switch on the police radio. But I got to Ashfordly without mishap and found the police station. I had to ask the way – I felt something of a fool, sitting on a police motor-cycle in full uniform, asking a little old lady the way to the police station. She told, but her eyes told of her alarm. She would tell a good tale over coffee that morning.

Ashfordly Police Station is a beautiful building. It is built of good-quality brick, and stands solidly on one of the nicer streets, just off the centre of this busy market town. Attached to each end of the office there is a police house, one being occupied by Sergeant Blaketon and the other by the senior constable, in this case Alwyn Foxton. In front of the station is an attractive garden, tidily kept by the sergeant or anyone else detailed to do so, while inside the place is immaculate. A daily cleaner pops in to do the brasses, to dust and polish and consequently the place reeks of polish and shines with the brilliance of a well-kept fire-engine. Police cleaning ladies are inordinately proud of their own buildings.

There is one garage and it was occupied by the official car, a neat black Ford Anglia. The place hummed with clean-cut efficiency.

I must admit that I trembled with anticipation as I walked along the path towards the front door. I had parked the motor-bike beside a convenient wall and entered to smell the cleanliness. I found a grey-haired policeman leaning on the counter, waiting for me with his red and jolly face.

"Alwyn Foxton," he extended a hand.

"Nicholas Rhea," I shook his hand.

"Sergeant Blaketon had to go out," he told me. "He won't be long. Take those leggings and things off, and I'll show you round. Not that there's much to see."

In fact, there was very little to see. To the left of the door was the tiny public office with a long wooden counter running from the inside of that door. To the right, was the sergeant's office. Alwyn explained there were two sergeants – Charlie Bairstow who was enjoying a day off and who lived at Brantsford, and Oscar Blaketon now on duty and somewhere in town. Bairstow was easy-going, he told me, while Blaketon stuck to the rules. I would meet them both in due course and make my own judgements.

The office contained bound copies of the *Criminal Law Review*, the *Justice of the Peace*, and some very ancient police law books. There was little else, save the weekly duty sheets. The duty sheet showed me as 'rural beat' for tomorrow and the following day, with a late route from 7 pm until 11 pm the day after that.

Alwyn showed me the Found Property register, the Lost Property register, the return of licensing premises, the return of explosives stores, bookmakers' shops, telephone calls register, postage book, the list of keyholders of places like banks and shops, and the names of local contacts. I would, from time to time, be instructed to perform duty in this town, and based on this office, especially when there was a shortage of men due to leave or sickness. In any case, I was expected to pop in at least twice a week to keep myself updated with affairs in town. Actually, the town boasted a population of only 3,000 but for us folks on the moors, this was a considerable centre of activity.

"Have we any cells?" I asked, thinking of prisoners.

"Two," Alwyn told me. "I'll show you. In fact," he went on, "the toilet is in one of the cells. We haven't an official toilet here, so we all use the cells."

He led me into the tiny cell passage where were confronted by two massive, studded doors with huge keys and gigantic iron hinges. No. 1 cell was on the left.

"Males in No. 1," he said. "Females in No. 2."

He pushed open the door of No. 1 and revealed the carcase of a fallow deer. It was lying on the stone floor.

"Killed in an accident with a milk lorry," he said. "This morning, just out of town."

"What happens to it?" I asked.

"We've an arrangement with a local hotel," he said.

"Arrangement?" I asked, wondering what sort of arrangement it could be.

"Oh, it's all above board," he smiled. "The deer about us, in the hills and forests, belong to the local estate, and his Lordship wants all those killed like this to be sent to the King's Head. He owns that hotel, by the way. When we've one brought in, we ring the hotel and the manager arranges collection. The estate gives us a useful donation for the Police Widows' Pension Fund. Deer are not reportable road accidents, as you know, but we take them in because too many bloody motorists insist on fetching them here. We get about two a week."

The deer's head, damaged on one side, lay on a piece of newspaper which absorbed the blood. There was the traditional wooden bed, boxed in all around, and a toilet in the corner. Nothing else furnished the place.

"Ladies in here," he said, throwing open the door of No. 2. This one was full of chrysanthemums. They stood around on

the bed, the floor, on a board on top of the toilet basin, and
on shelves which stood loosely against the walls. They were in
all colours, shapes and sizes, and they were beautiful.

"Mine," said Alwyn, proudly. "That's ideal for them,
especially when it's very hot outside. Lovely and cool in there.
I grow them for showing, you know. Get prizes all over.
Lovely flowers, eh?"

"Marvellous," I agreed, having never seen such a wealth of
colour in a police cell. "But what happens if you arrest
somebody? Where do you put your prisoners?"

"Arrest?" he sounded horrified. "We don't arrest people
here!"

Two

Having made contact with my colleagues at Ashfordly Police Station, one of my first duties was to acquaint myself with the public of Aidensfield and the residents of the surrounding villages which formed my beat. These were country folk, down-to-earth people whose ancestors had occupied these moors for generations and who had a built-in suspicion of strangers. This was coupled with a bluntness that was typically Yorkshire and yet it hinted at absolute honesty and integrity. Being moor folk, they also possessed a natural hardiness and a desire never to tangle with newcomers to the area. They called newcomers "off cum'd 'uns".

I was conscious of this because I had been nurtured in such a village at the other side of the moors and was reminded of a policeman colleague who was posted to a remote village in the depths of the North Yorkshire moors. Some weeks after his arrival, he was walking through Whemmelby when a man hailed him. The other was a retired gentleman, judging by his appearance, for he had grey hair, a somewhat stooping stance and a terrier on a lead.

"Are you the new policeman?" he'd asked Les, conversationally.

"I am," Les had replied, smiling.

"Well, you'll have the devil's own job with 'em round here," the man had said. "I've lived in this village for over thirty years, and they still regard me as an outsider."

He wasn't joking either. It was with this in my mind that I began my tour of inspection. It was a goodwill tour of my beat, my first and vitally important public relations exercise. It wasn't easy finding an excuse to drop in on people who had no reason to know me and who weren't accustomed to uniformed police officers calling unannounced at their homes. I was fortunate in having a reason for calling at Low Mires Farm, on the outskirts of Crampton. This was my very first port of call.

I knocked on the door and a young woman answered; her pretty face wore that haunted look that people acquire when they open the door and find a policeman standing there. Has someone died, or are we in trouble? I smiled in the hope it would lessen the tension, removed my cap and said, "I've come about Mr Bradshaw's firearm certificate. It's due for renewal."

The girl looked me up and down, nodded and shouted, "Father!", and vanished inside, leaving me standing on the doorstep. After a long, silent wait, a tall gaunt man appeared. He must have been in his late sixties and wore carpet slippers which scuffed the sandstone passage as he walked. He used the walls as supports along his short journey and his face bore a day's white whiskers but his brown eyes were alive and intelligent, the only bright spot in his weathered appearance.

"And who might thoo be, lad?" He leaned against the door pillar, slightly out of breath. He studied me carefully, those brown eyes ranging the full length of my build.

"The new policeman, P.C. Rhea," I informed him. "I moved into the police house at Aidensfield a couple of days ago."

"Oh, aye?"

"Yes, and I've come about this," I waved the application form at him. "It's your firearm certificate, it's due for renewal."

"Aye, thoo'll be reet. Thoo'll be yan o' them townies, eh? Sent oot here ti mak us country folks larn t'laws."

"Well, I . . ."

"Thoo'll have been in t'office, eh? A scholar mebbe? All book larning and syke? A young feller gahin up t'stee, heading for promotion, eh?" (*Stee* is the North Riding dialect word for *ladder*.)

I had indeed been stationed in the Accounts Department of Force Headquarters at Northallerton, a small thriving market town, but for Mr Bradshaw, it seemed I was one of the dreaded townies, sent out here to harass him. I wondered if he thought I'd come from the south, too.

"I'm just a policeman," I tried, wondering if they were all like this character. I was still on the doorstep and realised his daughter was watching me. She remained at the distant end of the long, dark passage playing with the apron she wore. "Shall we fill this form in?"

"It's nut oft I allows strangers inti my parlour," he said, shaking his head solemnly. "We've nivver seen thoo afoore, lad. Nivver. Thoo's a stranger in theease parts, thoo sees."

"I'm the village policeman." I made another attempt to convince him I was honest and trustworthy, and ran a hand down my uniform to emphasise the point.

"That's mebbe so, but thoo's still a stranger ti us. Ah reckons nowt ti strangers."

"All right," I compromised. "We'll stand here and fill it in."

I produced a pen from my tunic pocket and continued, "I'll have to see your current certificate and your rifle. I've got to enter the number of it, and other details, in the renewal form. It's your rifle I'm interested in, not shot-guns."

"It seems ti be a lot of fuss about nowt," he grumbled, eyeing me carefully. "Syke a lot of form-filling in as nivver was. Will thoo fill it in for me? My awd hands is a bit crammly wi' t'rheumatics."

"Yes, of course," I assured him. "That's what I'm here for – to help you."

"Aye, but thoo's new ti theease parts, and I'm nut yan for letting strange folks . . ."

I tried another line of approach. For this, I relied heavily upon my own village upbringing. Having been brought up in the dialect of the North Yorkshire moors, I spoke it as my native tongue. I had learned to be 'slape-tongued' when I left for the outside world of Northallerton. I therefore looked at him, and then at the daughter who by this time had crept forward a few paces, still fiddling with her apron. I addressed them both.

"Leeakster, maister, Ah's nut 'ere ti be kept ootsahde, yakking ti thoo and thi dowter when there's wark ti be deean. If thoo dissn't git this form filled in, ah'll etti git ower that hill and back ti my desk, and then tell 'em up at oor head office that awd Bradshaw's as orkerd as pump-watter, and that he weearn't sign up."

"Come in, lad," he grinned suddenly, his face breaking into a wide smile. "By, Mary, git t'kettle on. This un's yan of us."

And from that moment, I was always welcome at Sam Bradshaw's farm, whether or not I was there on business. He always found time to talk while his Mary produced a cup of tea and a slice of home-made apple pie with fresh cream. She looked after the house because her mother had died some years ago, and I knew there was no prospect of her marrying. She was very pretty in a rural sort of way and was shy to the point of embarrassment. She'd be in her early thirties, I guessed, and would have made some man a fine wife.

It was a cosy farm, run in a carefree but efficient manner and eventually Sam Bradshaw learned that my father was secretary to a fishing club on the Yorkshire River Esk, a river renowed for its salmon and trout. Mr Bradshaw was a keen fisherman and I told him I could get him a day ticket when he fancied a trip across to the Esk. For a stranger, I was suddenly very acceptable, although he never did take that fishing trip. For him, it was a dream for the future, something to look forward to.

I found that my dialect was an asset in my daily work, especially when dealing with farmers like him who insisted on using it in my presence. Many of them talked in their broadest tongue when strangers were about, either to confuse or impress them, and this was particularly evident in the pubs. But I could talk about swingletrees, nabblings, jauping and dunderheads, black-locks and bletherskites, pleeafing and ploating, owersetten and underhanded, just like the folk hereabouts. I knew the meaning of local proverbs like "As prickly as a prickly-back otchen", "As soft-hearted as a rezzil", "As warm as a sheep net", "As lonely as a mile-stone", and I could appreciate the thoughtful sayings like, "Maist folk can see t'wrang they've deean, but nut t'wrang they're deeing," or "He's nobbut half-rocked 'at believes ivverything, but he's clean oot of his head 'at believes nowt."

The uniform was a great asset, of course. It was, and still is, respected in this locality and I soon found myself being able to talk with the locals on level terms. I was not regarded as a rule-bound troublemaker from afar, but a friend to whom they could turn. I respected their confidence in me, and realised the "official" blind-eye had to be turned from time to time. Warnings, not summonses, were utilised where possible.

One example of the type of dutiful assistance I was expected to give came from old Miss Cornelia Harborough. She distrusted strangers even more than the others did, and led a life that made a hermit seem sociable. It was a long time before I realised she even lived on my beat. Her home was in the hamlet of Waindale, and I must have walked past it countless times without realising the place was inhabited. It was a tumbledown cottage, more of a ruin than the genuine ruins in the area. The upper windows were hanging from their frames, the front door was always open and the place bore an air of total neglect. The garden was overgrown and the path to the front door was merely a foot-trod through the tall, lanky growth of mixed weeds. The house next door to Miss Harborough's was derelict and the two dwellings resembled those drawings of ghostly ruins which appear frequently in Victorian topographical works.

My first meeting with Miss Harborough came when I was standing outside the telephone kiosk in Waindale one summer's afternoon, some six weeks after my arrival. It was a glorious day and I was basking in the warmth, clad in full uniform because I was on motor-cycle patrol. I became aware of a tiny old lady inching nervously across the road towards me. She wore a quaint little hat made of purple raffia with a huge flower in the front, and she sported a flowered pinny over a long, black dress. She looked like something out of a Dickens novel as she edged closer to me. Her face was elfin-like, pinched and wizened, but her teeth were beautiful. She must have been well over seventy.

"Are you the policeman?" she came very close before asking the question.

"I am," I tried to sound pleasant.

"There is a little matter I wish to discuss with you," she said solemnly.

"Can we talk here?" I suggested, wondering if she would step onto the footpath where I waited near the telephone kiosk for the call that may or may not come.

"It's very confidential," she spoke grimly. "Can you come into my house?"

"Certainly," I said. "Where do you live?"

"Over there, at Corner Cottage," and she pointed to the hovel.

"There?" I must have sounded horrified.

"Yes, over there. Come over, will you, when your call comes through," and off she paddled. I watched her negotiate the empty road and weave through the long grass towards her gaping front door. She squeezed through the gap and vanished inside. I waited at the telephone kiosk for my statutory five minutes in case I was needed by the sergeant, but no calls came. I was free to socialise with Miss Harborough. I crossed the road, plodded along the grassy path and reached her front door. It would not open any further, nor would it close. It hung from its hinges, rotten and slimy, so I squeezed through and found myself in a very dark living-room. The rear window was completely covered with greenery on the outside, utterly overgrown with rampant vegetation and the whole place reeked of dampness. The room was so full of furniture that some of it was piled on chairs and tables, and there was barely any space to squeeze between the items. Everything was Victorian, and was probably worth a fortune in a sale-room. Its condition here left a lot to be desired. Much of it was rotting and broken – it was such a pity. Then she appeared.

To this day, I do not know where she had been, nor do I know where she ate, slept or sat. The room was so full of furniture that it obscured all doorways other than the one I had used, and she appeared to pop from behind a pile of chairs. Perhaps she maintained a tunnel into a back room?

I had never seen the old thing before this day. I had never seen a vehicle call at the house to sell bread, meat or fruit, and there was no shop in this little hamlet. Buses never passed this way and she had no transport, not even a cycle. Her lights did not work and I guessed there was no toilet. I saw no taps either. But here she lived and, later, when I tried to interest the social services in her, she refused to leave. She could not be forcibly removed because she was not insane, nor was she a burden on the State, or a nuisance to anyone. I later tried to mend her door and to effect a repair upon her electrical system, but she would not hear of it. She was the epitome of independence. Stubborn, perhaps, but fascinating. How she managed to survive remains a mystery to me.

But her reason for calling me into her cottage that day was, in her mind, very urgent and very confidential.

"What do you want?" I asked.

"I have found this," and from the pocket of her pinny, she produced a sixpence. Today, in decimalised currency, it is worth 2½ pence.

"Where?"

"Outside my house, in the gutter," she told me.

When dealing with found property, the police must be extremely careful. A policeman who accepts property from a member of the public must always make a detailed entry in his notebook, give a receipt to the finder and ensure that the incident is fully recorded in his official notebook and in records at the police station. He must not forget to hand in the property at the end of his shift, otherwise he could be accused of stealing it. With items of no particular value or importance, like cash in small amounts, it is customary to let the finder keep the article and merely make a record of the finding, should the loser make a claim. The loser will then be referred to the finder. If property is unclaimed within a certain time, in our case three months, the finder may retain it and regard it as his own, always remembering that the loser has a claim of title to it.

It was my intention to deal with Miss Harborough's sixpence in that manner. I would tell her to keep it and if it was not claimed within three months, it would be hers. The chances of anyone reporting its loss were remote, to say the least.

"I'll make a note of it," I told her, but in reality I had no intention of noting this. No one would come seeking a lost sixpence and so far as I was concerned, she could keep it. I made a note of her name and address, and the fact she had found it three weeks ago. I said, "Keep it, Miss Harborough. If it is not claimed within three months, it is yours to keep."

"Oh, no," she insisted. "You must take it and you must make enquiries to find the loser. That is your duty, is it not?

Someone will have lost this coin and may be looking for it. Someone, may be, who cannot afford to lose money like this. That is why I called you in, to do your duty."

Inwardly, I groaned. If I took this to the office, the sergeant would half kill me. There would have to be entries in all manner of official places, a receipt would have to be issued, I would have to drive out here with the receipt for her and then, if it wasn't claimed within three months, the superintendent would have to write to Miss Harborough to ask if she wanted to claim the coin. I would have to motor down to Malton to collect it, against signature, and then drive out here to deliver it, against her signature, a round trip of thirty-three miles. Was a sixpence worth that?

"No, Miss Harborough, please. You must retain it." I tried to be firm. "I will make a record in our official books, and if the loser has reported the loss, we will send him along to you."

"No, officer, I insist. I do not want it in the house. It is your duty to accept the coin and to make enquiries to trace the loser."

Such tasks were not part of our duty, but she wasn't to know that. It seems I had no choice. I accepted the coin and was then compelled to go through the motions of recording it in our official system, much to the chagrin, and I suspect, amusement of Sergeant Blaketon. Three months later, I had to return to Miss Harborough because the coin had not been claimed. Even then, she refused to accept it. She wanted nothing to do with it, because it was not hers. I told her I would donate it to a police charity, and she agreed. The Widows and Orphans Fund derived a little benefit from her honesty.

My next contact with Miss Harborough was some time later, on the occasion of a forthcoming Government Census. She had received forms to complete and wanted help. She called me in and had the forms spread across a table. When she explained she wanted help to fill them in, I said, "Fine, let's do it now."

"Oh, no. You can't do that," she cried. "It asks for details of persons living in this house at midnight. It's only three o'clock in the afternoon now."

"That doesn't matter," I tried to convince her. "You know who'll be here at midnight. There's only you."

"You might be here," she corrected me. "You will come to help me, won't you? It definitely says midnight . . ."

"I can't come," I had to duck out of this one. "I've my own forms to fill in, you see, at midnight. I'll have to be at my own house, with my wife and children."

She looked a little sad but accepted the logic of my argument. She was happier than she had been a few minutes earlier, for I explained how to complete the paperwork. I later discovered, however, that she had called in a local farmer, asking him to fill in her forms at midnight. Knowing her well, he had obliged, and had sat in her house until the clock struck twelve. He had even put his name on her form, just to keep her happy.

I often wonder what the census officials made of that.

*   *   *   *

Another character with whom I made an early contact was a small scruffy individual of indeterminate age who went by the name of Aud George. No one used his surname and I learned eventually that he had retired from a life of farm labouring to live alone in a cottage at the edge of Aidensfield. I reckoned he must be about seventy, although he could have been anywhere between fifty and eighty, judging by his appearance and demeanour. He habitually wore black hobnailed boots, gaiters, corduroy trousers and an old rough shirt without a collar, albeit with a collar stud eternally in position at the neck. His jacket was fashioned from something resembling Harris tweed and it must have seen the passage of many years. He wore a cap, even when getting washed, and spent his days wandering up and down the village street, chatting to anyone who could spare the time. Aud George was a fixture in that street.

The prefix *Aud* is an old North Riding term of affection. Strictly interpreted, it means *old,* but it is seldom used in that sense. Way back in the seventeenth and eighteenth centuries, when witches were said to roam those moors, old women suspected of witchcraft were known by this prefix – Aud Nan, Aud Annie, Aud Meg and Aud Sue were examples. Even today, tales linger about Aud Nanny of Stokesley, Aud Nan

of Spittal Houses, Aud Mother Stebbins and many more. The
devil himself was known as "T'Aud 'Un" (The Old One), but
in recent times, the term Aud has come to mean something
approaching affection, possibly tinged with respect. Young
boys in my schooldays would call one another Aud Bernard,
Aud Alf, Aud Bill, Aud Fred, etc., as a term of affection or
friendship, and the practice has endured over the years. The
term is still heard in the moorland villages.

It was quite normal, therefore, that George should be
known by this prefix and everyone knew him by that name.
The story goes that a stranger arrived at Aidensfield seeking a
Mr Clotherstone, but the man had not been furnished with
Clotherstone's address. He had found Aud George in his usual
position on the seat in front of the church and asked where
Mr Clotherstone lived.

"Nay," George had said. "Ah dissn't know onnybody of
that name."

"He definitely lives here," the man had insisted. "I'm from
Adamson and Smythe, solicitors, and I must see him. I have
made enquiries and have traced him to this village. He is
known to live here."

George had shaken his head. "Nay, lad, thoo's foxed me.
There's neearbody called that in Aidensfield."

"He used to work on a farm, I'm told," the man persisted,
"and his first name was George."

"George?" asked Aud George. "Thoo dissn't mean Aud
George, doest tha?"

"Yes," beamed the man. "That's what I was told. Ask for
Aud George."

"Then that's me!" George had thrust out his chest. "I'm
Aud George, so that must make me Mr Clotherstone, eh?"

And so he was.

Because of our respective regular use of that street, my
contact with Aud George was frequent and invariably interesting. He was a fund of information, a veritable village
knowledge-box. Such a person is of inestimable value to a
policeman, even if much of his chatter is pure gossip. George
would chatter away quite amiably, giving me titbits of information which were useful to me in my work and which he
knew would be of value. He did not do so with any malice in

his mind, nor did he bear a grudge against anyone. He provided me with snippets simply because I ought to know what was going on. He would tell me, for example, that young Stan Fowler had taken up the hobby of throwing stones through greenhouse windows, or that Andy Merryweather's daughter was seeing rather a lot of a married man, or that Charlie Brett's lad was riding a motor-bike without a licence, or that young Ferrensby, aged seventeen, was supping ale in a local pub.

These snippets were of value, as was any other gossip, but occasionally he did provide very useful information. He had once noticed a car pass through Aidensfield at a slow speed, noted the number on the back of his hand, and then told me. It transpired that it was a team of confidence tricksters from Leeds who preyed on the elderly by offering to repair roofs or windows. Having done the work, which was shoddy in the extreme, they demanded exorbitant prices for the job, against veiled threats of violence if they refused to pay. This information was valuable and in fact, a colleague of mine on another beat arrested that bunch due to George's observations. They were awarded three years apiece for their crimes.

With regard to George's minor gems of news, I seldom took official action. For example, it was sufficient to stop Charlie Brett's lad and tell him I'd be checking his driving licence in a day or two, or I would pop into the pub to inform the landlord that young Ferrensby was under age. I maintained that this form of prevention was often better than taking the offenders to court, although such actions could be construed as being over-generous in the exercise of my traditional discretion. The ability to use such discretion is under attack by left-wing political elements who see it as favouritism and something to be enjoyed by privileged classes. Nothing could be further from the truth, for those helped in this manner are usually the modern under-privileged who, without this assistance from the police, would soon acquire a criminal record. Keen socialists are attempting to remove that valuable exercise of discretion from the policeman's armoury – it will be a sad day when it has gone. When it does go, the feared police state will have arrived when all rules will be obeyed, down to the last cruel letter of the law. Human policemen will no longer exist.

But back to George. My many talks with him revealed one charming habit which I don't think he realised he possessed. It concerned the passing of information about local deaths.

George would keep everyone, including me, informed about the latest deaths in Aidensfield and district. At first, the names he provided meant nothing to me, but after I had been in the area for a few months, they did begin to have relevance. I could associate names with houses, houses with faces and faces with the inevitable range of close relatives who lived hereabouts. Consequently, a death was important. It meant I could commiserate with the relatives of the deceased, should I chance to meet them in the street, and that sort of interest in other folks is useful Public Relations for any police officer.

After a while, I realised that George was unwittingly using a code when he passed on this information. He employed different phrases which were based on the religion of the dear departed, consequently it was possible to identify the religion of the deceased from the words used by George.

If a member of the Church of England died, for example, he would say, "He's seen t'last of his days," and for a Roman Catholic, he would gravely tell me, "He's gitten his time owered." For a Methodist, he would say, "He's gone to better things," and for members of the smaller churches, his phrase would be, "He's drawn his last."

Inevitably, there were those who professed no specific faith, but who would be placed to rest within the boundaries of the local parish church, officially enlisted in the great army of deceased members of the Church of England. For these, George's phrase was, "They've gone to their eternal rest, God bless 'em."

I enjoyed his chatter and we became great pals. He served the public of the district for many years and in all weathers. He was there when I left Aidensfield for pastures new, but I ought to add his own epitaph. I learned a few years ago that he had died. His own death was announced in his Anglican phrase, and I was sorry I was not there to learn of it first-hand.

I am told, however, that Aud George died slowly and very

peacefully, and that his own last words were "Ah's gahin to meet my Maker."

*   *   *   *

As I progressed around my beat in those early days, meeting people like Aud George, Miss Harborough and Farmer Bradshaw, I realised that those country folk were thoroughly decent people. They were good and they were harmless; there wasn't an ounce of evil in them. If they broke the laws of this land, then it was in a small way. They forget to renew their driving licences, got drunk on Saturday night, drove unroadworthy vehicles or let cattle stray on the highway. These are not evil transgressions like vandalism, violence and theft. Crime, in the real sense of the word was a rare part of my routine police duties. If I had to 'book' any of these people, that act of police duty was never held against me. They stoically accepted a court appearance or a fine and our friendship was never tainted. They considered errors on their part to be their fault, and knew that a constable's duty must be done. Once in a while, therefore, I was duty bound to take one of my 'parishioners' to court.

Such an occasion involved a local character called Dick the Sick. A dour Scotsman, he loved a practical joke and could be talked into all manner of japes after a pint or two of strong Yorkshire ale. Once a joke misfired because it involved the police in an official way.

I was on my weekly rest-day at the time, and the incident involved a famous greyhound which had been stolen. The Press was full of the story but it transpired that George, landlord of the Hopbind Inn at Elsinby, bred greyhounds. He used them in the popular sport of coursing and it was unfortunate that he had recently banned Dick from his bars, due to previous pranks. Dick had acquired his nickname of "Dick the Sick" because he never worked, always managing to exist on sickness benefits and other Government handouts. In spite of his multiple ailments, Dick and his wife had produced eight lovely children and a cottage garden as tidy as any for miles around.

On the occasion of the theft of the greyhound, someone

anonymously rang the nearest Divisional Police Headquarters to say the dog in question had been hidden at the Hopbind Inn, Elsinby.

As a result of information received, as we say in police jargon, a police car proceeded from that Headquarters with an inspector, a sergeant and two constables on board. In the jargon of newspapers, they swooped upon the unsuspecting Hopbind and its customers and mounted a very thorough search. They found many greyhounds, of course, but the stolen dog was not among them. From the ensuing conversation with the landlord, it became quite clear that the call had been a hoax. It also became clear from the distinctive Scots accent of the caller, that it had been perpetrated by Dick the Sick. George knew that, and Dick's motive wasn't difficult to imagine. Dick was interviewed by that army of officers, but he stoutly denied making the call.

Next morning, being totally unaware of this little drama on my patch, I booked on duty to find Sergeant Blaketon waiting on my doorstep. He provided me with a lurid account of the hoax call and of the alleged whereabouts of the famous missing dog. He went on to say the inspector had not been very pleased about it, and suggested we have another talk with Dick, in an attempt to secure an admission from him. We found him in his garden and when he saw the impressive bulk of Sergeant Blaketon, he wilted visibly. During the interview, however, he persistently denied responsibility for the call. I knew by his facial expressions and the way he ran his hand through his thick red hair, that he was guilty. But that sort of evidence is useless in a court of law. The more old Blaketon pressured him, the more firmly he denied our allegations. As we turned to leave, beaten by his Scots stubbornness, Dick tugged at my sleeve and said, "I'd like a word with you, Mr Rhea, please."

"Alone, Dick?"

"Aye, alone."

Blaketon gave me the nod and I went into Dick's tidy home. In the lounge, he looked at me, licked his lips and said, "It was me, Mr Rhea."

"I know it was, Dick, but why? Why make a bloody stupid call like that?"

"Aye, it was stupid. They got me tipsy, you see. They dared me to do it."

"Who did?"

"Them in the Brewer's Arms." That was a pub in Aidensfield.

"I'll have to book you, Dick," I told him and explained all about the fuss and the visits by other police officers.

"It'll get it off my chest," he sighed, and I thought I detected relief in his voice.

On his own admission, I reported him for summons and eventually he appeared at Eltering Magistrates' Court, charged with making an annoying telephone call. He was fined £5.

A few days later, I dropped into the bar of the Brewer's Arms where the place was alive with local men, still chuckling over Dick's dilemma. Dick was there, suffering them in a broody silence. As I walked in, the expected hush descended upon the assembly, as it always did when a uniformed bobby entered. Looking around the bunch of rosy, rural faces, I adopted a serious expression and said, "Well, gentlemen, Dick's been fined. Five pounds. It's not a lot, but it's a big amount for a chap with eight kids and no job. You've had your fun, all of you. I know you put him up to that joke," and I then adopted an even more serious tone. "It is an offence to aid, abet, counsel or procure the commission of an offence by any person. You're all guilty of that, each and every one of you."

They did not utter a word, but all looked at me steadily, wondering what was their fate.

"But," I continued, "I will not summon you if you do one small thing for me. I reckon you ought to contribute to Dick's fine, all of you," I had a quick count of heads and there were fifteen in the bar. "I reckon ten bob apiece would be about right, eh?"

No one moved. No one said a thing. "It could be a fiver each," I reminded them, "and your names in police files." I removed my notebook from the pocket of my tunic and opened it, as if to take names.

"We've had our fun, lads," said one farmer, as he dug into his pocket and produced some cash. "Ten bob's nowt."

He passed a ten shilling note to me and his action prompted the others into passing me a similar amount. I soon had £7 10s. 0d. (£7.50) in my hand. I passed this to Dick.

"There you are, Dick. You're in pocket and your fine's been paid."

"You'll have a drink on me, Mr Rhea?" he asked, smiling.

"Aye, I will," I said, for it's not often a Scotsman buys a Yorkshireman a drink.

But that's how the Dicks of this world exist without the need to work. Somehow, they always win.

* * * *

Another character I shall never forget is a nameless youth in a distant village. Soon after my arrival in Aidensfield, I found myself performing what we called 'routes'. In the early days of policing, these were undertaken either on foot or by pedal-cycle, and they were allocated to each rural policeman by a superior officer. Some routes were late at night and others very early in the morning, even starting at 4 am. Each route lasted about three or four hours and we had to follow a predetermined route around our area of responsibility. In the days before personal radios for policemen, we had to arrive at specified telephone kiosks at certain times, so that the office could contact us if our presence was required at an incident. The 'points', as we called them, enabled our superiors to find us and to check upon our whereabouts. Those points were used both as a method of communication and for supervisory purposes. The sergeant, the inspector or even the superintendent would get out of bed at the crack of dawn to drive out to one of our lonely points, hoping to find the duty policeman. A short conference would be held, and the superior would sign the constable's notebook to record the fact of that meeting. We nicknamed this curious little procedure as a 'chalk', probably from the days when the supervisory rank carried a little slate and chalked up the time of the meeting. If the visit was before 6 am or after midnight, the entry would be in red. It was considered quite an achievement to acquire two or three red chalks during a month.

The arrival of radio-equipped police motor-cycles sug-

gested that this ancient and mainly useless activity could be
dispensed with. But it wasn't. Old habits die hard and we had
to drive around those routes on our motor-cycles, continuing
to make points at telephone kiosks. This was insisted upon,
even though we had radio sets. Although modern equipment
was coming to the police, modern ideas were a long way
behind. I am reminded of a sergeant at a local station who,
upon receiving the first consignment of personal radio sets
worth around £100 each, refused to let the men use them.
"They're too valuable for you lads to mess about with," he
said, locking them in a cupboard.

As a result of this rigid thinking, therefore, I regularly
found myself motor-cycling about my beat either at the crack
of dawn or during the depths of night. The sound of the little
Francis Barnett two-stroke must have woken the populace,
caused dogs to bark, cattle to low and hens to cackle. Little
else was achieved by these patrols, simply because any self-
respecting burglar or poacher would hear the distinctive
sound of the bike long before the constabulary hove to. But
authority said we had to perform them, and so we did. I often
thought they were designed for supervisory officers to acquire
lots of red chalks, like a gunman of the wild west notching up
kills on his rifle butt. I wondered if some of our supervisors
ran competitions to see who could acquire the most red chalks
within a given time, with a prize at the end of the year. Like a
length of red chalk, maybe?

One evening, I performed a late route, working from 7 pm
until 11 pm, and then the following morning, I was allocated
another one beginning at 6 am. This was before the days
when we could demand eight hours off duty between shifts,
and so, at six o'clock that morning, I leapt aboard my little
Francis Barnett, kicked it into life and began a long,
cold and dark tour of lonely moorland and twisting lanes.
This particular route took me away from Aidensfield because
a neighbouring bobby was on leave. I had to cover his
beat.

I was rather concerned because my petrol was low. Because
I had to obtain my official petrol from a specified local
garage, I could not purchase any elsewhere; besides, garages
weren't open at that early hour. I knew I would have to be

careful, at least until eight-thirty when my local garage was able to supply me.

At my seven o'clock point, I received a phone call asking me to deliver a 'request message'. It meant a long detour to a lonely farm – it was to inform a farmer that Uncle Frank had died in Middlesbrough General Hospital and would he contact the sister on Ward 9. Having delivered this message (a task we often had to undertake before the increasing popularity of telephones in these remote places), I returned to my route, noting that my eight o'clock point was the hamlet of Whemmelby, at the telephone kiosk.

Whemmelby lies deep in the North Yorkshire moors at the top of a long glacial valley etched deep into the hills. In the spring-time, it is glorious with daffodils and bluebells which coat its nine miles of riverside, and in the autumn, the moors above glow with a rich, deep purple. It is a robust area, with long and low farm houses built snug into the hillsides. Its centre of population is a cluster of houses at the foot of a hill with a gradient of 1-in-3. There are several hills of this gradient in the North Yorkshire moors, and while they hold no terrors for the locals who use them daily, they do terrify town drivers and others from the flat regions of Britain who regard 1-in-12 as precipitous.

It was down one of these hills that I guided my Francis Barnett to make that eight o'clock point. Half way down, the engine stopped. I knew immediately what had happened, so I coasted into the hamlet and pulled up outside the kiosk. I inspected my petrol tank and, sure enough, it was bone dry. My fears had been confirmed and I was seventeen miles from my usual garage.

My radio would not function because of my location deep in the valley, so I went into the kiosk to ring Divisional Headquarters. I hoped they might arrange a car to fetch some petrol, but the phone was out of order. There was a small notice stuck to a window pane, but I tried the instrument just in case it had been repaired at the exchange end. It hadn't. It was stone dead.

What now? I knew Whemmelby from the past, and there was nothing here, not even a shop. There was a village hall with a small parking area in front, Methodist chapel, three farms and one or two cottages, all surrounded by steep hills and forbidding moorland. I looked at each building in the hope of seeing a tell-tale telephone cable running to it, but not one of them possessed a telephone. I could not push the bike up that incline and the nearest garage would be about eight miles away. I couldn't obtain my official petrol there, but I might be able to buy some at my own expense, hopefully just enough to get me home.

Another problem was the performance of my duty. Suppose that phone accepted incoming calls? Suppose Sergeant Blaketon rang me and instructed me to visit some house which had been burgled, or to attend a traffic accident or other calamity? I dreaded to think what his reaction might be when I said I'd run out of petrol, and I concluded that the only solution was to walk up the hill in the hope that a friendly motorist picked me up and transported me to a petrol filling station.

That course of action meant parking the machine in a safe place, not that anyone here would harm it but because Sergeant Blaketon might accuse me of carelessness with county property. I returned to the bike, sat astride it and began to propel it with my feet towards a parking place in front of the village hall.

It was then that I heard an approaching vehicle. As I manoeuvred my lifeless noddy bike across the narrow road, a tractor and trailer appeared from behind a farm house and moved towards me. It was driven by a roughly dressed youngster with long, straggly hair and a cheeky grin on his face. A large, square five-gallon can stood alone in the centre of the trailer. He stopped the tractor, jumped down from it and came over to me.

"What's up?" he asked with a friendly smile.

"Petrol," I said, feeling very foolish. "My bike's run out of petrol."

He looked at my crash helmet with POLICE across the front, examined the Francis Barnett with its radio set where the pillion should be, and peered at my uniform numerals.

"Thoo's nut our local chap?" he said by way of a question.

"No, he's on leave. I was working late last night, and I had to come out here early . . . "

"Thoo'll be wanting some juice then?" He didn't wait to hear my tale of sorrow and despair.

"I was going to walk up to Brantsford . . . "

"Neea need," he said, leaping onto the trailer. "Thoo can 'ave some of this," and he lifted the big can down. "Tak thy filler cap off."

"It needs two-stroke mixture," I said.

"This is two-stroke. Cap."

I obeyed, removing the cap from the petrol tank; he did likewise with the large red can and began to pour the precious stuff into my machine.

"Whoa!" I called. "That'll do. I just need enough to get me to a garage."

"I'll fill her up," he laughed. "Two-gallon tank, eh?"

"Yes, but there's no need . . . "

"This 'un's full, mister," and he kept on pouring. He filled my tank almost to overflowing, smiled and said, "There. That'll see thoo all right for a mile or two."

"I'll pay," I offered, starting to unbutton my motor-cycle gear. It took a long time to reach my wallet, tucked inside my inner tunic, but in the meantime, the cheerful lad had returned the can to the trailer and was sitting on the tractor seat, ready to move off.

"How much?" I shouted, still fiddling with buttons and press-studs.

"Nowt," he called back. "Thoo can have it for nowt. It's not mine, anyway."

"Not yours?" I cried, but he was moving away. I had a tank full of petrol, so I gave chase but he simply waved me away and shouted above the noise of our engines. "Have it on us, mister." He turned into a farm yard, leapt from the tractor and vanished indoors, waving me on.

I do not know who he was and I never saw him again. It was months before I made a return visit to Whemmelby, and I asked after him, but no one seemed to know who I was talking about. I never did know the true owner of that petrol.

But my petrol problems were far from over. Every month, we had to complete a mileage return which showed the places we had visited, the mileage covered and the petrol consumed. The return would be rigidly checked, as indeed it was, be-

cause of the milometer readings and the garage accounts.
This system meant I could not show the extra two gallons on
my return, for it was not part of the official intake. But my
mileage had to be shown correctly – the milometer ensured
that.

The result was that my motor-cycle that month registered a
somewhat staggering petrol consumption, having apparently
covered over 100 miles to the gallon instead of the usual 80. I
pleaded total ignorance for the cause of this astounding feat
of motoring and swore blind that I had never coasted downhill in my own economy drive. The next thing that happened
was that my machine was taken to Headquarters for a
thorough check by the county mechanics, and the garage
from whom I purchased my official petrol was asked to
carefully check its accounts. There were no discrepancies.
Officially, my motor-cycle had done remarkably well that
month, and all supervisory officers showed great interest in its
next performance. I had to disappoint them, because things
returned to normal.

Later, when I had time to reflect upon the incident, I did
wonder if a friendly farmer had sent that life-saving can on
the trailer. Was it coincidence that a tractor and trailer
carrying a five-gallon can of two-stroke fuel arrived just in
time to save me from a long, perspiring walk? Or had it been
neatly arranged by a friendly farmer who had witnessed my
dilemma from his breakfast table?

I shall never know, but if he reads this he will know that I
was truly thankful, even if the police garage manager did
grow a little more grey around the gills due to the strange
behaviour of the Aidensfield motor-cycle. If that manager
reads this, *he'll* know what happened too!

Three

The existence of the Slemmington Hunt was revealed to me shortly before eleven o'clock one morning. I had been on half-nights the previous day, i.e. working from 6 pm until 2 am, and had climbed from my lovely bed at ten o'clock. I had staggered bleary-eyed into the kitchen to find Mary had taken the car and the children, and had gone shopping in Ashfordly. I was alone, and it was time for breakfast.

After hunting in vain for the milk to add to my cornflakes, I realised it had probably just arrived and went outside to seek it. As I lifted the three creamy-tops from their resting place on the front doorstep, there was a thundering of mighty hooves accompanied by a deafening jangle of harness very close to me. I was rather surprised to see a massive horse leap across my garden fence. It galloped across the lawn and vanished over my far railings in a fog of minute pieces of flying earth, leaving my lawn like a recently used tank route. Sitting astride the animal was a man wearing a black riding cap, a red hunting jacket (called pink) and white jodhpurs and he shouted, "Tally-Ho" or something vaguely similar. Then silence descended.

I was not sure whether this was really happening and as I gazed after that apparition in an attempt to determine 'yes' or 'no', untold numbers of similar creatures accompanied by baying dogs, leapt the railings at the east of my garden, shouted in strange voices and vanished over the fence at the other side. They hooted and galloped down the hill into Aidensfield to disappear for ever from my sight. Straggling hounds followed, baying and sniffing, and one of them looked at me with baleful eyes, thought the better of it and ran to join his pals.

It probably took a mere second or two for this incident to

act itself out, but it seemed an eternity. I stood on my
doorstep, rubbing my eyes and wondering if I was in the
middle of a dream about the Valkyries but the battered
surface of my lawn bore evidence of genuine horses. The place
was riddled with hoof marks. A multitude of tiny sods littered
the place, rather like the main track at York Racecourse after
the Ebor Handicap is over. It had happened all right. I was
too tired and amazed to be angry; I simply stood and gaped
at the holes, all neatly shaped like horse-shoes.

It occurred to me, quite suddenly, that the fox might be
somewhere in my house. The front door was open, but I
didn't think it had darted between my legs. The garage doors
were open too, and so was the side door into the passage. I
hastily closed the front door, deposited the milk bottles and
made a hurried search of my premises. I saw nothing of a fox.
The hunt did not return, so I enjoyed a comparatively peaceful breakfast, wondering if this sort of thing was a regular
occurrence.

Perhaps one of the most mysterious aspects of the hunting
set is their ability to make strange noises via the mouth. Their
'yoiks' and 'tally-hos' carry a tone of unreality and some of
their yodelling is impossible to copy or impersonate with any
degree of authenticity. It seems that the ability to yodel is
something bred into that class of person, something which he
emits only when on horseback and only when the hounds are
milling around. Sometimes, as I sat in my kitchen listening to
them in the distance, I wondered if huntsmen practised their
calls. To be as proficient as that on a cold and frosty morning
must take years of practice and hours of devoted throat-
warbling. I believe Peter Ustinov had great difficulty
emulating the sound when filming "Lady L" at nearby Castle
Howard. He tried in vain to yodel like a North Yorkshire
huntsman and even though he was coached by some first-class
exponents in the art, the true sound eluded him. He spent
many an hour walking around the estate in full cry, and I
often wonder what the locals thought about him. For that
matter, I wonder what the foxes thought about him.

Be that as it may, those who participate in such pastimes
are a race apart. True huntsmen are born, not made. Robert
Smith Surtees in his *Handley Cross* sums it up by writing:

" 'Unting fills my thoughts by day and many a good run I have in my sleep. No man is fit to be called a sportsman wot doesn't kick his wife out of bed on a haverage once in three weeks." Although I had been born and bred in the fox-hunting and otter-hunting territory of the North Riding moorland, I never took part in any of those sports. Other than attempting to follow a hunt on foot, my only involvement in such matters was a shooting trip with my grandfather. It was during one of the annual February pigeon-shoots. Armed with a .410 shotgun, and aged only sixteen, I tramped the hills with him, shooting at hundreds of pigeons and hitting none. I don't think I was capable of hitting them, not because I was a bad shot – I wasn't – but somehow my love of birds and animals caused my aim to wander. My only hint of success came when I shot at an unsuspecting pigeon which was about to land on a distant tree. I released both barrels and the only result was the angry appearance of a man who had been sheltering beneath that very tree. In his moments of solitude, he had been showered with falling twigs and spent lead shot, but escaped with his life. So did the pigeon.

I was to learn that fox-hunting is almost a religion in Aidensfield and district. Because of the damage to my lawn, I made enquiries around the village in an attempt to establish my legal rights. I was told, quite politely, that the local hunt had the right to cross and re-cross my land, and indeed lots of other land in the locality. I failed to find anything to state otherwise and it seemed that this was one of those grey areas of law where no hard-and-fast rule existed. It had been happening for generations, and probably would continue to happen until the socialists banned the sport.

Thankfully, the hunters hadn't leapt into the lower part of the garden where it was thick with equipment and children's toys. I did wonder what would have happened if one of the horses got its head fast in the children's swing or put a foot through a cloche. It seemed I had to allow them access to my lawn. But after that occasion, they never leapt my way again. One of the reasons may have been that whenever I learned they were hunting in our area, I parked my car outside my garage, right in the path of any horse that might leap my garden fence. If a horse landed on that, it would be another insurance job.

That single brush with the hunt was my only personal complaint against them. I spoke to the Master of Fox Hounds about it, and he was polite but firm in his right to hunt across land in the vicinity. Like many other people, whether from town or country, I found the sight of the meet very thrilling. At times, there were as many as 25 pairs of hounds, 200 horsemen and upwards of 100 foot followers meeting in the grounds of the great houses of the district. The spectacle was fascinating, all colour and excitement, and the party would enjoy the traditional stirrup-cup before setting off in pursuit of old Reynard the cunning. It was a fine sight and one of the essential parts of the English countryside.

Whether or not one agrees with the hunting of foxes, the sight of a hunt in full cry is guaranteed to thrill. The cunning of the fox, the skill of the hounds and the uncanny knowledge of the hunters, all combine to make the day memorable for everyone. A kill is seldom of any great importance – the fun, they say, lies in the chase.

For centuries in these hills, men have pitted their wits against the fox. Today, there seem to be just as many foxes; it has been said that hunting them destroys the weaklings and therefore breeds a strong strain thus proving the adage 'only the strong survive'. The foxes are experts too – they win by 'going to ground', as otters 'go to couch'; some foxes are tempted by the skills of foot hunters too. For example, some foresters spotted a fox making towards them. They were down-wind of him, beyond his range of scent, so they tried to coax him into coming nearer. They did this by taking a blade of grass, placing it between the fingers and thumbs and blowing gently to make a whistling noise. Children often do this. The fox pricked up his ears at the sound. Was it a screaming rabbit? Something else he should investigate? But he was not fooled; he lowered his head and vanished into the undergrowth. Minutes later, the hunters arrived with their hounds, but he had gone.

On balance, I am not offended by either hunts or hunters,

and I have no personal grudge against foxes. They don't carve up my lawn.

* * * *

Fox-hunting was just one of the rural sports practised on my beat. The others included coursing, fishing, shooting, gliding, hiking, football, cricket, billiards and table-tennis. There were probably others. I frequently questioned the meaning of "sport" in this context – high bred rurals consider 'sport' includes blood sports, i.e. hunting, shooting and fishing, whereas others of more lowly origins think of football, cricket, dominoes and school sports days. I suppose I could add bare-fist pugilistics, bear-baiting and public executions. The list is virtually endless.

The point is that I, as the village bobby, had to know what was happening upon my beat. As I lived and worked in a lush green part of the countryside, full of large country estates, it was sensible to familiarise myself with the sporting events occurring about me.

Sergeant Blaketon frequently quizzed me about rural affairs of this nature, for the subject seemed to fascinate him. He had spent much of his police career on the industrial fringes of Teesside, where they bred racing pigeons and grew leeks, consequently our type of sport intrigued him. I could always answer his queries and this appeared to satisfy his curiosity, although I never did learn his true opinions on sport and the gentry. I suspect the truth was that he considered himself aloof from such matters. He enforced the law – he did not hold opinions. With a head of thick black hair, thick black eyebrows and a figure like a prize fighter, he was an impressive sight. Furthermore, he was honest, straight and completely trustworthy. But he was unbending, I was to learn. He disliked his men exercising what he termed 'loose discretion'. I learned he was rigid with the public too – there were no 'warnings' from Oscar Blaketon. If someone offended against the law, he booked them. The painful decision whether or not to prosecute offenders was therefore avoided by him, and his technique ensured that the problem rested with someone higher up the promotion ladder. That's what promoted people were paid for.

For example, if he found a motorist parked without lights, he booked him. If he saw a drunk, he arrested him. If he stopped a motor-vehicle, he checked every document it carried. Some of us weren't as keen as that – we would switch on the lights of parked cars, we would put drunks into a taxi and send them home, and we would give friendly advice to those who erred slightly. Oscar might adopt our rural ways in time, we felt, for I learned he had arrived at Ashfordly only weeks before I came to Aidensfield. We were both new to the locality.

Knowing of his rigid attitude, I wondered why he allowed Alwyn's chrysanthemums to flourish in the female cell. I learned, by way of an answer, that Sergeant Blaketon hated gardening; if Alwyn was not permitted to use the cell, his glorious display would have to occupy a prominent position in the garden next door to Blaketon's house. Blaketon must have realised that his wife would react violently to such a gorgeous floral display so close to her kitchen window, and he was happy that she never set eyes on it. It seemed he was content never to examine the female cell. No one saw him enter it. Knowing Blaketon, however, I knew that procedure would have been among his priorities upon arrival here. He'd obviously opened the door, seen the blooms and made a very rapid decision. He was a man with a fast-moving brain, I decided.

It was his attention to detail and his rigid adherence to the rules, that caused me to think twice when George Ward, landlord of the Hopbind Inn, Elsinby, asked if he could run greyhound races in a local field.

My initial reaction was to wonder why he had asked me and to say, "Go ahead", but the figure of Oscar Blaketon loomed uneasily in the background. We sometimes called him "Occurrence Book" because of his initials; this was an essential document at police stations, a record of every incident that happened, and it was known as the "O.B.". My knowledge of O.B.'s adherence to rules halted me.

"I'll let you know," I told George. "When do you want to run them?"

"Friday nights," he said. "We were thinking of having half a dozen races or so, around Harold's field down Ploatby

Lane. Starting at seven-thirty, I reckon, and finishing about half nine. One race every twenty minutes, give or take a minute or two."

"How many competitors?"

"Dunno," he shrugged his shoulders. "I've a lot of runners, and if we advertised it we'd get loads in from all over."

"A big affair, then?" I suggested.

"Oh, aye. We'd have traps and a proper track, you know. Electric hare and all that. Bookies too."

"Not just a bit of village fun, then?" I put to him.

"Not really. There is a demand for this, you know," he spoke seriously. "I've asked among my mates."

"The cars?" I asked. "Where would you park them?"

"In Harold's field. It's big enough to take a circular track, and there's room for a hundred cars."

"Noise?" I tried to anticipate the reaction of the village to this proposal.

"No problem," he assured me. "The field is nearly a mile out of Elsinby."

"It seems O.K. to me, George, but I'll check with the sergeant and let you know. When do you hope to start?"

"Three weeks on Friday."

I relayed all this information to Sergeant Blaketon and he frowned heavily. "Greyhound racing at Elsinby?" He rubbed his chin. "It can't be legal."

"Why not, Sergeant?" I asked in all innocence.

"Dunno," he admitted. "But it doesn't sound legal, does it? It's not in a proper stadium for a start."

"I can't see why a bunch of men can't race their dogs around a field," I put to him.

He shook his big black head. "It's never been done before," he said. "If it had been legal, somebody else would have thought of it."

"Maybe they have, Sergeant, maybe the big greyhound stadiums all began like this? They must have started in a small way."

"No, son, I can't accept that. They're in cities with big money behind them, they're big business right from the start. They don't begin in little ways, don't big business stadiums."

"This is just a bit of fun."

"No, son. There's summat funny here. They're up to summat."

I couldn't see what was bothering him. I went home and read my lawbooks but found nothing to disqualify those dog-lovers from racing their animals around Harold's field. Half an hour after I'd begun my studies, the phone rang.

"Sergeant Blaketon," said the voice. "Did you say they're having bookies?"

"That was the intention, Sergeant. They want to have bookies, just like a proper racetrack. There'll be hot-dog stalls, ice-cream and soup."

"They can't," he said triumphantly. "They can't have bookmakers. It's not an approved course."

I didn't answer for a moment or two. Without bookies, what fun would there be? That was the whole idea – the men and their ladies would proceed to Harold's field, place their bets on the few races and then adjourn to George's pub to drown their sorrows or to spend their winnings. Without bookmakers on the track, the whole idea was a non-starter.

"Are you there, Rhea?" I heard him call.

"Yes, Sergeant. I was just wondering if there was a way round it."

"A way round it? Our job is to adminster the law, not to find ways round it. No bookies. That's final. Tell them they can hold their meeting if they like, but without bookmakers. There must be no obstruction of the road outside the track, no noise and no trouble of any kind."

And having made that decision, he replaced the telephone. Sitting at my desk, I wondered if he was secretly smiling with immense satisfaction. I could almost see the smirk of inverted pleasure on his face. I felt sorry for George and his pals, for the notion seemed a good one. I lifted my phone and was dialling George's number at the Hopbind Inn when I recalled a visit to a donkey derby. There had been bookies there, and it had been held in a field. And it certainly wasn't an approved racetrack. If they could have bookies, why couldn't George?

I replaced the telephone and lifted my battered copy of *Moriarty's Police Law* from its shelf and began to examine it. There was a good deal of information about approved race-tracks and I learned that a 'dog race' meant "A race in which an object propelled by mechanical means is pursued by dogs." That was contained in section 20 of the Betting and Lotteries Act of 1934, then in force. A 'track' meant premises on which races of any description, athletic sports or other sporting events took place.

There was a lot of information about the procedures required to secure licences to authorise betting on tracks. I learned, however, that special rules appertained to dog tracks. For example, betting could not take place in connection with more than eight dog races and was restricted to one continuous period not exceeding four hours. George's proposal seemed to comply with this provision. I discovered that the Totalisator could be set up on a dog track on any appointed day while the public were admitted and it could be operated for persons resorting to the track, on dog races run on that track on that day.

All this appeared to be running in George's favour and I even learned that bookmakers could not be excluded from a track being lawfully run, and that space for bookmaking should be afforded them. But all this applied to "approved" racetracks. It seemed that the local councils were empowered to grant licences for racetracks and to authorise betting on them, provided two months' prior notice was given.

I began to accept the superior knowledge of Sergeant Blaketon. His long experience was his salvation. He knew what could or could not occur. George couldn't function with bookies! And then I found the salvation clause!

I learned that bookmaking could not be carried on on *any* track unless the occupier held a licence in force under the provisions of the Betting and Lotteries Act 1934, authorising betting facilities on that track. And I discovered that the prohibition did not apply to any track on which bookmaking had not been carried out on more than seven previous days in that year, beginning on July 1, provided seven days' postal notice of the intended bookmaking had been given to the chief officer of police by the occupier.

So there it was. Long-winded, but there in print. George would be the 'occupier' of the field for this purpose, and all he had to do was give written notice to the chief constable. This did not even amount to a request for permission. It was simply a notification of the event, so I rang George. I explained this to him and told him that he could hold no more than seven days racing in any year, starting each July, and that bookies could come and accept bets on the field. He was delighted.

Sergeant Blaketon did not express his feelings when I acquainted him with this piece of legislation. He simply said, "Oh, yes?" and put down the telephone.

I was off duty on the night of the first meeting in Harold's field and went along in my civilian clothes to enjoy an unusual evening's entertainment. As I entered the field, George waved me across for a chat.

"Nice gathering, Mr Rhea," he beamed his appreciation and gazed around the chattering crowd. The place was almost full and even on this small field, there was the unmistakable atmosphere of a racecourse. Bookies were calling the odds, people were talking shop and discussing the runners, a hot-dog stall was making a fortune and the car-parking fees would keep Harold happy – whoever Harold was.

"Have you many runners, George?" I asked, walking into the centre with him.

"Full house," he told me. "Thirty in all. Some good dogs among 'em too. Six races, five to a race. Having a bet, are you?"

"I'm not much of a betting man," I said, truthfully.

"Put ten bob on No. 3 in the fourth," he advised, winking at me. "My way of saying thanks. I rang your office some weeks ago, you know, before I spoke to you. They said I couldn't have bookies. I know you found I could and I appreciate that."

"It's all part of the service, George."

"Don't forget then, No. 3."

I left him to go about his duties and went to one of the bookies' stands where I learned that No. 3 in the fourth race was called Rob Roy. I put ten shillings each way on him and settled to watch the intervening races. Just before the start of the fourth, I spotted Sergeant Blaketon, towering above the race-goers. I was in two minds whether or not to approach him, but decided I should. I pushed through the crowds and hailed him by waving my race sheet.

"Good evening, Sergeant," I was very formal.

"All quiet?" he asked, as if I was on duty.

"A very well behaved bunch, Sergeant. Their cars are all off the road, and there's no noise. Just good-humoured fun, all around."

"I didn't know whether you'd be here, son, seeing you're off duty."

He started to walk into the arena and I fell into step at his side.

"I came to see what goes on, Sergeant. I've never been to a thing of this kind."

"Me neither," he admitted. "Have you had a bet then?"

"Just one. I'm not a betting man," I told him.

"Which dog?"

I looked at him as we walked. I wasn't on duty, therefore I was permitted to have a bet. Was he catching me out?

"Rob Roy, Sergeant, in this race."

"Is it any good?"

"I was advised to put my cash on that one, Sergeant," I smiled. "It's the only bet I've placed."

In a flash, he had his wallet out and was waving a pound note at me. "I can't place a bet when I'm in uniform – stick a quid on for me, ten bob each way. That dog, same as yours."

I hurried to a bookmaker and managed to place his bet just before betting closed. To our delight, Rob Roy won handsomely at four to one and we were nicely in pocket.

"You know, P.C. Rhea," he was always very formal. "I could have made a nasty mistake there, couldn't I? If I'd forbidden that meeting, someone might have discovered those sections in the Betting and Lotteries Act. They could have complained to the Chief Constable, eh? I'd have been in serious trouble. I'm pleased you sorted it out – you did a good job. And you did it without twisting the law. We administered the law, which is our duty. Well done, lad," and he strode off.

"Thank you, Sergeant," and I adjourned to the Hopbind Inn where celebrations were already being held. I had the reason, and the cash, to celebrate.

* * * *

One sport which I had never seen before and which was

totally new to me, was hare coursing. I had never been in
contact with it, but soon after my arrival at Aidensfield, I
learned that the headquarters of the Ryedale Coursing Club
was at the Brewer's Arms, Aidensfield. The pub was the
headquarters of almost every other village organisation, ranging from the Catholic Women's League to the British Legion,
so the identity of the Coursing Club's HQ did not surprise
me. Coursing meetings were held at Aidensfield during the
winter of each year.

My very first coursing meeting came one crisp November
day. I was on duty at the time, which meant I could officially
visit the scene; in fact, I was allocated that duty because of
the expected traffic influx and other associated problems.
There would be a bar, for example, and I had to be on guard
against youngsters buying ale. Such is the lot of the rural
policeman – he attends everything on his patch "just in
case".

I had read a good deal in the papers about the coursing of
live hares. It had, and still has, a lot of enemies, particularly
among Socialist Members of Parliament. Attempts have been
made since 1924 to place an Anti-Coursing Bill upon the
statute book but, to date, all have failed. I knew that the
political atmosphere surrounding the sport could lead to some
aggravation, but was that likely to happen at Aidensfield?

Against that background, therefore, I attended my first
coursing meeting. Sergeant Blaketon advised me to be on the
alert for trouble because he had learned of a similar meeting,
in Lancashire, where a crowd of anti-blood sport fanatics had
demonstrated. They had invaded the coursing field into the
bargain. Chaos had resulted, with some violence from all
parties and I was warned against a repetition of that. Chaos
must not occur at Aidensfield, ordered Sergeant Blaketon.

In uniform, with wellies on my feet, I walked down to the
course. It was held on the flat fields of Home Farm. These
were spacious grassy areas, although some were of stubble,
and all were bounded by trees and interesting copses. They
provided good running for both dogs and hares, and I was
happy to learn that there were adequate parking facilities,
with ample space for the roving crowds. Spectators at
coursing meetings do not stand still, but wander around to see

the action. The action depends greatly upon the location of the hares which are the focal-point of the sport.

Another feature of the place was the mobile canteen and its supplies of hot soup, meat pies and sausage rolls. Next door stood the mobile liquor bar, and although it was only ten o'clock in the morning, it was open and serving alcoholic refreshment designed to warm the cockles of anyone's heart. The necessary licence had been obtained – I checked that. The arena was growing busier by the minute.

The essence of this misunderstood sport is that of hunting a hare with a greyhound. The sport has persisted since the beginning of time and the first laws of coursing were drawn up in the sixteenth century. The modern sport, however, differs from the ancient in that the killing of a hare does not necessarily determine the winning dog. Many enemies of the sport believe that this is one of the rules – it is not, as I was to learn from that day's duty.

Mingling with the spectators and competitors, I watched the sequence of events and soon the objects of the sport and the marking system became reasonably clear. I was helped by the chap who served the beer on the make-shift bar and learned that he was secretary of the local club. It was affiliated to the Old Yorkshire Coursing Club which had closed forty-eight years before this meeting, but which had been revived only a year earlier. The headquarters of that club were also at a pub.

With the barman, whose name was Sid, I watched the prelude to the day's events. A long line of beaters, each equipped with a white flag and a good voice, were despatched into the distance. When they were some 400 or 500 yards away, each man smartly about-turned and began to advance towards the clear field before us. This was the coursing field, an area set aside for the purpose. The beaters spread themselves across the width of the countryside and began to wallop the undergrowth with the flags and short sticks, shouting and making a terrible din. Ahead of them was the coursing field where two competing greyhounds were held on slip-leads. The object was to locate a hare and drive it into the field so that it would be seen by the eager dogs. Only two dogs compete in each course. These fit, shivering animals were

therefore waiting for the first hare to come bounding into the
flat field, whereupon, at a signal from the judge, they would
be slipped from their leads by the slipper. The judge was
mounted on a horse to give clarity of vision and ease of
movement as the dogs chased the hare around that field.
From the moment the dogs are slipped, the course is on.

As was expected, there were several abortive beats and on
one occasion that day, a leveret was put up. For those not
familiar with rural life, a leveret is a young hare, but he was
allowed his freedom. Coursing is for fit, adult hares only.

Eventually, a suitable hare was put up. A signal came from
one of the beater's white flags which was held aloft for all to
see, and the beaters began to warble as only coursing beaters
can. The expectant crowd waited for the hare to bolt through
the hedge and into the coursing field. He was driven that way
by the oncoming beaters and their horrendous voices; finally,
he entered through the hedge, ears flat against his body as he
raced for his life. He legged it for all he was worth, heading
for the far side of the arena and darting across the frontage of
spectators. When he was about two hundred yards ahead of
the straining dogs, they were slipped. The first course was on.

At this point, I learned of the two great differences between
greyhound racing and coursing. Firstly, the hare in coursing
is a live one; he is on his home ground, unconfined open
countryside which he knows intimately and which he uses to
good advantage. The second difference is that the dogs operate only in pairs, and they are identified by colours. One
wears red and the other wears white.

Because the competition begins with the slipping, the judge
has the unenviable task of deciding the winner and it is
invariably a very close contest. The judge on this occasion was
a lady, the only woman qualified as a coursing judge in the
North of England. She had to award points for speed in
get-away, for the number of times the dog makes the hare
turn, for go-byes (overtaking of one dog by the other in the
chase), and for the lengths distant from the hare. Points are
also awarded for toppling the hare, but not for a kill. A kill
does not determine the winning dog. In fact, a kill can lose
the course because the other dog can gain valuable points
during the killer's excitement. If a kill does occur, the course

ends there, but it usually occurs when the hare escapes through the hedge and runs out of the coursing field. At this point, a trained coursing greyhound will return to its owner. Usually, coursing greyhounds are kept solely for this purpose and are not run in other races.

During all the meetings I attended in the course of my police duty, I never saw one hare killed or maimed. As a matter of interest, it is a strict rule that only wild hares are used for the sport. It is against coursing rules to breed hares or to use captive hares for this purpose. Another rule forbids the coursing of ground to which hares have been introduced within the last six months. This allows the animals time to acquaint themselves with their natural surroundings. Some clubs will not chase hares which are wet due to the rain. They like their hares to be in peak condition – it helps the hares and it provides a better test of skill for the dogs. Hares are always given between 150 and 200 yards start too.

I must admit that I was impressed by the rigid rules which govern the sport, and after talking to the followers I was pleased to learn that they do their utmost to obey those rules. They are very conscious of the propaganda being issued against the sport and ask only that the true facts be known to a wider audience.

The judge, at the end of each course, raises either a red flag or a white one to indicate the winning dog; if the result is a draw, the judge raises his (or her) riding cap. The judge wears hunting pink.

At this meeting, sixteen dogs were waiting to participate, and at £5 per entry, the prize money was good. The victorious dog is the only one who has beaten all others during the day's competition, having knocked out all competitors as the meeting progresses. The winning dog of each heat competes against the following dog, but on a bad day, not every dog will get his chance. It depends upon the number of hares found; hares are not always available and cannot be made to appear to order.

The ultimate in the coursing world in this country is the Waterloo Cup, held each February at Altcar, near Liverpool. This was instituted in 1836 by the proprietor of the Waterloo Hotel in Liverpool, and the winning of that cup is the dream of every coursing fanatic. But even our little meeting attracted its share of enthusiasts – they came from all over Great Britain, including Scotland and Ireland.

But, as O.B. had predicted, the meeting also attracted unwelcome attention. As the day progressed, I became aware of alien visitors, people carrying placards and waving banners which condemned coursing and all who followed it. I realised they were there about two-thirty in the afternoon and as it would grow dark before five, I was not too alarmed. The meeting would end about four o'clock, I felt, so I decided to keep a wary eye on the visitors. I would inform the organisers if trouble appeared likely. I noticed the protestors were long-haired, youthful and serious; they did not dress like country-folk, and they did not enter the coursing area. They remained on the road outside the farm, having apparently learned something of the laws of trespass on private property. Had they trespassed on that field during the day, the farmer would have been within his rights to eject them or at least ask them to leave. He allowed coursing spectators and participants upon his land, but did not permit enemies of the sport to enter, consequently they could be considered trespassers.

Clearly, they realised this and as the afternoon progressed, the little gathering of protestors grew to around twenty. They had chosen their location fairly well because everyone who left the coursing meeting, whether by vehicle or on foot, would have to pass them and read their messages or listen to their words of wisdom. The sporting Press were there too, but whether they would photograph these people remained in doubt. The local reporter was there, but he did not warrant the assistance of a photographer. It seemed that their protest would be limited to the spectators and a few villagers, and I knew they would all ignore it.

Happily, the demonstration was a peaceful one. I wandered over to the group to acquaint myself with them and found them charming and sincere, an interesting group of earnest youngsters, male and female, none of whom had ever attended a coursing meeting and none of whom had studied the rules. Nonetheless, they believed they had a right to make their protest and I could not forbid them, unless they obstructed the highway or broke the law in some other way. I did not wish to chase them away, for everyone must have the right to free speech and thought, so long as it does not infringe upon the freedom of others.

I returned to the meeting for the final minutes and then Sergeant Blaketon arrived.

"What's that lot at the road end?" he asked, indicating with his head.

"Protestors," I told him. "They've come to demonstrate against coursing."

"Are they a nuisance?" he put to me.

"No, Sergeant," and I explained their activities and intentions.

"They can't hang around here all night," he commented.

"They won't," I assured him. "The meeting ends about four o'clock and I'm sure they'll leave then. They've got scooters with them."

"Don't stand any nonsense from them," he ordered me. "Remember you can book them for obstruction of the highway if they block the road. And there's breach of the peace if they fight."

"I'll remember, Sergeant," and off he went to have a look at the final contest of the day. I remained near the gate, keeping half an eye on the protestors and half on the progress of the meeting. As the final race got under way, I saw the protestors group themselves into a formidable knot and squat right in the centre of the exit road! I groaned. This was exactly what I did not want. This could cause trouble.

This kind of thing had been done before. Demonstrators would squat in the middle of the road, a most effective ploy, and they brought traffic to a halt. With Press and photographers there, the situation could be guaranteed publicity and this was beneficial to their cause. Invariably, those protested against would react violently and that would damage their image. With only two policemen at this meeting, as fast as we removed one protestor, another would take his place. Two policemen could not forcibly remove twenty sit-down demonstrators. The spectators' cars would be forced to stop and frustration would build up into something serious. If the protestors were manhandled by anyone except the police, they would register complaints of assault. And this was the only exit route from the field. I couldn't direct the leaving crowds via another route. I was sure that if I left the sit-downers in position, the trapped and frustrated spectators would use their own methods of dispersal. And that would mean trouble – big trouble, with lots of unwelcome publicity.

I looked at my watch. It was ten minutes to four.

Already cars were forming a queue at the exit of the car park and within minutes, they would arrive at this blockage. I decided to address the group.

"O.K. lads," I began. "You've made your point. Now move on, please, and let these people go home."

"We're not moving until we get an assurance that there will be no further coursing meetings here,"m said their spokesman, a clean-faced youngster with freckles and bright blue eyes.

"I'm afraid you will have to move," I chose my words carefully.

"It will take more than you and your sergeant to shift us," said another, a thick-set youth with a bushy beard. He looked like a prop forward.

"You said it," I smiled, and returned to the field. Sergeant Blaketon came towards me, looking very harassed.

"They're there, Rhea, look at them! They'll sit there and block the road until they've got publicity. If we're not careful, there'll be a punch-up. Some of these chaps have had a skin full of ale . . ."

"We needn't worry, Sergeant," I said confidently. "They'll soon go," and I told him the reason why I was so sure. He smiled and nodded his approval to my idea. I then moved towards the first car in the queue and explained the situation to him, asking him to be patient for about ten minutes. He agreed. I told the driver of the car behind and got the motorists to pass back the word. They smiled and were happy at my suggestions.

And so the protestors sat in the middle of the exit road, with a queue of very patient, smiling motorists confronting them, with engines idle and with no blaring horns. I waited too, and I must admit I was a little apprehensive. The seconds ticked away. Four o'clock came and went. And then at three minutes past four, I knew I had won.

Farmer Joe Sculley was bringing his cows in. They moved

slowly and inexorably towards the little band of demonstrators, their horned heads down and their tails lashing as they deposited pounds of wet cow-clap behind them along their route. Those cows had no intention of stopping for this little party and ploughed on, thinking only of the blessed relief of the milking parlour.

In the face of this opposition, the demonstrators left their positions and the leading car moved deftly into position right behind the cows, spreading the fertiliser evenly across the highway. The queue of cars moved slowly away behind the trudging cows, and so we won the day.

It would take a very dedicated demonstrator to squat in a sea of freshly deposited cow dung.

Four

I became fascinated at the number of craftsmen who managed to earn a living on my beat. Almost every village or hamlet boasted one or more of these interesting folk. There was the cobbler of Elsinby, the woodcarver of Aidensfield, the blacksmith of Maddleskirk, the potter of Crampton, the furniture-maker of Briggsby and a host of assorted artists, writers and sculptors.

I found these people just as interesting as the farmers and rurals with whom I worked, and I respected them because of their independence, their love of hard work and their undying spirit. In their own way, they had discarded what is often termed the "rat race", and had settled in this rural paradise to earn their living in the way they wished. Pensions and status meant nothing to them, and they seemed to avoid the pressures of modern life. I was envious of them and their freedom.

I did not discover all these people at once. It took me some months to appreciate the wealth of talent that lay within the boundaries of my beat and I made new discoveries of this sort almost weekly. The first realisation that I had someone of note living nearby came with the arrival of a huge lorry. It parked outside my house one afternoon while I was off duty, enjoying a spot of weeding. The driver hailed me and announced he was seeking a Mr James Flagg who had a quarry.

"There's no one of that name with a quarry around here," I told him, racking my brains to recall such a person.

"Well," said the driver. "I've got a delivery note that says there is. 'James Flagg, Aidensfield', it says. And I've got a bloody great lump of rock for him."

He pointed to the rock in question. It was massive. I did wonder why he'd be taking rock *to* a quarry, but didn't ask – there must have been a logical reason.

"There's only one quarry around here," I pointed out. "It's down the road at Thackerston. It's a limestone quarry, getting rid of lumps like that after it's been broken down to powder."

"I've been there," he said. "It's not theirs."

Being new to the village, I decided to ask Mary if she'd heard of Flagg. She'd met many villagers socially. "Darling," I called through the door. "Have we anybody called Flagg in the village?"

"Yes," she replied. "I've met her, she's got a youngster at play-school. She plays with our Elizabeth. Nice people. They live in that little cottage at the far end of the village. Honeysuckle Cottage."

I knew the house. It was a gorgeous cottage built into the lee of a hill; it faced south with roses and honeysuckle around the doorway and was everyone's ideal country home.

"There's a Mr Flagg down the village," I pointed out the route. "But it's not a quarry. He's a sculptor – he carves things out of stone and wood."

I had seen him at work as I passed his house, but hadn't connected the name with him until now.

"How am I going to get this lump off my truck then? I thought I was taking it to a quarry – I thought there'd be lifting gear . . . "

I walked to the gate for a closer look at his load. Strapped onto the flat rear of his lorry was a huge oblong piece of stone. It was a good eight feet long by six feet high and six feet wide. It was secured with heavy ropes and stood on a pad of thick rubber material. It had come from somewhere in the Scottish Highlands and was beautiful to behold. I don't know what type of stone it was, but even in its square untouched state, it looked magnificent. Having made sure the driver knew the location of Honeysuckle Cottage, I waved him into a lane to turn his long vehicle.

"I hope that chap's got lifting gear," he shouted as he moved off.

"If he's expecting you, he'll have something fixed up, I'm sure," I called after him, hopefully.

I must confess that my curiosity had been aroused and fortuitously I had some mail to post. This seemed an ideal time to potter down the village and drop them in the letter box. I dressed in some passable clothes which were not full of soil and stray rose thorns, and meandered upon my little expedition.

From the distance, I could see the lorry parked outside Honeysuckle Cottage and could see the figure of the driver gesticulating; before him stood the squat shape of the sculptor, listening carefully. They walked around the lofty chunk of rock, each looking seriously at the vehicle and doubtless discussing mutual problems. I pushed my letters into the box and went into the post office to buy some stamps, a pair of bootlaces, some sugar and a bag of firelighters. When I emerged, they were still there, walking around the lorry like a pair of dogs sniffing a butcher's van.

I wished I dare walk closer, but refrained because it would seem I was snooping. But a shout from one of them halted me.

"Mr Rhea!" It was not the lorry driver's voice. I stopped, turned around and walked the fifty yards or so towards the unhappy pair.

"Mr Rhea? Our new policeman?" the man asked me.

"I am."

"James Flagg. I'm a sculptor, as you may know. I've a problem," and he looked at the vehicle and its load.

"Is it yours?"

"Mine," he smiled wryly. "All the way from Scotland and would you believe, they've sent it on a flat lorry. No crane. They always send a lorry with lifting gear. What can I do? It must not be cracked or chipped in any way. It's for a commissioned piece – a Madonna and Child . . . "

"How much does it weigh?" I asked.

"Several tons," said the driver. "I'm not sure really, except it's a bloody great lump of stone."

"You've not had this problem before?" I asked Flagg, hoping he might provide his own solution.

"Never. Mind you, this is the biggest chunk I've ordered for a long time, and they've always sent a lorry with lifting gear. Always. They know my requirements."

"There's Paddy Stone at Maddleskirk," I suggested.

"Stone? That's appropriate!" laughed Flagg. "Who's he?"

"He's got the timber yard there. I had him remové a fallen oak a few weeks ago. He came out with a massive crane and shifted it in no time. I'll bet that oak weighed as much as your lump of stone."

"Is he on the telephone?"

"He must be," I said.

Flagg rushed inside and made his call. It seemed that Paddy was at work in his timber yard and being the generous man that he was, he accepted the challenge. It was a ten-minute drive out to Aidensfield, and he came with two of his best men, plus an impressive crane.

The problem was finding something to grip the rock without damaging it and then to lift it sufficiently to slide a powerful sling beneath. But Paddy did the trick. He used a type of jack which lifted the stone very gently and then slid a second one beneath it. By pumping a handle, he lifted the rock high enough to slide a strong belt beneath it, and he repeated this with other strong belts until he had the chunk in a type of cradle.

It was then a simple matter for the crane to hoist it from the lorry and deposit it in Flagg's front garden, at a point selected by him. We all went inside for a noggin of whisky and Paddy got himself a few quid for the job.

When I showed interest in Flagg's work, he showed me around his studio. He explained how a figure was created and how moulds were made for copies to be taken. His work appeared in many churches, both in Britain and Europe, and from that day I was welcome to call at any time. It was an offer that I frequently accepted. I would stand for minutes at a time, watching him chip away at featureless lumps of rock or timber, to create beautiful figures in his own distinctive style.

Over the months, I saw that huge lump of rock change shape. It lost its squareness and began to assume a more rounded outline, and then the features of a head began to appear. This was gradually followed by the familiar outline of a Madonna and Child, and by the end of the year, the figure was complete. It was beautiful, two human bodies with skin as smooth as any advert for expensive soap whose clothing bore all the creases and wrinkles that one expects in real life. The expression on the mother's face, the innocence in the baby's gaze – it was all contained in that solid lump of Scottish rock.

The next problem was moving it out. It had to travel down to London to the buyer who had commissioned it, and I was pleased to learn that Paddy was hired for the lifting ceremony. With infinite care and tenderness, he used his experience to manhandle that heavy, boxed load onto a lorry for transportation to the big city, two hundred and fifty miles away. Before it left, Flagg opened the crate to inspect his work, to ensure it was undamaged before leaving Aidensfield. I looked inside too, and so did the lorry driver, a stranger to the area.

He looked at the child's face, and then at Paddy.

"That's you, innit?" he smiled and the case was bolted shut.

Paddy blushed; I hadn't noticed the likeness, and James Flagg merely smiled. The load arrived safely at its destination and Paddy got more jobs after that. But I could hardly regard him as a face of innocence.

* * * *

Samuel Cook looked like a cobbler, which he was. I found him by accident. When walking through Elsinby one afternoon, the heel of my boot fell off and my embarrassment was witnessed by an elderly gentleman on his way to collect his pension.

"Nip into Aud Sam's," he advised. "He'll fix it for you."

He issued guidance to Sam's workshop so I hobbled the few hundred yards to locate it. It was half way up a steep hill which led from Elsinby towards Waindale. It was a wooden hut painted a deep green and somewhat isolated. Sam seemed happy out here, a good five minutes' walk from his home.

I limped to the door, knocked and waited. There was no reply, but I knew he was inside because I could hear the whirl of his sewing-machine. I knocked again. The noise stopped and the door opened. A small man about sixty years old with thick ginger hair greeted me. He had heavy spectacles with thick lenses and they were covered in dust. How he could see through that heavy layer, I do not know. He wore a thick, long apron of strong leather and several tin tacks were clamped between his lips, like vampire's fangs.

He muttered through them.

"Come in, nobody ever knocks, Just come in," so I followed him into the tiny workshop. To the left of his door was his store of new shoes and wellington boots, all for sale. They were stored neatly on racks, brown on one side of the hut and black on the other. There were no other colours. The big shelves held huge boots, tough shoes and leather leggings, all the trappings of country folk, while the smaller shelves bore the cobbler's accoutrements, like polish, laces, heels, dubbin, brushes and a host of other items. The entire place reeked of leather – the woodwork must be saturated with the scent, but it was not unpleasant.

In the centre of the floor stood an ancient but efficient wood-burning stove. This was Sam's heating system and waste disposal unit; when winter descended, I found it most reliable and welcoming. He used it to burn his waste products and rubbish, and I later discovered that he mended Paddy Stone's shoes, and did other leather work for him, all free of charge. This was in return for free loads of end-cuts from Paddy's timber yard. Sam would drive up in his van, deliver a pile of boots and shoes which Paddy repaired for his family and workmen, and in return Paddy would load Sam's van with pieces cut off the end of his timber. It seemed a marvellous working arrangement, although I often wondered what the tax man made of it.

To the right as you entered the hut was Sam's working area, containing the bench at which he spent all his working days. Here he had spent all his working life, cobbling for all he was worth and it seemed he demanded no more from society than the grace to allow him to continue his craft. He had a very old but beautifully made sewing-machine which looked as if it would never break down, and which thrived on a diet of thick thread and thin oil. The bench was piled high with leather pieces of all shapes and sizes, and knives hung from the wall. These were razor sharp with blades hollowed by sharpening over countless years. Many is the time I've watched him shape a heel from a piece of thick leather, marvelling at his swift and uncanny skill. That first day, I watched him hammer one home on a boot, skim the edges with a polishing wheel and then dye the new leather to match the existing boot. It looked so simple, but this was his craft. He worked day in and day out, never complaining.

I showed him the heel of my boot and he examined it. "You could do with a new 'un," he said simply, his brown face expressionless.

"I'll leave it," I said stupidly, for I had no spare.

"Nay, I'll fix it now," and he did. I sat on a chair near the stove with one stockinged foot on a stool as he shaped a heel for me. He tacked it onto my boot and trimmed the edges.

"How much?" I asked when he'd finished.

"Sixpence," was his price.

"Sixpence?" I gasped. It would have cost me a few shillings in town. "Here, take two bob."

But he refused. "I know my terms," he said proudly. "I'm not one for making a big profit. Big money brings its problems, you know. I just want to earn a decent living – a fair day's work for a fair day's pay."

He steadfastly refused even to take a sixpence as a tip. Today, a sixpence is worth $2\frac{1}{2}$ pence in decimalised currency. Naturally, I returned there often, with my police boots, the children's shoes, leather bags and a host of other items which required his skill. His charges for sewing up a split handbag or suitcase would be 2d or 3d; the full repair of a pair of shoes would be fifteen shillings or so, all of which were about a third of the price in York or elsewhere. And he was good too – plus the fact, he provided personal service.

Through calling regularly, I discovered he was seldom alone in his little shop. Everyone popped in for a sit beside his stove and a chat, but he worked through their chatter. He talked freely about his life, about shoeing the monks at nearby Maddleskirk Abbey, about making hunting boots, clogs, leather aprons and saddleware. He could fashion almost anything from leather it seemed, but he had another talent. I learned he was a hairdresser.

Practically all rural cobblers were hairdressers and his charge was 3d (1½p) for a short-back-and-sides. I did not use him for this purpose, except on one occasion. I had been summoned to Police Headquarters for an interview with the Chief Constable. It seemed that the Chief Constable had telephoned my superintendent who telephoned the inspector who telephoned Sergeant Blaketon.

O.B. rang me and instructed, "Rhea. Get yourself over to Headquarters for two o'clock this afternoon. The Chief wants to talk to you."

At that stage, no one told me what the Chief wanted to talk about. O.B.'s instructions had been curt, and all manner of possible reasons flashed before me. I was being posted away from the beat. I had been promoted. I had made a mess of something. There'd been a complaint about me. My hair was too long . . .

Hair!

It was too long for an officer about to be interviewed by the Chief Constable, so I had to get it cut in a hurry. I thought of Sam and his cobbler's shop. He was salvation. I hadn't time to go elsewhere. I drove across to Elsinby, went in and explained the problem. He said he would cut my hair immediately and I settled on a chair. After covering me with the traditional checked cloth, he snipped away at me, chattering all the time and regaling me with tales about World War I. I paid my 3d and went home for an early lunch. As I walked in, Mary burst into fits of laughter.

"What on earth have you done!" she cried, with tears streaming down her face. "It's like one of those pudding basin cuts!"

And so it was. Sam didn't have the luxury of a mirror so I hadn't been able to view myself before leaving his emporium. In the comfort of my own home, the full horror of my hair style was plain to see. My hair was like that of a village yokel of the fifteenth century – and I was due to meet the Chief within the hour. I tried trimming it with scissors, but it was futile. I had to leave because it was a twenty-mile run on the Francis Barnett. *En route,* I determined that I would not show my back view to the Chief. If I was in trouble of any sort, this display would only aggravate matters.

With some trepidation, therefore, I waited hatless outside the Chief Constable's office door at Headquarters and was ushered in. I stood to attention, smart in my pressed uniform and clean shirt. I had done what I could with my hair at the front and I thought it had passed his scrutiny. He left his desk and came forward to shake hands with me. This surprised me.

"Congratulations, Rhea," he beamed. "You've done us proud. A splendid show. Excellent."

I must have looked surprised. Indeed I was, for I had no idea what I'd done to justify this reception. It was certainly not the hair-do.

"You don't know why you are here?" he must have recognised the look of bewilderment on my face.

"No, sir," I shook my head and felt the hair flop over my brow. I swallowed hard.

"The Gold Medal Essay. The Queen's Police Gold Medal Essay competition," he said proudly. "You submitted an essay on juvenile delinquency."

"Yes, sir," my heart began to thump.

"You've got second prize, Rhea. You were beaten by the Commissioner of the South Australia Police. It was a Commonwealth competition, Rhea, with entries from all over the world. And you've got second prize. Here is a cheque for £30 – I am delighted. I regard this as a triumph for the force."

The Home Office, who arranged the competition, had apparently notified my Force direct, and I had no idea of this success. I accepted the cheque gratefully, for it represented almost three weeks pay. With three little children, we needed every penny, so I was delighted. After a chat about the work I'd put into the essay, he dismissed me. I wheeled smartly about, stomped my feet and marched from his office.

Then a loud bellow halted me. "Rhea!"

"Sir?" I was only inches from the door.

"What the bloody hell's happened to your hair?"

I turned to face him. "I had it cut this morning, sir, in a rush."

"What a bloody awful mess! I'm amazed at you, reporting here like that. I'm amazed that you had the effrontery to enter my office in a state of that kind. God Almighty! I wouldn't be seen dead like that, man," and he proceeded to give me the bulling of my life. He was expert at this, being an ex-military man, and I left his office clutching my cheque for £30, but feeling as small and as helpless as a harvest mouse. His dressing-down made me shake for hours afterwards.

I often returned to Sam's workshop, where I talked to him and had my shoes repaired, but I never let him touch another hair of my head.

* * * *

I met another of my craftsmen friends during routine enquiries into a series of housebreakings in the locality. Someone had been travelling around the villages in the early afternoon of certain weekdays, and had broken into several houses over a wide area of the district. Individually, the thefts were not very serious – at each house, two or three pounds in cash would be removed from tins on mantel-shelves, or food would be taken from the larders. Occasionally, an item of clothing would disappear and very infrequently, something with a saleable value would be missed, like a portable radio or small items of jewellery. Taken as a whole, however, the crimes were serious and engendered considerable alarm among the people.

My detective colleagues had investigated these crimes, many of which had occurred well beyond the boundaries of my beat and concluded they were the work of either a tramp or someone on the run, living locally and stealing in order to survive. It could be the work of absconders from an approved school, but the pattern ruled out a professional thief bent on stealing high-value goods.

As time went by without an arrest, the women folk began to grow alarmed at the prospect of someone entering their homes and rifling through their belongings. I made a point, therefore, of visiting as many isolated houses as possible, in an attempt to alert the occupants to the criminal's activities. It was during one of those missions that I came across Stanley George Hatton.

I discovered his house after bouncing my motor-cycle along

an unkept lane for almost a mile. It was a very isolated place, and a sign on the gate said 'Brockrigg Farm'. I entered and drove the motor-cycle as far as possible along the muddy track, then parked it against a stone gate post. I removed my helmet and walked the final twenty-five yards to the house. I knocked on the door and waited. Soon I heard heavy foot-steps inside and a woman's voice told a dog to "Git oot o' t'rooad" before the door opened.

"Oh!" upon seeing me, she smoothed her rough hessian apron, known hereabouts as a 'cooarse appron', and said, "Oh, it's t'bobby."

"Yes," I said. "I've come to give advice about burglars."

"Here?" The dog appeared and sniffed at me. It was one of the black-and-white curs which are so prominent in the farms of the region.

"Hereabouts," I told her. I called the criminal a *burglar* whereas the term was strictly wrong. He was a *housebreaker* because he broke in during the daylight hours. Burglars were those who broke and entered houses during the night, but since that time, the law has changed. All those who break into premises of any kind are now legally entitled to the name of burglar. It is a technicality, but the word *burglar* has always been easily understood by the general public.

"Well you'd better have a chat wiv oor Stanley George," she suggested.

"Your husband?"

"Aye, he's roond there, in yon aud barn, working."

"Thanks," and I followed the direction of her finger.

The large double-sided barn door was open and I walked in. I expected to find a farmer hard at work, but instead I found a carpenter. The old barn had been converted into a comfortable work-shop and it was full of wooden articles. My first impression was that of a furniture store, but the scent of glue and polish, of wood shavings and of oak told me other-wise. There was a mass of wood shavings on the floor too, and rows of tools hung from the wall. This was a one-man factory.

A stiff man in late middle age got up from the bench and struggled towards me, limping painfully.

"Don't, I'll come over," and I crossed the floor towards him.

He smiled gratefully, and settled back on the stool beside the bench.

"Rheumatics," he said wryly. "In me aud legs. Gives me hell, it does."

"I'm P.C. Rhea," I said, holding out a hand. He shook it strongly.

"Hatton," he introduced himself. "Stanley George Hatton. Everybody calls me Stanley George. It's on account of my mother. She had three lads, me and two brothers. She called 'em all Stanley because it was her favourite name – I'm Stanley George, there's Stanley Eric and Stanley Peter. I wish folks would just call me George, but they never do, not around here."

I settled on a newly made chair at his side and explained the reason for my visit. He listened intently and said he'd make sure everything was locked up. In any case, he and his wife were always pottering about the premises during the day, and she'd notice any strangers lurking about. We talked happily and his wife, whose name I learned was Millie, brought us a cup of tea. She stopped for a chat, and I told her of my mission. She had heard about the thefts and house-breakings and promised to be a little more crime-conscious.

I had a look around his workshop and marvelled at the quality of his work. There were chairs galore, Windsor style in the main, which he had fashioned from the piles of wood stacked in one corner. But he had also made cupboards, wardrobes, even bedsteads and a whole range of large items like dining-suites and kitchen-fittings. He told how he had been compelled to give up farming because of his legs. He'd let his land to neighbours but not being a man for idling his time away, he'd turned to his life-long hobby of carpentry. Suddenly, the orders had boomed – he found himself making complete dining-sets for customers, and Windsor chairs which sold rapidly to the city stores, and a host of other items. He'd had offers of more than enough work and had been surprised to suddenly find himself in demand. He worked to suit himself and accepted jobs which meant he could remain seated for much of the time. All his work was hand-finished and polished with a care that bordered on the fanatical.

I began calling on him every time I was in Briggsby, once a

quarter or so, and we had long, interesting talks. Gradually, I realised his farm was not connected to the mains electricity supply; he had no electrical apparatus in his workshop and even his drill was hand operated. His wife cooked on a large Aga in her ample kitchen and the light came from oil lamps strategically placed about the premises. The whole farm had an air of calmness and peace, very reminiscent of the last century.

I grew very fond of Stanley George and Millie. He would chat away to me in the rich dialect of the locality, and I could chatter back in like terms. I told him about life in a modern police force, with motor vehicles, personal radio sets and improved facilities. He told me about the old days on the farm, before tractors came along and before combine harvesters had shortened the harvest period.

It was some months later that Stanley George sought my advice on a matter which was troubling him..

"Thoo's a man of the world," he said one day as we drank Millie's tea. "I'd like a spot of advice."

"Of course," I assured him. "Ask any time."

"Well, it's like this," he began, sipping slowly from his mug. "We've no 'lectric in this house. We've grown used to makking do wivoot it, me and oor Millie. Never missed it, you understand. Onnyrooad, some 'lectric fellers were fixing poles and cables just over that hill behind our house. Last week, this was. Yan on 'em come to me and asked if I wanted t'electric in this house. He's given me till this weekend to think it over."

"And do you want it?" I put to him.

"Nay, now I can't be sure," he admitted. "Just can't mak up my mind. I mean, what good would it be to me, at this stage of life?"

"It would make life easier," I assured him. "You'd have instant light all around the house, you could boil kettles of water much faster, you could have power tools in here, like drills and saws."

"It would tak me ages ti get accustomed ti it."

"What about Millie? How's she feel about it?"

"No idea," he shook his head. "She's no idea. She's got relations in Richmond with t'electric, but they burn t'toast, t'custard gits tak tiv it, and all soorts goes wrang. And them bulbs they use – they keep banging and flashing."

"Faulty wiring, I'll bet," I said. "If lights keep flashing or bulbs keep blowing, it'll be old wiring. They should get new wiring fitted right through the house. But back to you – I reckon you'd like it."

"Them 'lectric fellers said they'd fix me up wiv an estimate," he said. "What's that mean?"

"It means they'll come around your house and buildings to examine everything, and then tell you what's needed – how much wire, for example, how many plugs and sockets they recommend and that sort of thing. The Electricity Board will send you a letter telling you what it will cost."

"And would I have to get it?"

"Not if you didn't want to," I assured him. "The estimate will be free – they come along and measure up, that's all. For nowt."

"They said they would come this Friday, unless I said no."

"Let them come," I said. "At least you'll know what it will cost you. You might say no when you learn what the cost is, but at least you'll have an opportunity to be fitted with electricity."

Stanley George agreed to this. I left him and it was another fortnight before I returned to his farm. I popped into his workshop as usual, and the inevitable cup of tea appeared. Millie stayed with us for a chat.

"Well?" I asked him. "Did they estimate for your electricity?"

"By!" he said with feeling. "By, that was a to-do, that was. Two fellers came with rulers and instruments and they went right round that house of mine, and right round these buildings. It took 'em ages, I can tell you. They went through ivvery room doonstairs, and then upstairs. I was right behind, watching from t'bottom to t'top, and do you know, they started to measure every bedroom. Well, Mr Rhea, we've seven bedrooms in this aud house, and I can't see t'sense in having 'lectric in every room, can you?"

"It's the normal practice," I told him.

"It seems daft to me," he shook his head. "I reckon all I would need would be one light on t'landing. It would shine into ivvery room upstairs, eh? I can't see t'sense in having lights in every bedroom."

"It's convenience," I said. "You enter your bedroom, switch on the light and get ready for bed . . ."

"Aye," he said, "That's it. I like reading in bed, and so does our Millie. Just imagine – we'd get settled in, all nice and snug, and then we'd have to get out and paddle across t'floor to put t'lights out. By my way of thinking, if we had one light on that landing, it would show us upstairs and we could use candles at our bedsides, like we allus have. We could switch t'landing light off, take our candles across to t'bedside and read till we felt like nodding off. Then blow t'candles out. That way, you keep your feet warm."

Try as I might, I could not convince him that it was better to have lights in every room, nor could he appreciate the value of an overhead switch at the bedhead. I do not know what his estimated cost was, but he did tell me it was based on a full system downstairs, with power and light installed in his workshop, but only one light on the stairs. There were to be no lights in the bedrooms. He'd made his mind up about that, and the estimate was made on those terms.

He had the electricity installed to his desire. I called late one afternoon and learned it had been in working order for about ten days. The men had wired the house and he had a solitary bulb, without a shade, at the top of the staircase, from where it shone into all seven bedrooms. He had relented a little because the bathroom contained an electric bulb. Downstairs, the system was complete and Millie had a brand new washing machine, cooker, kettle, iron and other essential modern household goods. It must have cost Stanley George a fortune, but I knew he was well off.

"Well?" I asked, settling at his side. "How's the new electricity?"

"I don't reckon much to it," he said bluntly. "Our Millie still cooks on that Aga, it's hot all t'time you see. And that cup of tea – well, that aud kettle boils on that Aga, all t'time, so it's allus ready. Bubbling away all day, singing and warm. And she puts her iron on before she fettles my shirts and things . . . we don't use t'electric, you know. We don't need it."

"Not at all?" I cried. "Not after all that expense?"

"I can't use it in my workshop, Mr Rhea – I like a hand drill and hand tools. They've got feeling in 'em, you see. Power tools have no feeling, have they?"

"But surely you must make some use of it?"

"Aye," he acknowledged gravely. "We do. That light on t'top of our stairs. We switch it on before going up to bed. It lights our way upstairs and we switch it off before we go into our bedrooms. That's a very useful light, is that one."

I called upon him many times after that, but I never saw him, or Millie, make use of anything electrical.

Incidentally, the youth responsible for the housebreakings was caught a month or so after my first contact with Stanley George. He'd run away from home and was sleeping in a barn about eight miles away, living by his thefts.

* * * *

Perhaps my favourite craftsman was Aud John. Everyone knew him as Aud John and it was some time before I knew his surname was Frankland. John was the local blacksmith at Maddleskirk and he had occupied his smithy just off the High Street for over seventy years. It had been his father's place before that, and John continued to operate with huge bellows, a pile of coke and an anvil which must have shaped thousands of horseshoes over many dozens of years.

John was well over eighty. He was a thick-set man and weighed well over seventeen stone. He had a fresh complexion, a white moustache and white hair with sparkling grey eyes. He habitually wore a long leather apron which was scorched with heat and tattered from other labours. He worked day in, day out with his sleeves rolled up and I never once saw him wear a jacket. His feet always sported clogs; he was muscular and fit, as straight as the proverbial ramrod and he possessed a marvellous sense of humour. Everyone liked and respected Aud John.

In his heyday, the smithy had been the resort of horses from far and near, and that had been the sole living of John and his father. John had continued to earn a good living until that period after World War II when horses began to dwindle as a form of rural draught and transport. The motor-vehicle was taking over and John found business sliding from him. He was not one for letting things go and refused to give up his ancient craft. After all, it was his only skill. He began to fashion ornamental gates and other similar fittings, which he sold at the markets of Harrowby, Brantsford and Ashfordly. Business began to thrive once again, although he still shod the occasional horse when the occasion demanded. With a renewed interest in horses, John's business enjoyed a second revival and he became busier than ever in his declining years. He reckoned that hard work kept him alive and fit. I believe it did.

I enjoyed visiting John. It was a long time before he totally accepted me, and I learned very quickly that he hated being watched at work. If he had a caller, he would promptly cease work and talk for as long as he considered necessary. He would then dismiss the visitor. As he worked in the open air in a square yard which abutted a lane running off the High Street, he had frequent interruptions, although I did discover that his trusted friends and local colleagues were allowed to talk to him while he worked.

My visits to his yard were originally for duty purposes. I was checking for stolen scrap metal. Unscrupulous scrap merchants might attempt to sell stolen property to him, or they might attempt to steal his stock of metal, consequently I paid regular visits to his small establishment, just to keep an eye on him and his belongings. Constant reminders kept him alert to the possibility of visits by criminals.

The entrance to his tiny square yard was through two wooden gates, just wide enough to admit a lorry, and these were always closed when he was working. He would sit or stand in a small clearing among his heaps of metal and there fashion his exquisite gates, brackets, fireplaces and other objects, many of which had been commissioned. Gradually, he began to accept me; I knew I had 'arrived' when he continued to work in my presence.

At the back of the yard was his store-room and internal workshop; inside the workshop was the traditional blacksmith's shop, with the anvil, the coke fire, the trough of water and piles of horseshoes. There was the ever-present smell of hot metal, coke and horses. On cold days, I would pop into that shop to get warm because the fire was always burning.

There is nothing cosier than a working blacksmith's shop.

One late autumn day, I popped in for a warm-up, for I'd been on a long motor-cycle patrol and was chilled to the core. Aud John nodded me through and I went across his yard and through to the shop where I removed my motor-cycle gear. I settled before the glowing fire, pumped the bellows to bring up a blaze, and warmed myself before it. Outside, John was busy with a wrought-iron gate which had to be finished that day, so I did not try to talk to him. I sat in his smithy while he worked outside, even though there was a hint of frost in the air.

And as I enjoyed the growing warmth, I became aware of two young men. They were strangers to the village and were leaning upon his gates, watching him at work. For a long time, he was unaware of their presence and I wondered how he would react when he realised they were there. I began to observe them, realising I was invisible to them within the darkness of the forge. The confrontation could be interesting.

Each visitor was about thirty years old, smartly dressed and obviously of good standing. One had thick fair hair and rimless glasses, while the other was rather thick-set with a balding head. Finally, John realised they were there.

"What's thoo fellers want?" he demanded, downing his tools with evident determination.

"Oh, er, nothing," the fair-haired one answered. "We are just watching."

"I'm a busy chap, and I don't like being watched by strangers," he told them. "Can I sell you anything?"

"No, thanks," the fair one said. "Can we watch for a while?"

Grudgingly, John retrieved his tools and resumed work on the urgent gate. He was uneasy, I could sense that. He continually looked across at them and I knew he wouldn't normally have worked like this, but the job was pressing. They remained leaning across his gate for a few more minutes, quietly observing his efforts. Finally, he could stand it no longer.

"Look here," he pulled himself to his full height, a magnificent man for his age. "I can't abide folks watching me when I'm working. If there's summat you want, then get it and leave me be. I've got to finish this job."

The balding one spoke.

"We're sorry," he smiled gently. "We'll go in a moment. But we find it so nice to watch a genuine craftsman at work, especially a man like you, working in the open air. We are up here on business, you see; we're heading for Brantsford and we stopped here to stretch our legs. We have a factory in the south; we're from London and we manufacture precision instruments. For that reason, it's so nice to find a real craftsman, working in the old tradition and using his own hands."

"That's right," his fair-haired companion continued. "Mind you, our sort of work is very, very precise. We have to work to an accuracy of one ten-thousandth of an inch."

"In that case," said John with his eyes twinkling, "You'd better stay and watch. I'm exact."

Five

With about a dozen Acts of Parliament and other minor pieces of legislation to cater for dogs, I realised the rich man's guardian and poor man's friend would feature in my daily work at Aidensfield. My beat was the home of numerous dogs and in common with other rural areas, they ranged from tiny indoor pets like Yorkshire terriers to keen, working and sporting dogs, but included the inevitable strays, sheep worriers, lost dogs and perpetual wanderers, to say nothing of Claude Jeremiah Greengrass's lurcher.

So far as the law was concerned, there were dog licences to check, stray dogs to house, sheep killers to be concerned about and collars to examine. Almost every week involved me in some form of doggy problem.

Due to this regular commitment, it wasn't long before I knew many of the resident dogs by their first names. I began to accept the situation that it was not unusual in this type of rural bliss, for dogs to wander unaccompanied around the villages. Each did its own thing while its unseen master went about his unknown business.

One such wanderer was Rufus, a lethargic Golden Labrador, whose unquenchable lust was for dustbins. He roamed Aidensfield at all hours, up-turning the district's dustbins so he could ferret among the contents. His master was a hairy musician who knew of Rufus's craving and who had tried, many many times, to cure him of the habit. Practically everyone else in the village had tried and while most of them had resorted to concealment of their bins, one man had gone to the lengths of wiring his bin to a 12-volt car battery. His hope was that Rufus would cock his leg against it or otherwise attempt to overturn it, and thus give himself a severe shock in a painful region. But Rufus never went near

79

that bin. He must have realised it was dangerous and it was an unfortunate refuse collector who received a nasty kick from the lethal object.

As Rufus went along his merry way, leaving as his trademark many up-skittled bins and trails of rubbish, Sergeant Blaketon instructed me to check all dog licences. Everytime I saw a dog, I must interview its owner to check the necessary document. It was around this time that the law changed slightly in favour of those farmers who kept dogs purely for working purposes. Hitherto, they had been permitted to keep a number of unlicensed dogs, based on the number of livestock they kept. Each year, these farmers required a certificate of exemption and came to the police for issue of the document. The change meant that any dog used solely for tending sheep or cattle could be kept without a licence and no certificate was necessary. The onus rested upon the farmer to prove that his dogs were for tending sheep or cattle, and even pups might be included under that general heading if they were being 'brought on' by older dogs. Among the people who could (and still can) keep dogs without licences were blind persons who kept guide dogs, persons keeping dogs under six months old, shepherds who kept dogs in the exercise of their calling, and keepers of hound dogs under 12 months of age, not having run with a pack.

I knew it would take weeks to check every dog licence on my beat, so I went into the four village post offices and, casually in the course of our small talk, I told the men and women behind the counters that it was my intention next week to check all dog licences. I knew the outcome – word would spread like wildfire that the bobby was having a purge and there would be a sudden rush of applications. I knew my ruse had worked because in the days which followed, several farmers came for advice about the new rules, and I later discovered the post offices had done a roaring trade in new issues. To satisfy Sergeant Blaketon's desire for correct procedures. I did check a few and recorded them in my notebook. It kept the sergeant happy and also showed the village that I had meant business. This piece of strategy was necessary because there might, in the future, be a reason for letting a similar piece of confidential information loose upon the villagers. A follow-up, however minor, was important in any ruse of this kind.

To accommodate the numbers of stray dogs that roam the nation, many police stations possess what is conveniently known as a dog house. Some rely on local dogs' homes, but official police dog houses come in varying shapes and sizes. Unfortunately, architectural ignorance invariably sites them next door to the cells or beneath the windows of private houses which adjoin police stations. Because the captured strays howl their protests long and loud at all hours of the day and night, this leads to complaints from prisoners who say they cannot sleep and from neighbours who claim a reduction in their rates. Policemen, however, seem impervious to the howling of unhappy dogs and the occasional "shurrup" seems to achieve great things. One of the more important tasks of a police cadet is to take the captive animals for walkies and sometimes these youngsters are advised to 'let the dog escape', and to write up the books as 'dog escaped'.

Unclaimed dogs are destroyed after seven days so this ruse saves the lives of many. The escape procedure, highly unofficial though it is, solves a lot of other problems because stray dogs very often find their own way home, having never been a true stray in the first place, but having been incarcerated through the misplaced kindness of an animal-lover. Someone else might find the 'escaped' dog and be willing to retain it until the true owner turns up, or indeed to retain it for ever. Not many come back a second time, which proves the sense of this procedure. It is somewhat embarrassing, however, when the same person finds the same dog two or three times a day and insists on fetching it back into custody, even though his kindness can lead to the death of a very nice dog.

On one occasion, I was on office duty from 2 pm until 10 pm at Eltering when a minute and elderly gentleman wearing plus fours and brogue shoes entered the police office. He was carrying a tiny Yorkshire terrier and it would be around 2.30 in the afternoon. The dog was one of the miniature variety which shiver all the time, and this one wore a blue ribbon in its hair. It wore a collar but bore no name and address. Its tiny eyes looked around in horror as the gentleman placed it on the counter and said, "I've just found it wandering in Flatts Lane, lost."

"Lost?" I commented. "Are you sure?"

"Aye, dogs like this don't wander alone, they're pets."

"There was no one about, eh?"

"No, Officer. No one. It's criminal, letting dogs like this wander at large. All kinds of harm could be done."

The little man steadfastly refused to take the dog home with him, which meant it had to be lodged in the dog house at Eltering Police Station, pending the arrival of its owner. Like all strays, if it was not claimed within seven days, it would have to be destroyed. In practice, we tried to save good dogs by dropping a word in the ear of the local newspaper reporter in the hope he would print a sob story in his columns. Very often, strays were handed over to people who would love and care for them, and many have acquired beautiful dogs through this system. It saved the Force, and ultimately the ratepayer, the cost of destroying the animals. I could hardly let this one escape – where would it run to?

The dog house at Eltering police office was a huge one. It had been built from plans prepared by the County Architect who probably thought he was designing a buffalo cage for the local zoo. The kennel was well constructed, airy and clean, and could have accommodated something as large as a buffalo. This little Yorkshire terrier was destined to be its first occupant and after I had entered the necessary details and description in the Stray Dogs Register, I carried it through the office and out into the yard where I placed it in the brand new dog house. It stood and shivered in the centre of the huge compound, its beautiful fringed eyes pitifully gazing up at me. I wondered if it slept on a silken bed at home. It yapped despairingly as I left, but once I was back in the office, its high-pitched protestations were beyond my ears.

I made sure we had sufficient food for it; we kept a stock of dog biscuits and were allowed to purchase other forms of dog food if necessary, the cost being recovered from the owner or from the person who decided to accept the dog as a stray, with our compliments. I popped out to see the little creature after about half-an-hour, taking with me a bowl of fresh water and some biscuits. It yapped its thanks, gazing expectantly at the wire netting.

I was surprised that no one had come to claim the little animal; pets like this were seldom lost and if they did go astray, you could guarantee their owners would come rushing around to claim them within a very short time. But not so with this little dog. By tea-time, no one had called or telephoned and I began to grow concerned about its future.

At five o'clock, another problem presented itself. A little girl entered the office towing a donkey behind her. She was about ten years old and had found it wandering down the lane behind her house. Her dad had instructed her to take it to the police station, with orders not to fetch it back. I noted her name and address and suggested she take it home until the owner was traced.

"My dad says you must keep it," she said firmly. "We've nowhere, we only live in a little house."

"Surely your dad knows somebody with a field," I suggested, knowing there was no formal procedure for dealing with found donkeys.

"No, no one. That's why he said to bring it here."

It wasn't a very large donkey, but it was a genuine, living one nonetheless.

"We've no fields here," I said inanely, "and I can't leave the office to take it anywhere."

"I've got to get ready for Brownies," she smiled. "Bye".

And with that, she turned and hurried from the station, leaving the benign ass standing before the counter like a baleful drunk. It looked about its new quarters and began to walk around, trailing the rope which was attached to a hessian halter.

"Oh no!" I shouted at it. "You can't have the freedom of the station, you're coming with me."

Our commodious new dog house was the answer. It was cosy and certainly large enough. The County Architect had some sense after all. Because the donkey might stand on the little dog, I decided to fetch the dog into the office, at least for the time being. And so the animals changed places. The donkey entered the dog house quite happily and sniffed at the clean hay, while the dog pranced and yapped in its new freedom. It followed me back into the office where it continued to yap and bark with delight. Because it was my meal time, I made sure all the doors were closed and allowed it the run of the place while I settled down to eat my sandwiches.

I was the only man on duty, consequently there was no one to relieve me. This meant I had to eat my meal at the counter. I didn't mind – there was nowhere else in the station, other than the cells, and this place was cosy enough. Besides, I now had an interesting little companion. I ate my sandwiches and dropped crumbs for it. Having discovered it liked cheese and chocolate icing, I named it 'Topsie' and we had a long and earnest conversation over our meal. It was an engaging little creature and I grew fond of it.

At six o'clock, a rough looking character pushed open the door and demanded, "Where's my donkey then?"

"Your donkey?"

"Aye, I heard tell it was here."

"There is a donkey here," I confirmed. "What's yours like?"

"Like? It's like any other donkey. Donkeys is all alike."

"You'll have to sign for it," I smiled, pointing to a place in the Found Property Register. "Received, one donkey in good condition."

"Where is it then?"

"In the stable out at the back," I said. I daren't say 'kennel'. "I'll fetch it through. How did it get lost?"

"Just bought it," he said. "For the kids. Some idiot left the gate open and it got out. Been missing since three o'clock, it has. I heard a little girl had fetched it in."

I couldn't bring to mind any offence of suffering a donkey to wander at large in a public place, so I led the man, whose name was Joseph Purvis, through to the dog-house-cum-stable. There he saw his pride and joy. His bland face beamed with open pleasure as he led his beast out of its cell and through the police station.

"Thanks," he said, and I was surprised to see him stuff a pound note into a charity collection box on the counter. He asked for the little girl's name too, and I gave it willingly. She was in for a tip as well. I held open the doors and he took his donkey outside where a small Morris pick-up was waiting. A plank reached the ground from the rear and the donkey climbed this quite happily, and allowed itself to be tethered to a hook on the rear of the cab. The van set off and the donkey seemed to enjoy the ride.

I decided to leave Topsie in the office because she was good company, but Sergeant Blaketon had other ideas. He arrived about seven-thirty to check that everything was in order, and noticed the shivering mass of blue-ribboned hair in the hearth.

"What's that?" he pointed at Topsie.

"Found property," I replied.

"What is it? A muff?"

"A dog, Sergeant," and I told him the story.

"Dogs is for the dog house, Rhea. Dogs must not be kept in offices. There is a Standing Order about that. That's what dog houses is for, Rhea. Dogs. And we've just had an architect-designed dog house built here. So put that animal where it belongs, lad."

"Yes, Sergeant."

Somewhat reluctantly, I carried Topsie outside and lodged her, unprotesting, back in the dog house. She looked very sad, I must admit, and I was sure she was crying as I closed the wire mesh door and turned my back upon her. She whimpered softly as I walked away.

In the office, Sergeant Blaketon was examining all the books and as I entered through the rear door, a tall, rather haughty woman entered through the front. Blaketon saw her and stood upright, revealing the full splendour of his ex-guardsman figure.

"Good evening, madam," he spoke politely.

"Sergeant," she said without smiling "I need help."

"Certainly, madam."

She was clearly a discerning person because she addressed herself to the sergeant, the senior officer present.

"Sergeant, I am the Honourable Mrs Allerston," she announced, "and I live near Scarborough. I have been visiting a sick relative in Leeds and I left my little dog with some nieces here in Eltering. They don't allow dogs in the hospital, you see, and I didn't like leaving her alone in the car. So I left her

with relations. I have just returned to learn they have lost my
dear Susie. My dear, dear little dog. She's a Yorkshire terrier,
Sergeant. They have searched everywhere, everywhere. And
all to no avail," the lady's voice was beginning to crack and I
could see she might lose control. "My dear little dog, so clever
and well behaved. I have searched too, all over the streets and
lanes, and there are such horrid people about. I cannot find
her, Sergeant. I have to ask you – and your, er, gentleman
here, if you could mount a search for her. With police dogs,
maybe? They can follow scents, can't they?"

Blaketon looked at me and, to my surprise, winked
mischievously. "Madam, we shall be only too pleased to
help." He drew a pad of paper towards him and adopted a
very serious attitude. "Now, perhaps you can describe your
dog?"

"She's very small," began the Honourable Mrs Allerston,
"and she has a long, dark coat with silky ears. She is five years
old and has a blue ribbon tied in her hair, in a bow."

"Ah!" he beamed with benevolence. "Then I believe we
can help you. We have a similar dog in our dog house at this
very moment."

"Dog house?" she exclaimed. "My Susie in a dog house
with all those other strays?"

"Madam," he drew himself to his full and impressive
height. "This is no ordinary dog house. It is architect-
designed, and it is brand new. It was installed only last week,
and it is full of lovely fresh hay. If this dog is your Susie – as I
believe it is – then she is the very first occupant."

That was perfectly true. She had been the *first* occupant,
and the donkey had been the second. But I hadn't got around
to telling him of the donkey, and he had not reached the
Found Property Register during his routine inspection.

"That is all right then," she nodded towards me. "I
presume this, er, dog house is well disinfected after each
occupant? And I assume my Susie has been well fed and
cared for during her stay with you."

"Madam," O.B. drew himself to his full height again. "We
take great pride in the way we care for animals placed in our
custody. That dog house is pine scented, and I will personally
ensure that it is cleaned and disinfected to avoid diseases. But

as your Susie is our very first guest, there is no problem. She entered a virgin dog house."

"My Susie is very delicate you see, and she must not be exposed to doggie diseases."

"Madam," he boomed. "I am sure your Susie has enjoyed her stay with us."

"And you fed her? You didn't answer that."

"Police Constable Rhea fed her, Mrs Allerston. He gave her only the best of food that we possess and he tells me she ate like a horse. Isn't that true, P.C. Rhea?"

"Perfectly, Sergeant," I entered the spirit of the moment. "She ate like a horse."

"That is most unlike my Susie. She has a very small appetite and is very particular about her food."

"It must have been all the exercise and fresh air she's had today," he continued. "Now, madam, if you would sign for her and pay the cost of her upkeep, she will be returned to you in good condition. The cost will be five shillings. P.C. Rhea will be making out the receipt as I escort you to our dog house."

She paid and I wrote out the necessary receipt. I did not go out with them, and he told me later what had happened.

He had led the superior woman to the impressive new dog house whereupon Susie had leapt and barked with happiness at the sight of her mistress. O.B. had unlocked the door and the Honourable Mrs Allerston had entered the structure to collect her prize. And then she had screamed in horror.

"Susie!" she had cried. "What have you been eating?"

The dog had yapped happily at the sound of her voice, and as the Honourable Mrs Allerston had emerged, ashen-faced, Blaketon had looked in.

The other occupant had done a whoopsie right in the centre of the floor, and the pile of donkey manure dwarfed the tiny dog. The Honourable Mrs Allerston did not wait for an explanation, but rushed from the station gently stroking her dog and talking to it in a very soothing manner.

"You poor, poor darling," she was cooing. "What did they give you to eat then? Was it awful? It must have been painful too."

Sergeant Blaketon saw the funny side of this tale and

brushed aside my apologies for not informing him of the
donkey's stay in our showpiece. I recalled his words that Susie
had eaten like a horse and I often wonder what that lady
thought we had done to her little Susie.

* * * *

Superintendent Arnold, the Divisional Commander at
Strensford, kept a nondescript dog, a true Heinz-57 variety
type mongrel whose predominant colour was black. It was
hairy and had one lop ear, but in spite of its uncertain
background, it was a happy little dog upon which was bestowed much love and affection, especially by Mrs Arnold.

Jimbo, the dog in question, loved to accompany its master
upon his many supervisory perambulations and in its undying attempts to achieve this happiness, it would frequently
dash from the house in defiance of the Arnolds. Jimbo seemed
to know when the Superintendent was about to take a duty
stroll about town; he also knew his master did not like his
presence during those spells of police work. Jimbo would
therefore rush out of the house and lurk in dark corners,
waiting for his master to emerge, and once the Superintendent had left the house *en route* to the office, Jimbo would
secretly follow him at a safe distance. He would reveal himself
only when it was too late to return him to the house and
would then follow the Superintendent around the town,
steadfastly refusing to return home. This caused intense embarrassment to Superintendent Arnold but it delighted the
townsfolk, specially when the Superintendent tried to pretend
the dog was not with him. The public considered that a full
uniformed police superintendent faithfully attended by a
disobedient and scruffy mongrel was something of a prize
sight.

I was drafted into Strensford for a period of night duty
when the town was suffering from one of its regular and acute
shortages of men. Because I was not too familiar with the
town and its maze of alleys and back streets, I was allocated
office duty for the duration of my night shift. It was an old
police station of decidedly Victorian origin, and the office in
question was an elongated room with a wooden partition
running its length at one side.

The partition created a corridor for the public, and they told their tales of woe through a little window which had been built into it. On the inside of the window a counter ran the length of the partition. It had a sloping top formed by lots of desk lids. The space beneath the high counter was enough to accommodate the lofty stools and long legs of the policemen who sat there to minister to the public and to listen to their tales of human misery. The desks accommodated their paper work.

At the left-hand end of the wooden corridor was the entrance to Superintendent Arnold's office. Whenever he was supervising the night shift, he would stalk majestically along the corridor, poke his head around the end of the wooden partition and ask, "Anything doing?"

I was perched on one of those tall stools at eleven o'clock that night when I heard the unmistakable footsteps of an approaching policeman. He was heading towards the office. I waited and saw a figure pass the hatch and then the solemn features of Superintendent Arnold peered around the end of the partition and asked, "Anything doing?"

"No, sir, all quiet," I gave the traditional response, but he didn't withdraw his head. His eyes were glued upon something beneath the counter, something just beyond me. I looked down. There, lying blissfully asleep in the corner, almost out of sight, was a little black dog.

"That bloody dog!" he snapped. "It's followed me down again!"

At that time, I did not know of his perpetual battle with his dog, and merely said, "Really, sir?"

"You're not one of the regular constables, are you?"

"No, sir. I'm P.C. Rhea from Aidensfield, helping out."

"Ah, well, that dog is a bloody nuisance, Rhea. It persists in following me around the town, and dodges out of the house when it knows I'm on the way down here. It will follow me all around the town now, most embarrassing. It must be taught a lesson, once and for all. It must be taught that it must not follow me out of the house and it must not follow me around the streets."

And with that, he strode into the office, sailed right past me and seized the dog's collar. He hauled it towards his office.

The little dog, awake by this time and somewhat bewildered by this sudden turn of events, planted its feet firmly upon the wooden floor and refused to move. But Superintendent Arnold was a strong man. Gritting his teeth, he tugged and pulled the stubborn animal towards his office and eventually reached the door. He dragged the whimpering dog inside and slammed the door behind them. The dog was then subjected to what we might call the 'carpet treatment' – in other words, it was given a severe telling off.

But its treatment did not end there. There followed the distinctive sounds of someone beating the dog. The Superintendent's voice was admonishing it very loudly and very clearly, and his words were accompanied by the unmistakable sounds of a severe thrashing. The dog was howling loudly and this continued for what seemed an age, but in reality it was only a few minutes.

Finally, the door of Superintendent Arnold's office burst open and the pathetic figure of the little dog was hurled through the air to land near my feet. It wore a highly surprised look upon its tatty face, and its long black hair was considerably ruffled.

The Superintendent also looked ruffled.

"That isn't my dog, P.C. Rhea," he said, blushing furiously as he shrank back into his office.

It wasn't. This one belonged to a local sergeant. Arnold's own dog was still at home, sleeping soundly.

*   *   *   *

Claude Jeremiah Greengrass was always in trouble with the police. He had a formidable list of petty convictions, most of them acquired through blissful ignorance and carelessness, rather than by evil intentions. He was not a criminal in the strict sense of the word. He was just a bloody nuisance.

A small, pinched sort of man, he looked like an elf or an ex-jockey, and lived alone at Elsinby. He was brown-skinned due to a life in the open air, and earned his living in what I considered a dubious manner. He had no job, and performed small services for anyone who would pay. He gardened, washed cars, painted and decorated and cleaned out stables.

Everyone liked him, but no one trusted him. He was certainly light-fingered as his convictions testified.

Claude Jeremiah had a lurcher called Alfred. He had acquired this poacher's friend from a pal who had gone to live in the city. Claude Jeremiah had really done it as a favour, but nonetheless, took his duties and responsibilities very seriously. He set about training Alfred to the standard required of a domestic dog. He wanted him to stay, sit, heel and lie instantly at his word of command.

To accomplish this part of Alfred's training, he took him for long walks in quiet places where man and dog could become deeply acquainted with one another without the minor distractions of everyday life.

In Maddleskirk Wood, there is a small lake. A footpath runs around its shores and a number of cottages overlook the path. For Claude Jeremiah and Alfred, the place offered untold possibilities. It offered more for Alfred than it did for his master, for the area was full of scents, sounds and interesting creatures. It was while walking along that path that the trouble began.

Claude Jeremiah told me how Alfred had started to crawl through a hole in the hedge and how he refused to return in spite of his master's shouted commands. By the time Claude Jeremiah had reached the point, Alfred had gone through the hedge and there were the sounds of alarmed twittering from behind the shrubbery. The twittering burst into panic-stricken cries accompanied by the urgent flapping of many wings.

Claude Jeremiah had located a garden gate and had rushed through to find Alfred inside an aviary, thoroughly enjoying himself as he chased hundreds of budgerigars. The budgies weren't very happy about it, however, because Alfred ran, barked and jumped among them, causing them to crash against the wire netting in pathetic attempts to escape the excited dog.

One fell to the ground and Alfred seized it in his mouth, gripping it tightly and viciously shaking the poor creature just as the irate owner rushed from his house. Claude Jeremiah was, in the meantime, seeking an entrance to the enclosed area but found none, and suddenly found himself staring into

the florid and angry face of a large, powerful budgie breeder.
He had begun to apologise, but the man had said, "He's
killed one and look at all the others! Battered, bruised and
terrified out of their minds! All my years of work . . . " and the
upset breeder was fitting a key into the lock of the door of his
aviary as Claude Jeremiah shouted, "Sit, heel, lie down," all
to no avail.

Once inside the cage, he cornered Alfred and after removing the dead budgie from his mouth, began to beat the
wilful dog.

"I'll pay," he had said.

"You will that!" the angry fellow had shouted, looking
around at the discarded feathers which still floated in the air.
"Get yourself and that bloody animal out of here before it
does any more harm. It'll take ages for them to settle down.
And give me that dead one."

"He got in through a hole in the hedge," Claude Jeremiah
had bleated, pointing to the hole in the netting.

"Your bloody dog made it bigger, didn't it?" the man had
yelled. "Anyroad, my missus has called the police. They'll be
here soon. You'll go to court over this, mister, you can tell
your excuses to the police."

It was shortly afterwards that I entered the drama. I
examined the scene and paid close attention to the hole used
by Alfred. The aviary wall was in direct contact with the
hedge; Alfred must have nosed his way through the hedge
and forced his bulk through a hole in the netting, to find
himself in the middle of the unsuspecting flock. And then
he'd made the most of it. There's no doubt he enjoyed those
minutes of action.

I took possession of the dead budgerigar for evidence of the
crime and informed Claude Jeremiah that he would be
reported for summons. His offence was allowing a dog to
worry livestock on agricultural land.

When he appeared before the court, he pleaded not guilty.
Claude Jeremiah always pleaded not guilty, no matter how
the evidence was stacked against him.

The bench, chaired by Alderman Fazakerly, and comprising Mrs Pinkerton and Mr Smithers, listened as Sergeant
Blaketon outlined the alleged facts and presented the case for

the prosecution. The budgie breeder was first to give evidence and related how he'd found Alfred chasing his flock. He'd witnessed the death of one of his birds and had been present when the defendant admitted ownership of the lurcher in question. He valued the dead budgie at £2 0s. 0d.

I was next and told the court that, acting upon information received, I had visited Pond Cottage and had been shown the dead body of a budgerigar. It was within a wire-enclosed aviary, the floor of which was covered with feathers. Upon making an inspection of the walls, I had located a hole which led through the garden hedge and onto the footpath beyond.

I told their Worships how I had interviewed the defendant who admitted ownership of the dog. Upon being told he'd be reported for allowing his dog to worry livestock, the defendant had replied, "Livestock? A budgie isn't livestock – you can't get me for that one, P.C. Rhea." This response was duly noted by the magistrates.

Greengrass went into the witness box, took the oath and gave his version of the incident. He maintained the breeder should have known about the hole – there must have been a small one at least, and he accepted that Alfred had probably enlarged it. But, as he told the court, he felt the term *livestock* did not include budgerigars. The law was to prevent dogs chasing cows, sheep and other domestic animals.

When Greengrass stepped from the witness box, the Chairman sought the advice of his clerk, Mr Whimp.

"Is the fellow right, Mr Whimp?"

Whimp, as efficient as ever, had the necessary information to hand.

"The term is defined in the Dogs (Protection of Livestock) Act 1953, Your Worships. It means cattle, sheep, goats, swine, horses and poultry. Poultry is further defined as meaning domestic fowls, turkeys, geese and ducks."

"There is no mention of budgerigars?" asked the Chairman.

"None, sir."

"Could we include them within the term *domestic fowl*?" he asked.

"That is a matter for the court to decide," Mr Whimp smiled graciously at the assembled members of the bench.

"Damn it all, man," I heard the Chairman whisper. "There must be some guidance on this. What about domestic pigeons? Hasn't anyone had his pigeons worried by dogs? Or penguins at a zoo?"

"I recall one case, Your Worships, where hand-reared pheasants were regarded as livestock, but only during their captivity. There was another instance where doves were held to be *domestic fowls*."

"Doves, eh?"

"Those cases were not reported, sir. The decision is yours, I'm afraid."

"Hrrumph. I suppose we are all right about the *agricultural land* bit?"

"That term includes allotments, orchards, arable, meadow or grazing land, sir."

"But not aviaries?"

"They are not specifically mentioned, Your Worships, although they may be part of a meadow, orchard or allotment, of course."

"Thank you, Mr Whimp."

In a judicial huddle, the magistrates concluded that the case was unsatisfactory from two standpoints. Alderman Fazakerly addressed the court and the accused.

"Claude Jeremiah Greengrass. The court has very carefully considered this case and feels that budgerigars are not livestock within the meaning of the Dogs (Protection of Livestock) Act. Furthermore, there is some doubt as to whether an aviary can be classified as agricultural land. The case is therefore dismissed. You are free to leave the court."

The breeder jumped to his feet. "What about my compensation?"

"That is no longer a matter for this court," Alderman Fazakerly spoke with an air of finality.

After the hearing, Sergeant Blaketon said to me, "We slipped up, Rhea. We should have taken him for failing to keep a dangerous dog under control, and sought a court order upon him to keep the lurcher under control. That can include anything done by dogs. I thought we were taking a risk with a worrying charge."

"He'll come again, Sergeant," I smiled with confidence.

"Besides, he's really done that breeder a good turn. All his budgies could have escaped through that hole, once they'd found it. As things are, he's only lost one."

"And will you tell him that?" smiled Blaketon.

* * * *

Of the dogs which wandered around Aidensfield, the one which caused the most upset was an Alsatian called Emperor. It belonged to a gentleman called Hubert Fishburn who lived in a new bungalow and who was an "off com'd 'un", i.e. a newcomer to the community. Fishburn worked in York and from what I gathered during casual chats, he was something to do with insurance and worked in a managerial capacity. The tiny patch of land surrounding his miniature home was barely sufficient to keep a hamster, let alone a large Alsatian, so his agile and intelligent pet would take every opportunity to go for walks without waiting for his master.

I had spoken to Fishburn many times about Emperor and he was always most apologetic, usually blaming his wife and two small sons for the freedom enjoyed by the dog. In point of fact, it was not a great nuisance to the community of Aidensfield, but only to one poor old man. Unlike the musician's dog which loved dustbins, this one had only one passion, and that was the garden of a dear old character called Stumpy Sykes.

Stumpy had not worked for years because of leg trouble and coped admirably with his artificial leg. He spent his time in his garden which was superb by anyone's standard, and he earned a living of sorts by doing all kinds of odd jobs around Aidensfield. If anyone wanted a washer on a tap, a plug fitting to a kettle, a plot of land digging, a car washed or a kitchen painted, then Stumpy was their man. He was tall and lithe with thin black hair and a figure as slender as a child's. His teeth were brown with nicotine, but his eyes were piercing blue, sharp and alert. He was not married and, to my knowledge, never had been but lived in a delightful cottage which sparkled like new. It was a showpiece and was located in the older part of Aidensfield, being frequently photographed by visitors.

His garden was his pride and joy and in addition to

growing prize chrysanthemums and dahlias, he grew vegetables which he sold and flowers which he would fashion into
wreaths and posies.

Another of his talents was his ability to cure animals. In
this, he had a wide reputation and his secret was a large
brown pill, about the size of a walnut. He would shove that
thing down the throat of any sick dog, horse, pig, goat or
sheep and it always seemed to work. What it contained was a
mystery to me, but it never failed. He also cured smaller
creatures like cats, mice and hamsters, and even cage birds. In
short, Stumpy was a fascinating village character and a
stalwart of Aidensfield.

It was very unfortunate that Fishburn's Alsatian selected
Stumpy's garden for its daily visit. It would jump across the
wall and wander around Stumpy's plants, knocking them
down and destroying many in its tour of the garden, and then
it would leave its trademark in what was often a very obvious
place, like the centre of his beautiful lawn. After many
unsuccessful pleadings with Fishburn, Stumpy asked me to
talk to him.

I did, but it wasn't any good. Try as we might, that
Alsatian returned time and time again, and always to the
same place with the same smelly result. It can be argued that
it is no duty of a police officer to stop dogs fouling rose
gardens, but in a village the local constable must do all in his
power to keep the peace. I could see that this had all the
makings of a future breach of the peace. But the dog beat me.
Poor Stumpy grew desperate. The show season was practically at its height and although he loved animals, he began
to hate this one. But good will always triumph over evil, and
Stumpy did achieve his heart's desire. He stopped the dog
from entering his garden and he told me about it long after
the incident was over.

He knew the offending Alsatian came into his garden late
in the evenings, and as the early autumn began to draw its
cloak of darkness about the dale, the furtive visitations of the
dog were shrouded in gloom. Stumpy could sit at his bedroom
window and watch its arrival. He did this one night while
armed with a loaded shotgun. His love of animals compelled
him not to load the gun with a conventional cartridge.

Instead, he loaded this weapon with a sand cartridge. It was full of sand instead of lead shot, and they are not difficult to make from ordinary cartridges.

The big dog had duly arrived to carry out its intended purpose and from his vantage point above his garden, Stumpy took aim. With a tremendous bang, and at very close range, the gun was discharged and a wave of fast-moving sand hit the dog. It ripped every shred of fur from its hind quarters, leaving the front half of Emperor covered with normal hair but the rear was totally bare, like a plucked chicken. The dog howled in pain and surprise as it galloped home, its nudity embarrassing to behold.

Hubert Fishburn's surprise was total. He had no idea what had happened to his dog and he did not come to me. However he did go to see Stumpy, but only because Stumpy was the acknowledged expert on all animals and their ailments. Fishburn had no idea that Stumpy had caused Emperor's acute embarrassment. Stumpy had examined the dog.

"I reckon it sat in some lime," said Stumpy, seriously. "Up in them fields, you know, where they're liming t'land. Funny stuff is lime, it burns flesh and fur. I reckon your dog's done that, rolled in it, mebbe."

"Will it grow again?" asked Hubert.

"It might, with the right treatment," Stumpy advised him.

"You can treat it, can you?" There was a pleading tone in the man's voice.

"Aye, I reckon I can, but it'll cost you," said Stumpy, eyeing the anxious man.

"How much?"

"Depends," said Stumpy.

"On what?"

"On how long we've got to continue the treatment."

"But how much? I mean, do I pay per visit, or for the stuff you use, or what?"

"Each visit, two pounds inclusive should do it. I reckon ten or twelve visits will see him all right."

"Starting tonight?"

"Aye, if you like, fetch him up to our house."

It seems that Fishburn had a terrible job coaxing the dog

through Stumpy's garden gate and into the shed at the rear, but as the owner held the dog by its head, Stumpy began to smooth a thick, greasy ointment across the barren areas. It took him about a quarter of an hour, and he accepted the two pounds, saying, "Come back next week, same time."

I had seen Hubert once or twice, coaxing the unwilling dog into Stumpy's shed, and was told part of the story at the time. I knew better than ask Stumpy at that stage, but the weekly visits continued and the hair began to grow.

Finally, Stumpy said, "There we are, Mr Fishburn. I reckon that'll do now. The new hair's coming along fine, and that dog'll be back to normal very soon. That growth has a few weeks to go yet before it's fully grown, but it'll come along nicely now. There's no bald patches. You don't need me any more. It'll grow thick and fine in its own good time."

"I don't know how to thank you, Mr Sykes, really I don't. That lime must have been strong stuff."

"You never see cows sitting in it," smiled Stumpy. "I should keep your dog away from it in future."

"Oh, I will. He doesn't seem very keen on going out alone."

"Doesn't he now? I reckon he's learned his lesson, eh?"

"I think so. Well, thank you for all you've done. I really am most grateful. I'm amazed that you knew what it was and how to treat it."

"A lifetime of experience, Mr Fishburn," said Stumpy, accepting the final two pounds. "A lifetime in the countryside and a close knowledge of all animals."

And so Hubert Fishburn went off very happily. One evening, I popped in for a chat with Stumpy and he told me this tale, laughing until the tears ran down his cheeks.

"Has it ever been back to your garden, Stumpy?" I asked, laughing with him.

"Never, Mr Rhea. It never comes near the place now."

"That stuff you used to make the hair grow – what was it?" I put to him.

"It would have grown without it, Mr Rhea, but I thought I'd make him pay for all the damage his dog has done to my flowers. I got over £20 out of him for my cure. That makes us just about square."

"All right," I persisted. "But what was the stuff you rubbed on that dog?"

"Well, Mr Rhea," he said cautiously, "You won't tell him, will you?"

"I promise," I wondered what was coming next.

"Well, you see, my sister came to stay with me a few years back, and she left a jar of that stuff that women plaster over their faces. Cold cream, I think they call it. I used that on his dog."

Six

If Sergeant Blaketon was tall, severe and somewhat humour-less, my other sergeant, Charlie Bairstow, was round and happy with a bubbling sense of humour. He was an older man and had been a policeman all his working life. His pleasant nature led him to adopt a very philosophical outlook on life. It was his belief that no one should be arrested unless there was absolutely no other way of dealing with him. Although he was a very good practical policeman and a first-class sergeant, he liked the easy life. His pink face wore a perpetual smile and his hair always seemed to have endured a very stiff breeze. Jolly was a word which would describe him.

He was on duty one Sunday morning when I had to perform a four-hour stint at Ashfordly. I had motor-cycled in from Aidensfield and was working in the tiny office when I heard his voice. It called from the Sergeants' Office.

"This one's for you," he shouted from his sanctum.

I looked out of the office window to see a tall, smart woman approaching. She walked stiffly along the footpath towards the front door and as she came into the building, Sergeant Bairstow vanished with remarkable agility through the back entrance and hurried into the garden. I wondered why.

But the woman was standing before me at the far side of the counter and smiling sweetly into my face. She had a very 'peaches and cream' complexion, nice brown eyes, smart grey hair and horn-rimmed glasses. She stood very erectly before me, wearing a hat of deep cherry-red with matching shoes and handbag. Her coat was obviously expensive and I got the impression she was wealthy and influential. She might even be a magistrate and would be about sixty years old.

"Good morning, madam," I greeted her.

"Good morning," she spoke very pleasantly with a refined accent. "You're new, aren't you?"

"Yes, madam. P.C. Rhea, stationed at Aidensfield."

"Ah, well," she began earnestly. "It's about that man who's been pestering me. I've been here before, you know, he's a real menace. I've got to keep coming here to ask for your help. Jackson is his name."

I pulled a scrap pad towards me and began to make notes.

"Jackson, eh?"

"Yes, he's been at it again, Officer. Annoying me. He's always annoying me, you see."

"Could I have your name and address please?" it was always wise to begin at the beginning.

"Miss Fraser. Josephine Fraser. I live at 43, Prince Terrace. I'm a retired office worker, young man. Now, can you please do something about Jackson?"

"What's he done, Miss Fraser?"

"Done? He's sprinkled blue washing-up power all over my staircase. And it's not the first time. He must be stopped. He goes on and on, doing things like that all the time. It gets everywhere – I paddle it into my carpet . . ."

"How did he get into your house?" I asked, wondering whether he'd broken in. Had I a housebreaker on my hands? An arrest, maybe?

"I don't know. I just don't know," and an anguished look appeared on her calm face. "But he gets in all the same. I can't keep him out."

"Where does he live?" was my next question.

"Next door to me, Number forty-one," she said. "What an awful neighbour."

"It is not our policy to become involved in domestic issues," I tried to explain. "Have you seen a solicitor about him? If you arranged for a solicitor's letter to be sent, asking him to cease his activities, you'd surely find he would stop."

"Stop? He would not, young man. I've tried everything, I can tell you. Everything," and her voice began to rise in volume and pitch. "I'm about at my wits' end, you know. Everything that is possible has been done and he still keeps pestering me. All I want is for you to have a sharp word with him, and I know he'll stop, at least for a while."

Charlie Bairstow had not returned from his urgent mission, so I asked to be excused for a second and went to seek him. I wanted to ask if we, as the local police, got ourselves involved in Miss Fraser's troubles which appeared to be nothing more than a very localised domestic dispute. But he'd vanished completely.

"I'll pop around later this morning and warn him off, Miss Fraser."

"I would be most grateful," and with that she turned on her smartly dressed heels and left the station.

Half an hour later, still with no sign of Bairstow, I locked the office and walked round to Prince Terrace. I found No. 43. It was smart and clean with a bow window, a glass-fronted door and neat curtains. It was evident that Miss Fraser was a decent-living woman. Next door, however, was not quite the same. No. 41 was almost derelict. I walked up the path, knocked on the rotting door of No. 41 and it slid open beneath the touch of my hand.

"Anyone in?" I shouted inside.

No reply. I knocked again and entered, loudly proclaiming my presence and asking if anyone was at home. The place was deserted; there was no furniture and it was riddled with dampness and rot. I wondered if the villainous Jackson was a tramp, sleeping rough in this place.

I made a detailed search of the house. Apart from a stray cat, it was empty and there were no indications of recent human habitation. When tramps live in a house, there is always something to reveal their presence, like dirty cups, rotting food, cigarette ends, the foul smell of unclean humanity and so forth. But this place bore none of those signs. I left and decided to acquaint Miss Fraser with my action. It seemed that Jackson had left his address, possibly due to her threatened police action. I knocked on her door and it was opened almost immediately.

"Ah!" she beamed. "You're just in time for coffee. Would you like some, Officer?"

"I'd love one," I said and followed her inside. She kept a beautiful home, furnished with genuine antiques and interesting paintings. The carpets were thick and lush, the furniture of good quality and the decor of a very professional standard.

Everything in the house showed taste and discrimination. She led me into her beautiful lounge which overlooked the street where I noticed a tray already set with coffee and waiting on a low table. It bore a silver coffee-set, with delicate china cups. Two cups. And the coffee pot was steaming appetisingly.

Over coffee, she told me more about her running battle with Jackson. She agreed that today's visit to the police had terrified him, and he'd fled. That was her explanation of the empty house and I accepted it. But that was not all. Now she'd got a captive audience, she insisted on letting me know about his other activities. It seemed he would enter her house when she was out and move things around. He'd change the position of her ornaments, or tilt the pictures. He'd enter the bedroom too, and interfere with her clothing, hiding things so she couldn't find them. And, horror of horrors, he examined her underwear in the drawers and cupboards; she knew, because they'd been moved. He played drums at night and had sent swarms of invisible insects into her kitchen, where they'd contaminated the food. And then he sent rays through the walls, invisible rays which kept her awake at night and gave her bad dreams.

And as I sipped her delicious coffee from exquisite china cups, I realised she was crackers. She was clean, presentable, charming and well-spoken, but she was nuts. Judging by the house, she was comfortably off and money was not a problem. On the face of things, she was everything a favourite aunt might be. But she was as nutty as the proverbial fruit cake. I couldn't say whether she was batty enough to be certified, but she was certainly very odd.

It took me a long time to escape. She talked on and on about Jackson, regaling me with horrific tales about his interference with her life and his domination of her daily routine. When I began to ask specific questions, however, it transpired she had never seen him. She could give me no description at all. I wondered if he was a meths drinker or just a character who passed in the night. An hour and a half later, when eventually I managed to leave, I found Sergeant Bairstow back in his office. He smiled graciously as I entered.

"Well, Nicholas, did you kick Jackson out of that house?"

"Jackson!" I cried. "Who is that man? Why does he cause her so much trouble? I think she's imagining most of it."

"All of it," he said. "She imagines all of it. There is no Jackson; it's all in her mind. She's lonely, she likes male company and she's never had a feller. She's a frustrated virgin, Nick, and that's why she's like that. That's how they grow up when they're frustrated. She needs a bloody good man to sort her out, if you understand what I mean. Today, she's had a charming young man in for coffee and that will keep her going for a week or two. She'll go to bed with you, in her mind's eye that is, but she'll be back to see us, mark my words."

"You set me up for that one, didn't you?" I laughed.

"We always let the new lads deal with Miss Fraser, Nick, she loves them, you see. It gives her deep satisfaction – that's what we are here for, isn't it? To satisfy the public."

I gave a lot of thought to poor old Miss Fraser just in case I was on duty next time she called. As things worked out, I was on duty again at Ashfordly when she came to the station. It was about a month later.

"He's been at it again, Officer," she told me seriously. "Blue powder again."

"Not all over your stair carpet?" I cried.

"No, in the frying pan this time. All over my cooking utensils."

"I'll be around shortly to have words with him," I promised.

An hour later, I knocked on her door and she invited me in for coffee as before. I accepted because she was entertaining and the coffee was excellent. This time there were biscuits.

I told her I had dealt with Jackson once and for all. I told her he would never trouble her again, ever.

"What have you done with him?" she asked, her eyes wide with anticipation.

"I've arranged for a deportation order," I said seriously. "Jackson is to be deported to Australia. The order becomes effective at noon next Friday, when he will be transported to Australia. He sails from Southampton."

She did not speak for a long time. Then she smiled. "Thank you," she said. "Thank you very much."

"He'll never trouble you again," I assured her. I had no trouble leaving after imparting this news. She seemed numbed and I left her, having gained the impression that she was sad. Nothing happened for several weeks after that visit, and we saw nothing of her. Then an inspector from Eltering called me into his office.

"What the hell have you been up to, Rhea?" and he waved a letter at me.

"I've got this letter from the Home Office," he glared at me. "It concerns a complaint they've received from a Miss Fraser of Ashfordly and it has come to me via the Chief Constable. There's hell on in high places, Rhea."

I blushed deeply. I wasn't aware that I had done anything to justify a complaint, particularly one which involved the Home Office. I knew that the Home Secretary was responsible for all law and order in the country, so had I broken some golden rule?

"I didn't do anything wrong, sir," I said, not knowing the basis of her complaint.

"Do you know the rules about emigrating to Australia?" he asked. "They don't accept convicted criminals – if you have convictions for crime, you cannot begin a new life in Australia. They don't want convicts, not any more."

"I heard of something like that, sir. Isn't it connected with the ten-pound passage scheme?"

"Yes," he acknowledged, his face breaking into a smile. "It seems that you have arranged the deportation to Australia of a very dangerous criminal called Jackson. Miss Fraser is demanding an enquiry into the matter – she wants the Home Office to investigate the system which allows a notorious villain like Jackson to dodge the rules. How did he get through Customs? How did he evade the Special Branch? Why has Australia accepted him? The Home Office has asked the Chief Constable for a full report."

"It was like this, sir . . ." I stuttered.

"I don't want to know, lad! Just write the report, will you? I'm sure the Home Secretary will be very amused to know how you dealt with a man who puts blue powder into frying pans and who conjures up swarms of invisible insects from the air. But I think you had better arrange for the return of this man, Jackson, before we have a diplomatic incident."

"Yes, sir."

"You haven't got rid of him, have you, Rhea? You'll have to come up with another idea, won't you?"

"Yes, sir," and I crept away to write my report.

* * * *

A few months later, I was subjected to another of Sergeant Bairstow's orders. Technically, the mission was no part of my duty; it was an extension of my role as village constable, but he considered it important enough to justify particular action on my part.

I received his phone call just after lunch one Friday when he updated me with the daily messages. Having concluded that essential part of the conversation, he said, almost in passing, "Oh, Nicholas, there's a little job for you. It's just off your beat, in Maddleskirk, but as you're out and about this afternoon, I thought you might do it."

"Willingly, Sergeant," I agreed, having forgotten about his disappearing trick when Miss Fraser called.

"It's a Mrs Dulcimer and she lives at Acorn House. Audrey Dulcimer."

"I've got that, Sergeant," I wrote down her name and address.

"She's had another of her confrontations with a policeman in York, and she must produce her driving licence and insurance certificate. It's a regular occurrence with her – she's always getting booked for parking or for obstruction in York, and she dislikes coming all the way into the office, merely to produce her documents. It means a special journey, so she gives me a ring and I ask someone to call around. It's not a special journey for you because you're out and about anyway. So pop in, lad, it's a courtesy job. I realise it's her responsibility to fetch in her papers, but we do try to oblige where possible, eh?"

"Yes, Sergeant."

"Good. Glad to know you'll co-operate. Be kind to her, she's a barrister's wife. Nice woman, good house. And I'm sure she'll give you a cup of tea as well."

"It'll be a pleasure, Sergeant."

"I know it will. Do you know the house?"

"No, but I'll find it."

"It's a big place just off the main street, there's white gates."

"I'll find it," I assured him.

"I said one of our men would be there about three-thirty? Does that fit in with your plans, Nicholas?"

"Fine," I said.

Having dealt with my paperwork, I mounted the trusty Francis Barnett and began my afternoon patrol. With just over an hour to use before my appointment with Mrs Dulcimer, I visited one or two farms to check their stock registers and popped into some local stores to warn against a confidence trickster who preyed on rural shopkeepers. His trick was to ask for cash in advance, on the pretext that he could supply goods at huge discounts. He'd conned a local off-licence into parting with £50 for cut-price whisky and had done a similar trick on an electrical goods shop, taking £40 on the understanding he'd deliver cut-price radio sets. We knew the goods would never arrive and were surprised at businessmen parting so readily with their money to people they didn't know. It seemed that the opportunity to obtain something for nothing could be relied upon to make a man and his money easily part company. The possibility of gaining summat for nowt never fails to achieve results.

At twenty past three, I drove into Maddleskirk, a long sprawling village with rows of tiny houses, all built of mellow yellow stone with red pantile roofs. I drove slowly, seeking the double white gates of Acorn House and found them next to the church. I drove up the drive which twisted through rhododendron bushes and parked my machine on its stand outside the front door.

It was an impressive house, built in the style of the 1930s with attic windows and a double garage tucked behind the living quarters. The woodwork was pure white and the garden was a picture. The place bore an air of extreme efficiency, and had a colour supplement aura about it. I removed my crash helmet, rang the door bell and waited.

Soon I heard soft footsteps on the inside and the door

opened to reveal a very slender woman with greying hair and
a ready smile. Her face was lightly made up, showing off her
grey eyes, good teeth and fine skin. She was tall by feminine
standards, probably around 5 feet 9 inches, and wore high-
heeled shoes, a white pleated skirt and a light summery
blouse, open at the neck. I couldn't estimate her age with any
accuracy, but I'd say she was in her middle forties.

"Mrs Dulcimer?"

"Yes, do come in," she oozed. "I'm awfully sorry to drag
you all this way, Officer, but your sergeant is so good, isn't he?
He knows it means a special journey . . . "

"I was in the area," I lied easily. "It's of no consequence."

"I'm so pleased you could come. I always seem to get
myself into trouble when I visit York. It's a driver's night-
mare, isn't it? But do come in. You'll have a cup of tea?"

"Thank you," and I stepped inside. She suggested I hang
the motor-cycling helmet on the hallstand, but I wore no
other protective or waterproof gear because it was a fine
summer day. I followed her into the lounge, allowed myself to
be settled on her settee and flicked through a copy of *She*
while she wafted into the kitchen to prepare the tea. I heard
the kettle sing immediately; she had obviously been prepared.
Moments later she returned bearing a tray and teapot, with
cups, milk and sugar.

She settled at my side. I could smell the perfume as she
leaned forward to pour two full cups, asking if I wanted
sugar. I shook my head and accepted the cup from her. She
chattered away very amiably and told of her motoring frus-
trations in York, the delights of living in the country, the
benefits of this particular house and about her family. She
had two sons, grown up and now at university. She prattled
on about her boys, both studying law and destined to follow
in father's legal footsteps. Mr Dulcimer, I learned, was a busy
and successful barrister whose skills took him all over
England, a task which meant he was often away from home. I
enjoyed her tales; she was highly attractive and easy to
converse with.

As our talk progressed, she confided in me, saying she had
no money troubles and occupied herself with charity work,
church duties and other essential village affairs. She did this

to while away the time when her husband was absent, and to fill her lonely day-time hours. Having finished the tea, she went to a desk in the corner of the room and returned with a buff envelope.

"Insurance and driving licence," she handed me the envelope. "You'll find they are in order."

I examined them and wrote their data in my book. This was necessary because I had to transmit the details to the police officer who had stopped her in York. He would write to Ashfordly Police Station to request the information. I noted the number of the insurance certificate, its dates of validity, the registered number of her car, the conditions under which it was issued and the name of the issuing company. Similarly, I wrote down the details of her driving licence, noting that it was signed and that it was current.

"Fine," I said, pushing the documents back into the envelope. "All in order."

"With my husband being so involved with the law, I can't afford to take chances," she smiled. "More tea?"

"No thanks," I closed my notebook and slipped it back into my tunic pocket. "I'd better be going."

"Oh, must you?" she asked softly. "There's enough in the pot for another cup," and before I could refuse, she began to pour. I shrugged my shoulders in cheerful resignation and accepted the second cup. It tasted good, I must admit, and I found her a charming person. I could imagine her being the centre of attraction at any function, whether formal or informal, for her range of topics was remarkable. She seemed well read but soon she turned her attention to me. She asked about my growing family, my work and my impressions of this area, and it wasn't long before I realised she had steered the conversation around to her own home.

"We haven't been here long either," she was telling me, sipping delicately and smiling at me. "We had a house in York, then moved out to Stillington. We came here about five years ago. My husband likes this village – it's not so flat as York and we love the moors. They're so handy for walks, you know. We found this house quite by chance, motoring here one week-end, and it was just right for us. Spacious, detached and in very good order. We did a bit of work upon it, mainly on the interior, but the fabric was sound."

"It's a very nice house," and I told her how much I would like a house of that sort, when eventually I left the Force.

"Would you like a look around?" she asked pleasantly.

In all innocence, I said I would love to have a look around. She showed me the ground floor, the dining-room with its oak suite made by Mousey Thompson of Kilburn, the kitchen with its fabulous fitted range, the study with Mr Dulcimer's enviable law library and filing system, the veranda with its array of potted plants and the garden beyond. There I admired an ancient sun-dial, the goldfish pond and the crazy paving. To say it was beautiful was an understatement; it was worthy of inclusion in one of the Sunday colour supplements. She was a fortunate woman and I felt a twinge of envy as we returned to the lounge. I caught the occasional whiff of perfume as she walked close to me, sometimes very close.

"Would you like a look upstairs?" she ventured.

"Thank you," I said, with even more innocence. After a ground floor of such opulence and taste, what would the bedrooms be like?

She led me up the wide carpeted stairs, showed me the tiled bathroom with its pale green fittings and the shower unit in the corner, the boys' bedrooms, the guest room with its bathroom *en suite* and finally, her room. This was exquisite; the predominant colour was pink, with matching curtains, carpet and bedspread. I could sense she was excited, her voice trembled as we talked. She came very close to me.

"It's beautiful," I said with genuine feeling.

"Like me?" she cried and to my total astonishment, she literally threw herself onto the bed and in a single movement, flung her skirt across the room. She was naked beneath. From the waist down, she wore nothing at all as she lay on that gorgeous silken cover, smiling up at me.

But there are certain things that do not come within the scope of a policeman's duty, and that was one of them. I fled. In something of a daze, I returned to Ashfordly Police Station to enter the details of Mrs Dulcimer's documents in a register kept for the purpose. It took a long time because my mind was still reeling from this experience, or perhaps the lack of it! But we had been warned of women like this at Training

School, and all kinds of ghastly ends to one's career had been threatened if any of us succumbed. As I wrote the details in the register, Sergeant Bairstow entered the office.

"All correct, Sergeant," I trotted out the automatic response.

"Good," he returned. "Anything to report?"

"Nothing, Sergeant," I said.

"You, er, visited Mrs Dulcimer, did you?" he asked, his merry eyes watching me carefully. I noticed a definite twitch at the corners of his mouth, the beginnings of a smile, maybe?

"I did," I wondered if he knew what she was like.

"You found everything in order, did you?"

"Everything was in order, Sergeant," I realised what he was getting at, the crafty B! I decided to string him along for a while.

"Nice woman," he muttered eventually.

"Very pleasant," I was determined to continue this cat-and-mouse game for as long as possible. Dare I admit I hadn't accepted her generous offer? Or should I let him think I had? His questions told me he'd known what was in store for me, and I now realised why she wanted the policeman to visit her, in order to check her driving documents. How many had been there before me? Had he, I wonder?

"Alone, was she?" he continued.

"All alone, Sergeant. Nice house, too. A very nice woman," I said concluding my written entry with a flourish of my pen.

"Hmm," he walked about the small office, his chin cupped in his hand. "I'm pleased everything was in order."

"I'm glad I didn't have to book her for an offence," I said seriously. "She gave me a lovely cup of tea and besides, her husband is a barrister."

"Yes, he is, Nicholas. He's away a lot, they tell me."

"Yes, he's a busy man, and a prosperous one by the look of it."

There was another long pause.

"Did she show you round the house, Nicholas? She's very proud of it, they tell me."

"A nice place," I smiled at him. "They've done a fair bit to it, I believe, in the five years they've been there. It's beautifully situated, isn't it?"

"I've never been," he told me. "I've only heard, you know, from lads who've been up there, checking her credentials."

"It's the sort of place I'd love to own," I was thinking of the pittance that policemen earned.

I wondered how long he would question me in this oblique sort of way, so having completed the entry in the register, I closed the book, slipped it back onto its shelf and prepared to leave. He watched me and made small talk about nothing in particular, chattering merrily as I placed my helmet on my head.

"I'm going round by Briggsby, Sergeant," I told him as I started to walk from the office. "I've a call to make there – a youngster wants to join the police cadets. I'm seeing him after school."

"Cheerio, Nicholas, " he called as I walked out, and as the door had almost closed behind me, I heard him shout, "Did you get your oats then?"

I pretended not to hear his question. I simply waved a hand in reply, a farewell gesture as the door clicked home. I left him in blissful ignorance, which I reckoned was the best thing to do.

* * * *

Another interesting encounter with the fair sex occurred when I was on early duty in Eltering. It was my duty to patrol the town's streets between 6 am and 10 am, due to a shortage of local manpower. Eltering is a small North Yorkshire market town located on the southern edge of the moors. It is therefore appropriately known as 'Gateway to the Moors' but it was never busy during those morning hours. The only regular indications of early morning work came with people like the milkman, the postman and window-cleaners.

As eight o'clock came around, the town grew more active. People began to move. Some emerged from their homes to catch the shops, to buy papers, cigarettes, milk or coffee, while the policeman spent that time wishing them all 'Good morning'. It was pleasant, watching the town come to life. In some sense, I enjoyed this duty. It differed greatly from my own rural heaven, but it could be very monotonous from time to time, particularly during the dark winter months. Summer brought a welcome cheeriness to the place, however, and it was a late July morning as I made this early morning patrol around the town, using streets not yet aired. The very early morning workers had left – the eight o'clockers hadn't yet emerged. I had the town to myself as the church clock struck seven.

I decided to patrol the Aislaby estate, a new housing complex on the western edge of this charming town. I knew I could walk up there, do a circuit of the streets on foot and be back in town for eight o'clock, in order to make my point on the hour outside the post office.

With my cape over my shoulder in case of rain, I set off. It was a pleasant stroll. There was nothing criminal to worry me, although I did check a few parked cars to see if their tax discs were displayed. I examined a few lock-up premises *en route*, to establish that no shopbreakers had paid illegal nocturnal visits. But all was in order. All was quiet, as I would report to any sergeant or inspector who might ask. Having performed that perambulation, I made my way back to the town centre, noting that it was about a quarter to eight. The morning bustle was beginning.

As I made my slow, methodic way down the gently sloping gradient into the town centre, I became aware of some urgent activity ahead of me. A policeman can sense when something is happening – people begin hurrying towards whatever it is. Everyone wants to see it, so they can talk with authority in the pubs, clubs and offices, and there is a tangible scent of excitement in the air. Those symptoms were happening in Eltering right now. Men were hurrying towards some unknown incident just out of my sight. Whatever it was, it had literally brought the town centre to a halt. There was a car with its driver's door standing open, a butcher running with his blue-and-white striped apron flapping about his knees, a milkman dashing along with a crate rattling at his side, a pedal cycle lying in the gutter, its rear wheel spinning uselessly.

And so, quite naturally, I speeded up my regulation pace. I began to hurry. I had no idea what had happened, but the chances were that it would involve the police. Unexpected incidents usually did. I simply followed the growing number of hurrying men. Where they came from, I will never know, although the clatter of closing doors, the abandoned cars, the shops standing empty and the number of early morning businessmen provided me with a good clue. Somehow, word of the incident had spread like wildfire.

Just around the corner, I found the main clutch of men. They were standing around the entrance to an alley just off the centre of the town, so I used my elbows to good advantage. I pushed my way to the front.

"What's going on?" I asked in what I hoped was a voice bearing some hint of authority.

A shirt-sleeved man answered. "It's a young woman," he grinned. "Starkers. Down there – she's told us to keep out."

"Down there?" I pointed down the alley. It was a narrow passage between a shop and an hotel, and it had a corner at the distant end. She'd gone around the corner, and I heard her shout.

"Don't any of you dare come down here, not one of you, or I'll scream."

"Who is she?" I asked of anyone who might answer.

"Dunno," one of them said. "She's bollock naked, Officer. Not a bloody stitch on. She was running down the street, crying."

"When?"

"Just now," he confirmed. "A few minutes ago. She bolted down there, like a scared rabbit."

"And you all ran after her, eh?"

"Cor. Not 'arf, Officer," grinned one of them. "I mean, it's not every morning a naked woman runs down the street, is it? Not in Eltering, any road."

"How old is she?" was my next question.

"Early twenties, mebbe. Beautiful too, lovely knockers on her."

"All right, lads," I tried to defuse the situation. "The fun's over. Imagine this was your own daughter or wife, eh? It might be, mightn't it? She'd be scared, wouldn't she? With a lot of sex-starved blokes chasing her through the streets."

They murmured something non-committal and there were lots of bawdy comments about running in the opposite direction if it had been the wife, but at least I had gained their attention. They refused to leave just yet, however. They wanted to have another look at her. I had to save this slip of a lass from a fate worse than death.

"Hello," I shouted down the passage. "I'm the policeman. It's P.C. Rhea from Aidensfield. You can't stay there all day – the town's coming to a standstill."

"I'm not moving. Tell them to go away."

"You can't go through the streets like that!" I called to her, although I'd not yet had the pleasure of viewing her body. "I've got a cape, you can put that around yourself. It will cover you up, and we can get you home."

There was a long pause, during which the assembled men began to make ribald remarks about my intentions, and then she said, "All right. Just you."

This was one of the perks of the job, and so with wolf whistles and calls of encouragement, I walked the few yards along the alley to meet her. She was cowering behind the corner of the wall, in the lee of a tiny outbuilding of some kind, and her bare arms did their best to cover her nakedness. She had sandy hair and a face covered with freckles, but her body was young and luscious. She wore no shoes – she hadn't a stitch on.

"I'm married," I said as if that made any difference and with a flourish, I removed my cape from my shoulder. "Here," I offered it to her. "Try this for size."

With a weak smile, she opened it and draped it about her body. It came down to her knees. If she walked through the street wearing it, no one would know she was naked beneath. At this time of day, comparatively few people were about anyway – all those who were abroad were, at this minute, swarming around the exit of this alley.

"All right," I shouted at the waiting voyeurs. "The show's over, lads. She's covered up now. Off you go and let the lady through."

One or two of them drifted back to their jobs or morning chores, but the inevitable handful remained.

"Can you face them?" I asked her.

She nodded.

"Come on," I took her arm, holding it through the folds of the cape, and led her from the passage. A cheer went up from the assembled crowd and she blushed furiously, although recognising the good-humoured affection behind their noise. They drifted away as I accompanied her through the streets, using the quieter routes.

Once the initial audience had dispersed, no one paid any attention to us. The sight of a girl in a long cloak was not unusual, nor was it odd that a policeman should walk along the street chatting to a local person. By the time we reached her home, she was quite affable.

"Well?" I asked eventually. "What was all that about?"

She smiled. "Sex," she said. "I wouldn't let him, so he threw me out. The door's got a Yale lock and it clicked behind me. I couldn't get back in. I was crying and I panicked."

"Where?"

"Just round the corner from here," she pointed. "Up one of those alleys."

"Why run right through the town?" I asked.

"I've a friend down there," she said. "Janice. A good pal. I thought she'd let me in."

"But at eight o'clock in the morning? With the town just getting busy?"

"I didn't know it was eight o'clock" She laughed now. "I thought it was about five, and it wouldn't be busy."

"So what happens now?" I asked her.

"I'll go home. I'll show you where I live and then you can have your cape back."

"I thought you said it was along one of these alleys?"

"That's where I was last night, with this feller. I don't live there, I live further along."

"Boyfriend?" I asked.

"Sort of," she nodded. "He went crazy, honest, when I said no. I got out of bed and said I was going home, so he kicked me out. Pushed me downstairs and out of the door."

"What will your mother say when you turn up like this?"

"It's not my mother I'm worried about," she said frankly "It's my husband!"

"Husband?" I cried.

"Yeh, luckily he's away at sea. I hope he doesn't find out or he'll kill me."

"I won't tell him," I promised her.

We reached her house, a small cottage just off a side street near the Co-op, and I had to force a window with my pocket knife, because her key was at the other place, in her clothes. I managed to open a window, climbed inside and released her latch to let her into her own house.

"Thanks," she breathed, and thereupon removed my cape. She stood before me unashamed and proud, smiling at me. She asked, "Are you staying a while?"

"No," I had to say. "Duty calls."

"I think you policemen are wonderful," she winked at me, closing the door as I left. "Do call again, won't you?"

"I might," I said, knowing full well that I wouldn't go near the place. It would be several weeks later when I was patrolling the town during the evening. A pretty young woman stopped me outside the chip shop, offered me a chip and said, "Hello".

"Hello," I said, accepting the chip but not recognising her.

"You don't remember me, do you?" she smiled. "I'm all dressed up now."

"Ah!" I realised who it was. "Sorry, I didn't recognise you with your clothes on. You've had a new hair-do too?"

"You are observant," she grinned, offering me another chip. I accepted her chips, and learned her first name was Sylvia.

*   *   *   *

"I must stress that this is an informal chat at this stage, P.C. Rhea," said the Superintendent. "It might lead to an official complaint against the police, however. I am anxious to hear your side of the story."

"Yes, sir." I was in the Superintendent's office at Divisional Headquarters, wondering what was coming next. He lifted a file from his desk.

"This," he said, "is a complaint against you."

I'd always regarded myself as the epitome of good behaviour, and I was shaken by this revelation. I knew that a lot of police officers welcomed complaints about their men because it proved they were doing their job. But that didn't take into

account the mental anguish when one heard a complaint
about oneself.

"Do you know a Miss Angela Hamilton in your village?"
he asked.

"Yes, sir. She's a big chapel woman, a do-gooder and all
that. She's very pleasant – in her early forties, sir. A bit prim
and proper maybe, if you know what I mean."

"I sensed that from her letter. Now listen. She accuses you
of infidelity. She has been observing your movements, P.C.
Rhea, and alleges that you, a family man and father of three
children, have been visiting some of the ladies of the village at
late hours. Miss Hamilton has a record of those dates and
times. Your police motor-cycle has been seen in close proximity to their homes – there's a widow called Mrs Christian, a
young blonde called Kay who hasn't been in the village for
long, a woman whose husband goes away on business for long
periods, and several others. All, according to Miss Hamilton,
are ladies of doubtful virtue."

"Oh?" I replied. This latter snippet was news to me. They
were all nice women, so far as I knew.

"Is that all you've got to say?" he asked me.

"There's not much more I can say, sir, because my motor-
cycle will have been near or right outside everyone's house at
some time or other. How long has this supposed orgy been
going on?"

"Over the past four or five months."

"I can't remember all my movements, sir," I said honestly.
"Damn it all, I've kept observations in the village, I've made
crime enquiries, I've renewed firearms certificates and done a
host of other jobs which entail visiting other people's homes at
all hours."

"I am sure there is a perfectly logical explanation, P.C.
Rhea, so I want to hear your story before I decide whether or
not to take official action. But remember I've got this written
complaint about the conduct of one of my men, and it must
therefore be investigated. I'll supply you with the alleged
dates and I want you to go home and explain, in writing, the
presence of your motor-cycle outside those places at the
material times. Go home and write up your report, and I'll
decide what further action to take."

I told Mary all about it. Being a good wife, she sympathised and affirmed her trust in me, whereupon I adjourned to my office to find all my old pocket books. I now had the chore of checking every date mentioned in Miss Hamilton's letter.

"She's in the ideal position to spy on people, living right in the middle of the village," Mary observed. "And her a pillar of the chapel! Fancy spreading malicious rumours like that! I've a good mind to go and tell her what I'd like to do with her!"

"Hold on, girl, that would only make matters worse. Let's find out why I was at those houses, and why my motor-bike was around at the times she mentions."

It wasn't a long job to unearth the information because my pocket books told all. For each of the dates provided in Miss Hamilton's accusation, there was a true explanation – crime prevention advice to the young widow; Kay Hartford, the blonde newcomer, had a firearm certificate for variation, and the wife whose husband was away on business had twice found footprints in her garden and wanted police action. I had kept observations on her garden from another building and from time to time, called to acquaint her with my action to stop prowlers. And so it went on until I had a complete answer to all her charges.

I typed these into a full report and submitted it to the Superintendent.

"Thank you, P.C. Rhea, for your co-operation," the big man said. "I'll drive out to have a word with this woman myself. She's a mischief-maker."

But his action did not stop her.

The bishop of the Anglican diocese received a complaint from Miss Hamilton, who had reported that the vicar's estate car had been seen outside certain ladies' homes at strange hours. This resulted in the vicar being called to the bishop's palace for a down-to-earth chat. Similarly, it seemed the postman had been dallying too long at specified calling places and the Co-op van driver seemingly spent too long upon his deliveries.

The Head Postmaster of the area and the manager of the Co-op duly received letters from Miss Hamilton. As things tend to happen upon such occasions, it wasn't long before the Co-op driver happened to mention this to the postman, who in turn laughed about it as he talked to me. I thus became aware of the whole story. It didn't take much intelligence to realise that the complaints from the frustrated Miss Hamilton were all levelled against men in the public eye. The same ladies featured in all her letters. Invariably, they were attractive women. It was therefore in the course of my duty that I popped in to see the vicar, the Reverend Clifton, to ask about his chat with the bishop. His bishop, it transpired, had been most uncharitable about it, apparently more concerned about the tarnished image of the church than the personal dilemma of his vicar.

"She's a member of the chapel flock, isn't she?" I put to the vicar.

"Happily, she's not one of mine," laughed Roger Clifton. "I might have a word with her minister. She's got to be stopped."

"I think I could stop her," I suggested.

"You really think so?" beamed Roger Clifton. "I'd be most grateful if you could. How would you tackle the job?"

I said I'd prefer to be non-committal at this stage, and said I'd like to have a word with the minister of the chapel first. A lot depended upon his co-operation. After speaking at length with the minister, Pastor Smith, I next discussed my idea with the postman, the Co-op van driver and finally, the Reverend Roger Clifton. I told him how pleased they all were and he felt it was a sound suggestion.

A few weeks later, Miss Angela Hamilton found herself being summoned to the presence of Pastor Smith and the elders of her local chapel, all sitting in stony silence.

"Miss Hamilton," coughed the minister solemnly as she settled before them. "You enjoy a high position within this chapel, but I am afraid I have had a series of complaints about your behaviour."

"About me?" she cried.

"I have a list of dates and times when motor-vehicles belonging to certain men of this village have been seen outside your house at some very strange hours. Indeed, some have been noted outside your house for lengthy periods during the day. I need mention only the postman, the Co-op van, the policeman's motor-cycle . . . Now, Miss Hamilton, I know you are an unmarried lady, and I am not suggesting for one minute that you are leading an immoral life, but for a lady in your position, as warden of our chapel . . ."

When Pastor Smith told me of this chat with her, he said that it was at that stage of his conversation, that Miss Hamilton had ceased to listen. The frown of concern upon her face had become a quiet smile of success.

But she didn't write any more letters to my Superintendent.

Seven

The atmosphere at the Hopbind Inn, Elsinby was invariably
jolly. I paid many visits during the course of my duty, for it
was a fine pub. Its drinking accommodation was one long bar
with six oak beams, furnished with the inevitable dart board,
yards of ale, hunting prints, sporting trophies, an open fireplace and a stone floor. It boasted a landlord for whom
nothing was too much trouble and it was a foregone conclusion that his inn was very popular. An added bonus was
the fact that the beer was very good. That was understandable, because it was brewed in Yorkshire.

I popped in whenever I passed through the village at
lunchtime, and I popped in most evenings. I never drank on
duty, but went for a chat and an opportunity to learn local
gossip. At lunchtime, the locals would be swapping yarns and
playing darts, and it was the same crowd that frequented the
bar during the evenings. Those locals practically lived there.

Outsiders joined them for the evening sessions, but the
nucleus of life in the pub was that group of local men. I was
to learn, soon after my arrival that they were local farmers in
the main, plus a businessman or two, a racing journalist, a
doctor, the vicar, the postmaster and others of no specific
occupation. Due to the nature of the people who attended so
regularly, it was logical that village meetings be held in that
pub. The parish council met there monthly because every
councillor was in the place anyway. The British Legion
committee met here too, in the shape of the same group of
men, and if there was a special meeting or committee for any
village function, the same people would be appointed, the
meeting held and the function arranged.

In many ways it was an admirable arrangement and there
was the added benefit that I knew where to find these people

if they were required in a hurry, like the doctor, for example. Such an occasion arose with the death of Irresponsible John.

Irresponsible John was a tramp. He was a tall man with masses of very dark hair through which shone a scarred nose and two very dark eyes. He was like every man's idea of Fagin. His unruly mass of hair was covered by an old top hat and he wore a long, black coat with old boots and dark trousers. His hands were always gloved with a pair of very holey mits without fingers and I never saw him remove them, whether in the middle of summer or winter.

John lived in a derelict cottage on an elevated site on the edge of Elsinby, along the York road. He spent most of his time roaming the neighbourhood and earning a few shillings by casual labour, scrounging his meals from grateful farmers and smallholders. The village loved him too because he was totally harmless and honest. Everyone accepted him for what he was – a harmless old tramp of indeterminate age and unknown background. Very occasionally, he would pop into the Hopbind for a mild ale, but this was not a common practice. In the coldest spells, he would buy the occasional bottle of rum, a relic of his naval days.

I was in the Hopbind one Wednesday lunchtime when Gilbert, the postman, dashed in looking haggard and flustered. He asked for a double Scotch which was promptly handed to him and then he gasped.

"It's John, dead. At his cottage. I've just found him."

"Not Irresponsible John?" asked George, the landlord.

"Aye, John. He's up at his house."

"How did you find him?" I asked, not at that time knowing the village routine.

"Took his dinner as usual." He shrugged his shoulders and downed his drink. "Pork pie, peas and chips, done to a turn by my missus. He liked his pork pies, chips and peas, did John. I knocked, opened the door like I always do, and there he was, lying on the floor."

Doctor McGee, in his tweed plus fours, joined us. "Dead, did you say?"

"Flies all over," said Gilbert, wrinkling his nose.

"I'll go up there," I said, for I was on duty. My motor-cycle was outside, so I donned my helmet and left the pub. Doctor

Archibald McGee said he would follow in his car, and he rapidly swallowed his pint.

I knew the cottage. It was just off the York road and was a lovely place, or it had been a lovely place. It was the type of house that graces Victorian paintings, with honeysuckle around the door, roses climbing the walls, no footpath or garage, and a garden full of hollyhocks and red-hot pokers. Built of yellow limestone, it had a red pantile roof and a range of outbuildings adjoining the dwelling portion. Sadly, it was neglected and rotting, because no one admitted ownership so John had made his home there, many years ago. He demanded little of the place, save shelter from the elements. I leaned my motor-cycle against the rickety garden fence and walked somewhat apprehensively towards the front door. It was open. I inched it further against the wall and shouted, "John? Are you there?"

Wondering if Gilbert had made a mistake in his amateur diagnosis, I entered on tiptoe, feeling like a trespasser, but there in the middle of the floor of the tatty living-room was the stiff corpse of Irresponsible John. It was early autumn with a warm September day to compensate for the wet summer, and the flies were enjoying the gift nature had presented them. I have no idea how long he'd lain there, but pathologists can estimate this by the stage of development of maggots found in and upon bodies. I had no wish to determine this, nor even to examine him for their presence, but I touched the whiskery face and found it was stone cold. *Rigor mortis* had set in. That John was dead could be in no doubt.

Policemen always treat sudden and unexplained deaths with extreme caution, regarding them as murders until proved otherwise. The house did not bear signs of forcible entry, but an unlawful entry would barely have been evident here. The windows were hanging out, the doors tilted from their hinges and the place had a dark and dismal appearance inside. There was no way of knowing if anyone had broken in, but I could see no injuries upon him. It was not easy to be sure due to his mass of hair and the thick clothes in which he lay. We'd have to strip him to be absolutely sure.

A few minutes later, Dr McGee arrived, followed by the entire lunchtime population of the Hopbind Inn. As McGee entered the house, the others remained outside, silently waiting for news. It reminded me of the crowds that used to wait outside prisons for news of executions. McGee looked at me, wrinkled his nose and said, "He's a bit strong, isn't he?"

"Like Gorgonzola," I heard myself comment. "He's dead, Doctor."

McGee crouched at his side, felt the pulse, lifted the eyelids and touched the skin.

"Dead as they come," he said. "How, I wonder?"

"You've never treated him, Doctor?" I asked.

"Once, years ago," he confirmed. "He stuck a hayfork through his foot. Never since."

"So you can't certify the cause of his death?" I put to him hopefully.

"Sorry," he shook his head. "I can certify that he *is* dead, so you can set the ball rolling. But I can't certify the *cause* of death – it looks like natural causes, I must say. There's no indication of poisoning, no obvious marks of violence, no sleeping tablets lying around. I think he's just faded away, Mr Rhea, but I cannot certify that."

I groaned inwardly. This meant a post-mortem and I must set about the task of arranging it. I would have to make enquiries about his past and then complete reports. There would be relatives to trace, the funeral to arrange with a hundred other chores, to say nothing of stripping that smelly corpse to the bare skin in readiness for the pathologist's knife. John's remains would have to be removed as soon as possible and taken to the mortuary at Ashfordly, the nearest place which boasted one.

Having delivered his glad tidings, Dr McGee went outside and told the assembly that Gilbert's diagnosis had been correct. Irresponsible John was dead. Upon receipt of that news, they all adjourned to the pub to drink to his memory. I was left holding the body.

I radioed Control and asked for a message to be passed to Sergeant Bairstow, who was the duty sergeant that day. I asked that the van be sent from Eltering to John's cottage, complete with the shell. The shell was a fibre-glass box, shaped like a coffin, into which a corpse was placed for transportation, especially for a trip to the mortuary. Sergeant

Bairstow was out, and no one was at the office. I knew he'd be at lunch, and he never answered the telephone during his refreshment break. I asked Control to try at two o'clock.

That meant I had to wait around and I didn't relish the idea of standing like a sentinel at John's gate until help arrived. I went back into the house, made a careful search for signs of violence upon him, weapons, forcible entry and all the other routine matters appertaining to a sudden death. Then I left. John wouldn't go away, so I adjourned to the pub where I broke my rule about drinking on duty. I ordered a sandwich and accepted a pint from the doctor. Like the others, I raised my glass and said, "Here's to Irresponsible John. May he roam the heavens as he did the English countryside."

By two o'clock the regulars of the Hopbind Inn had done their best to speed him to eternal happiness, and I returned to the scene to await the shell. It arrived about half past two in a police van driven by P.C. Alwyn Foxton of Ashfordly. We carried it into the house, placed it at the side of the corpse and, holding our breath, lifted John and his entourage of buzzing flies into the shell. We rammed on the lid after forcing down a stubborn arm which insisted on rising like a flagpole from his side. Then we lashed the lid with ropes in case that arm lifted it off. A rising coffin lid, with an arm that looked like someone attempting to escape, could have caused embarrassment in town. We lifted the shell by its rope handles and lugged it into the rear of the van, sliding it along the floor. No one would know we had a body in there, except the cloud of hovering flies.

We transported him to the mortuary where I formally identified him as a tramp known to me as Irresponsible John. My search of his house had revealed nothing to indicate his true name and our records would show him merely as John. With Alwyn's help, we stripped the body, searched it thoroughly for signs of injury and listed all his clothing, together with odds and ends from his pockets. We placed everything inside a locker and recorded that we found no sign of injury upon the body. John now lay starkers upon the slab.

I arranged the post-mortem for next day at Scarborough Hospital and we took him in the van, once more using the

shell. The pathologist, a hawk-like fellow with staring eyes
and a weird sense of humour, performed the necessary operation and pronounced that John had died from natural causes.
His heart had given up its long, hard battle and he estimated
that John was about eighty years old. For a man of that age,
he was remarkably well preserved and surprisingly fit. He'd
had a good innings.

A natural death meant there would be no inquest, which in
turn meant that his funeral could go ahead. I reported this to
the committee in the Hopbind Inn the following lunchtime
and realised the burial was causing problems. John had no
known relatives, so who was going to organise and pay for the
funeral? By chance or by good fortune, the local carpenter-
cum-undertaker was in the pub. He assured us he could make
a coffin and carry out the funeral. The vicar said he would
bury John in his churchyard, even though it was not known
to which religion John had adhered throughout his wandering life. But who would pay? The assembled drinkers decided
that John had been too much of a friend to the village to
suffer the indignity of a pauper's grave.

It was Gilbert Kingston, the postman, who made a suggestion. He said the entire village should pay. The inhabitants numbered about four hundred and if they all paid ten
shillings each towards a funeral kitty, we could send off John
in a decent manner. Harold, the undertaker, reckoned that
sort of money would pay for a high quality coffin with
chrome handles and silver angels, a marble headstone, flowers
and funeral tea afterwards. The idea seemed feasible, so it was
proposed that a committee be established to make the arrangements for the interment of Irresponsible John. There
was no time to lose.

I was not elected to the committee because I was not a
resident of Elsinby, although it was stated that I could be
co-opted if the need arose. I agreed to this. Harold would set
about making the coffin and the vicar would begin the
funeral arrangements. It was decided that the funeral should
be at 3.30 pm the following Tuesday, at Elsinby Parish
Church.

Faced with the impossible task of tracing his relatives, I
told the Press who gave space to my problem in the hope that

someone would claim him. I assured the committee that John could lie in state at Ashfordly Mortuary until the day of the funeral. There was nowhere else for him; besides, the mortuary was an ideal resting place and some schoolchildren picked flowers to display on the window ledge above his head.

The whole idea of a village fund was a fine one, but even before that lunchtime session was over, the racing journalist came up with a better suggestion.

"Look," he said, swilling his brandy around the glass. "If you ask ten bob from everyone in the village, you're bound to come across those who are unwilling. There'll be those who are skint, and those who are too mean. There'll be some who reckon it's not the correct thing to do. Then there's all the bother of collecting it. Why don't we raise the cash in an enjoyable way? Why not arrange a dance or something? Some kind of social event? We hold dances from time to time to raise cash for the old folks' Christmas treat, or for the church repair fund. We always get a good turn-out because folks enjoy it, so I'm sure they'd turn out for John. We could lay on a supper, and I know George would see we got a bar."

"I would that!" enthused George.

"Lots of folks would come and we'd raise a few hundred pounds. There is that lad in the council houses and his mates, who play guitars. They'd make music for us, I'm sure."

"Is the parish hall free on Saturday, Vicar?" asked Gilbert.

"It's free today and Saturday," he said. "Does that give us time to get things fixed?"

"Sure! We can run a dance. Charge ten bob per person for entry, run a bar and a raffle, lay on a supper and we'll make enough to give John a decent burial. Great idea!" George was delighted with the scheme.

And so the function was organised. I have never seen a village committee work so quickly. I left because I had to see a man about a witness statement relating to a traffic accident in York, but the committee remained on the pub premises to work upon the idea. Before tea-time that Friday evening, posters had been handwritten and distributed, the lads seen about the music, the bar arranged, the vicar had checked the heating of the hall, and the W.I. agreed to provide the supper. Their terms were half the proceeds for themselves and the other half to be allocated to the I.J.F. – the Irresponsible John Fund.

And so the great dance was fixed. It would take place in the village hall, Elsinby on Saturday night, commencing at 8.30 pm. Tickets would be ten shillings each, with supper 5 shillings extra, payable on receipt. George, the landlord of the Hopbind Inn, agreed to let all his profits, less expenses, be allocated to the Fund. The cost of hiring the hall would be waived, and so a good "do" was assured. One village elder suggested that John should lie in state during the dance, with his clean body, probably with a shave and a haircut, on display in his excellent coffin. The notion was not considered viable because he wasn't president of anything, or an archbishop.

At eight o'clock that Saturday, I presented myself in full uniform at the dance hall and was staggered by the size of the crowd. With half an hour to go, a queue was forming. The waiting people were of all types and ages – pensioners, farmers, young folk, professional people and even a smattering of visitors who had come to pay their last respects to a lovable person. The three lads who formed the group called themselves Hot Potato and were on stage, fixing their electronics and amplifiers, and tuning their guitars. They fancied themselves as the Beatles, and although their music was amateurish and noisy, with a lot of wrong notes, it was ideal for this night.

In one of the ante-rooms, the ladies of the Women's Institute were frantically laying out plates of food, each plate bearing two quarters of a sandwich, one bun and one biscuit, with an unspecified number of cups of tea being allowed per person. They had arranged a raffle, with rapidly gathered prizes like fruit cakes, bottles of spirit, a chicken or two, and several prizes of a dozen eggs.

George had installed his bar in another ante-room and although all his produce was bottled, he was guaranteed a good trade. Drinkers of draught beer would come tonight – he had ensured that by the simple expedient of closing his pub in John's honour.

The dance began with the opening tune of "Johnny was a Warrior" and the excited crowd squeezed onto the floor. The

place was heaving with room only to shuffle around but
everyone seemed very happy. These rural dances seldom
caused any policing problems because they attracted a good
quality of person, youngsters who knew how to behave in
public and who respected the property and rights of others. I
had managed to park all the cars around the minor roads of
the village and some had squeezed onto the car park before
the hall. Sergeant Bairstow arrived about ten o'clock, just to
make sure things were running smoothly and he remarked
upon the good nature of the dancers and the lack of fights
and other trouble. He had spent a large slice of his time in
one of the local towns on the borders of Middlesbrough,
where trouble went hand-in-hand with Saturday night.

Out here, it was different. We had pleasant ways of enjoying ourselves. I wandered around the exterior of the hall,
showing my uniform prominently as I was expected to do,
and occasionally I popped in just to check that the bar wasn't
full of children and that no drunkenness would spoil the
evening. My worries were superfluous. The committee had
everything under control.

Myself and Sergeant Bairstow purchased our suppers when
the group broke for theirs, and by quarter to midnight, the
dance was over. The revellers made their contented way home
and I spent another hour in the village, checking that no one
had broken any of the minor laws that the Government had
inflicted upon us. I turned in, very happy.

When I called at the Hopbind the following lunchtime,
Sunday, the committee members were earnestly counting
cash. The bar was high with coins and notes, and there were
little boxes marked 'raffle', 'door', 'bar' and 'supper'. A repre-
sentative of the W.I. was there in the form of the husband of
one of the members, and when all was totalled up, the profit
was just over £800. In precise terms, it was £806 15s. 7d.
George had taken out his expenses for the purchase of beer
and spirits, which he allowed the committee to have at cost,
while the W.I. stuck to their guns by claiming half-crowns for
every supper sold. The £806 was profit after all expenses had
been deducted.

Harold the undertaker reckoned that his costs would be
little over £200, added to which would be the church expenses

and other incidentals, coming to around £50 at the most. Another item of expenditure was the funeral tea. It was customary in these moorland villages to have a funeral tea, and it was fashionable among the best people, to have ham. As one old lady said, "I've buried four husbands, and all with ham."

Some twenty years before this particular burial, the funeral would have been a long, drawn-out affair with everyone dressed in black, and a *cortège* drawn by a black horse. Bidders would go around the village, 'bidding' folk to attend, and another custom was that every one attending the funeral would pay a proportion of the cost. It was a relic of such a custom that helped bury John in a decent grave, although the method of raising the cash was a little at variance with past ideals.

The committee therefore decided to organise a funeral tea in the village hall and the W.I. accepted responsibility for that task. The costs would come from the fund already on hand. This was agreed. As the funeral was the following Tuesday afternoon, I made sure the body was released on Monday, in time to be laid in the coffin so lovingly prepared by Harold. On the Monday evening, it was taken into the church where it rested overnight on a bier before the altar.

By 3.30 pm on Tuesday, the church was full with mourners spilling into the churchyard as the bells tolled mournfully. Many were dressed in the traditional black, wearing clothes that had attended every funeral in this village for the past century or so. The committee had found six volunteers to act as bearers and John's grave had been dug in a peaceful corner. As the sexton told me afterwards, "Ah laid him in t'quietest spot, thoo knaws. Ah thowt that if he was gahin ti pong as mich in deeath as he did in life, we'd better put him somewhere oot of t'rooad. Ah disn't want my graveyard smelling' o' tramps."

With the body already in church, the vicar began his service as only Anglican vicars can. His sombre intonations echoed around the church and sounds of sobbing could be heard here and there, with elderly ladies sniffing into black-edged handkerchiefs. The Reverend droned on and on, using the formal service and then he delivered his tribute to the

dead John. He spoke in glowing terms of John's love of peace
and solitude, of his godliness, of his desire never to inflict
himself upon anyone and never to be a burden on society. He
talked in emotional terms, but failed to remind the congregation of the time he'd asked John to leave a communion
service because of the old wayfarer's pungency on a hot
summer day.

He then quoted a little from Milton by reading "A death-
like sleep, a gentle wafting to immortal life" and ended with
Byron's words,

> "How sweet this very hour to die!
> To soar from earth and find all fears
> Lost in thy light – eternity!"

Finally, the bearers lifted the superb coffin from its wheeled-
bier and carried it from the church. Everyone tried to follow
it into the churchyard where the interment occurred amid
more sobbing. Solemn prayers filled the air, a handful of
earth was thrown into the grave to rattle on the coffin lid, and
it was all over. The sexton, who was able to dig any grave in
any ground and achieve straight sides, began the long job of
topping it up. Everyone else made a rush for the village hall
where tea, with ham, was laid on. John had been finally laid
to rest. His tombstone, suitably inscribed, stood in the blacksmith's shop awaiting erection at the head of the grave.

The blacksmith was something of a stonemason too, and he
had carved an epitaph upon it. It read, "John, a friend of the
village", followed by the date and a small piece of prose
which read, "A tombstone can neither contain his character,
nor is marble necessary to transmit it to posterity". The
obscurity of this phrase made it very acceptable, because no
one really understood it.

The tea was a mountainous affair and it seemed that the
ladies of the W.I. had talked to their grannies and elderly
relations, because it was reminiscent of a funeral tea of the
last century. There was ham in abundance. It was a memorable day to say the least and it lasted from the beginning of
the funeral until about eight-thirty at night, with the final
moments of the tea providing beer for everybody who requested it and tea for the teetotallers. When the meal was

over, the drinkers adjourned to the Hopbind for further
opportunities to say farewell to Irresponsible John. I went
home.

I thought that would have been the end of my involvement
with John, save for the occasional burst of energy in attempting to trace his relatives, but this was not the case. About a
week later, I dropped into the Hopbind Inn at lunchtime and
found the committee still hard at work. They welcomed me
and offered to buy me a drink, but I declined because I was in
uniform. A drink was therefore set aside for me next time I
called off duty. It was a small 'thank-you' for my help with
the funeral.

"We've all this spare money, Mr Rhea," Dr McGee told
me. "Our total income from the dance was in excess of £800
as you know. The funeral costs came to £243. That left us
with a balance of £563 to be precise. We laid on that funeral
tea – and a right good 'do' it turned out to be. All that ham!
That cost us £120, leaving us with £443, which we have
placed in a deposit account with Barclays Bank. Now several
folk at the tea reckoned that John's Fund should not have
paid for it – they were old-fashioned folks who believed that
bidden mourners should pay towards the expense. So somebody started putting money in a jug. Others followed suit and
we collected £74 at the tea! That makes a balance of about
£517, give or take a bob or two. We're meeting now to discus
what to do with it. Damn it all, we didn't intend this. We just
wanted to give John a decent funeral. So how can we spend
it?"

"Have you considered a playing field for the village?" I
suggested. "You've no cricket field of your own, have you?
I've often talked to the youngsters of Elsinby and I know
they'd love a field where they could play football and
cricket."

"Now that's a grand idea," beamed George the landlord.
"Aye, that's a right good idea. Jim Friend has a field, hasn't
he? You remember, he tried to get planning permission to
build a couple of bungalows, but they wouldn't let him.
Summat to do with ribbon development, I think. It's no good
for grazing because it's too sour. He might sell it, eh?"

It was therefore decided that Dr McGee, as chairman of the

committee, should approach Farmer Friend with a view to buying the field. It was reckoned there was enough land to provide space for a pitch and changing rooms/pavilions. And there was sufficient cash for all that. As they deliberated the possibilities, I felt elated. John had done a lot for Elsinby.

I called in a week later, off duty and in civilian clothes, and Dr McGee was in the bar, as usual. I got my free pint this time.

"Ah, Mr Rhea. Just the fellow. We got that field."

"That's great news!" I was delighted. "When do we start making it fit for play?"

"We've started," he told me. "But old man Friend insisted we did not pay for it. He's made his money, and he felt it was a good donation for the village. We can't get rid of John's money, can we? Anywa,, we now have a sports field, and we are busy looking at suitable pavilions."

The plans went ahead. The local reporter heard about it and did a feature in the Ryedale Weekly. The formal opening of the field, with an inaugural if late cricket match, took place one September evening and a good crowd attended. Elsinby beat Aidensfield by three runs, a good result. A small charge was made to fund the newly formed Elsinby Cricket Club, and so that project was nicely under way.

As a result, the story of Irresponsible John's benefit to the village made headlines in some of the national papers. A local T.V. station made a short feature film about the village community and in all, Elsinby hit the headlines for a brief period. The field was named after John, and is now called John's Field.

The fund continued to grow in spite of efforts to spend it, and after everything had been paid for, there was still £400 left. And it was gaining interest all the time. The fact that our story had appeared in some of the national papers resulted in the inevitable.

People began to claim relationship to John. Some said the money was theirs by right, but none of the claims could be substantiated. The committee made use of a solicitor who had a cottage in Elsinby and he reckoned the cash did not belong to any estate of John's. It belonged to the villagers, for it had been contributed by them to a fund for use by the village, and not by John. The living John had never exercised control over it. We successfully resisted every claim.

The finale came late one evening as I was patrolling Elsinby. I decided to pop into John's old house. I often did this just to check that no more dead bodies lurked there. On this night I found three living bodies – three more tramps. They had a small paraffin stove in the middle of the living-room floor and were brewing soup of doubtful origins. It was evident they intended staying.

I checked their names with our Control Room but none was wanted for any crime or for service of summonses, so I allowed them to remain. Ownership of the house was in doubt; no one seemed able to say to whom it rightly belonged and I knew that if John had been alive, he'd have welcomed his brothers of the highway. I had no power to remove them and besides, if I let them stay there, I knew where they were and what they were doing.

"We've heard about this village," one of them smiled through toothless gums. "They like tramps here, eh? They look after them, so we've come to stay."

Before Christmas, two more turned up and soon there was a colony of them in John's old house. Looking at the state of them, I felt we'd soon need some of John's Fund to bury them! I reckon he would approve of that.

Eight

Having been recruited into a predominantly rural police force, it was understandable that I should be indoctrinated with the law, practice and procedure relating to animals. Like all other bobbies, I had a lot to do with dogs, but there is a whole range of other animals which are likely to cross the path of a patrolling constable.

Because of the infinite range of possibilities stretching across thirty years of a policeman's service, our training school days were heavy with lectures and practical displays on how to cope. We were told about epizootic lymphamgitis, cattle plague, pleuro-pneumonia, foot and mouth disease and anthrax, with sundry horrors like fowl pest and rabies thrown in. We were taught about cruelty to animals and provided with detailed explanations about *cruelly* beating, over-riding, over-driving, ill-treating, over-loading, torturing or terrifying any animal. How one could perform these deeds without 'cruelly' doing them, was beyond me. There were lectures on illegal operations on animals, about performing animals, about horses, stallions, knackers' yards, birds and pet shops. We got the lot.

It would be fair to say that the lectures covered most of the problems involving animals which we were likely to encounter during an average tour of duty in an average English county. Unfortunately, I was not given advice about coping with zebras, camels, elephants and wallabies, nor did we receive instruction about the problems of pregnant badgers and hedgehogs with their heads fast in treacle tins.

The basic training was sound, however, and one of its more enjoyable aspects was the practical demonstration. Such demonstrations were given by our instructors and one dealt with the subject of "Animals Dead or Injured in the Street".

For this, the instructional staff staged a traffic accident where a motor vehicle had knocked down and killed a domestic animal. A volunteer student had to deal with the situation from the traffic accident viewpoint and then deal with the dead or injured animal. We were told that a reportable road accident involved D. G. CHAMPS – dogs, goats, cattle, horses, asses, mules, pigs and sheep. Incidents involving other animals were not classified as "accidents" for road traffic purposes. Nonetheless, if a car ran into something pretty large like a stag or a fox, there would be work for a police officer, if only to clear the scene, to attend to any injured person or beast and to find a garage to tow off the damaged vehicle. In our dealings with animal accidents, we could be relied upon to provide nice business for the local knackers' yards.

In one of our staged incidents at training school, a pig had been run over by a car. It was dead. A pretty young policewoman was volunteered to be the "officer at the scene". She strode confidently towards the location as we stood around in a watchful semi-circle, with our pocket books open. We were to take notes too, as if we were also dealing with the matter. The procedure at a genuine accident is fairly routine and straightforward. The police take all the known details of the driver, including his name, age, occupation and address. They note particulars of the vehicle, such as its make, model, type, registration mark, details of tax and insurance, and any other factual matters which are relevant. Because the traffic flow must not be interrupted longer than necessary, the vehicle must be removed, although the animal victim must not be forgotten. If it is alive and injured, with no known owner around, a police officer can call in a vet to have it examined and, if necessary, destroyed. The expense lies at the door of the owner if and when he is found. If the vet thinks the animal can be removed without cruelty, the owner must remove it; if he refuses or is not there, the police can cause it to be removed and the owner is responsible for the bill.

It was with these considerations that our practical demonstration got under way. The instructional staff kept a large, pink model of a pig for this purpose and it lay in the road, mortally injured by a motor-car driven by a huge man, another volunteer student. This was the scene, therefore, as our little lady policeman called Susie, waded in to cope. She managed very well with the irate motorist, who blamed the pig for all his misfortunes. She calmed his shattered nerves, then took all his particulars, including measurements of the road and the position of the car. The owner of the pig was not known, nor was its place of origin revealed. She rang a vet who said he would come along to examine it and in due course, another instructor arrived, suitably clad in a white overall and plus fours. In the traditional Scots accent of a vet, he declared the pig dead.

"Now, W.P.C. Shaw," beamed the instructor, "you've made a good job of this. The pig is dead, so we are not worried about having to destroy it in a humane manner. What are you going to do with the carcase?"

"I'll have it dragged away by the knackers," she said, with all innocence.

Armed with training of that quality, I sallied forth into the vast empty spaces of the North Riding of Yorkshire. In the years prior to my posting to Aidensfield, I had dealt with one or two traffic accidents involving animals, usually dogs or cows, and these had caused no problems. Soon after my arrival at Aidensfield, however, a very harassed motorist knocked at my door late one night. I was on duty as it happened, working a late shift from 5 pm until 1 am, and was fortuitously in the house having my statutory three-quarters of an hour refreshment break. I was on my final cup of tea when the knock jerked my thoughts from the television, so I answered the door. A white-faced man stood there, leaning heavily against the door jamb. He was middle-aged with greying hair and I noticed his smart, polished shoes. He was breathing heavily and looked like a town gentleman. I could see he was perspiring slightly and wondered if he was ill.

"Good evening," I said, not being able to conjure up anything more sparkling.

"Ah!" the relief was evident in his voice. "You are a policeman?"

"Yes," I was in shirt sleeves, and he managed a thin smile when I confirmed my role.

"I've got to report an accident." He shook visibly as he spoke those words.

"Oh, come in," I stepped back and invited him into the house. "Can you manage a cup of tea?"

"Love one," he breathed, sitting heavily on a chair in the office. "Yes, I'd love one if it's no bother."

"There's one in the pot," I told him. I left him for a moment as I asked Mary to produce a cup for him, and I'd have another myself as I talked with him. I returned and found him smoking a cigarette, somewhat relieved.

"Now," I said, handing him the tea. "Accident? Was it a bad one?"

"The front of the car's all bashed in," he said. "One headlight's gone, mudguard dented, bonnet twisted slightly. This is the first police house I've found . . . "

"What did you hit?" I asked.

"A kangaroo," he said, looking at me and staring into my eyes, daring me to disbelieve him.

"A kangaroo?" My thoughts turned immediately to D. G. CHAMPS. Kangaroo was not one of the listed animals, so this was not a road accident. This meant I did not have to compile an accident report.

"It's not listed in the road traffic acts," I aired my knowledge. "You don't have to report it – accidents involving kangaroos are not reportable."

"But I hit one, officer, just down the road!"

"Are you sure it was a kangaroo?" I asked. "You are deep in the countryside, you know, and we have all kinds of animals here. Deer, badgers, foxes, hares . . . "

I'd once seen a camel striding purposefully across the moors in a heavy mist, but daren't mention that to him. It had astounded some drivers at the time, but had been hired from a local zoo by a party of schoolboys who rode it during a stunt. As I talked to him, I realised that a camel wasn't D. G. CHAMPS either, unless it qualified as 'cattle'.

"It was a bloody kangaroo," he almost shouted. "I saw it. It hopped right out of the hedge and I ran slap-bang into it. I don't know where it went – it just seemed to get knocked away and I couldn't find it."

"It's not dead, then?" I asked.

"I stopped and had a look," he said. "There was a spot of blood on the road, and on my car. But it's not around, I'm sure."

I wondered if our local vet would come to declare a kangaroo dead? Or would it have to be dragged away by the knackers? I went out to examine his vehicle and found it severely damaged, with splashes of blood here and there. I took his personal particulars and a precise location of the happening. He left me half an hour later, a little more composed. I could not put this one through the books as an accident having regard to D. G. CHAMPS. It was simply not a reportable road traffic accident. I would record it merely as an 'incident'.

But I puzzled over his kangaroo. When I resumed patrol, I decided to visit the location of his confrontation and in the headlight of my motor-cycle, found the spots of blood on the road. He'd told me of the direction from which it had leapt at him and I decided to have a look around. I guessed it had gone into the field opposite, so armed with my sturdy police torch, I parked the bike and climbed the gate, to wander across the grassy area beyond. And I found his kangaroo. It was dead, with its head badly injured. It had managed to leap this far before collapsing. But it wasn't a kangaroo. It was a wallaby, and wallabies are not part of D. G. CHAMPS either! I left it in the field, just as I would have done had it been a hare, a rabbit or other wild animal. Besides, it would be found by the farmer next morning, and it would provide a talking point in the pub for many an hour. They'd all wonder how it had arrived, and I would not tell them. It would be interesting to hear the speculation.

Next morning, I rang the motorist at his home near Middlesbrough to explain he'd been wrong. I told him it wasn't a kangaroo, but a wallaby. He laughed.

"Go on," he said. "Put me out of my misery. How can I run down a wallaby in the North Riding countryside?"

"They have some at a local zoo," I told him, "and several have escaped over the years. They've adapted to the countryside and some of them are breeding in the district. You hit a wild wallaby."

"And do you think my insurance company will swallow that?" he asked.

"Ask them to write to us," I advised him. "We'll confirm it."

That was my first brush with animals from the local zoo. Housed on a large country estate in the North Riding, the zoo was the home of a fascinating variety of animals, ranging from domestic poultry to lions and hippos, including crocodiles, flamingoes and dolphins. From time to time, some of the species did escape, although the officials were marvellous at arranging their re-capture. Because of this, exotic birds lived in the woodlands about me, and many a British ornithologist has been dumbfounded by the multi-coloured parrots, budgies and humming birds which somehow managed to survive in the bleak hills of the region, if only for the summer months. After all, it's not often you find vulturine guineafowl, scaled quail or variegated wrens in English orchards.

My next link with the zoo came as the circus arrived in town. It was a small touring circus which was scheduled to stage a series of performances within the grounds of the zoo. Many of its larger animals were to be transported by rail and this was part of a publicity stunt. The elephants would be walked from Eltering Railway Station, when they would lead a procession of other animals and acts. Some would be walked, like the monkeys and chimps, while the dangerous ones would be in cages and carried on the rear of their own transporters. They would be waiting at the railway station.

It was Sergeant Bairstow, with the usual twinkle in his eye, who called me into his office one morning.

"Ah, Nicholas," he beamed. "A nice day?"

"Very nice, Sergeant," I agreed, little knowing what he had in store for me.

"I've a nice little job for you this afternoon," he smiled. "You're to be on motor-cycle escort duty."

"Something important?" I asked.

"Yes, very," and he explained about the arrival of the circus. "You're to be at Eltering Railway Station at 2 pm. The train will arrive shortly afterwards, and when all the animals have been transferred from the train, you will lead the procession through the town. Take it along the main road and into the grounds of the zoo. It's about four miles, so it could take an hour. O.K.?"

I did not know whether to be amused or not. I'd never escorted a circus. I knew there'd be clowns, jugglers, monkeys, balloons and a host of ancillary publicity gimmicks. And I'd be escorting that lot! But orders were orders. Mounted on my trusty Francis Barnett with its aerial waving behind, I reported at the railway station. The place was alive with people, especially children, and already the waiting animals were being arranged in some sort of order. Whips were cracking, trainers were shouting, animals were calling, the music was playing . . .

"The elephant's going to lead the procession," said Sergeant Bairstow who had arrived by car. "It'll dictate the pace for the others. You ride your bike ahead of the procession – clear the route of sightseers, make a way through, prevent accidents, warn motorists of the oncoming procession. I'll be at the rear – if you meet trouble, radio for assistance."

"Yes, Sergeant."

And so I waited for the moment to begin my leadership of this curious procession. After a lot of shouting, fuss, general noise and re-arranging of vehicles and cages, the circus was ready to move. I was parked in the street, waiting for the signal to start. When I saw the column of marchers heading for me, led by a huge, grey elephant, I kicked the bike into life, waited until they were closer, and set off.

I knew elephants could walk with considerable speed and this one would dictate the pace of the entire march. Driving ahead, I soon found I had difficulty maintaining a balance upon my machine. This would be due to the very slow speed, but by travelling at a steady four or five miles an hour, I managed to keep it upright. Regular checks in the mirror on the handlebars told me the entourage was keeping pace, and I could see the bulk of the elephant immediately behind me, moving with surprising speed. I daren't look around in case I wobbled and lost my balance, and therefore relied on the mirror.

We passed several knots of people *en route;* entire villages turned out to see us pass, and motorists halted to let us through. As we approached each gathering of people, cheers rose high in the air and I felt quite proud. Then the bike wobbled again; in recent minutes, I had become aware of its liability to wobble more than it should. Perhaps my back tyre was flat? I tried to look down, but this caused me to wobble alarmingly, so I frowned and kept going, hoping that I was not going to have trouble. Finally, when I reached a long, fairly flat and straight piece of road, I ventured a careful glance behind.

The leading elephant was clutching my wireless aerial!

It had seized the slender, tough aerial with its trunk and was trotting behind, hard on my tail. Three more elephants were behind that one, all gripping the tail of the one in front, and I was leading the motley procession towards the zoo. I never lived it down. One newspaper printed a photograph of me and my elephant and captioned it, "Elephant Old Bill", while another headlined the item, "Lead Kindly Bike".

It was all good, harmless fun and besides, I got free admission to the circus for my wife and family, for my part in the publicity. All the same, I began to wonder what Sergeant Bairstow would involve me with next!

I ought to add that the zoo in question was not on my beat. It lay within the boundaries of a neighbouring beat, but I frequently found myself patrolling the locality, due to my colleague's absence on other duties, or when he was ill or attending a course. I enjoyed those duties because they were so different. On two occasions, however, I received a fright, and both occurred during the same night.

Sergeant Bairstow (who else?) asked me to visit the grounds of the zoo late one night because there was a barbecue on the site. Intoxicating liquor was being sold and the organisers had obtained an occasional licence for the function. I had to pop along to ensure they closed their bars on time and that the revellers dispersed quietly. The fun was to end at 2 am, I was told. As I was on night duty, driving a Ford Anglia car instead of my motor-cycle, I was allocated that duty. It was suggested that I make my visit fairly late, in order that my presence would jolt the memories of the organisers.

I decided to visit the barbecue at 1.45 am. I drove into the car-park and was surprised to see it was deserted. I left the police car there, placed my peaked cap upon my head,

grabbed a torch and walked towards the buildings of the zoo.
There was not a sound from the place, save the twittering of
birds and the grunts of sleeping animals. I reasoned that if
there was a barbecue, there would be sounds of people and
music; there'd be cars around the place and lights. But there
was nothing.

In the stillness of that night, I stood with ears straining,
listening for sounds of merry-making. But there was none.
The place was deserted. Even the animals were asleep.

Because I knew the zoo's geography fairly well, I had a look
around. I knew there were certain areas which were ideal for
such an occasion, like open fields, a picnic area or the lawns
before the mansion. I made a systematic search but found
nothing. I did not even find any trace of a recent event, let
alone a current one. I veered towards the big house, hoping
that lights inside might indicate a celebration of some kind,
but all was in darkness. From there, I searched the outbuildings, but again drew a blank. It was at this stage that I
began to wonder if this was one of Sergeant Bairstow's quiet
pieces of fun. To be completely sure in my own mind, I made
a second tour of the entire zoo, but drew another blank.
There was no barbecue here. I was sure of that.

I returned to the car because it was almost two-thirty in the
morning and I was hungry. My refreshment period was
overdue, and I was to take it at Eltering Police Station, where
there was a kettle.

I began to re-trace my steps in the general direction of the
car park and was cutting between some buildings when I
became aware that someone was following me. My own feet
made little or no noise because I wore brothel-creepers, boots
with thick crêpe soles. But I could hear a woman's footsteps
immediately behind me. The delicate clipping sound of high
heels moved along with me. My hair stood on end. I stopped.
So did the woman. I looked behind, and there was nothing,
only total silence.

I wondered if I had imagined it all and set off again. The
striking footsteps renewed themselves. Clip clop, clip clop,
right behind me. I stopped and whirled around. There was
nothing. By this time, a cold sweat was making my back most
uncomfortable and my hair was standing sharply upright

about the nape of my neck. No one had said the zoo was haunted, not even Sergeant Bairstow. And I didn't think he would lay on a ghost, especially at two o'clock in the morning. Or would he?

I walked again, rapidly this time, but the terrifying footsteps came with me, moving in time with my strides. I knew the sound of a woman's high-heeled shoes, and this was definitely that sound. There was no doubt about it. I had my torch and after stopping a few times, I decided I must catch the woman, or the prankster. I had decided it was one of my colleagues playing a joke. There was no other explanation.

To complete my plans, I walked rapidly along the narrow path which ran between a building and a wall. The wall was shoulder height and I strode purposefully along, then suddenly whirled around and shone my torch directly behind me. There was nothing. Not even Sergeant Bairstow.

I was almost at my wits' end to know what it was, when I heard a snuffling sound at the other side of the wall. I shone my torch over and found a zebra in its compound. I talked to it, switched off my torch and moved on. The clip-clop came with me. I stopped, shone my torch and there she was beside me. It was the zebra, moving along with me in her compound. Every time I stopped, so did she. I walked backwards and forwards along that wall, and all the time she repeated her trick. I wished I had some food for her, but I hadn't. I left her rather sadly, for she was infinitely more beautiful and far more interesting than the non-existent barbecue!

When I rang Sergeant Bairstow from Eltering Police Station and mentioned the missing revelry, he laughed and said, "I must have got the wrong night, Nicholas."

I didn't mention the zebra and wondered if he would bring up the matter at a later date, but he didn't. He went to bed and after my welcome breakfast, I resumed patrol at three-thirty. There were two-and-a-half hours before knocking off time. To fill in the lonely hours, I drove along the main road from Eltering and turned off beyond the Black Bull Inn. This would take me back into the general area of the zoo, albeit from another direction. I might just come across the site of the barbecue, in a field near the zoo, maybe?

As I drove along, I kept my eyes open for the bus shelter

which stands at the junction. I used that shelter as a kind of
landmark, knowing that I had to make a sharp right turn at
the point. As my headlights picked out the re-assuring shape
of the shelter, I was surprised to see it was full of dogs. They
were lying or standing in the bus shelter, and there would be
six or eight in all. I couldn't be sure of the exact number. As
my lights lit the interior, I realised they were Alsatians, so I
pulled up directly opposite as they watched me with baleful
eyes. Two of them came to the front of the car and sniffed at
the engine, then peered into the headlamps, which I had
switched off to leave only side lights.

As the engine ticked over, I racked my brains. Who bred
Alsatians around here? I thought of sheep worrying and the
chaos they could cause if they became savage. Clearly, someone's breeding kennels had been left open, allowing the
animals to wander off as a pack.

A pack?

My hair stood on end. For the second time that night, I was
terrified. One of those 'dogs' came to my window and peered
up at me. I saw that its eyes were yellow and that it wasn't an
Alsatian. There was some white about it, its tail was longer,
the slope of its legs was different, the coat was thicker – and
those yellow eyes . . . !

Wolves. This was a pack of wolves! I recognised them now.
It was a pack of Canadian timber wolves and I knew where
they'd come from. The zoo. I was horrified when I realised
what might have happened if they'd taken a walk near that
zebra, with me as an object of pursuit. It didn't bear thinking
about.

Feeling as if I was in a safari park, I sat in the safety of the
car as they sniffed around it before returning to their shelter.
They seemed content to remain there but I was in a quand-
ary. If I left them to seek aid, they could wander anywhere
and might harm cattle or sheep. If I remained here, how
could I inform the zoo? My thinking must have been rather
slow, probably due to the hour, for I remembered the car had
a radio. I called up Force Control Room and asked them to
contact the zoo, even though it was about four o'clock in the
morning. The message was that their Canadian timber wolves
were in a bus shelter just south of Eltering.

Within forty-five minutes, there arrived a van containing three men armed with two big nets. With remarkable dexterity, they coaxed the docile animals into the van, where they seemed like pets, and not in the least savage. It transpired they were not dangerous to humans, but I wouldn't have given them the chance. It seemed that someone had slipped open the door of their compound, but we never traced that person.

I clambered into my warm bed just after six that morning, and Mary muttered, "Had a busy night?"

"I've been trapping Canadian timber wolves," I said with as much nonchalance as I could muster.

"Wolves?" she murmured sleepily.

"Yes," I said, snuggling down against her warmth.

"Not polar bears?" she asked, moving away from my chilly feet and sinking into a deep sleep.

*　*　*　*

A persistent animal problem came in the shape of Miss Fiona Lampton's pony. Miss Fiona spoke with a horsy accent, dressed in horsy clothes and mixed with horsy people. She had a horsy face with matching teeth and it could be said that even her laughter had a ring of the equine. She was a spinster of the parish, aged about thirty-eight years, give or take a little, and she lived on private means. She had no known occupation but was never short of cash; somehow she contrived to run a large, sporty car which was seldom clean, but always in a hurry.

She kept several horses but one of them was a pony, a delightful creature with a long, straggly mane and an equally straggly tail. The unfortunate animal caused me lots of problems because it had mastered the ability to open the gate of its paddock. Having perfected this trick, it would regularly unlatch the gate and take an unaccompanied stroll down the village street of Aidensfield. Horses were not unusual in our village street, but this one, whose name was Topsy, had a liking for lawns, garden flowers and lettuce. This made it rather unpopular.

During its perambulations, it would push open garden

gates or simply wander through the new open-plan estate, there to feast upon the flavour of the month, sometimes tulips, sometimes dahlias and occasionally prize chrysanthemums. Many complaints were levelled at Miss Fiona but they seemed to slide from her masculine shoulders like rainwater from a plastic mac. She agreed that Topsy was a naughty boy, in fact a bloody naughty boy at times, and she promised she would make him behave. Several villagers suggested a change of both latch and field, but she explained that Topsy was like Houdini – he could open any latch.

Eventually the problem landed on my doorstep. One or two of the more vociferous villagers decided it was time to do something official. In their eyes, that meant action by the constabulary.

I listened to their listed complaints and suggested they sent bills for damage to Miss Fiona; several had already considered that action and had sent bills, which had been promptly paid. One or two had made their garden gates more difficult to open, but as Miss Fiona said, Houdini the horse could open them. The villagers had wisely decided that a padlock on Fiona's field was not a good idea because other people required access via that field to their own premises. Locks were therefore beyond consideration. Miss Fiona had tried placing Topsy in different paddocks, but he opened those gates too. If he wandered from the nearest paddock, into the village street, at least we knew where he was.

I promised I would do what I could, but the truth was I had no idea what to do. Everything that was possible had apparently been done, both by Miss Fiona and by the villagers. The pony seemed unstoppable.

I wondered if she should be asked to sell it, then a day or two later I met the lady in the street. She cried, "What ho, Officer," and slapped her thigh with a riding crop.

"Ah!" I hailed her. "Miss Fiona. Just the person – I'd like a word with you."

"Is it about that bloody animal of mine?"

"The pony," I confirmed. "Yes, there's been a complaint, from several villagers."

"He is a bloody nuisance, Officer, and no doubt about it. A downright bloody nuisance. I can't keep him in that field, or any field for that matter. Daren't put locks on, what? Might cause problems of rights of way and things. Damned nuisance, isn't he?"

"You've horses in that top field of yours," I reminded her. "Couldn't Topsy go in there? He might like the company of other horses, and that might encourage him to stay."

"Not on your bloody nerve, Officer," she cried, horrified. "I keep my best animals in there – they'd kick poor old Topsy to death. No, I can't do that."

"He's a danger to traffic," I said. "There could be an accident."

"Not with Topsy, Officer, not with Topsy," she boomed. "Marvellous on the road, you know, better than a dog even. Hears oncoming cars and gets in the side. No problems there."

"He eats people's flowers and growing vegetables. One chap reckons he lost an entire garden full of prize dahlias."

"I paid, I always do. Good compensation. They'll have to tolerate Topsy, Officer. There's nothing I can do, I'm sorry."

"You could sell him."

"Sell him? He was a gift from an admirer of mine! No, I couldn't sell him, he's a real pet."

"Miss Fiona," I said, trying to appear threatening. "I might have to consider a prosecution, for letting him stray on the highway."

"If you must, you must," she said, and stalked away, thrashing her thigh with the crop. I watched her stride down the street, her body swaying in time with her leg movements, and I wondered what the answer could be. I didn't want to book the woman, but if she persisted in allowing Topsy the freedom of the main street, it would be necessary. It would be necessary too, if I was to appease the villagers; at least it would prove I had done *something*. If Sergeant Blaketon heard about it, he'd start asking questions and he'd demand a prosecution. But would court action stop the horse?

It was perhaps fortunate that Sergeant Bairstow met me a few days later and asked if I had any problems. I thought it a fine opportunity to discuss the pony, as he was such a seasoned and experienced police officer.

He listened carefully with his gentle smile and when I had

concluded, he said. "I don't think we need report her for summons, Nicholas. I mean, it's a well-behaved animal, isn't it? It's not dangerous to people – it doesn't go around biting and kicking them. It knows what to do in traffic and it doesn't cause severe problems."

"It eats flowers and lettuce," I reminded him.

"That's a civil matter, lad, not a crime. And she pays compensation. What more can the injured parties expect? We must not involve ourselves with civil matters."

"I must do something, Sergeant. That woman must be taught that the pony is her responsibility."

He smiled faintly. "Suppose it wasn't a horse or a pony. Suppose you found it. What would you do?"

"I don't follow." I had to admit I was confused.

"Well, suppose it was a pet cat or a dog, or something like a hamster or little lad's rabbit. You found it in the street. What would you do?"

"I'd take it to the owner's house, if I knew where that was."

"Exactly, Nicholas," he smiled again. "And suppose the owner was out?"

"I'd put it somewhere safe until they returned."

"Of course you would," he said. "I mean, if the kitchen door was open, you'd probably pop it in there, wouldn't you? Or if a hen-house was open, you'd use that . . ."

"She has no hen-houses," I said. "And her stables are locked when the horses are in the fields."

"But she always leaves her kitchen door open, doesn't she?"

"Does she?" I asked, surprised at his local knowledge.

"Always," he nodded gently. "We had trouble with her once before – it was a randy stallion she kept. It fancied everything from articulated lorries to poodles, and I often called to see her about it. She sold it to a circus, I think. I've no idea what kinds of tricks it got up to. I seem to remember they had to keep the elephants out of its way."

"You're not suggesting I put it in her kitchen, are you?" I asked, horrified at the suggestion.

"I wouldn't suggest a thing like that, Nicholas!" he said, leaving me to my thoughts.

During that summer, I must have received a further half-dozen complaints about Miss Fiona's pony, and one day I was in the village street when Topsy came trotting along, utterly alone.

This was my moment of decision. I was faced with the problem in person.

"Topsy!" I shouted, and the pretty pony came willingly to me. It nuzzled its face under my arm and I patted its head, as it rubbed itself against me.

"You've done it again," I heard myself say to the animal. "Come along, it's time for action."

Holding its long mane, I walked the length of the street and several villagers smiled their greetings. I said I was taking Topsy home for tea, and they smiled, some with happiness and other with expressions of bewilderment. I reached her house. It was a lovely cottage with a large white gate opening onto the road. Inside the gate was a converted farmyard, with outbuildings all around, all locked. Her cottage was on the left as I entered. It had a white door of the old stable-door type, and this led directly into her kitchen.

I knocked.

There was no reply. I reached up for the latch of the top half of the door and found the pony's muzzle nudging my hand. It managed to press the sneck and the door swung open on oiled hinges, swinging with its own weight to rest inside the kitchen.

"Clever stuff," I stroked its head. "Can you smell the metal or something?"

I reached down for the lower sneck but the intelligent animal was with me. With its nose, it depressed the handle and the door swung open, to lodge beneath the upper half. The way into the kitchen was clear. I led Topsy inside and left him standing on the tiled floor, as I closed the door behind myself. I didn't think he could let himself out because the doors would only open inwards – whether the horse would reason that, I did not know. But I left the house feeling very happy. Fiona now had a horse in her kitchen. I was to learn later, that this had registered in Topsy's head. Each time he let himself out of his field, he made his unerring way to the kitchen, opened the door and let himself in.

It would be several weeks later when I met Miss Fiona.

"Ah, Officer!" she beamed. "I've good news for you."

"Really?" I wondered what it could be.

"Topsy!" she said. "He's with a riding school at Eltering now. I donated him on a permanent-loan basis. He remains my property, but they use him for lessons; they feed him and so on. Good wheeze, eh? He'd found a way of opening my kitchen doors you know. Let himself in, opened the bloody fridge and pinched all my vegetables and fruit. The bloody animal!"

"He's an amazing horse," I smiled. "Very intelligent."

"Too bloody intelligent!" she laughed.

When I told Sergeant Bairstow, he smiled quietly. "It was better than taking her to court over the pony," he said.

"Yes, it was," and I knew the villagers regarded my action as being very correct. Several asked if I had considered joining the Royal Canadian Mounted Police.

Nine

With an abbey full of Benedictine monks virtually on my doorstep, it was not unexpected that I should become involved with the church in one or more of its forms. Life within the shadows of an abbey was fascinating – the Benedictines of Maddleskirk are Roman Catholics but their philosophy is that all men are children of God and therefore to be treated with the respect due to them. There were precious few religious barriers and even members of the Wee Frees of Scotland would find a welcome within the portals of that mighty Christian church, an invitation that was not expected to be reciprocated. But true men of God are full of forgiveness.

Monks in long black cloaks, or tee-shirts and jeans, or sports gear, wandered about our countryside and were part of the scenery. Because they were a living part of the local populace, they had lost a lot of their mystique. The villagers found the monks very human, very kindly and very knowledgeable, as was expected of an ancient and historic teaching order, and it was not unusual to find oneself enjoying a pint of beer in the pub, with a monk standing next to one, also enjoying a pint.

Soon after my arrival in Aidensfield, I discovered that their local ecumenical movement had already started. The two chief faiths of the district, Anglican and Roman Catholic, were friends. They shared churches, they shared services and they even shared priests. The latter came as a surprise to me, having been schooled in the village the Reformation had missed, i.e. Egton Bridge in North Riding's lovely Eskdale. I had been reared in the ancient Roman Catholic faith which tended to isolate Catholics from other faiths, but out here, this thriving Catholic monastery was the centrepiece of rural

life where other faiths were openly accepted and the views of
their adherents respected.

This important lesson was given to me about nine-thirty
one Sunday. It was a bleak, wintry morning with sleet in the
air and a powerful easterly wind blowing across my exposed
hilltop. I was enjoying a week-end free from police duties,
when Sunday morning meant attending Mass with the
family. We had breakfasted and were washing up in the
kitchen when I spotted a bedraggled figure at my garden
gate. He was propping a pedal cycle against a gate post and
through my steamed-up window I watched him enter the
garden and make for the front door. His head was bowed
against the driving sleet and his clothes blew in the cruel
wind.

I dried my hands as I went to answer the door and found a
young man standing before me, sensibly dressed in heavy
cycling gear. He was saturated about the face and feet, his
outer clothes were dripping and he looked nigh frozen to
death.

"Good morning," he smiled apologetically, the words finding difficulty in leaving his frozen face. "I wonder if I might
use your telephone?"

"Certainly," I agreed, bidding him enter the house. He
did, and I closed the door. It was bitterly cold outside; the
temperature was dropping and it wouldn't be long before the
sleet turned to snow. And with this wind, there'd be problems
in this locality. Lanes would become blocked with drifts and
lonely farmsteads would be cut off. But all that was later . . .
now, I led him into the office where his dripping clothes
would not damage anything. He stood on my polished floor,
making pools on the shining surface.

"Are you going far?" I asked, surprised that anyone would
cycle in this weather.

"Crampton," he rubbed his hands to encourage circulation.
"At least, I was. My bike's got a puncture and I wanted to
ring the abbey for help."

"The abbey?" I wondered if he was talking about a pub.

"Maddleskirk Abbey. I'm a monk," and he opened his
waterproofs to reveal his dog-collar. "I'm on my way to
Crampton to play the organ for the ten o'clock service."

"Oh!" that explained his journey. "I see," and I then pondered slightly. "But you're Catholic monks, aren't you? Crampton Parish Church is Church of England?"

"That's right," he smiled. "The vicar rang us up in a panic. It seems his organist fell ill last night with 'flu, and he asked if we could help. The Abbot agreed, as he always does, so I'm *en route* to play their hymns like a good Anglican."

"I thought Catholics weren't allowed to attend Protestant services?"

"They weren't. It's a long story, as you know; the differences between our faiths are historic, and the Abbot regards our churches as two sisters who aren't on speaking terms. It's a temporary state of affairs, in his opinion. Eventually, they will learn to speak with one another and then I'm sure we'll find we have a lot in common. The Reformation did a lot of harm, but in the end it will be shown to have done a lot of good. In the end, we'll all be one church again, just as God intended. This is just one of the ways our Abbot has of making those two silly sisters take a long close look at each other, and to make them realise that they do share a lot of common ground."

"He sounds a very sensible man," I said.

"He is, he'll go far. Now, could I use your phone please? I'll get the monastery garage to send a car out for me."

"I'll run you down," I offered. "It's only a couple of miles."

And so I did. I said I'd ring the Abbey upon my return and arrange collection of his cycle, as I'd be at Mass myself, in the village Catholic church. I did that and later that afternoon, I mended the puncture in his back wheel. He called a day or two later and had a cup of tea, telling me he'd welcomed the experience of playing in an Anglican church. He'd enjoyed listening to the hearty Anglican singing. It transpired that the vicar hadn't announced him as a visiting Catholic monk, but had simply identified him as a visiting priest, without telling the congregation of his faith or place of origin.

"Isn't that cheating?" I asked. "Surely those good Anglicans should have known you were a Catholic? They would think you were a visiting member of their own faith?"

"Does it matter?" he asked me. "I was there to play the organ not to convert them or to argue about religion. I think one old lady summed it up afterwards – she came to me, shook me by the hand and said, 'That was fine playing, vicar'. She said it was plain to see I was a man of God. She was right, you know."

And off he went. I saw him cycle past several times in the future and he always waved.

My next spell of duty involving the church came with a telephone call from a passing motorist.

"Ah!" he said breathlessly into the mouthpiece. "Is that the policeman?"

"It is," I confirmed.

"Oh well, there's been an accident. There's a car on its roof between Thackerston and Aidensfield. It's in a field, just past the quarry," and he rang off before I could ask for more details.

It was about ten o'clock in the morning, and he'd caught me just before I left the office on my rounds. I told Mary I was just popping down the road to deal with an accident, and there I'd be for about an hour. The Sergeant could find me there, if he came visiting.

Mounted on my trusty motor-cycle, I drove slowly down the gently sloping incline which led from my house into the village of Thackerston, about two miles away. I sought indications of the accident, but arrived in Thackerston without finding any sign of trouble. Had it been a hoax call?

The fields lay to the south of the road and I'd kept my eyes peeled as well as I could while riding a motor-cycle and watching the road ahead, but there was nothing. There were no signs on the road, no broken glass, no deposited mud, no skid marks or other debris. I began to feel sure I'd been dragged out on a false call. I mounted the bike and made the return journey, remembering that the caller had mentioned the quarry. The quarry lay roughly between the two villages, so I parked my motor-cycle near its entrance and walked along the verge, seeking the accident.

And then, as I peered over the hedge at that point, I saw a car on its roof in the field. It was half-way down a steep incline and invisible from the road. I clambered over the drystone wall and ran down the grassy slope to the vehicle, but it was empty. It was a tiny black Austin A30, the successor of the Austin 7 and ancestor of the BMC Mini. There it was, finely balanced on its roof, rocking to and fro as I touched it. There was a distinct whiff of petrol but little sign of damage, other than a dented roof. I looked for the injured people, but there wasn't a soul around. I made a note of the registration number from which I could trace the owner, and returned to the road.

Once there, I sought indications of a battle with steering or brakes, but found none. Judging by its position, it had left the road, run across the wide grass verge and dived through the hedge without even attempting to brake or change course. Its point of entry into the field had been precisely where a drystone wall and a hawthorn hedge met – the car had bolted through them at that exact place. The hedge had parted and had closed after it, thus leaving no trace of its remarkable journey. It had nose-dived into the steep field and had rolled over several times, to end its trip upside down.

I rang Durham Taxation Authority, with whom the car was registered and learned that it belonged to a vicar from that part of the world. Having not heard from anyone about this accident, other than the anonymous caller, I rang his home address and a woman answered.

"Mrs Dwyer?" I asked, hoping I was talking to the wife of the Rev. Sidney Dwyer.

"Yes?" there was a question in her voice.

"I'm P.C. Rhea of Aidensfield, in the North Riding," I began.

"Ah!" she said. "My husband said you might ring. Is it about his car?"

"Yes it is, as a matter of fact."

"Well," she said. "He was on his way to Filey with three of his colleagues, where they are attending a conference. He ran off the road, near Thackerston, he tells me, but no one was hurt. They flagged down passing cars and got lifts to the conference. They're all very well, and he rang a garage to arrange removal of his car."

"Oh," I was pleased at his efficiency. "He's got it all organised."

"He's very good at organising," she said. "I do hope there's no problems."

"No," I assured her. "No problems, so long as you know about it."

"Thank you for ringing," she sounded very pleasant. "He'll call in on the way back for you to see his insurance and licence, by the way."

"He thinks of everything," I said.

"Yes, he does, doesn't he?" and she rang off. But even now, all those years later, I marvel that a car full of people could leave a road, cross a wide grass verge and plunge through a hedge without leaving a mark of any kind. And then to land upon its roof without causing any injury to its four inmates. It was a tiny car, so perhaps they'd been so tightly packed that they'd escaped injury?

It was almost as if the hand of God had lifted the little car off its wheels and plonked it upside down in the field. But why would He want to do that?

* * * *

Lairsbeck is a hamlet some miles off my beat, and it lies deep in the North Yorkshire moors, hidden in a timbered valley called Lairsdale. It comprises a scattering of farmsteads, a telephone kiosk, some ant hills, a pillar box and the chapel. The chapel is the dominant feature. It was erected in that upsurge of religious fervour that followed Wesley across these remote parts, and it stands on the road side just beyond the first clump of pines after the watersplash. The door is of oak and very strong but inside the walls are covered with flaking whitewash and the whole place smells musty and damp.

The chapel is not used very often, perhaps once a month at the most, which means that modern heating and lighting systems are luxuries the tiny congregation cannot afford. The full congregation totals eleven, and they rely on oil lamps and paraffin heaters for light and warmth.

The task of filling the heaters had long been in the hands of Joshua Atkinson while his wife, Martha, looked after the lights. Other chapel folks had jobs like dusting, sweeping, winding up the clock, storing hymn books and stocking the tiny place with flowers. Everyone had a job of some kind, which was one way of ensuring they attended services.

That ploy gave some indication of the wisdom of Pastor Smith. He was a cunning old character, I found, and I liked him. He did not live at Lairsbeck but commuted to this outpost once a month; I met him in Ashfordly from time to time. He once told me of his first days with this small congregation.

It seemed they did not want to stand as he entered the chapel to begin the service, and this was something he felt was a vital part of the proceedings, a show of respect for him and his office. He had spoken of this from the pulpit on one occasion, and asked them to stand up next time he entered. They did not obey. He repeated his request from the pulpit but the sturdy and stubborn congregation refused to get to their feet as he entered the body of the chapel. Then he realised they always stood up to sing their hymns, and he hit upon the bright idea of having an entrance hymn as he walked towards his pulpit.

Sure enough, as the organ burst into life, they all leapt to their feet and launched into their favourite hymn as Pastor Smith moved down the aisle with a smile of satisfaction upon his face. But that was the last time they stood up, even for hymns. He told me the tale, and one of his flock told me the same tale one afternoon, over tea at his farm.

"Yon's a crafty aud sod," the farmer said. "By, he thowt he'd tricked us inti standing up for him, but nivver again. He'll nivver trick us again like that – we allus sings hymns sitting doon now, just in case he's trying to catch us out again."

It would be late on autumn afternoon when Pastor Smith hailed me in Ashfordly. "I'd like a word with you," he said.

I stopped and listened.

"I try to get men and women from the professions to read a lesson in my chapel, at the Lairsbeck services," he began. "I've had doctors, shop keepers, veterinary surgeons, and many others. Would you read for me one Sunday evening, Mr Rhea?"

It was a bolt from the blue. I'd never been to a Methodist service in my life, and told him of my own faith. He seemed surprised to find a Catholic policeman, but was even more

surprised when, bearing in mind the monk and the organ
playing, I said, "I'll have a word with the Abbot of Maddleskirk. If he agrees, I'll read for you."

The Abbot agreed; in fact, he was very enthusiastic and
one Sunday evening in late autumn, therefore, I found myself
driving to Lairsbeck in my own car and off duty, but in full
uniform. I was on my way to read the lesson at Pastor Smith's
tiny moorland chapel. I arrived twenty minutes before we
were due to start and met him in what was akin to the vestry
in my own church. He showed me the relevant passages and I
read them to familiarise myself with the phraseology before
my moment of glory. I said I'd be fine. He thanked me and
wished me luck.

"Oh," he said, almost as an afterthought. "Be sure to sit in
the seat directly beneath the pulpit."

I didn't question the wisdom of this, but nodded and we
later entered the church. They were singing one of their
hymns, sitting down as was their practice, and I made my
way self-consciously to the seat he had advised. I noticed the
little church was cosy and the oil lamps flickered in the
draughts of the place, giving the building a very homely
atmosphere. I knew that Pastor Smith had a reputation for
long sermons, and hoped he would deliver a short one
tonight. I had no idea of the progression of a chapel service
but waited for the nod from him. Eventually, the signal
came and I entered his varnished pulpit, cleared my throat
and read the relevant passages. As I returned to my seat, he
mounted the stairs and began his sermon. It went on and
on. I knew I was in for a long session, for his theme was
"Christianity in Practice", a talk about the benefits of
ecumenism.

He spoke well, I must admit, and his words made sense, but
after half an hour, I could hear the restless sounds of shifting
feet, of rubbed hands, of coughing. He ploughed on regard-
less. I was nice and cosy beside the heater, and it wasn't an
unpleasant experience.

Eventually, it was all over and they drifted away, the
caretaker remaining behind to lock up and put out the lamps.
Pastor Smith bade them farewell until next month and
invited me to his home. "I've some explaining to do. Can I

tempt you to my manse at Ashfordly? For a bite of supper, perhaps and a cup of tea?"

I agreed and followed him home. His wife produced some home-made scones and cakes and we sat to enjoy a marvellous supper. His eyes twinkled as he told me the story.

"You'll know old Joshua Atkinson?" he asked.

"Oh, yes," I knew him all right. "Queer old character, isn't he?"

Joshua was a farmer in the area, a stalwart of his chapel and one of the old school whose life-style had not changed since Wesley's visit to these parts.

"Well," said Pastor Smith. "He looks after the heaters, and his wife does the lamps. On winter Sundays, when we have services, Joshua comes down to the chapel just before lunch and fills the heaters. He lights them so the church will be warm by evening. By seven on the chilliest Sunday, the place is lovely and cosy, and you can sit without a coat. But Joshua, I found, is very cunning. He's got it off to a fine art. He'll fill the heaters just long enough to last a certain time, time for one very short sermon. If I go on too long, the heaters dry up and the congregation begins to feel cold. So do I. It is Joshua's method of telling me to belt up and go home. The crafty old monkey tries to dictate the length of my sermons.

"When he got the television installed, he would put even less paraffin in! He wanted to get home to watch his favourite programme. Well, tonight, I took my own paraffin, and I filled the heaters in the pulpit and beside your seat. He'd already filled them at lunchtime, putting in enough for his purpose. But I put more in. As Joshua and his cronies sat shivering, you and I were nice and warm, Mr Rhea. I'm sorry I went on a bit, but it was done to teach them a lesson."

I laughed aloud. "You've got to be crafty to beat this lot!" I said. "It wouldn't surprise me if they realised what you were doing!"

"He doesn't know yet, but it won't take long," Pastor Smith laughed. "It's not the first time I've filled my heater to make it last a little longer, so I'm sure he'll work it out. He judges his own fillings by the little chapel clock."

"The clock?"

"Yes, on the wall. It's an old clock. He knows how much

paraffin will last per hour, and he fills the heaters accordingly."

"The crafty old blighter!"

"But I alter the clock!" chuckled Pastor Smith. "I always get here before him, in time to fix my heater and to change the pointers of the clock. That means that his timings for the consumption of paraffin are not accurate."

"What good does that do?" I asked, puzzled by the complexity of this.

"When he realises what I'm doing," smiled Pastor Smith, "He'll work out new amounts of paraffin for the heaters, and he'll base them on the clock. But the clock is always wrong, you see, so he'll never get it right, will he? I shall work things always to my advantage. Joshua will always shiver, Mr Rhea, and I shall always be warm."

I wondered where this little drama was going to end, and left the manse very amused by it all. As I drove home, I wondered what Pastor Smith would do next in his attempts to make them stand up as he entered. Perhaps he'd play the National Anthem? I decided to suggest this to him next time we spoke.

* * * *

Contrary to popular belief, the monks of Maddleskirk are a worldly crowd, closely in touch with our modern society and its attendant problems. They know about the public's concern over sin and sex, money and motoring, they take part in village affairs and county matters. Some sit on councils and one became chairman of the local District Council. Others take leading roles in teaching, sport, drugs education, religion and a host of other extramural subjects. In short, they know more about life than many of our so-called progressive society.

In spite of their many external interests, they are intensely religious and their daily routine centres upon their faith. It is probably fair to say that their Catholic faith is more important then any other aspect of life, and there are times when this overlaps with my duties.

On one occasion, I was summoned via the radio on my

motor-cycle to a fire in Aidensfield. A cottage was burning, with smoke pouring through the roof and upper windows. Someone had phoned my house; I was out, engaged upon a routine patrol and Mary had the presence of mind to contact me via Control Room. I was only five minutes away and arrived at the scene to find a gaggle of onlookers staring at the smoke which was permeating through the multitude of gaps about the cottage. It rose, black and thick, through the roof, the windows and the woodwork, but no one had entered to seek its occupants.

"Is anybody in there?" I shouted as I ran to the door.

"It's old Mr Blenkinsopp," twittered one old lady. "It's his house and it's locked."

During a two-week fire fighting course a member of the R.A.F. had taught me that the opening of a door or a window could introduce fresh oxygen to the seat of a fire and that could cause it to burst into flame. At the moment, the place seemed to be gently smouldering, producing lots of smoke but no flames. Should I break down the door or not? I had to get inside somehow, and in those precious seconds of indecision, the Fire Brigade arrived.

"There might be somebody in here," I shouted.

"We'll have to break in then," returned a leading fireman. "We'll contain any blaze that erupts."

As they organised themselves, I ran to a ground-floor window and cracked it with my gloved fist, opened it and climbed in. The place was full of choking fumes and I covered my face with a handkerchief as I raced through the downstairs rooms. There was no one here. I ran upstairs and as I reached the half-way stage, the front door collapsed behind me and a fireman appeared, silhouetted in the doorway. He ran upstairs behind me. I found a bedroom with billowing smoke pouring from it, and inside I could see the still figure lying on a smouldering bed. Poor old Mr Blenkinsopp.

Coughing madly, I went to him, but it was far, far too late. His body was the colour of brown varnish, his clothing smouldered to ashes and his extremities burnt away. He had no feet or hands, no hair and his hot body was swollen with a combination of fire, gas and intense heat. I heard a loud thump behind me; the fireman had fainted at the sight, but another rushed in with a hose and asked, "What shall I do?"

"Switch the electricity off," I shouted at him. "It's an electric blanket." The tell-tale cable ran from beneath the remains of the bed, and he switched off the mains supply.

"Shall I spray the bed?"

"Please."

No. 1 fireman had recovered and together, they sprayed the red-hot bed and the heated corpse with their small hose. Fortunately, nothing else was burning and all that had been destroyed was the bed. Nothing else had caught fire. Smoke had discoloured the upper rooms and some places downstairs; even the windows bore a covering of slimy brown fumes, but happily, the close atmosphere had prevented the flames breaking out. We later discovered that the bed had smouldered literally all through the night, and that poor old Mr Blenkinsopp took drugs. He was also an alcoholic. The postmortem later revealed he had gone to bed heavily laced with barbiturates and whisky, and had left his blanket switched on. He'd probably wet himself while asleep, an action which could cause an electrical short in the blanket, and that in turn could cause the smouldering. He'd died by inhaling the fumes of the burning mattress, and would have been dead long before the heat began to consume his body. He would have felt no pain.

The firemen extinguished the burning bed and doused the entire room with water, for it was hot all over. Even the wooden beams and floor were hot to the touch and the curtains might have blazed, the rugs too, or the bedding which had slipped to the floor. Miraculously, nothing had burst into flames, the house was intact and no other damage had been done. When the firemen left, I had to remain with the body until I could arrange its removal, and as I waited in the room, taking the necessary notes for my report, I was aware of footsteps on the landing. A monk appeared in the doorway. He did not faint, but smiled and made the sign of the cross.

"Hello, Father," I said, wondering why he had come.

"Oh," he said, "I'm pleased it's you, Nicholas. Join me in prayer, would you? He was one of our flock, although he never came to church in his later years. I'd like to pray at his side for a few moments."

And so I found myself kneeling before the charred remains of this unfortunate man as the monk began his prayers. It was an emotional moment, even though I had never known poor old Mr Blenkinsopp. As Father Egbert began the *De Profundis,* I felt tears coming to my eyes. The little ceremony was soon over, we shook hands and Father Egbert thanked me. Then he went away, leaving me to the police duty of dealing with a sudden death.

Looking back upon that moment, I often wonder what Sergeant Blaketon would have said if he'd entered the room during our prayers. What would he have made of a policeman kneeling beside a corpse, chanting the *De Profundis* in Latin with a Benedictine monk?

* * * *

Brother Franklyn was another interesting monk who had not been ordained into the priesthood. He was studying with that in mind. He was a keen rugger player and had been captain of his school XV and of his university team. Massively built, he was as strong as an ox and coached in his sport at the local public school, which was part of the abbey complex. A real man's man, he would take his victorious team into the local pub and sup pints with them in the cause of a just celebration. He liked a good sing-song too and knew most of the popular rugger songs.

His hobby, when not playing rugby football or chanting at Evensong, was breeding white doves. My knowledge of doves is poor and I am not sure of their breed, but they were beautiful, gentle creatures of purest white and they lived in a loft at the edge of the monastery's grounds. He ministered to them daily and knew them individually; he bred from them and sold the chicks to others of similar interests, and I believe his strain was noted for their excellence. He appeared to be an authority on the subject and judged at local shows.

Around April one year, I was off duty with influenza when the telephone rang one Sunday morning. Mary answered it, and came to me after dealing with the call.

"That was Brother Franklyn," she explained, and the expression on her face told me something was wrong. Lying in bed with red eyes and a running nose, there was little I could do for the monk, but I asked what had happened.

"How did you know something was wrong?" she put to me.

"Your face, darling! It tells a million stories. What's happened to upset you?"

"Brother Franklyn's doves," she said softly. "You know them?"

"Sure," I smiled through my running eyes. Everyone knew of the doves, for they flew around the village, their wings whistling as they twisted and turned overhead, as if by some spoken command.

"Somebody's killed them," she said, with tears in her eyes. "Most of them, anyway."

"Killed them?" I cried.

She nodded. "Yes, last night, during the night. They broke into one of his lofts and they've strangled them all, wrung their necks and smashed the unhatched eggs."

"Poor Franklyn," was all I could say. "All of them?"

"No, just one of the lofts, the big one. He's got the little loft left, untouched. He says he can breed again."

"What a bloody awful thing to do." I was angry and upset at the cruelty of the persons who did this.

"He'd phoned Ashfordly but got no reply, so he rang us, just to alert the police."

"You'd explain I was off duty with flu?"

"Yes, so I said I would ring Ashfordly Police Station as soon as I knew someone was in."

"There's not a lot anyone can do now, unless someone saw the culprits," I said. "Does he think the bastards will come back and have another go at his loft?"

"I'm sure the possibility was on his mind," she told me.

"O.K. Do your best to raise someone at Ashfordly. I'd love to catch the thugs that did this, and do the same to them."

"That's not allowed." She shook a finger at me. "Thugs can misbehave, but not policemen."

An hour later, the telephone rang again and I heard Mary's voice from my resting place upstairs, but I could not distinguish her words. She came up to me, announced the caller had been Brother Franklyn and that he'd changed his mind about requesting police action.

"That's typical of a monk!" I almost shouted through my thick throat. "Somebody does him a favour like that, kills all his livestock, destroys a loft that's taken years to accumulate and what's he do? He'll go into the Abbey Church and pray for them to be forgiven! And the vandals will escape Scot free!"

I laid in bed for a further three days until I felt fit enough to venture from the room. I spent a couple of days finding my feet and my increasing strength, and I returned to work three days after that. It would be another two or three days later when I found myself on a foot patrol near the Abbey of Maddleskirk. The first person I saw walking towards me, *en route* from the post office, was Brother Franklyn.

"Good morning, Brother," I hailed him. "Good to see you."

"And you, Nicholas," he smiled broadly. "Have you recovered from your bout of 'flu?"

"Yes, all clear now. It's good to be out and about. I hate being confined to bed."

"I'm sorry I rang you about my doves when you were ill. I had no idea, or I wouldn't have troubled you."

"You weren't to know," I assured him. "I was only sorry you changed your mind about calling the police."

"I called in the heat of the moment," he said. "After I'd discovered the carnage, the police were the first people who came to mind."

We strolled together along the road in front of the magnificent abbey and he said, "I'd like to talk about it. Fancy a beer?"

"I'd love one," so he took me into the monastery guest room where he furnished me with an earthenware pint pot full of deliciously cool beer. He had one too, then told his tale.

"After I'd tried to contact the police at Ashfordly, I rang your home and found you were ill. On reflection, that was a good thing – from my point of view," he qualified his remark. "It gave me time to cool off, to reconsider my action. I had a long hard think about what had happened and decided to call off the police. After all, what could you do? The culprits had long since gone and even if you had any idea of who they

were, you'd have a most difficult job proving it, for court
purposes. There'd be a lot of work for nothing, so I cancelled
your official involvement."

"I wanted to get my hands on those vandals." I sipped the
beer and it was delightful.

"And me," he smiled. "And me. Oh, I wanted to get my
hands on them too, and wring their necks!" and he clenched
his huge fists about his pint pot.

"Why call it off then?" I asked him.

"You are a trustworthy man, aren't you?" he asked me
suddenly. "I can trust you – I can talk to you in confidence,
even on delicate matters?"

I wondered what on earth was coming now. "Of course," I
assured him.

He drew a deep breath. "Well, Nick," he spoke seriously.
"It was like this," and he proceeded to tell me this story.

It seemed he'd been very concerned about his second loft
and had a gut feeling that the vandals would return for an
attempt upon that one. He'd discussed this with his pals in
the school rugger XV who'd been incensed and who had
produced a plan of action. The entire school rugger team and
reserves would lie in wait for the killers the following
Saturday night. At first, Franklyn had been reluctant to agree
but he knew his players were furious about the death of his
birds, and they might allow it to affect their playing. This
could purge it from their systems. So he agreed, in the
interests of the game.

They had examined the area about the loft and had
worked out the likely parking places for the villains' vehicles.
Having done this, they had evolved a plan to deal with one or
more unofficial cars that might arrive in the area. Once the
passengers had left any vehicle, they would let down the tyres
and remove the rotor arm, thus effectively immobilising the
vehicle. They would then wait until the culprits were approaching the loft; at that stage, the team would pounce.
They would set about dealing with the ruffians as only a
rugby XV can.

That was the plan.

According to Brother Franklyn, the villains did arrive.
Around one-thirty in the morning, a car crept into the

grounds of Maddleskirk Abbey, parked behind a wall and four youths emerged. This had been spotted by one of the concealed members who had promptly activated their 'peace plan'. They called it that because the dove is the emblem of peace.

Without exception, those boys were massive, powerful youths of seventeen or eighteen, and one of them removed the rotor arm of the car. Once the invaders were out of earshot, two of them let down the tyres, and so the trespassers were marooned within the grounds of the abbey. Meanwhile, the marauding gang had made their approach to the small loft as anticipated, although their movements were now monitored every inch of the way. And as they had begun their climb up the steps, their approach had been completely cut off. They found themselves surrounded by twenty powerful youths, all hell-bent on having a whale of a time at the expense of some ugly villains.

Brother Franklyn was in bed at the time, which I felt was a very diplomatic move because he could justifiably claim not to be involved in this episode. The four villains had been given 'the treatment'; they had been severely thrashed to say the least, and had then been cast fully clothed into the slime-covered disused outdoor swimming pool. After an enforced swim there, they had been allowed out, and their shoes had been removed. They had then been sent on their way home to the nearby market town of Harrowby, a walk of ten miles or so. It was rough treatment for a set of cowardly rogues. After minutes, their shoes had been returned, but it was still a long, long walk.

"So there we are," smiled Brother Franklyn. "That's what happened."

"I don't want to know about it," I said.

"They daren't tell you, dare they? You'd have them for killing my birds?"

"I would, but you'd best not mention this to a soul!" I advised.

"I won't, I won't," he breathed.

"I must be going, Brother," I stood up to leave. "Thanks for the beer, and thanks for telling me about it. I feel better now – my mind is at rest. Justice has been done.

Really, they have received their punishment, haven't they? Goodbye."

"Peace be with you," he said, showing me the door.

Ten

That year, Christmas arrived all too quickly. It seemed but a week or two since our arrival at Aidensfield and the changing weather, the darkening nights, the cooling of the air had descended upon us almost without warning. The clocks had gone back an hour, the summer birds had left our valleys and the land had reverted to its dullest clothing. It was as if the countryside had gone to sleep, and I was reminded of Keats who wrote:

"Ah, bitter chill it was!
The owl, for all his feathers, was a-cold;
The hare limp'd trembling through the frozen grass,
And silent was the flock in woolly fold."

But the countryside was far from trembling, even though the owl might be cold and the hare trembling. Like the dormant plants and the animals who hunt for survival, the weather means little to the policemen of Great Britain. They must work throughout the seasons – it means cold nights, wet feet, chilled hands and a longing for warm soup, hot coffee and cosy firesides. It means, after eight hours of frost-laden night duty, the heaven that is a snug bed containing a warm, soft woman.

Out there in the great chilly wilderness that is North Yorkshire, the work of the policeman must go on which means that policemen must tolerate the cold, and they must tremble, like the hare, in the chilly atmosphere. Motorcycling in such conditions was appalling, so I took my car as often as possible, hiding it from the sergeants behind haystacks and in the yards of friendly farmers. I could therefore embark upon rapid foot patrols of my area to keep myself warm. I risked being called on my official radio, for I had

171

none in the car, but I could always plead that I was in an area of poor reception, or engaged upon enquiries about current crime or missing persons, an act which took me away from the radio. In any case, I continued to make hourly points at telephone kiosks consequently I was never long out of contact with my Divisional Headquarters.

This highly unofficial strategy meant that my winter patrols weren't too bad. I took care to keep warm, I had lots of friendly calling places around my beat and I made sure that I had lots of enquiries to undertake, enquiries which took me indoors to sit beside warm fires and to enjoy numerous cups of tea and coffee, and/or glasses of proffered spirits.

Work under those conditions had considerable appeal, and I was aware of the old saying, "A good policeman never gets wet."

At home, the children were beginning to realise it was a season with something extra to offer. Father Christmas was very much alive in our family and even though a police house chimney is perhaps narrower than most, I ensured that letters were posted into its lofty darkness. I'm something of a traditionalist in that respect, for I love the joy that Father Christmas brings to youngsters during that season of goodwill and plenty. To abolish Christmas would be to abolish a slice of childhood.

Happily, by this time we had found a baby-sitter in a million, a steadfast lady of the moors who stood no nonsense from anybody, man, woman, child or animal, but who would sit till dawn if necessary and who would let us know in plain terms if something did not suit her. Her philosophy about children was "If they yell, I'll skelp 'em". Mrs Quarry was a treasure. It was fortunate we had found her before the Christmas season which, incidentally, begins at the end of October and develops into a hectic and expensive round of dinners, dances, parties and other associated functions.

My shifts did not allow me to attend every function, nor did my pocket, so we opted for the Ashfordly Police Christmas Dinner-Dance, held in the second week of December at a local hotel. Sergeants Bairstow and Blaketon had organised it with volunteers from the other lads in that town, and it was to raise funds for police widows and orphans. Being a late arrival in the district, I found myself free from official dance duties that night.

Mary and I decided to go along and to make this our sole Christmas fling. One reason was that we were hard up, a situation that has been with me ever since, for I had had a brain-storm a few months earlier and had purchased a brand-new car. What on earth possessed me to do such a thing on a police constable's pittance, with three youngsters and a fourth nearly there, I'll never know. But I had done it. It was a red Hillman saloon and it cost me, brand-new, £609 on the road. It was the first and last new car I've ever purchased, and it ran for well over 100,000 miles, We loved it. Naturally, we took it all over before the frosts and ice played havoc with the highways of the region, and it was our Christmas present to each other. For that reason, we had to economise, therefore we settled for one Yuletide function.

Mrs Quarry insisted that she baby-sat for us that night, even though the dance did not conclude until 2 am. We agreed to this. Mary had the statutory hair-do, but had to make do with an existing dress, while I dug out my only dark suit, brushed it, pulled in my belly and decided I must wear it. I had nothing else. Armed with a pocket full of cash, we left the children in the capable hands of Mrs Quarry and sallied forth into Ashfordly, very excited and looking forward to the dance. The car went beautifully and we arrived at Ashfordly at 7.30 for dancing at eight. We adjourned to the bar where we met our colleagues and friends, and in no time the function was going with the proverbial swing.

A tombola room was set aside from the dance hall and it was separated from the bar by a passage. It was like Aladdin's cave, piled high with prizes all donated by local people. There were bottles of spirits, boxes of chocolates, wines, Christmas cakes, game birds, silverware, glasses, cutlery *et al.* It looked almost like a display of wedding presents; we played tombola and won a box of chocolates.

Alwyn Foxton was the man in charge of this department and he said, "You can leave your prize here if you like, Nick. It'll save worrying about it during the dancing."

And so, like many other winners, we left our trophy on the table behind the glittering display and went off to enjoy the dance. The floor was excellent, sprung to take the rhythmic movement of skilled dancers, while the walls were decorated with original oil paintings by a local artist. They depicted our moorlands with purple heather and blue skies. High above was the buffet supper, served on a balcony which ran around the room and from where the diners could sit and view the dancing below. Supper was to be served at nine-thirty, a sit-down buffet.

The night disappeared in a haze of enjoyment and warmth. At functions of this kind, there is always so much to do, so many old friends to greet and to chat with, so much entertainment and so much chatting-up-of-pretty-women. The time flies without anyone realising. The leader of the little five-piece orchestra announced that it was time to eat, and we all adjourned upstairs for the feast of a lifetime. We were back within half-an-hour, to resume our merry-making.

Then I spotted Sergeant Bairstow, looking very harassed.

"Ah, Nicholas!" he spotted me in the middle of a Boston Two-Step. "Have you a minute?"

I led Mary to the side, bowed my ear against the noise of the music and heard him say, "It's bloody embarrassing, is this. But did you play tombola earlier this evening?"

"Yes, Mary won a box of chocolates. Black Magic, I think."

"Well," he coughed and ran his hand through his untidy hair. "Somebody's pinched the lot. They've cleaned out the whole bloody room – there's nothing left."

"That *is* embarrassing," I whispered.

"A lot of the stuff hadn't been won, so that's not too important, but what about all those prizes, like yours, that had been put to one side, for safe keeping? We'll have to replace them."

"Forget ours," I said. "But you can't replace them, Sergeant, can you? You don't know what they were. And if you announce what's happened, everyone will start claiming bottles of whisky or silverware, won't they?"

"Aye," he said dejectedly. "They will. We'll have to buy them all replacement prizes, and that'll ruin us. It'll take all our profit – and more."

"Why not announce that the tombola room has closed, as all the prizes have been won," I suggested. "Then ask the prize winner to see you, in person, to claim their prizes before they leave. Ask them individually what they won, and then tell them what's happened. Offer to buy a substitute tomorrow. I'll bet a lot of them will dismiss the affair and forgo their prize."

"I hope you're right," he sighed. "What a bloody thing to happen. I hope the Press doesn't hear about it."

They didn't, or if they did, they did not print anything. I was still amused by the incident as we left the dance at 2 am. By that time, word of the theft had percolated to most of the revellers and they thought it hilarious. Not many of them made claims upon the prize list, and if I know those folks, there'd be no false claims. The final outcome was not unpleasant, and we maintained a bank balance.

Outside that night, however, a covering of seasonal snow had fallen and it lay about two inches deep, "reg'lar away" as the locals term it. In other words, it was a level covering of that depth, unhampered by winds. For that reason, I drove with extreme care in my new car, the drink I'd enjoyed earlier having long since vanished from my system. The dancing and the superb meal had nullified the effects of any alcohol, and so I manoeuvred my shining vehicle through the forests and lanes as I neared my house on the hill top.

And then, as I negotiated a stiff bend about a mile from home, I felt the front wheels misbehave. The car refused to turn the corner. It was determined to travel in a straight line towards the tall hedge before me, and in spite of my wrestling with brakes and steering, it continued along its predetermined path. It mounted the verge on the nearside, climbed steeply towards its summit and threw light powdery snow in all directions. Then very gently, oh so very gently, it twisted across its path and toppled onto its side. My side. And there I was, sliding along a snow covered highway on the clean red doors of my new car. Mary was on top of me, cushioned by my body as we careered onwards with the engine roaring and the lights reflecting from the white expanse before me, and so close to my eyes. Everything seemed to be happening in slow motion and I was trying to lift my head away from my door window in case it shattered. I worried about our unborn baby too and all kinds of things flashed through my mind as we came gently to rest some yards further along.

"Are you all right?" I asked Mary, who was sitting on my head.

"Yes, are you?" came her voice from somewhere above.

"Fine," I tried to appear calm. She was moving somewhere above me and I saw her feet on the door beside my head. She was opening the window of the door above her, and once she'd achieved this, I helped her out. I switched off the engine but the lights were still blazing and there was an ominous smell of petrol. Then, in a blaze of light, another car pulled up.

"Have you had an accident, old boy?" asked a splendid voice.

"No, I always park like this." I wasn't feeling too affable, but he roared with laughter, expressed pleasure that we were not injured and offered to topple my Hillman back onto its wheels. With three more helpers from his car, we easily returned mine onto its four wheels and a superficial examination revealed very little damage. The thick snow had cushioned our fall and the only damage appeared to be the door handles on my side, plus a few minor scratches. I thanked him and off he went, chortling at the delight of finding a policeman in such a compromising situation after the dance. He laughed again at my ungrateful remark and I promised to buy him a drink if I saw him at another function.

I drove the final yards home and the car performed very well. It was very slightly damaged.

"Did you have a nice time?" asked Mrs Quarry as Mary entered, covered in snow, with her hair awry, her feet soaking and a patch of dirt on her cheek.

"Wonderful," she said. "Yes, wonderful."

* * * *

With my car at the village garage getting its doors corrected and re-sprayed, I had to return briefly to the chilly motor-cycle for some of my winter patrols. With ice always a possibility on the roads, I was never fully confident upon that machine; having only two wheels puts one at considerable risk and I think the car accident had shaken me more than I cared to admit. Nonetheless, I managed to patrol my beat in that wintry weather and I did not suffer any further mishaps.

As is customary on a rural policeman's beat, one is fêted with alacrity during the festive season, and I had offers of wine, Christmas cake, spirits, beer and frumenty. Because it was the Christmas season, I accepted these positive indications of appreciation, although I took great care never to over-indulge, especially with alcoholic drinks. If I took a drink, I walked home. I found this to be the safest way of patrolling and therefore the motor-cycle found itself spending more and more time in the garage. I patrolled my beat on foot, having in mind the very generous and very persuasive rural folk.

Christmas is a happy time for a rural policeman, and it should also be a happy time for his 'parishioners'. This came to mind one Friday evening as I patrolled Elsinby on foot. It was bitterly cold and there was a hint of snow in the air, coupled with what Yorkshiremen call a "lazy wind". It goes through you – it is too lazy to go round. I had walked from Aidensfield into Elsinby and was therefore quite snug in my winter uniform. I made my ten o'clock point at the telephone kiosk and was about to leave when the phone rang. It was Sergeant Blaketon.

"Ah!" The relief was evident in his voice. "Got you, Rhea. We've just had a telephone call from a lady in Elsinby. She's complaining about the noise at the pub. Very loud singing, apparently. It's disturbing the neighbourhood. Go and sort them out, will you? Tell them to shut up. I know it's the festive season, but we don't want complaints."

"Yes, Sergeant."

I walked the few hundred yards and as I approached the Hopbind Inn, I could hear lusty voices rising from it. The place was undoubtedly in fine song and the cheery atmosphere gave me a feeling of loneliness and isolation. I wished I was in there right now, warm and snug, with friendly folk and a nice drink. But the din was awful! I could hear a familiar tune whose title escaped me; it could be heard well away from the premises and there was little wonder the lady had complained.

I walked into the busy pub and George, the landlord, greeted me with a smile. Clearly, he was pleased with the music.

"By, that's a bit of grand singing," he clutched a full pint pot as he beamed with pleasure.

"It's too good, George," I shouted above the noise. "We've had a complaint. Somebody's rung our office at Ashfordly to complain about it. I've just had Sergeant Blaketon asking you to shut up."

"You're joking!" he gasped.

"I'm not," I said seriously. "They making a hell of a racket, you know. I could hear them half way up the street."

"But Nick, listen to them!" he pleaded and he held up a finger to indicate silence. I listened to the tune that came from the bar. It was a fine version of "The old rugged cross", a popular Methodist hymn sung regularly in these parts. For the Methodists of this region, it was almost an anthem.

"Hymns?" I asked.

"Aye, hymns. It's the carol singers." He lowered his voice. "They were singing out there and it's bloody cold tonight. Everybody in the bar invited them inside – they're chapel folks, Nick, and they don't touch a drop. They're just singing hymns and carols, that's all, inside my pub instead of on the street."

I laughed aloud. "If they thought they'd been the subject of a complaint about singing in the pub, they'd never live it down!"

"They wouldn't," he agreed. "Can you do summat about it?"

"I don't know who made the complaint," I had to tell him, "and I daren't ring Blaketon to tell him the truth. To him, a noise is a noise, whoever makes it and for whatever reason. All I know is that the caller was a woman."

"Oh, it will be Miss Allison just around the corner. She often grumbles and she's got the telephone in. She's the only woman living alone along there."

"I'll see if it was her," I offered. I went to her cottage and knocked. It was about ten fifteen by this time and she answered quickly. Behind me, the strains of "Silent Night" were now ringing forth.

"Did you ring our office at Ashfordly, Miss Allison?" I asked.

"I did, Mr Rhea, yes I did. I'm sorry if I am a nuisance, but the noise from the Hopbind was getting too much."

"It's the chapel carol singers," I told her. "Listen, they're there now."

Standing together on her doorstep, we listened to the verses of that popular carol as they filled the chill air of this December night.

"Oh dear, I thought it was someone in the pub," she blushed. "I had no idea it was carol singers."

"It is carol singers, but they are in the pub," I corrected her, and explained about the chapel folks, now firmly installed in the bar and singing their hearts out beside the regulars. She burst into laughter.

"Oh, dear, that's marvellous, isn't it? Really marvellous. I'm so sorry I complained . . . Do they know I complained?"

"No one knows," I assured her, "except me and George. I'm going back to put his mind at rest. Can they continue like that? It closes at eleven and besides, there are many chapel folk in there who will soon want to be going home."

"Thank you for telling me." She sounded sincere, and I got the impression she was wistful.

As she made to close the door, I said, "I'm going back, Miss Allison. Would you like to come across and hear them for yourself?"

"Oh, I'm not a drinker, you know. I never go into pubs."

"Neither are they. They're singers."

"Do you think I should? I mean, it's not the thing for a woman to go into a public house unaccompanied."

"I will accompany you. You could stand in the passage with me and listen to the carols."

"Thank you," she smiled, and in a second she had on a warm coat and a scarf. George was delighted and by the time we arrived, the singers, chapel folks and regulars, were in top form with "Oh Come All Ye Faithful".

I could inform Sergeant Blaketon that I had dealt with the complaint and that all parties were satisfied with my action. But I did wonder what the Catholics and Anglicans would do to cap this one!

* * * *

George Boston, his wife and son occupied Low Laithes Farm. Its fields spread smoothly across a lush and green part of the valley below my lounge window and in moments of silent reflection, I would often stand at that window to gaze across the dale far below. My view looked south across the deep rift in the hills where ranging conifers decorated the slopes. Christmas tree thieves would be a menace in there about now; I'd have to arrange patrols during the darkened hours. Lonely farmsteads dotted those slopes and their lights twinkled at night, lighting my view like glow-worms in the undergrowth. I could look down upon the spread of the whole dale.

Boston's farm provided an everlasting frontage to my view. There were times his spread was hidden in the mists of autumn. Sometimes his farm was totally obscured and sometimes I could see only the tops of the trees and the caps of spindly telegraph poles protruding from the dense white blanket. At other times the Boston farm lay revealed in all its symmetrical wonder, with neat walls, trimmed hedges and the tidiest farmyard for miles around. Even his animals seemed tidy – sometimes I could have sworn they grazed in drilled ranks.

From my vantage point, I could watch George at work and I began to recognise his wife's daily routine. White smoke spiralling from her chimney told me whether or not it was going to be a fine day, but it also told me whether Mary Boston was baking, washing the clothes or going out for the day. If she was baking, the fire would be lit early to heat the fireside oven she continued to use to such tasty advantage; if it was wash-day, the wash-house fire would belch forth a darker smoke from behind the main house, while a day's outing meant no smoke until later in the day, usually around tea-time.

The farm buildings were gathered about the dwelling-house like pups around a loving mother; they were homely, warm and inviting, so friendly and yet so plain. Their construction and furnishings were simple and provided a life without complications. The fields were the same, always neat, always well tended and up to date with whatever crop George had decided to produce. The place reeked of rural contentment.

Sometimes I stood at the window, wondering if the Bostons bothered about the village bobby being so high above them with such a splendid view of their territory. Did they have the feeling they were being watched? Did they think the village constable was spying on them? Did they feel that my binoculars were upon *them,* and not upon the wildlife that lived about their premises? It was like standing on a mountain top and observing the minutiae of life in a valley far below; but George's life and mine were really no part of each other.

My first visit to his farm was some six or eight weeks after my arrival, and it had been a routine check of his stock register. When a farmer bought stock, he had to enter details in a register, including facts like the date and time of purchase, the place they were purchased, the number of animals and a brief description. Cows and pigs were the chief livestock of this area and it was my job to ensure their entries were correct. If an outbreak of disease occurred, it would have to be traced to its source, consequently those records were vital.

My second visit was for a totally different purpose. It was strictly official and it reminded me of the risks attached to the nationwide practice of giving Christmas presents to village policemen. Policemen are always conscious of attempts to bribe them during their duties, and the acceptance of gifts, however small, is fraught with danger. Police Regulations are specific upon the subject. Some superiors interpreted these rules so rigidly that acceptance of a cup of tea on duty was seen as the acceptance of a present. Reliable sources of tea were therefore jealously guarded by policemen.

This second visit occurred on Christmas Day, when such temptations were placed before me. I had been off duty during Christmas Eve and my Christmas Day duties were from 10 am until 6 pm. This suggested a daytime patrol of the village and its surrounding area, and meant I was always available for despatch to any incident, large or small. In reality, it meant I stayed at home with my family, always on the understanding that if anything did happen, I must go out and deal with it. On Christmas Day therefore, I sat around the house in my uniform shirt and trousers, hoping nothing would happen. This system gave me Christmas Day at home.

Shortly after ten o'clock that morning, my telephone rang. It was P.C. Jim Finn from Ashfordly.

"Nick, I'm sorry, but we've got a job for you."

"I was out of bed," I laughed. The children had seen to that – Father Christmas had roused them about three this morning, from which time sleep had been impossible.

"It's not serious," Jim was telling me. "A hit-and-run accident in the early hours. Damage only, no injuries. We didn't get you up at the crack of dawn, but it needs attention."

It seemed that a worshipper had attended Midnight Mass at Maddleskirk Abbey. Mass had concluded about 1.15 am and the worshipper had turned his car towards Aidensfield, aiming for his home. Unfortunately, some of the local pubs had been making merry at the same time, and had thrown out their faithful just as the Abbey was ejecting its regulars.

A small Morris Minor had hurtled along the narrow lane between Maddleskirk and Aidensfield. According to an eye-witness, it had been driven erratically and had collided with a nice new car belonging to the said worshipper. The Morris had not troubled to stop, but had careered out of sight amidst a rending of metal and a tinkling of broken glass. The eye-witness, another home-going worshipper, had seen ·this incident from the relative safety of a wood, into which he had had the presence of mind to leap as the offending Morris approached. Nonetheless, he had had the sense to note the registration number of the Morris.

"So," concluded P.C. Finn. "There's a useful 'Careless Driving' for you, a 'Fail to Stop' and a 'Fail to Report'."

"Who was driving the Morris?" I asked.

"Dunno. I can give you its number, but the Taxation Offices are closed. They won't be able to supply the keeper's name until after the holiday. Maybe you know the owner?"

When he told me the number, I knew it was a local lad. The car belonged to George Boston's son, a lanky twenty-year-old called Samuel Victor. This revelation meant I was faced with a rather unpleasant Christmas Day task. However, sentiment and seasonal jollifications cannot be allowed to infringe upon the execution of one's lawful duty, so I put on my uniform tunic and cap, told my wife where I was heading and said I'd be back for lunch.

Although I often felt I could toss a pebble from my garden into the stackyard of Low Laithes Farm, it was about a mile from my house when using the conventional route. I decided to walk and enjoyed the clear, crisp morning air, with just a hint of frost. There was a suggestion of snow too, for snow packs were forming around the horizon and there was the distinctive smell of oncoming snow. It is a peculiar smell, one which is recognised by countrymen. I knew that smell. Snow was on its way and would fall before long.

I arrived at the gate of Low Laithes Farm just before eleven, having passed the time of day with one or two residents *en route*. I touched the latch and it swung open. They call this type of latch a hunting sneck, a wooden affair peculiar to this part of England and perhaps designed to be drawn by the lighest of touches from a riding crop, or by Miss Fiona's pony. It was simply a long wooden bolt, hanging from short chains and carved with nicks. When the gate is open, it hangs free but once closed, it is very secure. The Boston dogs began their well practised barking and, with my arrival thus announced, I walked across the clean farmyard, with its area of grooved concrete as clean as the front path of any semi-detached house in the land. This farm even lacked the traditional midden, a heap of dung and household waste which was once so familiar at the front door of every farmstead. I knocked on the kitchen door and Mrs Boston, a plump attractive woman in a flowered apron, opened it. She was smiling a welcome.

"I saw you coming, Mr Rhea. Fancy calling on Christmas Day?" and at that, she adopted a slightly worried frown.

"E'll have cum for 'is duck," growled a voice from inside the kitchen. "T'bobby allus comes for 'is duck on Christmas Day. Fetch 'im in."

"Well," I began . . .

"Don't stand oot there, it's cawd," said George's voice. "Bring t'lad in."

I entered and removed my cap, and was immediately inside the farm kitchen. A friendly fire warmed the room, casting bright and flickering glows of red across the furnishings, the tiled floor and the beamed ceiling so brown and stained with age. Meat hooks decorated the ceiling and horse brasses were crudely nailed to much of the woodwork. George Boston sat in a Windsor chair, the cushion bulging between the uprights. He wore a thick tweed jacket of mottled green and brown, a fawn waistcoat and heavy corduroy trousers, polished with regular wear and tear. His feet wore battered but cosy slippers, one of which had a hole in the toe, and a pet cur lay at his feet. Its head rested on the fender almost within reach of falling cinders, while its body sprawled across the thick clip hearth rug. It didn't rouse at my entry, and George didn't leave his chair.

"Noo then, lad," he beamed. "Thoo'll 'ave cum for thy Christmas duck, eh?"

"No, I haven't," I had to say. I knew nothing of such an arrangement. "It's about something else, Mr Boston."

"Get 'im 'is duck oot o' t'larder, Mary. Let's git this bit owered afoore he spoils things."

"No," I insisted. "Please, you mustn't. I'm here on business – you'll not want to give me a duck when you hear what I've got to say."

He studied me for a few moments and said, "Oh, it's like that is it? Sit down then," and he indicated a chair at the table. I put my cap on the scrubbed wooden top and Mrs Boston produced a mug of tea from somewhere. This was their break time, 'lowance time as they called it.

"Give 'im summat stronger than that, Mary," insisted George.

I held up my hand. "No, wait, please. I must tell you why I'm here."

"This lad's nut gahin ti be bribed, is he?" smiled the genial farmer. "Well, lad, oot wiv it. What's up? It must be summat important to drag you oot looking serious on Christmas Day."

I told him about last night's incident, or this morning's to be precise, and he listened without a word. Mrs Boston stood close to me, listening carefully and sipping from her mug which she clutched with both hands. I told them the story in what I hoped was a clear manner and left the identification of the alleged offender until the end.

"That Morris car," I said. "It bore the same registration number as your son's car," and I quoted the number.

"Aye," he said. "That's oor lad's car and no mistake. Is onnybody hurt?"

"No," I said to his relief. "Just minor damage to both vehicles."

"If he'd stopped, it might 'ave been sorted out there and then."

"Possibly," I agreed, wondering if Samuel had been drunk at the time.

"What happens next then?"

"I'd like to see the car."

"Me an' all," and he slipped his feet into a pair of waiting wellington boots and led me through the back of the house, the cur following without any bidding. We traversed a cattle shed or two with cows ruminating noisily in their winter quarters, the heat of their bodies warming the entire complex. Finally, we entered an outbuilding which served as a garage.

"There she is," he pointed to a car.

Out came my official notebook as I circled the little car, looking for signs of recent damage. I found them; the front offside wing had been dented and the surface paint was fractured. The bumper was twisted and the headlamp glass was broken, most of it being missing. There were clean, rust-free scratches along the doors too, and also along the rear wing, all on the driver's side. It had clearly been in a recent collision. I noted this damage and then, taking out my pocket knife, lifted a sample of paint from the damaged part of the car. I carefully placed this in a plastic envelope and then, upon the damaged portion of the car, I located an alien colour, a dull red paint. I guessed this had been transferred from the other vehicle during their contact, so I lifted this and placed it in another envelope.

"What's all this business for?" George asked with genuine interest.

"I might have to prove it was him," I said. "I have taken a control sample of the paintwork from Samuel's car, and another piece bearing a different coloured paint. That shows he touched something else, something bearing that colour of paint. We'll do the same with the other chap's car, then we will get our forensic wizards to examine all the pieces. They'll tell us whether the two cars were ever in contact with one another. I reckon they'll say 'yes'."

"You fellers leave nowt to chance, do you?"

"No," I said. "We don't."

After I had noted the excise licence details, I said, "I'd like to see Sam now. Where is he?"

"He'll be in these buildings. I'll shout him."

He bellowed Sam's name and soon the lad appeared looking pale and dishevelled, the legacy of his night out. He was very tall and thin, a serious-faced lad but pleasant to deal with.

"Now, Sam." I did not smile.

"Hello, Mr Rhea," and his eyes did not meet mine.

"You know why I'm here?"

"Aye."

"It's your car?" I had to ask the formal question for evidential purposes.

"Aye."

"And you were driving it from Maddleskirk towards Aidensfield in the early hours of this morning, past the Abbey about quarter-past-one?"

"Aye."

George interrupted us to address his son. "Leeakster, lad, when thoo's involved in summat like a traffic accident, thoo's got ti stop and tell t'folks who's there who thoo is . . ."

"Aye, Ah know," said Samuel, "but Ah was scared."

"Drunk, mair like," snapped his father.

"Ah'd had a few, not too many, not enough to stop me driving."

"Thoo'll nut be having t'lad for drinking and driving, Mr Rhea?"

"No," I said to his relief. This was before the days of the breathalyser and besides, this youth was stone cold sober now. "He's not drunk now, and I can't prove what he was like when this happened, can I?"

George smiled.

"Come inti t'house then, both on you."

We followed him inside and he produced a bottle of whisky. "It's Christmas Day, Mr Rhea, so thoo'll have a noggin wiv us?"

"Aye," I said, "I will, but I must see this lad's papers first – insurance, driving licence, test certificate." I hoped they were all in order, for I didn't want to get Samuel into deeper trouble.

"Get 'em, Sam."

I was relieved to find they were all correct, and I sat at the table to note their particulars in my notebook. As I worked, Samuel plonked a huge glass of whisky before me. It was neat and there must have been a third of a pint.

"Sup it up, lad, it'll warm thoo nicely."

"Samuel," I addressed him before I lifted my glass. "I've got to report you for various offences – it will probably mean an appearance at Eltering Magistrates' Court."

"Can't thoo settle it oot o' court?" asked George.

"This is a criminal court, it's not a civil case," I tried to explain the difference. "We've had a formal complaint about Sam's driving, so I've no choice. I've got to submit my report and Sam will get a summons in due course."

"It won't mean prison, will it?" The lad's eyes were wide and fearful.

"No, a fine perhaps, a smallish one. It's your first offence," and I tried to put the situation in its right perspective.

"Ah'll say it was my fault, 'cos it was," offered Samuel, white-faced and obviously worried. "Ah should 'ave stopped, Mr Rhea; Ah was bloody daft not to."

"Fair enough. Now listen to what I'm reporting you for," I advised. "First, there's bound to be careless driving. Then you failed to stop after an accident, and you failed to report it to the police as soon as practicable."

"Three, eh?" counted his father. "Three offences."

"Three," I confirmed.

"Not drunk driving?"

"No," I said once more. "I've no evidence to suggest he was drunk."

"Nobody said I was?" Samuel's statement was phrased like a question.

"Nobody suggested anything of the sort, Sam. It won't enter my report. You panicked, that's all."

"Aye," he smiled. "Fair enough."

"Thoo's a lucky lad, Sam," commented his father.

"You'll get a summons in about three weeks," I told him.

"Serves the young bugger right," said George when I'd finished. "Ah've had a go at him for gahin oot late and driving home. Yon pub needs checking, lad, for boozing late."

"It's not on my beat, Mr Boston, but I'll have words with the sergeant."

"Aye, well, sup that whisky. This is Christmas, thoo knaws."

Samuel and Mrs Boston joined us and we chatted as we always had before this incident. We talked of nothing in particular for this was just another friendly chat between the village bobby and one of his farming community. What we had discussed ten minutes earlier was now over and done with. I stayed longer than I intended and had two more massive whiskies. I found the room beginning to move about me, so I made a pathetic attempt to leave.

"It's a good job thoo's walking back, lad," George laughed. "Ah hope thy missus has a nice heavy dinner ready. Thoo'll need summat to sober thyself up, 'specially if t'sergeant turns up."

"She's busy with the dinner now," I muttered incoherently, aiming for the door. "Thankshh for being sho co-operative."

"Hod on, lad, thoo's forgotten summat," George called me back.

"Forgotten?" I wondered if I had left my cap, but it was perched on my head in approximately the right position. I looked at George. He was holding a massive, dressed duck, ready for the oven.

"It's thy Christmas duck, tak it."

"No, I couldn't, not after reporting Sshamuel."

"Oor Sam was a bloody fool; he's lucky he's not been takken off t'road for ever, drunk driving or summat warse. Tak this duck – it's thine."

"I can't," I managed to say, "I musshn't – I cannot accept gifts, it's againssht the rules."

"Who said it was for thoo?" he questioned me. "It's not."

"Then who issh it for?" I asked stupidly.

"Thy wife and kids," he smiled. "There's no law to say Ah can't give thy missus and bairns a duck, is there?"

I left, bearing the huge bare duck beneath my arm as I

wound my erratic way back up the hill and into my cosy house. I was just in time for dinner and spent the afternoon getting over that spell of duty. I sat around, at first in a haze of noise and fun, and then in a clearer atmosphere as I played with the children and their new toys. Nothing else turned up, except a sprinkling of snow. As George Boston would have said, "It snew on Christmas Day, just a strinkling."

But that 'strinkling' became a steady snowfall and I could see the features of his farm gradually vanishing in a desert of white. Walls disappeared against a background of pure white and I was reminded of the lines of Robert Bridges' poem, 'London Snow',

> "Hushing the latest traffic of the drowsy town;
> Deadening, muffling, stifling its murmurs failing;
> Lazily and incessantly floating down and down:
>   Silently sifting and veiling road, roof and railing;
> Hiding difference, making unevenness even,
> Into angles and crevices softly drifting and sailing."

With that snow, Christmas had truly arrived and the land about grew whiter as evening fell. It was a very pleasant Christmas Day.

We had the duck for New Year's Day dinner and it was truly delicious, and that Christmas and New Year, Mary received eleven pheasants, two brace of grouse, one hare, two Christmas cakes, several bottles, one umbrella and a bag of anonymous Brussels sprouts.

A month later, Samuel was fined a total of £32 and had his licence endorsed.

Constable
Around
the Village

I

"Ill customs influence my very senses."

Sir George Etherege, 1635–1691

Somewhere across the map of North Yorkshire there lies an invisible line which separates the north of that county from the south. People in counties Durham and Cleveland will accept a north North Yorkshireman as a northerner, but those unfortunates who live in the southern regions of North Yorkshire, in the soft warmth and built-up wilderness of cities like York and Ripon and boroughs like Scarborough and Harrogate, are considered southerners.

In every northerner's eyes, a southerner is suspect. There is something not quite right about them. If that southerner happens to qualify only because he lives in the southern part of North Yorkshire, then that makes no difference. Anyone unenlightened enough to live south of that unseen line is indeed a person to be pitied, more so if he happens to live in a town. *Pity* is perhaps not the right word; *tolerance* is not totally apt and neither is *deplore*. A feeling of despair may not be absolutely accurate, nor is excruciation, agony, passion, or anxiety.

If there is difficulty in finding a word suitable to describe that feeling, the north North Yorkshireman will come to the rescue by saying, "Ah can't abide southerners." Having said that, he knows what he means. He can't abide them; there's a lot that a Yorkshireman can't abide, but, as a group, southerners are definitely the least abideable of anyone.

The snag is that the all-important, but invisible line is very difficult to define or determine. No one is quite sure where it lies, least of all the self-appointed northerners.

In my capacity as the village constable at Aidensfield, I lived somewhere on that line. I appreciated that fact when I was posted there; having been reared *in a genuine* northern district, the moorlands of the North Riding of Yorkshire, I had been brought up in the knowledge that the area around Aidensfield was definitely "south". Even though the outer limits of Aidensfield beat encompassed the southern edges of the North Yorkshire moors and lay well within the North Riding's administrative area, the village was definitely "south" in the eyes of many.

Once I moved into Aidensfield, however, I did not consider it "south". In my view, it was north because the folks who lived there spoke the same language as my ancestors and adopted the same hard-headed attitude. In fact, the villagers considered themselves "north"; in their view, southerners lived at York or beyond and occupied those indeterminable areas of suburbia between there and London, which was a biggish town located at the bottom end of the Great North Road.

Having been nurtured as a northerner, finding myself working in what they consider a southern district was disconcerting. Even so, I was confident that Aidensfield really was "north". But who could decide the issue? There had to be some definitive method of settling the matter. Somewhere, somehow, there had to be a rule which clearly and permanently categorised North Yorkshiremen. Perhaps a road, a river or a parish boundary or two? By chance I stumbled upon the answer. It lay in the ancient custom of First Footing, a matter in which I, as the local constable, soon found myself deeply involved.

First Footing of the genuine kind does not take place in the south. That is a golden rule. Worse still, in some southern areas the people attempt to copy the custom by doing it on Christmas Day! That is sheer impudence. First Footing is purely a northern custom and, because the villagers of Aidensfield and district take part in the custom, they must be northerners. In those days the people of York didn't genuinely First Foot while those in the West Riding, at centres like Leeds and Bradford, certainly did not. Further away in the deep, deep south of Yorkshire, at Sheffield, (which is halfway to London), the matter was not even considered. Down there, they thought First Footing was a building term. But Aidensfield did First Foot. That classified it as north and that made me happy. It meant I had not trespassed beyond the bounds of true northern credibility by emigrating into unknown southern regions and, even if my old colleagues continued to categorise Aidensfield as south, I knew it wasn't. That the custom of First Footing occurred in Aidensfield assured me it was a northern village and for that I was eternally thankful. For a northerner to be mistaken for a southerner was akin to a Catholic being mistaken for a Holy Roller.

First Footing is a very ancient and noble custom. It is practised with alacrity on New Year's Eve and its misty origins matter very little to those who enjoy it in our modern society. Nonetheless, there are certain rules which must be obeyed.

First and foremost, it is a New Year ceremony, the purpose of which is to bring good luck and prosperity to the household. The method of First Footing is very simple, albeit undertaken within the accepted but unwritten code of conduct.

The term means "first into the house". A First Foot is therefore the very first visitor to a house in the New Year. He must arrive as soon as possible after midnight on New Year's morning and he must bring with him certain gifts which symbolise a lasting supply of food, warmth and prosperity. These items are fairly simple—there must be a piece of coal to symbolise heat and light, a coin to symbolise continuing wealth or perhaps a little salt in lieu, and a piece of bread to fulfil the food requirement. In Aidensfield and some other areas of North Yorkshire, a piece of holly must also be carried, this evergreen being an ancient symbol of everlasting life.

In addition to the required gifts, the First Foot must also comply with certain personal rules. He must always be a man. Women must never perform this task, otherwise it brings bad luck, and the Sex Discrimination Act has not yet been amended to change this rule. In order to qualify, a man must never be flat-footed or cross-eyed, and his eyebrows must not meet across the nose. In addition, he should have dark hair. In the ideal situation, he should be a total stranger who chances to enter one's house at the right time, but, as honest midnight visitors of this sex are rare and indeed open to close police interest, most northerners make do with someone they know, provided he is suitably qualified.

To ensure that each household is visited at the necessary time, plans are made well in advance. The selected First Footer is approached and asked if he will execute this noblest of deeds for the everlasting benefit of the household in question. Invariably, he says he will be happy to oblige. Thus committed, he must equip himself with sufficient bread, money or salt, coal and holly, for each house upon his itinerary and he will be expected to kiss every lady encountered *en route*.

The selection of a suitable First Footer, or Lucky Bird as he is often known, is therefore a matter of some importance. Tall, dark men are in demand as careful plans are laid. As zero hour approaches, the doors are locked until the arrival of the First Foot. It would be disastrous if someone else entered to ruin the luck of the coming year.

It ought to be said at this stage that there is another seasonal custom in the north. This also takes place over New Year's Eve and well into the early hours of New Year's Day, and it is known as Boozing Late. All the pubs and clubs work hard to cater for massive thirsts and seasonal celebrations and it is fair to say that a high proportion of the indigenous population inhabit these places as the Old Year changes into the New. Much singing and high-spirited jollification takes place and a great deal of last-minute First Footing is arranged at these celebratory gatherings.

It follows, therefore, that the role of the country constable is somewhat unspecific over those midnight hours. The pubs make brave attempts to comply with the law by seeking permission from Their Worships to open late. This is seldom refused, if only because Their Worships also enjoy the occasion, and the customers play their part by never drinking away from their home village at New Year. Thus they are all "friends of the licensee" which means they drink later than normal and this also obviates the constable's worries about drunks navigating ungovernable vehicles about the place. Everyone walks, or tries to. Another feature of this arrangement is that, by walking, one can call at many houses *en route*, ostensibly to check that the First Foot has performed his annual ritual. If he hasn't, entry is refused; if he has, everyone is welcome to take cheese and gingerbread, laced with ginger wine.

On my very first New Year's Eve at Aidensfield, therefore, I found myself on duty and having to perform half nights. It was a shift beginning at 6 pm on New Year's Eve and ending at 2 am on New Year's Day. This fact registered itself with horror on my mind, but as the newest newcomer to Ashfordly section it was my lot to be allocated this duty. It meant I would have to patrol my beat for eight miserable hours while everyone else was welcoming the New Year in the traditional northern manner.

The pubs would be full of merry-making and the houses noisy with parties. The streets would be deserted, at least for the final throes of the Old Year. My role would be to enforce the law that night, to patrol my wide-ranging beat on a cold, noisy motor-cycle and to return home in the early hours of New Year's Day frozen to the core and reeling at the absence of pure enjoyment. It threatened to be a miserable time.

But the general public had other ideas. Because I was almost six feet tall with dark hair and eyebrows that did not meet in the middle, plus the fact that I was, in truth, a stranger to the district and a person of the male sex to boot, I was deemed eminently suited for the role of a First Footer. Little did I realise, as I embarked on my evening patrol shortly after six o'clock, that my New Year's Eve would be both memorable and enjoyable.

As I began that final Old Year tour of duty, I made a mental note to First Foot at my own house on New Year's Day. I would be my own First Footer at two o'clock that morning. If all else failed, I would achieve that honour. But as I chugged into Aidensfield, parked my motor-cycle and embarked upon a foot patrol to the pillar-box a lady hailed me.

She was middle-aged with greying hair and wore a

flowered apron about her ample body. It transpired she had spotted me marching past her tiny cottage and had rushed to the door to call me. In the blackness of that early evening, I must have looked horrifying in my crash-helmet, goggles and motor-cycle gear, but it did not frustrate this determined woman.

"Mr Rhea, Mr Rhea," she called. "Have you a moment?"

I halted, turned and beamed at her from beneath my heavy clothing.

"Hello, Mrs Mitchell."

"I'm glad I caught you." She was panting slightly. "I wonder if I might ask you a favour?"

"Go ahead," I invited, wondering what lay in store.

"Tonight," she smiled. "It's New Year's Eve and I haven't a First Footer."

"Do you want me to find one?" I asked, innocently.

"Well, no, not exactly." She didn't lose her smile. "I thought you might do it for me."

"Oh." I must have sounded surprised, then realised I was being paid a compliment. "Well, yes, I will. I'm sure I can manage that."

"At midnight," she told me. "You must come at midnight, or as soon as you can afterwards."

"Let me see." I made a mental calculation of the conference points I had to make. I had one at eleven-thirty at Elsinby and my next was twelve-fifteen at Aidensfield.

"Yes, I can be there," I offered. "I'll do your First Footing."

"You'll need a piece of coal, some holly, money and bread," she said seriously. "I'll get them for you."

And with no more ado Mrs Mitchell returned to her home and moments later reappeared with the necessary items. I opened one of the panniers on the motor-cycle and popped in the coal and holly. I slid the £.s.d. penny and slice of bread into my overcoat pocket.

"Midnight," she said, "not before."

"I'll be there," I assured her.

Having settled that little issue, I completed my journey to the pillar-box, popped in a birthday card I had to post and began the return trip to my motor-cycle. As I did so, I reflected briefly on the honour she had bestowed upon me. I felt this request had come to me because of my comparatively recent arrival in the village, but at the same time it showed that I was accepted. It proved I was allowed into the homes of the people otherwise than in the course of my duty. I was part of the life of the community. That's how I interpreted this request and it pleased me.

Within the next three hours, I was approached by seven further villagers, all wanting me to be their First Footer. I was given lumps of coal which filled one pannier while sprigs of holly were pushed unceremoniously into the other. I had a coat pocket full of sliced bread wrapped in greaseproof paper and lots of coins jangling about my uniform. The situation had now arrived whereby I had to make notes about the precise timing of my First Footing activities.

Mrs Mitchell could be accommodated just after midnight, for I would then have returned from Elsinby in readiness for my twelve-fifteen point at Aidensfield telephone kiosk. This was no problem. I had also to remember that Sergeant Blaketon was on duty tonight and he was quite likely to pay me a call, so I didn't dare miss any of my rendezvous points. So it was to be Mrs Mitchell at midnight, Stan Williams at ten past, my point at quarter past, Mr and Mrs Collins at twenty-five past, Mrs Collins's mother next door at half-past, the elderly Misses Bush and Rowe at quarter to one, Alan and Sue Bentley at one o'clock and the Leech family at quarter past one. I would make my one-thirty point at Thackerston and that would get me home at two o'clock, there to perform my final and most important First Foot duty. My night of threatened misery had taken a turn for the better and time would fly.

It seemed a reasonable night's work. From eight o'clock until nine, therefore, I patrolled the beat with holly sticking from one pannier and a fair tonnage of coal in the other, ending my first half of the tour at home for supper. I tucked into a warm pie before the fire and laughed with Mary as I explained my forthcoming "duties". The children were tucked snugly in bed and Mary said she would go upstairs when I left home at quarter to ten.

It would be a lonely New Year for her, but with the children so tiny it was impossible to go out and baby-sitters were difficult to acquire on such an evening. Stoically, Mary accepted her domesticity and I kissed her farewell as I began the second and most arduous part of my tour of duty.

As there had been no sign of Sergeant Blaketon and no other official calls upon my time, I decided to pay an early visit to all the pubs on my patch. Sight of the uniform would remind the revellers of the presence of the law and that alone should cause most of the merry-makers to enjoy themselves within reasonable limits and to refrain from punch-ups and wild drunkenness.

I discovered that at every pub there was a party. As each had been granted an extension of hours, every bar, lounge, hall and passage was full to overflowing, with many of the landlords putting free food at the disposal of the customers. In addition, there was a stock of streamers, balloons, funny hats and kissable young ladies; even at this early hour, a good time was assured.

Cars and motor-cycles were noticeably absent; I was pleased to note the basic common sense of the merry-makers and mentally praised them for leaving such liabilities at home. In every case, the pub atmosphere was superb. Every building radiated happiness and *bonhomie* as its inmates worked towards the explosive climax that was 12 midnight. That would be the signal for everyone to kiss everyone else, for the champagne to flow, for First Footers to roam the streets and for all kinds of resolutions to be made. It would be a time of joy and fun.

Outside those doors, it was a different world. The bucolic lanes were silent. No one moved between these isolated centres of population. Everyone was at home, waiting for midnight. There was no moon and the countryside lay dormant with just a hint of frost. The only moving thing was my motor-cycle with me astride it. I began to ponder upon the value of this presence. Eleven o'clock came and went without incident. Other than the controlled revelry in the pubs, the countryside was at its most peaceful and serene. Houses with lights at the windows dotted the remote parts showing there was life beyond the pubs and, for five minutes, I sat astride the machine at the top of Aidensfield Bank and looked across the landscape spread below me. I felt no part of tonight's excitement. I felt as if I was a total outsider. I thought about the excitements, the friendships, the fellowship, the happiness and even the unsung misery being played out in the villages down there. From my hilltop vantage-point, I could see nothing but a carpet of darkness dotted here and there with pinpricks of light. Those lights however, represented happiness, distant lights with friendship behind them. And I was alone on my hilltop.

It's a miserable job being a policeman on such occasions. I knew I could not join the people in their merry-making because my uniform would immediately freeze any atmosphere of pleasure. I had to patrol alone. And so I did. I kicked the bike into life and moved off.

Occasionally I parked and walked the streets of peaceful villages in order to increase the circulation of my blood. It kept my fingers and toes warm and I made my allotted points at selected telephone kiosks. Surprisingly, the time passed quickly. It would soon be New Year.

After my eleven-thirty point at Elsinby, I paid a quick visit to the Hopbind Inn. I caught George's eye and waved at him across a sea of pink faces and hovering glasses. He beckoned me to the counter in the passage, leaned across and said in true landlord's style:

"Have one with us, Mr Rhea?"

I pondered. I did not normally drink on duty, but on this occasion he recognised my hesitancy and pressed home his advantage.

"Just a quickie. Small whisky? To see the New Year in?"

I looked at my watch. There was twenty minutes before Mrs Mitchell and my First Footing obligation. There was no sergeant about. I was cold and lonely . . .

"Aye, all right, George. For Auld Lang Syne."

He invited me into the packed bar but I tactfully declined, and he drew me a measure of finest malt whisky. In the passage, I raised the glass, toasted him and his customers and wished them all the happiness of the New Year, now only eighteen minutes away.

"Thanks, George," I returned the glass. "I appreciate that. Now I must dash—I'm First Footing at midnight."

"All in the course of duty!" he laughed and returned to his generous hosting.

The whisky had warmed me nicely and I felt the beginnings of a glow of happiness as I guided my little machine through the dark, deserted lanes. As I glided into Aidensfield, I could hear singing in the pub. All its lights were aglow as I parked the machine against the wall of the village hall. Like everyone else, I was in my home village for New Year. I checked my watch. It was two minutes to twelve. I waited. I knew I must not enter Mrs Mitchell's house before midnight, as that would bring bad luck. It was a long wait.

Finally, the church clock began to chime. Its long, measured tones brought the anxiously awaited news and the pub erupted into a cacophonous din. Trumpets blew, bagpipes wailed, voices were raised in song and a badly-tuned piano began to pick out the notes of Auld Lang Syne. Inside, it must have sounded heavenly. Outside, the racket was appalling. I waited and listened, feeling very very miserable and very very lonely. Then the door burst open and two men rushed out, each wearing a paper hat and carrying a balloon. At exactly the same time, both noticed me. I was about to move towards Mrs Mitchell's house but was too late.

"It's t'bobby!" I heard one of them splutter in slurred language and with some effort. "He'll do it . . . You ask him . . ."

"Yessh, . . . good idea, John . . . very, very good idea . . . you asshk him."

Brave with drink, the two men came towards me, both evidently about to ask me something serious.

"Misshter Conshtable," said one of them. "Your presshensh issh required insshide, immediately if not sshooner," and he giggled at his little joke. "Now, immediately," and he saluted.

"Trouble?" I asked.

"No trouble, offissher, just Firsht Footing. There'ssh no one who can Firssht Foot, you sshee, because they're all in there now. It mussht be a stranger."

"All right, all right," I said.

"Great, great," and in they ran. I broke a little piece of holly from the adequate supply in my pannier, broke a piece of coal to gain the necessary lump, tore off a corner of bread and found a penny of my own.

Thus armed, I sallied into the smoky, alcoholic and happy atmosphere of the Brewers Arms. A huge shout of welcome erupted as my uniform materialised through the haze and I was manhandled through the crowd, being kissed by countless women until I reached the fireplace. There I knew I must deposit the coal, bread, money and holly. Surprisingly, the entire place fell silent. There was not a word as I made an exaggerated action to perform the necessary First Footing act and straightened up to find a huge glass of whisky before me. To have refused would have been churlish.

Cheers erupted about my ears as I brought guaranteed good luck to the Brewers Arms for the coming year and I raised my glass to wish happiness to everyone. The job over, the singing resumed, the kissing continued and the music commenced to the accompaniment of much back-slapping and hand-shaking as I quickly consumed the fiery contents of the glass.

Refusing another whisky on the grounds that I had an urgent appointment, I left the pub to make my way towards Mrs Mitchell's little house. It was now ten past twelve. I was ten minutes late and I found that my head was noticeably light and my walking action somewhat erratic. I had drunk the whisky far too quickly and the cool night air was causing me to amble from side to side. Nevertheless, I collected the necessary goods from my panniers and reached the cottage.

I knocked.

"Come in," she called from inside.

"It's P.C. Rhea," I opened the door and announced myself in case she thought it was a burglar.

Holding the coal, holly and slice of bread before me, I walked into her cosy living-room and swayed ever so slightly across the rug. Carefully, I placed one hand on the mantelshelf to steady myself and even more carefully placed the coal, holly and bread in the hearth, followed by the coin. My head was swimming slightly, but I was able to stand upright and wish her "Happy New Year".

"And a Happy New Year to you, Mr Rhea," she beamed. I had done well. The silence before this exchange was part of the ritual. It has been deemed that as the First Foot enters with his traditional gifts everyone must remain silent until he has deposited them in the hearth. Only then can the silence be broken.

"I have your drink ready," and she passed a glass of sherry to me.

I hadn't bargained for this. When accepting all these commitments, I thought my duties were merely to enter with the gifts and break in the New Year, but at every house I was expected to join the compulsory toast. I didn't dare refuse in case my lack of courtesy brought bad luck to everyone.

I gulped Mrs Mitchell's sherry because my point time was due and, after making something approximating an apology to her for my hurry, I rushed out to stand swaying near the telephone kiosk. My face was warm now and my entire body was responding to the liquor. Inside that hot motor-cycle gear I was sweating profusely and decided that New Year duty wasn't too bad after all, even on half nights. No one rang me. Sergeant Blaketon did not make an appearance to wish me a Happy New Year and so I was left with the honourable duty of fulfilling all my other First Footing appointments.

At this stage, it was difficult to remember anything after Mrs Mitchell's sherry. I know that I did call upon all my other customers and a good many more besides. People kept pushing lumps of coal, sprigs of holly and slices of bread into my hands and I must have visited almost every house in Aidensfield, plonking coal, bread and holly into their hearths and downing indescribable concoctions as I offered slurred toasts to all and sundry. It must have been a happy time.

Instinctively, I knew I was in no fit state to ride the motor-cycle back to my house and somehow, during the festivities, it got forgotten. The passage of time was also forgotten. I had no idea what the time was and became aware only of other demands for me to First Foot. It seemed that the entire population of the Brewers Arms took me into their homes to bring them luck.

After it all, I made my slow, laborious and hiccuping way back up the hill to the police house. I managed to fit my key into the lock and staggered inside, sweating and panting. I wiped my brow and my feet but recalled sufficient about my responsibilities to go into the living-room and place the coal, bread, coin and holly in the hearth. I must have remembered to bring these from my panniers, but as I stooped and swayed above my own fireside I noticed my hearth already contained those objects.

They weren't mine. Someone else had been. I had been surreptitiously First Footed! My gifts were still in my hands, all black with coal-dust and cold after the night's excesses. I stood for some minutes, wobbling before the sight in the hearth. Some unknown person had First Footed in *my* house. While I had been diligently patrolling, solving major crimes and protecting the public, someone had crept into my home and First Footed. Who? How? It was all too complicated for my fuddled brain and I simply placed my gifts beside the others, turned and struggled upstairs.

Memories of that awful ascent are hazy to say the least, the stairs presenting an almost insurmountable obstacle to my progress. I can recollect opening the bedroom door as quietly as possible before tripping over a chair and crashing unceremoniously onto the bed. Mary said something about it being a Happy New Year and I fell asleep, fully clothed, on top of the coverlet.

Next morning I was in severe trouble. My coal-black hands and motor-cycle clothing had smeared the bed-clothes, the staircase, the walls and the living-room, to say nothing of the bathroom which had received me on occasions during those night hours. It looked as if a sweep had rampaged through the house. To make things worse, Sergeant Blaketon had come to the house at 2 am, expecting to find me booking off duty. On failing to find me, and thinking I had dodged in home early, he'd knocked on the door and had roused Mary and the children. He had then tried to overcome his error performing our First Footing, pinching my coal and breaking a twig off the holly-bush near the gate. From evidence thus acquired, it seems I had returned to base around 4 am, but I can't remember much about it.

On the credit side, my efforts did bring luck to the villagers. Later that year, Aidensfield Parish Council presented them with a street lamp.

*   *   *

If my start to the year did not please Mary and the sergeant, it did please the village. From being a comparative stranger, I was now accepted as a villager, albeit with further reservations. I knew that I was regarded as a local person. My efforts at First Footing had ensured that, but I still had to prove myself as a policeman in the old-fashioned sense of the word. There's a big difference between a "person" and a "policeman" and my next task was to firmly establish myself in my official capacity.

This is more difficult than it seems. For one thing, it is never easy for a policeman to prove himself in the eyes of other policemen. To achieve that rare distinction, he must have an infinite capacity for arresting villains, drinking copious quantities of ale, dealing with "hard" men and sorting out problems of every kind. Proving oneself as a policeman in the eyes of the *public* is a totally different matter.

Members of the public view policemen in a particular light. They view them firstly as people and secondly as law-enforcement officers. I was sure that my status in the village as a person had been deemed satisfactory—my first few months had helped establish me in that sense, with my wife and young children helping enormously to make vital contacts. I had sealed that side of the business with my First Footing. But how could I prove myself a truly capable rural bobby in the eyes of the great British public? I required an important event, a big issue or emergency of some kind.

I waited for a suitable opportunity. It might be a crime to solve or a major incident to cope with. There might be a tough villain to conquer or a rescue operation of some kind. As the weeks went by, nothing happened. No crimes were committed, no villains fought me and no damsels required my rescue expertise.

As I patrolled my beautiful beat, alternating between the motor-cycle and my own size nines, I remained vigilant as I anticipated the right opportunity. It almost became an obsession. I knew I had to show that I could be a policeman, as well as a person. But how? Nothing dramatic seemed to happen. No one got murdered or raped, no one had his house broken into or his car stolen, no one got lost on the moors or attacked in the street. Life was so unpleasantly peaceful. The sergeant grumbled because I didn't submit offence reports and the inspector nattered because I had recorded no arrests.

It was during one of my low spells, when I wanted drama to enter my mundane life, that I sensed a dramatic occurrence. I noticed a farmer, clad in carpet-slippers and corduroys, galloping along Aidensfield village street at six o'clock one morning. I was forlornly standing outside the telephone kiosk making a point, having been on an abortive motor-cycle patrol since 4.30 am, and wishing something would happen. This could be it! Trouble of some kind!

I watched his approach. He wove from side to side with his head down, his flat cap perched on the front of his head and his feet twinkling across the road surface as he panted towards me. Knowing I could help, whatever it was, I stepped forward and said, "Hello, Mr Stanhope, nice morning."

He slowed momentarily in his tracks, looked at me and said, "Aye," then darted into the kiosk.

Feeling snubbed, I stood at a discreet distance as he began his urgent telephoning. Several of the glass windows of the kiosk were broken and I could not help overhearing his words. It didn't take long for me to appreciate he was having trouble with the telephone. I could hear him shouting uselessly into the mouthpiece and it was evident there was a total lack of response. After two minutes of futile efforts, he emerged and addressed me.

"Mr Rhea, can thoo work this contraption?"

"I can, Mr Stanhope. What's the matter?"

"Ah've a cow aboot ti cawf and ah need a vetinary. Ah've nivver used yan o' these new-fangled telephoning contraptions. Ah'll etti git him there sharp, she's very nigh due."

"Well," I said. "It's quite simple. You call the operator, ask for the number you require and then she'll tell you how much money to put in. You can see the coin-box just there. When the money's in, she'll ring the number and when you are connected you'll be told to press button 'A'. That's on the side of the box. Then you can talk."

"Oh," he said, obviously failing to comprehend my advice. I knew I'd have to show him. I exhorted him to enter the cramped box and I followed, squeezing him inside as I stood at the entrance holding the door open with my foot. This was in the days long before decimalisation and long before STD became commonplace in telephone-boxes. Those kiosks were solid edifices with a large money-box inside and a little tray to help get your money back, if the call was not connected.

"Ah see's where Ah've been gahin wrang," he laughed. "Ah thowt there was a choice of prices. Ah thowt Ah'd 'ave t'cheapest on offer. Ah mean, a penny's nowt is it?"

I knew the coin-box had "penny", "sixpence" and "shilling" written on the top, with appropriate slots for each coin. I didn't know what he'd done so far, but he seemed to be coping. I dialled "O" to link him with the operator and left him to it. He had a pile of coppers on top of the coin-box and seemed content.

"Number please," I could hear the strident voice of the lady operator.

"Hello," he shouted. "Hello, Ah want oor vetinary."

"Which veterinary?" I heard her ask.

"That'un that cums tiv oor farm ivvery Thursday," he said blandly.

"Look, sir," the girl replied in a softer voice. "I need to know his number before I can put you through."

"Number?" gasped the farmer. "He hasn't gitten a number, has he? He's nut a convict or a policeman or owt like that. Our policeman's gitten a number on his shoulder, but oor vetinary hasn't . . ."

"No, sir, his telephone number . . ."

"Nay, lass, Ah knows nowt about that, that's your job. Look, just git hod on him and send him along. Ooor Primrose is gahin ti cawf and he's needed there right sharp. She's very restless, thoo knaws."

"Who is that calling, sir? I will try to find a veterinary surgeon for you . . ."

"Stanhope from Aidensfield."

"And where is the trouble, Mr Stanhope?"

"In my cow-shed. If he doesn't get there quick, I fear for t'awd lass."

"I appreciate that, but where is your cow-shed?"

"Next ti t'pig-sties. We've gitten fifteen pig-sties and yon cow-shed's right next door . . ."

"No, I mean your address! Where shall I send the vet if I find him?"

"Oh, just to our farm. Stanhope, tell him. Me and my family's been farming there for generations. Tell him Stanhope, he'll know where to come."

"But I don't know which is your vet, Mr Stanhope . . ."

"Oh, it's young Singleton from Ashfordly."

"Look, Mr Stanhope, you get along home and I'll ring Mr Singleton for you. It's a cow that's calving, and she's in your cow-shed. Now, what's your address?"

"High Brow Farm. He can't miss it, thoo knows and any rooad, he's been before."

"All right, Mr Stanhope. You get along and I'll ring him."

"Thanks, miss," he said.

He replaced the handset and emerged happily, collected his pile of unused pennies from the top of the coin box and grinned at me.

"Well?" I asked.

"Grand," he grinned wickedly. "Grand. Yon telephone lass is telling Singleton to get himself there as sharp as he can."

"So things will be right, eh?"

"Aye," he said, "things'll be right. Nice awd cow is our Primrose. Thoo'll be coming along to have a look at her, eh? There'll be a cup of tea about seven, I reckon, after t'vet's done his stuff."

"Thanks," I said. "I'll look forward to that."

"Think nowt on it," he said. "Yon phone call cost me nowt, did it?" He smiled craftily. "I reckon you and me's earned our cup of tea this morning."

As he stomped away, I wondered what this early morning encounter had proved. I hadn't dealt with a major police crisis but, somewhere, crafty old Stanhope had taught me a lesson in Yorkshire thrift.

2

"Men are suspicious; prone to discontent."

Robert Herrick, 1591–1674

Like any other organised body of people and equipment, the police service cannot afford to stand still. Progress must be allowed to intrude and interfere and, because many police officers are essentially conservative in their outlook and stubborn to boot, change comes by being forced upon them. Initially, many attempt to reject this but the mighty feet of officialdom stamp forward until, by dint of enforced usage and repeated orders from above, the necessary change is effected. By then, it is time for another.

Policemen everywhere do not agree that change or progress constitutes improvement. Progress implies a move forward, but that in itself is not necessarily an improvement. Within the service, changes are made frequently. Progress is moderately common and improvement a rarity.

It can be argued with some justification, therefore, that the concept of Unit Beat Policing and the accompanying Collator system was "progress", its arrival undoubtedly a useful change. For that reason it can be regarded as progress. Whether it was an improvement is for history and crime statistics to decide.

The system was designed for town and city policemen, but it was based upon the ideals of rural policing. The focal point of the system was a constable who lived on his patch. He was provided with a car in which to patrol and a back-up force to aid him in his duties. Basing this idea on the notion that rural bobbies know everyone and everything that happens on their patch, the pundits reckoned the same logic could apply to a city area if the area had its own constable. And so the Unit Beat system was born. To assist the constable living in pseudo-rural bliss among slag heaps and council houses, he was allocated a team of panda car drivers to patrol the area. They were to deal with matters of urgency and transport the resident bobby around and there was a plain-clothes man from the C.I.D. He sorted out the villains on the patch. Between them, these men policed their Unit and spent time getting to know everything and everyone. In theory, it was masterly.

The snag was that it didn't quite work like that. It is quite impossible to transplant rural systems into city environments. City people are a different breed and do not react or behave like countryfolk. And, furthermore, one car cannot do the work of five men. The result was that every police force developed its own interpretation of the Unit Beat system and few of them benefited from it.

One redeeming feature, however, was the Collator and his concomitant indexing system.

There was nothing original in having a comprehensive index and in fact most rural beat constables used their own excellent systems. The problem was that they filed most of the information in their heads. They knew who got up early, who came home late, which car belonged to whom and whose wife was seeing someone else's husband. They knew the villains and the goodies, the perverts and the businessmen. In short, they knew a lot. If a constable left the vicinity, he took all his information with him. That was the problem because the new man had to start all over again. If only all that information was recorded. . . . With this idea of bliss in mind, Home Office experts created the Collator. This was merely a man with a filing system. He used reference cards, strip indexes and other office requisites to keep tabs on the villains and ne'er-do-wells. The basic idea was sound. It said that every policeman who patrolled a Unit Beat area would make a written note of what he saw. If, for example, he observed Burgling Bert from Bridlington walking along Albany Street at 6 o'clock one morning and carrying a walking-stick, he would note that fact in his police notebook. He would then enter the fact in the Collator's files, probably under the name of Burgling Bert. Gradually a file would grow and the Collator would have a complete record of Burgling Bert's movements should anyone wish to run a check on his activities at any time. The system was useful because it could identify a villain, but, if correctly compiled, it could also clear a suspect. It might prove the alibi of an innocent person.

Most rural beat constables ran a similar system long before the Home Office came up with its mind-boggling advance and I kept my own record of events on Aidensfield beat.

It was through my system that I became very suspicious of John Henry Tyler. It must be said at the outset that, in spite of this new and revolutionary aid to common sense, I would have become suspicious of the fellow. Recorded facts cannot lie; John Henry Tyler was up to something and my files proved it.

He was a retired hill farmer in his middle sixties who had come down from a remote part of the North Yorkshire moors to retire to Aidensfield. His wife was called Ruth and they kept a collie dog called Wade, named after the giant who lived near their farm years ago. John Henry was a stout man with a walk like a sailor and his shortness, when in motion, served only to give him the appearance of a trundling barrel. His face was round and jolly and it always wore two or three days' growth of whiskers. I wondered when he shaved, or how he shaved, in order to preserve this unkempt appearance. His clothing was rough and rural, practical perhaps but never smart. To complement his rustic countenance, he reeked of farmyards, middens and cow-sheds. He was a walking example of the scents of the English countryside.

Not once during my first few months at Aidensfield did I have any reason to suspect him of illegality. He taxed his car, licensed his dog, paid his rates and ensured that all his firearms documents were in order. He was the epitome of a worthy villager, true as they come and as straight as a newly fletched arrow.

Having been a hard-working and poorly paid hill-farmer, he had been accustomed to rising very early and it was the continuance of this habit that drew my attention to him. Very early one morning, I was sitting astride my stationary motor-cycle at the junction of Aidensfield village street and Elsinby Road. I could hear approaching footsteps and was tucked nicely beneath an overhanging conifer. I knew I was practically invisible so I remained very very still in the shadows. I looked at my watch. It was 5.30 a.m.

Very soon, the oncoming footsteps materialised into the rounded shape of John Henry Tyler. His head was down against the fresh breeze of an early spring morning and he wore a muffler about his neck. On his feet were the traditional leather-topped clogs of the district and he wore the only coat I'd ever seen him use, a tatty, dull brown, sack-like affair with bulging pockets and a massive collar. His hands were deep in those commodious pockets, his chin was tucked into the ample collar and his feet were eating up the yards as he hurried about his early business.

He walked right past without seeing me. I observed that grizzled grey hair, the unshaven weather-beaten face and his rough country clothes as he hurried along the lane. John Henry hadn't changed in retirement. He still went about unshaven and smelling of cows and pigs. This morning was no exception. But he wasn't going to work, surely? Naturally, I was curious about his purpose, but didn't interrupt. Instead, I simply kept him under observation.

He turned right at the junction and hurried down the gentle gradient which led to Elsinby, two miles distant. I waited ten minutes before I left my vantage-point and took the motor-cycle to the hill top. From there, I could see John Henry's diminishing figure striding along the road. He was still heading towards Elsinby with his hands in his large pockets and his old head bowed against the chilly breeze. Where was he going? At this point, I never suspected his involvement in anything criminal. I took him to be an active countryman going for an early morning walk.

Over the following months, however, this event repeated itself many times. I noticed him on several occasions, always walking that stretch of road and always at this time of the morning. He was always dressed in his scruffy old clothes and clogs and never carried anything. Furthermore,

I never saw him make a return journey. Mentally I had noted these sightings but now decided to record them in writing. Maybe they could be linked with some distant crimes? Had he a woman? Once or twice, I waited in Elsinby village but always missed him there. He seemed to vanish somewhere on the road between the two villages. One or two of my colleagues reported seeing him during their early morning patrols around my beat, but none saw him actually in Elsinby. This created even more interest.

The frequency of his trips bothered me too. My awkward shifts did not allow me to see him regularly, but by dint of asking my colleagues and checking from time to time myself the fact emerged that it was a monthly outing, usually on a Thursday.

I could not believe that John Henry was a criminal. He was not a criminal type, he was a stolid rural character, a bit sharp perhaps, but definitely not a villain. I had no reports of criminal activities on my beat with which he could be associated but I did check my Crime Bulletins just to be sure that there was nothing suspicious along my beat boundaries. I was very aware that a series of burglaries had been committed in widespread rural areas over a period of about two years and all had been perpetrated during the early hours of the morning. Collators over a large area had pooled their information, and as a result, an early-morning worker from York was arrested. His practice was to hitch-hike out of town to his place of work, but this system sometimes provided him with spare time. He made profitable use of that time by breaking into houses. The mass of apparently unconnected intelligence gathered by the collators, eventually linked his movements with the burglaries and brought about his arrest. It was not impossible that old John Henry was perpetrating something highly illegal. Stranger things had happened, but I had to know. I had not to ask him directly, not yet. I must discover more about him and began discreet enquiries into his background. He lived in a rented house in Aidensfield with his wife and dog, and had never had children. His circumstances could be described as "poor". The farm he'd worked high on the North Yorkshire moors had also been rented, and throughout his life he had worked from morning until night, scraping the barest of livings from that tough moorland area. He'd kept a few sheep and half a dozen milking cows and he had grown root-crops in a small enclosure surrounded by a dry-stone wall. My sources told me his income had never exceeded £11 per week. John Henry was indeed a poor man, but proud. If he'd existed all his life in this manner, it was barely credible that he'd turn to crime in his retirement.

Nonetheless, the fact that he had retired meant he would have little to live on. So was the old devil going stealing at dawn? It seemed a feasible theory and one which would impress Sergeant Blaketon, so I decided to intensify my observations and enquiries.

I checked all the reported burglaries, housebreakings, shop-breakings, larcenies, poachings and other crimes in the district and compared their times with the known movements of John Henry. It is fair to say that none could be positively attributed to him, but in some cases they could have been. Rather sorrowfully, I began to grow worried about him. I knew that if I made a good arrest, especially one which cleared up a spate of serious crimes, I would be in Sergeant Blaketon's good books for a time. I found myself regarding John Henry's movements as a key to my future. Through him, I could make a name for myself.

I knew I had to be cunning. I had to catch him either in the act or with the stolen property. It was little use going about the place on the noisy Francis Barnett as that would alert him so I crept out of the house on several mornings and went about furtive foot patrols. I kept to the shadows, to the fields and woods as I attempted to keep an eye on this early morning clog walker.

Finally, there came a moment of triumph. I was concealed behind an old building alongside the Aidensfield-Elsinby road when I heard the familiar clip-clop of his clogs. It was a lovely summer morning with the birds singing and the scent of blossom in the air; it was most certainly not a time to be engaged in furtive criminal activities, but, sure enough, John Henry was heading my way.

I watched him from the security of the building. His head was down in that familiar style and his hands were tucked deep into those huge pockets as he stomped along the road. I waited until he was fifty yards ahead of me and began to shadow him. I used the heavily-leaved hedges and copses as my shelter as I moved stealthily along the fields. I readily kept pace with the active old man and he never once turned to look my way. I got the impression that he was deep in thought, his mind a long way from this peaceful stretch of England.

I shadowed him all the way to Elsinby where he arrived just before six o'clock. But instead of entering the village street he turned sharp left and for a moment I lost him. Blast! He'd tricked me! In order to catch him I had to scramble out of the fields and regain the road, and I did so with considerable effort and anxiety. Eventually, I landed muddy-footed on the highway, panting slightly and with my cap at an angle. I hurried after him into the village, but he'd vanished. He'd got away! The cunning old devil!

He could only have gone one way and that was along the lane to Ploatby, so that was the road I took. But even before I'd gone fifty yards a car emerged from one of the cottages along that road. It was a nice tan Rover 2000 driven by a smart gentleman and in the front passenger seat was none other than John Henry Tyler.

It was past before I could stop it and I was rewarded by a wave from both men as the car vanished through the village towards York. I knew the owner of that car—he was a Mr Eugene Peterson, a retired wealthy businessman from Croydon. It was a most unlikely partnership, so what was going on?

The mysterious pair vanished from my sight with no attempt to conceal their departure, so I now wondered if Peterson was a high-class villain, perhaps a con-man, using old Tyler as a stooge? It was not beyond the bounds of credibility.

Deflated, I was now faced with a long walk back home and my efforts had produced very little more information, except I now knew the identity of his partner in crime. Back in my office an hour later, I rang York's collator to see if there was any record of that car in their files, but there wasn't. It had never come to the notice of York police in a suspicious manner, nor had its occupants. Either they were very clever criminals or they weren't criminals at all.

I was now faced with several probabilities and several different ways of tackling the problem. Certainly, something unusual was going on. There was no doubt about that and it was my duty as the local constable to unearth the truth. If I told Sergeant Bairstow, he'd laugh it off, and Sergeant Blaketon would wheel them both in for interview. Neither seemed the right approach. I had to find out for myself and then tell the sergeants. I could be bold and ask them outright to account for their movements, but, if they were engaged in crime, that would alert them to police interest and we'd never solve anything.

The only solution was to make discreet enquiries in Elsinby and the finest starting-place for such delicate questions was the Hopbind Inn. Later that morning, I made it my first calling-place and George produced a cup of warm coffee. It was just ten o'clock.

"Busy?" he asked, by way of opening the conversation along official lines.

"So, so." I shrugged my shoulders, hoping he'd accept that as an indication of the non-urgent nature of my presence.

"You're early—it's usually dinner-time when you get here." Dinner-time for Yorkshire folk is lunch-time for other people.

"Aye." I sipped the coffee as I perched on a stool in his bar. He wiped many glasses. "Tell me, George, do you know Eugene Peterson, the chap with the Rover?"

"Aye, I do," he said, looking earnestly at me.

"What sort of chap is he?" I continued. We were alone.

"All right," said George. "Honest, quite well-off, I'd say. Grown up family, retired businessman. Pleasant enough chap."

"Honest?"

"I'd say so. I've never heard anything against him."

I didn't respond but savoured his coffee so now he came at me with:

—"Come along, Mr Rhea, what's on your mind? Is he up to something?"

"I don't know," I said wistfully. "I don't know, but I must find out."

"Why, what's he done?"

I knew I could trust George's discretion, so I unfolded my catalogue of early suspicions about John Henry Tyler and now Eugene Peterson. George listened carefully, wiping more glasses and sipping occasionally from his own coffee.

He smiled as I unfolded my yarn, his smile broadening as I enlarged my tale. I could see he was amused and knew, at that point, that my two suspects were not criminals.

"So, there it is, George. What's going on?"

"You've no idea, have you?" he grinned wickedly.

"No," I said, "I haven't."

"Well, every third Thursday in the month, John Henry walks down here and goes off in Peterson's Rover. They go to York Railway Station and catch an early train to London."

"Go on," I encouraged him.

"Well, you might believe this of Peterson, but not your John Henry. You see, they're both top chess-players; they play international chess at a club in London. Some are postal contests, some are live, and I believe some are played over the telephone. Peterson introduced John Henry to the London club, and they go there every month. John Henry's loved down there!"

"John Henry Tyler? You mean that smelly old farmer is a major chess-player?"

"One of the country's best; you'll occasionally see his name in the posh Sundays—last year, he beat a Russian grandmaster. . . ."

"But why doesn't he get dressed up?"

"He never dresses up for anything and he doesn't want the village to know about it. You won't tell anyone, will you? The club has agreed not to publicise his real identity, so don't let John Henry know that you're onto him. He'll kill me for letting his secret out."

Back in the office, I wrote "checkmate" on my file about John Henry Tyler.

It was the ubiquitous Shakespeare who called the milkmaid "Queen of curds and cream", while Sir Thomas Overbury in

1614 wrote, "In milking a cow and straining the teats through her fingers, it seems that so sweet a milk press makes the milk the whiter or sweeter."

These lovely rural ladies were considered the height of perfection and in days of yore were worshipped as the purest of creatures. When farms were run as highly competitive commercial enterprises, even ladies of standing regarded the job of milkmaid as worthwhile. It was never looked upon as a menial task and advice given to dairy farmers was to have a good breed of cow, to possess proper buildings and implements and to have an attractive and skilful dairymaid. One farmer, writing in the last century said, "It is a truly feminine employment and to their hands it (the milking) should be left." It was widely accepted that cows "never let their milk down pleasantly" to someone they dreaded or disliked and it was felt that cows enjoyed being soothed by mild usage, especially when ticklish and young. It was known that contented cows provided good creamy milk, and it was the job of the milkmaid to win the best from her bovine charges.

Although my beat embraced many dairy-farms, there were not many milkmaids in or around Aidensfield. To be truthful, I did not personally know one, but it seemed that there was such a beauty on a remote farm. One day I would meet her, I felt sure. The farm in question, a large dairy-farm on the moors beyond Briggsby, occupied a considerable but isolated site well away from the main road to Harrowby. I had called on a couple of occasions in the past to check the stock registers but never during those brief visits had I espied this renowned beauty.

Then late one evening, I received a telephone call at home. It was from Joe Camplin, the farmer in question. He sounded agitated and asked if I was on duty.

I wasn't, but asked if I could help.

"Aye, it's about Diane Ferguson," he said hesitantly.

"Diane Ferguson?" I didn't recognise the name.

"Aye, my milkmaid, the Scots girl, you know."

"Oh." I had never seen the girl, but the point registered. "Something wrong, Mr Camplin?"

"Aye, she's been attacked."

"Attacked?" I shouted. "Where?"

"Down our lane. Not five minutes ago . . ."

"Is she badly hurt?" I asked, wondering whether a rogue cow had attacked her or whether it was something else.

"No, but she's shaken. It was a man, grabbed her, he did. She got away though."

"I'll be there right away," I promised.

Although it was my day off, I jumped into my private car and rushed five miles to the lonely farm. As I drove through the countryside, I looked for a solitary man walking the lanes at night, but found no one. I hoped I might come across the culprit but out here a person can lose himself very rapidly. Near this farm, there is nothing but wide open moorland, interspaced with a few spruces and silver birch. He could be anywhere out there. My headlights found only dry-stone walls, solitary trees and the occasional cottage. As I turned down the lane to Crag Foot Farm, I discovered the unmade road was muddy and full of holes. It threatened to shake my car to pieces as I bumped and bounced along its terrible surface. Fortunately, the farm's exterior light was burning and guided me onto the concrete yard near the back door. It was a relief to come to a halt.

I hurried inside, pausing to knock but once and shouted my arrival. I knew the way and rushed inside. In the comfortable kitchen I found Joe and Mary Camplin fussing over a tearful girl. This was Diane Ferguson.

"Ah," said Joe as I entered. "Thank God I found you in."

"How is she?" was my first question.

The girl smiled weakly through her tears and wiped her red eyes with a man's handkerchief, doubtless supplied by Joe. "I'm all right, thanks. Just shaken."

"Cup o' tea?" suggested Mary Camplin. "I've made one for Diane."

"Thanks," I accepted her offer and pulled out a chair to settle at the table. The tea was lovely.

"I heard her come crying into the yard," began Joe before I could ask what had happened. "It was dark, and she'd run all the way . . . he got her by the throat . . ."

"Let's start at the beginning, eh?" I suggested, turning my attention to Diane. She was a petite girl, about twenty years old, very pretty with mousy hair and a face bearing a suggestion of freckles. Her delightful grey eyes were sharp and alert, her smile tantalising, and all were complemented by her figure which was charming and full. She looked more like a farm secretary or a shorthand typist than a milkmaid, but her appearance and demeanour reminded me of the charm of her Shakespearian counterparts. If poets and writers said that milkmaids were charming, this one proved the truth of their words.

"Tell me, Diane. What happened?"

"Well, Mr Rhea." Her accent contained a beautiful Lowland lilt. "It was like this. I got off the bus at the lane end," and she indicated the direction with her hands. "I always get off there, you see . . ."

"It's her afternoon off," butted in Joe. "She goes to Harrowby for the afternoon and gets that bus back. It stops at the lane end, just up the road from here."

"I see," I smiled and bade her continue. "You got off the bus. What time?"

"Half past eight, Mr Rhea. It was right on time."

"Go on."

"Well, it was dark, you see, and I had a torch. I got off like I always do, and began to walk down the lane to the farm . . ."

"I've often said I should put a light at that lane end," commented Joe. "I'll do it now, by God I will."

I smiled at Diane. She understood and we tolerated his well-intentioned interruptions.

"Well," she continued. "I got as far as the haystack . . ."

"I always put a stack in that field," said Joe. "It's handy for my cows when they're up there . . ."

"Joe, shut up," ordered his wife. "Let Mr Rhea talk to Diane."

"Oh, sorry," he said, picking up his cup of tea.

"I'd just got past the stack when a man jumped out at me," the girl said slowly. "I didn't know what to do. . . . I didn't run. . . . I think I was too frightened. . . . I just didn't know. . . ."

"What did he do?" I put this important question gently but firmly. I had to know whether there'd been any attempt at rape or indecent assault. It mattered for my subsequent action.

"He tried to put a sack over my head," she said, wiping away a tear. "A dirty old sack . . ."

"A sack?"

"Yes, it sounds so silly, but he had a sack. It was a rough hessian one, all smelly and horrible, and he tried to put it over me. . . . I began to run, but he grabbed me by the arm. . . he was very strong, so I shouted and screamed . . ."

"He didn't touch you?" I asked. "Indecently, I mean? Or say anything?"

She shook her head. "No, nothing like that, thank God. It was just that sack. . . . I fought and fought, but he was very strong."

"And you screamed?" I sipped at the tea.

"Yes, but the farm's too far away for Mr and Mrs Camplin to hear me and the bus had gone by then. No one heard me. There was nobody."

"So what did you do?"

She hesitated. "I kicked him, right between the legs," and she laughed. "I knew it hurt—he called out in pain, and then I hit him with my torch." She showed me the cracked glass.

I smiled at her bravery. "Great! That'll teach him a lesson. Then what happened?"

"He ran away," she smiled at the memory, "and I came in here, crying. Mr Camplin went out. . . ."

"I did that, with my shotgun. If I'd seen him in our lane he'd have got both barrels right up his backside, I can tell you."

"And you found no one?"

"Not a soul." He shook his head.

"And the sack?"

"Nay, lad, I didn't see that. I was too concerned about Diane."

"Did he say anything to you?" I asked her again.

"No, nothing. He just panted and grunted as he tried to put the sack over me. It's so silly . . . maybe he didn't mean any harm . . ."

"It was an assault if nothing else," I said. "Now, Diane, you had your torch. Was it on?"

She nodded.

"And could you see him? I need a description if you can give one."

She had no trouble providing me with a marvellously detailed description of her assailant. He was about 50 years old with thick grey hair, about average height, and he wore a dark donkey jacket with leather shoulder-patches. He had dark trousers, dark shoes, and a flat cap, checked style, with the press-stud undone above the peak. And he had a squeaky voice. She'd noted that as he'd cried out with pain. He was clean-shaven, she said, but whiskery, as if he'd not shaved for a day or two. He wore a white scarf and gloves with string backs, like racing drivers wore.

It was a first-class description and if this man lived in the district I would have little trouble tracing him. We'd trace him in no time.

"Have you any idea who it was?" I put to her. Quite often, unprovoked assaults of this kind were an outcome of some recent disagreement with a boyfriend or prospective suitor. Diane was a very pretty young woman, and must have had lots of suitors, so this could be some form of revenge.

"Yes, I think so," she said quietly.

"Aye," said Joe. "We think we know who it is. Nasty business, Mr Rhea. I don't want to be one to cause trouble, but it'll have to be stopped. Innocent girls can't be put at risk, you know. . . ."

"So who is it?" I ventured.

"You know that Frenchman who lives up the hill, on the road to Harrowby?"

I shook my head.

"No, you wouldn't, he's like you, not been here all that long, but he took Blackamoor House as a studio. He's an artist, a clever chap, but a bit weird."

"Weird?" I asked.

"Well, not like us. Dresses queer, dyes his hair, smells of scent and stuff. It wouldn't surprise me if he had a bath every day neither."

"Artists often do dress individually," I said. "Has he been a nuisance before?"

"No," she said. "No, he never bothers me."

"So you're acquainted?"

"Aye," said Joe. "He comes here for his milk. Two pints a day—he collects them himself, in a little can like they do in France."

"What's his name?"

"Edouard Sannier," said Mary Camplin. "Monsieur Edouard Sannier. He's quite nice, I think. At least, I used to think he was."

"Now, Diane, listen carefully," I put to her. "Are you sure it was him? If I had to get you to swear on oath that it was Edouard Sannier would you say it was?"

"Yes," she said with a determined clenching of her teeth. "Yes, I would . . ."

"OK," I said. "I'll go and talk to him."

"What can you do with him?" Joe asked me.

"It's difficult to know what we can do," I said. "There was no indecency, and no attempt to rape Diane. He didn't say he was going to rape you, did he? There's no cuts, bruises?"

She shook her head.

"We're left with common assault, in which case you could take your own action against him. Common assault is not a matter for the police," I told them. "You go and see a solicitor and he'll fix it to go to court. If we consider he is a public nuisance," I added as an alternative, "we might get him bound over to be of good behaviour."

"I thought they'd send him to prison for what he did!" gasped Mary.

"For rape or attempted rape, yes, but for something like this, no. There's very little in law that can be done. Mind," I continued, "if he admitted he was going to rape Diane, or touch her indecently, we could consider a more serious charge. But first let me talk to him. I'll let you know how I get along. If I have to take him to the police-station, it'll be morning before I see you."

"Aye, all right. I reckon Diane needs an early night," considered Joe, "with a drink of hot milk and whisky. She'll sleep on that."

"Couldn't be better. Now, Diane, is there anything else I should know? Did he say anything or do anything else? Have you angered him at all? Led him on, teased him?"

"No, honest, I've never given him any encouragement. Never . . ."

"These Frenchmen are very romantic, you know." I tried to make the incident sound light to reduce its seriousness, but I failed. For these people, it was a most serious event.

"It's not romance when they put bloody sacks over lasses' heads!" growled Joe.

I left them and drove the few hundred yards to the lonely cottage on the hill top. A light was burning, which pleased me. I had never been into this house although I had passed it several times. Feeling apprehensive about the interview, I parked my car on the main road, walked to the studded front door and knocked. A pretty middle-aged lady answered, smiling up at me. She was very petite and charming.

"Yes?" she said pleasantly.

"Oh, I am P.C. Rhea," I introduced myself. "Is Monsieur Sannier in, please?"

"Yes, do come in." There was no trace of a French accent. In fact, she had a very English voice and I estimated she would be in her late sixties.

She led me into the lounge where I saw a grey-haired man sitting on the settee, sipping coffee. He rose as I entered.

"I am P.C. Rhea, the village policeman at Aidensfield," I announced. "I wonder if I could have a word with you, sir." I probably sounded very formal.

"But of course," he smiled and indicated an easy-chair. "It is always nice to meet the local policeman, eh, Alice?"

"Yes, dear," smiled his wife. "Would you like a coffee, Mr Rhea?"

"Er, no thanks," I refused as I settled in the chair. "I've just had one actually. Now, it's a very difficult enquiry for me . . ."

"We are very civilised," he said graciously. "It is trouble?"

His English was impeccable too, but he did have a high-pitched voice.

"Mr Sannier," I anglicised his title. "Where were you tonight, about eight-thirty?"

"Tonight? Why here, of course. With my wife."

"You didn't go out?"

"No, he did not," she said grimly. I paused deliberately as I looked around the small room. A piano stood against one wall and on top was a flat cap with the press-stud undone, a pair of gloves with string backs and a long white scarf. Hanging on a hook behind the door was a dark donkey jacket with black leather shoulder-patches and he had a thick mop of grey hair. Diane's description was perfect. It fitted him absolutely, although I'd have placed his age nearer sixty than fifty.

But was it too perfect? Everything matched and she had said he called regularly at the farm for his milk.

"Mrs Sannier, could you swear your husband did not leave the room this evening?"

She regarded me seriously. "We both went out, in our car, down to Ashfordly and returned in time for tea, just before five o'clock. Edouard went out to fill the coal-scuttle at six o'clock, and we've not been out since, neither of us. I will swear to that." She spoke in a fiercely protective manner.

"I believe you," I said, for it was true. I did believe them. This man was no putter of sacks over the heads of young nubile girls.

"What is it?" he asked, with a genuine interest. "Have I done wrong?"

I was in two minds whether to tell him. I didn't want to give the impression that I believed he'd do such a thing and yet I did owe the couple some explanation. As I dithered for a moment, Mrs Sannier poured a coffee and said, "I think this would help." She passed it to me and I relaxed in the chair.

I told them the full story as Diane had related it, and included the description she'd given. When I had finished, he laughed, "She described me, eh? You had to come."

"I had to come," I said. "But it seems a strange tale for a girl like Diane to concoct, Mr Sannier. I'm sure she was attacked."

"Maybe she is telling the truth," said his wife. "When I was washing the tea things, I saw a young man walking down the road towards the dairy-farm. He wore a dark donkey jacket, just like Edouard's, and a flat cap, and a long light-coloured scarf with string-back gloves. I remembered thinking how like Edouard he looked."

"What time was that?" I felt excited.

"Six o'clock," she said. "Perhaps a minute or two either way, but near enough to six."

That was two and a half hours *before* the attack. "Tell me more," I said.

"Well, he comes down the road every Wednesday night. He walks into Ashfordly to the pub. I think he works on the Forestry Commission land near Sutton Bank Top."

"Do you know his name?" I asked.

"Sorry," she said. "I don't."

"Well, I'll have to make some more enquiries," I said. "Look, I'm very sorry to have troubled you like this—I feel very guilty about ruining your evening."

"Think nothing of it, young man," said Monsieur Sannier. "In some countries, I would have been dragged off and clapped in jail for less. I hope you find the man."

There are times one has to trust a man almost on sight and I trusted this one. I was convinced he had nothing to do with the attack on Diane.

To cut a long story short, I went straight to the private address of the Forestry Commission boss for the district and explained my problem. He told me he knew the lad, a twenty-two-year-old who lived with his parents in a woodland cottage a mile from the top of Sutton Bank. The parents kept a smallholding with hens and pigs but the lad was very shy with girls. He was totally unable to communicate with them, so he was a likely candidate. The description supplied by Mrs Sannier fitted him.

Knowing I would have difficulty locating him tonight, I went to the cottage in the woods first thing next morning. I found Jeremy Morley at home. His dad was labouring on a farm nearby and mother was out. He allowed me in; it was a hovel and filthy with it, but for this unfortunate lad it was home. And there, on a hook behind the door was a dark donkey jacket, a flat cap with the peak button undone, a dull white scarf and, on the table, a pair of driving-gloves with string backs.

Almost before I began my questioning, the lad readily admitted trying to capture the girl. He knew it was best to put sacks over the heads of captured birds to calm them; he'd seen his dad do it many times with hens. And he'd seen the television, where men carried off the girl of their choice. He thought he'd do the same. He'd waited two hours behind that haystack, knowing Diane got off the Harrowby bus each Wednesday, and said he liked the look of her. He'd never spoken to her—he didn't dare, and he'd dressed up like Monsieur Sannier because he liked the Frenchman's style and confidence. That man knew how to treat girls, he felt, so he copied his idol for style and his father for action. I don't think he realised it was wrong.

After speaking to Sergeant Bairstow about it, we took the lad to court and he was bound over to be of good behaviour. The court persuaded him to seek treatment for his loneliness and appalling shyness in the face of girls. Diane forgave him too, which helped, and she went up to the Sanniers' cottage to apologise for implicating the unfortunate man.

Although I was pleased we found the culprit, I was even more pleased that I hadn't prosecuted the wrong man. It would have been so easy to ruin the Sanniers' life but I did wonder about the calming influence of hessian sacks upon one's head!

3

"Is there anything to which you wish to draw my attention?"
"To the curious incident of the dog in the night-time."
"The dog did nothing in the night time."
"That was the curious incident," remarked Sherlock Holmes.

When I walked in the garden of my hill-top police house, I could look upon the expanse of the valley between and watch the passing show. One outcome of my elevated rural studies was an appreciation of the variety of farm animals that lived and worked on my patch.

There were horses of every kind. They ranged from the massive Shires and Clydesdales being bred for show purposes, to the diminutive Shetland ponies loved by little girls having riding-lessons. The cows included everything from Red Polls to Friesians with bulls to keep them content, and there were pigs and sheep, dogs and cats, hens and guinea-fowl. Some farmers even bred rabbits, hamsters, goats and donkeys. One striking fact was that all these beasts lived happily side by side and seemed in joyful communion with the wild creatures that occupied the same parcel of countryside.

It would be nice if all races of men could live in such harmony, but we must recognise that animals are not emotional creatures. They eat and sleep, they make love and they make war, but they do not worry about their image, neither do they stalk their portion of England believing that brown cows are superior to whites, that stallions should wash up, or that moles should fight for equal rights with squirrels. In spite of their minor quarrels, they are a happy bunch, and it is fair to say that no animal, of its own volition, caused me professional anxiety. Interest, yes; curiosity, certainly, but apprehension—no!

Some of their owners did and some of the animals did when affected by the behaviour of their humans. One professional problem surrounded a beautiful black labrador called Nero. Really, it wasn't his fault at all, but it was alleged that he became savagely involved with a flock of sheep owned by a fiery farmer called Fairclough. This was Donald Fairclough of The Grange, Thackerston.

During the early months of my constableship at Aidensfield, I had experienced very little contact with Donald Fairclough because Mr Fairclough had taken it upon himself to be a gentleman farmer. He wore hacking-jackets, plus-fours and brogues. Locally, the term "gentleman farmer" suggests a rich man who owns a farm but who pays someone else to do the work and talk to policemen. Mr Fairclough's wealth allowed him to spend a lot of time overseas or riding about the countryside in his Daimler with two golden retrievers and a shotgun at his side. Had anyone witnessed his demeanour, dress and dogs, he would immediately classify him as a gentleman farmer. He was that sort of person, although I believe he grew up in Middlesbrough.

Being Mr Fairclough of Thackerston Grange made him feel rather important and he perpetuated his personal image by talking loudly, telephoning incessantly and writing incomprehensible letters to newspapers and parish councils. His turnover of domestic and farm staff was rapid, and it was rumoured that sometimes he had to return to his lovely farm personally to feed the pigs or muck out the cows when a walk-out occurred. But such events were rare—he had enough money to find someone to do the job in return for a quick pound or two in cash. Donald Fairclough always got by.

It was during my first spring at Aidensfield that I experienced the wrath of his tongue. My telephone rang in the middle of a Wednesday afternoon when I happened to be at home between shifts. Mary answered it and informed me it was a Mr Fairclough who sounded important and upset.

"Hello!" boomed the voice. "Is that the policeman?"

"P.C. Rhea," I identified myself.

"Sheep-worrying," shouted Fairclough. "Some bloody dog's attacked my flock of black-faces."

"When?" I asked.

"Recently, very recently," returned the voice. "My man's just come down from my ten-acre. There's five sheep mauled and one dead. Savaged by a bloody dog. Get yourself down here straight away."

I was tempted to reply "Yes, sir" but resisted. Fairclough wasn't going to have me running around in circles.

Even so, sheep-worrying is one of the most terrible of rural happenings and I felt sorry for him. Anyone who fails to appreciate the horror of this all-too-common tragedy should take a look at a savaged sheep. They should think about a living animal with its intestines torn from its throbbing body by bloodthirsty domestic dogs whose normal senses have evaporated in a mist of raw meat smells. They should witness the terrified huddle of mangled animals who survive the onslaught, they should see the aborted lambs, dead even before they see separate life, and they should witness the tears in the eyes of tough, unemotive farmers who weep at the appalling sight. The agony is everyone's.

Sheep-worrying is much more than dogs running after stupid woollybacks. It is unbridled savagery at its worst; it is flocks of sheep which can be literally terrified into death; it is individual animals being eaten alive and it is humans claiming, "My dog could never do that." But it can, and so often does.

Fortunately, most rural folk understand the horrible nature of sheep-worrying and seek effectively to control their dogs. Some do not care, however, and, in addition, many newcomers to the countryside do not comprehend the dangers caused by roaming Fidos and wandering Fluffs. In recent years, it has been observed that sheep who live near towns and city suburbs are being savaged by urban dogs whose owners turn them loose for walkies. Nationwide, it is a massive problem; for anyone living near sheep, it is a harrowing and ghastly crime.

I knew the problems only too well, having been nurtured

in a moorland sheep-farming district, and I knew just how difficult it can be to locate the guilty dogs. If they are not found, they kill again and again. It is sometimes possible to analyse the stomach contents of suspect dogs or examine the hair about their muzzles in an effort to prove they had eaten living tissue from sheep. Positive proof is required but so often the guilty dogs escape and are never found, even though they return to savage the flocks time and time again.

It is a harrowing period for the farmer when a killer dog is at large and for the rural policeman it can prove a severe test of his skills in tracing suspects, even those of the four-legged variety. It is a battle which must be won. It was with some trepidation, therefore, that I motored along the lane to Thackerston Grange.

Fairclough must have heard the distinctive note of my motor-cycle because he was waiting in his farmyard. I parked the machine against a saddle, removed my crash-helmet and left it on the pillion.

"Fairclough." He held out his hand and we shook on this, our first official encounter. I had seen him striding about Ashfordly from time to time and we'd nodded a kind of greeting on occasions. But this was business.

He indicated a tractor and said, "Jump on."

Soon he was guiding the noisy machine down the lanes between his expansive fields with me perched on the back, hanging on for grim death to a mudguard.

"Glad I caught you in," he shouted above the noise.

"You caught me between shifts," I shouted back. "Normally, I'd have been out and you'd have missed me."

"You fellows are fully modernised these days, what with radios and motor-cycles. I'd have found you. But I miss the copper who walked. Sad days when those chaps disappeared. Ah, here we are."

I hadn't time to point out it would have taken half an hour for me to walk to his farm, because we had arrived at a gently sloping field on the western limits of his farm. He shouted at me, "Open the gate, will you?"

I dropped from the tractor, opened the wooden gate and

admitted the noisy machine. He brought it to a halt just inside and stopped the engine before climbing down.

"Over there." He pointed to a corner of the field where the hawthorn hedge was sufficiently robust to frustrate penetration by the most determined fleeing ewe. As we walked towards the corner, I could see the mass of blood-stained wool, some of it writhing painfully in a weird silence.

"There," and his voice softened. The most hard-headed farmer would show genuine sorrow at such a sight, and we both knew there was no way to save the lives of these mutilated animals.

"The vet's coming to put 'em to sleep," he said, "but I know you need to record what happened, for court."

"Of course. When did this happen?"

"Today, sometime between eleven this morning and two this afternoon."

Out came my notebook and I noted that there was one dead ewe, with its belly eaten away and its flesh torn into shreds. It had died an agonising death and it was possible to see the teeth-marks on the remaining skin. Protruding from its body was the half-eaten carcase of an unborn lamb.

The other five victims were lying in a huddle where they had fled, all severely mutilated about the belly region, with their innards protruding and their unborn lambs killed. All were in a state of severe shock and terror. It was impossible at this stage to say how many more of the remainder, now huddled beneath a clump of trees in a far corner, would suffer abortions as a result of being stampeded by the killer dog or dogs.

I made note of the injuries to thse ewes and, with Fairclough's permission, cut a small strand of wool from each savaged sheep. I placed these into six plastic packets, all labelled.

"What's that for?" he asked with genuine interest, his voice subdued.

"If we find the dog and the owner denies it was loose at the material time, we might find traces of wool about its mouth or teeth. This can be matched with the wool I've taken from these animals."

"Thanks," he said.

"Well," I said. "These poor creatures will have to be put out of their misery."

"They'll not be feeling much pain now—the shock's numbed them. You'll see how they didn't try to flee from you. Poor devils—they're finished."

"But the vet will see to them?"

"He will, and soon."

We turned and walked away from the carnage. The brisk spring breeze wafted a nauseating smell towards me, the stench of death mingled with the unmistakable aura of sheep. It was gone in a second, but ever since that day I have linked the scent of raw mutton with sheep-worrying of the most horrifying kind.

"Well," I said as I regained the platform of the tractor. "All I need is a dog."

"It's a black labrador," he said firmly. "Come into the house and we'll talk."

His house was a picture. It was beautifully furnished with exquisite antiques and expensive carpets, all combining to produce an impression of opulence and style. For all his reputed faults, the fellow had taste. He led me into the kitchen and we sat at the long scrubbed wooden table. A girl appeared without being called.

"Coffee, or something stronger?" he asked as she hovered.

"I wouldn't say no to a good stiff whisky," I admitted, for the sight and smell of those suffering ewes had made me queasy.

"And me." He nodded at the girl and she obeyed his wish. Soon we were enjoying large whiskies in tumblers of cut glass.

"You mentioned a labrador," I ventured.

"Yes," he sipped appreciatively, "a black one. It's the first time I've had sheep killed or mauled, but not the first time they've been chased. Around Christmas, a neighbour reported that a black labrador had been chasing my sheep around the field, but it got away. Since then, several farmers have seen the dog wandering about their land, sometimes alone and sometimes with a young lad."

"You know the lad?"

"I do," he said. "Mind you, Mr Rhea, I'm not saying it has killed my sheep. All I'm saying is that I *suspect* it has. I now pass those suspicions to you."

"Who is the boy?"

"You know Sidney Chapman?"

"Chapman?" I puzzled over the name. "Sorry, no."

"He doesn't get about, he's confined to a wheelchair. He lives in Valley View, the cottage with honeysuckle over the front door, just down the road from here."

"Right on the roadside?"

"That's the one."

"I know it." I knew the house, but not the man. "And that's the home of the dog?"

"Yes, his son, Jeremy, often takes it out. He's at school, a lad in his teens. Fifteen, I'd say."

"And the dog often goes out alone, eh?" I put to him.

"Aye, it does. Mrs Chapman works part-time in Malton, mornings, that is, and I do know the dog gets away from poor Sidney. I appreciate his difficulty but I must consider my stock."

"You don't commit yourself, yet you seem positive it is that dog." I sipped from the glass.

"It's the only black labrador in this village," he said firmly, letting me draw my own conclusion.

"I'll have words with him," I promised. "You'll be prepared to let us prosecute if necessary?"

"I'd be happy to see the dog destroyed first," he said firmly. "If he does that, I'll not worry about him going to court. I just want the dog stopped."

"Fair enough."

A prosecution under the Dogs (Protection of Livestock) Act of 1953 could not proceed without the written consent of either the Chief Constable, the owner of the livestock worried or the occupier of the land where it happened. Accordingly, I obtained a written statement from Mr Fairclough which I wrote in my notebook, and incorporated his willingness to authorise proceedings, if the dog was not destroyed.

Having attended to both that matter and the massive

tumbler of whisky, I adjourned to the village and walked to Valley View. It was an old cottage with Yorkshire sliding windows and a rough rustic porch overgrown with honey-suckle. There was a green front door and green woodwork, but the door was standing slightly ajar. I knocked.

"Come in," called a voice from the depths. "First on the right."

"It's the policeman," I announced as I pushed open the door.

"It's about time you called to see me," he said even before I entered the room. "Your predecessor always popped in when he was passing. Made himself a coffee and one for me too. Regular caller, he was."

I pushed open the door of the living-room and found Mr Chapman before the cosy fire. A black labrador lay curled at his feet, wide-awake, and its dark eyes watched me as I entered the room. It flapped its tail on the fireside rug as I walked in, then closed its eyes.

"He likes you," said the man. "Sit down, Officer."

He was reading a heavy volume on the History of World War I and placed it on his occasional table to greet me.

"Sidney Chapman," he said. "Forgive me not getting up. I leave the door ajar so I can shout at visitors."

"P.C. Rhea," I introduced myself and shook his hand. "I'm fairly new here."

"I knew we'd got a fresh bobby and was hoping you'd pop in. I like company, you see, being stuck here all day. I lost the use of these legs eight or nine years ago. Car accident—I'm lucky to be alive, they tell me. Look, if you want a coffee, the kettle's in the kitchen . . ."

He was a neat man in his middle fifties, I reckoned, with a head of sleek hair which was neatly trimmed. His face was narrow and sharp, with prominent cheek-bones and just a hint of pallor. He wore spectacles and seemed an intelligent man. I wondered how he'd earned his living before the accident. He was cheerful and affable and I liked him immediately.

"No thanks," I said, "but I'll get you one . . ."

"No, I've just had the electricity meter reader in, he had a coffee with me. Thanks—but next time . . ."

"Mr Chapman." Sorrowfully, I had to notify him of the unpleasant purpose of my visit. "I'm afraid I'm not here on a social visit. It's business."

"Oh dear, something wrong?" he looked at me with concern.

"I'm afraid so. I'm sorry we have to meet like this, but there's been a nasty case of sheep-worrying at Grange Farm, Mr Fairclough's place. He tells me a black labrador has been wandering around his fields."

"But Nero wouldn't harm a fly!"

At the sound of his name, the dog's head rose and his ears became alert as his eyes scrutinised the man for signs of further activity. His tail thumped the rug as he waited for developments.

"Has he been out this morning or this afternoon?"

"No, Mr Rhea, he hasn't. I can swear to that."

"Your front door was open—could he have gone out without you knowing? Maybe sneaked out for ten minutes and back again before you realised it?"

He thought carefully, then shook his head.

"No, I could swear to it. I've been here all morning, and he's been with me. He never leaves me, Mr Rhea, unless our Ian takes him out for a run. He's my sole companion during the day. . . . he's not a killer."

"Do you mind if I examine him?" I hated to imply that I didn't accept his word.

"No, of course not."

I approached the waiting dog and noticed his brown eyes upon me, but a word from Mr Chapman kept the animal on the floor. As I touched the broad top of his head, he rolled over onto his back, with his legs in the air and I obliged by tickling his stomach. He lay there, tongue lolling out and those dark, trusting eyes upon me as I quickly surveyed his underparts and legs. They were clean—there was no sign of mud or blood. I was pleased.

"Can I open his mouth?"

"He won't bite," said the owner with confidence.

I gripped the dog by his jaws and opened his mouth, pressing the flaps of skin away from his sharp white teeth and clamping my hand over his tongue. There was no blood and no wool adhering to his mouth area. The dog was as clean as a whistle. This was no killer.

"Well?" he asked.

"Clean," I said.

"Does that mean he's innocent?" he asked.

"It means I'm sure he is, Mr Chapman. I understand that a black labrador has been roaming those fields, unaccompanied, and yours is the only one in Thackerston."

"Yes, he is. But he's not been out this morning. I'd swear to that in a court of law."

"Thanks. I'm obliged." I made as if to leave his home.

"Mr Rhea, I'm not one to hold this against you—you are doing your job, and I respect the law and all it stands for. You'll call again?"

"I will, Mr Chapman, and under better circumstances next time."

When I informed Fairclough of my actions and decision, he almost burst a blood-vessel.

"P.C. Rhea! You are failing in your duty if you believe that rubbish! Of course he'd say the dog hadn't been out! He would, wouldn't he? It would go home covered in blood and dirt, so he'd clean it up! Of course he would, anybody would, if only to check the dog for injuries . . . it's a natural action . . ."

"I'm sure it was never out of that house during the times your sheep were attacked," I stood my ground. "A cripple couldn't wash a dog clean, not a dog that size and not as clean as that one. I even had its mouth open—it was clean too. No wool about the teeth, nothing. That dog didn't worry your sheep, Mr Fairclough."

"So what happens now? What does the law propose to do about my sheep?"

"I'll report this to my superiors," I said, "and our men will keep observations. If you see any dogs on your land, perhaps you'd let me know."

"I'll shoot the bastards first," he said. "I can, can't I?"

"You can shoot a dog actually in the act of worrying sheep, or one which you know has been worrying them and is about to renew its attack. You can't shoot one which is running away afterwards."

"Why not, for God's sake?"

"It might not be the culprit, not if it's only seen running away. It could be another innocent dog."

"Aye, well, we all know the way to get round that, Mr Rhea. Now look, if any of my sheep are damaged again, I'll be in touch with your Chief Constable and I'll tell him of this conversation. I know that dog killed my sheep. It's your job to prove it."

He was building up for a shouting match, so I left him. There was little point in continuing the argument. I could understand his view, but I was convinced Mr Chapman was telling the truth. I could not ignore the fact, however, that Nero might have sneaked out through that open door. Chapman could have cleaned up the animal too. It was quite possible, but I couldn't work on surmise. I needed absolute proof.

For a week there was peace, and then, one Sunday morning, my telephone rang. It was Fairclough again and he was extremely agitated.

"Mr Rhea? That dog's been back. One sheep attacked and torn this time. The flock terrified out of their wits. . . . get yourself right down to Chapman's and see that dog of his. It was seen again."

"What time did this happen?" I asked.

"Between ten o'clock and half-eleven."

"I'm on my way," I told him. It was quarter to twelve.

Fairclough was parading up and down his farmyard as I entered, and his face was a picture of anger and frustration. As I parked the motor-cycle, he marched across with eyes blazing and in a foul mood.

"It's that bloody dog again, Mr Rhea, one of my men saw it." He pointed to a clump of distant sycamores. "It went over there—he gave chase but lost it. A black labrador—*that* black labrador, the one you cleared last time. It's it, right enough."

"I'll see Mr Chapman straight away," was all I could promise.

I left my motor-cycle in his farmyard as I intended returning, and found the cottage door open as before. I knocked, shouted and was bade enter.

"Mr Chapman? It's P.C. Rhea."

"Come in, Mr Rhea."

As before, I found him in the cosy living-room with a warm fire blazing cheerily in the grate. And, as before, the big black labrador lay at his feet, with its head on the hearth. It pricked its ears and thumped its tail on the rug, apparently its regular welcome to its master's callers.

"It's about the same subject as before," I told him and he pointed to a chair.

"When?" was all he asked.

"This morning, between ten o'clock and half past eleven."

"He's not been out Mr Rhea, I swear it. He's been here all the time."

"The door was ajar," I said. "He could have sneaked out—it would take only ten minutes to worry a sheep—less in fact. He lives very close to the farm."

"Look at him," and the unhappy man pointed to his dog. I crouched on my haunches to examine the animal and at my touch it rolled over and asked for its stomach to be rubbed. I obliged and at the same time examined its body for signs of blood and dirt. There was none. His fur was dry too, indicating it hadn't been recently washed.

"Are you alone?"

"Sally's in the kitchen, doing lunch," he said. "She and Ian went out to church this morning. I was alone from quarter past ten until half past eleven, and Nero never left this room. I'd swear to this in court if necessary. You must believe me."

"You were here *every* minute?" I put to him, quietly.

He paused and looked steadily at me. "No, to be honest, I wasn't. I went to the toilet about eleven o'clock."

"Upstairs?"

"No, out at the back. I can get there and back with my chair."

"And, without wishing to be crude, how long did that take?"

"Five or ten minutes," and I could see the sorrow growing in his eyes. Like me, he realised that Nero had had enough time to gallop out, worry a sheep and return to the house. It was highly unlikely, but it was possible. Practical policemen must always consider the possible. I knew, and Sidney Chapman knew, that Nero could be the culprit in spite of his cleanliness. Perhaps he'd licked himself clean, or maybe never got dirty.

I looked again at the magnificent dog. There was not a mark upon him to suggest he'd been chasing sheep within the past hour or so. In spite of Fairclough, I was convinced this was not the guilty dog.

"Is it nasty, this sheep-worrying?" Sidney Chapman asked me.

"It's one of the most appalling things that can happen to an animal," I said and, with no further ado, I provided a graphic description of the sights I'd witnessed. I stressed the emotional anguish and financial problems it presented to a farmer, and the continuing threat if the guilty dogs were not halted.

"But Nero couldn't do that . . ." he said. "He couldn't. He's gentle and tame, a family pet. He's my companion, my only real pal, Mr Rhea. When everyone's out and I'm left alone, he's all I've got. I know he hasn't done this horrible thing. I know."

"I believe you," I said. "There's nothing on Nero to make me even suspect him. But a black labrador's been seen near the attacked sheep, and he's the only one around here. He's the prime suspect."

"Mr Fairclough wouldn't make this up, would he? About it being a black labrador, I mean."

"No, he'll be as anxious as anyone else to find the right culprit. If he blames the wrong one, the right one will return and continue its work, won't it. He'll not blame the wrong dog, Mr Chapman, that would be foolhardy."

"I'd like him to call and talk to me," said Mr Chapman, "perhaps you'd ask him to pop in?"

"I will," I promised.

I honestly felt this would be a good idea and within minutes I was back at the Grange talking to Mr Fairclough. I told him of my visit and of my opinions, which he ignored, and I then invited him to visit Sidney Chapman. If he went now, I suggested, he'd see the dog for himself.

He agreed. He stomped away without a word and I decided not to intervene at this stage. If there was to be a prosecution, I would play my part, but I could never believe this dog was the worrier.

I do not know what transpired between them, but two days later I received a telephone call from Mrs Chapman. She rang from a kiosk and asked me to pop in to see Sidney when I was passing. I made a point of calling that same day.

In the same room beside the same glowing fire, I found him alone. He was clearly distressed and in a very emotional state.

"Mr Rhea," he said. "I couldn't bear the thought that my Nero might be killing sheep and lambs. I know he was not the guilty dog, I know it, but he could have been, eh? He could have sneaked out when my back was turned, or done it when he was out with Ian. . . ."

"I don't think it was him. . . ." I began.

"I've stopped it all," he said, sniffing back unshed tears. "The vet came this morning."

"The vet?" I cried.

"He took him away, Mr Rhea. It will be painless, he said," and Sidney Chapman burst into a flood of tears. I didn't know what to do, and took the line of least resistance. I left him to his misery.

I told Mary about it and we both felt deep sorrow for the poor man. In my heart of hearts, I could never believe Nero was the culprit, but Sidney Chapman had taken a wise course. He'd had the dog destroyed, and so removed the cause of any future aggravation.

Four days later, Fairclough hammered angrily on my front door. I was in the middle of lunch and found him spluttering furiously on the doorstep.

"That bloody dog again!" he said. "Less than five minutes ago. . . ."

"Which dog?" I asked him.

"That bloody black labrador of Chapman's! Caught in the act! Two sheep this time, one dead. But I got the bastard, Mr Rhea. Both barrels. It's in the Landrover."

And he stalked away to his Landrover which was parked in my drive. I followed and, sure enough, there was a dead dog, a large handsome black labrador. It had been killed by two blasts from a 12-bore gun and was a bloody mess around the head and neck.

"You've solved your problem, then?" I smiled at him.

"I have, and I want that man prosecuting. He ignored me."

"Which man?" I asked.

"Chapman—it's his bloody animal."

"It isn't," I said softly. "He had his dog put to sleep four days ago, Mr Fairclough. His only pal, his only pride and joy. But because you said it was his dog he had it put down by the vet. This isn't his dog."

Deep among the hairy mess, I found a collar and there, hidden beneath a thick coat of fur, was the owner's name and address. It was a newcomer to Elsinby, two miles away across the fields, a retired lady from Leeds.

"I'll prosecute her for allowing her dog to worry your sheep," I said.

"No." He shook his head and I could see he was shaken. "No, there's been enough damage. It's over—I'll seek compensation from the dog's owner, that'll do me. I'll go and see her now."

And he turned and drove away, a sad and thoughtful man.

A week later, he presented a new black labrador pup to Sidney Chapman. When I called to see him a few weeks later, it had its head on the hearth and its tail thumped the rug, but only for a second.

It jumped up and fussed over me with all the vigour of youth. "He's called Caesar," Sidney told me as I went to make the coffee.

Although my professional duties involved all manner of farm animals, I did involve myself with canine matters more than any other. It is true that dogs are an essential and integral part of village life, but the same could be said of cows, horses, pigs and sheep. I had to inspect small groups of these animals from time to time, either to count heads for record purposes or to see if I thought they had some disease that necessitated a veterinary surgeon's attention. I found it strange that a policeman's opinion was sought on such matters but invariably the problem was solved by ringing a vet.

It was one such problem that intrigued me at Cold Hill Farm, and it involved another dog. This was a cur, a common breed in these parts. They are used to guide sheep and are the hill farmer's constant companion. They are black and white dogs, tough and intelligent little animals with a natural instinct for herding sheep.

The resident cur at Cold Hill Farm was an elderly dog called Shep and he belonged to Mr and Mrs Ambrose Lowe. He had endured a long and hard life on this remotest of farms, spending his years herding moor sheep into their pens and rounding them up for their quarterly count. Year in, year out, poor old Shep had done those tasks and many more. Now he was twelve years old and I think he'd made his own decision to retire.

The snag was that Ambrose wouldn't let him retire. There was always a great deal of work to be done, always some pressing matter for attention. It was during a busy time that I called at the farm one Friday morning to check the latest intake of pigs for the stock register. As always, Mrs Lowe, whose Christian name I never knew, invited me in for a coffee and a sweet biscuit. As I settled at the rough kitchen table with the couple I noticed Shep asleep near the door which led into the back of the house. He ignored my presence.

After the introductory small talk and a brief chat about the quality of his latest acquisition of pigs, Ambrose asked:

"Does thoo reckon to know owt about dogs, Mr Rhea?"

"Not a great deal," I admitted.

"Oh," he said, without further comment.

"Something wrong?" I recognised the countryman's hesitation to lead into the problem. He wanted me to take the initiative, and turned his head to look down upon the sleeping dog.

"Aye, mebbe. Ah'm not sure."

"Something to do with Shep?"

"It could be his age," he said.

Mrs Lowe next spoke up. "He's twelve, you see, and he's had a hard life."

"Is he lame or something?" I ventured, thinking the dog might have a form of rheumatism.

"Nay, lad, nowt like that," and Ambrose paused to drink from his cup. "I reckon he's gone deaf."

"Deaf?"

"Aye, deaf. Dogs do go deaf, thoo knows, quite young sometimes. But awd Shep's getting on in years. . . ."

"Has the vet seen him?"

"No, he hasn't, and Ah didn't feel like calling him all this way if it was nowt."

"He would tell you one way or the other," I said seriously. "And he might be able to treat the condition."

Mrs Lowe spoke again. "You see, Mr Rhea, we don't think he's really deaf. We think he's pretending."

"Pretending?" I almost laughed aloud. "Dogs can't pretend; they can't tell lies or be devious, can they?"

"Ah reckon thus 'un is, Mr Rhea," said Ambrose, who now seemed relieved that his wife had opened up the conversation by mentioning their private worry.

"You must have a good reason for thinking that," I put to them both.

"Aye, we 'ave, Mr Rhea," said Ambrose. "It's not a sudden idea, like. Me and our missus have been watching Shep of late, and Ah'm positive he's up to summat."

"Tell me more." I sipped from my cup.

"It's like this," he began carefully, speaking slowly with emphasis on the key words. "Ah've noticed, over t' past few weeks, that when Ah tell Shep it's time to start work, he just lies near yon door and never moves. We've both tried him. . . ."

"Aye," confirmed Mrs Lowe. "Ah've told him it's time to fetch t' cows in, or round up a few sheep, and he just lies there, never twitching an eyelid. We've had to kick him into life, you know. Clout him with a mop or summat, and then he'll stir himself. Bone-idle he is."

"He could be deaf," I said. "If he's always been a good worker before . . ."

"Aye, lad," Ambrose raised a finger to emphasise the

point, "but when oor missus tells him it's dinner-time, he hears that all right! By gum, he does that! He's up and at his dinner like a flash. We tried whispering, real quiet like, and he never missed a meal. Not once. But you try and tell him its milking time and he has to fetch t'cows in, and he'll doze there like it would take a bomb to shift him."

"He thinks it's time we got another dog, I reckon," Mrs Lowe offered her opinion. "I mean, in human terms, he's turned eighty, isn't he? He should be retired and he knows it."

"Let's see how he reacts now," I suggested. "Will he behave like that while I'm here?"

"He won't dare do otherwise if he doesn't want to be caught out!" and Ambrose Lowe put on a coat, took a crook from the corner and made all the noises he would have made under a normal excursion to locate sheep. Then he said, "Come, Shep, come lad."

I watched the inert form at the base of the door. The dog never moved, not even a flicker of an eyelid or a movement of an ear.

"Shep, come on, time to get sheep," called his master.

Nothing.

"It's a rum soort of a gahin on." I momentarily lapsed into the dialect of the area. "Is he allus like this?"

"Aye, just now. Now Ah'll get outside and pretend Ah've gone, leaving him there. Ooor missus will tell him it's dinner-time and thoo see what he does."

I waited as the little drama was acted out. Ambrose left the farmhouse and made the normal noises for such an occasion. Shep slept on. Then Mrs Lowe began to prepare a dog's dinner. She found his old enamel plate and opened the pantry door to produce some old bones and dog-biscuits from a tin. She placed these on the plate then put it on the floor, making a small noise. I saw Shep's ears prick at the sound.

"Come, Shep," she said in a normal voice. "Dinner."

And he was on his feet in a split second. Wagging his long tail, he moved quickly across the floor and began to wolf down his meal, showing sheer enjoyment and every sign of fitness.

This dog was certainly not deaf and he was most certainly not suffering from rheumatics. But could a dog feign deafness in order to avoid work? I doubted it. Surely dogs didn't possess that sort of cunning?

When he was midway through the meal, Ambrose returned and smiled at the active dog.

"Well?" he asked me.

I shook my head. "He heard Mrs Lowe all right. He must know when you're going out to work, eh? By the noises you make. He just lies there, waiting for you to call him, then ignores you. . . ."

"He makes a good draught-excluder for yon door, and that's about all he's good for these days," commented Mrs Lowe. "What can we do, Mr Rhea? He's bone-idle—look at him. He's getting fatter all the time and more and more lazy."

I shook my head in bewilderment, then asked, "Have you come across this before, either of you? In other dogs—yours or anyone else's?"

"Never," he said firmly. "Never."

"A vet might have," I ventured. "Maybe if you rang the vet, he'd have a simple answer. It's maybe a common condition."

"Them fellers cost money, and Ah've enough trouble making ends meet as it is. Nay, I wanted a second opinion and you happened to come along. You've confirmed what we thought. So now, would you say he's having us on?"

"It looks very much like it." I didn't dare commit myself totally. How could I say, in all honesty, that this dog was nothing more than a confidence trickster or at least, one of the nation's shirkers?

I looked at Shep. He had finished his hefty meal and had returned to the space at the base of the inner door, where he lay down, sighed loudly and closed his eyes.

"It's milking time at half past four," Ambrose told me. "Ah'll warrant Ah'll nivver shift him then unless I clout him. By, he's takkin a lot of waking up these days."

I continued to watch the inert canine form and wondered if Shep could understand what we were saying. He gave no indication that he could hear us or understand us, and then an idea came to me.

"I've an idea," I said. "I think we could teach him a lesson!"

"Ah've yelled and cursed him, and we've both knocked him to his feet," said Ambrose. "Ah don't think there's owt a policeman can do."

"Why don't you both convince Shep that he really *is* deaf?" I suggested.

For a moment, there was no response from the couple, then Ambrose looked sideways at me. "How do you mean, Mr Rhea?"

"Well," I began, "I noticed that you made a lot of noise getting ready to go out. Banging doors, tapping your crook on the floor, that sort of thing. And your missus, well, she banged his plate down, there was a noise when she opened the pantry door and got the stuff out . . . and there's the words you use, like dinner, food, cows and so on. He knows what they all mean. He's a clever dog."

"Aye," agreed Ambrose.

"Well, whenever he's lying there, you should do everything very, very quietly. Make no noise at all. And if you talk to him when he's awake just shape the words, don't speak them. Put his dinner down silently and don't tell him it's ready . . . make him *think* he's gone deaf."

"By lad, that's a capper!" grinned Ambrose. "Aye, we can do that, can't we, oor missus?"

"It won't be easy, Mr Rhea, will it? I mean, he'll hear other noises, won't he, and we might forget sometimes. . . ."

"I don't think it will take very long to get him puzzled about it," I ventured. "A day or two. It might cure his idleness."

"Right, we'll try it."

I hadn't time to remain behind on this occasion in order to see how this middle-aged rural couple went about their deception. Knowing the pair, it would have been a treat to observe them both mouthing silent words at each other and putting everything down in total silence when the dog was there—which was most of the time. When I told Mary about it, she laughed until the tears ran down her face, and said she thought I was crackers. I began to wonder who was daft—me or that lazy dog!

The Lowes weren't on the telephone so I couldn't ring them to ask about Shep's deafness cure, so I was delighted when I had to pop over to the farm later that week to see about a movement licence for some pigs.

I arrived at my usual time, just before eleven, and knew there'd be a cup of coffee and biscuits. Mrs Lowe saw me coming and, as I parked the motor-cycle against a wall, she beckoned me to enter. She also placed a finger across her lips, indicating silence. She then came out to meet me, closing the outer door very, very quietly.

"By," she said, "our Shep's right puzzled."

"You're still giving him the treatment?" I exclaimed.

"We are," she confirmed. "Ambrose said we should keep it up until you came next time, so you could see if it worked. So here you are."

"It should be interesting," I smiled. "Where is Ambrose?"

"He'll be in any minute for his elevenses," she said. "Any road, he'll have heard your bike."

She took me into the kitchen where Shep lay in his usual place at the base of the door, performing his role as a draught-excluder and forgetting he was a working farm dog. As I entered, he looked quizzically at me, but Mrs Lowe smiled and mouthed the words, "Would you like a coffee?"

Feeling something of an idiot, I answered "Yes" in an exaggerated silence.

She went about the chore and I noted that she did everything in total silence. She had become expert at her new skill. The cups and saucers made not a sound, the kettle was boiled in the kitchen and everything was done completely without noise. Within five minutes, Ambrose entered and it was like watching a silent film. The couple went about their daily domestic chores in a remarkable way and I saw the puzzled dog watching this charade. He shook his head several times, and looked at me as if to ask what on earth was happening. Ambrose smiled, sat down and carried on a weird conversation with me, saying absolutely nothing and

I responded in like manner. If Sergeant Blaketon came in now. . . .

To complete the performance, Mrs Lowe got Shep's dinner ready. Out came a tin of dog-biscuits, some old bones and scraps, and a tin of dog-meat. His old enamel plate was placed on the floor in total silence and then she looked at him. He looked at her and shook his head, and she mouthed the words, "Come, Shep, dinner."

Shep looked at me and then at her, struggled heavily from his prone position and ambled across to eat the meal. As he licked the plate there was a faint noise as it scudded about the floor, but he appeared to ignore this. Then, having eaten, he returned to the door, curled up and lay down, but this time kept his large brown eyes open, watching us all in turn.

Ambrose smiled at me and mouthed the words, "Now, let's see if all this performance has fettled him."

Getting up from the chair, he went over to the crook in the corner, banged its ferrule on the floor and, in a normal voice, said, "Shep, come along. Time for work."

The dog lay there for the briefest of moments before leaping to his feet with a delighted bark. In no time, he was panting at the door wanting to be out. The ruse had worked perfectly. Or had it?

That weekend, in the Brewers Arms at Aidensfield, I heard Ambrose telling the tale to his drinking companions.

"By," he was saying, "oor dog was that glad he'd gat his hearing back, he ran inti my fields and rounded up all oor sheep and cows half-a-dozen times. He's never been idle since, Ah can tell you."

Nonetheless, I think Shep did win in the end. A few months later, Ambrose bought a young dog called Bob to take over from Shep, and Shep was honoured with the duty of showing the young dog how to work on the farm.

Before long, Shep would be officially retired. He'd earned his rest, and I knew that dog was far from stupid. But I did wonder what kind of tricks he would teach young Bob.

4

"Money is like muck, not good except it be spread."

Francis Bacon, 1561–1626

It has been said that if a ten-pence piece fell over the side of an ocean liner in a storm, the first man to reach the water after it would be a Yorkshireman and the second a Scotsman. The Jews are not in the race. It is difficult to assess the truth of this bold statement without actually testing it on location, but it is fair to say that where money is concerned a Yorkshireman does exercise considerable care.

Right across this massive county, the natives possess an inbred cunning where finance is involved and I think this yarn illustrates the point.

In a remote moorland village, the local simpleton found a half-crown lying in the middle of the road. This occurred in the days when a half-crown was of considerable value and the lad was delighted with his luck. It represented more than a day's wages. Off he went into the local pub to spend it and announced to the landlord that he wished to buy a pint of best bitter. The landlord, knowing the lad wasn't in the habit of spending his workaday pittance on beer, asked if he'd come into money.

"Aye," beamed the youth. "Ah've found a half-crown."

At this, a local ne'er-do'well approached the bar and said:

"Well, fancy that, Roger, that'll be that half-crown I lost this morning."

"Will it?" replied the finder sadly. "Did you lose it out there, in the street?"

"Aye, I did," agreed the trickster.

"And did your half-crown have a little hole drilled through it, just near t'date?"

"Aye, as a matter of fact it did!" smiled the villain of the piece.

"Well, this 'un hasn't," grinned the simpleton, handing it to the landlord.

Natural craftiness of this quality is perhaps the result of long and careful grooming in matters of finance, and there is little doubt that a close-fisted Yorkshireman is one of the meanest of creatures. He doesn't see it in that light, of course. He sees the issue as one of care coupled with necessity, and he does not believe in parting with his brass to anyone who hasn't earned it. It is no accident of history that a Yorkshireman's motto is:

> Hear all, see all, say nowt,
> Eat all, drink all, pay nowt,
> And if thoo does owt for nowt,
> Do it for thyself.

The county is replete with legendary yarns about the characteristic stinginess of Yorkshiremen and it is impossible to quote them all in these pages. To further illustrate Yorkshireman's niggardly attitude, the following parables are but examples.

There was a farmer's wife who sat beside her husband's deathbed, waiting for him to pass away. His customary meanness had infected her and it had been a long vigil. A candle burned at the bedside, for this was the only form of light in the house.

The long hours passed but the old man clung to life with all the grit and determination of his Yorkshire breeding. Then he turned to his wife and said, "I could use a nice cup o' tea, Martha."

"Nay, Sam," she said, "Ah'm not gahin to waste food on you now. Thoo mun do without. Thoo'll nut need food where thoo's gahin."

"But Ah's fair thosting for a drink," he said.

"Then Ah'll fetch a glass o'watter," and she rose from the bedside.

"Thanks," he managed to gasp in a sudden fit of coughing.

At this, she stopped at the door and said, "Sam, if thoo feels thysen slipping away while Ah'm downstairs, blow t' candle oot."

Another example occurred in our village post office before decimalisation came to harass the older folk. A local farmer entered to draw money from his Post Office Savings Account. The post-mistress produced the necessary forms and he completed them.

"Oh," she said when she read his words, "you can't draw out sixpence. You can only withdraw amounts of one shilling or greater." For those no longer familiar with £.s.d. money, a shilling was twelve old pennies, now worth 5p.

"I only want to buy six pennorth o' stamps," he retorted.

"I'm sorry, it'll have to be a shilling," she told him firmly and so he completed another form for that amount. He received his shilling, bought six pennyworth of postage-stamps and then said, "Right missus, now I'd like to make a deposit."

"Certainly," she smiled. "How much?"

"Sixpence," he said and this time she had to accept his cash. There was no such rule about deposits.

Many local farmers and small business-people nurtured an open mistrust of banks. They utterly failed to understand the system and could never equate money with pieces of paper in cheque-books. Complicated matters like investments, securities, interest rates and the like were gibberish to these people, for they dealt always in cash, buying and selling everything in ready money and somehow managing to amass massive quantities of cash.

I have personally witnessed milk-churns full of old £5 notes, some of which had been there so long the money had gone green with damp and mould, and there is the classic tale of a son who tried to convert his old dad into depositing his money with a bank. After much explanation and pleading, the old man agreed to deposit £10,000 with the bank in town and he asked the son to fetch the milk-churn from the pantry.

They loaded the churn into the rear of the car and drove to the bank, where they manoeuvred this unusual purse into the building. There they stood and watched as the bewildered clerk counted out the money. Finally, she stopped.

"There's £9,997," she said, smiling at them.

At this, Dad turned to his son and grumbled, "Thoo silly young buffer, thoo's brought t'wrong churn!"

Then there was the miller who was eventually convinced that a bank account and a cheque-book was a good idea, and accordingly he deposited his £1000 with a local branch. After instruction from the manager, he went home with his brand new cheque-book and began to pay his bills. At the end of the month, the manager called him in and informed him that he was overdrawn.

"What's that mean?" asked the miller.

"It means you've overspent," explained the manager. "You've spent more than your £1,000."

"Don't be so daft!" retorted the miller. "I've never seen a penny of it!"

Knowing the true Yorkshireman's attitude to his money, it is interesting to spend time in one of the local markets, watching and listening to them as they wheel and deal among cattle, pigs, sheep and hens. Even today, there are many weekly markets in the small country towns of North Yorkshire, and it is traditional that the pubs are open all day for the service of suitable refreshment to those attending the market.

Attending market is one of a rural policeman's multifarious duties and, in my time, it was a regular task to attend for the sole purpose of issuing pig movement licences. These documents were vital if it was necessary to trace the movements of any pig thought to be affected by disease, and the farmers themselves knew and appreciated the value of this security. It was a simple system and it worked very well, both for the benefit of the police, the farmer, the vets and the Ministry of Agriculture.

The duty had many benefits, one of which was the pleasure of listening to the haggling that went on between farmers buying and selling. Even before they began, each knew the price he would either pay or receive, but, traditionally, there was, and still is, a great deal of good-natured haggling before reaching that figure. In addition, there is "luck money", a vital part of any deal.

A conversation might go something like this.

"How much for them pigs?"

"Fifteen quid apiece, and I'm letting you have 'em cheap."

"Fifteen quid? There's no such price for pigs! Nay, lad, thoo's not on wi' that sort of game."

"Fifteen or nowt. That's my price."

"I'll settle for ten."

"Ten? For these? Nivver. These are good pigs!"

"Ten is my figure and nut a penny more."

"By, thoo's a difficult chap ti deal with. These pigs is grand . . ."

"Twelve. Nea mair than twelve apiece."

"Push it up to twelve pound fifty and we might start talking."

"We'll talk when thoo comes down to eleven."

"Thoo just said twelve."

"Twelve was ti start thoo talking sense. Eleven apiece and that's my final offer."

"Twelve then, mak it twelve apiece."

"And luck money?"

"Aye, all right. A quid apiece for luck, then."

So he got them for £11 each. Such a deal can be a long-drawn-out affair, but luck money is always the concluding part of the deal and is always handed over in cash. It is not knocked off the price or added on. It is a cash transaction quite separate from the main deal, and marks the continuance of a very ancient custom in local cattle markets. Its origin is simply a method of bringing good luck to the transaction and the actual amount of money is a matter for negotiation. The conclusion of a deal, and the payment of luck money, is marked by the buyer and the seller slapping the palm of each other's hand. It is neither blackmail nor corruption, but a long-standing local custom that fills a few back pockets.

Such a purchase, with luck money, found me involved

with one of Claude Jeremiah Greengrass's business enterprises. Most of his ventures concluded with my giving evidence against him in court, and I wondered if this was to be different.

It seemed that Claude Jeremiah had decided to enter the bacon business and he set about purchasing a dozen small pigs to make the foundations of his new enterprise. He knew that Joshua Sanders of Stang Farm, Maddleskirk, had a suitable litter for disposal and therefore went to see the dour farmer.

Joshua Sanders was noted as a hard and cunning businessman with a shrewd eye for a bargain but with a deep suspicion of those who never paid in cash. He disliked banks and, although he was now beginning to reluctantly accept cheques at the markets, he preferred to deal in ready money.

It must have been with some apprehension, therefore, that he opened his front door one Friday morning to find the notorious Claude Jeremiah Greengrass on the doorstep. Everyone knew of Claude's reputation as a small-time crook; he was untrustworthy, shady and should always be treated with caution. Joshua faced his potential customer with true Yorkshire grit.

"Noo then, Claude Jeremiah," greeted Joshua blandly.

"Good-morning, Mr Sanders." Claude smiled at the big man, his tiny pinched brown face wrinkled in the morning sun. "I hear tell you've a litter of pigs for sale."

"That might be right." Joshua was exercising his traditional caution. "There again, it might not. Who wants to know?"

"Me. I'm after buying some pigs," beamed the little man. "I'm getting established in the pig-breeding business, you see, and I need some good stock. Bacon's always a good investment."

"Well, now then." Joshua rubbed his bristly chin. "That's a capper," he was flummoxed for a moment or two. "Ah've more or less promised yon litter to a bloke from t'far side of Thirsk. Ah daren't let him down. . . ."

Joshua was stalling. There were two reasons why he didn't want Claude Jeremiah to have these animals.

One—he probably wouldn't pay for them, and two, if this was one of Claude Jeremiah's enterprises, everything connected with it would go wrong. The miserable little pigs would probably die from neglect and starvation. . . .

"I can pay good money for them. . . ." began the little man, pulling out his wallet. It was full of personal papers, and a cheque-book lay inside. "I've a bank account."

Knowing Joshua as I did, I guessed his brain was working very rapidly at this stage, desperately seeking some cast-iron reason for not selling his stock to Claude Jeremiah. But Claude Jeremiah was also cunning.

"Ah allus deals in cash," Joshua said by way of dismissing the nuisance.

"I've an old aunt in Australia who's left me a large amount of money," announced Claude Jeremiah. "She always wanted me to enter a business of some kind, and I've now got enough money to stand any loss I might make during the first couple of years. I want to employ a man to help me, and I intend to learn all about pigs."

"Old aunt?" Joshua's eyes opened wide at this revelation.

"Yes, on my mother's side. Aunt Jemima. You'll have seen her about the place, Mr Sanders. She's a tall woman with a bun at the back of her head, always voted Liberal and kept Yorkshire terriers. Loaded, she was. She went to live in Australia about nine or ten years ago. . . . bought a sheep-ranch out there and made thousands. Well, she died and I've inherited a share of her money. I know you'll keep this to yourself, but I got over £15,000. Naturally, I want to put the money to good use. . . . I've had sties built at my place and need some good stock to start my enterprise . . ."

Claude Jeremiah's well-rehearsed yarn would not have tempted a city businessman but, in spite of his caution and in spite of his knowledge of Claude Jeremiah's past, this talk of wills, big money, faraway places and deceased aunts weakened the resolve of Joshua Sanders. But it was not completely weakened—that was impossible.

"Well, now young man," he said gently. "We might have a deal. If thoo reckons my pigs is good enough for you, and thoo pays a bigger price than that other chap was reckoning on, thoo can 'ave 'em."

Claude Jeremiah's pinched face broke into a happy smile.

"Come, Ah'll show thoo yon litter," offered the farmer.

It seems that Claude Jeremiah was highly impressed by the pink piglets as they ran and grunted about their large cosy home in a dry building. Accordingly, the traditional bidding began.

"Ah can't take less than £12 apiece," Joshua leaned on the gate and solemnly shook his head.

"I was thinking more on the lines of £8," came in Claude Jeremiah.

"There's no such price for decent pigs, not like these," and Joshua made as if to leave the building.

"Nine?"

"Mr Greengrass, thoo's very near insulting me with offers like that. £9 for these pigs? Nay, lad, thoo'll have to think harder than that. Thoo'd better try Aud Yeoman rather than me. His scrawny animals might fit that price."

"His pigs die after eight or nine weeks," said Claude Jeremiah. "He's got the kiss of death on pigs, has that chap."

"Well, that's the sort of pig thoo can expect with an offer like this. Nine quid a pig! Ah've never heard sike rubbish."

"Ten, then?"

Joshua rubbed his bristly chin once more.

"Mak it eleven and we'll begin talking."

"That's a lot of money for a chap to find for starters, Mr Sanders. What about me taking just half a dozen then? That would be £66. . . ."

"Nut a chance. It's all or nowt. A dozen or nowt, Claude Jeremiah. Twelve quid apiece."

"Tak eleven pounds ten bob each?" he queried.

Joshua leaned on the gate and pulled a large briar pipe from his jacket pocket. He began to poke and prod it and eventually lit the fearsome machine to produce clouds of sweet-smelling smoke.

"Ah'll tak eleven pund ten bob apiece then, on one condition."

"Condition?" Claude's eyes beamed with satisfaction but seconds later changed to a hue which indicated suspicion. Joshua was up to summat.

"Aye. At that price, thoo sees, Ah's letting them pigs go for next to nowt. It's a giveaway price."

"It's a fair price, Mr Sanders. The market price isn't as high as that. You can get good store pigs for £10 each. . . ."

"But not of this quality, young man, not of this quality," and he waved the pipe around like a conductor's baton as if to emphasise his claims.

"What's this condition then?" asked Claude Jeremiah, cautiously.

Before announcing the condition which he was to impose upon Claude Jeremiah, Joshua had recognised the little man's anxiety to buy the pigs; he'd also taken account of his reputation as a confidence man and concluded that the tale about Aunt Jemima's fortune did not sound true. Joshua therefore needed some kind of surety, for he knew Claude would try to dodge paying cash. It was to be a dreaded cheque transaction.

"Well." Joshua puffed at the pipe. "Ah've an awd donkey down them fields. Nice friendly donkey, it is, used at the seaside for giving kids rides before it came out here to retire."

"Yes?"

"If thoo wants them pigs at eleven and a half quid apiece, thoo'll have to buy yon donkey an' all."

"But I don't want a donkey. . . ."

"And Ah don't want to sell them pigs at £11 10s.0d. apiece."

"What would I do with a donkey?" asked Claude Jeremiah.

"Sell it, mebbe, in time."

"What sort of price were you thinking for the donkey then?"

Joshua pursed his lips. "A giveaway price really, fifty quid."

"Fifty!"

"Aye."

"Look, Mr Sanders, I don't want a donkey. . . ."

"But thoo dis want twelve good pigs, for a knockdown, giveaway price. . . . them's my terms, Mr Claude Jeremiah Greengrass. And cash for t'donkey."

"Now look, I can't find that amount of money. . . ."

"Then thoo dissn't get my pigs."

A long silence then descended as Claude Jeremiah gave this proposal his most earnest consideration.

"Forty," he said. "Cash, for t'donkey."

"Forty-five," countered Joshua.

"Right, £45 for the donkey, cash. And a cheque for the pigs?"

"Twelve pigs at £11.10s.od each. That'll be £138," said Joshua like lightning, puffing at his pipe.

Out came Claude Jeremiah's cheque-book and he wrote a cheque for that amount. Then he delved into an inner pocket of his old coat, well away from his wallet, and surreptitiously produced £45 in notes, which he passed to the waiting farmer.

"What about my luck money?" asked Joshua.

That cost Claude Jeremiah another £5, cash.

"Right," said Joshua. "Thoo can take them pigs when thoo's ready, but t'donkey stays here."

"Stays here?" cried Claude Jeremiah.

"Aye, until that cheque gets through yon bank. That story aboot a rich aunt dissn't seem true ti me, so yon donkey stays put until that cheque is paid inti my bank."

"But you can't do that . . ."

"Ah just have," grinned Joshua. "Good-morning, Mr Greengrass."

Claude Jeremiah returned later in the day with a cattle-truck and loaded the twelve pigs. Joshua however had been active during Claude's absence. Realising that Claude might not take them home, but might instead sell them immediately for a profit, he had effectively prevented this by charging a very high price. Claude would have to keep them for a month or two in order to make any profit, upon his payment for the donkey, but just in case the cheque did bounce Joshua rang all the dealers that afternoon to warn them that the Greengrass pigs had been vomiting and seemed to have diarrhoea. That was enough to put any farmer off a deal; swine-fever was the last thing they wanted on their premises.

The outcome was that Claude was compelled to keep the

pigs for a month or so, whether he liked it or not, and meanwhile the donkey remained on Joshua's farm.

As Joshua had anticipated, a week after the deal the cheque bounced. There were no funds. It had been a confidence trick after all and, when this became known, I was called in.

Mr Sanders invited me to join him in a large whisky and a slice of gingerbread as he explained how he'd been conned into parting with £138 worth of pigs for a worthless cheque. I was not told of the donkey at that stage. So far as I knew therefore, I had a case of false pretences on my hands, and a ready-made suspect for the crime.

"Ah doesn't want this to go to court," said Sanders when he'd finished his tale.

"Hang on, Mr Sanders," I said. "If you report this to me on an official basis, I'll have to take Claude Jeremiah to court. He's committed a criminal offence."

"But if Ah *knew* he'd try it on, and took steps to deal with it myself, Ah've not been conned, eh?"

"Er, no," I had to admit.

He then told me about the donkey deal and I laughed at the notion. I wondered who'd conned who—Claude had unwittingly paid for the pigs at a moderate price.

"So what do you want me to do?"

"See him and put the wind up him," said Joshua.

"That'll do no good!" I laughed. "Claude Jeremiah's my one regular court attender. He knows more about dealing with the court than anyone I know. You'll not put the wind up him."

"Well, Ah thought you might do summat, just to cap him."

"Come on, Mr Sanders. You've got something up your sleeve. What is it?"

"Well, Ah sees it like this. He's not paid for them pigs, so that makes 'em still mine. Right?"

"It might need a civil court action to definitely state that," I told him.

"Nay, be damned," he growled, "Ah'll not have that. Them's my pigs, Mr Rhea, and mak no mistake about it."

"So what's your plan?"

"Tell him you know about his dud cheque, tell him he might go to court for false pretences or whatever you said it was, and then give him another month to pay me. Cash."

"He'll never pay you! You shouldn't have sold him those pigs!"

"But you'll do that, for me, eh?"

"It might get him off the hook, and I'll forget about the donkey?"

"Aye, for now."

Claude Jeremiah Greengrass had won so many battles against me and my colleagues that I felt justified in going along with Joshua's little scheme. After all, if he had not been deceived in any way by Claude Jeremiah's stories, the episode was nothing more than a bad business transaction and therefore of no interest to the police. So I went along to Claude's home and told him what I knew.

From the little man, I got a tale of woe and sorrow. He told me how he'd bought the pigs knowing of a ready market for them, but old Joshua had stopped all that by telling everybody for miles around that there was summat wrong with the animals. And no one would pay the price he'd paid.

"So, Mr Rhea, I can't sell the pigs to get my money back. If I'd sold them straight away, I'd have made enough to pay Mr Sanders and a little bit for me on the donkey deal."

"Claude Jeremiah," I said. "I know you too well. You would have made a profit, but kept the lot for yourself and you never would have paid Sanders. I know that, and he knows that. But he's made a very generous offer—he'll allow you one month to pay. You've a month to make £138 and square up with him. Otherwise it's court for you."

"A month? I'll never make that sort of cash in a month, Mr Rhea, besides, he's got my donkey."

"If you choose to let your donkey graze on his land, that's a private deal between yourselves," I dismissed the problem.

I left Claude Jeremiah to his worries and told Sanders what I'd done. He smiled and asked me to go and visit the farm in a month's time. I made a note in my diary.

A month later to the day, I made the bumpy journey to

Stang Farm and found Joshua in the stackyard, smoking his pipe.

"Ah heard yon bike coming up our lane," he said. "It'll be about Greengrass, eh?"

"Has he paid?" I asked.

"Not a penny. I knew he wouldn't. Right, Mr Rhea, my cattle-truck's ready. Let's go."

"Go where?" I cried.

"Greengrass's place, to pick up my pigs."

"You're retrieving them?"

"Aye, they're still my pigs. You'll be needed to prevent a breach of the peace, I reckon."

And so I followed his rickety old vehicle down to the Greengrass abode and there we confronted the little man. He had no money; he had been cleaned out of cash by Sanders' actions in selling him the donkey, and his expenses on food had not allowed him to make up the deficit. So the pigs were herded squealing and protesting into the cattle-truck and Sanders smiled at me.

"There'll be no court case, Mr Rhea?"

"Not on this occasion," I smiled.

"What about the cost of feeding those pigs?" asked Claude Jeremiah before we left. "I've had your twelve pigs on my premises for over a month, and I've fed them all that time. . . ."

"And they look very well on it," smiled Joshua.

"You'll pay me the going rate for boarding them?"

"That just equals the rent of that field of mine where you graze your donkey," smiled Joshua. "I reckon we're square."

"But you've had a month's free accommodation for those pigs!" came in Claude Jeremiah. "You can't do that."

"Ah've just done it," grinned Joshua. "Call for your donkey when you can. The rental goes up next week. If you can't pay, I could always sell the donkey to settle your overdue account."

And off he drove, very happy with himself.

Claude Jeremiah Greengrass looked miserable in the extreme. He'd been beaten by this crafty old farmer and I was delighted.

"You wouldn't like to buy a nice donkey, Mr Rhea?" asked Claude Jeremiah as I climbed aboard my motor-cycle.

"From you? It might have epizootic lymphamgitis!" I laughed as I rode into the sunshine. I left the little man with a very puzzled frown on his weathered features and learned later that it was impossible to catch that donkey. It had lived for years in that field, defying all attempts to get it into a halter or a vehicle.

"If anybody can catch yon donkey, Mr Rhea," smiled Joshua a week later, "They can have it."

It could be said that police officers are the dustmen of society, many of them spending their days cleaning up the offal left by the baser forms of humanity. It is true they do spend a lot of man-hours dealing with matters that no one else would cope with, even if they were ordered to. Happily, there is a list of things which must not be done by policemen in the course of their duties and this includes the collection and recovery of money under affiliation orders, the collection and recovery of money under maintenance orders (except the acceptance of monies paid to a police-station) the collection of market tolls, the duties of mayor's attendant, or town-crier, the regular cleaning of police-stations when the Home Secretary has directed that it is not a police duty, and any other work not connected with police duty which the Home Secretary decides is not to be performed by the police.

Strangely, we are allowed to perform a weird range of other duties, like enforcing cinematograph acts and regulations and borough byelaws; then there are billeting duties, the inspection of domestic servants' registries, common lodging-houses, hackney carriages, licensed boats, beach trading, markets, fire appliances and street lamps, and we may also issue pedlars' certificates.

In addition, there are diseases of animals, licensing matters, duties under the Shops Act and a host of other miscellaneous odds and sods that no one else seems anxious to do. So the police have to do all these things, as well as fight crime, keep traffic flowing, and battle with pickets, demonstrators and yobbos.

It is difficult to specify the most unsavoury of our duties, but for my mind the execution of a distress warrant is one of the worst. This document was not uncommon in under-privileged urban areas but I scarcely expected to be faced with one during my spell in rural Aidensfield.

It was with some interest therefore that I answered the call to attend Ashfordly Police Station one fine morning for a chat with Sergeant Bairstow. When he spoke on the telephone, he gave no indication of the turmoil that was to come, but I should have realised it would be something very complicated. He loved giving me the awkward jobs.

"Ah, Nick," he said as I walked in, removing my helmet with a flourish.

"Good-morning, Sarge." I used the diminutive of his rank, an indication of my progress on the beat. I might even be allowed to refer to him by his Christian name during off-duty moments—only time would tell.

"Nick," he said smiling with what I discovered was an evil grin. "I've a nice little job for you."

"Something special?" I wondered if I had to interview the Lady of the Manor, or talk to a lovely girl about something fascinating. Maybe, he'd solved a crime and wanted me to arrest the suspect. . . .

"Yes," he said as he lifted a file from the desk. "A distress warrant. We've got one to execute in Crampton."

"A distress warrant?" I opened my mouth with astonishment. "Here?"

"Yes, here," he said, showing me the document in question.

Every warrant is a directive signed by a magistrate, and the policeman must read it with a view to learning what his duty is to be. This one said that the Police in Ashfordly must distrain goods to the value of £107.15s.8d because of the non-payment of rates by a Mr Charles Edward Hatfield of The Bungalow, Church Lane, Crampton.

I read it carefully, scarcely believing my eyes. I had no idea these things were actually issued; we had been told about them at Training School and we had been given a good grounding about the problems and routine of executing them. It was rather like learning about Henry

VIII or Napoleon—we knew they had existed but never expected to meet them.

But this document was real enough, and it was signed by Alderman Fazakerly to give it authenticity.

"What shall I do with it, Sergeant?" I reverted to the formal mode of address.

"You will deal with it," he smiled wickedly.

I studied the terrifying piece of paper for a long time, wondering how I would cope. Charlie Bairstow watched me and I knew my hesitancy was amusing him, but I was determined not to allow him better me this time. I'd had enough of his pranks with zebras, ghosts and the like. This was a real job.

"I must get the money out of him," I said. "Otherwise we seize goods to the value of £107.15s.8d."

"He won't pay up, he never does," came the reply.

"He's a regular?" I asked.

"One of the regulars, perhaps *the* most regular of the regulars," Charlie Bairstow told me. "Mr Hatfield never pays his rates. The Council always send people around, they cajole him and bully him, but he never pays. Then we get lumbered with a distress warrant to seize goods to the value of the outstanding amount."

"I'll need more than the stated amount, won't I?"

"Yes, much more. You must arrange to sell the seized goods at a local auction, leaving enough profit to pay expenses and to ensure there's enough to pay off the rates."

"I might frighten him into paying cash?"

"You might," he laughed.

Tucking the offensive piece of paper in my pocket, I sallied from the office and journeyed over to Crampton, about six miles away. I had never encountered Mr Charles Edward Hatfield and wondered what kind of person could leave his rate payments so that they accumulated into impossible amounts.

I soon found out.

Before actually knocking on his door, however, I popped into my own office to swot up the rules and procedures on distress warrants. My memory did not produce the precise rules, and I knew my notes taken at Training School would guide me.

Certain items had not to be seized when I swooped on The Bungalow; they were the wearing apparel or the bedding of the person and his family, and I was not allowed to seize the implements of his trade to the value of £5. This was to allow the fellow to continue to earn. I was not allowed to seize goods which he did not own or which were the subject of hire-purchase agreements and rentals. I could not break into the house to carry out this duty, and I had not to raid him during the night hours. All this was coming home to me now; my training had been sound.

I had to mark the seized goods in a manner which was clear and conspicuous; this was for the benefit of the removal men when they arrived in due course, and it was an offence for the householder to delete my marks. I decided the best way was to take a pile of sticky labels and fix these to the seized items, endorsing each one with my signature.

Having marked all the goods, I had then to leave them in the house until I could arrange a sale. This meant contacting the local auction room on the understanding that the sale had to take place not earlier than the sixth nor later than the fourteenth day after I had marked the goods, unless the householder agreed in writing to an earlier sale. I knew the saleroom at Ashfordly held weekly sales on a Friday, so that seemed not to present problems.

If the fellow had no goods, or there were insufficient to cover the costs, I had to endorse the warrant and return it to the Justices' Clerk. That seemed simple enough. What the Clerk did thereafter was not my problem, I hoped.

Armed with this useful information, I continued my journey to Crampton and parked my motor-cycle in Church Lane. The Bungalow was not difficult to find.

It was a rickety construction of dark green hue, comprising timber and corrugated-iron sheets rusting about the metal edges and needing a coat of paint upon the wooden bits. A short red-brick chimney protruded from the roof and clouds of black smoke were belching from it. The smoke rose straight into the sky, which, to my countryman's eye, indicated a fine day tomorrow. All the windows were closed and needed cleaning, while the garden resembled a rough shoot or a haven for harassed weeds. An untidy thorn hedge bordered the premises and there was a little wooden gate leading into the grounds. A rough path led through the weeds to a rustic porch with honeysuckle climbing about it. It was picturesque in a grotty sort of way.

I let myself in, marched along the path with the determination of a constable under orders and knocked on the battered old door. I could hear movements inside and eventually a scruffy man with a grey beard revealed himself.

"Mr Hatfield?" I asked.

"That's me, son," he smiled through the untidy mop of hair.

"P.C. Rhea," I introduced myself. "From Aidensfield."

"Aye, I guessed as much. You'll have come with one of those distress warrants, I'll guess."

"I have, yes. It's for a large amount, non-payment of your rates . . ."

"Come in, son. We'll talk about it. I don't believe in paying rates. Would you, for a spot like this? I know it's my home, and I know it's falling down, but rates? I never use the library, I don't send kids to school, I never drive a car along the roads, I don't spend any of the ratepayers' money, so why should I pay rates, Mr Rhea? Answer me that."

By now, we were inside and it was dark and dingy. There was no one else in the house and he led me towards a wooden table with a dirty top overflowing with cups and milk-bottles.

"Cup of tea?" he invited.

"No thanks, I've just had one," I lied. I couldn't face drinking from one of those cups. The whole place was filthy and almost devoid of furniture.

"How much is it?" he asked.

"One hundred and seven pounds, fifteen shillings and eightpence," I informed him, reading from the warrant.

"That's accumulated over four or five years," he smiled. "They don't know what to do with me. They daren't put me in prison. Every year, I get my rate demands and every year I fail to pay. Then, every year, the bobby calls with one of those bits of paper and tells me I'll be for it if I don't cough up. But I never do, Mr Rhea. Have a look around. What can you take? Clothing, no. Bedding, no. Implements of my trade? I have none. That table? It's my sister's—she loans it to me. Cups and saucers, pots and pans—they're hers. You can't take them. My radio and television—I rent them. I've nothing, Mr Rhea."

"You haven't a job?"

"Not me! Why work? I can get money from the State, enough to feed me and keep me warm. Why work, eh? Look at you, doing a job like this. You can't like it. . . ."

"I don't, not this sort of thing."

"Then why do it? Why not live every day as if there's no tomorrow, eh?"

"I couldn't. . . ." I found myself beginning a discussion with him and knew I'd lose. You can't argue with folks of fixed opinions and it was clear to me that this character had very fixed views on life. "Look, Mr Hatfield, I'm here to seize goods in this house to the value of the warrant. May I now look around?"

He indicated the living-room door and I walked in. It was almost bare. The floor was uncovered, showing bare sandstone with a worn rug upon the area in front of the empty fireplace. A battered old armchair occupied a corner—in a sale it might fetch five shillings. And that was all, except for the television and the radio in the corner near the window.

"Rented," he said, shoving his hand under the TV set. He pulled out a rental agreement for each item and I had to agree. I could not seize those.

"Bedroom?" he asked me.

I nodded and he showed me into a small room at the rear. There was a single bed neatly made and covered with a faded eiderdown. Beside it stood a cane chair painted blue, while a wardrobe had been built into one wall. I opened it; it contained his clothes, such as they were. There was not even a chest of drawers. Next to the bedroom there was a crude bathroom albeit with an electric heater for the water and a water-closet.

And that was it. My seizures were:- living-room, nil; kitchen, nil; bathroom and bedroom, nil.

"Nothing, Mr Rhea, like I said," and he smiled wickedly at me. I knew I was beaten. How long would the Council tolerate this, I wondered? He might be threatened with imprisonment if he failed to pay this time.

"Look," I tried to be firm. "It'll mean prison for you, Mr Hatfield. You can't keep on like this for ever. The Council has been very, very tolerant with you. . . ."

"I wrote to 'em, a long time ago, Mr Rhea, and suggested they send me to prison. I'd be fed and clothed in there, eh? And I still wouldn't pay my rates."

"Why have you stopped paying them?" I decided to ask. "You must have paid until four or five years ago."

"I did, young man, and was pleased to pay my way. But it's these scroungers, you know, folks who live off those who are daft enough to work and pay taxes. Well, I couldn't see why an old man like me should have to pay for idle sods who can't be bothered to earn their keep. So I stopped my rates, a form of protest, you see."

"If everybody stopped, Mr Hatfield, there'd be no education for the kids, no roads, no future for anyone."

"Get the scroungers back to work and I'll pay up," he said with an air of finality.

"I'll call back tomorrow," I said. "I'll expect the cash. I can't accept cheques."

"There'll be nowt for you, young man. Sorry. It'll be a wasted journey."

He was right, but I had to go through the motions of exhausting every possibility. Besides, Sergeant Bairstow would want me to account for my actions, and he'd want money.

While I was in Crampton, I decided to undertake a short foot patrol about the village and was soon chatting to the locals over garden walls, in house doorways and in the street. This was rural policing at its best—a friendly type of person willing and happy to pass the time of day with the local bobby. And it was an old man who hailed me from his greenhouse.

"Here, Bobby, come and see this," he beckoned.

I let myself into his neat garden and entered the well-kept greenhouse. It was full of cacti; large and small, plain and decorative, and he pointed to one with a huge red flower at the end of a thick stem.

"How about that?" he beamed.

"Very, very nice," I enthused. "Did you grow it?"

"I did," he said proudly. "And do you realise it flowers only once every seven years. And this is it. Seven years and she's flowering today, my birthday, would you believe. By, I am capped."

He then told me all about cacti and quoted lots of weird foreign names. He kept me there nearly half an hour but I enjoyed his prattle. Finally he said, "My missus will have a kettle on. Come and have a cup."

I learned his name was Albert Peacock and we had a very enjoyable cup of tea and a chat.

"Now then," he said after I'd met his wife, drunk his tea and looked at more cacti on his window-ledges, "I asked you in for a reason."

"Trouble?" I asked.

"Nay," he said, "but I seed you up at old Hatfield's spot."

"Yes, I called just now," I confirmed.

"Rates, again, I'll bet. The old sod never pays, you know, and you fellers keep coming with warrants. We know what he's like, and the village reckon it's time he was made to pay. We all pay up."

"There's very little anyone can do," I said. "He has nothing to sell . . ."

"He's worth thousands," said Albert. "Mebbe tens of thousands. He's got money all over, because he never pays for owt. He's the tightest bloke I've come across, is yon."

"Is he? His place looks terrible. . . ."

"It is terrible because he neglects it, and won't pay for a tin o' paint or tools to fettle his garden with. He'll tell you a load of rubbish about spongers, but that's all tommy-rot."

"I can't raid his bank account," I smiled.

"Nay, but you can raid his loft," he nodded knowingly.

"Loft?"

"You didn't see it?"

"There's no door into a loft in that cottage," I said.

"There is, thoo knows," he winked. "In t'bedroom, far corner. Loose boards, they are, looking just like the others

in the ceiling. No handles, nor nowt. Just a flat board sitting
in place. Push it up and a ladder'll come down, folding
down over."

"How do you know this?"

"Late one night, I thought I heard somebody in my
garden, so I crept out. Well gone midnight, it was, and I saw
a light in Hatfield's spot. So, being nosey, I had a look and
saw him climbing up. He hadn't drawn his curtains, 'cos he
hasn't any."

"And what's up there?" I put the obvious question.

"Paintings," he said. "Lots of paintings."

"Valuable ones?"

"They'll be valuable, or he wouldn't have 'em," said
Albert. "Then I saw him one day at a sale, buying up all the
old oils and watercolours."

"Thanks, Mr Peacock," I smiled.

"No saying how you knew, eh?"

"Not a word," I promised.

I went back immediately.

He answered the door and was clearly surprised to see me
so soon.

"Hello, Mr Hatfield," I beamed. "I just got down to the
bottom of the village when I realised I hadn't looked in your
loft."

"Loft?" he blanched.

"Yes, looking at your cottage from down the village,
there's clearly a loft. I wondered if you had anything up
there that we might sell to raise the money."

I could see his mind working. For a person who collects
or hoards, money is of less value than the goods in question, and I knew his brain was working rapidly.

"You said you'd call back tomorrow?" he put to me.

"I did."

"Will you do that then? It won't be a wasted journey this
time. How much is it?"

I told him once again and emphasised that I must be given
cash, for on occasions of this kind cheques were not acceptable.

"I'll have it ready," he said frowning. "You won't want to
be in my loft, will you?"

"Not if the money is available tomorrow at this time," I told him.

I called again as promised and it was there, in cash, down to the last penny. I endorsed the warrant in his presence. This effectively killed the document and I issued him with a receipt.

The formalities over, I smiled.

"I might see you next year, Mr Hatfield?"

"I'll have the cash ready," he said, "but I might give them a run for their money, like this time."

"I don't mind the trip," I said.

Afterwards, I wondered what kind of pictures he had collected and I speculated upon their value. But it seemed I would never know the answer.

But I reckoned that Charlie Hatfield would pay his rates so long as I was the village bobby.

"Did he pay?" smiled Sergeant Bairstow, but the smile vanished as I produced the cash and the endorsed warrant.

"How did you manage that?" he asked.

"By causing a little distress," I said.

5

"What a pity it is that we have no amusements in England but vice and religion."

Rev. Sidney Smith, 1771–1845

When the Reformation swept the valleys and moors of the North Riding of Yorkshire, it missed one or two areas. These became known as hotbeds of Papists or Centres of Catholicism, depending upon which God you worshipped. The statutory new Anglican religion did its best to fill the pews wrested from the Catholics but in the passage of time this failed. Anglican churches are emptying as the Catholic are refilling. Wesley had to go too; he tried to reform the reformed and his efforts produced a crop of chapels right across the hills, many of them nestling in remote places to echo with the voices of song-happy dalesmen.

Eventually they too began to lose their fervour. History repeated itself and the Catholics returned to build new churches. They built a monastery at Maddleskirk and monasticism returned to the dales. As time went by, the old religious wounds were healed and the various faiths mixed in business, in pleasure and in matrimony, but seldom in church. Inevitably, a little of the old misunderstanding and antagonism remained, so the Catholics went to Mass in their churches or abbeys, the Anglicans attended services in their ancient places and the Methodists went to chapel and sang with great gusto. The many other little faiths did their stuff too. Everyone seemed content.

No one made any real attempt to understand the other's point of view, all believing God was of their faith, but as the

second half of the twentieth century entered the history-
books there did appear a softening of attitudes. The new
movement became known as ecumenism which really
meant Catholics could attend services in Protestant
churches, and Protestants could join Catholics in prayer.
Real and sincere efforts were made by those in charge of the
various religions and places of worship, and it was pleasing
to see all faiths joined together in prayer on occasions like
Armistice Day or the induction of vicars or welcoming of
priests.

While all this ecumenical chat was being encouraged by
religious leaders, no one bothered to tell those of their faith
who seldom attended church. Those in the happy circle
knew all about ecumenism, but that great mass of the public
who didn't go to church were not informed about the new
developments. Many stalwart members of every faith therefore steadfastly refused to bend their opinions, and this
caused me something of a problem at a local funeral.

My official role in the affair was that of traffic policeman.
The deceased, a man called James Bathurst, was well known
around Elsinby and Aidensfield, having served on the
parish council, the county council, the Police Standing
Joint Committee and the parochial church council. A
widower of seven or eight years, Mr Bathurst had lived
alone in a lovely house which had been his family home for
generations.

There had been Bathursts in Elsinby for hundreds of
years, proof of which was very evident upon the gravestones
and upon the various rolls of honour affixed to the sturdy
walls of the parish church. The family was Anglican
through and through; Bathursts had supported the church
in all its troubles, donating pews, stained-glass windows,
altar-cloths and many other things as and when necessary.
Verily, they had been a marvellous family and generous
benefactors.

I did not get to know James Bathurst very well, for he died
soon after my arrival at Aidensfield. I did know, however,
that he had not been in very sound health for some months
and that he had been more or less confined to his house. A
lady from the village went in daily to feed him and clean the

premises, and it seems he had had a very pleasant and fulfilled life.

The one problem was that he never produced an heir, male or female. This meant he was the last of the Bathursts, for he was an only son. Finally, therefore, the Bathurst dynasty ended and I was privileged to direct traffic at the funeral of the very last member. I was present during a moment of local history.

Money for the funeral came from the provisions of his last will and testament, and the house was to be sold by auction. I knew all this and I was told by his solicitor that the funeral would be a massive affair. It was he who requested my presence to ensure that the hearse got to the church, that the mourners found parking-places and that the passing traffic flowed freely on its way. I agreed, for this was part of my duty as the village constable.

What I did not realise was that Mr James Bathurst had upset Elsinby and district in such a way that many of the residents felt deeply snubbed and very hurt. On his deathbed, he had decided to join the Roman Catholic church.

Some local Anglicans, distant relations and other interested bodies were later to attempt to contest his will because he had decreed that he be buried within the grounds of the little R.C. church of St Francis of Assisi, and that the proceeds from the sale of his house and other belongings be given to various Catholic charities.

In the days before the funeral, I learned of the various rippling undercurrents but felt such problems were not my concern. My sole duty was to attend the funeral and ensure the smooth flow of traffic and easy passage of people.

In spite of parish mutterings, the funeral was fixed for 2 p.m. one Saturday in April at the Catholic Church of St Francis of Assisi at Elsinby. It is a pretty little church with a neat graveyard nearby and is almost opposite the Anglican parish church. I visited the locality before the funeral, making my decisions about who should park where, and what to do with the hearse. There was plenty of room; I could foresee no problems.

In spite of the parochial upset, a large crowd comprising faithful of all denominations was anticipated, along with various dignitaries from the organisations he had supported. The Catholics, of course, were cock-a-hoop with pride that such a noted person had joined them albeit in the final moments of his long life. They totally rejected the suggestion that he had become a Catholic simply to prevent the death of an Anglican. And, being a Catholic myself, I was also pleased about it, and knew dear old James would find peace in the long silence that was to come. It was Abraham Cowley who said, "An eternal now does always last."

At 1.15 p.m., therefore, I positioned myself outside the church and was vaguely aware of the grave-digger, old Dusty Miller, wandering into the pub with a shovel over his shoulder. He had completed his part in the event. Minutes later, the mourners began to arrive, all wanting a front seat as Father Brendan O'Malley watched over them. Suddenly, I was busy. I parked cars, bade "Good-afternoon" to lots of solemn folk and ushered them all into the tiny church which soon boasted standing room only.

The coffin and its contents were already inside, having been previously brought into the building. The hearse had long since gone, for the graveyard lay just behind the church. James would be speeded to his eternal rest with the full splendour of a Requiem Mass, intoned by a priest in black vestments. It was truly a moving occasion, and even some hardened atheists, Methodists and Anglicans were moved to tears by the Irish eloquence of Father O'Malley's tribute to the deceased. In the Latin parts of the Mass, he spoke with rare feeling and, even though the Latin was incomprehensible to most of those present, it sounded fine and noble.

Then came the interment. Six powerful lads of Elsinby, dressed in sombre black, prepared to carry the coffin to the grave. Seated at the back, I made my move—I hurried outside to ensure the little gate was open, and found the undertaker looking somewhat harassed.

"Mr Rhea," he breathed in sepulchral tones. "There's no grave!"

"No grave?" I cried.

"No," he said. "I've been right round the churchyard,

looking for somewhere to put the flowers, but there's no grave. They haven't dug one. . . ."

"But I saw Dusty Miller with his spade. . . ." I cried.

"They're coming. . . ." and he galloped into the grave-yard once more to make a final search. I didn't know whether to tell Father O'Malley or not; after all, the under-taker might have been mistaken. So I decided to let the procession pass.

With Father O'Malley leading the way and with six sturdy red-faced lads bearing the coffin the procession was moving towards me and my little gate. I stood aside to let them through. I tried to catch Father O'Malley's eye, but his head was deep in prayer and he was intoning aloud from a Missal as he led the mourners through the tiny opening and along the side of the church. He was heading for the graveyard beyond. I joined the procession, being swept along by a tide of mourners and all the time stretching my neck for sight of the foraging undertaker. I saw him dodging about, ducking behind tombstones as the multi-person crocodile crept around this sacred ground.

Luckily, he spotted me and ran towards me, tugging at my sleeve.

"I've been right round the place, there's no grave!" he hissed.

"How long's it take to dig one?" I asked him, thinking we might get Dusty to dig a large enough hole.

"All day," he said. My heart sank.

"I'll get Dusty," I said. "He's in the pub—maybe he's got the day wrong, or the time."

"What'll I do?"

"Keep 'em going round the churchyard until I get back," I said. "Father O'Malley's got his head down, so if you go in front and lead him round in circles he'll never notice. He'll just follow your heels."

"Those lads will drop the bloody coffin!" he cried. "It's heavy, you know, good solid oak. And Jim was a big bloke."

"They're tough youngsters," was all I could say as I hurried away.

I dashed from the churchyard and held onto my helmet as

I ran down to the pub. George was just locking up and seemed surprised at my perspiring and panting figure.

"Thirsty, Mr Rhea?" he smiled. "I've just closed."

"Is Dusty here?" I panted.

"Nay, he went over to the church," he said. "Said summat about filling in Bathurst's grave."

"There is no grave!" I called. "He's forgotten to dig it."

"Forgotten?" cried George. "Not Dusty, he never forgets. It'll be there. . . ."

So I left. I was running back when I recollected my earlier sighting of Dusty with his spade. If he had been going to the pub, which he was when I saw him, he hadn't come from the Catholic Church of St Francis of Assisi. A horrible thought dawned on me. I halted my gallop, turned on my heels and ran into the grounds of the Anglican parish church of St Andrew.

The place was full of tall tombstones and crosses, but in seconds I located him. He was standing against the wall at the far end of the churchyard. He saw me and waved his spade to draw my attention.

"Over here, Mr Rhea," he shouted.

"Dusty!" I was breathless as I came to rest before him. "Is this for James Bathurst?"

"Aye, it is," he confirmed.

"But it's in the wrong churchyard!" I panted. "It should have been over there, at St Francis."

"Nay, lad, it shouldn't," he clenched his teeth, placed the spade against the wall and crossed his arms. "This is t' right spot."

"No," I said, gaining my breath. "He became a Catholic on his death-bed, and his funeral is over there. Father O'Malley's looking for his grave right now."

"Then tell him it's here," said Dusty.

"But it's the wrong place, wrong religion . . ." I tried to explain.

"Nay, Mr Rhea. This is Bathurst territory, this piece of land. All his ancestors are here, every single one of 'em. This is where yon Mr Bathurst gets buried, not over there among all them Papists."

"But he became a Papist . . . er Catholic," I tried. "It was his personal choice."

"On his death-bed, not in his right senses at the time. Nay, Mr Rhea, I can't accept that. Here he's buried or not at all," and his jaw jutted in an act of personal defiance.

I dithered for what seemed an eternity, then dashed back to the other church. The procession had done one complete circuit of the churchyard to the music of Father O'Malley's intonations—up one side, across the bank and down the other with everyone seeking the elusive hole in the ground. They were now setting off upon their second exploration and the lads bearing the coffin looked all in. Sweat was pouring from them and they would soon have to have a rest. . . .

"Father." I hurried to the front of the queue and spoke quietly to him.

For a moment, he ignored me and I thought I'd get an Irish blasting, but he recognised the concern in my voice.

"Yes, my son?"

"The grave," I whispered. "It's over in the Anglican churchyard, with the Bathurst ancestors."

"Holy Mother of God!" he burst. "That bloody man Miller!"

"The lads with the coffin are nearly all in," I warned him. "What shall I do?"

"Keep walking beside me, my son, while I ponder this one," he said in his thick Irish brogue. "Now, what would God do in a situation like this? God would never get Himself into a situation like this, would He now? There's a hole in the ground over there and all holes in the ground are the same. Earth to earth, dust to dust. But it's not Catholic consecrated ground. It's Protestant land, fit only for sheep and hens. But he's a man, and a man needs a decent burial. . . . most of us like to be with our loved ones in our eternal rest. . . . but the Anglicans will be claiming him as theirs. . . . but we get the proceeds of the will, eh? We sell the house for Catholic charities. . . . we can use money to put a plaque in our church, so we can, telling the world where he's buried and how he was converted. . . ."

I listened to his one-sided conversation and turned to

look at the poor bearers. They were buckling at the knees, their eyes were bulging and their faces were red with the pain of their burden. Strong fit farm lads they were, but there is a limit. . . .'

"Rest awhile on the stone bench beneath the Anglican lych-gate," he said to them. "'Tis apparent he's to be buried at the other side."

Most adroitly, he guided the long, straggly procession around the graveyard and out onto the road. The grateful bearers placed the coffin on the slab beneath the lych-gate and the entire procession halted. Father O'Malley addressed them.

"It seems there's been a bit of poaching," he said. "Dusty's dug the grave at the wrong side of the road, so he has. So we'll bury him there, poor man. May the Lord have mercy on his soul."

And so, after a brief consultation with the vicar, James Bathurst was laid to rest among his ancestors and relations. I knew that Father O'Malley would erect a memorial plaque on the wall of St Francis of Assisi, so the truth would prevail. As we adjourned to the house for the traditional ham tea, Dusty lovingly filled in the grave and arranged the floral tributes about the new earth. He came into the house an hour later, ready for his refreshments and I saw one or two of the villagers congratulate him. I wondered if this had been Dusty's own idea, or whether some of the stalwarts had put him up to it.

But it didn't matter. With the coming world of ecumenical understanding was one grave any worse than any other?

The last word went to Father O'Malley. I was fortunate to be nearby as he cornered Dusty Miller over his cup of tea.

"Dusty Miller," he breathed at the little fellow. "This was all your doing, I'll be bound."

"He's resting in his rightful place," stated Dusty.

"Then you'll rest in my churchyard, Dusty Miller," said Father O'Malley. "If I can convert a Bathurst, I'll make short work of you, my lad. Mark my words, and like it or not, you will be buried in the churchyard of St Francis of Assisi. I'll get you, so help me!"

Dusty fled and I saw the glint of amusement in Father O'Malley's eye.

No worse fate could befall poor Dusty, for he was a very protesting Protestant.

That little incident served to bring together the two faiths, Anglican and Catholic, in Elsinby. The Rev. Simon Hamilton and Father Brendan O'Malley became even more friendly towards each other, although it must be said they had never shown any real antagonism. They served together on committees, lunched together regularly to discuss mutual problems and ambitions, and loaned each other various items of religious significance. All this had evolved long before the Bathurst funeral, but it was that burial with its last-minute compromise which sealed the friendship. One immediate result was that the Catholics traipsed into the Anglican churchyard on a regular, organised basis to pay open tribute to their celebrated convert, James Bathurst. Some had misgivings over this, but Father O'Malley dealt with their worries by buying the grave from the Anglicans. He paid a nominal sum, but it thus became Catholic ground. James Bathurst was now buried in a patch of Catholic ground, an island of saintly refuge in the middle of an Anglican graveyard. But at least he was among his Protestant forebears and friends, an ideal situation.

While Catholics could be seen pottering up and down those paths of Anglican ground, the Anglicans had no reason to do likewise so far as the Catholic church was concerned. Their reticence continued; the only occasion they entered the walls of St Francis of Assisi was for a local wedding or funeral, or when the two ministers of religion held a joint service, such as an ecumenical gathering or on Remembrance Day. Officially, a state of bliss existed but in practice the two faiths were poles apart.

A real test occurred late one summer. My first intimation was a telephone call from the Reverend Hamilton asking if I would pop in to see him next time I was on duty in Elsinby. I agreed and within a week I was in his study, enjoying a pleasant coffee.

He was a fine man, the Reverend Hamilton. With a faint

Scots accent, he stood an impressive six feet tall and boasted an athletic past, having once played football for a Scottish First Division team. He was married to a lovely wife who happily joined the multifarious affairs of village life. The vicar considered himself very much part of the North Riding population even though he had been here a mere eight years. He reckoned he had adopted the county as his home.

But there was one grey cloud on his horizon. In spite of his popularity and his earnest efforts, the congregation of St Andrew's Parish Church continued to dwindle. Young folk didn't bother to attend, the middle-aged were too busy and the elderly too tired. Mr Hamilton relied on a regular attendance of some twenty faithful, swollen to fifty at times like Easter and Christmas, but this was in no way a proportional representation of the population. With over 350 people in the parish, his church looked miserably empty at most times.

Father O'Malley, on the other hand, had a Catholic congregation of some 180 souls, young, old and middle-aged, and he ensured they attended Mass every Sunday. They also came to other services as and when required. He averaged a hundred and ten each Sunday for Mass and this made the poor Anglican church look very poorly attended.

The unhappy Simon Hamilton told me all about this aspect of his work and he wondered how the Catholics managed to fill their church with youngsters when he failed; I told him I was a Catholic and attended Mass regularly at Aidensfield, and he raised his eyes to Heaven.

"You know, Mr Rhea," he said, with that faint Scots accent lingering in the air. "I could do with your faithful in a fortnight's time."

"Really?" I didn't quite understand his comment.

"Yes, I've called you here to discuss a small matter." I thought he'd gone off at a tangent, but he continued. "My bishop is coming a fortnight on Sunday. It's his first visit since his appointment three years ago, and that's why I called you in. I want to ensure everything goes well, and I need your advice on car-parking and traffic arrangements."

"I'll help, of course," I assured him, for supervision of such events was part of my duty.

"There's no car-park at the church, as you know, so I'm afraid the bishop's car will have to park on the road outside."

"That's no problem," I said. "The road is wide enough to allow that."

"Yes, I'm sure it is. And there's the congregation's cars, plus the other clergy who come from neighbouring parishes. There might be a lot of cars, Mr Rhea, and I wondered if I could prevail upon you to ensure the bishop is parked as near as possible to the gate."

"I'll get here half an hour before the service," I assured him, "and I will make sure things go according to your wishes."

We discussed the outline plans for the day and I learned he was to prepare a feast in the parish rooms, at which the bishop would attend for the purpose of informally meeting the parishioners. Clearly, Mr Hamilton had a lot of work ahead, and I could see that he wanted the day to be a huge success.

Having explained everything to me, with details of timings and anticipated numbers, I could see he still looked rather apprehensive.

"You're not very happy about this?" I put to him.

He shook his head. "No," he sighed. "No, Mr Rhea, I'm not. It's the apathy."

"Apathy?"

"Yes, people don't come to church any more and I've tried to talk those who never come into attending on that day. This church was once a flourishing community, full every Sunday with lots of activities, but now, well, I get my regulars—only a dozen or so—but no more."

"Surely they'll all come to meet the bishop?" I said.

"Ah, yes, they'll come, the regulars. But no one else. Well, I'm lying there—one or two extra people have expressed a desire to come, but I'll have more clergy there than lay congregation if I'm not careful. I would have liked a full church that day. . . ."

"Is it just a social visit?" I asked, wondering whether this came under the heading of ecumenism, or whether it was a confirmation visit.

"Not really. It's an official inspection really, disguised as a social 'meet the people' outing. Bishops go around checking on us, very discreetly, to make sure we do our job. My God, Mr Rhea, I've worked, but I never seem to make headway . . ."

"If it was an ecumenical service, Father O'Malley's lot would come," I smiled. "They would fill your empty seats."

He rubbed his chin and smiled at me. "If I didn't know better, I'd swear you were trying to convince me that Catholicism was the answer to everything."

"It's not the answer to everything, Mr Hamilton, but it might be the answer to your immediate problem."

"You're not serious?" he cried, staring at me over his coffee-cup.

"Why not?" I returned. "Why not fill your church with Catholics?"

"The bishop would object. . . . he'd know. . . ."

"Not if you didn't tell him, not if Father O'Malley provided them with. . . . er. . . . how shall I put it. . . . their terms of reference."

"But suppose the bishop talked to a Catholic who let the cat out of the bag and said he was from St Francis' across the road. . . ."

"Then you talk to the bishop about the spirit of ecumenism. You tell him how the faiths mingle in the village and quote the Catholic presence as an example of the interest in his work by the Catholic community. . . ."

"My church will seat nearly three hundred," he mused. "With a handful of locals and a few clergy hangers-on, it will look deserted. How many Catholics could he muster?"

"A churchful," I smiled. "If you issue that as a challenge to Father O'Malley, he'll fill your church with religious folk who will listen to your bishop and eat your sandwiches like good Anglicans."

He smiled, "You know, Mr Rhea, I find this very tempting. I would not wish to lie to the bishop, but a churchful of worshippers would look fine, and it would be impressive."

"Shall I intercede with Father O'Malley?" I suggested.

"No," he said. "No, I think this had better come from me.

Look, I'll talk to him and let you know what transpires. Can I be in touch again about the car-parking?"

"Of course," and I left him.

Hardly had I got outside when I saw Sergeant Blaketon sitting in his official car with the window down. He was looking up and down the High Street and when he saw me emerge from the vicarage he left the car. He strode stiffly towards me.

"Good afternoon, Rhea," he greeted me. "I saw your bike. Busy?"

"I've been to a meeting with the vicar," I told him. "He's got an official visit by his bishop shortly, and wanted me to help with car parking."

"Do you anticipate problems?" he asked. "We can fix you up with parking cones or another constable if you wish."

"No, I'll manage," I said and added thoughtlessly, "I don't anticipate a lot of cars."

"Oh, does that mean a poor congregation?" he asked me. "Even for a bishop's visit?"

"He's working on ideas for filling the church," I said. "He's a man of great imagination, is our vicar."

"What he needs is a few Methodists to help out," I heard him say. "Now, I'm a keen chapel-goer, and in these days of ecumenism it's good for the faiths to mingle."

I began to wish I'd accepted his cones and additional policeman.

"I'm sure he will fill the church." I tried to steer him away from his topic, but he was not to be swayed.

"Not with Catholics?" he looked at the modern outline of the St Francis of Assisi Church just behind.

"I think there are enough Anglicans hereabouts to provide him with a full house," I said.

"Not on your life," he retorted. "I'll speak to our local minister at the chapel. We might come along to support him. When did you say it was?"

I provided him with the date and groaned inwardly. I hoped he'd stay out of this. We went for a long walk around Elsinby, with Sergeant Blaketon expounding the merits of inter-religious exchanges and the need for more discipline among the young. I wondered if the two were connected, but he lost me in a sea of hazy words as I worried about the possible outcome of his idea. I tried to deter him but he was not to be deflected.

A week later, I was back in Elsinby and decided to call upon Father O'Malley. I found him making wine in his kitchen and he invited me to sample a glassful of last year's vintage. It was beetroot wine, a beautiful red colour, and it tasted like fine port.

"Your health, Nicholas." He raised his own glass. "What brings you here?"

"I was passing," I said, "and thought I'd pop in."

"You did right, so you did," he smiled through his strong teeth. He looked a typical Irishman, with bushy black hair and firm eyebrows set in a strong face, full of character. "How's the wine?"

"Fine." I sipped appreciatively. "Father, has Mr Hamilton seen you about a service at the parish church?"

"He has, yes he has. And a nice idea too."

He paused and sipped the wine, then added, "He tells me it was your idea."

"Well, I thought we might do a little for ecumenism."

"And so we will. I've already mentioned it to some of the faithful here and we'll fill the church for him, to be sure. It's a challenge to these people, Nicholas, and it's a way for them to get their own back for Jimmy Bathurst's funeral. But I've asked them all to behave like good Anglicans that day."

"I hope it doesn't backfire on him."

"No, it won't. I'll see to that. I'll be there too."

"In your collar?"

"No, I will dress as an Irish labourer that day, so help me. Never you worry, Nicholas. We'll give his bishop a day to remember. We've already agreed on the hymns that will be sung, and my lot are in full training. They'll sing some lovely Anglican hymns, mark my words."

So far as the arrangements for the service were concerned, I knew I had no worries. The two clergymen had come to a fine, sensible agreement and my next involvement was on the actual day of the bishop's visit.

The service was to begin at 3 p.m. that Sunday and it

would last for an hour, with twenty minutes being allowed for an address by the bishop. Tea had been arranged in the parish rooms during which the bishop would mingle with the faithful on an informal basis. Those Catholics who felt they might behave erratically need not attend, for the tiny room could not accommodate everyone.

On the big day, I took my motor-cycle into the grounds of the Hopbind Inn and left it there with George's permission, replacing my helmet with a uniform cap. At two-thirty, I took up my position outside the St Andrew's church gate to keep a space free for the visiting dignitary. Cars began to arrive about twenty minutes to three and all greeted me warmly. Mr Hamilton came out to check that all was well, and the sun shone upon his little castle. I bade "good-afternoon" to many good Anglicans and lots of equally good Catholics, all filing into the sombre walls of the church to be issued with hymn-books upon entry. Father O'Malley was there too, dressed in rough clothes but beaming all over his rugged face.

"'Tis good to understand the ways of the Lord, Nicholas," he smiled as he strode towards the imposing entrance.

I looked at my watch. Ten minutes to three. The bishop was due in five minutes.

Mr Hamilton came along the path ready to meet him and we stood together, looking anxiously along the High Street.

"Will he be on time?" I asked.

"I'm sure he will, he's been to a morning service south of York, and he lunched in the city with the archbishop. He'll be on time."

"The last bishop never visited Elsinby?" I put to him as we waited.

"No," he said. "All those occasions when a bishop was needed, like confirmations, were held in Aidensfield, so we never got a visit. But this chap's changed all that, he's visiting every church in his diocese."

At five minutes to three I heard an approaching vehicle.

A large, luxury coach materialised around the corner and I was horrified to see Sergeant Blaketon's huge figure standing near the front door. The bus halted right before us with a squeal of brakes and Sergeant Blaketon, in full uniform, clambered down. It had parked right in the bishop's place.

"Afternoon, Vicar, afternoon, Rhea," he beamed at us.

"Mr Hamilton, this is Sergeant Blaketon from Ashfordly, my section station. Sergeant, the Reverend Simon Hamilton, the vicar of Elsinby."

They shook hands, and Blaketon said, "I heard you needed a congregation, Vicar, so I've got a bus-load of Methodists with me, all from Ashfordly."

"A congregation, Sergeant?"

"Yes, young Rhea let it drop that you couldn't fill the church, so I thought it would be a nice gesture of working Christianity if I brought along a few of my friends, just to fill the gaps, in a manner of speaking."

"Er, it's very kind of you, Sergeant, but I think you'll find my church is full. But go in, please—it might be standing room only."

"Come along, you lot," bawled Sergeant Blaketon in a good-humoured way. "Fill up that church like good Anglicans."

And as they descended from their coach I saw the oncoming procession with its Austin Princess at the lead. The bishop was here.

"Sarge!" I cried. "That bus is on the bishop's parking-place."

"We won't be a minute, lad."

"But he's here, coming up the village now!"

There was a moment of confusion, as Sergeant Blaketon tried to get the driver to move before everyone was out, but he failed. The slow-moving stream of Methodists held up the coach and the result was that the bishop's car had to park a few yards away. I was upset but the bishop didn't seem to mind.

He and his attendants dismounted and I saw he was a little, jovial man with a round happy face and dancing eyes.

"Full house, eh?" he beamed, looking at the coach. "Am I early?"

"No, Your Grace," smiled Mr Hamilton. "When they get inside, I will take you in."

"Let us not hurry those good people," the bishop said, looking at me. "And this is your local policeman?"

"P.C. Rhea, from Ashfordly, Your Grace." I extended my hand and he shook it warmly with a firm grip.

"It's nice of you to help us out," smiled the bishop as he watched the last of Blaketon's faithful enter the church. The bus moved away and the bishop's chauffeur slid into his correct position. Everything was just as it should be.

"Are you going in?" asked the bishop of me.

"I am, Your Grace," and I went ahead, leaving the bishop and the vicar to enter last. As I edged my way into the packed church, I could see people everywhere. The place was packed and Sergeant Blaketon's Methodists were standing in the aisles down the side and at the rear. It was a wonderful sight.

Sergeant Blaketon saw me enter and I was compelled to stand close to him. "Rhea," he whispered hoarsely, "This place is full of bloody papists."

"Is it, Sergeant?" I smiled as the organ struck up with the first hymn.

As the bishop walked down the aisle, the Anglicans, Catholics and Methodists burst into a rousing hymn of welcome, each faith trying to outsing the other. The harmonious Methodists sang with their usual blend of religious fervour and elegance and perhaps theirs was the better music. But it was a joyful welcome and everyone settled down for the start of this memorable service.

It was a splendid occasion by any standards. The singing was good enough to lift the ancient roof of this church, and everyone joined in with the utmost enthusiasm. The Catholics almost forgot to add the tailpiece at the end of the "Our Father", but Father O'Malley's stentorian tones led them into that final act of homage. By four o'clock it was all over, and the congregation reckoned the bishop's address had been first rate. He had talked wholeheartedly of harmony between Christians and I wondered if he knew how apt his words were on this occasion.

During the tea afterwards, everyone mingled and ate happily, and I was pleased to see local Catholics chatting with local Methodists interspaced with Anglicans. The bishop in his purple mingled too and I saw him chatting earnestly with several of the catholics of St Francis. But it all went very, very well indeed. Mr Hamilton beamed benevolently upon everyone.

His Grace was scheduled to leave at five fifteen and I positioned myself near his car to ensure a smooth departure. He was five or ten minutes late leaving and I saluted him as he came through the door. There he paused a moment, and said, "You know, Officer, the Pope would have been proud of that turn-out, eh?"

"Yes, Your Grace," I smiled as he departed. As the car swept along the village High Street, I turned to find Sergeant Blaketon standing at my elbow.

"I don't suppose you had anything to do with this, Rhea?" he growled.

"With what, Sergeant?"

"Packing that church with papists?"

"If I was an insurance agent, Sergeant, I would record it as an Act of God," I said, turning back to find another cup of tea.

I never really knew whether Sergeant Blaketon disliked members of the Roman Catholic Church, or whether his remarks were deep-seated jokes understood only by himself. In truth, there were few occasions when religion entered my work as a village policeman, but I must confess that on one occasion the rigid faith of a little old lady completely thwarted me.

To put the story in perspective, it began with the death of a Mr Abraham Potter whose home was a lovely cottage in Aidensfield, just up the street from the pub. Awd Abe, as everyone affectionately called him, had been a lifelong Methodist of the strictest kind, never drinking liquor, never smoking, never swearing, never gambling and never working on Sundays. He led an exemplary life and was a true pillar of the chapel. There, he cleaned and gardened, painted and decorated and wrote the notices for Sunday in his beautiful copper-plate handwriting. Then he died.

My arrival at Aidensfield coincided with his death, so I

never met Awd Abe. From his reputation, I guessed his name would live on as an example of righteousness and Christian standards. His death meant that his little cottage would be sold and, within a few weeks, the "For Sale" signs appeared in the garden. His relatives had been traced and had agreed to sell the house, but no one had foreseen the conditions he'd imposed upon the sale.

I learned of these by pure chance, for I was patrolling the village street as the estate agents were erecting their "For Sale" boards. As village constables are wont to do, I stopped for a chat.

"Will it sell?" I asked, for rural properties at that time were not fetching very high prices. It was before the boom in country cottages.

"It would, if it wasn't for Awd Abe," said the man.

"He's dead," I remarked, wondering if he knew.

"Aye, we know, but he's left a will saying what's got to be done with this spot, if his nephews sell it."

"Has he? What's he said?" I was interested now.

"You knew him?" the man put to me.

I shook my head. "No, he died just before I was posted here."

"Big chapel man, he was," I was told. "Very straight sort of a chap. Lived by the Bible, you know."

"So I've heard." Awd Abe's reputation lived on.

"Well, he's put conditions on the sale of this spot," the man told me guardedly. "I reckon we'll have a job selling it."

"What sort of conditions?"

"Well," he said. "First, it mustn't be sold to or occupied by a Roman Catholic. And the person that buys it must not read Sunday papers, mustn't play cards, mustn't drink alcohol, mustn't have children, mustn't keep animals, mustn't smoke, mustn't gamble and mustn't work on Sundays. And they must be regular attenders at chapel, not church."

"He *will* have a job selling it here!" I laughed. "Practically every other family is Catholic and I imagine most folks nowadays read Sunday papers. . . . why the Sunday papers bit?"

"He didn't believe in working on the Sabbath," said the estate agent's man. "Anything that had been created on the Sabbath must not enter his house. He didn't even wash up on Sundays, he was that pernickety about his faith."

"But the papers are printed on Saturdays," I said.

"Aye, lots of folk told him that, and they told him about factories making furniture on Sunday, or canning food, farmers working, doctors and so on. . . ."

"But he wouldn't give?"

"Not him," said the man. "And when we got this house to sell, well, we all laughed. I mean, who's going to buy it? Who can truthfully agree to those conditions?"

"Search me!" I smiled and went on my way. Lots of the locals would have loved his cottage for it was pleasantly located and well-built, but Awd Abe's conditions immediately placed it beyond the reach of local folks.

But it did sell.

Word must have spread far afield because a little old lady called Miss Sarah Prudom arrived to inspect the cottage. I didn't see her arrival, but learned she came from the Doncaster area and was seeking a place in the country for retirement. She'd worked as a laundry manageress, I was told.

As things turned out, Miss Prudom perfectly fitted Awd Abe's specification. Furthermore, she was an unmarried lady of spotless virtue, and we all felt Abe would have been proud of her. I wondered if they might have married, had they met in life, but perhaps such associations could lead to sins of the flesh. Anyway, Miss Prudom bought Awd Abe's cottage.

One fine spring day, she moved in with her furniture and books and there is little doubt that her arrival in Aidensfield brought hope to the tiny chapel flock. Abe had gone but his place had been taken by an equally enthusiastic worker, as indeed she was. Miss Prudom soon busied herself about the chapel and fussed over the congregation, visiting them, talking to them, praising them and arranging prayer meetings from time to time.

As the weeks rolled by, it was quite evident that she fitted perfectly Awd Abe's specifications. She was a lovely little woman, both in charm and in appearance. Her trim figure graced the village as she went about her daily business, for she was always smartly dressed and wore rimless spectacles which seemed to shine beneath her grey hair. Rose-coloured cheeks and a ready smile completed her charming appearance and everyone liked her.

Then, one day, she appeared to break her strict rules, because she appeared in the village store one Sunday morning. The store opened from 10.30 a.m. until 12 noon, and was patronised by the Catholics as they left Mass, and by others who forgot bits and pieces on Saturdays. The uncharacteristic appearance of Miss Prudom in the shop caused something of a stir, and I was in at the time, just passing the time of day.

She blushed as she entered, for she must have known that all present knew of her strict beliefs, but the shopkeeper calmly asked, "Yes, Miss Prudom?"

"I have friends calling for tea," she said confidentially, "and they have just telephoned to inform me. I have nothing in the house. Could I have a tin of smoked salmon please, and a lettuce and some tomatoes?"

"Certainly."

She wanted other items too, and ticked them off a handwritten list as the shopkeeper busied himself with her order. Finally, her basket was full.

"How much is that?" she asked smiling.

"One pound, five shillings and threepence," he said.

"Will you take a cheque?" she asked him.

"Of course, I will be pleased."

She opened her cheque-book on the counter and wrote in the correct amount, then said, "I have dated it for tomorrow, will that be all right?"

"Yes, of course, Miss Prudom."

After handing over the cheque, she smiled graciously at him and said, "Thank you, Mr Woodall, it is most kind of you to allow me to do that. You see, I cannot buy goods on the Sabbath, so this means I've bought them tomorrow, Monday. You have got me out of a dilemma, and I appreciate it deeply."

"I'm always pleased to help," and she was gone.

I was amazed at her logic, but have since come across similar faithful who bend the rules, such as those who refuse to drink alcohol, but who buy in bottles of brandy or whisky for medicinal purposes.

But it was Miss Prudom and her religious beliefs which caused me a headache.

Several months later, her house was burgled. I do not think she was wealthy, but her prim little home did contain some pleasing items of crockery and glassware, in addition to several good pieces of silver plate. These were family heirlooms. Sometime between nine o'clock one Saturday night and six o'clock the next morning, Sunday, a villain broke into her home and stole silver and crockery worth about £200. He entered through the rear kitchen window, which he broke in order to release the catch, climbed in and ransacked the downstairs rooms while she was asleep.

As Miss Prudom rose early on the Sabbath, she discovered the horror just after six and the shock was so great that she did nothing until nine o'clock. As I learned afterwards, she'd simply sat and wept at the sight of her personal belongings strewn across the floor, and at the thought of a strange, uncouth man rifling her treasures as she slept. At nine o'clock, she rang Ashfordly Police Station to report the crime.

Alwyn Foxton was on duty and chanced to be in the office. He listened sympathetically and asked her not to touch anything. He told her he would despatch a policeman immediately to the scene. Alwyn then telephoned me, for I was on duty that Sunday.

"I'll go straight there," I said.

Within minutes, I had donned my crash-helmet and heavy coat against the threat of April showers and within two minutes of leaving my hill-top house I was drawing up beside Miss Prudom's cottage. She came to the door to greet me and her ashen face and red-rimmed eyes told of her solitary distress.

"I'm P.C. Rhea," I announced. "Your local policeman—we haven't met formally."

"You were in the shop the other morning," she said seriously.

"Yes, I often pop in to talk with Mr Woodall."

"It's awful, Mr Rhea, the mess. Just to think that some-body has been in there, while I was in bed, going through my belongings. . . ."

"I'll examine the house first, to give a quick assessment, and then I'll call the C.I.D. They'll come to fingerprint the house and examine it for other clues. . . ."

"Oh, you can't come in," she said pertly. "I'm sorry."

"But I need to, Miss Prudom. It's vital that the police come in to examine the scene of the crime. We can't make a proper investigation without seeing for ourselves. . . ."

"No, you don't understand. Mr Rhea, you are a Catholic, aren't you?"

"Yes, I am," I confirmed.

"But you see, I do not allow papists into my home. I never have and never will. And today is Sunday too. You must know of Mr Potter's conditions of sale, about Catholics not entering or buying this house. . . ."

"But, Miss Prudom, it is my job. If I am to have even the remotest chance of detecting this crime, I must come inside to see how the criminal has gone about his work. And I need to talk to you, to take a statement from you, to ask about identification of the stolen goods and a host of other things, like values and detailed descriptions. . . ."

"I'm sorry, Mr Rhea," was all she said.

I stood on the doorstep looking at her. She was a sad picture; her eyes were rimmed with red and her pretty face was pale and drawn. She was wringing her hands before her frail body as she kept me at bay and I must admit I didn't know how to tackle this problem. I felt desperately sorry for her.

"Can I see the window then, at the back? I can examine it from the outside. That will be a help."

"Yes, that will be all right."

She led me to the rear of the house and I examined the smashed window-pane. It had been broken with some heavy object, and pieces of glass lay inside, on the window-ledge. Chummy had opened the latch, climbed in and ransacked the place, leaving by the front door with his loot.

I made notes of this, which was all I could see.

Back at the front door, I smiled at her. I remembered one little item.

"Miss Prudom," I said. "You were in the shop the other Sunday and you bought some food."

"Yes."

"That was an emergency, wasn't it? And I noticed how you paid by cheque, dated Monday, to avoid buying them on the Sabbath."

"Yes, but it was a dire emergency. . . ."

"Then so is this. The police might be able to catch the criminal if we can come inside. . . . I could always date my reports tomorrow, you see. . . ."

"You miss the point, Mr Rhea. The point is that papists must not enter my house. That is the point, it's nothing to do with the Sabbath."

"If Christ lived here, would He let me enter?" I asked her.

She remained very silent and her bright eyes regarded me solemnly, before adding, "But He doesn't live here. I do."

I felt like quoting the Parable of the Lost Sheep but knew I was fighting a losing battle. "Well, Miss Prudom, what can I do? A crime has been committed on my beat, and I am responsible for recording the fact and investigating the matter. I cannot do my work, which could lead to the arrest of the criminal, without examining your house."

"Mr Rhea," she smiled sweetly. "I have nothing against you personally. You must realise that. It has long been the practice in my family never to associate with or to encourage popery in any shape or form. You must allow me to exercise my principles."

"Even if it means post-dating a cheque to allow you to buy goods on the Sabbath?" I was angry now and utterly failed to understand the hypocrisy in her. I could have argued all day and all night but it would not have made any difference to her bigotry. I knew it would be unchristian of me to begin a pitched theological battle on her doorstep, and besides, she had suffered the ignominy of a burglary. I did not wish to add to her obvious distress.

I left, saying, "I'll get another officer to call on you."

It was with some sadness, therefore, that I returned to my house on the hill and telephoned the office at Ashfordly. As

Alwyn Foxton answered the telephone, my experience of the bishop's visit to Elsinby came to mind.

"Is Sergeant Blaketon there?" I asked.

"I'll put you through," he said.

"Blaketon," came the solemn response. "Something wrong, Rhea?"

"I've a problem I think you might solve for me, Sergeant."

"Oh, something you can't cope with?" I thought I detected a faint hint of sarcasm in his voice.

"Yes," I said, "a woman."

"Women are always problematical," he propounded. "I thought a young lad like you would be able to charm a woman."

"Not this one," I said. "She's a fierce chapel-going Methodist."

"So?" he boomed.

"So she won't let me into her house to investigate a burglary," I said, "and if any of the CID are Catholics they won't be allowed in either."

He roared with laughter. I could hear him at the other end of the line, chortling in his happiness as I explained the problem.

"Nice one, Rhea, yes, a very nice one. Serve you right for getting our Anglican church full of papists the other week. Right, leave it to me. I'm with Miss Prudom on this one. I'll sort it out."

And so he did. She allowed him to enter her premises whereupon she provided all the necessary help and information. The CID were called too and Sergeant Blaketon first warned them not to bring a Catholic—she'd know if they did, he warned them. She could smell 'em. Through his help, the crime was reported in the formal way and the necessary documents were completed. Miss Prudom provided a very detailed list of all the stolen goods and in the course of the next few days we circulated the information to all police offices in the locality. This was standard procedure.

Sadly, the burglar was never found. He committed several similar crimes in and around the North Riding over the next few months, and then he stopped. His hallmark was the method of entry and exit, and the type of property he took, but we never caught him. Perhaps another police force came across him, perhaps he was arrested elsewhere. We shall never know.

The sequel to the yarn, however, was the criminal's return of a photograph. It showed a very young Miss Prudom with her father and it was endorsed to that effect on the rear. The picture was probably fifty years old or more and I'm sure it was of sentimental value to her. For that reason, it was returned to her through the post.

She called at my police house to inform me of this event and I invited her in so that I could amend the list of stolen goods. She entered my house without hesitation and we concluded that piece of official business. I considered questioning her ethics on this occasion, but decided against it.

She'd probably say the police house didn't qualify in her rule-book due to its official function, so I didn't ask. There seemed to be no point.

6

"What is this that roareth thus?
Can it be a motor-bus?"

Alfred Denis Godler, 1856–1925

One of the inescapable features of a police officer's life is to be told incessantly about parking tickets. In company, the moment one's true occupation is known, out come all the harrowing tales of parking problems; he is told how the speaker parked only for the briefest of moments while he changed his library book/bought himself underpants/waited for the wife/suffered from dampness on his coil or got involved in some other accident of history. Never is a motorist at fault in such circumstances; everyone else is, especially the police.

Police officers who suffer from such ear-bending sessions can sympathise with doctors who are bored about operations, solicitors who are cornered by convicted innocents and plumbers who can't get away from rattling taps or overflowing cisterns. For this reason, policemen who go on holiday seldom admit their true occupation—only a masochist would do that. Holidaying constables announce to their audience that they are variously employed as clerks for the government, officers in local authority employment, out-of-work salesmen, bingo callers or members of other sundry occupations. I know one policeman who, when on holiday, always tells his new-found friends that he is a button salesman. He reckons that's the best conversation-stopper there is—after all, what can anyone ask about that?

One of my constabulary pals was on holiday in Scotland

when this problem arose. Paul was with his wife and they had booked into a beautiful bed-and-breakfast farmhouse in the Highlands intending to stay overnight. So nice was the place that they stayed the entire week, and found the only other residents were another gentleman and his wife. They became friendly, especially over the evening meal and at breakfast. As the week progressed, Paul realised that the other gentleman never once gave a clue to his own occupation. Moreover, he never asked Paul how he earned his living.

The state of unspoken bliss continued through the week and on the final breakfast morning, that Saturday, Paul decided to tackle the other about his job. All through the week, he had realised the other was being overcautious about his work and decided to put him to the test.

At breakfast, therefore, he said, "Look, Jonathan, let's be honest, eh? You and I have been carefully avoiding any discussion about our jobs, haven't we? All this week, you have carefully avoided talking about your work and so have I."

The other smiled agreeably. "I don't like to talk about my job when I'm on holiday."

"Neither do I," smiled Paul in return. "But this is our last morning together. By lunchtime, we'll be on our way home. Let's tell each other."

The other smiled again. "All right," he nodded. "Who's first?"

"I raised the matter," Paul admitted. "So I'll start. I'm a policeman."

"And I'm a bishop," said his friend.

For the country constable, however, such anonymity cannot be enjoyed. If he walks into the shop, pub, church or meeting of any kind, he is always "the policeman" and his wife is always "the policeman's wife". When visiting one's local pub, therefore, it is impossible to be anything other than the local bobby, even when dressed in gardening clothes and covered in non-artificial farmyard waste products.

This being so, the talk often turns to motoring adventures in alien cities, of being stopped for speeding, booked for parking, checked for one's driving licence and insurance or pulled up for faulty windscreen-wipers. But at least in Aidensfield, I had a variation of this eternal theme.

I had a man who talked about buses.

It was soon very clear that he could talk about nothing else. For that reason, it became something of a trial to enter the pub knowing he lurked in the shadows, waiting to pounce on someone with his latest piece of juicy information about a 52-seater with reclining seats. I did my best to avoid him, as did every other regular in the bar of the Brewers Arms. They had had their fill of Plaxton Shells, Wallace Arnold tours and United Express runs with rural bus-stops.

At first, the fellow was interesting. I listened enthralled as he discussed the merits of demisters on side-windows and emergency exits near the front, tool-boxes under the offside exterior and double-deckers on rural routes, but when one has this indigestible manna during every visit it does begin to pall. I didn't know a great deal about buses anyway, but wondered how much this fellow really knew. Was it all conjecture and legend, or did he really know a lot about buses?

His name was Arnold Merryweather and he would be in his early fifties. He was a genial fellow, heavily built with a thick head of ginger hair and bushy side-whiskers, and he loved Irish jokes and Guinness. He was the life and soul of the pub, and his stories were funny, even if they were all about buses.

Arnold drove the bus which crept around our lanes day after day, week after week, to collect passengers at Ashfordly and transport them through the picturesque lanes and villages into York. His bus left Ashfordly at 7.30 a.m. and trundled through Briggsby, Aidensfield, Elsinby, and then beyond the boundaries of my beat and eventually into York. It did a return trip around lunchtime and turned about immediately for York. It arrived in time to turn round in the City at 5.15 p.m. to bring home the diminishing army of workers. Every day, week in week out, Arnold's bus undertook those journeys.

On Tuesdays, Thursdays and Saturdays, he left York

immediately upon first arrival and did a special market-day run, collecting at Ashfordly at ten o'clock and getting into York around 11.30 a.m., having done a circuitous tour of Ryedale to get there. He was just able to fulfil his timetable with this extra trip and there's little doubt he earned his money on those important three days. Those earnings probably lasted him all week.

I learned eventually that Arnold owned the bus. He did not operate for any company, but earned his living entirely by his bus. During the evenings, he would arrange tours to cinemas in York, or to the theatre, and he did runs to the seaside and works outings to breweries and other places of interest. He did a school run too, collecting a rowdy horde of children from isolated places and risking his bus and its passengers on gradients of 1-in-3 as he visited outlying farms and hamlets. But Arnold always got there and very rarely was he late. His purple and cream bus, with "Merryweather Coaches" emblazoned across the rear, was a familiar sight in the hills and valleys of Aidensfield and district.

To fulfil his many commitments, he had two coaches, and had a standby driver employed to assist when necessary. But if it was possible to use one bus and one driver for his complicated timetables then Arnold did so.

I made use of his bus once or twice. Sometimes, if the weather was atrocious and if Mary was using the car, I would catch Arnold's bus at Aidensfield if I had business in Elsinby or Briggsby. I always paid, although he did offer me free transportation, for I reckoned he must be struggling to earn a living for himself and his colourless wife called Freda. He had to maintain his vehicles and premises too.

To partake of a trip on Merryweather Coaches was an experience which could be classed as unique. Each bus was identical and I think they were Albion 32-seaters. The seats were made of wooden laths set on iron frames and bolted to the floor. There were no cushions and other comforts, and the door was at the front. It was hinged in the middle and required a good kick from Arnold both to shut it and open it. Arnold acted as driver, conductor and guide as his precious heap of metal navigated the landscape.

My infrequent trips on his coaches proved to be an education. In the few flights I had, I saw him take on board one pig on a halter, three crates of chickens, a sheep and its lamb, a side of ham, several parcels and packages, a bicycle for repair, umpteen suits for cleaning or laundry for washing in York, and on one occasion he transported an unused coffin from Elsinby's undertaker to a man at Ashfordly who wanted it for timber.

These assorted objects were loaded into the bus via the rear emergency door and I learned that Arnold was paid for these sociable services. In addition to being a carrier of people, he was a carrier of objects and this was accepted quite amicably by his human cargo. If Farmer Jones wished to send a pig to Farmer Brown twenty miles away, Arnold would deliver the said animal by bus for a small fee. It seemed a perfectly sound system, but its legality was in grave doubt.

I knew Arnold had been in buses since leaving school and I reckoned he'd put himself on the road long before officials like the Traffic Commissioners appeared with their P.S.V. licences, certifying officers, certificates of fitness and road service licences. Nonetheless, he displayed in his windscreen the various discs which proved someone knew he was operating a bus service. Even so, the other rules and regulations seemed to be superfluous so far as Merryweather's Coaches were concerned.

His transportation of goods for hire or reward, for example, seemed to put him in the category of a goods vehicle rather than a bus, but it would be a stupid constable who attempted to stop that. After all, the fellow had to earn a living and he was doing a service to the community. I knew lots of house-bound folks depended upon Arnold for their weekly shopping, for he also spent his non-driving hours in York carrying out shopping requests for pensioners, invalids and others. He dealt with the parcels and packages on his bus, suits for the tailor to repair, carpets for the cleaners to clean, sewing-machines to mend, bikes to sell—the whole of society and its well-being made use of Arnold's bus.

Late one winter evening, I was pleased I tolerated his

unofficial enterprises. My little Francis Barnet motor-cycle broke down due to the driving rain which had penetrated the electrical circuits, and the faithful machine completely refused to go. The savagery of the storm meant I could find no place to dry the connections, then salvation arrived in the shape of Arnold's bus. He had taken a trip to the Theatre Royal in York to see a pantomime and his returning head-lights picked me out in the appalling weather. Realising my predicament, Arnold hauled his laden coach to a halt and shouted:

"Stick it in t' back, Mr Rhea."

The rear door was flung open and several willing villagers leapt out. In a matter of seconds, they had manhandled my dripping motor-cycle into the back and we rode home in triumph with the inactive bike held upright by pantomime visitors in their best clothes. Arnold refused to accept pay-ment for this assistance, so I promised to buy him a pint in the pub. For me that would be a real penance because he'd bend my ear for an hour or two on the merits of diesel oil for buses or left-hand-drive models for continental tours.

Even I failed fully to appreciate Arnold's complete service to the public until I took his bus into York one market-day when I was off duty. Mary had a lot of shopping to do and Mrs Quarry took the children; the car was due for a service and it seemed a great idea to make use of Arnold's com-prehensive bus service. Armed with baskets and money, therefore, we waited at Aidensfield one Tuesday morning for Arnold's market-day special. We were surrounded by little old ladies and retired gentlemen, all wondering why we had chosen this mode of transport, and we said it was because of Arnold's world-wide reputation as a busman.

Halfway between Aidensfield and Elsinby, Arnold halted and switched off the engine. We were parked in the middle of nowhere—no houses, no village, no bus-stop. Nothing. No one spoke. They all sat there very quietly and I watched Arnold in his driving-seat. He was reading the *Daily Mirror*. I checked my watch. We were running according to schedule. The fuel was all right, as he'd switched off the engine.

"Why have we stopped?" Mary ventured to ask in a whispered voice.

"I don't know," I had to admit. I didn't dare make a fool of myself by asking the others.

Nothing happened. We must have waited a good ten minutes and by this time we were running late.

Then, as one, the assortment of passengers sighed with relief. I looked out of the window to my nearside and noticed a distant figure hurrying along a winding farm track. It was a farmer's wife, laden with baskets.

I recognised her as she approached.

"It's Mrs Owens," I said to Mary.

"She always goes to market on Tuesdays," breathed Mary. "I've heard her talk about it in the shop. I didn't realise she lived down that lane."

I learned that Mrs Owens travelled on Arnold's bus every Tuesday and he always waited for her. Today she was a little late, but then that could happen to anyone. And so the bus continued.

The next diversion was about a mile out of Elsinby. Suddenly, we swung off the road and along a narrow tarmac lane. We trundled along this winding track for nearly half a mile and then Arnold turned his bus through a farm gate. We were now on a muddy track full of potholes and thick with half-buried rocks. Grass grew down the centre but Arnold's groaning, bouncing old bus negotiated this rough terrain and came to rest in a grubby farmyard.

At this point, he began to crash the gears, seeking reverse. Eventually, with a shudder, the gear slotted home and he began the difficult manoeuvre of turning the bus within the confines of the farmyard. Chickens and ducks scattered, dogs barked and a horse stared in amazement as the purple and cream vehicle moved slowly forwards and backwards, turning gradually until it was facing the way it had come.

"Now what?" Mary grinned.

"A load of manure?" I ventured.

The engine died and someone threw open the rear door. Out jumped about a dozen passengers, just as they had done for my motor-cycle, and I watched them march towards a

small outbuilding. The door was opened and they collected
trays of packed eggs. Dozens and dozens of eggs. They bore
these to the rear of the bus and began to stack them carefully, each tray bearing a dozen fresh farmyard eggs.
Gradually the pile grew until it was as high as the shoulders
of the seated people, and a second pile began. I lost count
but I knew there was an awful lot of eggs. Without a word,
all the volunteer loaders climbed aboard and closed the
door.

But Arnold did not move yet. He waited until a tiny farm
lady appeared. She wore a dull green mackintosh, black
wooden clogs and a headscarf about her head. She carried a
butter-basket in one hand and a hessian bag in the other,
climbed aboard, asked for a "York return" and settled in a
front seat.

And so it continued. We took children to catch trains, old
folks to visit relatives in hospital, but the most amazing was
Arnold's action in York City. The eggs were bound for York
market which is tucked behind the city in a narrow market-
place. Because of sheer numbers, it was impossible to carry
them from Arnold's terminus, so he took his bus and its
load right into the market-place and halted near a stall.

There, the reverse procedure was adopted; the rearmost
passengers flung open the door and the clog-shod little
woman masterminded the operation from outside. Every
tray of eggs was delivered to the market trader who counted
them and paid in cash, as Arnold sat in his seat, ignoring the
hoots of protest from cars and vans around him. As the job
was under way, he disgorged his other passengers and
retreated to his official bus-stop, there to offload his grocery
orders, parcels and messages.

After that first trip, it was a regular sight to see the
familiar shape of Arnold's bus jolting along farm tracks, or
turning around in stackyards, as it took aboard the produce
of the district. Arnold's contribution to the economy of
Ryedale was immense. Although he was supposed to follow
a prescribed route, he totally ignored it and went wherever
he was needed. Somehow he knew who was waiting on any
particular day and he provided what amounted to a house-to-
house bus service. Furthermore, it was expected of him.

With a service of this nature, coupled with his un-authorised diversion into the city centre, it was inevitable that the Traffic Commissioners would learn of his methods. I waited for that day with some trepidation. But it wasn't the Traffic Commissioners who caused my first legal brush with Arnold—it was Claude Jeremiah Greengrass.

Arnold halted his creaking bus at my shoulder one morning as I walked through Aidensfield *en route* to the post-office. His face was like thunder and he was in a highly agitated state. This was most unlike him—Arnold was usually the epitome of pleasantry and *bonhomie*, but it was clear that trouble was afoot.

"Mr Rhea," he hailed me by leaning out of his window.

"Morning, Arnold. Something wrong?"

"I'll say there is." He left his seat and emerged from the bus. On the street, he took my arm and steered me from the flapping ears of his passengers. "It's that bloody man Greengrass."

"Claude Jeremiah? What's he done to you?"

"He's pinching my customers, that's what."

"You don't mean to say he's bought a bus!" I cried, horrified at the ramifications of this and remembering the problems of the pigs and donkey.

"No, he's got an old car, a right old heap it is, Mr Rhea. He's running it ahead of me on my market-day runs, picking folks up and charging them less than me. He's ruining me."

"He can't get many in his car, surely?" I said, wondering what sort of enterprise Claude Jeremiah had evolved.

"I've seen him with seven packed into that old Austin," Arnold growled. "And he comes back before me, charging each customer sixpence less than me. He's taking trade off me, Mr Rhea. He'll have to be stopped."

"I'll have a word with him."

"He needs stopping, Mr Rhea, words are no good. He's behaving illegally, so he is."

"What law is he breaking?" I had been taught a good deal about public service vehicles at Training School and knew sufficient to appreciate that Claude Jeremiah could be running an unlawful public service vehicle. In those days, it was illegal to charge passengers separate fares in private cars, because this brought the car within the realm of a public service vehicle. Besides, ordinary motor-car insurance didn't cover such use so it seemed there'd be an insurance offence too.

I wanted to know if Arnold knew the rules. He did. He promptly reeled off a list of rules and regulations likely to be broken by the enterprising Claude Jeremiah.

"You won't have mentioned this to anyone else, have you?" I put to Arnold.

"No, but I've grumbled a lot, to my passengers, my regulars."

"I was thinking of the Traffic Commissioners," I told him.

"No, should I tell them?" he asked in all innocence.

"They might investigate your affairs too, Arnold—like your carriage of goods for reward. . . ."

"Oh." He saw what I was driving at. "Oh, aye, well. I see. Can this be dealt with quietly, Mr Rhea?"

"If I take Claude Jeremiah to court, Arnold, he might hit back at you; he might complain officially to me about your activities, or he might drop an anonymous line to the Traffic Commissioners about the goods-carrying affairs of Merryweather Coaches."

"I am allowed to carry parcels, Mr Rhea, and passengers are allowed to fetch parcels on board, you know."

"I wouldn't classify a hundred dozen eggs as a parcel, Arnold."

"It's serious, Mr Rhea, I am insured, he's not. You'll have a word with him?"

"I will," I promised. "But you should be more careful about carrying parcels, eh?"

In the seclusion of my office, I settled down with my books to refresh my memory on the laws about public service vehicles, or PSVs as we knew them. I knew they fell into three groups—a stage carriage was one which carried passengers at separate fares while not fulfilling the definition of an express carriage. The ordinary town service bus or a rural bus were typical examples. An express carriage was a PSV carrying passengers at separate fares none of which was less than one shilling or some other prescribed greater sum. Long-distance express coaches fitted this definition, like the overnight runs to London or Liverpool. The third was a contract carriage which did not carry passengers at separate fares—like a bus hired to take a party to the theatre or a football match.

The other rules and case law on buses were highly complicated with many exceptions and provisos. I concluded that if Claude Jeremiah was charging his passengers separate fares for their trips he was operating a public service vehicle. The appearance of his vehicle was immaterial. This meant he was breaking umpteen rules of the road, including motor insurance offences, public service vehicle licence offences and a host of others.

The first job was to prove that Claude Jeremiah's old banger was a bus, and that meant catching him with a full load of paying passengers. After having words with Arnold about the most beneficial time to halt Claude's motor, I arranged to position myself one morning on a wide stretch of road at the far boundary of my beat. This was the route taken by Claude Jeremiah, and it was an ideal place to halt a moving vehicle. Furthermore, he would have a full load by the time he reached this place.

Sure enough, soon after quarter past nine, the distant rumble of the ancient car reached my ears as it laboured towards the lofty boundary of Aidensfield beat. I was in full uniform and stepped impressively into the centre of the road as the rattling machinery approached. With a screech of brakes and a multitudinous banging and clattering, the old car groaned to a halt and Claude Jeremiah wound down his window.

"Morning, Mr Rhea." His tiny brown face creased into an uneasy grin as he regarded me from his driving-seat. "Want a lift?"

"Morning, Claude Jeremiah. Full load, eh?" I stooped to peer inside. The car was packed with people and I counted nine heads including the driver. They were chiefly grey-haired ladies, as tight as baby wrens in their nest.

"Aye, just giving some friends a lift into York," he said.

"Do you mind if I have a word with them?" I asked.

"Summat important, is it?" shrilled a woman's voice from inside. "We've a busy day, Mr Policeman. We go like this because it's quicker than yon bus, trundling down farm tracks and the like, delivering eggs and pigs. Mr Greengrass gets us there on time. . . ."

"Are you a taxi then?" I asked him.

"No, just a friendly cove giving pals a lift—being community-spirited, in a manner of speaking, Mr Rhea."

"What is the cost of your trip?" I asked the passengers.

"Half a crown apiece," said a woman. "Two bob if you get on at Elsinby."

"Look, Mr Rhea." Claude climbed from his car and stood on the road, facing me. "I'm doing a public service. I can do a return trip cheaper than Merryweather and I get them there quicker. Tell me what's wrong with that."

"By doing what you are doing—" I tried to sound professionally knowledgeable and adopted an official tone— "you are fulfilling the role of a bus. That means you need licensing as a bus. You are therefore operating without the necessary licences. And you are not insured."

"He's doing us a favour, Mr Rhea, giving us a lift. If we decide to tip him a half dollar or pay for the petrol, that's up to us. . . ."

"It's not as easy as that, Mrs Prescott," I said. "There are rules to obey and careful safety regulations to follow. . . ."

"If an accident happened to any of you in this car," I said, "your families would not get compensation. Claude is not insured for paying passengers—he's running a hell of a risk because he can't afford to pay for your injuries or loss."

"He's a taxi. . . ," bellowed a deep-voiced woman from within.

"He's not a taxi, not when he charges separate fares and picks you up at stages, and he's not licensed as a hackney-carriage either. If he wants to do this sort of thing, he could get licensed as a hackney-carriage. . . ."

"Look Mr Rhea. . . ."

The situation was getting out of hand. By now, all the irate ladies had disembarked and were standing around glaring at me and their voices began to rise with irritation and anger as I pathetically tried to explain the rules and to point out the risks to themselves. But it was futile. No one wanted to know the intricacies of public service vehicle licensing laws—all they wanted was to get into the shops as quickly as possible.

"Right!" I shouted. "Listen to me," and I banged on the roof of the car to emphasise my words.

Silence fell.

"Claude Jeremiah is breaking the law in several ways, and I intend to take action against him," I said sternly. "And if you agree to go along with him in this you are also aiding and abetting him. That means you could all go to court, everyone of you."

Their gabbling stopped and now they listened carefully as I explained their liability, but as I talked I heard the approaching music of Arnold's bus. It was heading this way, as I knew it would, and it was making hard work of climbing the hill towards our present position. I kept the women there, talking in graphic detail about the fearsome penalties that could be inflicted upon those who aided and abetted the functioning of illegal buses.

As the bus appeared in view, I told them it would take me an hour to interview Claude Jeremiah about the miscellaneous offences that had been disclosed, and at this juncture the strident voice of Mrs Prescott shouted:

"Claude Jeremiah—give us our money back. We're catching that bus. . . ."

"But. . . ." He stared at me and then at them.

"It could prevent you going to court," I added slyly.

He began to fumble in his pockets and by this time the bus was upon us. I raised my hand and halted Arnold's onward progress.

"Morning, Arnold. Going to York?"

"Aye, Mr Rhea. Got some passengers for me, have you?"

"There's a few ladies in need of urgent transport to York," I said.

"There's room enough in here," he told me and I climbed in for a look.

"Your aisles are not blocked, I see," I smiled. "No crates of eggs or manacled pigs blocking the exits?"

"No, Mr Rhea, I run a properly conducted public service vehicle."

And I happened to see that all 22 passengers had on their knees four or five egg-boxes, all full. A hundred dozen eggs. . . .

"All these ladies and gentlemen are taking eggs into York market," he said, smiling at me.

"I don't want to know about their private arrangements." I left the bus and watched Claude's passengers clamber aboard. They paid their fares and with a double hoot of the horn the old bus rumbled on its way.

"That was nasty of you, Mr Rhea," Claude grumbled.

"I've saved you from a fate worse than death!" I countered. "If the Traffic Commissioners had got hold of you, my lad, your feet would never touch the ground. I'm not taking you to court on this occasion, Claude Jeremiah, although I should do so. Regard this as a warning—no more pinching bus passengers. If you want to make money with your car, get yourself licensed as a taxi."

"Yes, Mr Rhea."

He looked dejected, but I think it was for the best. If I'd taken him to court, there would have been a long, involved and highly controversial case about what constitutes a bus, and I was happy to let him go with an unofficial warning.

"Do I need a licence to carry other things then?" he asked me with a crafty gleam in his eyes.

"Other things?" I asked.

"Well, folks keep asking me to deliver things in York, you see. . . . carry stuff for them. . . ."

I stared at him and said, "Open your boot, Claude Jeremiah."

He gingerly opened it and it was full of cartons of fresh eggs.

"If you convey goods for hire or reward, you need a goods vehicle licence," I informed him. "And you need a special excise licence. . . ."

"I'll have to take those back then," he said.

"I haven't seen those, Claude, not today. I might stop and inspect your boot another day. . . ."

"Thank you, Mr Rhea, thank you."

He locked the boot, jumped inside his old car and roared away in a cloud of oily fumes.

Perhaps it seemed a little unfair to let Arnold's bus continue to carry eggs, pigs and the like, but Claude was too much of a risk to allow loose upon the public with his car. In his case, people could suffer awful consequences—in Arnold's case, only Arnold could suffer.

If the soft-glove treatment worked on this occasion, I would be pleased, but I wondered how long it would be before we had the Greengrass Taxi Line. A shudder ran down my spine.

For the next few months I had little contact with Merryweather Coaches and, so far as I know, Arnold never experienced a visitation by the Traffic Commissioners. I felt it unwise to check too closely upon his goods-carrying activities because he did provide a service to isolated rural communities. For Arnold, therefore, business began to boom. Contrary to the national trend, his bus service gathered more and more passengers and he felt obliged to employ a conductress to ease his burden.

He had found that his precious time was being consumed at every stop; he spent many useful minutes issuing tickets or delivering change and reckoned that if he paid for the services of a conductress much time and effort would be saved. Furthermore, his passengers would receive a swifter service. He placed an advert in every post-office window of the district and some eight or nine ladies made rapid application for the post. This was long before the days of the Sex Discrimination Act and it is possible that Arnold envisaged a delightful creature of exceptional beauty parading the length of his coach, but in this sense the sun did not shine on Arnold.

None of the seven hopefuls could even be described as remotely attractive, although five could count money and one knew how to change a wheel. After interviewing each woman, Arnold settled for Miss Hannah Pybus, whose name led to many nicknames aboard the coach. Some of the children called her Fly-Bus or Hannah Wide-Bus, the latter being due to the somewhat extensive measurement of her hips.

Hannah was a spinster of the parish of Thackerston and was in her fifties. She had lived with her retired father for years, never working at a normal job but spending her time looking after the old man. He had died several months ago and she now needed an outlet. The opportunity of a job which took her free of charge into conurbations like Ashfordly and Elsinby, and into that far-off place of York, was a godsend. A whole new world opened for Hannah Pybus.

It was sad that Hannah was not in the least attractive in her appearance. From a distance, there could be considerable doubt as to whether she was male or female, for she was almost six feet tall, with a frame like a battleship and hips like the proverbial rear-end of an African bull elephant. Stout, trunk-like legs supported her massive frame and she walked with a strange, sailor-like motion, as if throwing her body forward in an attempt to keep it mobile. Her shapeless, outdated clothes concealed any semblance of breasts or waistline while her face was heavy about the jowls with sandy-coloured tufts of hair sprouting from all manner of odd places. She had a freckled face with pale brown eyes and a mop of sandy-coloured hair on top, the strands held in place with tortoiseshell slides with a thick red ribbon at the back.

Being a lady of leisure, therefore, she embarked on her new job with characteristic gusto, cycling daily from her cottage at Thackerston to Arnold's depot at Ashfordly, some six or seven miles. Her cycle had a basket on the front and a wire skirt-guard at each side of the rear wheel. Somehow she forced the pedals of her gallant machine to carry her up the long incline to Aidensfield Bank Top before gathering speed for the remaining four-mile run into Ashfordly.

After Arnold had explained the intricacies of his ticket machine and accounting system, he took off for York with Hannah aboard. She was clad in a shapeless gown coloured purple and cream to match his coaching colours and looked like a statue awaiting its unveiling ceremony. In her enthusiasm as the first passenger entered, she pounced on him and demanded his destination. He paid all the way to York, even though he only wanted to go to Elsinby.

Within a week, she was totally in charge. Arnold told me he'd never seen anything like it. Hardly had the last passenger boarded at any given stop, than Hannah rang the bell to send him along his route. There were no delays now. She proceeded to allocate seats to the passengers, leaving them no choice in the matter, and demanded their fares while making sure they behaved. Children quaked when she appeared, old men didn't dare smoke their foul pipes and the village gossips watched their language as Hannah hovered around, eagle-eyed and always anxious to please her boss.

There is little doubt that Arnold and his finances benefited from her presence. He was able to concentrate upon his driving and maintenance, while Hannah cared for the interiors of the two buses. She polished and washed, swept and tidied, and she seldom made an error with the cash. The general behaviour of passengers, especially children and drunks, improved tremendously and the net result was that more people used Merryweather Coaches. They seemed happy to obey Hannah when on board. Arnold was in his sixth heaven and, whenever I saw him in the Brewers Arms, he talked incessantly of bus-conductresses, buses and bus routes. For him, Hannah provided a new dimension in his life, but for the regulars in the pub they grew just as sick of Hannah as they did with every other facet of bus-lore. Even so, they all agreed that it was nice to see Arnold so happy.

There was even talk of a romance between the unlikely pair, although it was universally agreed that the man who took Hannah in all her prime showed gallantry of the highest order or foolishness of the most awful kind. Nothing developed along those lines while I was at Aidensfield, although I did note Arnold's starry eyes as he talked about Hannah's role in his coaching enterprise. Maybe there was something there? Maybe he did drive her home after the last trip, with her cycle in the rear and his hands on the wheel?

It is quite true to say that the entire community was delighted at the success of Arnold's venture. The little bus company with its huge conductress did a roaring trade and Hannah did allow some parcels to be carried. She had studied the *Conduct of Drivers, Conductors and Passengers Regulations 1936 and 1946*, consequently she knew which goods were permitted and which had never to be brought aboard. She knew that she must never talk to the driver when driving, unless for safety reasons, and she appreciated that it was her duty to enforce the regulations relating to the conduct of passengers, and to see that the route, fare and destination notices were properly displayed.

Hannah enforced the rules most carefully. She enforced those which said passengers had not to be disorderly, that they had to enter and alight in the correct manner and not through skylights or windows, that they had not to distract the driver's attention, nor distribute notices or advertising matter aboard the bus. She had learned that they must not play noisy instruments or throw bottles, coins and litter about the place, nor allow any banners, flags or streamers to overhang the road outside. She made sure they did not soil the vehicle or be offensive, either in behaviour or clothing. Loaded firearms had not to be taken on board, nor had any other offensive article and no one could bring an animal aboard without the consent of an authorised person. Hannah reckoned she was authorised to refuse the pigs, lambs, hens and goats although she did tolerate such creatures if the accompanying adult would clean up the mess and keep the creature under control.

Hannah knew that she had wide powers to enforce the observance of these rules, and that a constable was also given like powers. If any passenger contravened the regulations, he had to give his name and address on demand to the driver or conductor, or to a constable, and such a person could be removed from the bus by either the driver or the conductor, or by a constable if requested by those officials.

It was difficult to envisage an occasion when I would be called to act officially, for I knew Hannah would quell any riot by the merest glance of those pale eyes, but one Wednesday afternoon I found myself involved in what appeared to be an infringement of the *Conduct of Drivers, Conductors and Passengers Regulations*.

I was in my office at home, writing reports, when Arnold's bus halted outside and a very distraught Hannah hurried down the path. I opened the door to admit her, for she was clearly distressed. I gathered from her first words that a passenger had infringed the rules in a rather peculiar way.

"Calm down, Hannah!" I said. "Take a deep breath and then tell me about it."

She took a huge breath, enough to drain a hot-air balloon, and her colossal bosom swelled behind my counter and threatened to dislodge the typewriter. But the trick worked, for her face lost its initial look of horror and disgust, and she sighed.

"By jove, Mr Rhea, it was a nasty shock, I can tell you."

"Come in and sit down." I lifted the flap on the office counter and invited her in for a seat. She settled down and refused a cup of tea; Arnold was waiting outside in the bus and would take her home. She'd give him a cup in her house and would have hers then. He wouldn't come in, she said, as he found it all too embarrassing.

"So what happened on that bus?" I asked.

She swallowed hard and I could see she was acutely embarrassed.

"It was a man," she said. "He. . . . er. . . . well, he broke the rules about the conduct of passengers. . . . he was offensive," she added quickly.

"Dirty clothing? Been cleaning out his pigs, had he?"

"No," she said, gritting her teeth. "It was worse than that, Mr Rhea, much, much worse."

"Go on, I must know what he did if I am to take action."

She swallowed again.

I waited.

"He. . . . look, Mr Rhea, I'm not very good at explaining things. . . ."

"I'm good at listening," I assured her. "Take your time."

She paused, clearly trying to select the right words to describe her ordeal, and all the time my curiosity was increasing. What on earth had happened aboard Merryweather Coaches to create such an effect upon the redoubtable Hannah Pybus?

"He was indecent." She managed to spit out the word.

"Indecent?" I asked. "How? Did he swear at you?"

She shook that pale gingery head.

"No, it was worse than that. I'm not fussy about a swearword or two, Mr Rhea. This was worse than any swearword."

"Go on." I was getting interested now. Had he taken a grab at her? Some passengers weren't slow in smacking the shapely bottoms of conductresses, but I couldn't imagine anyone being so fuddled as to smack Hannah's spacious rump regions. Maybe a drunken passenger had done that, or seized her by some other part of her towering frame? The thought was astonishing.

"He exposed himself at me." She lowered her head and blushed furiously as the words emerged.

"Indecent exposure?" I asked. "On a bus?"

"Yes," she said, relaxing now she had clarified the situation.

Immediately, my Training School knowledge began to click within the farmost regions of my mind. Indecent exposure was a public nuisance if it was done *publicly*. If Hannah alone had seen the object in question, it might not be an indictable common law offence. There being no public viewing. The Vagrancy Act, 1824, section 4, offered a possible solution because it created a summary offence for a man to wilfully, openly, lewdly and obscenely expose the person with intent to insult a female. Nothing said what "the person" meant here, but most of us had a good idea. If the fellow intended to insult Hannah, that provision might fit the circumstances. The Town Police Clauses Act 1847 also created an offence of indecent exposure if it occurred in any street to the annoyance of residents or passengers. Arnold's bus wasn't a street, so I had to rule out the latter offence. Because the Common Law offence must be proved to be a *public* display I was left with the Vagrancy Act and its quaint Victorian phraseology.

On a bus? I knew there were no buses when the Vagrancy

Act came into force, but happily that old law, still in force, left the situation sufficiently open to cater for such crimes. Besides, the *Conduct of Drivers, Conductors and Passengers Regulations of 1936* and *1946* would cope with the fellow, if all else failed. I felt I could proceed with the matter.

"An indecent exposure on a bus, Hannah. Would you say you were insulted?" I had to ask this in order to prove the case, should it ever reach court. It was part of the Victorian wording of the statute.

"Insulted! I was mortified!" she said, hurt at my question.

"I have to ask, as it's an essential ingredient of the offence. The lady must be insulted if I am to take action."

"I was grossly insulted!" she stressed.

With her use of words like this, I was reminded of the police recruit who defined Gross Indecency as "Indecency between a large number of persons, 144, I think".

"Who was the man?" I asked next.

"I don't know his name, but he got on at York. He was all right until I went for his fare. He got off at that lane end, just before you get into Elsinby from York."

"You'd know him again?"

She nodded. "Oh yes, I'd know him again!"

"Did you tell anyone at the time?"

"No, I didn't want to upset the passengers. I told Arnold when we got to the terminus and he said I'd better mention it to you."

"Certainly. Well, it looks as if he lives on my beat. What's he like?"

She described a man about fifty years old, with grey hair and an unshaven appearance. He was a small man, she said, wearing a dirty raincoat and heavy black boots. All flashers wore dirty raincoats, I thought. This one fitted the traditional pattern.

Having described him quite well, I had to ask her precisely what he had done. It was important from the prosecution point of view.

She blushed furiously once again and asked, "Do I really have to tell you?"

"I'm afraid so. I must know precisely what he did, Hannah, if I'm to take any action."

"Well," she said. "Er. . . . his trousers front was open and . . . it . . . his thing . . . it was sticking right out."

"Did he draw your attention to it?"

"Yes, he did!" she snapped.

"How?" I asked.

"He placed his fare on it, for me to take."

"His fare?" I almost doubled up with laughter at this latest technique, but managed to keep a straight face.

"Yes, he spread the money out, right along it."

"And how much was his fare?"

"A shilling," she said. "He laid it out, right along his thing."

"What sort of coins were they?" I was fascinated now.

"Pennies," she said calmly. "Twelve pennies."

My mind boggled. Side by side, they'd cover a large area, but twelve £.s.d. pennies laid out in a line covered an enormous distance, nearly fifteen inches. I made her repeat this. I had to be sure I got it right. Who was this man, I wondered? It looked as if we had a world record-breaker in the locality.

"And?" I asked.

"Well, I refused to accept them. . . ." she said pertly. "I made him collect them himself and pay his fare."

"And did he?"

"Yes, he did!"

"And then he put it away?"

"I don't know. He was all alone on the back seat and I didn't stay a minute longer."

If my report of this event reached Force Headquarters, the place would be in uproar and every member of the police service would be jealous. I could imagine a stampede to check the veracity of this claim, but one's constabulary duty must be done.

"Thanks, Hannah. I'll make enquiries and I'll let you know how I get on. You go home now and have that cup of tea with Arnold."

She left the office and, as the bus rumbled out of sight I

collapsed in a fit of laughter. I'd never heard anything like this before and felt sure Hannah had made a mistake. What had she seen? I racked my brains to identify the fellow and then I realised who it was.

Poor Hannah!

But, first, I had to check my theory. I jumped aboard the little Francis Barnett and chugged over the valley to Elsinby. Through the village, I turned left along a rough lane until I arrived at Bankside Cottage. I knocked, for I knew old Bill Firby was at home. Smoke was rising from his chimney. Soon the green door was opened and Bill stood there, his jacket open and his face registering surprise when he saw me.

"Hello, Mr Rhea." He stood back to invite me in. "You're a stranger at my door."

"Aye," I agreed, entering his cosy home. "It's not often I have cause to call on you."

"Summat up, is it?" He led me into his sitting-room where a cosy fire burned, and pointed to an armchair. I settled with my crash-helmet on my lap.

"Bill, you're going to laugh when I've finished this tale, but I need your answers first. Were you on the bus out of York today?"

"Aye," he said. "Yes, I was."

"And Hannah was conductress?"

"She was."

"And did you pay your fare all in pennies?"

"Aye, I hadn't a shilling piece, so I used pennies. Nowt wrong with that, is there?"

"No, there isn't." I laughed now. "You've cleared up a massive problem for me."

"I have?"

The truth was that Bill had only one hand. His left hand was missing at the wrist, and that arm terminated in an irregular fleshy stump. He wore no covering and no false hand. On the bus, his fare had been in his right-hand pocket and in order to count it he had pulled up his left sleeve to expose his arm from his elbow down to his wrist. To gain stability for his stump, he had placed his elbow on his lap, tucking it firmly into his groin, and he rested his wrist on his right leg. He had then laid out the coins for Hannah to count, placing them along his arm.

Hannah, poor unmarried woman, had totally misunderstood this innocent action.

When I told him the essence of her complaint, he laughed until tears rolled down his eyes and asked if I was going to tell her the truth.

"Yes, of course," I assured him.

"Nay, lad, don't do that. Think of my reputation if she spreads that tale around. I'll be the envy of all the blokes for miles around!"

But I had to tell Hannah the truth. I did and she listened intently; happily, she laughed when I explained Bill's fare-paying technique. Whenever he travelled by bus or paid in a shop, he always used that system, I explained.

"Oh," she said. "Silly of me. I'm sorry to have troubled you Mr Rhea. I will apologise to Mr Firby when I see him."

"He's not worried," I said. "There's no need to bother yourself any more about it."

"Thank you, Mr Rhea," she beamed and I left her comfortable house.

On reflection, that little episode raised more questions about Hannah's past than it solved. Until then, we had assumed she had never had a man friend, but perhaps she had.

We all wondered who it might have been.

7

"Crabbed age and youth cannot live together;
Youth is full of pleasance, age is full of care."
   William Shakespeare, 1564–1616, "The Passionate Pilgrim"

It has been said that the duties of a police officer do not include social work. In theory, there are skilled professionals to undertake such responsibilities, but in practice the work of a police officer does include a whole range of jobs which could be classified as social work. The conscientious constable visits the sick, the lame, the infirm and the aged because one of his basic functions is to protect life and property. If he can call upon those in need of help, he might save a life or prevent damage to property. His presence is often reassuring to the lonely and frightened.

The rural bobby in particular spends a good deal of his time, on and off duty, visiting the aged upon his beat. I was no exception.

During my daily tour I would drop in, unannounced, upon many pensioners and have a cup of tea with them. I think Sergeant Blaketon frowned upon this; he never said so because I had pre-empted any criticism from him by stressing that I considered this to be an important part of a rural constable's work. He suffered my cups of tea in silence and I got the impression he resented my free tea rather than the time I spent indoors chatting for no apparent constabulary purpose. Sergeant Blaketon was one of the old school; he liked policemen to be seen and he liked them to be always asking questions about unsolved crimes or seeking criminal information from likely sources. He failed to appreciate the very basic social requirements of the job.

While law-enforcement is a vital part of the constable's task, it is no more important than the welfare of those under the constable's care, and I made certain he knew how I felt.

Gradually, I learned of the whereabouts of the lonely aged on my patch; I was not too concerned about those who lived with their families, or even those with families living nearby. I needed to know about the widowed and lonely, the isolated person with no relatives to call upon. These were my concern—they might be suffering from illness, or they might have fallen and hurt themselves; they might be plagued by stupid vandals or be the butt of confidence tricksters . . . all kinds of social evils can befall an elderly person living alone and I wanted no villainy against those residing on my beat.

Visiting these marvellous old folks was a wonderful experience. There was a man of 92 who had made ornamental buttons for Queen Victoria; a lady of 87 who recalled seeing Queen Victoria when she visited the district in 1900 and a man of 83 who fell down an apple-tree and who pleaded me not to tell his wife how he'd hurt his back. I liked the man of 88 who was ill and, when I asked if he wanted me to tell anyone, he asked me to notify his school-teacher, a Miss Wilkinson. She'd taught him as a boy in primary school and, thinking he was senile, I checked—she was still alive and enjoying the sunshine in Eltering, aged 98!

Yorkshire folk are noted for their contemptuous attitude to old age. It is merely a nuisance to them, something like a nagging illness. No self-respecting Yorkshireman will admit to being ill. They fight illness by pretending it doesn't exist, and will continue working through ailments that would fell lesser mortals.

This stubborn attitude is shown in a lovely tale about a young lady newspaper reporter who called to see a Yorkshire villager. He had reached 100 years of age and was inside his house as the reporter talked to his daughter.

"You must be very proud of your father," the reporter commented.

"Oh, Ah don't know," replied his daughter. "He's done

nowt but grow old, and look how long it's taken him to do that!"

The elderly crack jokes among themselves, such as "Awd Sam's refusing to die because it saves funeral expenses", while another in his nineties commented, "When Ah was a lad, Ah used to get oot o' bed ivvery morning at five, but now Ah's gittin on a bit, it's very near six before Ah stir."

Those with a literary turn of mind might consider the words written by the poet Edward Spenser which so aptly sum up the feeling of creeping senility. He wrote:

> "The careful cold hath nipt my rugged rind,
> And in my face deep furrows old hath plight;
> My head besprent with hoary frost I find,
> And by mine eyes the crow his claw doth wright;
> Delight is laid about and pleasure past;
> No sun now shines, clouds have all over-cast."

One wonders what he knew about old age, because he died in 1599 at the ripe old age of 46.

In reality, however, I found the aged had minds of their own. Their opinions, which had been nurtured over many generations, were so firmly established that no amount of argument or discussion would shift them. I had to accept this as a fact of life. Change is not welcome in the land of the aged. Memories of loved ones do feature in this tough, inflexible attitude and can lead to a softening manner or even a change of opinion. Such a case involved old Mrs Ada Flanagan of Aidensfield and her easy-chair.

The chair was nothing special to look at. It was of simple design and rather old-fashioned for it had wings at the back and castors beneath which squeaked every time it moved. The upholstery was dull grey but this lack of glamour was concealed by a faded cover of deep-blue material, offset with a floral design. Mrs Flanagan had made the covers herself some ten or fifteen years ago and was undoubtedly proud of her handicraft. She called it Bill's chair.

That the chair needed a new cover was obvious to me, but

I sensed it was imprudent to even suggest it. Although she'd asked me not to sit in that chair, I think she welcomed my visits for she would make me a cup of tea when I called, usually around eleven o'clock on a morning. In respect for her wishes, I would never sit in that chair to drink it, always using a dining-chair at the table. Bill's chair was always in the same position, I noticed, just to the right of the fireside. There it was close enough to the mantelpiece for Old Bill to have reached out for his pipe or tobacco, or his racing papers.

Through those regular visits, I learned all about Bill's chair. He had occupied it every evening after work and in retirement had used it during the day as well. He liked it exactly where it now stood, and she was determined that it should remain there.

I whiled away many hours drinking Mrs Flanagan's tea and listening to her constant chatter as she either ironed or baked on the table before me.

She would talk about her childhood in Ireland and how she went potato-picking on her father's farm. I knew it had been a struggle to earn a living; then, when she was twenty, she had married Bill Flanagan. He'd always wanted to go to Scotland—and so he had, with his young wife.

That old chair had been one of their first possessions as man and wife. Sometimes she would laugh as she told me how they would both use it—they would sit in it together because they had nothing else! She would sit on Bill's knee and they'd chat together as only a young couple can; this chair had been their joy until they could afford more furniture.

In Scotland, their fortunes had improved and Bill had found a good job on a farm; gradually they built their little home, with this chair always occupying the prime position near the fireside.

As my first year as the village bobby passed, it seemed as if I was an old friend to Mrs Flanagan. Perhaps I was because I knew all about her wishes, hopes, sadnesses and past history. We knew each other very well, I felt. I also felt I knew old Bill; although he'd died long before I came to Aidensfield, her stories had made him live anew. Sometimes I could almost see him in that battered old chair, so vivid were her memories.

Then, quite unexpectedly, Mrs Flanagan started to go out to work. I was quite surprised, but she told me she did this to occupy herself and to earn a few coppers. Her new part-time job was to cover chairs and furniture, or make curtains. She told me she used to do that sort of work when she was younger but in those days her skills had been confined to the family or for the benefit of close friends. She'd never thought about doing it professionally, but had seen an advert in the local paper.

It had been placed by a department store in Ashfordly who sought a seamstress capable of covering chairs and making curtains on a part-time basis. The work entailed some travelling to take measurements in the homes of customers, all of whom lived locally, while the actual sewing could be done at the seamstress's home.

For Mrs Flanagan it was the ideal job and she was appointed. I could see it was the making of her.

Then, quite suddenly, I noticed the chair had gone. One morning as I called, I could see that Old Bill's chair was no longer before the hearth and in its place was a modern chair with slender wooden arms. I'd seen this one before, in Mrs Flanagan's front room when I'd been in for sherry and Christmas cake.

So from that day forward I sat in that new chair for my cups of tea, but I didn't dare ask the whereabouts of the old blue one. Perhaps some bygone memory had upset her? I didn't dare risk an upset by referring to it, so left my questions unasked.

Nowadays she chatted to me and made my usual cups of tea as she told me of the people she met during her travels and how nice they all were. She used the buses, or a taxi if it was urgent, and I knew the job had given her a new lease of life.

Sometimes I found her ironing chair-covers and curtains as well as her own washing. But I still wondered what had happened to Old Bill's chair?

Where had it gone? Why had she moved it? It was really no concern of mine although I often felt like asking about it.

Maybe it was linked with her acceptance of this job? But I never asked.

Then one summer morning, I called as usual but she didn't hear me enter. I had knocked and walked in like I always did, but she was busy in the front room. I could hear her old but efficient sewing-machine whirring away, so I stepped across the floor to tap on the front room door.

She stopped her work; the door opened and I saw the old treadle machine with yards of material strewn about it. She had a mouth full of pins and the floor was covered with paper patterns and cut pieces. I was surprised to see such a large amount of cloth but I was equally surprised to notice the material was the same colour and pattern as that battered old cover on Bill's chair. Was she covering his chair? Here was a new design, an exact copy of that old one, but all this material for one chair?

She smiled as I entered and took the pins out of her mouth.

"Go and sit down," she said. "I've got to finish this edge and I'll be through."

"Don't rush and spoil it," I told her. "I'll make the tea!"

Her quiet smile told me that this was a good idea, so I left her to continue her work. I knew where everything was and before long had the kettle boiling. When I made the tea she came to join me and brought a length of cloth which she hand-stitched as we chatted.

We talked about the weather, the news, the village problems and a young couple down the road who were expecting their first child. Occasionally we lapsed into silence as she came to a tricky part of her work; throughout, I watched her quietly.

In some ways, my time in her house was like stepping back half a century—there were the worn beams, the ponderous tick of the grandfather clock, the black-leaded iron grate and its glowing fire which invariably crackled and spat with logs newly cut. The brasses shone and the windows glittered after years of methodic housework.

I enjoyed the peace and atmosphere of this place. Mrs Flanagan had captured the slow-moving rhythm of her life and her mode of existence was the epitome of country life. I liked it.

"You know," I spoke after a spell of silence, "I'd miss this cup of tea and chat, Mrs Flanagan. I really look forward to it. I'm pleased you don't work full-time."

"So am I," she said, "and it's nice to talk to somebody who doesn't pass on everything I say!"

These confidences were clearly something she treasured and yet we had never reached the Christian-name stage. I always called her Mrs Flanagan and would no more dream of using her first name than she would of using mine. We were friends but kept our distance and our chats were confined to these occasional visits. Maybe that's why our talks were so successful—in some way, I was like one of those anonymous people who answer letters and give advice in magazines and newspaper columns. I was someone she could trust with her innermost thoughts and I knew we had a fine platonic relationship and eventually I knew that I could safely broach the subject of Old Bill's chair, more so because she was working with material which was an exact replica of that which covered his absent fireside friend.

"That's nice material." I pointed to the piece in her hands. "Is it an urgent job?"

"For the weekend," she answered. "The van is coming for it on Friday afternoon. It's for a young couple over at Fernley. Their parents gave them an old three-piece suite to start their home and they wanted it covering. It'll look nice when it's finished—it's a real good suite, you know. One of the type which seem to last for ever."

"They made things to last in those days," I said.

She nodded and there was another pause.

"It's exactly the same as the pattern on Bill's chair," I spoke slowly.

Perhaps I shouldn't have said it! Immediately the words were out, I regretted having said them. But I needn't have worried.

"I know," she spoke quietly. "It's funny really. Here I am, covering furniture for a young couple with material which is exactly the same I used for our first chair—the very first bit of furniture we had, me and Bill."

There was no finer moment to ask about Old Bill's chair.

"Where is his chair, Mrs Flanagan? You haven't sold it, have you?"

She shook her head. "It's upstairs, in the spare room."

"I liked that chair," I told her. "It looked so comfy and warm."

"It was Bill's," she said simply.

I didn't answer. Perhaps she didn't want to talk about it any more, and that last brief sentence told me everything. Because it was Bill's, she wouldn't want to give it away or sell it, and yet for the same reason she wouldn't want it in this room where it would constantly remind her of his absence, especially when others tried to sit in it.

But she was talking again.

"I always wanted to cover it for him," she was saying. "I did it years ago and he liked it so much that he didn't want any other pattern on it."

"It was nice," I said briefly.

She was in full flow now. "It became very shabby, you know. He would sit in it after work, often in his working clothes and it got awfully dirty. I washed the covers time and time again to try and keep them fresh-looking."

"It was always nice when I came," I added.

"Yes, but it was so worn, wasn't it? Faded and thread-bare."

"And he didn't want another cover! Was that why you moved it, because it was getting shabby?"

She shook her head. "No, not really. It was my Bill's chair, you see. He didn't want me to touch it—he loved it just as it was, you understand. Well, if I'd had it in this room, I'd be itching to re-cover it. And Bill wouldn't want that."

"So you put it out of temptation's way?"

"Yes. I wouldn't part with it, not for the world, so the spare bedroom was the best place. I use it sometimes myself, when I'm dusting upstairs. I use it to have a sit down, you understand, and it gets dusted regularly."

"Why didn't he want it re-covering?" I asked, feeling that we could talk freely.

"He didn't tell me."

"Can't you guess?"

"I think I can," she answered slowly. "I covered that chair specially for him. He found the material in a shop years and years ago, and it was just what he wanted. He grew attached to it—he wasn't a fellow for changing things without good reason."

"I know," I sympathised, "men get like that. But you could cover it now, couldn't you?"

"Do you really think so?" Her eyes sparkled with new interest and I knew she'd been wanting someone to say that.

"With this new material," I continued. "It's exactly the same as Bill's chair—he would love that, wouldn't he?"

"It's just what he always wanted," she whispered. "We looked in all the shops for this colour but never found it. Not in all our years. All the shops said it was too old-fashioned and out of stock."

"That was a few years ago," I reminded her. "And now that same pattern is right in fashion again. That often happens—I know Bill would agree now, wouldn't he?"

"Thank you," for her only reply, and I rose to leave, then she said, "Would you like to see the finished covers?"

Puzzled, I followed her into the workroom and there I saw a fourth cover, shaped differently from the rest, and admired the style and loving workmanship it contained. When I called the next time, Old Bill's chair was back in its place before the fire, looking regal and splendid in its new cover.

It was a perfect complement to this room.

"I'll make the tea now," she said. "You sit there."

And she pointed to Old Bill's chair.

One of my favourite characters was Simon Rawlings, a gentleman of 87 who lived with his daughter in a tiny cottage at Elsinby. Tall and erect, he had a guardsman's figure and even though his broad back was stooped with his great age he always tried to walk upright. It was a display of his deep personal pride.

Awd Simon, as the village knew him, was a retired railwayman. He had retired 22 years ago, long before the railways were nationalised, and lived quietly, his wife having been dead nine or ten years. Awd Simon passed his time by gardening and enjoying a pipe of tobacco, plus the occasional pint in the Hopbind Inn. For his age, he was impressive to behold. A good six feet tall, he must have weighed seventeen stone and was built like an ox. The village was full of stories of his young strength, but he was a gentle giant with a lovely touch of humour and a kind word for everyone and everything, man and animal alike.

I got to know him because he spent some sunny afternoons on the seat near the War Memorial and I made myself known to him very early in my period at Aidensfield. I quickly discovered he still lived for the railways, but not the modern diesel engines with their rows of anonymous coaches and hooting horns. Awd Simon worshipped the lovely polished green of the LNER and the maroon livery of the LMS, the romantic days of steam and high-quality service.

As I got acquainted with him, I found it easy to get him reminiscing about his time with the London and North Eastern Railway Company, where he'd worked his way up from track maintenance to fireman, and he'd even been a guard. He told me of the beautiful engines with their own names and distinctive personalities; coaches with splendid first-class compartments and brass fittings. There were pictures of landscapes to interest the passengers and it was essential that the timetables be maintained at all costs. Fear of competition from the maroon giants of the London Midland and Scottish Railway was always present and the company served its customers as a faithful servant would obey his master. Everything had to be right. Second-best would not be tolerated.

He told me about the coal fires in the waiting-rooms, the huge watering-tanks for engines to take on supplies, and the gorgeous floral gardens of the rural stations as they competed for the annual Best-Kept Station prize. Awd Simon would talk for hours about his days with steam-trains and he clearly exuded pride at his part in the history of the railways of this region. He had once seen the Flying Scotsman in Elsinby Station and had actually been on the footplate, the purpose of its visit being a publicity venture in the region. The Mallard too with its distinctive shape had

come this way, and he'd seen the King aboard the Royal
Train parked overnight in one of the sidings near Elsinby
Station.

I often wish I'd written down everything he told me; he
was a fund of historic knowledge while his anecdotes and
love of the LNER were nothing short of phenomenal.

He had no time for the nationalised British Railways; the
stations had become seedy and grimy and no one bothered
to light the fires any more. The trains were grubby too, and
it was soon after nationalisation that they turned to diesel
engines which weren't any better than buses and couldn't
cope with the deep snows of the moorland lines. The con-
trast for Best-Kept Station had ended and all the stations
became areas of weeds and overgrown rubbish. Paintwork
was allowed to deteriorate and then they began to close the
stations. One by one, the rural lines ended. . . .

During my conversations with Awd Simon, the process
of rural closure was underway. Many branch lines in the
north had closed and stations lay derelict in many areas. The
newspapers were full of the story, with cries about rural
communities being deprived of their lifelines. Some of the
villages were so hilly and isolated that no bus company
would risk its vehicles on the steep hills or narrow twisting
roads. The public joined the general outcry, but the wheels
of a determined government were not to be halted. More
lines would close; more jobs would be lost and more rural
districts would suffer.

No one ever thought this could happen to Elsinby. The
busy little station must have paid its way because the locals
used the rail service to commute to York or to go shopping
to Leeds. They went off to Scarborough or Whitby for the
day while the truly adventurous travelled to London and
other distant cities. Even though the trains were now drawn
by diesel locomotives and bore the British Rail insignia,
they were used frequently by the public of Elsinby and
district. With its coal business too, the station surely paid
its way.

The tiny station, with its signal-box, level-crossing and
two platforms was beautiful to behold, for the station-
master, a Mr Benjamin Page, made sure it was maintained

in an immaculate condition. He boasted white-washed platform front edges, clean oil-lamps, painted seats and offices, a glowing fire in the waiting-room and flowers to adorn the brickwork. For Awd Simon, this was a haven of comfort and he spent many happy hours helping about the station. Mr Page welcomed his presence—he left the responsibility for the appearance of the station in the hands of Awd Simon who weeded between the lines, watered the potted plants, cleaned windows and kept the place at its traditional peak of cleanliness and beauty. Mr Page made good use of Awd Simon.

And then the axe fell. Elsinby Station and the entire branch line through here via Maddleskirk to Thirsk was to be closed. Every possible avenue of reprieve had been examined, and every attempt made to keep the line, but the decision had been made by Parliament. Elsinby Station would close.

Awd Simon blamed the inefficiency of the nationalised system, saying no one had had any heart in the job right from the start. No one cared. For a long time, he looked pale and drawn and, during my regular chats with him on the seat, he was a picture of misery. He could not visualise life without his beloved railway line and the one bright spot was Mr Page's thoughtfulness towards the old man.

He gave him souvenirs, objects which would disappear once the line closed for ever. I know that Simon treasured his square-based oil-lamp from one of the platform lights, the seat with "Elsinby" written across the back and several small items from the booking-office, like a ticket, a pass, a book of rules and so forth.

With his little collection of railway souvenirs, Awd Simon looked rejuvenated. His colour returned, his zest for life reappeared and his general outlook seemed infinitely more hopeful. Even though the line was not reprieved he appeared to have accepted the inevitable. He spent less time around the station although he continued to regale me with the tales of his beloved green engines and the LNER. I was no longer bothered about his health. Awd Simon had accepted that life must go on, and that changes must occur.

I thought no more about his love for the vanishing railway until firm news came of the closure date. It was to be one Friday morning in September.

On that day, the last train would run along our branch line. It would call at all the stations *en route* as it travelled from York via Scarborough, and then through Ryedale via Eltering, Brantsford, Ashfordly, Crampton, Ploatby Junction, Elsinby, Maddleskirk, and eventually into Thirsk where it would join the main London-Edinburgh line for its return journey to York. Passengers would be carried and souvenir tickets would be issued. There would be a restaurant car on the train, with other entertainment, and the sad occasion would be made memorable.

Not wishing to miss any chance of a celebratory occasion, the regulars of the Hopbind Inn at Elsinby formed a committee to arrange suitable festivities in the village. The railway station was to be the focal point and Mr Page agreed. I was duly informed and assured the committee I would attend in my official capacity to control crowds and direct traffic.

What would normally have been a sad occasion for Elsinby became a festive one and I admired the stalwarts of this place for their ability to turn any affair, however sad, into something exciting and enjoyable. For the next few weeks, the place was alive with industry and ideas. I was pleased to see that Awd Simon had been drawn into the arrangements and he was given the special task of informing the new generation about the merits of LNER, LMS, GWR and all the other great rail names of bygone times. He identified engines on postcards and in books, he told historians how they operated and how much coal and water they used . . . notes were made, publicity brochures were printed and, in all, Elsinby was going to lose its station and trains in a blaze of local glory.

When the day came, I motor-cycled into Elsinby and parked my Francis Barnett behind the pub, where I left my crash-helmet and motor-cycle gear. I donned my regulation-issue flat cap and walked towards the station. Although the last train was not due to pass through until 12.35 p.m., the place was alive with colour and gaiety at 11 o'clock. It seemed that half the village population was already present, few of whom were to travel on the last train. True Elsiners preferred to attend their own celebrations rather than joy-ride with strangers.

I remember that I was suddenly very busy. Somehow I was inveigled into the last-minute organising and it seemed that everyone had a job of some kind. Then quite suddenly it was 12 noon. There were thirty-five minutes to go, if the train was on time.

Everyone was now on the platform; cars were neatly parked, the pub had shut for the occasion, although George did manage to arrange a makeshift bar in the waiting-room, and everyone queued on the twin platforms. I looked around the gathering, smiling at the young faces, the middle-aged ones and the elderly, all with memories and personal impressions. For the children, it was the start of a new era; for the old, the end of a bygone style of life.

Then I realised I hadn't seen Awd Simon. I thought about it—I'd been here since 11 o'clock and had not once set eyes on the old fellow. I wondered how he was feeling—maybe he'd gone to another station to secure the final ride into Elsinby? Or maybe he was at home, sad and moist-eyed at the thought of this final chapter of his life? Perhaps the emotion was too great, too overpowering, for him to face among crowds?

I was not unduly worried, but when I saw his daughter, Jane, on the up-platform I asked.

"Your dad's not here then?"

"He's somewhere about, Mr Rhea," she smiled. "He said he was working, helping out, and got dressed up in his old clothes."

"Old clothes?" I asked.

"Yes, his railway clothes. You know, his flat cap with a peak, his railway coat and boots. He wore them years ago and never got rid of them. And he took his bait bag with his sandwiches and flask. He got done up in those and said it was something special."

I smiled. Someone had clearly asked a special favour of Awd Simon and, knowing how the committee of the Hop-bind functioned, I guessed it would be some set piece for him to perform, some final act and some positive way of making Simon feel needed and useful. I knew, and I'm sure they knew, he'd never see another railway train after today.

Prompt at 12.35 p.m., the diesel with its garlands and gleaming bodywork rumbled into Elsinby Station. It hooted and hooted; the people cheered and several disembarked. Others climbed aboard, there were photographs and singing, paper chains were thrown and flowers tossed at the engine. Photographs were taken as the driver kissed several pretty girls on the platform and the guard did likewise, even including some grannies. It was a glorious ten minutes, and then with a long hoot on the horn the last train from Elsinby drew out of the little station.

Now there were tears. Many spectators, men and women, wept as the full stop was written at the end of this important chapter. Suddenly, and with remarkable simplicity, it was all over. No more trains would pass this way. For over a century, they had used this bonny little station and it had ended so suddenly. It all seemed so unreal. Later the rails would be lifted, the station closed and all its contents disposed of. No longer would the signal cabin be required and the level-crossing gates could be left permanently open for road traffic. No more children would have to be warned of trains and those who wished to shop in York or Leeds would have to find alternative transport.

We all walked away feeling sad, but luckily the bar was open on the station and almost everyone drifted inside for sandwiches. The liquor and food would dispel the feeling of melancholy. I looked around but failed to locate Awd Simon.

"Have you seen Awd Simon?" I asked several people and all shook their heads.

Between one o'clock and three, the celebrations continued and I left the noisy bunch to have a walk around the village. Away from the station, it was strangely silent, almost like a village after a funeral. I sought Awd Simon, but failed to find him. I tried all his pals and all his haunts with no success. I couldn't understand it at all.

I returned to the festivities and found his daughter, but she hadn't seen him. She told me he'd been very secretive about his proposed trip, and not in the least morbid or sad.

He seemed elated, she told me, and she guessed he was doing something confidential and very personal.

I must admit I felt worried. No one else appeared to be in the least concerned about his whereabouts, but I felt it odd that the old man had not taken part in the celebrations. He had certainly dressed up for something connected with today's events.

I went home about four o'clock and had tea with Mary and the children. They had attended the festivities, albeit not at Elsinby. They'd been with friends from Aidensfield and had gone down to Ploatby Junction to see the manoeuvres of the engine as it transferred itself from one end of the train to the other for the rest of the trip. The children had secured a grandstand view from a field near the line and I was pleased they'd been present on this historic date, even though they'd probably never remember it in adult life.

I told Mary about Awd Simon but she could shed no light on his behaviour and had not seen him at Ploatby. After tea, I changed into my civilian clothes, for I was off duty at five, and we watched the television news of the train's final trip. People had turned out right along the route through Ryedale and made it a colourful and emotional occasion.

At half-past seven, the telephone rang and Mary answered it.

"It's for you," she said. "I said you were off duty and she should ring Ashfordly, but she insisted she talks to you."

"Who is it?"

"Mrs Jobling."

"Awd Simon's daughter?"

Mary nodded and I went to take the call.

"It's Jane, Mr Rhea," she gasped into the telephone. "It's my dad, he's still not come home. I'm worried now. We've been all over the village and Mr Rawlings says he didn't buy a ticket to go to York or anywhere. . . ."

"I'll come right away," I promised.

I spent an hour seeking him in the village, asking members of the committee and everyone else, but no one had seen him. He'd left home this morning in his old railway clothes and had not been seen since. He'd vanished completely.

My professional problem was whether to mount a full-scale police search for the old man, or wait in the hope he'd return home. We had no real reason to think he was lying hurt anywhere, but my instinct told me something was wrong. I began to fear the worst.

I went into the pub and hailed George.

"George." I talked quietly over the counter in the passage. "It's Awd Simon."

"Aye," he said, "they tell me he's missing."

"I reckon we'd better search the place," I said. "Can you rustle up any volunteers?"

"There's a barful right here, Mr Rhea," he smiled and within minutes I had thirty men on the car-park, all volunteering for the hunt. I told them the situation and provided a description of the old man. As it was dark by this time, we needed lights and this caused no problem. All were local men and each could produce a torch.

I allocated teams of two men to every path and road and allowed them two hours for their search. As it was almost nine o'clock, I said we'd all meet back in the pub at eleven to compare notes. I felt sure we would secure a drink apiece, being friends of the licensee. I had a map in the car and would cross off the examined sections as they were cleared. I told Jane Jobling of our actions and she was pleased; I said that if this spontaneous search, by local men who knew the terrain, produced nothing I would call in a police search team, complete with dogs. That would take time to arrange.

We went to work as only a team of volunteers can, and I found myself paired with a youngster called John Fellows, an apprentice plumber.

"Did you know Awd Simon?" I asked John as we began our search.

"Yes," he said fondly. "He told me all about trains, Mr Rhea. I got a Hornby train when I was a lad, and he told me all about signals, engine types and so on."

"Where do you reckon he is, then?" I asked.

"We were talking in the pub before you came in," he said seriously. "Some of us reckoned he might have gone onto the line."

"The line?"

"Aye, he often went down the line, walking the sleepers like he did when he worked."

"I never thought of that!" I had to admit. "Which was his favourite part of the line?"

"Down near the beck. There's a level-crossing down there, near Marshlands Farm. He sometimes went there."

"Let's go," I said.

The walk across the muddy fields and farm tracks took us about twenty minutes and eventually we had reached the area known to the lad. The line was a single track here, running through narrow openings and thick with shrubs and trees, and there was a farm crossing. Here the line was open with no gates. This meant farmers and their workers had to be alert to the possibility of an advancing train, but to my knowledge there'd been no accidents.

"You go east, I'll go west," I said.

John obeyed. Together we gained access to the railway line and I began to walk along the sleepers, quickly acquiring the necessary pace as my feet adjusted to the regular small steps.

"Five minutes that way!" I called and John waved his torch in reply.

I walked along the line, my torch picking out the railway furniture, the glistening metals, the rows of wooden sleepers like an eternal staircase leading nowhere, while in the darkness of the vegetation tiny pinpricks of light showed. Glow-worms were abroad—it was Walter de la Mare who wrote: "But dusk would come in the apple boughs, the green of the glow-worm shine. The birds in the nest would crouch to rest, and home I'd trudge to mine."

And then I found him.

Quite suddenly, quite horribly, I found Awd Simon.

He was lying between the rails, quite dead, battered and bloody. Poor, poor man. He was clad in his railway clothes, with his bait bag across his shoulder while his peaked cap lay several yards away, knocked from his head.

I stood for a full minute looking upon his battered and torn body, wondering why. Was this an accident or was it deliberate? Had he donned his workaday clothes of yester-year for the sole purpose of undertaking his own final sentimental journey? Was it so impossible for Awd Simon to tolerate life without his beloved railways?

I shall never know.

He could have sprung from these thick bushes without the driver ever realising.

"John," I shouted to the lad, for we had to return to the village.

I had work to do.

8

"Even a child is known by his doings."

Book of Proverbs, XX 11.

It was William Blake who wrote "when the voices of children are heard on the green, and laughing is heard on the hill", but I suspect that the author of that resounding phrase "Children should be seen and not heard" lived in a village. Playing children do make a terrible noise and the larger their numbers the greater the noise. In play, children display a desperate desire to shout louder than their friends and their high-spirited physical antics tend to annoy those residents whose gardens receive footballs, whose greenhouses swallow cricket-balls and whose chimney-pots fly badly routed kites.

Rural children are better off than their city and suburban cousins because they have acres of fields and lots of open space to use for the noisy release of their excess energies, but this does not encourage them to play away from home all the time. Somehow they contrive to play where nobody wants them. All children love playing near their homes or, better still, near someone else's home. While most adults will tolerate their good-natured noise and their unintentional vandalism of rose-beds and windows, there is a hard core of householders who persistently telephone the village constable to complain about playing children.

Since the beginning of constabulary duties, policemen have suffered from this incessant complaining. They have been told loudly of children sliding down icy roads, jumping on rickety roofs, torturing cats or plaguing dogs, building houses in unsafe trees, killing each other or demolishing valuable property. . . .

And always, by the time the policeman arrives, the children have vanished and the misdeeds have ended. Policemen know how the system works, consequently they do not rush to the scene of a complaint in a flurry of blue lights and rising dust. Instead, they proceed at a leisurely pace, knowing full well that the subjects of the irate complaint will have scarpered into prearranged hiding-places at the first hint of trouble from long-suffering adults. By arriving at an empty scene, the police officer preserves everyone's dignity. The system operates something like this. The children have succeeded in annoying their victim, which is what they require; the victim has called in the police, who have responded, so he is happy, and the policeman is content because, knowing human nature somewhat better than most, he realises that his leisurely "action" keeps everyone sweet. There are no upset parents, no children to brag about being nicked and no reports or summonses for him to waste time in submitting. It is a very diplomatic arrangement, practised over the nation by discerning police officers. It keeps politicians happy about the incidence of juvenile crime and professional social workers happy that their skills are producing fruit.

It is true, however, that children's games can get out of hand. This is frequently the case when children discover a victim who responds violently to their taunts. The more he responds, the better the children like it, and the more he will be taunted by them. They knock on his door and run away, they smear paint on his windows or pull up his plants, they perpetrate all manner of hooligan pranks upon the unfortunate person who rises to the occasion for their entertainment.

Children like nothing better than an outraged adult threatening hell, fire and thunder from the safety of his curtilage. And another thing, no sensible adult will attempt to chase the children—this hasn't a hope in hell of achieving anything, other than a grievous loss of dignity by the adult and a repeat performance by the kids in the very near future.

It is far, far better to ignore their taunts. Children whose actions do not raise a flicker of interest from their victim rapidly lose interest. Quite often, the teasing of adults by children is a psychological battle which the youngsters win due to their instinctive understanding of human nature. Adults do not react in quite the same instinctive way and very often provide a memorable display of free entertainment.

The policeman must always bear in mind that children can get out of hand and wreak damage or injury if not checked. Old people can get hurt or shocked by youthful actions, but somewhere in the centre of this long-running conflict there is a level of tolerance which can be achieved by all parties. It is the duty of the village bobby to find that middle course.

I found myself seeking such a course in Ashfordly one autumn afternoon. It involved a formidable lady who stood almost six feet tall in her silk stockings and had a nose as long as Saltburn pier. Domineering and undoubtedly severe, she lived alone in a rambling house on the outskirts of Ashfordly and dressed characteristically in tweed skirts with pleats, brogue shoes with the tongues sticking out and hats that looked like fish-wives' bonnets. Her dark hair was severely styled with large slides holding it back above the ears and she spoke with a heavy accent which suggested a lineage of high-class breeding. She was Miss Deirdre Finlay who may have been in her mid-forties and who drove a little Morris estate car which was always full of plant pots and fertilizer sacks. She strode about the town as if she wore seven-league boots.

I do not believe she had a job of any sort. I understand she existed on a legacy from Daddy although she did grow plants of all kinds which she sold to the local greengrocers, fruiterers and market traders. Certainly this activity alone was insufficient to support her but it kept her occupied and probably brought in a few pounds cash every week, tax-free.

Her garden was one of the old-fashioned enclosed type, surrounded entirely by a tall brick wall a good eight feet high. Inside, it was suitably secluded and private and within those high walls Miss Finlay grew her widely assorted plants. One corner was devoted to apple-trees, all neatly pruned and all expert at producing a wide range of Bramleys, Cox's Orange Pippin and other soundly established varieties. She sold these too and made a useful income from her stock of sixty trees.

Late that autumn afternoon, it was fortuitous that I was patrolling the Ashfordly area. I had parked the motor-cycle and was enjoying a leisurely foot patrol around the market square, admiring the shops, the pubs and the pretty women who always seemed to be going somewhere important. During those blissful perambulations, I wandered through the streets away from the town centre and found myself patrolling along Water End. This was where a small stream, which meandered from the surrounding hills, joined the river and it was a very pleasant and pretty part of the town.

Miss Finlay's house was upon the side of this beck and it was by sheer chance that she poked that formidable head around her gatepost just as I was passing.

"Constable!" she called loudly as she noticed me. "A minute, if you don't mind."

I approached her with a smile on my face. Although we had never spoken before, I knew of this lady and her fierce reputation. I decided to be pleasant to her.

"Yes?"

"You are new?"

"I am. I'm P.C. Rhea from Aidensfield. I'm patrolling the town this afternoon."

"Then I have work for you. I have caught a thief."

"A thief?" I must have sounded surprised.

"Yes, a thieving youth, a good-for-nothing layabout. He was stealing my apples."

I looked around the gate-post and into her spacious grounds but saw no captured youth.

"Where is he?"

"I have locked him in my potato store," and she suddenly grinned. "That'll teach him, what?"

"Take me to him," I suggested. I wondered what sort of thief this was.

She took me into the well-kept grounds and at the side of her beautiful home there was an array of outbuildings, one of which was resounding with loud thumps and frenzied cries of "Let me out."

"In there." She pointed to a closed door. It was of solid

wood with a padlock slipped neatly through a stout hasp, securely imprisoning the villain.

"Who is it?" I called through the door before releasing him.

"I cannot say." She shook her notable head. "I have not seen him before."

The door rattled and banged as the incarcerated rogue attempted to regain his freedom, so I shouted, "It's the police."

The banging stopped and I heard a whispered voice inside say, "Oh, bloody hell."

"Who's in there?" I called through the wooden panels.

No reply.

I began to slip the padlock from the hasp, so she warned me. "He's quick, Officer, you'll have to watch him. I had trouble, you know; it's a good job I'm fit. Hockey, you know. It keeps me trim."

I smiled an unspoken answer to that claim and carefully unbolted the door. It opened easily and there, blinking in the sudden flood of daylight, was a diminutive youth with carroty hair and elfin features set in a freckled face. He made no effort to gallop to freedom, possibly because both I and Miss Finlay occupied the doorway of the potato-house and effectively prevented any exit. To this tiny lad, the opposition must have looked formidable.

"And who are you?" I put to him.

"Ian Fenwick," he said with a faint Scots accent. He didn't look into my eyes, but spent most of the interview contemplating the dusty stone floor of his cell.

"How old are you?"

"Sixteen."

"You're very small for sixteen," I said, for he looked no more than fourteen, perhaps even less.

"I'm an apprentice jockey," he said. "Jockeys are small."

"And where do you live?"

"Here, I'm with the racing stable round the back."

I knew the place. It was a successful racing stable on the outskirts of Ashfordly, positioned literally a stone's throw behind Miss Finlay's house. Some good winners had been bred here and the proprietor, a big Irishman called Brendan

O'Shea, was building himself a useful reputation in this highly competitive field. He employed around a dozen stable-boys and apprentices and inevitably they found themselves in trouble from time to time. But I'd never caught one stealing apples before.

"O'Shea's place?" I asked, waiting for his confirming answer.

"You won't tell Mr O'Shea, will you?" He raised his brown eyes from the floor and looked at us both. I recognised a genuine look of sorrow on his face. This was no regular thief.

"Let's hear your story." I decided I must know a little more about this curious episode. "Miss Finlay says she caught you stealing apples. That's a crime, you know, and at your age it could mean a court appearance."

"Oh, Jesus!" He blanched. "Not that . . . not for apples. . . ."

"You must admit it then?" I put to him as we contained him in the shed.

He hung his head.

"I'm sorry, it was for the horse."

"The horse?" I said. "What horse?"

"The one I ride most, Nature's Signal. She loves apples and there are times she won't behave unless she gets one. I didn't have one so I came over the wall. She was getting stroppy, sir. . . ."

"And I was waiting," came in Miss Finlay. "Caught him red-handed, I did."

"Did you get any?" I asked the lad.

"Aye, three," he said. "She took them off me."

"It is not the first time my apples have been attacked," she countered. "It seems that some children regard my walls as a challenge, Constable. . . ."

"Is this your first time?" I asked the little youth.

He nodded. "We usually have a good stock of apples for the horses, and for Nature's Signal in particular, but, well, there weren't any and she was getting stroppy . . . all I needed was four or five. . . ."

"If he'd asked, would you have given him some?" I asked Miss Finlay.

"I'd have sold him a pound or two, perhaps," she said without batting an eyelid.

"You know it's wrong to steal?" I put to Fenwick, still treating him like a child in spite of his age. His diminutive stature was off-putting.

"I didn't know whose they were and it was urgent," he explained. "I'm not a thief. . . ."

"I've a good mind to tell your boss!" Miss Finlay suddenly interrupted, and I wondered if she was softening a little, perhaps regretting her hasty action and hard attitude.

"Please, no. He'll sack me, I know he will. He's tough, sir, very tough with us."

"If you go to court, it will be all over the papers anyway," I pointed out, knowing I'd have to interview this youth formally in the presence of some adult if I was to take official action.

"What are you going to do with him, Constable?" I couldn't help noticing that Miss Finlay's voice had softened considerably.

"Well." I decided to put a little bit of pressure upon her. "There are several courses open to me. If you are prepared to attend court as a witness and give evidence, I will take him to the police-station. His guardian will be called and charges of larceny will be preferred. He will appear at a juvenile court in due course. That's one course of action."

She swallowed, but did not commit herself to being a witness.

"The second is for me to report him for summons. You would still be required as a witness in court during the hearing, but I would not have to arrest the lad. I would simply take his name and other details, visit his guardian's home. There I would report him for the offence of larceny in the presence of Mr O'Shea."

"And what will happen to him?" she asked with genuine interest.

"Who can tell?" I shrugged my shoulders. "The maximum penalty for simple larceny is five years in prison, but in this case we would probably proceed under Section 36 of the Larceny Act 1861, which is purely a summary offence with a small fine as the penalty. If this is Ian's first offence—

and it seems it was a sudden urge as he says—the court may let him off with a conditional discharge or probation."

"Is it really necessary for him to go to court?" she asked and I knew now that she was weakening greatly.

"Miss Finlay, you have arrested a thief, and you have handed that thief over to me, having accused him of a serious crime. I am duty-bound to take official action." I thought I'd let her stew awhile with those thoughts.

She licked her lips and I saw the lad's eyes turn away from us. He resumed his worried contemplation of the flagged floor.

"You just happened to be walking past. . . ." she began, almost apologetically.

"There is another way of dealing with the matter," I said slowly and she regarded me quizzically.

"Tell me," and there was a note of appeal in her voice.

"If you decide not to press charges, it would be possible for me to deal with the matter here and now." I played my trump-card.

"Really? I wanted him taught a lesson, people must learn that they cannot help themselves to other's belongings. . . ."

"I won't do it again, I promise. . . ." cried our prisoner.

"What must I do?" she turned to me. I knew she'd abandoned the idea of a prosecution.

"You've a lot of apple-trees." I turned and regarded them.

"Sixty," she said. "All fruit-bearing as you can see."

"And you pick all that fruit yourself?"

"I pay someone, it's a long job working alone. Too long when I'm busy."

Now I turned to Ian.

"Do you like picking apples, young man?"

He didn't answer. I think he knew what was going through my mind.

"Miss Finlay, if this young man agreed to pick all your apples without payment, would you drop your charges of larceny?"

For a moment, her face did not crack, and suddenly she smiled, showing acres of large brown teeth.

"I think that's an excellent compromise, Constable. But how can I be sure he picks them?"

"If he doesn't, we will tell Mr O'Shea what he's done."

"And if he does pick them?"

"We do nothing else. We don't tell Mr O'Shea, we don't trouble the courts with this, and you will not have to take time off work to give evidence."

She looked at the shivering lad, still held in the potato-shed, and said, "Well?"

"I'll start tonight," he whispered. "I'll do it— I'll pick them all for you, honest."

"Right," I said. "That's it. The problem is solved."

I told the lad to leave us immediately and when he had galloped out of sight I said, "Make sure he does it, Miss Finlay. Make him pick all your apples. If he doesn't, you must come back to me and I'll speak to Mr O'Shea."

"I like your idea, Constable. To be truthful, I couldn't bear the thought of him going to court. . . ."

I couldn't tell her that I didn't relish the idea of prosecuting the lad for stealing apples; what the inspector would have thought if I had, I daren't even consider. I left her garden feeling confident that Ian Fenwick would return to begin the long chore of picking stones of apples.

A fortnight later, I was in Ashfordly again and decided to check with Miss Finlay, just to ensure the deal had been carried out. She was delighted to see me, so much so that she invited me in for a coffee. As I sat at her scrubbed table in the rustic kitchen, she produced a hot coffee in a large mug.

"Mr Rhea, isn't it?" she asked, as if reminding herself of my name.

"Yes," I confirmed.

"Mr Rhea, that apple-picking idea was marvellous. That young man has carefully picked all my apples, and in fact comes round to work in his spare time. I pay him, of course, for this extra work. He's excellent, and a real nice young man. And that horse—she's a beauty, a real temperamental filly, and he knows just how to handle her. . . . I give him apples, for the horse, you know . . . and he has tea with me sometimes. . . ."

And as she prattled on I could see the light of lost motherhood in her eyes. Miss Finlay had become a very happy woman.

One eternal problem for the police officer is the gang of youths who persist in misbehaving. Such gangs are found everywhere, in all nations and in large cities or small towns. They are often male-dominated although girls are known to join them and indeed the so-called gentle sex can prove formidable leaders.

Even villages produce gangs of youngsters and the effect upon the neighbourhood is the same as that produced by their larger and more violent counterparts in the city. They worry the public. Policemen know that these gangs are inevitable; every year new gangs form as the older ones decline and, in the urban areas, they often call themselves by distinctive names as they compete for power against others of similar background. Such competition is rare in the small villages of North Yorkshire; occasionally, a rival mob from a market town will descend upon a dance in a peaceful village and wreak havoc among the local youths but juvenile demonstrations of this kind of strength are seldom a real threat to the peace and tranquillity of a community. They are little more than a temporary nuisance.

Aidensfield had its own gang. I could see it blossoming as the warmer nights took control. Several youths began to congregate around the memorial seat beside the telephone kiosk and this became their meeting-place. Each evening around six-thirty, six or seven of them would gather, some with motor-cycles and others without. Several of them showed their masculinity by smoking and laughing loudly as the citizens passed by, and the gathering was little more than a typical youthful show of collective strength. On their own, these lads were fine, but when placed within a gang they could be led into all kinds of situations, chiefly those of mischief and trouble.

From the policeman's viewpoint, these gangs are an interesting phenomenon. Every year, the pattern repeats itself—youths gather, dress alike, act alike, make a lot of noise, ogle girls and upset older folks. They make noise and laughter, leave litter and beer-cans around and within two years disappear as their maturing members make their way in the greater world. Then another gang takes its place; younger youths begin all over again and the pattern is repeated. . . .

Head-shrinkers and clever people attempt to find reasons for such assemblies, but I'm sure it is a natural phenomenon among the youths; they meet their own kind for social reasons; they show off, brag about their strength and powers, challenge adults and the law, and generally let off steam. If vandalism creeps in, then it is part of the charade of youth and never a serious threat to society, albeit, very annoying at the time.

It is part and parcel of a police officer's duty to deal with such gangs and it can be a shade daunting for a young officer to confront a fierce and threatening gathering of youths in order to curtail their more effusive outflowings. As a young bobby, before coming to Aidensfield, I had had my share of such gatherings and somehow managed to escape unscathed. In those days, people did not physically attack policemen and the gangs of youths nurtured a grudging respect for the policeman who moved them along or who compelled them to pick up their waste chip papers or empty bottles.

My early days of coping with rebellious urban youths was excellent training for the time I might have to cope with similar problems at Aidensfield. Sure enough, the occasion did arise.

I had watched the growth of the Aidensfield gang soon after my arrival. The summer nights brought them out and these teenage lads began to assemble near the memorial seat, as generations of previous lads had done. They did nothing alarming, although one or two elder folk did express concern. This was inevitable—a collection of high-spirited lads in outrageous clothes kicking a football about the road or chasing empty beer-cans to the accompaniment of loud shouts and curses was a little disconcerting, albeit harmless.

Their ages would be from fifteen to seventeen or eighteen, chiefly schoolchildren or sometimes those unable or unwilling to find work. Boredom brought them together and bravado compelled them to elect a member to visit the pub in an attempt to buy cider or beer. The landlord knew them and refused, so they drank lemonade or bottled shandy.

The problem was what to do with them. If they were not checked, their boisterous fun could lead to trouble. From a policeman's point of view, his duty is to maintain law and order and when assemblies of big lads begin to cause alarm he must do something about it. Inevitably, there are complaints from the residents if the situation gets out of hand, and occasionally the parish council sounds off by writing to the Press or to the Chief Constable. But what can a policeman do against a pack of cunning lads who behave when he's there and who promptly retaliate the moment his back is turned?

Some police officers have started youth clubs, others have created sporting clubs for football or cricket and all kinds of youth organisations have grown in an attempt to keep bored teenagers off the streets and away from situations of conflict with society. Such schemes had been running in and near Aidensfield for some time. There was a very good youth club in Ashfordly, a billiards club in Maddleskirk, several football and cricket teams, and still the lads congregated in villages with noisy bikes and foul language.

I had words with them; I even threatened to take them to court and for a time peace reigned. But the moment I was away the villagers began to complain. The lads were playing football in the street, upsetting motorists and kicking balls into gardens. Beer-bottles and waste paper were left around or smashed on the footpaths, old folks were jeered and vandalism began to materialise. On two occasions, car aerials were broken and windows smashed. . . .

This was now serious. I decided to take a hard look at the members of this troublesome set-up. Most of them were ordinary decent lads, somehow caught up in the relentless pressure put on them by more senior and more forceful characters. Each time I patrolled Aidensfield, I noted the names of the lads gathered in the village street, sometimes stopping to talk with them and sometimes merely passing by. If I became too strict with them and too niggardly about their behaviour, they would react against me and cause even more trouble when my back was turned. So I had to find another way. And my earlier days at Strensford helped.

There was one youth in the Aidensfield gang who was clearly the leader. Every gang has its leader and this was a dark-haired youth of striking good looks but whose personality was defective in some way. He was always at the centre of trouble, I noted, always making a noise, always shouting the loudest. I learned that his name was Alan Maskell.

I wanted to learn more about the lad. Over the next few days, I learned he lived in a council house, that his father had run off with a bus-conductress from York and that his mother spent her money and her time in the pub. Alan had gone to the local secondary school and had achieved moderate success in spite of his background, but at the age of sixteen there seemed no real future for him. He had no desire to leave the village and no real chance of a worthwhile job here. He could become a labourer on a building site, or a washer-up in a local hotel, but little more. It wasn't a bright future and his rebellion could be understood.

Tall and good-looking, he was a powerful lad. His active eyes told me he had a natural intelligence, if no great academic qualities. I could imagine him displaying a manual skill of some kind—bricklaying perhaps, or metal-work of some sort. When I talked to him man to man, alone and without his audience of adoring youngsters, he was fine. I liked him and in some ways felt sorry that his family background had let him down. With help and encouragement, this youth could do well. But who was to spend the necessary time and energy sorting him out?

I learned he was fond of animals and that he bred white rabbits; alone at home as a younger child, he had spent his spare time with his rabbits and now had a very good collection. At home, with his rabbits, he was a totally different character. Gentle and loving towards them, he worshipped the creatures and it was difficult to link this gentle lad with the toughie who ruled the others in the village street.

During that summer, I had repeated complaints about the

conduct of the lads, and indeed the gathering was growing. Others from afar came to join them and I knew that if I wasn't careful I'd have serious trouble on my hands. The matter came to a head late one August evening.

I was on duty in Ashfordly and was unaware that some two dozen lads had congregated in Aidensfield, many with motor-cycles. They had started to race up and down the street and this bit of fun had developed into a noisy and dangerous battle. Cheering, drinking and shouting abuse at the villagers had developed and the incoming bunch had virtually taken over. The local lads were jealous of their hard-man image too and so a battle of pride developed.

I received a telephone call about it; someone in the village had telephoned Mary who managed to trace me in Ashfordly and I drove in the section car to my own village. When I arrived, Alan was still there with the local lads, and one or two outsiders remaining, chortling at my presence.

My first job was to check all driving licences and insurance for their motor-cycles, and then to check the machines themselves for noisy exhausts and other legal defects. Next, I warned the motor-cyclists about the illegality of dangerous driving, careless driving and racing on the highway, and threatened court action against anyone found in the future doing any of those actions. And a court appearance could lead eventually to disqualification of their hard-won driving licences. I made a list of all their names and addresses, motor-cycle registration numbers and their own appearances. I then told them I would circulate those details to all my colleagues in the district—any more motor-cycle problems would result in heavy penalties against the offenders.

Next, I turned to the local lads without motor-cycles. They had been carried away by the excitement of the situation and continued to laugh and swagger about in group bravado as I lectured on their behaviour. Finally I turned to Alan Maskell.

"Alan," I said loudly, "I've a special message for you."

Before his adoring audience, he swaggered over to me, chewing something and winking at his friends.

"Yeh?"

"I'm putting you in charge of these lads," I said.

"Me?"

"Yes, you."

"In charge of them?" The swagger had gone already.

"Yes, in charge of them." I had to get the message firmly home, and they all listened.

He looked about them all and grinned. "Hey, you lot. I'm the boss."

"Yes, Alan, and that means you are responsible for their behaviour. If anything happens in this village—broken windows, litter, complaints about trouble, vandalism— then you will go to court. You, Alan. I'm making you responsible for the conduct of this lot. If they behave, you don't go to court. If they misbehave, you will have to answer in court for them. Do you understand?"

There was silence as Alan and the others began to comprehend the magnitude of the situation.

"You mean if he puts a window through, you'll have me, Mr Rhea?"

"Yes, Alan, that's what I mean. I've had enough of you and this lot. People are always complaining, and I've got to leave more important things to come down here, like tonight, and give you a bulling. So, as from today, you're the boss. It's your job to keep them straight. I'm going to pass the word around my colleagues and, if there's any more trouble in Aidensfield, they'll come looking for you."

"Bloody hell, Mr Rhea, you can't do that. . . ."

"I've just done it, Alan. It starts now. I mean it—every word."

"I could be fined or sent away?"

"You could, so you'll have to sort them out, eh?"

I could see the lad was shaken by his responsibility. Whether it would work, I didn't know. Alan was certainly the ring-leader, but whether the others would obey him when he called for *good* behaviour was a different matter. I knew some of the younger element worshipped him and I felt they would behave out of respect or admiration for him, not wishing him to suffer on their behalf.

As I stood my ground, the crowd of youths began to disintegrate. The motor-cyclists drove away, not revving and roaring out of the village as was their normal practice, but driving sedately through the houses. Next time they came, I would check their documents and vehicles again. . . . and so would my colleagues. We'd soon sicken unwelcome troublemakers.

Alan and his crowd of locals drifted away too, wandering towards their homes as I remained near the seat.

The next night, no one turned up at the seat. I walked around Aidensfield seeking them and wondered where they'd gone. Eventually I found them on the cricket field. They were playing a practice game and Alan was organising them into two teams. He saw me and came across.

"I asked the cricket captain for permission, Mr Rhea, and he said. . . ."

"Fine, Alan, you're doing a good job. Why not challenge the village team to a game one day? When your lads are practised up, eh?"

His eyes lit up. "Aye," he said. "Aye, I'll do that."

Alan and his pals caused me no further trouble. They did congregate near the telephone kiosk from time to time, and they did ride their motor-bikes around the place, but always in a reasonable manner. Later that year, Alan joined the Army and was subsequently posted to Germany. His gang caused me no further trouble because they had grown up.

Next year, another set of noisy lads would take their place and that meant I'd have to find someone else to take charge.

I would start my search immediately.

Another problem child was young Stephen Matthews. He was six years old with a round, cheeky face and mischievous blue eyes. His hair was sandy in colour and his fit little body spent its time galloping everywhere noisily in the sheer exuberance of youth. He was not a criminal; even if his activities had been of the kind that could be classed as criminal, he would not have been prosecuted due to his tender age. His problem was simple—he kept getting lost.

Stephen had a propensity for running away. If his beleaguered mother took him shopping in York or Ashfordly, it could be guaranteed that Stephen would lose her. The poor woman must have spent hours seeking him and the police officers in the area knew Stephen by name and description. His longest period of absence was one full day; on that occasion, he went with a school outing to Scarborough and promptly got lost among the trippers. His mother was there to supervise him, but he managed to give her the slip; she knew him well enough to remain where she was, and that he'd return eventually. But on that occasion he did not, for he spent the afternoon sitting in the police-station until mother arrived distraught and anxious.

At home in Aidensfield, his disappearances were monotonously regular. He would vanish on the way home from school, or from the pack of cubs he had joined; he wandered off into the woods and fields, looking for rabbits or birds, seeking excitement in nature. Time and time again, Mrs Matthews called me to help in searching for the little lad, and time and time again we found him wandering the lanes blissfully unaware of the panic about him. No amount of tellings-off and advice seemed to penetrate his mind, for Stephen would always get lost. I felt sorry for his parents and wondered what his maturity would be like. I could see his wife would have problems.

It was natural that I rapidly grew acquainted with both the little lad and his parents. I developed the practice, whenever I saw Stephen alone, of asking him where he was going, whom he was going to see and whether his mother knew where he was. This oft-repeated dialogue gradually resulted in Stephen's telling me the answers before I asked the questions, and if he saw me in the village he would say, "Mr Rhea, I'm going to see my Aunt Phyllis and Mummy knows about it." or "Mummy sent me to the shop, Mr Rhea, for some tea and bread. I'm going home now and won't be late. . . ."

He was a marvellously confident little chap, and most likeable, but in the summer he performed yet another of his vanishing tricks. Mrs Matthews telephoned to ask if I'd seen Stephen because he had not come in from school. I had to say I had not seen him. As things were, I was about to walk down the village to talk to a farmer about a movement licence for his pigs, so I promised Mrs Matthews I'd keep an eye open for her errant child.

As I entered Norman Berriman's farmyard, the very first person I saw leaving was young Stephen. He had a pup with him.

"Now, young man." I adopted a stern attitude. "I've had your mum ringing me about you. You didn't go home from school and she's worried. . . ."

"I'm going now, Mr Rhea. I just called in to see Mr Berriman about this puppy, you see. . . ."

And off he went. I watched the pair of them walk along the village street, the lad towing the disinterested pup with a long piece of string until they turned down the road towards Stephen's home. I thought no more of the incident until I had concluded my business with Farmer Berriman and happened to mention Stephen's name.

"Aye," said Berriman. "Yon little chap came in and asked if he could have a pup."

"I wonder if his mother knows?" I said, almost to myself.

"Now, that's summat I don't know," the farmer said. "He told me his mam did know and said it was all right. I gave him yon dog—it's a mongrel dog pup, and grand little animal. I can't do with more dogs than I've got and was pleased to give it a home. . . ."

"Has Stephen been here before?" I asked.

"Aye, more than once. He oft comes in after school, checking the dogs and seeing to the cows. Canny little lad, isn't he?"

"He drives his mother up the wall," I laughed. "She never knows where he gets to. . . ."

"He seldom stays long," smiled Norman Berriman. "Comes in here, feeds the hens mebbe or watches me milking sometimes, then off he goes, running down the street. Always at a gallop, isn't he?"

As I talked, I got the distinct feeling that Mrs Matthews would know nothing of the acquisition of that pup. Knowing of Stephen's cunning, he would have chatted to Mr Berriman until the farmer had given him the dog. But it was no problem of mine. It was something the Matthews family would have to sort out with the farmer. However, when I returned home, I rang Mrs Matthews to inform her that I had seen Stephen and that he was heading for home.

"Yes," she said gently on the telephone. "He arrived home safe and sound, Mr Rhea—and he had a pup with him. He said the farmer gave it to him."

"He did, I talked with Mr Berriman about it."

"I knew nothing of that, Mr Rhea. The young monkey's gone and got himself a dog without our permission, and now he won't part with it. . . ."

"It might keep him at home," I said wryly. "If he has to feed his dog and exercise it, he might come straight home from school."

"But we don't want a dog, Mr Rhea. I don't know what my husband will say when he comes home."

"I'm sure Mr Berriman will take it back when he knows the truth. He thought you knew all about it."

"I'll have words with him. Thank you, Mr Rhea."

I have no idea what transpired between father and son, father and mother, or mother and son, but the outcome was that Stephen kept the dog. Thereafter, I often saw them together, with Stephen eternally running and the growing dog galloping at his side. Sometimes the dog was on a lead and sometimes it ran free beside its young master. They were a happy sight.

Although the dog was a mongrel, it had the appearance of a black and white cur, typical of the sheep-dogs in this area. It was a pleasant and lovable animal and Stephen named it Skip. Over the weeks, the pair became inseparable. Where one went, the other followed. I never spoke to Stephen's father about the animal as I seldom saw him, although Mrs Matthews did chat with me from time to time as she went about the village. I learned that the unexpected acquisition had caused a lot of friction in the home, especially from Stephen's dad, who disliked animals at the best of times. But the lad's pleas and his mother's backing had beaten Dad, and the dog became part of the family.

The other bonus was just as I had anticipated—Stephen did not get lost quite so often, especially on his journeys home from school. He always galloped home to take Skip for a walk, although he was sometimes late from these expeditions. Mrs Matthews rang me less and less, for now she had a growing boy and a growing dog to get lost, but between them the wandering couple always returned home.

I wondered if the dog was responsible for taking Stephen home. A hungry dog will find its way to a known food supply and as the dark nights of autumn approached I received fewer calls about Stephen's disappearances.

But when I was next asked to help it was a very serious matter indeed. I don't think anyone realised at the time just how worried I had become.

I was on duty late on Friday evening because the Slemmington Hunt was holding its annual Ball in Aidensfield Village Hall. This was one of the highlights of the year. The Ball was always held on the first Friday in December in Aidensfield's beautiful village hall. This spacious building has a sprung floor which makes it ideal for ballroom dancing, and there is also a balcony, lots of anterooms and space for a bar, and although it is a somewhat remote village it has been host to many important functions. I had to be on duty in case of public order problems and at nine o'clock began to patrol the village on foot. It was bitterly cold, with a hard frost and a forecast of snow before dawn. I was well wrapped up and it would be around 9.30 that evening when Stephen's father, Desmond Matthews, hailed me outside the dance hall.

"Mr Rhea," he said and in the light of the doorway I could see the worried expression on his face. "It's Stephen again."

"Another absence?" I asked.

He nodded. "He went out about seven o'clock and hasn't come back. It's dark, you see, and he never stays out in the dark. . . . I've searched everywhere, and my wife too. He's taken a torch and just vanished—and the dog with him."

"Did he give any idea where he was going?" I asked, and a fleeting thought crossed my mind that it was unusual for Mr Matthews to come to me. On every previous occasion, his wife had set the ball rolling.

"No, nothing," was all the man said.

I could sense the concern in his voice and instinctively knew I had a major problem on my hands. A search for a child at any time is harrowing, but on a bitterly cold

December night it has much more relevance and urgency. Cold can be a vicious killer.

The problem was where to begin and who should conduct the search. Could one father and one policeman adequately search the wild and expansive acres of this area in the dark? Even if we had some clue as to his whereabouts, it would not be easy, but with no idea of his probable location it seemed impossible. The sheer size of the area and the time element combined to produce immense problems.

"Wait here, Mr Matthews, I'll ring Sergeant Blaketon at Ashfordly to see if we can get reinforcements."

I went to the Brewers Arms next door to the village hall and asked if I could use the telephone. Consent was immediate and I rang my section office. There was no reply. I next decided to ring the Sub-Division and managed to raise a constable on the enquiry desk.

"It's Nick," I announced. "Have you any idea where Sergeant Blaketon is, Harry?"

"He booked off the air at Eltering about half an hour ago," Harry told me. "Shall I ring him?"

"Please. I've got a missing child at Aidensfield—I'll begin the hunt now, and will return to the village hall on the hour. I reckon we might need help."

"What about police dogs? Delta Four-Seven is on the air with two dogs. I can send them over if you like."

"Yes, fine. When can they be here?"

"Twenty minutes I reckon. Can you wait?"

"I'll make a point of waiting. Can they meet me outside the village hall at Aidensfield?"

"I'll fix that, Nick. And I'll get Sergeant Blaketon to rendezvous with you as well. I take it you'll need volunteers?"

"I'm sure I will, but I think we'd better make a preliminary search of the village. I don't want to drag everybody out if he's lying asleep in a local barn. I'll ring you back if I need more help."

Now that the official wheels had started to turn, I told Mr Matthews what I'd done. I asked him to return home to make a further thorough search of the house and its surrounds, and also Stephen's known haunts. I said I'd do a quick recce of the village territory, including Norman Berriman's farm buildings and other likely places. There were the school grounds, the cricket pavilion, the churchyard, the river-banks and so forth.

I couldn't ignore my other responsibility and already, the dance was beginning to warm up. Dinner-jacketed men and ladies in flowing gowns were arriving thick and fast, so I entered the hall and found the organiser, Colonel B. J. Smithson. I told him of the development and asked him to excuse my absence, saying I'd return as soon as possible.

"Not a bit, old boy, good hunting." He dismissed me with a wave of his elegant hand.

I spent a hectic half hour searching the village and calling Stephen's name, all to no avail. I returned to the village hall and found the police dogs had arrived with two handlers. I decided we should visit Stephen's home first, to see if the parents had any further news.

Mrs Matthews was at home, waiting in case the absent pair returned, and Mr Matthews was out with a neighbour, searching some nearby woodland.

"I've got two police dogs, Mrs Matthews," I said. "We're just deciding where to deploy them."

"Will they hear Skip bark, Mr Rhea?" she asked.

"They might make him bark. Now, what time did Stephen set off?"

The dog-handlers and I listened to her story and we learned he'd eaten his tea about half past five and had then watched television for a while. At seven he had left the house and hadn't been seen since. We obtained a description of the clothes he wore, together with the dog's particulars, and I decided it was time to circulate them to all our mobiles and fixed stations. Some patrolling police officer might see them on the road somewhere. A lorry could have picked them up—anything could have happened.

I was not satisfied about the reason for Stephen's departure. Mrs Matthews did not give a reason and I found it odd that a child of six would suddenly take his dog away from the house in the dark. I wanted to know why he had left the house.

I began to probe and she broke down in tears; it seemed
her husband had lost his temper with the dog because it
kept scratching the paintwork of his newly painted front
door and he'd threatened to shoot the bloody animal if it
persisted. . . .

Stephen had cried for a long time about this and at seven
o'clock he'd slipped out of the house with Skip. At the time,
mother was washing the pots and Dad was attending to
something in the garden shed.

This news made the search even more important. On a
cold December night, a child could perish from
hypothermia if left out in the open, and I recognised the
urgency of our actions. There was no time to lose, but
where should I begin?

As I knew the village terrain very well, I suggested areas
of immediate search by each of the two dogs, while I continued to examine the open buildings about Aidensfield. At
eleven o'clock, Sergeant Blaketon materialised with five
more officers, having been told of our lack of progress by the
dog-handlers over their radios. By now, the matter was
growing desperate. Stephen and his dog had been missing
four hours with no indication of their whereabouts.

We asked questions around the village, but no one had
seen the lad and his dog. Darkness and the fact that many
villagers had been indoors preparing for the dance meant
they had managed to wander off without being noticed.

With Sergeant Blaketon now in charge, the hunt assumed
new proportions and I was pleased to have the vital
assistance of my colleagues from the Sub-Division. I
secured a map of Aidensfield and district and we
apportioned a given area to each police searcher, with me
providing local information about the dangers of deep
waters in the streams, dangerous and ruined buildings,
likely woodland hiding-places, little known routes and so
forth.

Through our police radios, we were able to keep closely
in touch with each other and by eleven thirty the inspector
arrived, having been told of the unsuccessful search. Now
Aidensfield was alive with police vehicles, dogs and vans;
men with powerful torches and loud-hailers patrolled the

outer areas, all searching to a pattern and all desperately anxious to find the little fellow before the awful chill of winter took its inevitable toll.

Inside the dance-hall, the huntsmen and their followers were unaware of the drama being played nearby. At half-past midnight, I decided to tell Colonel Smithson of the importance of our search and to apologise for my continued absence from his function.

I found him doing a waltz with a titled lady from an adjoining hunt and I waited until he drifted past in a cloud of her expensive perfume.

"Colonel, could I speak with you?"

"Ah, Mr Rhea, of course. Found that child, have you?"

"No, we haven't," I said. "I'm just explaining my absence from your function. . . ."

"What child is this?" asked her ladyship, with deep interest.

I told them both of the extent of our search and of the desperation now setting in. Her ladyship asked some very sensible questions about our methods of searching and the numbers involved, and Colonel Smithson did likewise. Their interest was intense

"You know," he coughed, "here we are, all enjoying ourselves and that poor child is out there, on a bloody cold night. . . . Mr Rhea, let us help."

"That's most generous of you," I began. . . .

"Generous be damned! It's a public duty! Look—all these people know this district like the backs of their pampered hands! They've all hunted over these fields and rivers, every inch of them . . . I'll stop this bloody dance for you and ask for volunteers . . . how's that?"

"Excellent idea, Benji," beamed his lady companion. "Yes, let's join your hunt, Constable."

I was somewhat taken aback by this response but before I knew what was happening the colonel had stopped the orchestra and was addressing the assembly through the microphone. He told of the little boy's absence and of the hunt now in progress, then asked me to detail precisely what the police were doing. I took the microphone from him and gave the whole story of the missing boy and his

dog. I provided a brief description of young Stephen and the
clothes he was wearing, and informed the gathering that
the inspector's official car, parked on the garage forecourt
higher up the village, was the focal point. He had radio
contact with all searchers and with Force Control at Headquarters, so this made his car the ideal Command Vehicle.

The colonel took over again.

"Right, gentlemen," he spoke into the microphone. "I
think this is an occasion for us to volunteer to join the
search. Everyone here knows this countryside intimately,
and I'm sure the police would be grateful for any assistance.
Have I any volunteers to report to the inspector's car and be
allocated an area to cover?"

In the moment of silence that followed, I thought no one
was going to raise a hand, but as if on an unspoken
command a sea of hands was raised and he beamed with
obvious delight.

"Right, that's it. Go home and change into something
more useful for tramping across the landscape. And, P.C.
Rhea, if we don't find the lad tonight, we will continue
tomorrow on horseback. . . ."

What followed next was truly amazing. Well over half the
dancers reported to the inspector's car in their evening-
dress, ladies in their long flowing gowns and fur coats, and
gentlemen in dinner-jackets with wellingtons drawn from
their car boots. The colonel took charge of his contingent
and I could see he was thoroughly enjoying himself being
back in the field of action. Others had gone home to change
into more suitable attire.

By one o'clock that morning, we had well over two
hundred people searching for Stephen and his dog. We
allocated one policeman to each party of hunters because it
meant we could maintain radio contact with our base,
should the lad be discovered. I was with a party of young
huntsmen and their girls from the York area, and we
combed the district bordering the parish boundaries
between Aidensfield and Maddleskirk. That comprised
some rough landscape, thick with thorn-bushes and laced
with dangerous marshland, all interspaced with deep
streams and expansive open fields. We combed the area

intensively by torchlight, thrashing bushes with sticks, calling the names of both boy and dog and examining every possible hiding-place. We found nothing. Even in spite of our activity, the cold was striking through our clothing.

I knew from the response on my personal radio set that the others were experiencing the same result. Nothing. There was not a clue; no sightings, nothing. It was as if the child and his dog had been spirited away.

Meticulous attention was paid to the stream which ran along the valley floor. It meandered gracefully through the fields and woods, sometimes spilling over the edge to form dangerous marshes and pools which were traps for the unwary. One team, plus a police dog, were given the specific task of searching the entire length of that stream for three miles each way. They found nothing.

Heart-warming response came from the caterers who had been booked to feed the dancers. Mr Humphries, the proprietor of the catering firm in question, had dashed home in his van to return to the scene with hot soup and sausage rolls. Although the search was of a most serious nature, it was gratifying to see the *esprit de corps* that was generated by these willing people. It was evident they were enjoying themselves, although carrying out their task with a high degree of professionalism.

None of us went to bed that night. The bitter chill gave way to an even colder dawn and as daylight broke we were a tired and bedraggled sight. Those who had not gone home to change looked a sorry mess, suits mud-spattered and torn, long elegant dresses stained and ripped and the people red-eyed and weary. We had been searching for twelve hours without a break.

At nine o'clock that morning, the inspector had to make a vital decision. His men needed rest. They needed sleep, refreshment and warmth if they were to continue; without that, there could be further casualties among the searchers. He knew the risks and I saw him look at his watch.

He called me in for a conference and we sat in his car.

"Nine o'clock, Nick. And not a bloody sausage."

"These people have been marvellous, sir," I said. "They

said they would go home and get horses at dawn, if he hadn't been found."

"They're incredible. And our lads too—they've tramped miles tonight in appalling weather. . . ."

"Where is everyone now, sir?" I asked.

"Still out there. Have you seen the parents?"

"The father's out somewhere and Mrs Matthews is still at home, standing by the window. I saw her as I came in."

"Let's give it another couple of hours, Nick. Can you stand it?"

"Sure," I said. "Thank God for Jack Humphries and his grub!"

I returned to my little party and left the inspector to relay his decision to the troops. We moved our group another half mile to the west and began yet another systematic search of the scrubland upon the foothills which rose towards the grim moors behind. It was tiring in the extreme.

And then, at half past nine, came some marvellous news. Stephen had been found and he was still alive—and so was the dog.

I was thrilled to hear the cheers rising from the hunters spread all over the countryside as the news was passed over the police loud-hailers and radio sets. We were all asked to return to base. It was all over.

By the time I returned, Stephen had been whisked off to hospital in one of the cars belonging to a huntsman, and his dog had been taken home. As everyone gathered around the inspector's car, he decided to thank everyone there and then, and explained how the discovery had occurred.

Miss Gabrielle Gladstone, a member of the Slemmington Hunt, had gone home to get her horse at dawn, and had decided to ride back to the Control Point via the fields. Her home was in Ploatby, several miles by road but a short ride across the fields. She was a pretty young woman of about twenty-five and as she had ridden through the fields in daylight she had recalled some of her own childhood adventures. There was a derelict mill deep in a wood, well off the beaten track, and she had decided to examine that during her trip.

And there was the boy. He had somehow found his way

into that awful place in the darkness, lost his torch and fallen. He had broken an ankle, she said, and had been unable to move. He had lain all night on a pile of sacks and the fact he was indoors helped him survive. But, she said, he owed his life to his dog. It had remained with him all the time and, when she found them, the boy was curled up asleep with his arms around his faithful friend. The dog had kept the boy's body temperature sufficiently high for him to survive.

Afterwards, Mr Matthews praised the dog, he praised the hunt and he praised the police. He was overwhelmed and overjoyed at the response by the public of Aidensfield and their friends.

I never knew how the youngster had managed to find that remote place at night and I don't think he knew himself. It was so far off the beaten track that it might have escaped our attention, and I found myself wondering whether we'd have found the lad if he'd chosen to run away on a night when there was no Hunt Ball.

That Hunt Ball was a success in many ways and, thereafter, young Stephen didn't wander very far. I do know that later in the year he was a guest of honour of the hunt, who took him around the kennels to see the puppies and the foxhounds. In fact, he was presented with a whip by the Master of Foxhounds, but with strict instructions never to use it on his own dog!

9

"All happy families resemble each other, each unhappy family is unhappy in its own way."

Leo Tolstoy, 1828–1910

There is no doubt that families of children can lead to friendships and understanding between their respective parents and in a village community many lasting relationships have developed because parents met at school events. When our three children were too young to attend primary school, we sent them to play-school. The eldest, Elizabeth, started by going once a week. There she met and played with other youngsters and this developed her ability to mix with those of her own age before attending school. We felt it an important part of her development and it helped at primary school.

Two of her little pals were Paul and Sarah Parker, instantly recognisable as twins. Mrs Parker was then a frail slip of a girl and she lived with her twins in a council house at Maddleskirk. Her no-good husband had left her when she was nineteen, having presented her with these bairns at a very tender age. They had now reached school age and started the primary school with my Elizabeth.

Julia Parker had to be admired. Somehow she managed to earn a few pounds each week and, although she depended heavily upon the State to maintain herself and her family, she did her best to keep her youngsters well-fed and neatly clothed. Both Mary and I had a deep sympathy for her in her plight; alone, she had to support those youngsters, run the house, pay her bills and somehow retain her sanity. I do not think her awful husband ever paid a penny towards their keep in spite of repeated court orders. Certainly, he never came near the village.

Julia herself was thin and wiry; she looked eternally underfed and hungry, although she was a pretty girl with delightful eyes and a lovely face. She was never heard to complain about the plight in which she found herself, and there is no doubt that the entire village liked her. Even her twins were nice—they were pleasantly mannered kiddies and seemed able to mix well with others of their age. She had every right to be proud of them as they came towards their sixth birthday.

It was with some horror, therefore, that I received a telephone call from York Police one Saturday afternoon to ask if I knew a woman called Mrs Julia Parker of Maddleskirk.

"Yes," I said to the unknown constable at the other end. "I know Julia Parker."

"Describe her, can you?"

I did my best, emphasising her dark hair, her slenderness and her general appearance. I put her age at about twenty-three. I followed this with, "Why are you asking?"

"We've a young woman in the nick," he said. "She says her name is Julia Parker from Maddleskirk, but can't prove her identity. She named you as somebody who can identify her."

"Does my description fit the girl you've got there?"

"It does," he said. "Thanks."

"What's the matter with her?" I asked.

"She's been nicked for shoplifting," he said flatly. "She's pinched some kids' toys from a shop in town."

I groaned. "Are you sure?"

"Positive," he said. "The manager caught her and she's admitted taking the things. We're going through the necessary procedures right now—she'll be at court next Tuesday."

"You'll be bailing her?" I put to him.

"I see no problem, she says she has twins with a baby-sitter in your village."

"Yes, it'll be Mrs Hird," I guessed.

"That's the name she gave. She seems a nice kid," he added.

"She is," I said and then gave him a genuine account of Julia's family circumstances and the problems she had surmounted. He expressed sorrow but we both knew the law must take its course. I asked the constable to pass a message to Julia, asking her to pop in to see myself and Mary when she returned. She had to know she had friends.

That evening, a tearful Julia knocked at my door and we admitted her. Mary took her into the lounge where our three children were being entertained before bed and, once inside the house, she burst into tears.

"I'm so embarrassed," she began. . . .

Mary made a marvellous job of comforting the girl. As the tale poured from her, we learned it was the twins' birthday next Wednesday. They would be six years old and she'd had no money to buy them anything; everything had gone on food and clothes and, in a last desperate act, she'd tried to steal a couple of toys. Other children got toys for their birthdays, she said, but hers wouldn't on this occasion. . . .

It was a very sad case, and so out of character. I knew there was no answer to it—she had stolen the toys, worth about £1 each, and had admitted it. I knew she would go to court and be fined a small amount; the magistrates might, however, decide upon a conditional discharge. Whatever happened, though, it meant Julia would be dragged through the courts and her name bandied about as a common thief. We did our best to comfort her and Mary said we would try to find some toys for the children before Wednesday. At least, they'd be happy.

Julia remained with us as our youngsters were taken upstairs and we all settled down for a coffee, all the time trying to find some way of helping Julia to accept her fate and to take a positive grip on her future. She had done so well up to date, but this one slip threatened to destroy all her past efforts. She had cracked under intolerable strains and would need help and guidance over the coming weeks. Mary took it upon herself to help this slip of a girl. Eventually, she left us with a smile, and I felt happier about her. She appeared to be calm in the face of her coming ordeal.

That all occurred on the Saturday evening and, on Monday night, my telephone rang. It was the same constable from York and he told me his name was Geoff Lewis.

"It's about that girl, she's due at court tomorrow," he said. "I would like you to make sure she comes, Mr Rhea."

"We've already talked to her," I told him. "I'm on day off and my wife has some shopping to do, so we'll fetch her through. She'll be there, you can rest assured on that."

"That's good of you. Could you fetch her into the police office first? The inspector wants a word with her."

This was unusual, but I agreed.

On the Tuesday morning, we stopped the car outside Julia's tidy home and she ran to join us, having arranged for the children to visit a neighbour if she was late. No one knew of her secret and I hoped the newspapers wouldn't make too much of a fuss about it. Although she was tearful, she seemed to be in control of herself as I told her about the message from York Police. I parked at the police-station, close to the River Ouse, and escorted Julia inside. I asked for P.C. Lewis and he appeared, smiling when he saw me. I guessed it was with relief at her presence.

He recognised Julia and said, "Can you come upstairs to the inspector's office?"

She looked at me and I said, "I'll come with you if you like," and turned to the policeman for his approval. He nodded. Mary and I followed them up the steep, winding staircase.

P.C. Lewis introduced me to the inspector and explained my presence; I told him of our links with Julia. He looked at me and smiled his understanding.

"Sit down, all of you," he invited.

"Julia," he addressed the worried girl. "We have been doing a bit of research into your background, and we now know that what you told us on Saturday is true. P.C. Lewis has spoken to P.C. Rhea about you."

Julia merely nodded and I've no doubt she regarded this as just another portion of routine court procedure. I didn't, but I had no idea what was happening.

"Julia," continued the inspector, "we have spoken to the manager of the shop about you. He has decided not to prefer charges—if he fails to give evidence, we cannot proceed. He will not come to court."

Tears came into her eyes. "Does that mean I will not be fined?"

"It means there will be no court case at all," he said gently. "You are free to leave and," he delved under the desk, "here are the toys. Give them to your children with our best wishes."

"But I must pay for them. . . ." She began to open her handbag.

"No," he said. "We've something else for you."

He pushed an envelope across the desk and it bore her name.

She regarded it solemnly and glanced at me. "Open it," I said.

She did, and inside were fifty £1 notes.

"Money. . . ?" she said.

"We had a collection among all the policemen here," said the inspector. "We paid for your toys. There's about two hundred of us and every man has given five shillings, so there's money for future presents for your family. We want you to put this money into a post-office account, and use it only for Christmas and birthday presents. You'll get a little bit of interest on the money and I know P.C. Rhea will help you to open the account. So your twins will always have presents like other children. . . ."

Julia was sobbing as she clutched the money to her thin chest and I put an arm about her. I felt my own eyes grow moist and I know the inspector was feeling very emotional about it. Julia didn't know what to say so I suggested she write a letter to thank them when she returned home. There was no fuss about it, no formal presentation, no publicity, just a show of genuine affection and understanding from two hundred policemen towards one girl who'd been badly treated by a man.

Later, my own family was about to increase. Our fourth child was almost due and I knew that in the very near future I would have to drive Mary to the Maternity Home near Malton. I didn't want a last-minute panic like the previous occasion and, sure enough, the warning signals began late one evening. I rang the hospital and they accepted her;

within half an hour, Mary was in my car and we were driving swiftly but carefully across the valley to the country-based maternity home. A neighbour had come into care for the other children.

We left it closer than I'd realised. Mary said the contractions were beginning and I realised that a birth was imminent so it was with infinite relief that I reached the hospital in time. The sister suggested I wait, for surely I would be a dad yet again within a very short time.

I entered the plain waiting-room full of old magazines and hard chairs and found another young man sitting there waiting. He was clearly a farm labourer, having come straight from some smelly job in his old clothes. He sat on one of the chairs, twisting a flat cap in his powerful hands and gazing at the floor. He smiled briefly as I entered and I settled down opposite; I felt very much the experienced dad with a score of three to my credit so far.

I greeted the young fellow with "Now then" as we do in Yorkshire and he nodded a brief response, all the time wringing his cap.

"It's not like a sow, is it?" he suddenly spoke.

"Er, no, I suppose not," I responded to his odd statement.

"Sows eat theirs, eh? If you don't do summat quickly, they eat their young. Cats do an' all," he commented.

"Humans aren't like that," I said by way of saying something constructive and helpful.

"My first." He squeezed the hat until I felt it must fall apart in those massive hands.

"My fourth." I felt a glow of parental pride as I realised we'd not eaten any of ours.

"It's not like horses either, is it?" he resumed after a break in our conversation.

"Horses?" I puzzled.

"Aye, foaling. Horses foaling. They've got to get ropes on the feet and drag 'em out. I've done it many a time. . . . nasty business. This won't be like that, will it?"

"No, it won't," I assured him, feeling it wise to refrain from explaining that some human births weren't all that easy.

There followed a long period of silence, during which he

mangled his cap until it looked like a battered dish-cloth. Then he smiled and said:

"It'll not be like cows either, will it?"

"Cows?" I must have sounded baffled by this time.

"Cows roll on their calves sometimes. Big hefty cows, lashing about. They roll over and smother their calves if you're not there. . . ."

"The nurses will look after ours," I assured him, wondering about the size of his wife.

He smiled at my blithe reassurance and settled down, then suddenly paced the floor and put the mangled hat on his untidy hair. He stopped right in front of me and peered at me seriously.

"It's not like lambs, is it?" he asked, those anxious eyes boring into mine.

"Lambs?" I shook my head.

"If the mother dies, they give the lamb to another ewe; they skin a dead lamb and hide the smell and put the skin over the orphan. . . ."

I visualised mothers wearing wigs to confuse babies; I visualised babies being painted with some fluid to disguise their smells so that foster-mothers would accept them. . . .

"It's not a bit like that," I said, and he returned to his chair where he recommenced his wringing motions.

We waited another five minutes and he smiled at me.

"I'm glad we're not like cuckoos," he winked. "Crafty old birds, those, eh? Laying their eggs in another nest and letting somebody else feed them and bring them up. . . ."

"I think a lot of humans are just a bit like that," I laughed with him.

The sister came through and addressed him. "Mr Winford?"

"Aye?" he leapt to his feet and clapped the mangled cap on his head once again.

"You've got a son," she smiled. "And he and his mother are both well."

"I reckon he'll be a thoroughbred sire like his dad," and he followed the nurse with gleeful pride in his eyes.

I waited, musing over his curious view of natural birth, and within half an hour the sister called me in.

"A daughter, Mr Rhea," she announced. "And both are fine."

For some reason, I thought of a fawn.

Constable
Across
the Moors

I

"O villainy! Ho! Let the door be lock'd;
Treachery! Seek it out."

William Shakespeare 1564–1616: *Hamlet*

In crime fiction, there can be an element of drama and suspense when secret missions are undertaken by sterling heroes. For this reason, if for no other, I suppose it is the wish of every budding constable to become operationally involved with secrecy, spies, M.I.5, invisible ink and all the other trappings of undercover missions.

My first involvement was nothing like that. It began with the intolerable and incessant jangling of the telephone somewhere in the depths of an icy cold, dark and miserable office. That office lay at the foot of my staircase, and the start of my staircase lay pretty close to my bedroom door. My bedroom door, however, lay some five or six feet from my snug bed, across a large expanse of very cold linoleum. On top of all that, it was pitch dark and the hour was about five o'clock on a chilly winter morning.

These factors, plus the warmth of a loving wife beneath the cosy blankets, amalgamated to declare the telephone more than a nuisance. But shrilling police telephones cannot go unheeded, and as I lay in the darkness contemplating my next action, it became very evident that the person at the other end was another policeman. Other people, reasonable creatures that they are, would have stopped ringing ages ago; other people would have had infinite compassion for someone who'd been working late, whose family were infants and likely to be fully aroused at any minute, whose wife was cosy and warm and who personally wasn't too fond of climbing out of bed at five o'clock to answer silly questions.

But policemen aren't noted for compassion towards fellow officers, especially those of subordinate rank. When they ring other policemen, at whatever hour of the day or night, they keep the instrument active until somebody is compelled to do something about it. As I slowly realised my caller was a policeman, Mary also realised it was ringing.

"Telephone," she burbled from a deep sleep. "Telephone."

"It's ringing," I said, my voice talking to an empty black room.

"It might be urgent," she managed to convey to me.

"It probably is," I agreed, turning over. It was about this time that I realised it must be Sergeant Blaketon. No other person at Ashfordly Police Station would be so persistent. No other policeman in my section would ring like this; if someone's presence was required, they'd ring Control Room or get the night duty man to attend. No member of the public would ring like this, not for anything!

"Oh, for heaven's sake . . ." Mary turned over. "It's not the alarm clock, is it?"

"No, the telephone," the house was full of strident ringing noises and I had horrid visions of Sergeant Blaketon hanging on to the other end, and equally horrid visions of him driving out to Aidensfield to knock on the door. That really would rouse the four children.

"All right, all right," I snarled. "I'm coming."

Protesting, grumbling and angry, I slid my feet out of bed and my warm soles met the bitterly cold floor. The chill raced up my spine and did something to arouse me; I shivered violently. I couldn't find my slippers, and therefore elected to descend in my bare feet. I daren't switch on the bedroom light because Mary would hate me even more, so I made my erratic, bleary way from the room and down the stairs, unerringly guided to ground level by the nerve-shattering din.

I fumbled my way across the hall and found the light switch. My frosted feet made their way across the bitterly cold composition floor of the office and I stretched a hand towards the noisy contraption.

It stopped ringing. A weird silence sat among the darkness of my house as I blinked in the light of my office.

I had heard many legends about telephones ceasing to ring just as the recipient reached it, but in circumstances like this?

I stood and stared at it. I dared it to recommence. My feet had started to turn into blocks of ice, and the awful cold was producing goose-pimples in very strange places. Nothing happened. And so, as I waited for the next sequence in this domestic drama, I could look out of my office window. The light showed a vast area of white and I groaned. Snow had fallen. Beyond my four walls, several inches of moorland snow had arrived unannounced and graced my weed-ridden garden. If this was a call-out, I could justifiably say I was snowed in. I realised today was Candlemas Day, February 2, and my mind quoted the local weather prognostication — "If Candlemas be fair and bright, winter shall have another flight. If Candlemas be dull with rain, winter will not come again". I wondered what sort of summer we could expect when Candlemas was thick with snow.

I must have waited for five long minutes because my feet appeared to be growing detached from me, and the telephone sat very still. So, it hadn't been a policeman after all. It must have been somebody else, somebody who'd given up, somebody who'd dialled 999, or who'd changed their mind.

Smiling, I turned towards the beckoning stairs. I thought of my welcoming Mary in her cocoon of bedclothes; she was just lying there with an overwhelming desire to warm my feet with her lovely back. This made me hurry up stairs. Out went the office light as I galloped back to bed, thankful for the consideration shown by this unknown caller.

As I reached the bedroom door, it began again. The incessant ringing resumed with evident determination and this time I raced down stairs, angry and upset that the world was so full of inconsiderate, demanding people who should know better.

"Police!" I snarled into the mouthpiece.

"Rhea?" It was Sergeant Blaketon. He sounded very wide awake, and I wondered for an awful moment if I should have been on early patrol route, but a glance at my diary revealed the truth. I was shown as late turn, starting at two this afternoon.

"Yes, sergeant."

"Did I get you out of bed, Rhea?" he asked blandly.

"No," I growled. "I was taking the budgie for a walk."

"There's no need for insubordination, Rhea, this is urgent."

"Urgent, sergeant?"

"Very urgent and very important. Get yourself down to this station for six o'clock, bike and all. Bring a packed lunch and some hot soup. It's an all-day job, and it might take us until night. Be equipped for snow."

"Snow, sergeant?"

"Snow, Rhea. There's five or six inches out here."

"What sort of job is it, sarge?" I dared to ask.

"I can't discuss it on the telephone," he informed me. "Just be here at six."

He put down his phone and I looked at my office clock. It was ten past five. For a few moments, I stood on the cold floor and stared outside. I could see snowflakes descending in the patch of light cast from the office window, and their beautiful smooth movements mesmerised me. Then Mary was shouting at me from the top of the stairs.

"What is it, Nick? Is it my mother?"

"It's worse," I called back. "It was Sergeant Blaketon."

"What's happened?" There was genuine concern in her voice.

"I've got to go out. It's something important and he won't tell me over the telephone. I've got to be at Ashfordly office at six, equipped for an expedition of some kind. I need soup and a packed meal, and snow shoes by the sound of it, or skis."

"I'll pack something, you get ready." She was a picture of composure as she switched on the stairs light and descended. How she managed to look so calm, I'll never know, although it might be linked with the fact that she'd had to discipline herself to wake at all hours to night-feed four children over several years.

I trudged upstairs and entered the bathroom. The mirror was frosted over, so I breathed on it and my breath frosted over too. I shivered violently and decided against shaving. A miniature beard would keep me warm – I'd seen "Scott of the Antarctic" and the frosted beards of his courageous crew. I might be like that.

By quarter to six, I was dressed for an Arctic expedition. I wore my pyjamas beneath my uniform, a device employed by generations of policemen who'd patrolled in sub-zero temperatures for twenty-five winters or more. On top of it all, I had dressed in my official motor-cycling suit. This was a large black rubbery outfit which smelled of oil and made me look like a paunchy grizzly bear. It was a two-piece suit with seamless trousers and a long tunic which concealed almost everything. Gauntlets protected my hands, and I sported a large round crash helmet with POLICE across the front. This was to protect what few brains I had. On my feet, I selected leather boots with rubber over-shoes. Thus clad, I had great difficulty in walking normally, but felt no one would notice me at this early hour. I was ready for my mission of mystery.

"Where are you going?" Mary asked, hugging her dressing-gown around her slender body.

"I wish I knew." I meant every word. In my arms, I carried my packed lunch and three vacuum flasks, two with soup and one with coffee. Apples and chocolate bars were stuffed into sundry pockets and I had managed to find a packet of dates in the pantry.

"I'll try to find a telephone." I wondered if they had telephones where I was going.

"Bye," and she tried to kiss me across the paraphernalia which cluttered my frame. I stooped awkwardly and plonked a chilly kiss on her forehead.

"Bye," and I opened the front door.

A huge drift had gathered against the door and nearly fell in as the stiff breeze whipped small whirls of floating flakes into the house. Outside, the garden was a white desert, endless and fascinating, but definitely not the sort of conditions to encourage the riding of motor cycles. But orders were orders and one's constabulary duty had to be done. I slammed the door before Mary was overcome with drifting snow and had to kick the drifts away from the garage doors.

After twenty minutes of hard labour, I succeeded in scraping away sufficient snow to permit the doors to open and I slid my meagre rations into one of the panniers of my bike. A line of drifting snow followed me into the garage, so I hurriedly straddled the machine and kicked it into life. It fired first time, a tribute to our police mechanics, and I guided the Francis Barnett from its cosy home. Together we braved the fierce black morning with its blanket of pure white, and it was a daunting experience.

The doors blew shut behind me and the resultant clatter must have told Mary I was on my way. The tiny machine phut-phutted into the deepening snow and I hoped I knew how to cope. There's an art in riding motor cycles in snow, and it is an art acquired painfully by many years of falling off or skidding into ditches. By use of gears, feet, body weight and accelerator, it is a marvellous experience to safely negotiate a well-tuned motor cycle through heavy drifts, up and down slippery slopes, past other vehicles and across wide expanses of virgin snow. But there was no guarantee I would achieve any of those aims.

Sometimes I stood on the footrests to allow the bucking, slithering machine to perform its gyrations beneath me, and at other times I lifted my feet off the rests and carried them slightly above the surface of the road, to keep me upright if the wheels decided to travel away from me. Surprisingly, my bike and I remained upright.

I moved steadily and enjoyably through the falling snow. The headlight picked out weird and grotesque shapes among the drifts, the heavily clad conifers, the smothered hedgerows and the undulations of the highway. But I was alone, so utterly alone among virgin snow, and knew care was vital. My exertions in maintaining both movement and balance made me perspire heavily beneath the heavy clothing, and by the time I reached Ashfordly Police Station, I was lovely and warm from my five-mile struggle against the best of winter snow. The fact that I was warm made the journey less onerous.

I parked my precious machine against the office wall and entered the welcoming brightness. A flickering fire glowed in the grate and the place reeked of warmth and cosiness. I stood in the entrance and Sergeant Blaketon bawled,

"Get out, Rhea! Look at you . . ."

I looked. I was caked in white. In spite of the windscreen, my motor cycle suit was frozen solid with a thick layer of crusty snow and my unshaven face bore icicles in abundance. But already, the heat was making them melt, and they began to drip on his clean, polished floor.

I went outside and jumped up and down to try and shake off my winter coat and managed to dislodge some of it. Then I re-entered and in the porch, removed my suit, managing to drop lumps of snow all over the door mat.

"You're late," said Sergeant Blaketon as I entered anew.

"I had to dig my way out of the garage, sergeant, and the road down here is full of drifts and is treacherous in places."

"Then you should have set off earlier. I do not like shoddy timekeeping, Rhea. You should plan ahead."

"Sorry, sergeant," I said, knowing better than to argue with him.

There was no one else in the office and I wondered if I was the only participant in this curious enterprise. I went behind the counter to look in my docket and there was no correspondence, but Sergeant Blaketon had vanished into his own sanctum.

"Come in here," he bellowed, and I obeyed.

I stood smartly by the side of his desk and he handed me an envelope. It was a small buff one with my name neatly typed on the front and it had the word SECRET in red ink across the top. If this was a red-ink job, it must be important.

"Open it, Rhea." He smiled fleetingly.

I did. Inside was a piece of paper with SECRET splashed in red across the top. It was addressed to me in person.

I read it most carefully, for I'd never read a secret document before. It told me to report to Sergeant Blaketon at Ashfordly Police Station at 6 am today.

I looked at him, and he looked at me.

"It says I've got to report to you, sergeant," I said foolishly.

"Yes, well, here you are and you have reported." He saw nothing odd about this initial encounter, for his rule-bound mind never looked for the odd or the strange. He obeyed orders and never questioned them.

"Right, Rhea," he said. "Remember this and don't write it down."

He coughed, cleared his throat and faced me squarely across his desk.

In these moments of history, I stood before him and tried to look interested. I hoped to God I would remember what he was about to impart.

He coughed again. "This is secret," he said, looking anxiously about himself. I wondered if any more snowmen were about to arrive. "We have learned from reliable sources that the Russians are very anxious to infiltrate our Ballistic Missile Early Warning system. They have already made several attempts, and one of their reported techniques is for a Russian ship to signal our coastguards with a report that a man on board is ill. They say he suffers from appendicitis or something which requires urgent medical attention, and the man is brought ashore. Several of his colleagues accompany him and we have learned that they don't all return. There are no Customs and Excise Officers on the remote parts of this coast, Rhea, and detailed checks are impossible. We believe the Russians are coming ashore to do something to the Early Warning Station."

He paused. I wondered if he'd been reading too many spy thrillers, although I had read of this attempted infiltration method in the newspapers.   •

"Last night, Rhea, at ten o'clock, such an incident happened. It was observed by the coastguards and they report that twelve men arrived with the sick sailor, but only eleven returned. One is still ashore."

"So we've got to find him?" I realised my mission for today.

"Yes. We have mustered men from all over the county, and each man has been given specific instructions. Your duty is to proceed to the area of Swairdale Forest. You must make a search and remain there until you are dismissed. Keep searching, checking, looking for footprints, meeting places, cars, anything that might suggest a link-up between the Russian immigrant and his contact. He might be meeting an accomplice, placing a letter in a collecting place, anything. You know what spies are."

"And if I find him, sergeant?"

"Arrest him, of course!"

"With my bike? Where do I put that? I can't sit him on the pillion . . ."

"Radio in, duffer! What's the radio for? Radio for help and we'll send a car."

"In this snow, sergeant?"

"Look, Rhea, you are not paid to think. Just get out to Swairdale Forest and start looking."

"What's he look like?" I dared to ask.

"We don't know. Just stop all suspicious characters and question them. If in doubt, raise Control. Oh, and prefix your calls for this mission with the code word 'Moorjock'."

"Moorjock, sergeant."

"Good. You've got it?"

"Is anyone else in Swairdale Forest?"

"Just you, Rhea, and a few animals and birds."

"No more men?"

"No, there's acres of pine trees. Your boundary is the forest itself and it includes the minor roads which join the main road from Strensford to Eltering. It's a big area, Rhea. It's just below the Early Warning Station which means that if he gets past our lads nearer the coast, he could confront you. A lot could depend upon your professionalism."

I asked him all kinds of questions, but it seemed I was on my own. I had a long period ahead of me, a period when I'd be climbing mountains, riding across moors, dodging bogs and marshes and winding my way between rows of Forestry Commission conifers. I knew the forest well. On a fine day, it was gorgeous, loaded with the scent of pines and replete with a multitude of wild animals and birds, ranging from deer to dormice and jays to jackdaws.

I had an Ordnance Survey map in my panniers, one I always carried, and after a quick cup of tea with Sergeant Blaketon, I climbed into my cold, stiff motor-cycling outfit and trundled into the bitterness of this cold February morning.

Outside, I had the world to myself. The roads were covered with a smooth white layer of new-fallen snow and they stretched interminably ahead of me. Riding carefully and treating my expedition as a test of motor-cycling skill, I covered the long miles at a reasonable pace. The heavily trod tyre on the rear wheel bit into the soft, virgin snow and the delicate surface presented no real hazard. The disturbed snow flew about me in a fine cloud, clinging to my suit and my face, and enveloping most of my machine in the purest of shrouds.

Surprisingly, I was not cold. Although the morning was bitter in the extreme, it was a dry cold, something on the lines I imagined in Antarctica or Alaska, and my unfailing efforts to retain my balance and to keep the Francis Barnett moving forward made me perspire deep inside my heavy layers of protective clothing. My face, however, was cold; the biting wind of a new dawn attacked my cheek bones and nose, and it battered my ears.

· But I cared not, for I was enjoying myself. I gloried in the experience of an uncluttered highway, for there was not a vehicle to be seen. I wondered at the silence beyond, the privacy of a new dawn in the moorlands of the North Riding, and I was flushed with pride at winning my contest with the slithering bike beneath me.

Soon after six thirty, I left the valley and climbed to the heights. Knowing how rapidly the winter snows obliterated the elevated landscape, I turned off the main road with some trepidation, and as the dry winds moved the light snow around in whirls and drifts, I found myself having to take fierce survival action. When I was confronted by a thick drift, I would kick my way deep into it while astride the bike, somehow holding it upright with the other foot. Then I would trundle the bike backwards, and accelerate many times towards the obstruction, literally bulldozing my way through.

Usually it worked. I would hurtle into a deep drift at a fair speed, and after repeated efforts, the bike often carried me to the other side. Through this kind of energetic progress, I reached the turn-off point for Swairdale Forest.

This was one of the extremities of the boundary in which I had to patrol to hunt the Russian during the coming twelve hours. I turned into the narrow, snow-filled lane and this took me deep into the forest. The road was bordered by tall pines and soft larches, interspersed with bare silver birches and some heavy broom shrubs. As I dropped from the exposed moorland road, there was less snow on the ground, much of it being caught in the evergreens above me. The trees were thick with suspended snow and as my motor cycle roused the sleeping birds, they moved off, startled by the noise but more startled when large dollops of snow fell on them. They fell on me too; it was like being bombarded from above by dozens of children hiding aloft with arms full of well-aimed snowballs. Maybe the Russian was up there? Perhaps he was aiming snowballs at the defending forces? I'd get him if he was!

I glanced skywards with a smirk on my face and fell off my motor cycle.

Through not concentrating on my route, I was late into a twisting corner at a point where the road turned left and dropped suddenly and steeply. The whole episode was deeply embarrassing. I hoped the Russian wasn't watching.

The motor cycle, with its engine roaring, back wheel spinning and lights blazing, began its independent descent of that hill. I was nowhere near it. It slithered away, and was kept on the road by the high sides and the drifting snow. As I staggered to my feet, I watched my transport hurtling noisily down this one-in-three gradient and I began to follow. In my eagerness, I moved far too quickly. My feet left me; by some unaccountable feat of gymnastics, both my feet left the ground at the same moment and elevated themselves to waist level. Somehow, they stuck out in front of me and pointed at nothing in particular. Momentarily, therefore, I was suspended in mid-air surrounded by snowflakes, and then I abruptly descended. My well-cushioned rump connected with the slippery slope and the smooth rubbery nature of the motor cycle suit was totally incapable of gripping the ice beneath me.

I started to slither down the hill. I was in hot pursuit of my motor bike and wondered if I would gain on it, or even catch it! Its weight and roaring engine kept it sliding majestically onwards but I was moving at a fair pace too. I was kicking my legs in the air, waving my arms and trying my best to seize something which might act as a brake. But I was too far into the centre of the road. Nothing came to my aid, and there was no way I could halt this downward race. In fact, I think my automatic gesticulations served only to speed me forward.

The wind rushed about my face and ears, and I remember seeing hints of daylight through the thick trees. I remember noticing the flashes of its headlight as the plunging motor cyle followed its pre-determined route and I realised there were better ways of spending my time before seven o'clock on a morning. Then there was a tremendous crash as my bike collided with a milk stand.

Three large milk churns were standing like sentinels on that stand. They were empty and awaiting collection this morning, but as my rampaging motor cycle assaulted the stand, two of the churns rolled off some yards ahead of me. They now began to roll down the hill. They rattled and bounced until their lids fell off and rolled in their wake. The din was awful. The clanging of the churns, the roar of the motor cycle engine and my shouting caused wild birds to race to safety from an unknown enemy, and their urgent flappings sent huge dollops of snow from the trees. It was snowing snowballs that morning.

I sailed past the milk stand in fine style. I must have been doing a good twenty miles an hour on my bottom, and I was reminded of my childhood sledging days, except I didn't have a sledge. I could not stop; I followed the erratic route of the milk churns and noticed one of the lids bounce into the woodland and vanish. The other continued to roll downhill, bouncing like a child's runaway hoop.

As I continued downhill, I realised the motor cycle had stopped and I could hear its engine behind me. It was now stationary in its garage beneath the milk stand, and eventually I halted. I terminated my journey quite sedately and quite smoothly in a dumpy holly bush which grew from the side of the road. As I closed my eyes to lessen the drama, I vanished into the depths of this prickly-leafed plant and found myself wrapped awkwardly about its sturdy trunk.

The milk churns continued for a further distance and rattled to an eventual halt somewhere out of sight. I ceased worrying about the churns and concentrated upon extricating myself from the embraces of the holly bush. It was not too difficult because I'd smashed a lot of branches on the way in but the road surface was treacherous. This was the root of my continuing problem. It was like glass; I guessed rain had fallen last night, or snow had melted on the road surface, and the night's frost had frozen it solid. The light covering of snow had done the rest, and tons of snow remained up there, to be knocked down by terrified birds. Dollops continued to tumble from the pines as I gathered myself together.

I could hear my motor cycle phut-phutting somewhere out of sight, and began to make my panting, breathless way back up the hill. I fell several times. My feet refused to grip the surface under any circumstances, and I spent several minutes propelling myself forwards with rapid movements of my feet, only to find I hadn't progressed at all. So I took to the trees.

My eyesight had become adjusted to the gloom of the forest, and by using healthy young conifers as bannisters, I gradually hauled myself up the slope towards the bike. By now, it had stopped phut-phutting, but the lights still burned and guided me towards it.

My only problem was getting across the road. Gingerly, I left the security of my trees and stepped on to the steep, treacherous surface. And my feet whipped away once again. Down I went, hitting my backside on the ice and once more spun down the icy slope. This time, I was twisting and turning like a spinning-top as my arms and legs acted like flails and completely failed to halt me. I thought of milk churns, holly bushes, holes in the seat of my pants and Sergeant Blaketon's Russian as I hurtled once more to the foot of the slope. I concluded this second journey in the same holly bush in approximately the same state as before. I spent some time sitting in that bush pondering my next move.

I couldn't leave the bike because it contained my soup and flask, and it also bore the radio which was my lifeline. I could wait until dawn and the possibility of a snowplough and gritter, although I knew the ploughs arrived here about twelve noon. They had to clear miles of major roads and visit umpteen villages before bothering with such remote areas as this. I could spread gravel or salt upon the ice, but I had no shovel . . .

Besides, it was still dark and I could not see very well, although dawn was not far away. I made my decision. I would try again.

This time, I made my nervous crossing of the road at a point very close to the friendly holly bush, and found I could make progress if I walked on all fours. If one foot slipped, the other and my two hands coped with the situation, and so I gained the other side of the road. There, I copied my earlier climb. I clung to the trunks of small conifers as I hauled myself through the thickening snow towards my precious flasks of soup and coffee aboard the stricken motor bike.

I made it. In the grey light of the coming dawn, I could distinguish the outline of the rough wooden table which had borne the milk churns, and beneath it was my fallen machine. The headlight and tail light still burned brightly and spread a patch of warm orange and red on to the snow. The lights also showed that it was still snowing. I gingerly stepped on to the verge and by holding on to the side of the stand, found I could maintain an upright position. I was making good progress.

My next task was to haul the bike from its resting place. Luckily, the Francis Barnetts of that ilk were not too heavy and the ice beneath it enabled me to drag it clear of the stand. By pressing my body against the milk stand, I could lever myself into a position where I could seize the fallen machine and haul it to its wheels. I coped surprisingly well and propped it against the milk stand. So far, so good.

Next I examined it. With a torch taken from the panniers, I found the machine had fallen on to the side which contained the tools and spare clothing, and so my soup and coffee flasks were intact. There was a scrub mark down one of the leg shields, and the windscreen was broken about half way up. I never found the missing bit.

But otherwise, the machine was in surprisingly good condition, and perfectly capable of being ridden. Dare I ride it down the hill? Or should I wait until the roadmen came with grit and salt?

But when hunting Russian spies, one does not wait for British workmen. So I decided, in the interests of the security of the nation, to guide my motor cycle to the bottom of this tricky slope.

It would be best to ride it, I decided, but I would sit astride in a low gear with my feet on the road surface, and allow the gears to hold the machine at a low speed as I allowed it to find its own way to the bottom. Gravity would achieve a lot, I reckoned.

And so, having checked it thoroughly once more, I gingerly sat astride, by using the security of the milk stand, kicked it into life and moved off. I eased it most carefully on to the snow-covered ice which now served as a road, and smiled to myself. Everything was going fine, just fine.

Then it slipped. Without any warning, the front wheel slithered away and I clung to the handlebars as the bike fell over yet again. It dislodged me, but I wasn't going to be deterred so easily. I hung on.

I am not sure how I managed it but I found myself squatting on my haunches, with both feet firmly on the ground, hanging on to the handlebars of the bike which lay beside me. Its footrest, pannier and leg shield were bearing its weight and it was sliding smoothly down the hill, taking me with it. And so we moved like that.

The bike continued its descent through the trees with me steering from my squatting position almost beneath it. I partly supported its weight as I hung on for grim death, and we sailed down that slope in fine style, the bike's light picking out the trees, a milk churn lid half way up a fir tree, the trail of one churn leading deep into the forest and the lofty trunks which supported a canopy of thick snow. But we made it.

My bike and I safely negotiated that steep hill in our outlandish style and we glided to a smooth standstill at the base, very little worse for our experience. I must have lost some material from the seat of my pants and from the soles of my boots, and the bike had shed half a windscreen and some slivers of paint. Some petrol had spilled out too, but the engine worked and the lights lit my route ahead. I was mobile.

I had no idea how I would climb back up that hill or up any other hill, but that was some time in the future. Right now, I could continue my journey deep into the forest, hunting the Russian and serving my nation with unstinted loyalty.

The Forest of Swairdale occupies a large tract of land in the bottom of that valley. Planted by the Forestry Commission, it comprises row upon row of immaculate pines, spruce and larch, all in symmetrical rows. Nothing else grows beneath them, and they cover the land with a deep blanket of dead pine needles, through which very little grows, other than a few fungi and blades of brave grass. As a moorland valley, it would be no good for agricultural produce, so its reclamation years ago from heather and bracken had been beneficial due to the timber it currently provided.

Indeed, a little village community flourished here. Due to the work brought to the valley by the Forestry Commission, a group of people live and work deep in the forest. They occupy cosy wooden homes which look like log cabins, and the community has a post office-cum-shop with an off-licence for liquor. Having arrived safely in Swairdale, I parked my machine near a gate and performed a walk-about patrol. It was half-past seven and the place was coming to life.

I spent an hour or more in the village, drinking coffee in a forestry worker's cosy home, finding the farmer to whom to apologise about his milk churns, and asking everyone to let me know if they noticed a Russian skulking in the woods. By eight o'clock, I had warned everyone, and returned to the motor cycle.

The radio was calling me.

I responded; it was Sergeant Blaketon.

"Location please, Rhea," he asked, speaking through the courtesy of Control Room via a system known as Talk-Through.

"Swairdale," I said.

"Down in the valley, you mean?"

"Down in the valley, sergeant," I confirmed with some pride.

"I never thought you'd make it this weather," was his remark.

"Neither did I, sergeant."

"Look, Rhea, you know the Moorcock Inn?"

"I do, Sergeant."

It was not far from here as the crow flies, but in fierce moorland weather, it would be isolated and beyond the reach of anyone. It would be like riding to the North Pole.

"I want you to call there," he said softly.

"I'll never get there, sergeant, not in these conditions," I protested.

"It's vital, Rhea, very important. You must make the effort, and that's an order."

"Is the Russian there?" I put to him.

"No, but there's a bus load of businessmen lost up there. They went to Strensford last night for a conference at the Royal Hotel, and haven't returned home. We checked, and they've left the Royal Hotel, but they haven't got home to Bradford. We can't make contact with the Moorcock Inn because the telephone cables are down, due to the weight of snow. Seeing you're in the area, we thought you might pop in to see if they're there. Lives could be at risk if they're not located."

"But it will take hours, sergeant!" I tried to protest.

"Then get going immediately, Rhea. Look, you'd better do something – one of those missing men is the Chief Constable's brother."

"I'm on my way," I said.

At first, I thought there was no way to the Moorcock other than by the hill down which I had travelled so dramatically with the milk churns and burning trousers, but I pulled the map from my pannier and examined it. My boundaries were clearly defined, and as I pored over the details, I discovered a forest track which led from Swairdale high on to the hills. It cut through the dense trees and then crossed the open moor at a point close to the summit, emerging at the top of a steep hill. The Moorcock Inn lay mid-way down that hill on the main road to Strensford.

I knew the forest route would be rough and for that reason it would provide traction for my wheels. Beneath the trees, there would be a minimum of snow. Having satisfied myself that the Russian was not lurking in Swairdale, I set forth upon my diversion to the isolated inn.

Surprisingly, the trek was possible. The heavy snow had failed to penetrate the ceiling provided by the conifers, and although a light covering did grace the route, it was negotiable without undue difficulty. I trekked high into the forest, standing on the footrests and using the machine in the manner of a trials rider. The action kept me warm and cosy, and after two miles of forest riding, I saw the summit ahead of me. A tall wire fence ran across the skyline and this marked the end of the woodland; beyond were untold square miles of open moor.

My forest track ran towards a gate in the fence and I halted there to open it. I checked again for the Russian – there was not a mark in the snow; no spies had passed this way. In fact, no one had passed this way. I went to open the gate.

It was locked.

A stout iron chain was wrapped around the tree trunk which formed the gatepost, and the chain was secured with a gigantic padlock. There was no way through. And the fence stretched out of sight in both directions.

I was completely stuck. I could ride all the way back to Swairdale but would never negotiate that steep hill to regain the main road; besides, that route emerged miles from here. I hoisted the bike on to its stand and walked along this perimeter fence, but there were no breaks. It had been erected recently and was totally motor cycle proof. Then I had an idea.

I looked at the hinges of the gate. Two large hinges were secured with long screws, and they were fastened to the other post, the one which did not bear the chain. With no more ado, I found the screwdriver and began to remove the hinges. It was the work of moments. In no time, I had both hinges off and swung open the gate, its weight being borne by the massive chain at the other end. I wheeled my trusty machine through, and returned the hinges to their former place. So much for moorland fences.

I mounted my bike and felt contented. I wondered how someone might interpret the footprints and wheel marks in the snow – there was a single wheeled track to the fence, a lot of untidiness around the gate and a wheeled single track leading from it. Once through, the terrain was terrible. I was crossing wild moorland, with my wheels bouncing and the machine bucking. I rode the bike in the style I'd now come to adopt, standing on the footrests and allowing it to buck and weave beneath me, trials style. I had a horror of falling off and breaking a leg, for no one would find me here. I would freeze to death, and for some two and a half miles, I carefully rode through snow which was smooth on the surface, but which concealed an alarming variety of pot-holes, clumps of heather, rocks and other hazards.

But I won. With my motor cycle and myself completely enveloped in frozen white, I managed to navigate that awesome moor. As I reached the distant edge of the moor, I saw to my right the three gleaming white balls of the Ballistic Missile Early Warning Station. They looked duck-egg blue against the pure white of the snow-covered backcloth, and dominated the surrounding moorland. The huge structures towered majestically above everything and looked surrealistic in this ancient moorland setting. The old and the new mingled in a fascinating manner.

Somewhere in the hollow which lay before the Balls, but which was invisible to me due to the snow, there stood the sturdy moorland inn to which I was heading. I reached the main road and was pleased to note that traffic had passed this way. A snowplough had pushed its way through, and there was evidence of other vehicles. Sergeant Blaketon's message was therefore rather odd, because if a snowplough had forced its way along here, and if other traffic was passing, then it was difficult to understand how a bus load of businessmen had come to be marooned in the blizzard.

It would be about nine o'clock as I carefully descended the steep, twisting gradients of Moorcock Bank, and sure enough, a bus was standing on the car park of the inn. It bore a Bradford address, Bradford being some eighty-five miles away. Having parked my bike, I knocked on the door and a lady opened it; she smiled and her pretty face showed some surprise at my snow-clad appearance. I wondered if she knew I was a policeman – the POLICE legend across my helmet was totally obliterated.

"P.C. Rhea," I announced, removing my gauntlets.

"Good heavens!" she stood back to allow me inside. "What on earth are you doing here?"

"It's a long story," I said, stamping the snow from my boots. It fell on to her door mat.

"Come in for a warm, for God's sake," and she stepped back to permit me enter. The interior was comfortably warm, and I was shown into the bar area with its flagstone floor and smouldering peat fire. The place was full of men, some dozing and other sitting around quietly playing cards.

"Oh," I said. "Company?"

"Marooned," she smiled. "A bus load."

I began to unbutton my stout clothing, my hands warm and

pliable after the exercise of controlling the bike, and she asked, "Coffee?"

"I'd love one."

"I'm doing breakfast for that lot. Forty-two of them, bacon and eggs. How about you?"

At the mention of food my mouth began to water and I assured her that a delicious bacon and egg breakfast would be the best thing that could happen to me. She told me to remove my outer clothing and sit with the others. She'd call us into the dining-room when she was ready.

Some of the men glanced at me, and it was only when I peeled off the heavy jacket that they realised I was the law. I could see their renewed interest.

"What's this, Officer? A raid for drinking after time, or before time?"

"No," I struggled with the ungainly trousers and rubber boots and was soon standing with my back to the fire, warming my posterior and rubbing my hands. My face burned fiercely and my ears began to hurt as the sudden warmth made the blood course through them. I hadn't realised my extremities were so cold.

"Breakfast then?" a stout man smiled. "You've called in for your breakfast?"

"I am going to have breakfast, as a matter of fact." I looked at them. "Are you the businessmen from Bradford?"

There was a long silence and then the stout man nodded. "Aye," he said. "How come you know about us?"

"I'm searching for you," I lied to make the matter seem more dramatic. "There's a hue and cry out for you – there's reports of missing men snowed up in the North Yorkshire moors, men dying from starvation and exposure, buses falling down ravines and bodies all over . . ."

"Gerroff!" he laughed. "Go on, what's up?"

"I'm out here on another job . . ."

"Not working? They haven't made you work out here, in all this snow, on a bloody motor bike?" One of them stood up and addressed me.

"They have. It's important," I tried to explain without revealing national secrets.

"It must be – I'd have a strike at my factory if I even suggested such a thing," and he sat down.

I tried to continue. "I was called on my radio. Our Control Room said your bus was thought to have got stuck, and it was felt you might be here but they couldn't make contact because the telephone lines were down."

"No, not down, officer. We've taken the phone off the hook."

"Off the hook!" I exploded. "You mean I've come all this way . . ."

"Look," the stout man stood up and came towards me. "We're businessmen, and we're always on call, always being rung up and wanted for some bloody thing or another. When we got here last night, for a drink, it was so nice and cosy that when the weather took a turn for the worse, we decided to stay. We took the telephone off the hook because we didn't want to be disturbed and we intended staying, didn't we, lads?"

"Aye," came the chorus from the assembled group.

"This is our holiday, officer. A sudden, unexpected and excellent holiday. Can you think of anything better than being snowed up in a moorland pub miles from civilisation? The landlord and his lady are marvellous and they've a stock of food that'll not get eaten unless they get crowds in. The beer's fine and we can play dominoes and cards to our hearts' content. We can drink all day because we're residents, and we've no worries about driving home or getting in late. Our wives will be happy enough that we're safe, and we'll stay here as long as we want, away from business pressures, telephones, secretaries, bank managers, problems and wives. We were going to ring today to tell them we're safe, but snowed up. Now you've gone and ruined it."

"Sorry," I said. "As long as you're safe, my job is over. I'll report back by radio."

"Don't say we're *not* snowed in, will you? I mean, we could leave now because the plough's been through, but we don't want to. Tell 'em we're safe, but stuck fast."

"I'll simply radio to my Control to say you are here and you are all safe. Am I right in thinking none of you wants to be rescued?"

"No," came the murmured chorus. "For God's sake don't rescue us. Leave us, officer. In a while, that telephone will mysteriously be reconnected and we'll convince our loved ones we're fine, sitting here in eight-foot drifts and suffering like hell, and then the telephone cables will come down again!"

"I get the message," I said.

"Then join us for breakfast. Cereals, bacon, eggs and tomatoes and mushrooms, toast and hot coffee . . ."

I joined them. I couldn't refuse, not after my appetite-raising morning. They chattered about their meetings, their businesses, their twelve-hour days and hectic travelling, and I could see that this enforced holiday was perfect for them. They could relax totally, and I would not reveal this to anyone.

After breakfast, I told them I must leave. I got invitations to visit them and pocketed many address cards before buttoning up my motor-cycle suit. Now it felt cold and damp, and the thought of leaving this warm place with its beams, open fires, smell of smoke and peat was awful. But I had a mission of national importance and I must not dally a moment longer.

As I fastened the zips and buttons, a young man in a fine suit and sleek blonde hair came forward for a chat.

"You didn't come all this way just to find us, did you?"

"No." I was honest. "I've another job here."

"I reckon it must be important to your people," he said, puffing at a pipe, "otherwise they wouldn't have made you risk life and limb by motor cycling here."

"It is," I confirmed, sliding my head into the cold helmet. I pulled the strap under my chin and it was wet with melted snow. I grimaced as I tightened it.

"Something to do with that chap that I saw crossing the moors, maybe?" he smiled knowingly.

"Aye." I knew he'd seen my Russian!

"I saw him from that back bedroom," he said. "A tall chap dressed like a bloody Russian. Snow suit and big fur hat. He was crossing the moor on that track behind the pub."

"What time?" I asked.

"Not long before you came," he said. "Quarter to nine, maybe."

"Which way was he going?" I had fastened my chin strap and was ready to leave.

"Out towards the moor heights. I reckon he'd been sleeping in one of the outhouses of this place, officer."

"Thanks," I said. "I appreciate your interest."

"And we appreciate your discretion," he said.

I waved farewell to them, and thanked the lady for a superb breakfast. I'd been there well over an hour and was feeling fit and ready. I radioed a brief report to Control and merely confirmed their presence here. I said they were fit and well, with adequate food and warmth, and there was no risk to them.

To cut a long story short, I guided my faithful Francis Barnett towards the track in question and there I found a single trail of footprints. They emerged from an outbuilding close to the pub and it was easy to follow them in the snow. By now, the flakes had ceased falling and a wintry sun was trying to force a way through the heavy grey clouds. I thought again of Candlemas Day and wondered if the sun would shine.

It was said locally that, "If Candlemas be dry and fair, Half of winter's yet to come – and mair!"

Perhaps the rest of winter would be better than this?

After a mile and a half, the footprints wove erratically towards a grouse butt. I could see the boot marks etched clearly ahead of me as they climbed towards the lofty butt. Boris must be hiding there now! A grouse butt is like a three-sided square, it is made of stone with walls about four feet high. Grouse shooters lurk in there to blast at birds which are driven over their heads . . .

I decided to park and inform Control of this development. It seemed I had succeeded where others had failed. Upon receiving my message, I was instructed to await further orders. I waited for quarter of an hour, and this caused me to feel the cold for the first time. My feet, hands and face were icy and a bitter wind whipped the dry loose snow into small heaps and drifts. If the wind strengthened, this place could soon be well and truly isolated. Those businessmen might be there for days!

Then came the response from Control.

"Proceed to arrest," I was ordered. I was a long way from the hiding man and decided to take the bike. At least, it would get me closer to him in a swift manner. I kicked it into life, and began to climb the rough track, with the wind biting into my face and driving loose snow into the goggles and among the engine parts. I wobbled in the fierce wind but kept my eyes on that distant grouse butt.

Suddenly, the man stood up. His head and trunk appeared above the rim of the butt as he stared in disbelief at my approach. Then he began to run. At that instant, a Landrover materialised from somewhere, having been hidden down a dip in the track and it also raced towards the fleeing Russian.

God, it was like something from a spy film! So those films were realistic after all!

I accelerated, but the snow-bound track caused the rear wheel to skid; I fought to maintain my motion and my balance as I saw the man running towards the Landrover. I was roaring towards them both. I had to get there first, this being my first major arrest. A spy!!

I stood on the footrests and allowed the little bike to buck and roar beneath me as I closed in; now I could see the fellow's eyes beneath his furry white hat and the Landrover was a similar distance at the far side of him. It was neck and neck. I must win! I couldn't let the nation down at a time of such need. I would have to abandon my bike, I would have to leap off as I neared him, and allow the machine to fall into the snow, but I *must* make this arrest. For the country's sake, for the Chief Constable's sake, for my own sake.

I climbed the rising ground as the Landrover hurtled towards me with clouds of snow rising behind. The fugitive moved closer towards it. I was only yards away; I could see his thick leather boots, his snow suit, his furry hat . . .

He was mine. I had him!

But he wasn't, and I hadn't.

The Landrover did not stop at him; instead it came directly for me, with its rear wheels skidding violently and the front ones bucking against the rough terrain. God, I was going to be killed!

I swerved aside; I tore at the handlebars and yanked the front wheel to one side, but I was too late. The motor cycle toppled over as the heavy wing of the Landrover clipped the handlebars.

I was thrown right off. I rolled clear and felt myself falling down a hillside. I curled up into a protective ball, with my helmet, suit and gloves providing ideal protection as I gathered speed down a snow-filled, bracken-covered and heather-clad moorland slope. I could hear the victorious Landrover roaring away, and my motor-cycle engine had stopped somewhere out of sight.

I came to rest at the bottom, shaken but not hurt. The heather, with its springy tough stalks, had bounced me down that hillside like a ball, and when I got to my feet, I saw that the Landrover had stopped further along. Several faces peered at me and I waved my fist at them.

They waved back, and as I started to climb the slope, tugging at heather roots for support, they vanished over the horizon.

I had lost my Russian.

*   *   *

Six weeks later, we were in a classroom for a one-day course. The subject was "Liaison with the C.I.D." A detective inspector from Headquarters was laying down the rules about communication between departments, and liaison between officers and men.

"Exercise Moorjock was a perfect example of confusion," he said.

Was that an exercise? I thought it was the real thing! I'd given my all on that occasion, I'd risked my life and my limbs!

"There was no communication, no liaison. We shot a film of the exercise to highlight some of the problems," he said. "It speaks for itself."

And when the lights went out and the film hit the screen, I saw myself riding towards the camera; I saw the pseudo-Russian waiting for me, and I saw myself tumbling down a moorland hillside in a cloud of winter snow.

I could not forget those Candlemas Day events, but did remember the old Yorkshire saying, "Look for nowt in February – and you'll get it."

2

"This only is the witchcraft I have us'd"

William Shakespeare 1564–1616 *Othello*

"Rhea? Are you there?" It was Sergeant Blaketon and I was retrieving a heap of files from the floor of my office. I had lifted the telephone to answer and had dislodged a heap of paperwork with the cable.

"Sorry, Sergeant," I responded. "Yes, I'm here."

"Get yourself out to Ellersfield," he instructed me. "Go and see a Miss Katherine Hardwick of Oak Crag Cottage. She's got a complaint to make."

"What sort of complaint, sergeant?" I was still struggling to hold the telephone with one hand and pick up the files with the other. It would have been easier to leave them on the floor, but they annoyed me.

"Mischief makers," he said. "She's being plagued by somebody from the village, one of the lads by the sound of it."

"Kids!" I snorted. "What's he doing to her?"

"Daft things really, knocking on her door when she's in bed and running away before she opens it, tapping on the window when she's sitting alone, pinching tomatoes from her greenhouse and cutting the tops off all her cabbages. That sort of thing. Nuisances, Rhea, nothing but bloody nuisances."

"Is she a regular complainer?" I asked him.

"No, she's not. She's a decent hard-working woman who lives alone and she earns her keep by growing flowers and vegetables, or doing odd jobs for the folk of the area."

"I'm on my way," I said.

"Good. It'll keep you quiet for the rest of the morning. Anything else to report?"

"Nothing, sergeant, it's all quiet." It was extremely quiet. My beat had lacked any real trouble or serious incident for the past six weeks, but this lull may have been due to the weather. The winter snows and gales tended to keep people away from the moors and its range of villages, but now the spring had arrived, my workload would surely increase. Life was beginning anew, and I wondered if this lad's activities with Miss Hardwick were a sign of rising sap.

I departed from my hill-top house on my trusty Francis Barnett, clad up to the eyeballs in my winter suit, goggles, helmet and gloves. The crisp air contained a definite chill, but the brightness of the morning and the clarity of the views across the valleys and hills were truly magnificent. I was faced with a journey of some eighteen miles each way, and braced myself for the long, cold ride. There would be none of the gymnastics I'd enjoyed during Exercise Moorjock.

I dropped into Ashfordly, rode through the sleepy market town and out towards Eltering before turning high into the moorlands which overlooked Ryedale. Here, the roads were reduced to tracks and I marvelled at the new growths blossoming from the depths of dead vegetation. The grass was showing a brighter green, new leaves were bursting from apparently lifeless stems and animals romped in the fields, glad to be rid of winter's burden and looking forward to the joy of spring.

My machine and I climbed across the ranging hills with their acres of smooth moorland, and I enjoyed the limitless vista of steep slopes, craggy outcrops and deep valleys. They combined to produce a beauty of landscape seldom found elsewhere. And there was not a person about. I had the moors to myself.

True, I did pass one or two cars, and in the villages I noted ladies going about their daily shopping or cleaning their cottage windows, but beyond the inhabited areas, there was a sense of isolation that was intriguing. It was like entering a deserted world, an area devoid of people and houses but full of living things like birds and plants and animals. In some respects, it was like a fairyland, with wisps of mist hanging near the valley floors and shafts of strong sunlight piercing the density of the man-made forests and natural woodland. The smell of peace and tranquillity was everywhere.

Ellersfield lay snug in one of these deep valleys, a cluster of stone-built houses nestling at the head of the dale. All had thatched roofs, and they were sturdy dwellings, somewhat squat in appearance but constructed to withstand the fierce winters of the moors. Oak Crag Cottage stood at the far end as I rode into the community, using a road which ended in a rough cart track as it climbed steeply on to the moors before vanishing among the heather.

It was a neatly kept house. The thatch was carefully maintained and an evergreen hedge acted as a boundary between the cottage and the track by which it stood. The wooden gate was painted a fresh green and bore the name of the house in white letters. I parked the motor cycle on its stand and opened the gate, walking clumsily in my ungainly suit.

The house had three windows along its front with two attic windows above, all with tiny panes of glass and all neatly picked out in fresh white paint. I knocked on the door and waited. There was no reply.

I tried again, with the same result, and guessed the lady of the house must be around because she'd called in the police to solve her problem. As policemen are wont to do, I moved away from the front door and walked along the sandstone flags to the rear. At the back was a long flat garden with sheds and poultry runs, and I saw a woman repairing a wire netting fence at the far end.

"Hello!" I shouted.

She stood up, placing a hand on her back to indicate some form of backache. She smiled a welcome.

"Oh, hello. Is it the police?"

"Yes," I confirmed, realising my gear made me look like a refugee from the Royal Flying Corps of World War I. "I'm P.C. Rhea from Aidensfield."

She came towards me looking pleased as she removed some rubber gloves. She wore a headscarf which almost concealed her face, and I wondered if she was pretty.

"Katherine Hardwick," she introduced herself. "Miss," she added as an afterthought. "I'm sorry to trouble you, but I thought I'd better put an official stop to my unwelcome visitor."

"You did exactly the right thing," I endeavoured to comfort

her a little. "You know who it is?"

She shook her head and said, "Come inside, I'll make a coffee. You'll have a coffee?"

"There's nothing I'd like more." The spring air had given me a healthy appetite and thirst, and she led me through a rear door into the dark interior of her cottage.

It was very dark inside and I noticed the rear windows were very small, so typical of these moorland houses. They aided warmth and security in the harshest of weathers. Her kitchen was a long narrow room with modern electric equipment, but she led me through and into her lounge.

As the kettle boiled, she settled on a Windsor chair and smiled pleasantly, removing the headscarf as she talked. She was a very tall woman, with an almost angular body and she appeared to be shapeless beneath her rough country clothes. She had a long overcoat which was all tattered and greasy, corduroy trousers and wellington boots, but as the headscarf came away, I saw that her face was beautifully smooth and pink. Her eyes were bright and alert, her teeth excellent and her hair as black as night, cut short but not severely so. I estimated her age to be less than forty, but probably beyond thirty-five. She was very attractive in a rural way, and I wondered what she'd be like in an evening dress or a summer frock. Did she ever wear nice clothes? I wondered.

The kettle began to whistle and she took off her old coat to reveal a well proportioned figure clad in a rose-coloured sweater.

She vanished into her kitchen and returned with two cups of steaming coffee, a jug of fresh cream and a basin of sugar. Some home-made fruit cake and ginger biscuits adorned the tray.

"This is lovely," I congratulated her. "You shouldn't have bothered."

"It's nice to get visitors, and besides, it's 'lowance time anyway. Now, Mr Rhea, did your sergeant tell you what this is about?"

"Somebody's playing pranks, being a nuisance, frightening you?"

"That's about it, Mr Rhea. I'm not one for calling the police,

I usually sort out my own troubles but I felt this one ought to receive the weight of the law. There's other folks who live alone up here, you see, and some are elderly. I don't want them terrified."

"There's not many folk live out here is there?" I sipped my hot coffee. It was delicious.

"Seventy or so, it's not many," she confirmed.

"You have an idea who's doing these stupid things?"

"I have," she said, "and I've warned him off. He says it's not him, but things keep happening."

"Such as?" I wanted her to tell me more.

"It's nothing serious. Last back end, for example, he opened my greenhouse door after I'd closed it for the night and the cold air ruined some young plants and flowers. He's let the hens out of their run and they ruined my garden when I was in Middlesbrough for the day; he knocks on windows and runs off when I'm alone in the house. One day, he cut all the heads off my cabbages and ruined them, and another time took the seat off my bike and threw it into a field."

"Are you frightened?"

"No," she said. "No, I'm not frightened. It's just a bloody nuisance, Mr Rhea, and I wonder if he's doing it to others in Ellersfield, others who are too shy or old to report it. People are shy out here, you know, they don't like making a fuss."

"I know," I knew enough about the stolid Yorkshire character to fully understand her remarks. "Right, who is it?"

"It's a youth called Ted Agar," she said, with never a doubt in her voice.

"You've seen him doing these things?" I put to her, enjoying the cake.

"No," she admitted. "But it's him."

"How can you be so sure?" I had to ask.

She hesitated and I wondered if I had touched a sensitive area. I allowed her to take her time before replying. She drank a deep draught from her cup.

"Mr Rhea, I'm a woman and I live alone. I'm thirty-six, and I'm not bad looking. Ted's been pestering me to go out with him – to the pictures, for walks, over to Scarborough for a Sunday trip, that sort of thing. He's only a child, Mr Rhea, a lad in his early twenties I'd say. I've turned him down every time and these things started to go on."

"Over what period?"

"Maybe a year, no longer."

"Is he a local lad?" I asked.

"Not really. He came from Eltering, looking for farm work and Atkinsons took him on."

"Atkinsons?"

"Dell Farm, at the bottom of the hill on your way in. That big spot with double iron gates."

"I know it," I smiled. "O.K. Well, Miss Hardwick, I can have words with him for you. I can threaten him with court action – we could proceed against him for conduct likely to cause a breach of the peace. That way, we could have him bound over to be of good behaviour, and if he did it again, he'd be fined or sent to a detention centre of some kind."

"I don't want to take him to court, a warning from you would be fine," she said. "I know he'll think I'm using a sledgehammer to crack a little nut, but he won't stop when I ask him. I thought a word from you might help."

"I'll speak to him. Will he be in now, at Atkinsons?"

"He'll be about the premises somewhere," she acknowledged.

I drained my coffee and stood up. "I'll let you know how I get on – I'll come straight back."

Before I left, I briefly admired her home. The kitchen was a real gem. The fireplace, for example, had an old stone surround with a black-leaded Yorkist range, complete with sliding hooks for pans, and a side oven. It was set in an inglenook and to the right was a wooden partition beyond which was a passage into a further series of rooms.

"It's a fascinating house," I observed.

"It's an old cruck house," she explained. "It used to be a longhouse, that's a farm house where the family lived at one end and the cattle at the other. The living quarters were warmed by the animals as they wintered next door. The crucks are like tree trunks, and they support the building. It's very old – I couldn't hazard a date."

"Did you move out here?"

"No," she smiled. "It's been in our family for generations. There's always been a Hardwick here, as long as anybody knows."

I walked around the spacious kitchen, and expressed delight at the ancient woodwork, so crude but effective, and then I noticed the carved wooden post at the outer end of the partition. I ran my hands down it, fingering the delicate workmanship.

"This is nice – what's the carving?"

"That's a witch post," she informed me. "Lots of houses had them installed."

"What's it for?" I had never come across this type of thing before.

"They were built into many houses in this area to protect the occupants against witches," she smiled. "They date from the seventeenth century mostly, but I've never dated ours."

"Was witchcraft practised here?" I was intrigued by this decorative post.

"A good number of old women were reputed to be witches," she said. "They were supposed to make the milk go sour, or cause the fruit not to ripen – stuff like that. Nuisances more than anything. There wasn't your dancing naked bits or rituals in lonely woods. They were just old ladies who terrified the superstitious locals and got blamed when things went wrong. Those posts protected the inhabitants against them."

After my obvious interest in her house, she showed me the rest of the layout of the fascinating building with its nooks and crannies, beamed bedroom ceilings, sandstone floors and rubble walls. It was a house of considerable age, albeit modernised to meet her modest needs.

I left my motor cycle near her gate as I walked down the steep hill to Dell Farm. This was a neat homestead with freshly painted gates and a scrupulously tidy farmyard. I made for the house, although I could hear activity in one of the outbuildings, knocked on the door and waited. At my second knock, a woman's voice shouted, "Come in, the door's open."

I entered a spacious farm kitchen with hams hanging from the ceiling and the smell of new bread heavy in the air. An old lady sat in a chair beside a roaring log fire. I think I must have aroused her from her slumbers.

"And who might you be?" she demanded, looking me up and down.

"P.C. Rhea," I said. "The policeman. From Aidensfield."

"You're a bit off your area, aren't you?" she quizzed me sharply, her keen grey eyes alert and bright. I reckoned she was well into her seventies, or even older.

"Not any more. Now we've got motor cycles, we go further than we did on bikes. We share the area."

"You'll have come for our Reg, have you? Summat to do with his guns, is it?"

"Are you Mrs Atkinson?"

"I am, but Reg is my son. He's the boss here – I'm just an old lady who lives in. Our Reg's wife, that's young Mrs Atkinson, is down at Ashfordly, shopping. Susan, that is."

"It's really young Agar I want to see," I explained.

"Why would you want to see him, then? He's not in trouble is he?"

"No," I said, "but I hear he's been making a pest of himself."

"Pest? What sort of pest?"

I provided brief details of his alleged misbehaviour and she listened intently, leaving me standing in the middle of the floor. She smiled fleetingly, and when I'd finished, she said, "Lads will be lads, it'll be due to his sap rising, Mr Rhea!"

"I agree it's nothing serious, Mrs Atkinson, but his behaviour is unnerving for Miss Hardwick."

"Hardwick, did you say?" she threw the question at me, with those eyes flashing brightly.

"Yes, up at Oak Crag Cottage."

"Then she ought to know better than to bring you in, should that one," the old lady said. "Fancy bringing you all the way in for a trifling thing like that . . . she ought to be ashamed."

"It's not nice, Mrs Atkinson, having unknown lads making nuisances of themselves when you're a woman living alone. I don't mind coming out to help put a stop to it."

"Nay, it's not that, Mr Rhea, it's that woman. Hardwick. It's the first time I've come across a Hardwick woman that couldn't sort things out by herself."

"Why?" I asked, intrigued. Katherine Hardwick seemed a perfectly ordinary young woman.

"They're witches," she said with all seriousness. "All Hardwick women are witches."

I laughed. "Witches?" I said, thinking she was joking.

"You'll have heard of Nan Hardwick, haven't you? Awd Nan
Hardwick, who was a witch in these hills years ago?"

"No," I had to confess.

"Then just you listen, young man," and she motioned me to a
wooden chair. I sat down, interested to hear her story. I knew
that old ladies tended to ramble and reminisce, but Mrs Atkinson appeared totally in control of her senses, and deadly serious
too. She spoke with disarming frankness.

After leaning forward in her chair and eyeing me carefully,
she unravelled her extraordinary story. She was in her late
eighties, she told me by way of introduction, and then related
the fable of Awd Nan Hardwick. She was a witch whose
notoriety was widespread in the North Yorkshire moors when
Mrs Atkinson was a young girl; everyone for miles around knew
Awd Nan.

She told me a story about a farmer's wife who was expecting a
baby. One afternoon, Awd Nan chanced to pass the house and
called in for some food and a rest as she was several miles from
home. She asked for a 'shive o' bread and a pot o' beer'. The
food was readily given to her and during the conversation, she
let it be known she was aware of the young wife's condition. She
wished the girl well and said, "Thoo'll have a lad afoor morning, and thoo'll call him Tommy, weeant thoo?"

The girl replied that she and her husband had already
decided to name the child John if it was a boy, but Awd Nan
replied, "Aye, mebbe thoo has, but thoo'd best call him
Tommy. And now, Ah'll say goodbye," and off she went.

Both the husband and the girl were determined to name the
child John, and later that evening, the prospective father drove
a pony and trap across the moors to collect his sister-in-law. She
had offered to help with the birth. Three miles from the farm,
he had to cross a small bridge, but the horse stopped twenty
yards before reaching it and steadfastly refused to move. Try as
he might, the farmer could not persuade the animal to proceed,
so he tried to leave his seat on the trap. To his horror, he found
he was unable to move. In his words, "Ah was ez fast as owt."

Eventually he concluded that Awd Nan had put a spell on him and shouted into the air, "Now, Nan, what's thoo after? Is this tha work?"

To his amazement, a voice apparently from thin air replied, "Thoo'll call that bairn Tommy, weearn't tha?"

The husband, still determined to select his own name, shouted back, "Ah'll call ma lad what Ah wants. Ah weearn't change it for thoo or for all t'Nan devils in this country."

"Then thoo'll stay where too is until t'bairn's born and t'mother dies," came the horrifying response.

The poor young farmer was placed in a terrible dilemma. He could not move his pony and trap, nor could he climb from the seat, and he was faced with the death of his dear wife, all for the sake of a lad's name. As he sat transfixed, he reasoned it all out, and decided there was an element of uncertainty because the child might be a girl. For that reason, he capitulated. He agreed to call the child Tommy if it was a boy. And at that, he found the horse could move and he went on his way.

My storyteller did not tell me whether the child was a boy, and I did not ask in case she was talking about her own ancestors, but she went on to relate more stories of Awd Nan Hardwick, all showing belief in the curious power of these local witches.

As I listened, it was evident that she believed the stories, and I could imagine her family relating these yarns as the children gathered around a blazing fire during the long dark evenings of a moorland winter.

"Is Katherine Hardwick a descendant of Awd Nan?" I asked.

"She is," the lady nodded her grey head seriously. "All those Hardwick women were witches, and she's no better. Mark my words, young man."

"What sort of things does she do then?"

"Turns milk sour if she comes in the house, makes folks ill by looking at them. Little things like that, like her mother and the other women folk did. Milk would never come to butter if a Hardwick was around."

"Is that why you said she could sort out her own trouble with this mischief maker?" I asked.

"Aye," she said, "any witch worth her salt could sort out that kind of trouble."

"But with all due respect, Mrs Atkinson, witches don't exist . . ."

"Balderdash!" she snorted. "Do you know what they did in a situation like this? When folks upset them, angered them, scandalised them?"

I shook my head.

"The witch took a pigeon, Mr Rhea, a wild pigeon, a wood stoggie we used to call 'em. They made pigeon pie, but they took the heart out and stuck pins into it, into the heart that is. They put as many pins in as they could, lots and lots, and then put the heart into a tin and cooked it. Then they put it near the door, out of reach of cats and things, out of sight."

"And?"

"Well, it made the mischief maker want to apologise for what he'd done. He went to the house and made his peace. It allus works, Mr Rhea." She spoke her final words in the present tense.

"And you think Katherine should do that?" I put the direct question.

"Nay, lad, Ah didn't say that. Ah said she *could* do that, because her previous women folk did that sort o' thing. If she wants to bring you fellers in, then that's her business." She spoke those words with an air of finality.

"Is Ted Agar in, Mrs Atkinson? I ought to talk to him while I'm here."

"Try those sheds at the bottom of our yard, he's down there fettling t'tractor."

"Thanks – and thanks for the story of Awd Nan."

"It's true," she said as I left the warmth of the kitchen to seek Ted Agar. I found him working on the tractor. He had the plugs out and was cleaning some parts with a wire brush, his face wrapped with concentration as I entered the spacious building.

"Ted Agar?" I spoke his name as I walked in.

He glanced up from his work and smiled at me. "Aye, that's me."

"I'm P.C. Rhea from Aidensfield," I announced, thinking this would give him notice of the reason for my presence.

He continued to work, acknowledging me with a curt nod of his curly black head. He was about twenty-two or three, I guessed, a sturdy youth in dirty overalls and heavy hobnailed boots. His face was round and weathered with a hint of mischief written into his smile.

"Summat up, is it?" he asked.

"Have you been annoying Katherine Hardwick?" I decided to put the matter straight to him. "Playing jokes on her, messing up her garden and so on?"

"Me? No," he said without batting an eyelid, and without stopping his work.

"Somebody has," I said. "She's upset and if I catch the person, it'll mean court."

"It's not me," he said firmly, furiously rubbing at a piece of rusty metal with the wire brush.

"Then don't do it," I said, leaving him. I felt it would be a waste of time, pressing him further. Denials of this kind rarely produced anything beyond those words, so I left him to his maintenance work. I poked my head around the kitchen door to inform old Mrs Atkinson that I'd found him, and said I was leaving. If Agar was the culprit, I felt my brief visit would halt his unwelcome attentions.

I walked back up the village to my motor cycle and popped over to Katherine Hardwick's house to explain my action. I went around to the back but she was not in the garden, and I noticed the kitchen door was open. I knocked and stepped inside a couple of paces, shouting "Miss Hardwick? Are you there?"

There was no reply, so I continued to shout as I entered the kitchen. Her lunch was in the course of preparation, so she must be around. I called again, "Miss Hardwick?"

"Upstairs," she shouted. "Who is it?"

"The policeman," I shouted back. "P.C. Rhea."

"Oh, I'll be down in a minute," she replied. "Sit down."

I sat on a kitchen chair, holding my crash helmet in my hands. And as I waited, my eyes ranged across the half-prepared meal. A pigeon lay on the kitchen table, plucked clean except for its head. Its innards lay beside it, having been expertly gutted and I saw the tiny heart set aside from the other giblets. There was a small tin beside the heart, and a pin cushion, thick with pins and needles. I thought of Mrs Atkinson and her tales of Awd Nan . . .

"Hello," she returned, smiling broadly. "Sorry, I was upstairs. I was changing out of my working clothes, I'm going into Eltering this afternoon."

"I just popped in to say I've spoken to young Agar," I announced. "He denied making mischief, but I'm convinced it was him. I warned him about the consequences of repeating any mischief at your house, so I reckon we've seen the last of him. If he does come back, or if anybody else starts those tricks, let me know."

"It's most kind of you, Mr Rhea. I really appreciate your help."

After some small talk, I left her to her cooking, my brain striving to recall the details of Mrs Atkinson's story. It was definitely a pigeon's heart on that table, and the pin cushion was so conveniently positioned next to it . . .

Three days later, my telephone rang.

"Is that P.C. Rhea?" asked a woman's voice.

"Speaking."

"It's Katherine Hardwick," the voice told me. "You called the other day, about young Agar."

"That's right," I recalled. "Has he been troubling you again?"

"On the contrary," there was a smile in her voice. "He's been to apologise. He said he did it for a lark, but didn't realise the upset he would cause. I've accepted his apology, Mr Rhea, so there won't be any need for further action, will there?"

"No," I agreed. "No, that's all. There will be no court action. Thanks for ringing."

I replaced the phone and reckoned the previous generations of Hardwick women would be very proud of their Katherine.

* * *

Happily for the Hardwick women and those of their ilk, the Witchcraft Act of 1735 had been repealed, albeit not until 1951.

England had had a long history of cruelty and antagonism towards old ladies who were regarded as witches, and before the

1735 Act, witchcraft had been a capital offence. The last judicial execution for witchcraft possibly occurred at Huntingdon in 1716, when a woman and her nine-year-old daughter were hanged, and the last recorded committal was at Leicester in 1717 when an old woman and her son were charged with casting spells, possessing familiars and being able to change their shapes.

It was not until 1951, however, that witches were safe from prosecution in England, and the statute which brought about this change was the Fraudulent Mediums Act, 1951.

The provision of that Act which was of interest to the police was Section 1. It created the offence of acting as a spiritualistic medium or using telepathy, clairvoyance or other similar powers with intent to deceive, or when so acting using any fraudulent device when it is proved that the person so acted for reward.

Those who reckon they can perform miracles of this kind purely for entertainment need have no worries, but those who seek to make money from their so-called powers can expect a file of their activities to be sent to the Director of Public Prosecutions and they can also claim right of trial by jury if things go that far.

In the bucolic bliss of North Yorkshire's Ryedale, I hardly expected to consider a prosecution under the Fraudulent Mediums Act of 1951, but my eyes were opened at the Annual Whist Drive and Jumble Sale held in Aidensfield Village Hall. This was an early event in the year, the social occasion of the spring equinox, when everyone in the village took mountains of junk for someone else to buy, and obliged by buying mountains of someone else's junk in return. Thus the junk of the village did a tour of the households and much money passed hands for worthy causes such as the church steeple fund, the old age pensioners' outing fund, the R.S.P.C.A. and other animal charities, including charities for children. Much money was made, and much junk was disposed of, to be returned for re-sale after a suitable period in someone's home.

The system was illustrated perfectly when my tiny daughter purchased for one shilling a box camera I had given away five years earlier for another jumble sale not far away. She bore her purchase proudly home, only to find the shutter didn't work because it was bent. She kept it and donated it to the sale the following year. I imagine that camera is still being bought and sold and I'm sure it now qualifies as an antique. If I see it around, I might buy it as a keepsake.

Because of the large volume of traffic expected at the function, Sergeant Blaketon telephoned and instructed me to perform duty outside the hall that Saturday afternoon. I had to control the crowds, prevent indiscriminate parking and keep an eye open for pickpockets and other villains. I parked the five cars without much ado, I controlled the perambulating crowds which swarmed the street, and kept vigil for local villains. I was not unduly busy.

The only villain likely to make an appearance was Claude Jeremiah Greengrass, and I was somewhat surprised and, I dare admit, disappointed, when he failed to put in his anticipated attendance. Claude Jeremiah liked jumble sales because he bought most of his clothes and furniture from such places, and I know he managed to earn a little extra cash by re-selling items of interest. I liked him there because his presence gave me work – I had to keep an eye on him to stop him stealing things.

With the grand opening neatly performed at 2.30 pm by the vicar's wife, and with my public order and parking duties enforced without incident, I entered the hall for a survey of pickpockets and ne'er-do-wells. Mary had brought the children, all four of them, and our family formed a crowd in its own right. The Rhea procession had entered some time earlier, and satisfied that crimes were not being committed, I looked about to see what I could purchase. The tiny hall was full, a pleasing sight, with nice people making faces at each other and complimenting the ladies for baking cakes, mending old clothes and manning stalls.

I found Mary and our little entourage and helped her guide the family around the stands, examining vintage baby clothes, looking at battered furnishings and cracked crockery, and deciding not to buy anything. And then I spotted the fortune teller.

This was a new idea. As my eyes settled on the ornate tent in a corner in front of the stage, I found it most impressive. The tent had the appearance of a small Arabian structure, circular in shape with a tall centre pole and flags flying from the top. The drapes were open down the front and the mysterious interior was coloured deep purple enhanced by golden curtains with a green centre support. In front of the opening was a table, also covered with purple and gold drapes, and upon the table was a crystal ball and several other implements used by a gypsy fortune teller. A large notice pinned to the tent told us this was Gypsy Rose Lee.

Behind the ball sat the gypsy herself. She was a small woman with a deeply tanned face, most of which was smothered by a veil which covered the nose and mouth. Her head was swathed in brilliant silken bands which cascaded down the rear of her neck, and her voluminous sleeves billowed as she sat before the crystal ball. Her hands were heavy with jewellery, and a tiny bowl of incense burned inside the tent, sending a strong aroma about the hall.

It was a most impressive display, and I watched with fascination because every woman in the place seemed to want her fortune told. I heard the chink of silver as money changed hands, and was surprised to see the growing queue of women, all eager to have their palms read or their fortunes told for the princely sum of five shillings.

I was kept fairly busy during the sale. Children got lost, people misplaced belongings, old ladies lost keys and purses, some teenage lads became a shade too boisterous and an exploding fuse put all the lights out. Mary and the children appeared to enjoy the occasion, but left early because the youngsters had exhausted themselves as only tots can. I helped Mary take the family up to my house on the hill and returned to the Hall to be present at the conclusion of this momentous event.

By five o'clock it was all over. The cake stall was deserted, and only crumbs remained; the soft drinks now comprised many crates of drained bottles, and the assorted stalls of junk had little left, other than the annual complement of totally unsaleable rubbish. This would come out again next year. I chatted to Miss Jenks, the secretary and treasurer of the Village Hall Committee and expressed my pleasure at a well conducted event.

"Thank you, Mr Rhea." She was a retired school-teacher of the old kind, stern and humourless. "We have done well, but then we always do."

"What's the profit? Do we know yet?"

"Not yet, but I imagine it will be around the £150 mark, an excellent result. It is going to the church steeple fund this year."

"I liked the gypsy idea – a real novelty," I nodded in the direction of the heavily clad woman who was demolishing her tent and packing her fortune-telling impedimenta.

"Yes, it was a good crowd puller. She rang me rather late to be mentioned in our posters and advertisements, but word got around."

"Who is she?"

"Gypsy Rose Lee," smiled Miss Jenks. "The real one, the one you see at Blackpool in the summer. She rang to ask if she could hire space from us."

"Hire space?"

"Yes, she rang me and asked what I'd charge to rent a corner of the room."

"And what did you say?" I asked gently.

"I said we didn't hire space, but if she really wanted to come and entertain us, she could give us ten per cent of her takings, and they would go to the steeple fund."

"And she could keep the rest?"

"Yes, the committee felt it was a nice idea. I telephoned them all when I got the request, and Gypsy Rose rang back for our decision. We all agreed, Mr Rhea . . ." her voice trailed away as she explained this to me. "Oh dear, I say, I haven't broken the law, have I?"

"No," I smiled. "No, but the gypsy might have. If she's been taking money for herself, by professing to tell fortunes with the intention of deceiving the public, then she might have committed a criminal offence."

"Oh, Mr Rhea, it's all a bit of innocent fun."

I would have agreed had it not been for my recollection of lots of cash dropping into the palm of that gypsy. If every woman had had her fortune told this afternoon, with some children, that gypsy would have reaped a fortune. I made a hasty calculation in my head and reckoned she'd collected about £70.

If she gave £7 of that to charity, it left a huge profit – over £60 – more than a month's wages for the average man.

The tent had by this time been reduced to a pile of flimsy material which was being packed into a large suitcase, along with the ornate pole. That was now in short sections. The crystal ball had gone, and the other materials were in a large leather bag. Only the woman remained and she was still in her heavy fancy dress. I found that rather odd. Why hadn't she changed into everyday clothes?

I stared at her, busy with her packing, and the provisions of the Fraudulent Mediums Act 1951 flickered from the dark recesses of my memory. She had taken money . . .

I stood alone, racking my brains, as Miss Jenks counted piles of money into a tin at my side. I was vaguely aware that the gypsy woman was heading for the cloak room, no doubt to change out of her ceremonial dress.

She walked across the floor before us, weaving expansively through the rubbish which remained, and she vanished into the cloakrooms. I chattered to Miss Jenks for a few minutes, and then decided I needed to use the gents. I made for the cloak-room too. One of the cubicles was occupied, showing the "Engaged" sign. And on the floor, I found a pile of flimsy silk and chiffon. I heard a window click . . .

I rushed out and ran down the alley at the side of the village hall. I was just in time to see Claude Jeremiah Greengrass, with his face the colour of chocolate, squeezing out of the gents' toilet window.

"Hello, Claude Jeremiah," I beamed. "Going far?"

He said nothing. There is very little one can say when one is caught climbing out of a gent's toilet window with one's face coloured chocolate, and with ornate ear-rings dangling from one's aching lobes. I seized his shoulders and hauled him through, placing him squarely on the ground before me. His wizened, pinched and elfin face twitched as I said, "Pockets – open them all up, turn them out."

Still without speaking, he obeyed. To give the fellow his due, when he was caught red-handed, he was most co-operative. He produced £62 10s 0d in cash, and there was a further £5 in his wallet.

"The wallet money's mine, Mr Rhea," he said, and I believed him. The other was in a separate pocket, and I knew enough of my local villain's behaviour to realise he'd keep today's cash takings separate from the other.

Standing there in the back alley, I chanted the provisions of the Fraudulent Mediums Act to him and told him he was being reported for contravening its provisions. I felt sure the Director of Public Prosecutions would be fascinated to learn of this incident at our Jumble Sale, and firmly gripping Claude's collar, I steered him back into the room to face Miss Jenks.

"Miss Jenks," I said, "this is your gypsy. Claude Jeremiah Greengrass to be precise, and he has a donation to make to your charity. Isn't that right, Claude?"

I shook his collar.

"Yes, Mr Rhea," and I handed her the £62 10s od.

She was sufficiently fast-thinking to appreciate the situation, and I noted the quick smile as she looked at the abandoned suitcases and unpacked tent.

"There was the question of rent for that space, Miss Jenks," I said. "Mr Greengrass and I had a discussion outside, and we agreed that £5 was a reasonable sum for the afternoon. Mr Greengrass will be happy to oblige, I'm sure."

"But Mr Rhea, there's all that money . . ."

"Rent, Claude, or it's a file to the D.P.P. my lad . . ."

"Yes, Mr Rhea."

He pulled out his wallet, extracted five pound notes and gingerly handed them to Miss Jenks. She smiled, issued a receipt and pushed the cash into a money box. "Mr Greengrass, this is most generous. I do believe this jumble sale's profits are the best we've ever had, thanks to you. I must make a note in the minutes. Maybe you'd come again next year?"

"I'm sure he will, Miss Jenks, and on the same terms, Claude Jeremiah?"

And, as we say in the force, he made no reply.

3

"Oh, dry the starting tear, for they were heavily insured."

Sir W. S. Gilbert 1836–1911

One of my greatest delights was to ride the sturdy little Francis Barnett across the wild acres of stirring moorland which lie to the north of Aidensfield. Lofty roads and rough tracks interlace across the more accessible regions of the heathered heights while prominent summits dot the horizons to mark the extremities of the more remote parts of the unpopulated portions. But even those far-flung borders conceal beauty and mystery, and are worthy of exploration.

Many is the time I have parked my little machine on the roadside at some eminent outcrop, to sit and admire the panoramic spread below. Mile after mile of uninhabited land, some of it moorland but much of it comprising green valleys, can be seen from countless vantage points. A succession of artists have attempted to capture the expansive attraction of the moors and dales, but few have painted a memorable reproduction. One or two have captured the exquisite purple of the heather, and some have caught the sheer enormity of the emptiness within the ranging hills. A true picture of the landscape eludes many. The hardiness of the residents has also defied interpretation by striving artists and the region is virtually ignored by novelists.

I have often considered myself fortunate to be paid a salary for touring these moors and valleys, whereas visitors pay substantially to explore them. That is the chief perquisite of the country constable in North Yorkshire.

But if the countryside is replete with attractions, then so are the people who scrape a living from these hills. Sheep farming dominates but in the lowland districts, the farmers manage to eke out a living through versatility and hard work. Few of them take a holiday or even a day off because their work and responsibility makes full-time demands upon them and their families. Because their work is their entire life, they are utterly happy and deeply content, a rare thing in any era.

On my visits to the more distant areas, I made regular calls at the lonely farms. These were chiefly to inspect stock registers or to renew or verify firearms certificates, and it meant I was known to every farmer in the district. The homesteads comprised every kind of farm from the huge, multi-owned premises run by a manager, to the tiny single-cow farm with a few hens and pigs, but which somehow maintained a man and his wife.

I learned to negotiate cattle grids, unmade tracks, water splashes, woodland ravines and every type of obstruction on the way to these premises, and I could cope with all sorts of gate, bulls, pigs and abandoned farm machinery. But almost without exception, my admission was friendly and courteous. At every place, I could expect a cup of tea or coffee with a slice of fruit cake, and in most cases something seasonally stronger, like whisky or brandy if warranted by the occasion.

Many of the farmers expected more from me – they expected me to sit down and eat their huge dinners, called lunch in less civilised areas. These are invariably massive, the logic being that the working man's body is in need of powerful fuel to keep it going correctly. The bigger the man, and the heavier his workload, the more fuel he needs to sustain him during a long working day. This logic seems eminently reasonable, because most of the farmers were huge, muscular men who kept working without a rest from dawn until dusk, their only sustenance being repeated doses of massive meals. As one farmer explained, "Thoo needs mair petrol for bigger, faster cars than for little cars, and they go better an' all. Ma lads is all like big cars, so Ah need ti feed 'em well."

It appeared to be the custom to offer a seat at the table to any stranger who chanced to arrive at meal time. Inevitably, there was enough food to cater for an army of unexpected visitors, and the meals were never made from fancy food. It was all good plain Yorkshire grub, substantial and tasty, comprising local dishes like potato and onion pie, or roast beef and Yorkshire pudding, or joint of lamb with roast potatoes. Home-made soup was invariably offered, with sweets like steamed treacle puddings, apple pie and custard, or fruit pies of most kinds. Rice pudding was common, as was any milk pudding, and a cup of tea concluded the meal, with buns, ginger bread or fruit cake. These were everyday meals, not feasts for special occasions.

This typical farm dinner (lunch) was followed by a light tea around five o'clock which was something like a fry-up of sausages, black puddings, potato, bacon, eggs and tomatoes, with a light sweet like tinned fruit and a cup of tea with buns, cakes or biscuits. Supper was similar . . .

Because the farmers of the moors ate so well and so bounteously, they beamed with health and the hard slog of their daily toil never appeared to have any ill effects. The volume of their unceasing toil would shame today's so-called workers, and their appetites would make a Roman feast look like a Sunday School tea party.

After a few months of patrolling and visiting my friends on the moors, I learned never to pack myself a meal. I also learned not to return home for my refreshment breaks. I ate with whomever I called upon around midday or at any meal time and it was deemed discourteous to refuse this hospitality. Thus I had many superb eating houses on my daily rounds, and my moorland patrolling became a gastronomic delight.

This applied equally to other routine callers, like the postman, the vet, the electricity-meter reader and similar officials. It was during this merry round of epicurean duty that I became aware of another regular visitor to my farms.

Sometimes, the fellow was leaving as I arrived and we would hold gates open for one another; sometimes he followed me in and we would eat at the same table with eight or nine farm workers, but no one bothered with introductions. I began to wonder who he was. He appeared to visit the farms with the same frequency as myself, and always availed himself of the mountainous meals.

He used a small grey Austin A35 car, immaculately kept with its chromium shining and its coachwork polished in spite of frequent muddy excursions. He was a smart man in his forties with neat black hair, who was invariably pleasant and courteous. We passed the time of day many times, without progressing beyond that basic formality.

Inevitably, we would meet one day with sufficient time for an introductory chat and this happened one spring morning shortly before twelve noon. I arrived at Howe End Farm near Langbeck after a tortuous ride up a stone-ridden incline, and my mission was to check the particulars of Farmer John Tweddle's firearm certificate, which was due for renewal. As I parked my motor cycle against a pig-sty wall, the little grey Austin chugged into the farm yard and came to a halt at my side. The neat man with black hair climbed out, clutching a briefcase in his hand.

"Morning," I smiled, removing my crash helmet. "You've survived the bumps, then?"

He laughed. "Aye," he said. "I've grumbled at old John about his road, but he never does anything about it. He reckons if folks really want to visit him, they won't mind a few bumps and buried rocks, and if they don't want to come, they deserve to suffer a bit."

"I'm P.C. Rhea," I introduced myself. "I'm the new policeman over at Aidensfield."

"This is a bit off your beat, isn't it?" He closed his car door.

"Not now," I said. "Since they issued us with motor bikes, they've closed some beats and extended the boundaries of others. I cover a large patch now, including this end of the moor."

"And me," he said, offering me his hand. "Norman Taylor, insurance man."

We shook hands warmly.

"I've noticed you coming and going, and having those massive meals," I laughed. "It seems all and sundry can just stop and eat with them."

"They're offended if you go away unfed at dinner time. It's as natural to these folks to feed their visitors as it is for, say, a policeman to give advice to a lost motorist. I think it stems from the days when visitors took days rather than hours to reach these remote places. If anyone came, they'd need feeding before they left, and I reckon these folks are continuing that custom. They haven't realised that our cars and bikes get us from place to place within minutes rather than hours."

Together, Norman and I walked to the back door which was standing open and he entered without knocking. He walked straight to a teapot on the mantelpiece, lifted the lid and took out a £1 note. He made an entry in a book which lay beside the teapot and smiled at me.

"Monthly insurance premium," he said. "She always leaves it here."

"They're trusting folk," I commented.

"They are; they trust those who call, as if they were their own family. Mrs Tweddle is a good payer, she never forgets to leave her £1 for me once a month."

"I'm looking for John, his firearm certificate's due for renewal."

Norman looked at his watch. It was twelve o'clock, and he said, "He comes in for his dinner at quarter past twelve. Elsie will be here soon – there'll be a potato and onion pie warming in the Aga."

And he sat down.

I pondered over my next action; I ought to go into the buildings to seek my customer and Norman recognised my hesitation.

"Sit down," he advised me. "They'll be in soon, and it'll save you chasing about the place."

I settled in one of the Windsor chairs and he occupied the other. We talked about our respective jobs, and it transpired he lived at Milthorpe, a hamlet on the northern edge of my beat. His agency embraced the whole of the North Yorkshire moors, a huge slice of countryside with scant population, and he told me how he enjoyed every minute of his work.

As we talked, a large rosy-cheeked woman entered the kitchen.

"Hello, Elsie," greeted Norman.

"Hello, Norman. Nice morning," she smiled happily. "By, Ah've just been down hedging in our five acre. Ah'm famished – have you checked the pie?"

"No, P.C. Rhea came and we've been talking."

"Oh," she said, looking at me. "Thoo'll be after our John?"

"Firearm certificate," I told her. "It's due for renewal."

"He'll be in soon," and she went about her business of examining the pie in the Aga. A delicious smell wafted into the kitchen as she opened the door and examined her handiwork. There were no introductions, no fuss over me, no false niceties. I was here, and that was it.

She lifted the steaming pie from the oven and prodded the thick, brown crust with her finger. It was contained in a huge brown earthenware dish and there was enough for a table of eight or nine people. She placed it on the Aga to keep warm and laid the table. She set four places, I noted, four knives, four forks and four spoons. No table cloth and no condiments. There was a good deal of pleasant small-talk between herself and the insurance man, and then big John entered. He saw me and Norman, nodded briefly and went to the sink where he washed his hands thoroughly with a grease-removing agent, then swilled his face with cold water.

"Bin greasing machinery," he informed us. "Spring time comes fast, eh? Winter's gone and next thing we know, it's time to get cracking, and my awd tackle allus gits rusted up."

Having washed, he plonked himself in a chair at the table and his wife pulled a hot dinner plate from her Aga and filled it with a massive helping of steaming potato and onion pie. The crust must have been an inch thick, and the pie filling consisted of sliced potato, onions and gravy, masses of it. The pie had no bottom or sides – just the rich food with a heavy lid of luscious pastry.

"Norman," and she filled a plate for him, and then looked at me. "Sit there, Mr Rhea," and she pointed to the fourth chair. It was not a request and not really an invitation. Because I was here, it was understood I would eat.

I was not used to this hospitality and my face must have registered surprise. Even though I knew of this custom, its manner of execution was strange to me.

"Come on, Mr Rhea," said John munching at the crust. "There's no time to waste."

And so I found myself tackling a gorgeous pie. It needed no flavouring with salt or pepper, but there was far too much. I

daren't leave any, and was on the point of finishing the first
helping when she ladelled a second dollop on to our plates. How
Norman coped I do not know, but I must admit I struggled.
Eventually, I cleaned it all away. I saw Norman and the others
cleaning up the gravy with a lump of pie crust held in their
fingers. Luckily I had some left, so I copied them. The result
was four very clean plates.

Mrs Tweddle took our plates and placed them on the Aga;
then she lifted an equally large glass dish of rice pudding from
the oven. It had a tough brown skin on top, and the contents
beneath were creamy and thick. She spooned generous helpings
on to our first course plates and I now knew why we'd cleaned
them so thoroughly. I must admit I was surprised at this but I
later learned it is a widely practised custom on moorland farms.
And it saves washing up!

After the final cup of tea with cakes and biscuits, Norman
bade farewell and I was left with John. He produced a whisky
bottle because it was our first meeting, and over a strong
draught we completed his application form for renewal of his
certificate. I collected the half-crown fee and left the farm,
having made new friends.

As things often tend to work out, I bumped into Norman
many times during my farm visits. His little grey car would be
negotiating tricky farm tracks and moorland roads as he went
about collecting his premiums and offering advice to his many
customers. I learned that his honesty was such that everyone
left their doors open, from big farms and houses to tiny cottages
and bungalows, and he knew where each person left his premiums. I never knew the name of his company because everyone called it Norman's Insurance, and this is how I came to refer
to it. The money left on tables or doorsteps was always for
Norman's Insurance.

But his activities began to interest me. He appeared to be
something of a general dealer because I often saw him carrying
rolls of wire netting, hunting boots, old pictures or other objects
to his car. On one occasion he carried a brace of pheasants, and
on others I saw him variously with a three-legged stool, a brace
and bit, a clip rug, two hunting prints, a car tyre, some brass
lamp holders from an ocean-going liner, a garden bench, a

scythe, a butcher's bike, a side of ham and a Victorian fire screen.

During the times we passed or met one another, he never enlightened me about his extra-insurance activities, and I did not ask. One does not pry too deeply because it indicates a betrayal of trust, but I did consider asking around to discover what he was up to. But, in the event, that course of action became unnecessary.

By chance, I was called urgently to Norman's village of Milthorpe because a visitor had reported his jacket and wallet stolen. It seems he had removed them while changing the wheel of his sports car, and when he'd finished the job, his sports jacket, and the wallet it contained, had vanished. I was on patrol at the time, astride my Francis Barnett, and the radio summoned me to the scene of this foul crime.

It took me thirty-five minutes to arrive, and I found the irate motorist waiting near his Triumph Spitfire. I eased to a halt, parked the motor bike and removed my crash helmet. I left it on the pillion.

"P.C. Rhea," I introduced myself. "Are you the gentleman who has lost a jacket?"

"Not lost, constable. Stolen," affirmed the man. He was tall and well-spoken with expensive clothes which spoke of a nice line in tailoring. His hair was plastered across his scalp with some kind of hair cream and he seemed totally lacking in humour. On reflection, it's not funny having your belongings stolen while changing a car wheel.

"Tell me about it," I took out my pocket book. He told me he was Simon Christie from Southwark, having a touring holiday alone in the moors. His wallet contained some sixty pounds in notes, together with his driving licence and other personal papers. The jacket, he explained, was of Harris tweed, tailor-made in London and worth a lot of money. I didn't doubt it.

I asked how on earth he'd managed to get it stolen.

"That is something you are here to establish," he said haughtily. "Look, I got a puncture in my front offside tyre, and stopped right here to change wheels. I removed my jacket and placed it on the railings at the rear of the car. I worked on the wheel at the front, and when I'd finished, my jacket was gone."

"How long did it take to change the wheel?" I asked.

"Ten minutes, maybe less," he said.

"And did anyone walk past while you were working?"

He shook his head. "I'd swear that no one came past, constable. I'd swear it."

"Are you sure it's gone? It's not in your boot, is it?"

He sighed the sigh of a man who'd hunted everywhere, but raised the boot lid. No jacket. I looked in the car, under the car, over the hedge and everywhere. It had vanished.

"I'll make enquiries in Milthorpe," I promised. "Can I contact you locally if I find it?'

"You sound hopeful, constable?" There was almost a smirk in his voice.

"This is a very small community, Mr Christie," I said in reply. "If anyone has stolen your jacket, someone here will have seen the culprit. These folks have eyes everywhere."

I made a deliberate attempt to sound confident, for I imagined his coat had been lifted from the verge by a passing tramp or hiker. If so, the locals would know where he was. I had complete faith in my ability to recover this property and emphasised that point.

"I'm staying at the Crown Hotel in Ashfordly," he said. "I'll be there for a further four nights, constable."

"I'll be in touch before you leave," I assured him.

Having obtained a detailed description of his jacket and of his wallet, I watched him leave with a roar of his throaty exhaust, and set about detecting Milthorpe's crime of the century. When beginning enquiries in any village, it is prudent to begin at the Post Office. Village post offices are replete with gossip and information about local people and their affairs, so I strolled into the tiny, dark shop with its multitude of scents, dominated by soap and polish.

At the sound of the door bell, a young woman appeared and smiled sweetly. She would be in her late twenties, I guessed, and had pleasing dark hair and a ready smile full of pure white teeth. She was very young to be a village post mistress, I thought.

"I'm P.C. Rhea," I announced, conscious that my helmet was on the pillion of my bike some distance away, and my motor cycle suit bore no insignia. I could be anybody.

"I saw you arrive," she said, as if to confirm my belief in the all-seeing eyes of village people. "You were talking to that man with the sports car."

"He's had his jacket stolen," I informed her. "It's odd – it was taken during the few minutes he was changing his wheel."

"That'll be Arthur," she said immediately. "He's always stealing – he once stole a pair of slippers I'd left outside, and he takes anything – trowels, flower pots. We daren't leave anything lying about."

"Oh, I see," I now had a name. Just like that. I hate to admit I didn't know Arthur, but I had to ask where he lived.

"Where's he live?" I asked.

She pointed out of the window. "Of course, you're new," she smiled again. "You won't know him. He's at Heather Cottage, next door to Mr Taylor, the insurance man."

Until now, I had forgotten that this village was the home of Norman the insurance man, and was pleased to be reminded of the fact. I followed the line of her pointing finger and saw a neat cottage built of mellow brick. It had bow windows at the front and a red pantile roof, typical of the area. Next door was a larger house standing in its own grounds, and she confirmed that the latter belonged to Norman.

I left the little shop just in time to pause at the edge of the road for a tractor and trailer to pass. Behind I noticed Norman's little grey car and waved an acknowledgement. He saw me, and the procession pulled up at his house. He got out and shouted,

"Hello, Mr Rhea, good to see you."

"And you, Norman," I walked across to him.

"What's this then?" he asked. "Business?"

"Yes," I said. "A theft."

"Here in Milthorpe?" he asked, eyebrows rising.

"A motorist stopped to change a wheel," I explained, "and took his jacket off to work upon it. Someone stole it as he worked."

"That'll be Arthur, next door," beamed Norman. "You'll find the jacket there, I'm sure."

"Yes, the girl at the Post Office said so."

"Come in for a cup of coffee when you've got the jacket

back," he invited. "I'm just taking delivery of some bantams."

I glanced at the tractor and trailer, and noticed a farm lad standing beside the trailer, awaiting Norman's instructions. On the trailer stood a large wire-netting cage containing a dozen white bantams.

Recalling his other acquisitions, I said, "You're a bit of a dealer, are you?"

"It's more of a bartering system," he told me. "These are insurance premiums. This lad's father is hard up at the moment, so I've accepted these bantams as his monthly payment."

"It seems a good system!" I laughed.

"I've got all sorts," he said. "Look, you go and find Arthur, and then come in. By then, we'll have this crate of bantams off and my good lady will brew us a cuppa. I'll show you round my garden, and you can see some of my better insurance premiums!"

I chuckled at the notion, and opened the gate of Heather House. At the sound of the sneck, an aged black and white cur dog ambled from the rear of the cottage and wagged his tail in greeting. I patted him and approached the front door, the dog following closely with his old grey muzzle nudging my legs and his tail lashing backwards and forwards in happy greeting.

I knocked and waited. Soon, a grey-haired man with a big white moustache and rosy cheeks opened the door.

"Yes?" he demanded.

"P.C. Rhea," I said. "I'm the new policeman at Aidensfield."

"Oh," he said. "And Ah'm Dawson. Edgar Dawson."

So this wasn't Arthur. I wondered if Arthur was the fellow's son, perhaps someone who was a bit simple. The dog fussed about as we talked, and I patted his head, an action which caused the tail to wag even more furiously.

"I've come about Arthur," I said.

"What's he pinched now?" the man stood on the top step and glared at me.

This was an easy interview. "A jacket and wallet," I told him. "You might have seen the sports car down the village? The driver changed a wheel and had his jacket and wallet stolen as he worked."

"Ah'll skin him, so Ah will!" snapped the man. "If it's not one thing, it's another. He never stops. Ah've thrashed him and belted him, but it's no good, Mr Policeman . . . come with me."

Sighing the sigh of a weary man, he led me and the dog around to the rear of the cottage, and into a shed. The shed door stood wide open and he beckoned me to follow inside. And there, lying on the floor beside a grubby rug, was the sports jacket. He picked it up and handed it to me. I looked inside the pocket – the wallet was there and when I checked inside, the cash and the driving licence were present. Nothing had been touched, and the name inside the wallet confirmed it was Simon Christie's property.

"Thanks Mr Dawson, I'm delighted. Now, I'd like to talk to Arthur about it."

"It's not damaged, is it?" he asked me.

I examined the jacket, but other than some flecks of dust from the floor of the shed, it appeared undamaged.

"No," I assured him, "it's not damaged. Now where's Arthur – I'd like to talk to him."

"He'll not understand a word thoo says, Mr Policeman." There was a twinkle in his eye.

Suddenly, I began to feel uncomfortable. I could write off the whole affair but felt duty-bound to talk to Arthur and to ask him for an explanation. Larceny was larceny, even though the property had been recovered intact, and I was obliged to take legal proceedings. In those days, it was unlawful to conceal a felony, and larceny was classified as a felony.

"Can you take me to him please?" I asked, speaking with authority.

"He's right beside thoo, lad," beamed Mr Dawson, and I turned to see the happy dog thrashing his tail as I caught his eye.

"You mean this is Arthur?"

"Aye, Ah thought thoo knew that. He's my dog, twelve years old he is, and a real rogue. Now if yon jacket's damaged, go and see Mr Taylor next door, and he'll settle up with t'loser."

"Mr Taylor?"

"Aye, t'insurance man. Arthur's allus been one for pinching things so I've got him insured. He once pinched a workman's trowel and chewed t'handle to bits. He loves gardening tools. Spades, rakes, owt with a wooden handle. Clothes an' all. He'll get on his hind legs and pull clothes off t'washing lines, knickers, stockings, trousers, sheets . . . you name it, and Arthur's pinched it. So Ah got him insured and if there's any damage, Norman's insurance pays out."

"Is there anything else that's stolen in here?" I asked, looking at the objects that filled the place.

"No, Ah've looked. Ah checks it reg'lar at night before Ah turns in, and if there's summat that's not mine, Ah leave it at t'Post Office. Ruth puts it on t'counter and whoever's lost it gets it back. It's only strangers that doesn't understand, Mr Policeman."

"I'm not surprised," I laughed, and the dog's nose nudged me. I turned to address Arthur, the thieving dog. "Arthur, you are not obliged to say anything, but what you do say will be taken down in writing and may be given in evidence!"

The tail thumped my leg as Arthur acknowledged the official short caution, but he made no reply. I wondered what Sergeant Blaketon would make of this – I wondered about writing a full report and charging Arthur as a joke. I wondered if it would pass through our administrative system and get filed at Headquarters?

Having recovered the jacket, I returned to my motor cycle and tucked the clothing into my pannier before visiting Norman. The tractor and empty trailer was just leaving, and Norman was at the gate.

"You've seen Arthur?" he laughed.

"Nobody said he was a dog!" I grumbled. "I could have made a right fool of myself."

"Sorry, we all know him. Every time something is stolen in Milthorpe, we know it's Arthur. Did old Dawson tell you I've got his dog insured for causing damage?"

"He did," I let myself through his gate. "He sounds a real character, that dog."

"He is! He's always chasing lady dogs too, so I had to insure him against getting bitches pregnant. He once put a pedigree bitch in the family way and there was hell on about it. So Mr Dawson has him comprehensively insured against causing

damage and distress of all kinds. Only last year, I paid out twice
for getting bitches into trouble – if that dog was human, he'd be
doing umpteen prison stretches by now. As it is, we accept him
for what he is, a likeable old rogue. His love life would cripple a
lesser dog. He's incredible!"

Norman's wife, Eva, was a charming woman who produced a
hot cup of strong tea and a plate of scones, and soon we were all
chattering like old friends. Norman told me of his bartering
system, explaining how the hill farmers upon the moors had
very little cash. All their work went into real estate and property, so when they died, their families inherited a great deal,
while the unfortunate farmer had worked for a pittance all his
life.

Norman's system involved many deals. He told me about one
farmer who did all his gardening, one who did his painting and
plumbing, another who repaired his car and others who regularly donated eggs, bacon, ham, milk and potatoes as methods
of payment for their insurance premiums.

After the cup of tea, he led me down the garden. The bantams
were pecking happily at their new piece of earth, and a peacock
stalked majestically up and down in a cage. "From the big
house," he said confidentially. "Times are hard all over."

Two goats and a Siamese cat were shown to me, and a new
pedal cycle graced the garage. The real gems were in a long
narrow shed at the far end of the garden. He opened the doors to
reveal a veritable treasure trove of objects, most of which would
be ideal curios for a rural museum. The walls were hung with
old advertising signs in enamel, house signs and shop signs;
every kind of gardening implement and carpentry tool was
there, many of them obsolete, and along the base of one wall
there were stone troughs and foot scrapers set in stone. It was an
Aladdin's cave of rural objects, of obsolete items which would
never again grace the homes of our people and which would, but
for Norman's care, have disappeared for ever.

"All these have been collected in lieu of insurance premiums," he told me. "I could sell some of the things, but if
anything's got historic or sentimental value of any kind, I like to
keep it. I've a three-seater tandem in that shed at the bottom of
the garden, and a 1927 motor cycle in full working order. I can't

sell stuff like that, can I? But I do sell a lot – I've got to, to keep my books right!"

I spent a fascinating hour with him, and wondered how many rural insurance agents traded in this way.

But it was time to leave.

I thanked Norman for his interesting tour and assured him we'd meet again. I invited him and Eva to pop into my hill-top house any time, and off I went.

While driving through Brantsford on the way home, I noticed Mr Christie's sports car parked outside a small café and decided I should reveal to him the results of my enquiries. I pulled up and parked the motor cycle on its stand before entering the café. I left the jacket in my pannier for the moment, just in case he was not in here.

But he was drinking a cup of tea and as he recognised me, his eyebrows rose sharply.

"Ah, constable! And have you detected the crime of the century?"

I smiled diffidently at him.

"Yes," I said. "I saw your car and thought I'd mention it. I have your jacket and your wallet – and the cash. It's all there."

He drained the tea and said, "No, really?"

"I'll fetch it in for you."

"No, I'm leaving. I've paid, by the way," and he followed me outside where I unstrapped my pannier and lifted out his precious belongings. He readily identified them as his property and checked the contents of his wallet at my request. Nothing was missing, and I then asked him to check everything for damage. There was none.

"Constable, this is marvellous. You've traced the thief too, I take it?"

"Yes, and I have cautioned him about his future conduct!" I smiled.

"You'll be proceeding to court though?" he queried.

"Not on this occasion," I told him with all seriousness. "The matter has been dealt with and my enquiries are over."

"But constable, I am a solicitor, and I know that it is an offence to conceal a felony . . ."

"There was no felony, Mr Christie," I interrupted him.

"There was a theft . . ." he began.

"It was no felony," I continued.

"Who took my jacket?" he demanded. "Are you covering up for a local thief or something? This is serious."

"His name is Arthur," I said, "and he is a twelve-year-old cur dog."

Christie paused as if not believing my words.

"A dog?" he grinned suddenly, not sure whether I was joking.

"A dog." I told him about the insurance scheme which catered for Arthur's incurable kleptomania.

He laughed loudly in the middle of the street, and slung his jacket over his shoulders. "Well done, constable, well done. Yes, I like it – a nice one. A dog, eh? Called Arthur?"

"Yes, Mr Christie."

"I don't believe you!" he chuckled. "But I like your style. Wait until I tell them in London about this."

And off he strode towards his waiting car. I watched him drive away in a flurry of exhaust fumes and wondered what he would tell his sophisticated colleagues about law enforcement in rural North Yorkshire.

4

"There are two classes of pedestrians in these days of reckless motor traffic – the quick and the dead."

Lord Dewar

In my extreme youth, lady drivers were a rarity and when one witnessed a member of that fairest of sexes driving a motor-car, the sight was enough to make one stand and stare, before broadcasting the sighting to one's friends. Ladies as passengers were not uncommon, but it is fair to say that the skill of guiding a moving motor vehicle from place to place was usually entrusted only to the male of the human species.

Gradually, however, the ladies began to assume the mantle of masculinity and independence, and in addition to smoking or wearing slacks instead of skirts, they took lessons in the art of driving motor-cars. It wasn't long before ladies were driving all sorts of vehicles but I cannot recall my first sight of a lady behind the wheel. It cannot have been that unusual or important.

Certainly, this form of emancipation occurred long before I joined the Police Force, consequently by the time I had passed through training school, ladies were frequently seen at the wheel. We were taught diplomacy when asking their age, and admittedly, there was jokes or tales about their driving. One instructor told us how he'd stopped a lady motorist in Middlesbrough for driving at 40 miles an hour in a built-up area, to which she retorted, "Don't be ridiculous, I haven't been driving for an hour, and I certainly haven't done forty miles."

There were those who hung their handbags on the chokes and wondered why the car engine throbbed and smoked; there were those who pointed at scenic things through open windows and

confounded those driving behind into thinking all manner of
things which were far from the truth, and there were those who
depended upon a man to keep the machine roadworthy after
their exertions.

It must be said that there were many ladies who coped
admirably with the motor-car and its moods. One lady who
thought she fitted into this category was Esme Brittain, a lovely
looking woman in her late forties who drove a white Morris
Minor. She was blessed with a pneumatic figure, jet black hair
and lovely white teeth, all enhanced by dark eyes and gorgeous
legs. She had been married but the outcome of that association
was something of a mystery because the male half had vanished
long ago, leaving Esme with her little cottage and a Yorkshire
Terrier. There were no children of the union, and Esme earned
her living by teaching pottery and selling her distinctive products to tourists and craft shops.

Esme was a charmer. Of that there was no doubt, and many a
hunting male had attempted to change her tyres, check her
batteries and clean her plugs but she politely and firmly rejected
and resisted all approaches, however oblique. Although she
never said so, the villagers felt she'd been let down by her erring
husband to such an extent that she trusted no man. It must be
said, however, that she never criticised her missing husband,
nor did she grumble about his absence. She lived as if he'd never
existed and perhaps she had the ability to blot him from her life
and memory. I shall never know, but she certainly kept all men
at a respectful distance, particularly from her emotions.

Nice as she was, and beautiful as she looked, Esme in a car
was a threat to society. She reduced the most innocent of
motor-cars to the status of a guided missile, and floated through
heavy traffic as if she were a balloon which would bounce off
obstructions. How she avoided accidents was never known,
because her driving ability was appalling in the extreme. She
had no idea of road sense, car care or any of the niceties of
motoring. She just climbed in and set off, heedless of other road
users. Yet she survived.

Such was her reputation that the local people kept well out of
her way. The moment Esme was mobile, everyone kept off the
streets until her little Morris Minor was safely beyond the

outskirts of Maddleskirk. What happened beyond those boundaries was none of their business, and they had the sense not to find out.

The trouble was that Esme's adventures frequently became my business. Her erratic excursions invariably had a startling conclusion, and if she entered any of the conurbations within striking distance of the village she could be guaranteed to collect a summons for obstructing the highway, illegal parking, lack of proper lights, careless driving or some other trifling traffic infringement. Esme's trouble was that she never reported to the local police as advised in the tickets which were plastered about her windscreen after such indiscretions, consequently when the distant police traced her through the registration number, I was given the task of interviewing her for her regular and multifarious misdeeds. In this way, I became acquainted with the lovely Esme.

She constantly and charmingly admitted her errors and got fined by many magistrates, yet her adventures never made any obvious impression upon her. She never altered her ways or improved her driving, and yet she was never involved in a serious accident. I considered that to be miraculous.

It is not to say, however, that she was not a danger, because she did occasionally cause people to jump off their pedal cycles or motorists to abandon the road in order to preserve their own lives or safeguard their vehicles. But she avoided most collisions.

One exception involved three visiting ladies from a Women's Institute in County Durham. One lovely Sunday morning in late April, a bus load of them had travelled from the pit villages up north, and had ventured south to North Yorkshire in order to visit Rannockdale and its acres of wild bluebells. *En route*, the coach had stopped at a remote moorland hamlet called Gelderslack so that the ladies could form a queue at the toilet and buy coffee at a local café. The driver told them the break would be for three quarters of an hour, because he'd calculated it was the shortest time that a bus load of chattering women could each visit a single toilet. Such is the wisdom of bus drivers.

The first three ladies in the loo queue, having achieved their purpose, were also first in the coffee queue and therefore first out of the tiny village café. To while away the time until the last of their kin had taken on coffee and poured off water, they settled on a seat in the village. The seat in question had been presented to Rannockdale by Sir Cholmely Brown, and it occupied a prime site at the eastern side where it overlooked Surprise View. The place was visited by tourists, cameramen and Americans, all of whom admired the stupendous views from this summit. The three satisfied ladies managed to occupy that hallowed place for a few blissful minutes; for them, it represented rural solitude, because here they could sit and admire the view while their friends queued.

But they had reckoned without Esme and her doubtful driving ability. Through one of those awkward coincidences, Esme arrived in Gelderslack at the same time as that bus, because she was thinking of trading her little Morris Minor in part exchange for a large Humber Snipe. Gelderslack garage had a gleaming black Humber for sale, and so Esme arrived that day to inspect and test it. The benevolent garage proprietor, on seeing the immaculately polished Morris, readily consented to Esme taking the Humber for a test run. She climbed into the driving seat, coped with the starter and the gears, and drove the huge car into the spring sunshine.

All went well until she reached Surprise View. At that point, she recalled that she was not very good at descending steep hills, so decided to turn around and go the other way. To achieve this about-turn, it was necessary to execute a three-point turn and Esme succeeded in guiding the front wheels of the Humber into the side of the road as the prelude to her change of direction. This meant that the nose of the Humber was a very few inches from the back of the seat upon which sat the three unsuspecting ladies from the County Durham W.I. In their state of happiness, they failed to register any alarm at the proximity of Esme and the big car.

She stopped without any trouble, placed the gears in reverse and let in her clutch. Sadly, she'd erroneously engaged a forward gear and the huge car nudged forward and touched the rear of the seat. Esme halted its forward rush, but it succeeded in tipping the seat forward and toppling the three ladies into an 'untidy and ungainly heap on the ground overlooking Surprise View. Highly apologetic, Esme rushed to their aid, returned the seat to its correct position, and dusted down the surprised trio. Rather baffled by this turn of events, they re-settled on their seat and gazed airily across the moor.

Her apologies accepted, Esme resumed her position in the driving seat and had another crack at selecting reverse. As she let in the clutch for the second time, the car misbehaved yet again and leapt forward to tip up the seat. Once again, the three surprised ladies slid off and crumpled into a pitiful heap with the seat resting on top of them. Esme blushed furiously. She rushed out of the Humber and re-positioned the seat yet again, dusting them down with her hands and expressing her most profuse apologies. She tried to explain about the gears, but they glared at her angrily; gone was their northern *bonhomie* as they sat heavily upon their precious seat, furious at the indignities they had suffered. One had even laddered her stockings.

Very nervously, Esme re-entered the waiting Humber and with extreme care, and selected reverse. Most gingerly, she let in the clutch but this car was enjoying itself. It moved forward for the third time, and before she could halt its short progress, it once again touched the back of the seat and tipped it forward. For the third time, the W.I. ladies slid to the ground, a miserable, angry heap of feminine wrath. Now, they could endure no more and chased Esme from the Humber. She managed to reach sanctuary in the garage and sought protection from the man who'd loaned her the wilful vehicle.

But luck was on Esme's side because the loo queue was dwindling rapidly and the bus driver, who had witnessed the whole affair, had a sense of humour. He tooted his horn and drew his passengers back to the coach, but this did not prevent the aggrieved three from making a complaint. A day or two later, I had to interview Esme about it. Although I submitted an official report against her for careless driving, the Superintendent authorised 'No action', his reasons being, I suspect, that any magistrates listening to this complaint would dissolve into laughter and that would be undignified in a court of law.

Happily, my regular official visits to Esme did not sour our relationship. She continued to regard me as a friendly caller and never once complained about the frequency of my visits, nor did she grumble about the regular fines she attracted. She probably thought all motorists suffered in this way.

I must admit I liked her. I remember one terrible winter morning when five or six inches of snow had fallen overnight. The roads were treacherous and the small amount of traffic had compressed the snow into a sheet of dangerous ice. Maddleskirk village was blocked at both exits, for there are steep hills climbing out at each end of the village street. The early morning traffic which comprised lorries, bread trucks, tankers, post office vans and commuters' cars had all come to a standstill because each hill was impassable. I arrived on foot to have a look, and borrowed a shovel from a farmer who lived on the main street. With the shovel over my shoulder, I trudged through the blizzard conditions, intending to spread gravel across the glistening surface, and get the queue of traffic moving.

As I walked to the base of the western hill, I heard a car engine behind and turned to see Esme in her immaculate white Morris Minor. She halted at my side and wound down her window.

"Good morning, Mr Rhea," she breezed, her lovely face wreathed in smiles and framed in a fur bonnet.

"Hello, Esme," I greeted her. "You're not going out today, I hope!"

"I must get to Leeds," she said. "I have an appointment at a craft shop this morning and can't let them down."

"You'll never get through," I pointed to the queue of patient drivers, all sitting at their wheels or helping to spread gravel.

"Oh, I don't worry about snow," she said. "I pretend I'm on a motor rally and it gets me through every time," and with that she set her wheels in motion. Two lorry drivers who'd overheard this remark launched into a polite cheer as the gallant little Morris approached the base of the steep hill. No one had climbed it that morning; it was like glass and the skid marks etched wildly across its surface bore testimony to their efforts.

We all watched and wondered how long it was going to take to dig her out, but the little white car chugged forward and started to climb. Everyone watched in sheer amazement as Esme's car stolidly climbed that treacherous incline and vanished over the top. Others tried, but all failed.

To this day, I do not know how she achieved that, but it dawned on me that I'd never seen Esme stuck in the winter. Faith must be a wonderful thing.

I began to think Esme was invincible. Somehow, she blazed a trail through life in her little Morris Minor and never seemed to ask help from anyone. Then, one fine morning in May, she called at my office in Aidensfield. She rang the bell, and I answered, very surprised to find her there.

"Come in, Esme," I opened the door and she strode in. "You've come to produce your licence and insurance again?"

"No," she smiled. "No, I'm not in trouble, Mr Rhea. I *can* drive without getting fined, you know. I'm not one of those silly women drivers who are always in trouble."

"Of course not," I pulled out a chair for her. "Well, what's wrong?"

"I am going down to Stratford-on-Avon," she said. "I'm taking a friend and we are going to see some of the Shakespearian productions at the Stratford Theatre."

"You'll enjoy it," I smiled, for I'd seen several of their skilled interpretations of the Bard's works.

"I do have a problem," she lowered her voice. "I need directions to Stratford, I cannot work out my own route."

"That should be no trouble," I pulled a road atlas from the bookshelf in my office. "I went a couple of years ago, and know the route well."

"Oh, I know the route," she said, pausing for effect.

"You do?"

"You've not heard of my problem?" she asked me solemnly.

"No." I wondered which problem she meant. "What problem?"

"I'm surprised no one has mentioned it to you," she continued to talk in a low voice. "And I'm surprised you have not noticed for yourself, Mr Rhea. I thought policemen were supposed to be very observant . . ."

"I haven't been here long," I began to make an excuse.

"My driving," she said. "It's the way I drive."

"Oh, yes." I thought of all the catastrophes she might create between Aidensfield and Stratford, and wondered if I should warn all constabularies *en route*.

She laughed and appeared able to read my thoughts, for she said, "It's not my parking problems, Mr Rhea, or my reversing difficulties."

"No?" I could not think of anything else right now.

"It's my inability to turn right," she said, pausing for the awesome implications of that remark to sink into my skull.

"Turn right?" I questioned.

"Yes, I cannot turn right off a road. I go everywhere by making left turns," she told me in all seriousness. "I·can cope with right turns off one-way streets, but not on ordinary roads. Surely you've seen me coming home different ways?"

"I had no idea that was the reason," I said. "So you are telling me you intend to drive to Stratford-on-Avon without ever turning right?"

"Yes, that's why I came to see you. Last year, I set off to go to Harrogate to the theatre and things went fine until I came to a new one-way street in Ripon. I got hopelessly lost . . ."

"What happened?" I asked, suppressing a chuckle.

"I got to Middlesbrough, miles from where I intended, and had to get a train back. It's all very embarrassing, Mr Rhea, and I cannot help it."

"I don't know whether I'm capable of producing a route for you all that way, Esme; I wonder if there are other people like you?"

"A cousin of mine could never go around a roundabout," she said. "He always took the right-hand route instead of the left and got into no end of bother from the police. He blocked the whole of Newcastle upon Tyne one Saturday morning because he hit a bus on a roundabout. He was fine if he drove on the continent."

I did not want to let her down and promised I'd do my best to find a route to Stratford-on-Avon, a distance of some two hundred miles, without her having to turn right. She was going in a fortnight's time, she told me, so there was no great rush.

With Mary's help, I settled down to work out a route and it was not as difficult as I had anticipated. Working along the main roads, I could plan the basic route bearing in mind one must make huge circular tours from time to time, and that the exits from motorways are all to the left anyway. The tricky bits were the towns, especially Stratford itself on the final lap, although I did suggest she parked on the outskirts and caught a bus into the town centre.

I calculated the length of this circuitous journey and felt she would travel at least twice the true distance, but on the appointed day she sallied forth full of confidence with a grey-haired lady passenger beaming hopefully from the front seat.

She allowed herself two days to reach her destination, and I was somewhat surprised when she rang me from Penrith in Cumberland, and then from Chester, to find out where she'd gone wrong. But she arrived safely three days later, having covered nearly eight hundred miles in large circular routes.

My plan hadn't helped because she'd missed several turnings and I'd not counted a new one-way system in Leeds. I couldn't remember including Leeds in my route, but did not argue.

I did wonder how she'd get back.

She returned a fortnight later and in the following days, I received twenty-five requests from police forces to visit her and report her for parking infringements, one-way street offences and careless driving on that trip, and they included places as far apart as Lancaster, Lincoln, Huntingdon, Warwick, Chippenham and Gateshead. But her Morris Minor hadn't a scratch, and neither had she.

*   *   *

In communities as small as Aidensfield, Maddleskirk and the like, there is usually one eccentric motorist whose deeds are widely known to the local people, and they contrive to keep well out of the way when the said eccentric is in motion. But these villages had Esme and another. Two of them in such a small area seemed destined to bring chaos.

Cedric Gladstone was the other's name, and he lived in a nice bungalow on the edge of Aidensfield with his lovely wife and two spaniels. Cedric was a retired motor engineer, a short, tubby gent with rimless spectacles and a bristling white moustache who had, in his working life, been something of an expert at his craft. In his retirement, he spent a lot of time in his workshop, making objects which no other craftsmen would tackle due to the time and patience needed. He fashioned objects like keys for grandfather clocks or winding handles for gramophones, small tools for specialist tasks and knick-knacks for household use. He did this for fun, although he was not averse to accepting gratuities in the shape of bottles of whisky as payment for his craftsmanship.

Cedric ran an old Rover car, a lovely 1949 model in a delicate shade of tan with darker brown mudguards, and this was his pride and joy. He had spent years with this car, having bought it new, and upon his retirement had managed to acquire a comprehensive stock of spares. By this prudent advance planning, Cedric was able to keep his car on the road when others fell by the wayside or ended their life on waste tips and scrap metal dumps.

I liked Cedric. I loved to chat with him in his workshop as he filed and soldered precious little pieces of metal together to create some implement useful for an obscure task. Even in his advancing years, a pride of creation and inventiveness remained. He showed me some of the things he'd produced – trowels, a ball-point pen, thousands of keys for hundreds of jobs, a toasting fork with a shield to protect the hand from the heat of the fire, all sorts of gadgets for working in car engines, a rack for shoelaces, a toothbrush holder and so forth. It's fair to say I spent many a happy hour watching him at work in his hessian apron and battered old flat cap.

But in that beautiful car, Cedric was a changed person. His big problem was drink, and I must admit it was a long time before I realised he was an alcoholic. I might have guessed because his home was stacked with an infinite variety of whiskies, collected over many years from the Highlands of Scotland, and drunk deeply every day by a thirsty Cedric. He was a frequent visitor to the local inns where he happily drank their whisky, or the whisky of anyone who would pay for the pleasure of seeing it vanish down Cedric's throat.

It is difficult to recall exactly when I became aware of this black side of Cedric's character. Certainly, his lovely Rover was at large most days, always immaculately polished and chugging beautifully along the lanes or through the villages as Cedric and his wife, Amelia, went about their business and pleasure. I had often seen the car during my patrols, and there was never any reason to halt it or to check the driver for illegalities. It had always been carefully driven, then one spring morning, some time after arriving at Aidensfield, my professional attention was drawn to the car.

It emerged from the drive of Cedric's house and someone was grating the gears. There was an awful noise as metal fought with metal, the gears doing their best to mesh under some intolerable handicap. I stared at the immaculate little car, wondering if it was being stolen, but saw that Cedric was driving.

I watched in considerable horror, wincing at the thought of unseen damage as the lovely vehicle emerged on to the road to groan its way into the village. As I was on foot, I was not in a position to chase him, although I did follow its path, listening to the clonking noises and the agonising screeching of the protesting gears. The din ceased somewhere along the village street.

Minutes later, I found Cedric's car. It was in the car park of the Brewers Arms, neatly parked and driverless. I checked my watch – it was ten thirty, opening time. I decided to pop in to see if Cedric was ill or in need of help and found him perched on a bar stool chatting amiably with Sid, the resident barman. He looked very content and relaxed, and in his hand was a double Scotch.

"Ah, Mr Rhea, can I tempt you?" he held the glass high, his grey eyes glistening with evident pleasure as he scrutinised the bronze contents.

"No, thank you, Cedric, not when I'm on duty." I couldn't face a whisky or any alcohol at this time of morning.

"I'm having a coffee, Mr Rhea," Sid offered. "There's some in the pot."

"I'd love one, Sid," and with no more ado, he produced a coffee pot and poured a steaming mugful. I removed my uniform cap and settled on a stool at Cedric's side. He looked in the bloom of youth now, sitting high on that stool with his back as straight as a ramrod, and his white moustache bristling with energy. His thick white hair bore no signs of thinning and his eyebrows matched his hair, thick and white, all set in a healthy pink face. His clothes were neat too, all cavalry twills, Harris tweeds and wool shirts with brogue shoes and green woollen socks.

As I talked about nothing in particular, I realised I'd often seen his car here, never thinking he was in the pub. I thought he parked it as a matter of convenience for the shop or the post office, because at home I'd never seen him drink heavily. True, he'd shown me his collection of malt whiskies, but I'd never seen evidence of alcoholism. But now, sitting at his side as he rhapsodised over the drink and recalling the method of the Rover's arrival, I realised I had a hardened drinker on my patch – and a motorist into the bargain.

This was long before the days of breathalysers and samples for laboratory analysis. In order to secure a conviction for drunken driving, it was necessary to prove beyond all doubt that the driver was under the influence of drink or drugs to such an extent as to be incapable of having proper control of the vehicle when driving or attempting to drive on a road. This was done by doctors; they were called by the police and conducted hilarious examinations of suspects by making them walk along white lines chalked upon the floor or asking them to add up sums of figures which not even the doctor could calculate correctly. The outcome was that many grossly drunken individuals managed to survive those primitive tests to escape conviction for an offence which so easily caused death to others. This was the reason for the introduction of the breath tests and the need for scientific analysis of the blood or urine to determine the alcohol level in the body. Thus, the guesswork and favouritism was eliminated.

But none of this affected Cedric. He was drinking long before such progress came to harass drunks. I looked closely at him. There was no sign of drunkenness. He was sitting unaided on a bar stool, with no back rest and he was not swaying nor was his speech slurred. He was conducting a most rational conversation with myself and Sid, and it was certainly not feasible to consider him drunk in charge of his vehicle. This differed from drunken *driving* because a person could be in charge of his van or car even when asleep in the back seat. Cedric was in charge of his car right now, sitting at that bar with the keys in his pocket . . .

But he was not drunk.

Once more, I recollected the pained howls from his car as it negotiated our village street and concluded something must be wrong with it.

"Is the car all right, Cedric?" I ventured to ask during a lull.

"The car? It's fine, Mr Rhea. Why do you ask?"

"I was walking up the village as you left home. It sounded as if the gears were fighting to jump out of their little box."

"My fault," he laughed. "I'm not at my best first thing, you know. I'm getting like my old car, I need a few minutes to get warmed up."

I laughed it off, but did notice Sid gave me a sideways glance. At the time, I failed to read any significance into his action, but some time later I came to realise what he was trying to tell me.

On several occasions afterwards, I saw Cedric leave the pub at closing time after lunch, each time manoeuvring his lovely Rover out of the car park with the smoothest of motions and the utmost skill. There was never a rattle or a grating of gears; his driving was perfect. No drunk could achieve that standard of driving, I told myself.

It would be four or five months later, when I was again walking in the village in civilian clothes, enjoying a day off duty. I overheard the noisy approach of a car. The din was terrible; gears grated, brakes screeched, tyres fought with the road and sometimes the horn blared. I turned to find Cedric's immaculate car bearing down on me. I stood aghast, watching the lovely old car struggle along the main street, and then it turned into the pub car park. I watched.

Cedric climbed out. Or rather, he staggered out. He ambled haphazardly across the empty park towards the front door of the Brewers Arms, and vanished inside seconds after the stroke of ten thirty. I was off duty, but Cedric had been drinking . . .

I hurried inside, and was in time to see him struggling to mount the bar stool. Sid was helping him and in moments, Cedric was perched high on the stool beaming at a full glass of whisky on the counter. Before I could climb the few steps into the bar, he picked up the glass and drained it at a gulp.

I rushed in.

"Cedric," I cried. "For God's sake no more . . . the way you drove that car . . ."

"Ah, Mr Rhea," he turned to greet me, smiling all over his

rosy face with his eyes full of happiness. "Good to see you. Have a drink – I see you're not on duty."

"No thanks," I declined, partly due to his state. "I can't drink that stuff this early. Look," I tried to talk to him. "I've just seen you drive in here, Cedric, and you must have been drunk, the way you drove your car . . ."

"No," he beamed at me benevolently. "I've not had a drop – not until this one," and he lifted his empty glass, and handed it to Sid for a refill.

Sid poured a generous helping and passed it back to Cedric, who tossed it down his throat with a smile.

"Nectar of the Gods," he addressed the empty glass. "Water of life, aqua fortis, aqua vitae, eau de vie, usquebaugh, perfume of Arabia . . ."

"Cedric, you must not drink and drive, it's dangerous – and illegal," I added.

"No one has ever seen me the worse for drink when I'm driving," he said quite coherently. "And no one ever will, Mr Rhea, I assure you."

"But I saw you just now, Cedric . . ."

"Stone cold sober, Mr Rhea. I was stone cold sober. I've told you before, it takes me a long time to get warmed up on a morning."

Sid interrupted. "He's right, Mr Rhea. You'll never see him worse for drink – he drinks whiskies, nothing else." Again, I noticed the sideways glance from Sid and knew I was wasting my time. Whatever had caused Cedric to drive so awfully was not drink. Maybe he was genuinely slow at getting mobile on a morning. He must be all of seventy and it did occur to me that he might be suffering from an illness of some kind. Perhaps he was rheumaticky and needed time before his ageing limbs functioned correctly.

I left the Brewers Arms and continued along the village to do some shopping for Mary. Later that day, we placed the four children in the rear of our battered Hillman and set sail for the moors, there to enjoy the space and beauty of this fine scenery. And as I motored through Aidensfield after lunch, I saw the lovely Rover emerge from the car park of the pub. I slowed a little, and turned down my window to listen for those awful noises but it moved beautifully along with never a murmur and never a fault in its driving technique. Cedric was on his way home. He'd been in the pub since ten thirty, and it was now two thirty, with four hours of heavy drinking a distinct possibility.

I watched as the exquisite little car motored happily out of sight, and I never saw a hint of illegal motoring.

It would be four or five days later when I next called at the Brewers Arms. It was late one evening, and I was on a routine pub visit, dressed in uniform to show the presence of the law. Sid was behind the bar, dispensing his wares on behalf of the landlord. He smiled as I entered.

"There's no trouble, Mr Rhea, not tonight. We're a bit on the quiet side."

Sid was a pleasant chap in his mid-thirties, but something of a mystery man. Always pleasant, smart and affable, he was not married and lived on the premises, where he earned a small wage for his bar tending duties and seldom left the building. He was contentment personified.

I told him about a thief who was trying to sell cheap cigarettes; we'd received information that he was attempting to get rid of stolen cigarettes by selling them to pubs and clubs, so I was warning my own landlords to be careful. Sid listened and told me the fellow had not called here; if he did, he would ring me.

As he chattered, he beckoned me to come closer.

"It's about Cedric," he whispered confidentially.

"Is he ill?" I asked.

"Alcoholic," Sid told me. "He drinks pints of whisky, and often spends all lunchtime in here, when his wife is out shopping as a rule."

"I was sure he was drunk the other morning," I said.

"On the way here? No, Mr Rhea. He's like that *before* he gets a drink. Once he gets himself well tanked up, he's normal. With umpteen whiskies inside him, he returns to normality. Without a drink inside him, he's a liability."

"Are you sure?"

"I'm positive, Mr Rhea. Ask about the place, ask his wife. Without his whisky, he can't do anything properly. He shakes and garbles, and is worse than useless. Honest. He rushes up here, downs a few and within minutes is back to what we'd call normal."

"That's crazy! How could I explain that in a court of law? How could I tell a court that Cedric's sober state is a damned sight worse than others when drunk, and when he's got a skin full of whisky, he's as normal as the most sober of judges . . ." I shook my head.

"We all keep out of his way when he drives here," he said.

"Why doesn't he walk to the pub?" I asked what I thought was a sensible question.

"He'd never get here," said Sid in all seriousness.

"But he's got loads of whisky at home, hasn't he? I've seen them – he collects bottles of all kinds, there's hundreds in his house."

"All locked in cabinets, Mr Rhea, by his wife. I reckon she keeps him short, and she's got them locked up for emergencies – like when visitors call, and he's got to be made presentable. She'll ration him to just enough to meet the requirements of the occasion."

"I only hope he doesn't have an accident when he's sober!" I laughed, but was assured the villagers knew his motoring movements sufficiently well to keep out of his way. I had my doubts about visitors to the place, or holiday-makers, though.

And so I became like one of the local people. I accepted Cedric for what he was. Based on the strict wording of the Road Traffic Act 1930, Section 15, he was not committing any offence when full of whisky because the wording said, "Being under the influence of drink or a drug to such an extent as to be incapable to having proper control of the vehicle . . ."

When under the influence, Cedric had full and proper control.

I could evisage a legal puzzler should he ever collide with some other person, animal or car, but he never did. In his happy state of aqua vitae, he was in perfect control of himself and his car. When sober, he was a terrible liability.

*　　*　　*

I must admit I was concerned about my pair of unusual motorists. Esme went sailing through life in her immaculate Morris, getting eternally lost and turning left at every junction or crossroads, while Cedric cruised about with his veins full of aqua vitae. Then the inevitable happened. They were both driving along the same stretch of road at the same time.

No one will ever be sure what happened, but it seems that Cedric's Rover had emerged from his gate with Cedric in a stone-cold sober state. It was shortly before his ten-thirty trip to the Brewers Arms. At that precise moment, Esme was chugging happily along in her little car, intending to visit York and its maze of one-way streets, there to collect a few parking tickets and make many left turns.

But as Cedric clanked and jerked out of his drive, Esme was horrified to see a pheasant run into the middle of the road immediately ahead of her. Had she been able to make a swift right turn, she would have missed the stupid bird, but Esme could not make a right turn. She therefore attempted to turn left.

This put her Morris right across the path of Cedric's Rover as it surged out of the drive, and he was either lucky enough or alert enough to take avoiding action. Faced with the oncoming Morris Minor, he did something to the steering wheel which put him through the hedge at the opposite side of the road, while Esme careered straight down his drive and on to his lawn.

She knocked over his sundial and sent a rustic bench into his ornamental pond, while he staggered out of his scratched car and asked if anyone had a whisky. Esme was unhurt, if shaken, and decided not to visit York that day.

My problem was whether to classify that incident as an accident within the meaning of the Road Traffic Act, but Sergeant Bairstow's advice was invaluable. It was on occasions like this that he excelled, and I was pleased I was not reporting to Sergeant Blaketon.

"A pheasant is not an animal within the meaning of the Road Traffic Act," Sergeant Bairstow assured me, "and besides, the damage to both cars, slight though it was, was not caused on a road. The Rover suffered minor scratches by a hedge growing on private property, and the Minor's dents were the result of colliding with a sundial in someone's garden. Take no action, Nicholas, old son. We don't want to get involved in that sort of thing, do we?"

"No, Sergeant," I agreed with some relief.

5

"And solitude; yet not alone, while thou
Visit'st my slumbers nightly . . ."

John Milton 1608–1674; *Paradise Lost*

Quite distinctly, two shots rang out. They echoed through the peaceful valley as I patrolled on foot. My mind was far from police matters as I marvelled at the spring colouring along the length of Rannockdale, and at first, I paid no attention. The entire countryside in his area is riddled with gunmen shooting; they shoot grouse during their season, pheasant and other game during their permitted times, and vermin all year round, consequently a couple of bangs were of no immediate interest.

But they came again. Two very clear shots rang out, and they came from a shotgun, not a rifle. It wasn't until I heard a shouting match somewhere beyond my ken that I recognised something more than a dispute over who'd shot which animal. There were the unmistakable sounds of vocal threats, so I increased my pace and listened for more indications of the precise location.

I soon found it. As I rounded a heavily wooded corner in the higher reaches of Rannockdale, I saw a track leading across several fields. At the distant end was a solitary farmhouse, and running like fury along that track was a little man in a smart grey suit. He was carrying a briefcase and holding on his trilby hat as he raced towards the Ford Prefect parked at the gate. He was clearly escaping from something.

I could hear the sound of a man's angry voice emanating from the farm house, and wondered what had prompted this confrontation. I increased my pace, anxious not to place myself in the firing line, but keen to discover whether or not this was a criminal matter in which I should take a professional interest.

As I drew closer to the Ford Prefect, the little man saw me and the expression of utter relief on his face was a pleasure to behold. I was his saviour and he continued to run as if his very life depended on it, ending this gallop to freedom by clambering unceremoniously over the gate.

There he halted and leaned on his car roof as he gasped for breath. I could see that his face was pale and drawn, and sweat was flowing down his cheeks in rivulets. Clutching his chest, he stared at me with an open mouth, unable to speak of this recent horror. The words refused to come and I waited at his side, all the time conscious of the silent house across the fields. Happily, there were no further eruptions from it or its occupants.

After a good five minutes, the little man got his wind back and found he could speak.

"Officer," he panted. "Officer, thank God . . ."

"Trouble?" I asked.

"You know that man in there?" he put to me.

I shook my head. "Sorry," I had to tell him. "I'm fairly new, and I've never had to call at this house. Who lives there?"

"A lunatic called Chapman," he said. "Charles Alexander Chapman."

He continued to draw in deep gasps of breath, and wiped his forehead with a coloured handkerchief after removing his trilby hat. He opened the door and placed his hat carefully on the rear seat, with his briefcase at its side.

"Inland Revenue," he told me. "I'm Eric Standish."

He held out a hand for me to shake, and his grip was surprisingly strong for such a small man. I smiled and introduced myself.

"They warned me about him," said Standish. "It's my first visit."

"What happened exactly?" I asked. "I thought I heard shots back there, and shouts."

"You did," he confirmed. "Shots from a twelve-bore. He was having a go at me; shooting at me!"

"I knew you chaps weren't the most popular of visitors," I tried to cheer him up. "You're probably more unpopular than us!"

"I accept that no one likes paying more Income Tax than necessary, but when a fellow ignores all letters and personal visits, there comes a time to call a halt. Head Office sent me to see him, to reason with him, but it's impossible, Mr Rhea. Totally impossible. He simply won't let anybody near the place."

"You've been before – not you personally," I corrected myself, "but your people?"

"Regularly for years. Not one tax man has ever managed to speak to Chapman, not one. God knows how much he owes."

"Maybe he owes nothing?" I suggested.

"He manages to live without a job," Standish said. "He's got investments, we're sure of it. Property too, we suspect, and we need to make an assessment of his income and his tax liability."

"It's a very effective way of avoiding tax!" I laughed. "Has he never paid?"

He shook his head. "Not for years and years. He moved here from a good position with a firm in Newcastle upon Tyne twenty years ago or more, and he's lived alone ever since. Our people have tried and tried to make contact, and we fail every time."

"I hope we don't have to visit him," I said. "Our uniforms might attract more target practice."

"I'll just have to report a failure," he spoke with a resigned air. "I don't like reporting failures, Mr Rhea. I like to announce success in my operations."

He entered his clean little car, started it and left me standing at the gate. I waited a few moments to see if there was any reaction and sure enough, a head appeared from an upstairs window as the car vanished along the forest road.

I could see it was a man with long grey hair and a matching grey beard, but at this distance I could not distinguish his facial features. I did see, however, that he wielded a shotgun.

"And don't you try it!" he bellowed at me, threateningly waving the gun. "Keep off, all of you!"

And he slammed the window to withdraw into the darkness of his isolated home. I smiled to myself, marvelling at the character of a man who could keep authority at bay for so long. I wandered along my lonely route and into the tiny moorland village where my motor cycle was parked.

For me, this was an exploratory visit, my first trip to Rannockdale village in an official capacity. I was keen to learn about its people and peculiarities, so as always on such visits I had parked the motor bike to walk the streets. On this occasion my action had been rewarded by the encounter with Mr Standish, the tax man.

It was important that I learn more about the eccentric Chapman, and the ideal place to begin was the village store. I pushed open the glass-fronted door and inside, a bell rang. A middle-aged man with a white apron appeared, smiling at me as he wiped his hands on the hem.

"P.C. Rhea," I introduced myself. "I'm new here, and it's my first trip to Rannockdale. I thought I'd say 'hello'."

"It's good of you to bother," he finished his wiping. "I've just been tidying some shelves at the back. Jim Freeman. My wife's called Ann, but she's out shopping for clothes, she went over to York this morning."

"I'm at Aidensfield," I said, removing my cap, "but now that they've issued us with bikes, we're covering bigger patches."

"I'm always pleased to see you chaps – fancy a coffee? I was about to have one."

"Thanks," and he escorted me through the shop to the living quarters where he motioned me to sit in a cosy armchair. He told me about the village, its amenities, problems, characters and gossip. I listened with interest, realising he was justifiably proud of the place and its people.

Over coffee, during which he answered the bell twice, I took the opportunity to mention Chapman and the income-tax man.

Freeman laughed loudly. "Oh, then you've been quick to meet our prize character, Charlie Chapman, the Recluse of Rannockdale."

"Is he really a recluse?"

"He never leaves that house – or at least, no one ever sees him leave. Rates, electricity, income tax, social services – they've all tried to get in to see him, and he gives everyone the same answer. A shotgun through the window."

"Doesn't he ever let anyone in?" I was amazed at this.

"What's he do for food or medical supplies? Money? The essentials of life?"

"There are two people he trusts. I'm one," he said with some pride. "The other is Miss Stanton. She's a retired schoolteacher who lives in a cottage near the church."

"How's he trust you? Do you get inside?"

"No, we take things up to the front door. There's a dog kennel outside the front door, and we place our things in there for him. I leave groceries once a week, and when I get there each Wednesday afternoon, he's left a note outlining the following week's requirements. I take other things for him – the mail, milk, stuff like that. I always leave them in the dog kennel with the note of the price, if any, and next time I go, the money is there, exactly right."

"He's got a gun," I said. "I know a shotgun doesn't need a certificate, but has he a rifle?"

"Yes, he's got a .22 rifle which he uses for killing rooks and wood pigeons. The policeman comes once every three years to renew it. I take it up, leave the forms in the kennel and next time, I collect the filled-in forms and the money."

At that time, a shotgun could be held without a shotgun certificate, although a gun licence was needed if the gun was taken outside the home; today, gun iicences have been abolished and a shotgun requires a shotgun certificate to authorise its possession by anyone, and other firearms, except air weapons, require firearms certificates. From what I'd seen already, I knew I'd have problems with Chapman if I had ever to renew his firearms certificate. That day would surely come.

Over the following weeks, I learned that Chapman had earned his nickname "Recluse of Rannockdale" due to his habit of writing reams of letters to people in authority. All his letters were written on beautifully printed notepaper in green type-written characters. He claimed he was Lord Rannockdale, a cousin of the Queen, and rightful heir to several estates in the North Riding; on some letter headings, he styled himself MP, and others comprised various business letter headings, happily of fictitious firms. The recipients of his letters must have wondered who was producing such gems, but I did learn that many were aware of his activities because of constant attention by the local and national press.

It was a local newspaper which had christened him "Recluse of Rannockdale" and the title had stuck. Every time he received wide publicity due to some idiot testing his defences for a giggle, the result was more people attempting to gain access to his house or visiting his farm with crazy notions. Some took along pressmen or cameras, for the Recluse had become something of a national celebrity. All this began some years before I arrived on the scene and in recent times, the publicity had dwindled considerably. The village people knew of his desire for the utmost privacy and respected it, and these days he lived his life almost as he wished. He was out of the nation's limelight.

That was until two burglars called.

Late one winter's evening, they decided to break into Charlie's farmhouse. What prompted them to embark upon an enterprise of this kind, in remotest Rannockdale on a winter's evening, is still something of a mystery, but it seems they had popped into the village inn for a quick drink. They were a highly professional team of burglars from Middlesbrough and their skills had earned them a comfortable living beyond the law.

It was that same skill that almost cost them their lives. Somehow, they managed to get into Charlie's house without him realising, a feat which had defeated every caller for years. Perhaps the passage of time had helped, for there'd been no concerted attack on his home for years. We reckoned he had been lulled into a false sense of security. Be that as it may, the skilled pair had broken in and had started to rifle Charlie's precious belongings.

He had a lot of things worth stealing, like antiques, jewellery, silverware and cash, and he kept them in a bedroom. It was to that very bedroom that the hapless pair went by the light of a torch in the very early hours. They reached the room, picked the lock and entered. And there lay Charlie's treasure. They could scarcely believe their luck; it was a veritable treasure trove.

They began to place these riches into pillow cases which they used as sacks, and then Charlie approached. They heard him coming; just in time, they heard his quiet steps and saw the glint of his torch as he moved along the long corridor.

One of them, Ginger Mills, slammed the bedroom door just in time, and rammed home the lock on his side. He and his pal, Cat Christon, were locked in.

Being professionals, they appreciated this gave them time to think and plan; the householder would go downstairs to ring for the police, and while he was down there, they'd sneak out with the loot. They'd go downstairs and, if necessary, tackle him and immobilise him. So they waited; time was on their side.

Suddenly, the door panels were splintered into fragments as the twin barrels of Charlie's twelve-bore discharged themselves and his voice called, "You can stay there, you bastards. If you climb out of the window, I'll be waiting . . . if you move along here, I'll be waiting . . ."

And as if to emphasise those words, he released a further barrage at the door. The little balls of lead shot peppered the door and blasted the interior of the room where two very alarmed burglars now crouched in fear of their lives.

He kept them there for two whole days and two whole nights, sometimes enforcing his threats with barrages of lead pellets at the shattered door. Naturally, the burglars kept out of the way, using a wall as a shield.

Then Charlie sent for the police. Early one morning, he placed a note in his kennel and this was intercepted by Mr Freeman at the shop and he rang me.

"Where are they?" I asked, surprised that Charlie's burglars had not been encouraged to leave with their backsides peppered as mementos of their visit.

"He's got them locked in the bedroom," he told me over the telephone. "Two, he thinks. He'll allow you to call and arrest them. He says you must be there at twelve noon today, and he'll deliver them to you at the front door."

"Is he sure they're burglars? They're not just daft youths who got in for a dare?"

"He says burglars in his letter, Mr Rhea, and I'm sure he's right."

"O.K." I assured him. "Tell Charlie I'll come with a police car."

I rang the section office at Ashfordly and Sergeant Oscar Blaketon answered.

"Sergeant," I said, "It's P.C. Rhea. Can I use the section car today?"

"You've a motor bike, Rhea. Has it broken down or are you just feeling idle?"

"No, Sergeant," I reasoned with him. "It's needed to carry two burglars. I want to go up Rannockdale to arrest them."

"Rannockdale? Who bothers to get burgled up Rannockdale?" he asked aghast. "There's nothing up there to be burgled."

"They're being held in a farm house," I informed him. "That old man who's known as the Recluse of Rannockdale has got them," and I explained the curious circumstances.

"Oh, well, in that case you can use the car." There was a hint of reluctance in his voice, "but I'll come with you. It's not often we arrest burglars out here, Rhea, so you'll need support. You're coming down to the office now, are you?"

"I am, Sergeant."

Ten minutes later, I eased my Francis Barnett into the police station yard at Ashfordly and parked it against the wall. I took my crash helmet inside and hung it on a peg, replacing it with the flat cap from my pannier.

"You drive, Rhea," said Sergeant Blaketon, standing majestically before me in his superbly fitted uniform. He was ready to go, eager to be moving into action, but knowing him as I did, I made a careful check of the essentials. I checked the oil, water, battery and tyre pressures of the car, I made sure the lights worked, and the horn, and the windscreen wipers, and then I checked all the doors, the bonnet and the boot to ensure they closed properly. Sergeant Blaketon was a stickler for rules and routine, and I dare not omit anything. Having made a rigid check of this drill before moving out, I drove sedately across the moors in strict accordance with the driving system taught at police motoring schools.

On the way, I explained about the Recluse. I told Sergeant Blaketon how I'd learned a good deal about his life style, and he listened carefully, sometimes chuckling at the antics of Charlie Chapman, and sometimes tut-tutting at Charlie's law-breaking enterprises. Blaketon had heard about him, of course; most of the local people had read of his exploits and the police, in one form or another, often caught the brunt of his anti-social behaviour.

"So what's the arrangement, Rhea? If this madman shoots everybody who puts a foot on his drive, how are we going to get the burglars out?"

"It's all arranged," I assured him. "We must arrive at his front door at twelve noon precisely, and he will pass them out to us."

"Twelve noon?"

"Yes, Sergeant," I confirmed.

"You've obviously established some sort of rapport with this character, Rhea," and before I could tell him the truth about the note in the dog kennel, he said, "You know, this will make the Superintendent very happy. He's been nagging about our lack of arrests, Rhea. When compared with other sections, we are not in the same league – no arrests for crime, no public order troubles or travelling thieves. But this is a good one – two burglars at one go, Rhea. Yes. It's good, and it will improve our figures."

It was very clear that I was in his good books, and for this I was grateful. To be on the right side of Oscar Blaketon was considered an honour, however short-lived it might be, and for a few minutes I basked in this unaccustomed glory. In his benevolence, Blaketon rambled on about the value of making arrests, of the effect they had on local villains who quaked in their shoes in anticipation of police swoops, and the need to show the public that we were, after all, a law-enforcement agency and not a charitable institution.

At one minute to midday precisely, we arrived at the entrance to the Recluse's farm. I opened the gate as Sergeant Blaketon sat stolidly in the passenger seat, then I drove through, closed the gate and climbed in beside him for the final trip. I could sense that Charlie was watching our approach, and at least he could not complain about the timing. We were accurate to the second so I had no reason to fear his shotgun.

I did realise the car was unmarked as indeed all police cars were in this region. All were a highly polished black colour with uniformed men inside, and it was this distinctive hue which identified them to the local folk. I trusted Charlie was sufficiently *au fait* with our systems to recognise our car. Happily, he did.

As we pulled up, I saw that the front door was standing wide open and two very sorry individuals in rough clothes waited just inside, with their hands on their heads. They looked awful; they looked tired, hungry and dirty as they waited in the large entrance hall of Charlie's farm. They also looked terrified because the wild and bewhiskered Charlie was standing right behind them with his shotgun at the ready.

Even as we stopped and emerged from the little car, the two men were thrust forward with the barrels of that dangerous weapon, and Blaketon said, "Cuffs, Rhea. Handcuffs, quickly man!"

I dragged my handcuffs from my pocket – we always carried handcuffs in our left trouser pocket and the truncheon in our right – and I waited as the bearded recluse ushered them completely from his home. Sergeant Blaketon held open the driver's door and pushed the seat forward, to give them entry to the rear of the Ford. Our cars were two-door saloons for this very purpose – it was a sound idea by our Purchasing Department to buy such cars, except that it was with great difficulty that we could encourage drunks and quarrelsome folks to clamber into the confined space.

However, these two characters were in no mood for arguing. Meekly, they shuffled out of the house, prodded forward by the twin barrels of Charlie's gun. With his nose twitching in disgust at the smell that accompanied them, Sergeant Blaketon stood back as they climbed with evident relief into our rear seat.

They sat down and Charlie slammed the door of his house.

"Mr Chapman?" Sergeant Blaketon called through the closed door. "I need to talk to you."

No reply. Blaketon shouted several more times, but the Recluse had returned to his lair. I knew why the sergeant wished to talk to him – we needed a statement from him, a written account of the events which preceded this arrest. Without it, there was no evidence to put before a court and we might not be able to substantiate a charge of burglary, which was then a very serious crime.

"Clear off!" came the voice after Sergeant Blaketon's repeated knocking had made his knuckles sore. "Clear off, and take those ratbags with you."

Sergeant Blaketon, straight as a ramrod and immaculate in his appearance, had no alternative. He turned away from the door, whirling around like a sergeant-major on parade, and made for the waiting car. I got in to the driving seat as he headed for the passenger side. The stench from our prisoners was appalling, more so in the confined space of the little vehicle.

"My God!" cried Blaketon, winding down his window. "What's happened to you two?"

The one with short, grizzly hair answered. "He wouldn't let us go to the toilet, sergeant. He kept us in that bloody room without any food, heat or toilet . . . the man's a bloody nut-case . . ."

"You're nut-cases to think of burgling the old fool's house," snapped Blaketon, holding a handkerchief to his nose. "Anyway, you're both under arrest for burglary."

"We can't deny this one," the other said. "I'm only relieved to be out of that spot, I can tell you."

With the stinking burglars continuing to fill the car with pungent fumes, we drove through the pure countryside air with our windows wide open. To cut a long story short, they were placed in our cells and we found clean sets of clothing for them. They readily admitted housebreaking, a lesser crime than burglary, and made voluntary statements to that effect. They told how Charlie had caught them and detained them, but we got no supporting statement from him. The Detective Inspector felt the courts would accept the men's own voluntary admissions as valid evidence.

These young burglars from Middlesbrough were each given a three-month Borstal sentence due to their age and previous record, and it was a good crime to be written off against our sectional record. For several weeks Sergeant Blaketon re-lived the moment of that arrest, telling all his pals and superiors about it, and there is no doubt it was the highlight of his month.

Then there came a note from Force Headquarters. It was to

remind us that the firearm certificate held by Mr Charles Alexander Chapman of Rannockdale was due for renewal. It asked that an officer visit Mr Chapman to inspect the .22 firearm in question, that he supervise the completion of the relevant forms and obtain the requisite fee.

"Rhea," said Sergeant Blaketon, "I think the time has come for us to visit this man. I know his past record, and of his obsession with keeping people out of his premises, but this is a matter of law and we are officers of the law. I intend to visit Mr Chapman to discuss the renewal of his firearm certificate. I am sure he will look favourably upon us due to our recent part in the arrest of his burglars."

With no more ado, Sergeant Blaketon instructed me to accompany him and we set off to enforce the law upon the impudent recluse. Sergeant Blaketon was at his bristling best, eager for the opportunity to come to terms with the eccentric man and he had the necessary forms in his briefcase. With the confidence of his kind, we could not fail. I enjoyed the trip across the forbidding moors, through avenues of pines and silver birches and across rippling streams. I had time to admire the outstanding views as we cruised into the remote valley which was the old man's home.

We pulled up at the farm gate and parked the car on the spot I'd found the Income Tax man's Ford Prefect all those weeks ago.

"You remain here, Rhea," instructed Sergeant Blaketon. "This is a task for a mature officer. It needs the skill of someone with deep experience and an understanding of the human mind. If two officers walk to that door, it will unnerve the fellow, so I will approach alone. I will take the renewal forms with me, and I will politely ask him to complete them as prescribed by the Firearms Act, 1937. Observe my approach, Rhea, and learn by my manner."

"Certainly, Sergeant," and I watched with bated breath as he tried to open the gate, but it had been tied with rope after our recent visit. He had to climb over, not the most impressive of actions by a man of his calibre, but soon he was striding manfully and majestically along the track to the distant front door. I watched with fascination and anticipation. Men like

Sergeant Blaketon, with a wealth of experience beneath their belts, could certainly teach youngsters like me how to deal with the great British public. I had a lot to learn.

I observed him striding confidently towards the house, but as he approached, I noticed the familiar grey hair and beard emerge from an upstairs window. I did not shout a warning – I couldn't, for I was in the car some distance away, but Charlie must have said something to the striding sergeant because he halted in his tracks and looked up at the bedroom window.

I saw the barrel of the shotgun appear across the window sill, and it was quite evident that Charlie was issuing threatening words towards my sergeant. It was equally clear that my sergeant thought he was joking.

As a multitude of past visitors had come to appreciate, the Recluse of Rannockdale never joked with people who trespassed on his land, even if they were clad in the resplendent uniform of a British police sergeant. Having given Sergeant Blaketon his marching orders, and having had those orders repudiated by a stubborn, rule-bound sergeant, Charlie resorted to the only means at his disposal. He pulled the trigger.

A barrage of lead shot spattered the ground alarmingly close to Sergeant Blaketon's feet and it caused lots of little eruptions of earth. It was rapidly followed by a second barrel, at which more earth erupted about Sergeant Blaketon. Charlie shouted something at him and I saw Sergeant Blaketon change his mind about staying to talk. I saw him do something I've never seen him do before or since. He started to run.

To see a figure of the majesty of Oscar Blaketon in full flight with repeated barrages of lead pellets spurring him on his way, is indeed a rare sight. It was more so because he was holding his cap on with one hand and clutching the firearms certificate renewal forms in the other. He reached the car by leaping across the gate with a single bound, and he collapsed at my side as I moved into the driving seat. He was panting like a broken-winded horse, and perspiration was swilling down his cheeks and neck. I've never seen him in such a state of panic, and his breathing was tortuous as he signalled me to drive rapidly away. I drove off and saw the grey-haired old buzzard waving his gun in triumph.

"The man's an idiot," Sergeant Blaketon gasped when he regained some of his breath. "An absolute idiot. I'll get him certified, Rhea, so I will."

He lapsed into a long silence as I drove steadily back to Ashfordly where I knew his wife would have his lunch ready. He didn't speak any more until I pulled into the police station car park.

"Rhea, if you mention this to anybody, I'll have you transferred to Gunnerside."

And with that parting remark, he walked away, not quite so erect and certainly more dishevelled than he had been at the start of this enterprise. I wondered what I had learned from his demonstration of human understanding, but I never told a soul about it.

6

"It is a silly game where nobody wins."

Thomas Fuller 1608–1661

It would be remiss of me to suggest that a rural policeman's job is all work and no play. Certainly, in my time as a village constable the position demanded a twenty-four-hour responsibility even though our duty sheets showed that we worked eight-hour shifts. In truth, an eight-hour day was a rarity because people called or rang with problems, and it was understood that we attended to all matters that came our way, even though we were officially off duty or on leave.

Only for special tasks were we instructed to work more than eight hours. The public didn't know this – they simply arrived at the door to complain of being raped or robbed and we had to attend. To win time off in lieu, however, was most difficult. Supervisory checks were made of our daily tally of hours worked and woe betide us if we were shown to have worked less than an eight-hour day. The bits we worked over the eight were lost to us; we donated them to the uncaring public.

Even so, we were allocated days off duty. On the duty sheets, they were shown as RD which means Rest Day, and they moved forward two at a time, being Monday/Tuesday one week, Wednesday/Thursday the next, Friday/Saturday after that, with Sunday/Monday to follow, *ad infinitum*. As this ritual progressed, it became a great achievement to secure a Saturday/Sunday weekend off duty. On this kind of rota system, Saturday/Sunday weekends came around very infrequently, and were consequently cherished as a gift from the gods, or perhaps from Sergeant Blaketon. In practice, however, something al-

ways happened to cause our Saturday/Sunday weekends to be
altered. Some incident would occur through which it became
necessary to work on those sacred days, and this served only to
galvanise us into positive action designed to secure that cherished time off.

Sergeant Blaketon was noted for his ability to find excuses to
cancel our weekends off. He had a thing about policemen
working when no one else did, such as Sunday evenings,
Monday mornings very early, Good Fridays and a host of other
occasions which he dredged from his years of compiling police
duty sheets. He appeared to think it was good for us. After a
while, we learned to tolerate his quirks and we came around to
the notion of never expecting a proper weekend off. When one
did arrive, it was a bonus rather than a right, and we all know
how pleasant it is to receive the occasional bonus.

Through working almost every Saturday/Sunday, however,
the discerning constable begins to yearn for a weekend off and
contemplates the best ways of getting his weekends free. One of
those ways was, and still is, to participate in police sport. Basing
my logic on the understanding that if you can't beat 'em, join
'em, I renewed my acquaintanceship with the sporting section
of my local constabulary.

Being a Yorkshireman, this meant playing cricket. All Yorkshiremen are supposed to play cricket and any who fail to reach
a passable stage in this most remarkable of rural games are not
considered genuine Yorkshiremen. I had reasoned that if I
wanted a Saturday off duty now and again, to be with my
growing family, the easiest guarantee was to join the Divisional
Cricket Team. If I did this, I would be sent to play at selected
rural pitches within our Division, and I could take along my
wife and four tiny supporters. We'd all get an airing.

With this devious plan at the back of my mind, I singled out
the cricket captain of our Division. I had to wait several weeks
in the spring, but one fine April evening, I came across him in
Eltering Police Station. I had popped in to record someone's
production of an insurance certificate and driving licence.
Sergeant Alex Benwell was there, checking some Court Sheets.
He was my passport to free weekends.

"Evening, Sergeant," I removed my cap and hung it on a peg

near the back entrance, trusting my greeting was affable and warm.

"Now, lad," he grunted while fingering down a long list of defendants due to appear at next week's Eltering Magistrates' Court.

I felt it unwise to disturb him for he was clearly engaged upon a matter of grave importance, but he broke the ice by saying, "Put the kettle on, will you?"

"Yes, sergeant," I acquiesced for the sake of free Saturdays. In no time, the leaky station kettle was singing and I had found some stained mugs and a tin containing tea leaves. I produced a useful brew in an earthenware teapot with a cracked spout, and waited for him to leave his Court Sheets. Soon he came into the tiny rest room, smiled and sat on a rickety chair.

"Now, lad," he said for the second time. "Good brew, is it?"

"Like my mother makes," I said, realising he had no idea what sort of tea my mother makes. I poured a generous mugful which he inspected carefully before sipping noisily.

"Not bad," he said. "Aye, not bad at all. Your mother sounds as though she knows summat about making tea."

"She likes a strong pot," I agreed. "The sort that a spoon can stand up in."

He laughed loudly, "Aye, we used to call it tonsil varnish when I was in the Army. It was powerful stuff."

He sipped again, and then eyed me carefully. "Rhea, isn't it?"

"Yes, sergeant. I'm at Aidensfield, the new man there."

"You sound like a Yorkshireman?" he said, his heavy face studying me.

"I am," I confirmed with deep pride. "Born and bred in Eskdale, I'm as Yorkshire as anyone can be."

"Then you'll play cricket," he said by way of a statement rather than a question.

He'd introduced the subject! Him, not me. I recognised my golden opportunity to get into the team.

"Yes," I said confidently. "I was captain of our village lads' team, and used to play in the second team as an adult."

I daren't admit I'd never scored more than fifteen, and wasn't a very good fielder or bowler . . .

"If you're a Yorkshireman," he was saying, "you'll do for us. Next Saturday? What are you doing next Saturday?"

"Has the season started?" I asked.

"Week after," he slurped his tea and smacked his lips. "By, you make a sound brew, young man. Next week, we're practising. Down at Eltering nets here, on the town playing fields. Saturday afternoon."

"I'm on late turn," I told him. "That rules me out."

"Who allocated that shift to a cricketer?" he bellowed. "No cricketer gets a late turn on a Saturday. I'll have words with old Blaketon. From now on, you don't work late on Saturdays. So be at the nets at two o'clock."

"Yes, sergeant, but suppose Sergeant Blaketon won't change my duties?"

"He will," was all he said, draining the dregs with his customary noise. "Thanks for the tea, lad. What's your first name?"

"Nick," I said.

"Nick," he repeated, getting up from his chair. He was a massive man with a huge girth and legs like tree trunks. He almost waddled from the tea room, but his jovial face revealed a soft, gentle nature beneath his hard exterior. He seldom visited our stations, for he was the town sergeant over at Staddleton, a market town just inside our Divisional boundaries. Only infrequently did he venture into our Section, and I'd been fortunate enough to meet him.

I found myself wondering how he could run and field, for men of this size were notably ungainly, and he seemed to move with ponderous lethargy across the office. But he was a contact worth cultivating and I chattered away to him, discussing the job and his views on how rural bobbies should operate. He talked a lot of sense and I liked him from the start.

Later that evening, I met Sergeant Blaketon at a point in Thackerston, and told him all was quiet. I must be brave and broach the subject of cricket . . .

"Oh," I said, hoping my expression would excuse the nature of my forthcoming request. "Oh, Sergeant, I met Sergeant Benwell at Eltering earlier this evening."

He eyed me with considerable suspicion.

"And?" He gazed at me through those dark eyes and fierce eyebrows, his face not revealing one iota of his thoughts.

"He wants me to play cricket for the Divisional team," I rushed out the words, "and says he wants me to attend practice at Eltering nets next Saturday afternoon."

"Did he now?"

He lapsed into an unhealthy silence, and I didn't know how to continue. Was I supposed to press home my point?

I waited for what seemed an eternity and decided I must make the next move. "He asked if you would change my duties," I said weakly.

"Rhea, you ought to know better than listen to Alex Benwell. You know what he's like . . ."

"Like?" I asked, innocently.

"Yes, like. You've seen him? The size of him?"

I nodded.

"Beer. That's the result of years of drinking gallons of beer, and all at cricket matches. Cricket's not a sport for him, Rhea, it's an excuse to go boozing on a Saturday night. That's how he gets out of Saturday night duties, Rhea; puts it all down to sport. Just because the Superintendent's a member of the Yorkshire Cricket Club . . . you didn't approach him, then? You didn't seek him out to fix this for you?"

"No, sergeant."

"Not like some I know," he said without halting for breath. "Some less honourable members of this section always wheedle their way into the cricket team to avoid Saturday duties, Rhea It means the rest of us, me included, have to do their duties for them, week in and week out . . ."

"He asked if I could attend the nets, Sergeant. I suppose he wants to see me play."

"All right, if that's all. Nets it is. Next Saturday – you don't play football, do you?"

"Not really, sergeant," I had to admit.

"Now that's my game, Rhea. Pure English football. I play football in the winter, you know. To keep fit. That's a real game, a real sport, a real contest . . ."

He was making a note in his pocket book, reminding himself to change the duty sheets. "Don't make this a habit, Rhea. I know you are not a skiver who wants only to have each Saturday off . . ."

"No, sergeant, not at all. It's just that Sergeant Benwell suggested it . . ."

"I don't like that man," said Sergeant Blaketon, closing his book. He drove away with a heavy and worried frown on his handsome face.

I enjoyed my session at the nets. There would be some fifteen off-duty policemen there, all testing their new boots, their freshly laundered whites and their muscles. I had a go at bowling and found my old skills returning, although my efforts with a bat weren't particularly promising. I fielded one or two nice balls and spent a very enjoyable three hours. Mary had come with me, chiefly for the outing in our car with the family, and the three elder ones spent the afternoon running about while I kept half an eye on them. Mary and the baby popped into town to do some shopping.

It wasn't a bad arrangement, but Mary was quite firm about accompanying me. She was determined to come with me upon every trip because it would give her a Saturday outing with me, and in some senses it would make our life resemble that of normal weekend people.

However, the outcome of my first practice was that I was selected for the Divisional Police team to play in the Ryedale League. Our opponents would be teams from the villages of the district. Because the police had no home ground, we begged and borrowed fields from other clubs and because Eltering was the most central, we were allowed to use it whenever Eltering had an away game. That became our Home ground, the Away grounds being remote villages and hamlets in the moors and dales.

It would be impossible to describe the sheer enjoyment we experienced at those villages, but our match against Brantgate First Eleven one Saturday in June typifies our experiences. This can be taken as the sort of match in which we engaged. It was an Away match for us, which meant we had to tolerate Brantgate's unique pitch. I had never played there, but my colleagues assured me a treat was in store.

Sergeant Benwell collected several of us at Eltering Police

Station and I was surprised to find myself being transported in a battered old ambulance. This was his cricket coach, the vehicle he used to ferry himself and his pals to distant matches. Mary had decided not to come because Elizabeth was feeling off colour, so I decided to travel with the others and give her the use of our car, should she need it.

The retired ambulance rumbled and rolled across the countryside and we climbed steeply into the depths of the moors. Half an hour later, we were trundling merrily across the heights with staggering views spread below our lofty route. We could look down upon a multitude of deep valleys and admired the sheer breathtaking splendour of it all. The glaciers of old had done a wonderful sculpture job on those hills.

"Down here," announced Alex Benwell, as he turned into a narrow lane. His route dropped sharply from elevated moorland road, turned left down the sheer side of a valley, then twisted and wove between high drystone walls. We drove slowly down the 1-in-3 gradient, the old truck groaning in low gear towards the bottom. Down there nestled the hamlet of Brantgate, a sleepy moorland collection of farms and cottages.

Suddenly, we rounded a blind corner and there, right across the road, was a five-bar gate. Its purpose was to prevent the free-ranging moorland sheep from invading the village gardens, and as we approached it, Sergeant Benwell pressed his foot on the brake. Nothing. Nothing happened.

"Brakes have gone!" he shouted as we began to gather speed. The monster gate loomed closer and I saw him grip the steering wheel firmly between both hands. Then I felt the ancient vehicle rapidly accelerate. He'd put his foot on the accelerator and we roared towards the stout gate. The nose of the heavy vehicle rammed it amidships, and the gate flew open with a crash. The force of it sent the latch flying over one wall and while the gate stood wide open for a fraction of a second, we hurtled through. The gate, as if on springs, rebounded from the wall and slammed shut. But we were through and were now careering headlong down the continuing gradient. Benwell knew the road and he was a first-class driver; he had to be, to guide the brakeless old truck down this steep, winding lane. By the grace of God, nothing was coming up the hill; there was no

room to pass even a bike. By knowing his vehicle so well, and
being such a fine steersman, he suddenly turned the wheel and
we roared off the road into a long field. He allowed the low gears
to control the forward rush and after about a hundred yards, the
ambulance eased to a smooth halt. Seven cricketers emerged,
some feeling sick and others marvelling at his motoring skills.
But Benwell was unruffled.

He kicked the front wheels and said calmly, "It's never done
that before," then walked off to the pavilion.

We followed, the other police players having made their own
way to Brantgate. The pavilion was little more than a decorated
hen-house, but we managed to change into our whites and find
somewhere to spread open the cricket bag with its pads, balls,
bats, bails and score book. As we busied ourselves for a practice
session, the Brantgate captain came in.

"Now then," he said gruffly. "Most of you fellers are newcomers, aren't you?"

"Eight or nine of 'em," confirmed Alex Benwell, tying his
laces.

"Then you'd better come with me," said the captain, "and
I'll explain the rules."

"Rules?" I queried, wondering if I had heard the word
correctly. I was under the impression that all games of cricket
were played with the same rules.

"Local rules," said Alex Benwell. "Go out and listen to
him."

We obeyed and the dour Yorkshireman, whose cricket gear
comprised a white shirt and grey flannels fortified by a pair of
stained white boots, led us away. We followed through long
grass for a considerable distance and he halted on a neatly shorn
piece of land. It was twenty-two yards long by about ten feet
wide. All around was long grass, knee high in places and I noted
the outfield was surrounded by an electric fence. Furthermore,
it was impossible to see one of the boundaries because the pitch
had been hewn out of a steep sloping hillside. The pitch was the
only flat part of the field; above it, the outfield rose steeply
towards a wooden fence several yards distant, and the electric
fence was mid-way up that slope.

"Now then," said the captain. "I'm Jake Foston, captain of

this team. This is our cricket pitch – I allus fetches new lads out to have a look at it because it's not a normal one. It's a good pitch, mind, takes spin very well and is as level as a billiard table top. Our lads have done some good work. But yon outfield is a bit brant."

I knew this was the dialect word for steep, and could see how the village got its name.

"Now, we can't help that. Nature's made this field and nature's got to be respected. Out in mid-field there's an electric fence, that's to keep cows off this pitch. It's switched off now, but you'll have to watch it if you have to chase a ball. Leap over it if you can – it's nobbut a couple of foot high. Beyond that there's the real boundary, and yon railings mark it. Through there is six."

"You mean over there, surely?" asked someone from our side.

"Nay, through is six. If a ball goes through there, our lads could run ten or fifteen while you find t'ball among t'nettles. So we play fair and allow six. If you clout it *over* that fence, then it's eight."

I began to wonder what sort of signals the umpires would use to signify these scores, and also how our scorer would record these runs, but Jake thundered on.

"Down t'hill," he said, "you'll not see t'boundary because it's out o'sight. You'll need a feller down there to call back the score. He'll have to be a bit sharp because he'll not be able to see t'batsmen nor can he know when t'ball's heading his way. So you lads will have to yell at him. 'Ball's coming,' or summat like that. 'Left or right a bit.' He'll soon cotton on."

Jake paused to allow us to think about that part of the game, then he continued, "Beyond yon electric fence there's lots of cow-claps. If a ball goes in one and stops there, we give you five runs. That's to let you have time to wipe it clean before chucking it back at your wicketer and we reckon that's fair. Cow-claps are five. That hen-house," and he indicated a hen-house tucked in the upper corner, "if you clout that hen-house it's a six. If it goes inside, it's eight."

"It won't be easy, fielding in this long grass," a policeman player said, guardedly.

"No, it's not, but we're used to it," smiled Jake. "And we can't cut it just for a cricket match or two, our cows need feeding, and this is good cow grass."

We followed upon a brief circuit of this unique cricket field and had no alternative but to agree with Brantgate's interpretation of the rules. We were assured that their scorer, who would sit in the pavilion alongside ours, would keep us informed, and that he was an honest as a new babe.

"Now," he said, "there's one other thing."

We waited with bated breath.

"We're a team member short, lads, one of our best players had to rush off to hospital with his missus. She's calving, he reckons, and he had to take her on his tractor."

I tried to visualise the farmer's pregnant wife sitting on a tractor and being rushed off to the maternity ward. I also wondered what the hospital authorities would make of it when the pair arrived.

"So?" asked Alex Benwell.

"We've a player to stand in for him, from another team."

"I've no objections, have you?" Alex faced us.

We all shook our heads.

"Then that's him," and the host team's captain pointed to a sturdy farmer in his sixties. Ebenezer Flintoft wore thick hobnailed boots, corduroy trousers lashed around the knees with bits of string, a thick working shirt with no collar and the sleeves rolled above his elbows, red braces and a flat cap. He beamed at us as we stared at him, and I noticed his mouth was devoid of teeth. He needed a shave too, for his chin bristled with grey hairs.

"It's t'father-in-law of our opening bat," announced Jake. "He's over for t'day, helping out with some pigs, but said he'd help us out if we were stuck."

We agreed to this last minute substitution, but didn't really see that it mattered. The fellow was clearly a non-cricketer and had come along as a goodwill gesture.

The rules having been explained, we tossed and lost. Jake elected to bat, and I knew why. We'd have an awful job coping with stray balls in that outfield, and so we did. They knocked our bowling all over the field, causing the ball to get stuck in cow-claps, to get fast in the hedge, to get lost in long grass, and to vanish over that hidden boundary below us.

It is difficult, due to the passage of time, to highlight the most memorable aspects of that enjoyable game, but one character does stand out above all the others. It was the last minute addition, Ebenezer Flintoft with his flat cap, hobnailed boots and braces.

He came in at No. 5 and we then realised their best batsmen had performed. If they were putting Ebenezer in to bat at this early stage, the remainder must be rubbish. Sergeant Benwell decided to give our opening bowler another crack at them, fully expecting him to skittle out the remainder for a very low score.

But they had expected nothing like Ebenezer. He flung the bat around like lightning, hitting everything that moved. He kept scoring fours, sixes and eights with monotonous regularity, and nothing seemed to beat him. He was very evidently having a whale of a time. The others came and went, but Ebenezer returned to the pavilion not out and beaming all over his whiskery face. "By gum," he said, "I right enjoyed yon knock about. How many did I get?" He'd scored 125 out of a total of 187.

We broke the proceedings for tea, and it was magnificent. The wives of the Brantgate team laid on a gorgeous tea worthy of any moorland funeral, and we resumed the game shortly after five o'clock. We didn't stand a chance of reaching their score, although sixes and eights could soon rattle up a useful total.

Sergeant Benwell was our opening batsman and I was amazed to see that Ebenezer was their opening bowler. The large, heavy Yorkshireman took a short run, whirled his arm in a peculiar sideways motion and delivered a ball that utterly beat poor old Benwell.

By some good luck, he survived the first over and began to score off the second bowler, but when Ebenezer returned, I could see that poor old Sergeant Benwell was struggling. He was clean bowled with the fourth ball of the second over, and this signified our impending collapse.

We did manage a creditable 56, all scored off the other bowlers, because Ebenezer was totally unplayable. We limped back to the pavilion, beaten and trounced by this village team from the moors.

But they treated us well. We were invited to the local pub for a friendly drink, and the blacksmith did something to Sergeant Benwell's brakes which made his old truck mobile once again. The way home was jolly and happy as we sang loud songs and told countless jokes. I certainly enjoyed that day's cricket, and all that followed.

I was to learn later that Ebenezer played for most of the moorland village teams. He lived in an isolated farm which did not belong to any village, consequently he was invited to play in several teams. He invariably won the match when they played outsiders, and I wondered how the teams coped if he was supposed to play for both. Knowing how these fellows played, he probably did play for both sides, just to even things out!

Some weeks later, I was chatting to a farmer from the moors and mentioned that match, with special reference to Ebenezer's role.

"Aye, Mr Rhea," he said, "if awd Ebenezer had taken t'game seriously, he might have been some good at it."

*   *   *

I did not play cricket every Saturday, for my performances were by no means memorable. I was unreliable as a batsman, erratic as a fielder and moderately useful as a bowler, so I played only when the best could not be spared from their shifts and unexpected duties. But I enjoyed my games. They did provide me with several opportunities to take Mary and the family into the country and they did introduce me to other members of our widespread Division. The social life was fine.

My own sport, which I had practised as a youngster before marriage, was cycle racing. It was not a sport which was encouraged within the police force, and I sold my trusty drop-handlebar special ten-speed lightweight Tour de France model. I could never envisage myself aboard such a machine in full uniform, with my backside elevated, my head down and my big boots turning lightweight pedals. This meant I no longer partook in cycle races or time-trials.

Furthermore, I never expected to use my cycling skills in the police force, but one night, I was instructed to take the Ashford-ly official police cycle and patrol the main road. The reason was that the county car had broken down and my motor cycle was due for a service. And so it was with great amusement that Sergeant Bairstow allocated me a cycle beat from 10 pm until 2 am.

I found the huge black monster and trundled it from the garage, where I dusted it down and tested things like tyres, brakes and lights. Everything worked well, thanks to the immaculate attention of P.C. Alwyn Foxton. He kept every-thing in fine working order. With some trepidation, therefore, I mounted the massive cycle with its double crossbar and straight handlebars and sallied forth upon my cycle patrol. It was, in truth, the very first, and indeed only, cycle patrol I performed in my career.

It wasn't long before I was enjoying the experience. I could feel the wind against my cheeks and I enjoyed the solitude and silence. Memories flooded back as I pressed those heavy pedals round and round.

I patrolled the main road and took little sojourns into the lanes at the side of the highway, calling at villages and inspect-ing out-of-the-way lock up properties while on patrol. I had lost a little of my racing ability but the old techniques soon returned as I steered the heavy cycle about its business. I found hill climbing difficult because of the straight handlebars, and found the heavy gears rather clumsy but a bonus did occur due to the weight of the cycle. Once I had encouraged it to speed along in top gear, its own momentum kept it going and it was possible to reach a moderately high rate of knots. I liked this sensation, and concluded that Sergeant Bairstow had unwittingly done me a favour tonight.

I paused at a telephone kiosk to make a midnight point and as I stood in the silence, I heard the distinctive swish of oncoming tyres. Another cyclist was approaching – could it be Sergeant Bairstow?

I peered from behind my kiosk and saw the approaching light. It was weaving slightly from side to side as the cyclist pressed towards the conclusion of his journey, and when he passed me, I noticed it was a racing cyclist. He had his head low over the handlebars and was clad in all-black gear, comprising a sweat shirt and shorts, topped by a black cap. The cycle was a racing machine, and I guessed he was clocking himself to compete in a time-trial at some future date.

But as he passed my vantage point, I saw that his back light was not working. As he rode away from me, he was rapidly lost in the darkness and his black clothing made him virtually invisible. The fellow was a risk to himself and to motorists, and I could foresee an accident of a horrible kind. I imagined some motorist running into the rear of this cyclist and killing him, or at the least severely injuring him.

"Hey!" I shouted, emerging from my waiting place. "Hey, stop!"

There was no response. The cyclist kept his head down and tore away into the night.

Not liking to be ignored, and angry that my call had been unheeded, I mounted my trusty old police cycle and gave chase. The heavy machine seemed like a tank, and it took an awful lot of pedal pressure to persuade it to move at speed. But within a few minutes, I was hurtling along in pursuit of the unlit cycle, hell-bent on reporting this thoughtless character for riding without lights.

The thrill of the chase spurred me to great efforts, and I felt as if I was riding in a time-trial, striving to catch up with the chap who would have one full minute's start on me. But this character had only a few seconds lead, and I succeeded. My own headlight caught the reflection of his pedals and I urged my sturdy steed to even greater efforts as I drew closer.

"Hey!" I shouted. "Police, stop!"

I was panting by this time, but my legs were holding out and I was certainly drawing closer to him. "Hey, you!" I began to call. "Police, stop!"

The fellow did not respond. His head was low over the handlebars as he pressed his pedals and I thought he was trying to get away from me. I called upon my reserves and all my past cycling skills as I forced the old police bike to draw level with him.

"Hey!" I shouted across at him, for I could see his ears now. "Hey, stop. Police."

He looked across at me and I could see the pain and anguish of competition on his face.

"What is it?" he panted.

"That back light of yours. It's not working. I've been trying to halt you . . . you ignored my orders . . ."

"Look," he said. "I'm sorry. I didn't hear you," and he continued to forge ahead. "I'm in a desperate hurry, officer, can't you see? I'm breaking a record . . ."

"A record?"

"Doing a fifty," he said in racing jargon. "I've only a mile to go . . . I daren't stop . . ."

"You're a danger to yourself!" I shouted, but my cycling days had also taught me the agony of attempting to better one's own time, and the thrill of breaking other people's records.

"I daren't lose precious seconds fixing that light," he pleaded, head down again. "Please bear with me, it's not far now."

"You could get killed," I snapped, and then I realised I could help him.

"One more mile, officer, then I've done it . . . the fifty record will be mine, I'm ahead on time."

"Right," I decided. "Keep going. I'll tuck in behind you, and my light will act as a warning. Keep going, and don't flag . . ."

And I moved into his slip-stream. I followed him for that final mile, he breaking some record and me urging the old police bike to its utmost speed as I kept pace with the record breaker. Towards the end, I knew he was flagging; I most certainly was, but I think my presence immediately behind helped to keep him going. After all, it would look rather odd if a fully uniformed policeman on a police cycle crossed the line ahead of him, so I reckon I did him a service.

He achieved his record by knocking some 50 seconds off the local record and he thanked me for my help. He fixed his light – the bulb had worked loose and I did not report him. I doubt if I could have spoken the necessary words. It took an age to regain my breath and cool down.

I did wonder how that old bike would have performed over the full fifty miles, but decided against making the attempt.

After all, a quick sprint over one mile is exhilarating, even on a police cycle, but it would have been impossible to sustain that pace for much longer. He deserved his record.

*   *   *

If there was one sport in which I had no interest, it was Association Football. I had played at school but completely failed to understand the off-side rule. In my teens, I had never felt inclined to attend Saturday afternoon matches, either of the village variety or at Middlesbrough which was then a top-class First Division team. Consequently, upon my appointment as a constable I had never expressed the slightest interest in playing football for my Division, my Station or the village team. Even if this did promise time off on Saturday, less night duty and more beer swilling, the appeal of the sport in all its facets was lost on me.

Following my first cricket season, therefore, I was somewhat horrified when Sergeant Blaketon sidled up to me one Wednesday morning and asked,

"Rhea, are you busy on Saturday?"

In my mind, this was a loaded question. I was supposed to be on Rest Day, and I knew that Mary was hoping for an outing of some kind; if I said I was busy, he'd ask what it was, and if I said I wasn't busy, he was likely to put me on night duty.

"Why, sergeant?" I replied with a question, a useful form of defence.

"I need help, Rhea," I detected the tone of a plaintive cry in his voice.

"What sort of help, sergeant?" I was still being very guarded.

"I note you are on Rest Day, Rhea," he said, his eyes swivelling towards the duty sheet which was pinned to the wall, "and I thought if you hadn't anything special to do, you might come to my rescue. After all, I did allow you to play cricket."

"If it is something serious, sergeant," I heard myself saying, "I'll be only too pleased to help."

"It is very serious," he informed me sternly. "You've heard of the Ashfordly Veterans Club Football Team?"

"No," I said truthfully, not being a football fanatic.

"I thought you were a sportsman, Rhea?" he put to me. "All

this cricket and that cycling of yours."

"I wouldn't call myself a sportsman, sergeant," I admitted. "What's this got to do with the Veterans?"

He coughed. "I am playing for the Veterans this season," he flushed ever so slightly. "In fact," he smiled weakly, "I'm captain."

"Congratulations." I didn't know what to say, or what I was expected to say.

"This Saturday is a very important game," he went on. "We are playing in the final of the Ryedale Veterans League Challenge Cup, here at Ashfordly Sports Ground. It's against the Brantsford side."

I wondered if he wanted me to write up an account of the match for the local paper, or to act as linesman maybe?

"You're playing too?" I smiled.

"I'm in goal," he said proudly. "My old position. When I was a young man, Rhea, I was a crack goalkeeper. My height was useful and I kept for the Force on twenty occasions; indeed I was short-listed for the British Police Football Team, as goalkeeper."

"Then your team will have no trouble winning," I beamed at him. I had no idea that he'd been so skilled and he must have been outstanding to have been short-listed for the British team.

"We're a man short," he said quickly. "Full back. I wondered if you would play for us?"

"Me?" I laughed. "Sergeant, I've never played football since I was at school. I hardly know one end of a pitch from the other."

"I can't find anyone. We're short as a general rule, but this weekend it's desperate. Two of our members have gone down with rheumatism, and one's got flu. We can't play unless we turn out a full team."

"But I'm not a veteran!" I protested. "I'm only twenty-six."

"Anyone over twenty-five qualifies," he beamed. "That's a rule, I checked before asking you."

To put it mildly, I was talked into playing for Sergeant Blaketon's creaking team. Mary laughed and said she would attend the game, for she could do with a good laugh. The thought of me running around a football pitch, however amateurish the game, was more than a giggle – it was hilarious.

That Saturday afternoon, therefore, I reported to Ashfordly Sports Ground and found Sergeant Blaketon prancing up and down in a dark blue jumper and white shorts. My kit was in the changing room, and it was the same colour. As I changed, I felt awful; the men around me, most of whom were in their forties and very fit, were clearly addicts of the game and I hoped Oscar Blaketon had acquainted them with my total lack of know-how. If youth was on my side, experience was not.

I remember where full-backs were supposed to play, having dredged that fact deep from my school memories and I swotted up something of the game in one of my reference books. I also learned that Blaketon's team had conquered all competitors prior to this game. This was the final. The thought that the fate of the League Challenge Cup lay at my feet was horrifying. I had agonised for hours before the game, worrying myself sick as to why he had selected me and what I'd done wrong to find myself in this awful position. The duty sheet told me – the three best footballers of the Section were all on duty, and Oscar could hardly change their duties to play when he'd been so critical of the cricketers and their time off. Local police politics were very much in evidence on this occasion. None of the civilians in town were interested in the game – they were too busy watching professional matches or doing their own Saturday things. Such a lot depended upon me.

In the changing rooms, he rallied his team and welcomed me to the game, never mentioning my amateurism. He punched a few pieces of advice at them, and spent time telling them about his favourite moves, his tactics, the weaknesses in the opposition and the strengths of their forward line. He did a good job, I felt, for he managed to demoralise me totally. I stood with the others, goose-pimples on my legs and a lump in my throat, as the clock's pointers ticked irrevocably towards two-thirty.

Then we were running on to the pitch. I kicked a spare ball around, and leapt up and down like the others. I tried to head one or two practice shots, but missed the lot and before I knew what was happening, we were lining up for the kick-off.

I was nicely out of the way in my full-back position, but the opposing team looked ominous and threatening. Brantsford

Veterans had the reputation of being a formidable side, and as we lined up, they galloped noisily around the pitch in their bright red strip, threatening us with total annihilation. Sergeant Blaketon won the toss and elected to play into the wind, hoping they would tire themselves out by the time they had to do likewise. Then he made his way between the clean white goalposts, there to defend the reputation of Ashfordly Veterans.

I noticed that everyone was trotting on the spot so I did the same, then the whistle blew. It shrilled loudly, and I started to run about knowing that in the very near future, I would have to attempt to stop the onward rush of the opposition. I was the last line of defence before the goal, and Oscar Blaketon was in goal, I couldn't let him down. I daren't let him down.

The first half went rapidly. I kicked the ball several times which made me feel moderately useful, and I didn't appear to do anything that caused groans and contempt from the others. In fact, one of my shots landed right at the feet of our centre forward and he raced towards the goal, being narrowly defeated on his run. I was congratulated because I had almost made a goal, and I felt proud. I could see Mary on the touch-line, mingling with the handful of spectators, and she applauded that piece of skill. Suddenly I felt confidence flowing through my veins.

By half-time, I was feeling even better. My patrol duties and my cricket during the summer had kept me fit and the exercise was not too strenuous. Age was on my side and I found I could outrun most of the Brantsford team members, although I must admit their skills were infinitely greater than mine. But I enjoyed the first half and walked off the field feeling very pleased. I waved to Mary as I entered the changing room for a drink of orange and a towelling.

The score was nil-nil at this stage, and everything depended upon the second half. We were now playing with the wind, an undoubted asset and I could sense Sergeant Blaketon's confidence as we took to the field for the second half.

We were certainly the fitter team. In that second half, we ran rings around their men, and I thoroughly enjoyed myself. I raced up field with the ball and kicked it to our own men time

and time again, our efforts being thwarted only by the anticipation and good luck of their goalkeeper. Time and time again he
saved powerful shots, and then one of their men fouled our
centre forward.

It was a dirty foul, the action of a desperate man, and our
player fell to the ground in agony as his shin took the force of a
well-aimed kick. My team exploded with anger because our
man had been racing towards the goal as the goalie had come
forward to vacate his position. We couldn't fail to score – then
we were fouled. The referee awarded a free kick, not a penalty
and I didn't know enough about the game to worry about the
difference, but it angered our lads. Shouts and cat-calls filled
the air and Sergeant Blaketon had a difficult job calming them
down. The tension was intolerable.

But Blaketon succeeded. As our centre forward hobbled off
the pitch with his leg bleeding nastily, we were compelled to
continue with ten men. There were no substitutes. We had
about thirty-five minutes to play before full time, and while our
earlier efforts should have produced results, it was now doubtful whether we could maintain that pressure. The centre forward, a butcher called Andy Storr, was a gallant and skilled
team member and he would be missed. Their viciousness had
hit us where it hurt most.

When all the fuss had died away, the game resumed and quite
suddenly, I had the ball. I have no idea how it arrived at my feet,
for I was still angry about the foul, but I thought of Sergeant
Blaketon and the honour that could be his. Forgetting I was a
full-back, I side-stepped a player who tackled me and tore down
the right wing with the ball bouncing at my feet. I felt the thrill
of the chase as players milled around and tackled me; I saw
Mary on the touch-line, her hands waving and her voice calling
to me, and I flew across the grass. Nothing could stop me now; I
was on wings of happiness and success.

Someone attempted to intercept me, and I did a quick
body-swerve to deposit him on the ground as I continued my
racing run. Never before had I experienced such a thrill and I
could hear the cheers of the spectators as I raced towards the
goal. I beat all comers; I was in a haze as I switched into skills I
never knew I possessed. I thought of Sergeant Blaketon and the

cup, my eyes filled with tears of happiness as I raced those final yards to the goal. I was unstoppable. Then a hush descended. The ground bore an air of expectancy and I knew it all depended on me.

I was before the goal-keeper; he crouched between the posts and my misty eyes could distinguish his dark figure with arms outstretched as I took my careful aim.

I have never kicked a football with such power and accuracy. It flew from my right foot and the goalkeeper didn't stand a chance. He dived across the goalmouth in a desperate bid to beat my shot, but the driving ball crashed into the net with a resounding thud of leather against netting.

I wiped my eyes. I had done it. And me a full-back too!

"What the bloody hell are you doing, Rhea?" cried Sergeant Blaketon as he picked the ball from the back of the net. "This is *our* goal!"

He didn't ask me to play again, for his team lost by that solitary goal, and I daren't ask him for time off to play cricket the following year.

He retired from football after that game, and I must admit I felt sorry for him.

I hope he didn't think I'd done it on purpose.

"If you want to win her hand,
Let the maiden understand,
That she's not the only pebble on the beach."

Harry Braisted 19th century

As I settled in my office to compile the quarterly return of
farms visited and inspections of stock registers, I discovered
I had omitted one busy establishment. According to the record
maintained in my office, my predecessor had called there
at least once a quarter and I had been lax in not continuing the
practice.

On that May morning, therefore, I decided to rectify matters.
I began my journey on the little Francis Barnett with the fresh
breezes of May stirring the blossomed trees and the growing
grass along the lanes. May must be the most beautiful of the
English months for the landscape is bursting with fresh life,
with flowers, leaves, insects and birds, all enjoying the warmth
that comes from the strengthening sun. To be paid for patrolling through such splendid environs is indeed a bonus, and I
enjoyed my ride across the valley.

I was heading for Slape Wath Farm, a lonely homestead
buried deep in the moors over by Whemmelby. I had to consult
my Ordnance Survey map before leaving the house, but established that I had to descend the steep 1-in-3 hill into Whemmelby, drive out towards the summit of Gallow Heights and turn
left about a mile before reaching the Heights. This took me
along an unmade track which climbed across the heathery
landscape before descending dramatically into a small valley.
Deep in the valley lay the homestead called Slape Wath Farm,
so named because the track crossed the mountain stream near

the farm, then wound its way across the moors, eventually leading to the main road from Eltering to Strensford. In our Yorkshire dialect, slape means slippery and a wath is water-splash or a ford, so the farm was aptly named. The crossing would be treacherous in winter.

I had to open several wooden gates, a tricky job with a motor cycle, but eventually found myself entering the yard of Slape Wath Farm. It was clean and nicely concreted, and I placed the machine against the wall of an outbuilding before walking across to the farm house. The time was shortly before eleven one Wednesday morning.

I halted before knocking on the door in order to check my records, and reminded myself of the occupants' names. The owners of this remote spread were the Misses Kirby, Frances and Irene to be precise. There was no other explanatory note in my records and I had never heard anyone mention these ladies; their farm, I appreciated, was far too remote for casual callers and I doubted if the two ladies in question enjoyed much of a social life.

My memory refreshed, I knocked on the kitchen door.

"A minute!" called a voice, and I waited. Presently, the door was opened and a huge masculine woman stood before me. She wore a hessian apron, a long working dress buttoned up to the neck and a curious dust-cap on her head. She was nearly six feet tall, with a head of ginger hair peeping beneath her headgear; her face was red with the effects of the weather but her eyes were unusually bright blue and bored into me as I stood on the doorstep. She was hefty and muscular, and wore heavy welling-ton boots which peeped beneath her long dress.

"Oh," she said, eyeing me. "It's t'policeman. Come in," and she stepped back to permit me to enter. I noticed she had a large broom in her hands and she appeared to be in the middle of sweeping the sandstone floor of her kitchen.

"That's a useful brush," I said by way of making an inane introductory comment.

"Aye," she said, looking at it with pride. "We've had it for thirty-five years, and all we've had for it is three new heads and two new shafts."

I didn't know whether I was supposed to laugh at this

statement as a joke or treat it as a piece of moorland feminine logic, but my embarrassment was avoided by the timely appearance of another lady. She was much smaller than the first but with the same ginger hair and masculine appearance. Her eyes were a paler blue and her face a trifle less colourful, but it was easy to deduce that the big lady was the man-about-the-farm, and her sister was the woman-about-the-house.

"I'm P.C. Rhea from Aidensfield," I introduced myself. "The new policeman."

"Oh," said the big one. "Thoo'll be calling about our registers, then?"

"Yes," I confirmed. "I've been rather busy . . ."

"Think nowt on it, young man," the big one said. "Sit thyself down and Rene, fetch him a cuppa tea. Sugar?"

I shook my head and said, "No thanks. Milk, no sugar."

"Mak it three, Rene," ordered the big lady. "Thoo come as well."

Rene never spoke as she drifted across to an oven at the far end of this large kitchen and busied herself with pots, pans and bottles of milk. I placed my helmet on the scrubbed kitchen table and sat on a bench. The big lady, who I reasoned was called Frances, sat on the bench opposite and peered steadily at me.

"It'll be about them pigs, is it?" she put to me.

"You got some at Malton Mart last week," I said. "I've got to check to see everything's in order, and that you've entered them in your register."

Without a word, she left her seat and went across to a cupboard hanging on the wall. She produced the register and flicked it open – an immaculate entry graced the pages and I said, "I'll have to see the stock in question."

"Thoo's a keen 'un, eh?" she grumbled, heading for the door.

"Just doing my job," I said softly, following behind.

"We're off to t'sties, Rene!" she bellowed, her loud voice blasting my ear-drums. "Three minutes, no more."

She led me in silence down to her pig sties and showed me the store pigs she'd bought. I leaned over the bottom half of the door, enjoying the sight of young pigs grunting in happiness as they nosed among the straw and potato peelings which covered the floor of their pen.

"Nice pigs," I commented, for they were lovely.

"The best," she said with some force. "Me and our Rene nobbut buys t'best, thoo knaws. We show pigs and sheep, so we've got ti have t'best."

"You show them?" I expressed interest in her remark. "Do you win prizes?"

"Win prizes?" she bellowed. "I'll say we win prizes. Great Yorkshire, Stokesley, Egton, Danby, Castleton, the Royal, you name it, and we've won there. We've got the best pigs this side of the Pennines."

"You don't show these though?" I gestured towards those in the pig sty. "These are for fattening, aren't they?"

"Aye, they are, young man. No, we breed our own show pigs."

The kitchen door opened and the smaller edition said, "Tea, Cis."

"Tea, constable," said Cis striding towards the house with me almost trotting to keep pace. She led me inside. Rene had placed a green patterned oil cloth on the rough table, and there were three cups, some scones, jam, butter, three slabs of fruit cake and a pile of chocolate biscuits.

This was a typical 'lowance, as they called it here; tea break is the word elsewhere, or elevenses. To these folk, it's 'lowance time, or allowance time.

"Thank you, ladies," I settled down and signed the book with a flourish. "You keep a very nice tidy farm."

"We've a man in," said Cis. "Jack Holtby."

"He's employed full time, is he?"

"He lives in, Mr Rhea, gets fed and bedded here, all found. He looks after my pigs."

"And my sheep," said Rene quickly. "Jack looks after my sheep as well."

"She breeds sheep. I do the pigs."

"They win at all the shows, Mr Rhea," said Rene, getting into top gear now her tongue had been loosened. "Good stock, is ours. You'll have heard of t'Kirbys of Whemmelby?"

I didn't know whether to acknowledge my ignorance by

shaking my head or to tell a white lie and pretend I knew all about their successes, but Frances saved the day by saying,

"Don't be stupid, Rene. Of course Mr Rhea knows about our showing. I've told him, and he reads the papers. Kirby's a famous name among showing folk; my pigs and your sheep are noted the country over."

"I always get first with my blackfaces, Mr Rhea . . ."

"And me with my saddlebacks . . ."

I listened as the two sisters prattled on about their wins, each talking about her own speciality, and I began to realise I was witnessing a curious phenomenon. Once they left the subject of their pigs and sheep, their conversation followed a peculiar pattern. Each contributed to a sentence by apparently knowing what the other was going to say.

"They tell me you're married, Mr Rhea . . ."

"With four children, eh? How nice, your wife . . ."

"Must be very busy, looking after them and cooking and cleaning. Big families are nice, but . . ."

"I couldn't cope, not with four, not here. Animals are enough and . . ."

"They're just like children, keeping us out of bed at night and wanting feeding when . . ."

"They're little and in bed . . ."

"So we always work shifts, four hours on and four off, especially . . ."

"In the lambing season . . ."

And so it went on. I listened in amazement at this curious form of communication, and it appeared only to manifest itself when they were talking about subjects other than their pigs and sheep. It seemed that the pigs and sheep were individual matters, with Cis the big one looking after the pigs, and little Rene concentrating on the sheep. I left the premises feeling very amused and wondered which of them was the elder. I guessed it was Cis, the larger of the pair, for she was the dominant one and certainly had the appearance of a man. It was difficult to estimate their ages – they could be anywhere between thirty-five and fifty, and I reckoned they were probably in their early forties.

During that visit, I did not see their man. Jack Holtby was

nowhere to be seen, but evidence of his skills, or of their supervisory capacity, was everywhere. The farm was beautifully maintained; its woodwork was gleaming, its glasswork polished, the yards swept clean and the loose pieces of hay and straw tucked firmly into place. It was a picture of professionalism.

It would be about five weeks later when the name of these curious sisters cropped up in a casual conversation. I was in Aidensfield chattering to Joe Steel in his grocer's shop, and he asked, "You'll have come across the Kirby twins, have you?"

"Twins?" I puzzled, and then remembered that Rene and Cis were called Kirby. "You mean those ladies out at Slape Wath?"

"Aye, that's them. Twins. Rum lasses."

I told him of my first visit to their establishment and of my fascination with their mode of speech. He laughed.

"They've always been like that, Mr Rhea. Get 'em talking about their own animals, and they'll be normal, but get off that subject and they both talk like one person. You should hear 'em in here, ordering groceries . . . one says, 'bread' and t'other says, 'butter', and they go on like that, right through a shopping list."

"Do they ever go their own ways? They're not identical twins, are they?"

"No, they're not. They could be, if they were t'same size, but little Rene's the quiet one and she often goes off alone, showing her sheep."

"I get the impression they're hard working," I commented. "Salt of the earth and all that."

"They've no need to work, Mr Rhea. That father of theirs left 'em thousands. Did you get into their living-room?"

I shook my head.

"You're not an artist, are you?" he appeared to change the subject and I shook my head again.

"But you'll have heard of Reynolds, have you?"

"The portrait painter?" I asked. "Sir Joshua Reynolds?"

"Aye, that's him. Well, they've five or six Reynolds paintings in that house, and antique furniture too, silver, jewellery . . ."

"Up there?" I cried. "In that old farmhouse?"

He nodded solemnly. "They're loaded, Mr Rhea. They've no

need to work, but they stick it out there in the hills, working themselves hard day and night."

He prattled on about their inherited wealth and their total ignorance of its capacity to give them an easy life, and then said, "I reckon they ought to have burglar alarms fitted, Mr Rhea. That's why I thought I'd mention it. If somebody broke in and took those pictures alone, they'd lose thousands . . ."

"I'll pop in and see them next week," I promised.

"And look out for their latest man," he waved a finger at me.

"Latest man?" I asked, smiling at him.

A broad grin flitted across his face and he ran his hand across his bald head. "Aye," he laughed. "They've had a succession of men working for them, year in and year out."

"Doing what?" I asked.

"Tending sheep or pigs, and general labouring," he told me. "Heavy work, mainly, but some skilled fellers have been through their hands. They never stay long."

"Don't they? Why?" I asked in all innocence.

"They fall in love with the fellow," he laughed. "Cis and Rene each fall in love with the poor devil at the same time. It always happens – within five or six months of the new bloke being there, they both start falling for him. Then there's jealousy, and Rene has a go at Cis's pigs and Cis has a go at Rene's sheep, and if it coincides with a show date somewhere, there's hell on . . ."

"And?"

"The poor chap is driven out. I've lost count of their fellers," he laughed. "Every poor sod finds himself fighting their battles and protecting their animals against the other's vicious attacks . . . then they both blame him for falling in love with the other and for sticking up for the other's animals."

"Does it ever reach my official ears?" I asked, visualising domestic turmoil out at Slape Wath Farm.

"No, it rarely gets out – they seldom go anywhere, and the fellers come and go quietly."

But I did get involved with them and their current love affair with Jack Holtby. I saw him for the first time when I went along to discuss the treasures in their house. He was having his 'lowance and I was invited to join them at the kitchen table, where I tucked into a meal large enough for the average man's lunch.

He was a dark-haired man in his fifties, with a heavily scarred face which was apparently the result of being trapped in a tank during the war. A small man, he was wiry and sparsely built, but had a ready smile for me as I joined him at the table. He was dressed neatly, albeit in working clothes, and appeared to be slightly on the shy side. As I talked to the ladies, he made an excuse and left, saying he was just popping up to his room before returning to work.

Two pairs of blue eyes followed his progress and I could see the signs of unrequited love. I wondered what problems it would bring to him.

But I was here to talk about security.

After my scones and coffee, I broached the subject of the paintings and the ladies agreed they were valuable, although neither had any idea of the total worth of their treasures. Neither had I, for I lay no claim to knowledge of antiques or works of art, but when I saw the array of Reynoldses and other valuables, I knew that this house was a veritable museum, a treasure trove of remarkable interest.

Following my visit to the downstairs rooms, they showed me around the upper floor, including all six bedrooms and the attic of their rambling old home. Every room was richly endowed with solid antique furniture and I noticed lots of pictures, large and small, but all of considerable age.

All about the house was the smell of age and dampness, except in Jack's bedroom where I discerned a different aroma. I could not identify the scent, but it was not pipe smoke and not old socks or sweaty feet. I dismissed the question as I continued to survey the house and its contents.

Downstairs, I told the curious pair that I intended to call in the Crime Prevention Officer from our Divisional Headquarters, and he would undertake a professional survey of the house, free of charge, with a view to recommending some form of protection. I also advised them to consult Norman Taylor with a possibility of taking out some insurance. While discussing the protection of their inheritance, I did worry somewhat about the presence of Jack Holtby, for I knew nothing of his past or of his character.

My first impressions were that he was an average farm worker who would never appreciate the wealth of treasures around him, and I felt they were secure in his presence. He would not talk about them because he would not recognise them for what they were, but there is a breed of villain who preys on innocent or elderly people. These are like ravenous wolves, pitiless and cruel, for they rob their elders and their descendants of their rightful inheritance. It was such scoundrels from whom the Misses Kirby must be protected, and that was my duty.

I could not ignore the presence of their 'latest man' however, and resolved to keep a watchful eye upon him and his contacts. I'd check his background too. Meanwhile, the official wheels could be set in motion, and our Crime Prevention Officer would be told.

Some weeks later, the survey was complete, and a recommended burglar alarm company arrived to fit their clever device. I was not there during these operations, although we did note the car numbers and the names of the workmen just in case they turned out to be less than honest. However, the deed was completed and the Misses Kirby were fully equipped with a modern and highly sophisticated burglar alarm.

To set it, there was a box of tricks on the wall at the foot of the stairs, and after locking the doors and windows, the box itself was activated by locking it with a key. That key was then removed and stored in a secure place. Upon leaving the house, the key was also removed and the outer door was locked, thus sealing the system. After this, any severance of a contact, either by opening a door or window, would cause loud bells to ring at the farm and a little light to flash in our Divisional Headquarters. At last, the Kirby treasures were in care.

The system was fine, moderately expensive and highly efficient. But it lacked one important factor. It did not contain the brain of a woman, and furthermore, it could not cope with the female habit of losing keys. Women the world over lock themselves out of houses, offices and cars, and it means that a burglar alarm in any female environment is something of a hazard.

Frances and Rene were no exception. They lost innumerable keys of their alarm system. The angry machine rang bells across the moors and flashed lights in the police station; it summoned countless frustrated technicians to the remote farm to re-set the device and to supply them with a new key. In time, everyone involved – police, crime prevention officers, the insurance and the burglar alarm company – lost count of the number of times they attended these false alarms and re-set the system. The ladies could not learn to safeguard the precious and all-important key.

Eventually, the insurance company put its foot down. Norman had the job of telling the ladies that his company would not accept further liability for the contents of their home because the ladies themselves were a bigger risk. Norman talked to me about it, and I talked to our Crime Prevention Officer; together we studied a long missive from the insurance company.

The problem was all to do with lost keys. The insurance company was not at all happy about the security of the key for the lock which was the nerve centre for the entire system. The company was even more upset when one of their inspectors called unexpectedly and found the key left in the lock, with a long piece of string reaching from the key to a nail in the wall. It seemed they'd decided to keep the key there, where everyone could use it and from where it would never stray. If it remained on that piece of string, it would never get lost.

The insurance man was not at all happy with that system. There were long discussions with the ladies, and then Frances chanced to mention their safes. It seemed each lady had a safe built into the wall of her bedroom, tucked well away behind the bed. These contained personal cash and private things, and were used for their trophies, for cups and medals won at agricultural shows. Each safe was operated by a numerical code known only to the owner. If each kept a key for the burglar alarm in her own safe, the problem might be solved. It would mean the introduction of a new rule for the company, i.e. two keys for this one alarm, but by issuing each with a key, the system might function correctly.

Norman put this to his company and they agreed. After inspecting each safe and studying their individual security systems, which were designed to prevent one another from snooping, the insurance company agreed to continue the ladies on risk. I was happy too, and for a while there were no more ringing bells, flashing lights and emergency calls from Slape Wath Farm. Each lady kept her personal key secure in her own safe and they learned to use these to set the alarm each night upon retiring, and each time they vacated the farm.

Peace reigned, and the treasures were protected.

It would be several weeks later when I received a sad telephone call from Frances Kirby. She rang about ten thirty one Friday morning, and just caught me before I vanished into my hilly beat.

"Mr Rhea," she burbled into the telephone. "You've got to come, it's Jack."

"Jack?" For a moment I'd forgotten about their live-in handyman.

"You know, Jack that works for us."

"Oh, that Jack! What's happened?"

For one horrible moment, I thought he must have absconded with their best silver, antiques and money, but she was speaking gently and with some feeling. Her voice was about to crack and I wondered what awful thing had happened to Jack. I thought of accidents, sudden death, electrocution, drowning, maiming by cows . . . all sorts of ghastly occurrences flashed through my mind.

"He's gone, Mr Rhea. He's gone and left us. It's our Rene's fault, the silly bitch . . . she won't leave him alone. I've told her and told her again and again, but she's been chasing him like a love-sick virgin . . ."

She prattled on about Jack's absence and I found myself suppressing a smile. I remembered what Joe Steel had told me about them driving away their menfolk and guessed this was just another in a long line of absconding lovers. Jack must have grown heartily sick of coping with two of them.

"How old is he?" I interrupted her chatter.

"Fifty-two," she said without hesitating.

"Then there's nothing I can do," I began to tell her. "If a grown man wishes to leave home or his place of employment, it is not a matter for the police . . ."

"Ah'm worried," she cried. "Mr Rhea, Ah'm so worried. It's not a bit like him, not like him at all, and Ah think he might have come to some harm. Oh dear, Ah wish that silly sister o' mine would lay off . . . he'll never marry her, Ah could see it in his eyes. He wasn't in love with her, Mr Rhea, not Jack. It was me, really, thoo knows, Ah was t'one he favoured . . ."

"Look, Cis," I said. "Shall I come up to see you? Maybe he's just gone off for the day?"

"No, he's gone for ever. He's locked his bedroom door and bolted. Gone."

It happened that I was about due to visit Slape Wath Farm for a routine stock check and I decided to pop in today. After all, I could make a cursory search of the premises, just in case poor old Jack had got his head fast in some machinery or fallen into a midden. It would show interest from me.

I shouted through to Mary that I had changed my intended destination and would not be back for lunch. One of the farmers in those moors would feed me before nightfall, I was sure. I was just heading out of my little office when the telephone rang again. I was tempted to ignore it, but realised it might be something more urgent than Frances's missing man.

"Aidensfield Police, P.C. Rhea," I announced myself.

"Mr Rhea? This is Rene Kirby. You must come at once."

"What's the matter, Rene?" I wondered if Cis had now fallen into the midden or got her head fast in a pig trough.

"Jack," she said with tears in her voice, "He's gone, Mr Rhea."

"Yes, I know. Frances rang a few minutes ago. I'm coming up to see if I can help."

"Rang? She rang? The scheming bitch! She's driven him away, Mr Rhea, so she has. All that courting and lovey-dovey slop she's been dishing out to him. She's after him, Mr Rhea, she won't leave the fellow alone, poor sod. Double rations of apple pie, more custard than a fellow can cope with, best crockery at tea-time – name it, she's done it for him."

"Has she?" I was astounded by this revelation. What more could a fellow want if he was getting double rations of custard?

The more she ranted about her sister, the more I appreciated the words of our village shopkeeper. Now I knew what life was all about at Slape Wath Farm.

I had no idea how many men the quaint pair had driven away, but I did appreciate that Jack was just one of a long, long line. I would go to the farm to express my sorrow and show interest in their dilemma, then maybe if I talked about agricultural shows and prize-winning pigs or sheep, I'd get them to forget the departed Jack.

But it didn't work. When I arrived at the farm, I found them both in the kitchen, sitting at opposite sides of the table with a pot of tea between them and three mugs awaiting. Big Cis saw me first and came to greet me, her eyes red with crying. Rene also sported two red-rimmed eyes, and sniffed into a lace handkerchief.

"Mr Rhea, oh, Mr Rhea, Ah'm so glad you've come . . ."

Rene added, "because we've not seen him for hours and hours and there's been no call, no letter . . . and it's not like Jack . . ."

"He would have said something, you know, left a note for me . . ."

"For me, you silly bitch, for me."

"Ladies, ladies!" I cried, settling down at the table. "All this bickering will do no good. Now you both love him?"

I was relying on Joe Steel's past assessment to deal with this situation.

There was a long silence, then Cis nodded.

"Yes, he was such a nice, kind man . . ."

"And so good to the animals, Mr Rhea. The way he handled a . . ."

"Pig or a sheep was magic to watch. Superb, he was, Mr Rhea, a real man . . ."

"And a friend, Mr Rhea, a real friend."

I listened to this double-sided conversation, and remembered what Frances had said when ringing me this morning.

"Frances," I said, "you told me he'd locked his bedroom door and bolted?"

She nodded fiercely.

"She's driven him away, Mr Rhea," butted in Rene. "He's

cleared off, never to return. Every time Ah find myself a nice man-friend, she gets her claws into him and frightens him off . . ."

"She frightens him off, not me. Throwing herself at him like that . . . baking cakes for his birthday, I ask you! And sending Valentine cards!"

"Hang on, hang on!" I shouted above their banter. "Look," I raised my voice and caught their attention, "did you set your burglar alarm last night?"

My change of tactic surprised them and both regarded me with puzzled expressions.

"Burglar alarm, Mr Rhea?" asked Rene.

"You mean our alarm, Mr Rhea?" followed Cis.

By this time, I was heading towards the control-box of their system and saw the familiar key in the lock, with a length of string dangling from it. A cotton reel hung on the end.

"Ah!" I said, spotting this. "This should not be here, should it?"

"It was awkward, going upstairs to our safes, Mr Rhea . . ."

"We kept forgetting and t'alarm kept going off, and so we hid a key in t'knife drawer . . . that's t'one, t'key we all use, us and Jack that is, it's t'only one left . . ."

"If Norman's insurance company saw this, they'd never cover you again, you know. There's no point in having a burglar alarm if you leave the key in all the time . . ."

"Nobody's going to burgle us, Mr Rhea, nobody . . ."

"Our geese and dogs will stop 'em, Mr Rhea . . ."

Then I guessed where Jack was.

"Look," I said, "when you go to bed, you turn the key and set your alarm. Is that right?"

"Yes, Mr Rhea, we do that," they both spoke at once.

"And you leave the key in?"

"No, we put it in the knife drawer, so we both know where it is."

"Would Jack know where it is?" I put to them.

"No, he thinks we put the keys in the safes, because that's what we told the insurance man," again they spoke together.

"So if Jack had come downstairs last night and crept away, he'd have set off the alarm, wouldn't he?"

Cis nodded and so did Rene.

"Yes, Mr Rhea."

"Yes, Mr Rhea."

"But he didn't set it off, and Cis said his bedroom door was locked, so that means he's still in the room, doesn't it?"

As I said it, I visualised him lying dead on his bed, having suffered a massive heart attack during the night. I'd dealt with many sudden deaths of this kind and this sounded like another. It looked as if I was going to be busy.

They were already galloping upstairs, their voices shrill and harsh as they careered towards the bedroom of the object they worshipped so dearly. Both were hammering on the door as I reached it, panting slightly from the steep climb.

They stood aside, gabbling incessantly and wiping their flooding eyes as I stepped forward and turned the knob. Nothing. It was locked and I guessed the key was on the inside. I knocked many times and shouted loudly.

"Jack? Are you there?"

There was nothing, not even a groan of pain or a half-hearted attempt to reply. I looked at my watch. Eleven thirty. And as I hammered on the door and shouted, I could faintly discern the peculiar smell I'd noticed previously when looking around the rooms. Now, I thought I knew what it was. If I was right, Jack wasn't dead.

"Well?" they both asked at once, expecting me to perform a miracle.

"Have you a ladder?" I asked.

"Ladder?" they chorused. "What for?"

"To look into his room," I said seriously. "I think he's in there and I think I know what's the matter."

"He's there?" they shouted. "You mean he hasn't left us?"

"I'll have to see." I didn't promise anything, but we all trooped downstairs and out into the foldyard. There hanging on a wall inside a shed was a long ladder, and I carried this to his bedroom window. Propping it carefully against the wall, I began my climb of exploration.

As I reached the bottom pane, I peered inside and knew my diagnosis had been correct. I could see Jack laid on the cover of his untidy, unmade bed, and he was out like the proverbial light. His head lay on the pillow and his mouth was wide open, an invitation to flies and passing spiders, while his hands lay palm upwards at the end of outspread arms. His feet, bare and black, hung over the end of the bed, and he was dressed in blue striped pyjamas. He was not a pretty sight.

From my position on the ladder, I could peer right into the room, and saw evidence of my suspicions. That smell had been alcohol, gallons and gallons of it, the sort that reeks when poured down human throats without ceasing, year after year, and which fills rooms like this when empty bottles are left around. Jack Holtby was an alcoholic. Even from this distance, the room bore the classic signs. There were bottles everywhere. Stout, beer, spirits, full ones and empties, all littered about the place, filling every spare inch of space. The window ledge, the mantelpiece, the top of the wardrobe, the drawers, the dressing-table – all were full of bottles, standing or lying, empty and full, and the floor was similarly littered. The fellow was as drunk as a newt.

I opened the window in the manner used by enterprising burglars and clambered inside, knocking bottles aside. The stench was appalling. Holding my breath, I raised the window to its full height to allow some fresh air inside, and noticed the two anxious faces below.

"I'm checking," I yelled at them. "He's here."

"Oh!" they cried, putting their hands to their mouths. "Is he ill?"

"I think so," I deigned to answer, and picked my way through the minefield of bottles towards the bed. I felt him; he was warm. He was therefore alive and I could just hear his faint breathing. I slapped his cheeks, but got no response. He was out cold, stoned out of his mind and I wondered if the ladies had driven him to drink . . .

Probably not. Probably, he was well on the way to alcoholic oblivion before getting this job, and this made it easy for him to avoid prying eyes. To be tucked away out here with two doting spinsters must have been a gift from the gods. No wonder he'd kept himself to himself.

I unlocked the door with the key left in the lock and made my way downstairs. They were hurrying towards me with worried expressions.

"Is he ill?"

"Or dead? Fallen and hurt himself?"

"Has he ever asked either of you for drinks?" I put to them.

"Yes," each said in perfect unison, "but he told me not to tell my sister. I got him drink from the village when I went down . . ."

"As a secret? A special favour because you loved him . . . ?" I smiled.

They didn't answer. Each was blushing, each had been skilfully used by this chronic alcoholic and each had served only to keep him well stocked up with booze of every conceivable kind. And last night, he'd reduced his stock by a fair margin.

"He's drunk," I said. "He's out like a light, totally and finally sloshed. He's an alcoholic, ladies, the room is full of bottles."

They looked at each other and didn't speak.

"I'll call the doctor," I said. "I think he needs medical attention of some kind. Can I use your telephone?"

"Of course, Mr Rhea."

When I called again three months later, Jack had gone. They introduced me to another man, a grey-haired slim man in his fifties. He sat with them at their kitchen table, sipping coffee and I saw the familiar light in their eyes.

"This is Ernest Wallace," beamed Cis. "He's been with us a few weeks . . ."

"He came from Waversford Estate, Mr Rhea, with very good references . . ."

"I know he'll be well looked after," I smiled, pulling up a chair. "Welcome, Mr Wallace."

I made a mental note to check his character and I wondered how he'd cope with a moorland burglar alarm and two love-sick spinsters.

8

"In works of labour, or of skill,
I would be busy too;
For Satan finds some mischief still
For idle hands to do."

Isaac Watts 1674–1748

Because it was Saturday, the grandfather clock had to be wound up. I opened the ancient glass door which covered the face and reached to the top of the case for the key. I kept it there because it was out of reach of the children and I knew where to find it each winding day. The key was a curious shape, being a tiny tunnel with a handle welded at one end, and it was used to wind the eight-day clock. It looked something like a miniature starting handle for a car.

As I wound up the faithful old clock, the key suddenly broke in my hand. The delicate handle had come away from the barrel of the antique key, and I could see it was nothing more than a straightforward welding job. The repair could be quickly affected.

At first, I thought of Awd John the blacksmith, but on second thoughts appreciated that his skills were more directed towards the repair of larger objects like ploughs and gates. I had never seen him tackle anything of a delicate nature, and I wondered if anyone in this village could fix my key. It was more than a soldering job, I realised, otherwise I would have done that myself. Welding was the only sure way of effecting this repair. The garage might have done it, but they closed on Saturday afternoons.

Accordingly, I decided to ask around the village, and the first man I saw as I patrolled on foot about the village centre was Stumpy Sykes.

"Now, Stumpy," I made the traditional greeting. "How's tha gahin on?"

"Middling," was his reply. Everything Stumpy did was middling – never good, never bad. If he was ill, he was middling; if he was fit and well, he was middling. If he won a prize in the flower shows, his plants were fair to middling, and whatever the weather, it was middling.

"Stumpy," I said, taking the broken key from my pocket. "Is there anybody who can fix this?"

He solemnly regarded the key and nodded slowly. "Deearn't trust Awd John wi summat like that. Welding ploughs and fixing rainwater pipes is right up his street, but fixing delicate things like yon is not in his line at all. Try Awd Alex."

"Alex?" I puzzled.

"Aye, that cottage yon side o' t'garage. He's a retired clock-maker, well into his seventies, but he can fix owt."

I'd not come across Awd Alex and learned his surname was MacDonald. Mr Alexander MacDonald to be precise, and he lived with his wife in a lovely cottage with a porch and climbing plants all over the front. The place shone like a polished cream-strainer. I knocked on the door, using a brass knocker in which I could see my own reflection, and soon a smart lady in her sixties answered. Her pretty face expressed surprise at the sight of my uniform but she rapidly gained her composure and said, "Yes?"

"Oh, I'm P.C. Rhea," I introduced myself. "I'm looking for Mr MacDonald."

"Oh, nothing's wrong, is it?" she asked the question every-one asked when finding a policeman at the door. I noticed she carried a yellow duster.

"Oh, no," I smiled and pulled the key from my pocket. "It's this – I'm told he can fix it."

"Well, yes, I suppose he can, officer." She spoke with a faint Scots accent. "But he's out just now. You can find him up at Miss Crowther's – you know her place?"

I shook my head.

"Stone House," she said, pointing along the village. "You

could leave the thing if you want – he's got a workshop up the garden."

"No, I'll explain how it needs fixing," I smiled. "I'll find him. Miss Crowther, eh?"

"Yes, he went there a long time ago – I hope you find him – if you do, officer, can you say tea will be ready at five o'clock?"

"Yes, of course," and I left her to her cleaning.

I walked along the main street, bidding "Good afternoon" to several residents and finally reached Stone House, Miss Crowther's home. It was a large, Victorian building of sombre grey stone and boasted a rather genteel but unkempt appearance. I had to lift the garden gate to open it, for it needed new hinges, and made my way to the front door. I rang the bell and it sounded somewhere inside, upon which I eventually heard inner doors opening and closing as someone came towards me. Then the front door opened.

A short, dumpy and smiling woman answered; she was clad in a long purple dress with a knitted shawl over the shoulders and smiled a warm welcome.

"Ah," she said, "You must be Police Constable Rhea?"

"Yes," I acknowledged.

"It's so kind of you to call," she oozed, "I'm delighted you have found the time. I do like the policemen to call on me, to make themselves known so that when I'm in trouble, I know who they are. That makes it so much easier to approach you, and it gives us all that much more confidence . . ."

As she ushered me inside her rambling home, she babbled on and guided me into a large lounge expensively furnished with Indian carpets and complementary furnishings. She motioned me to sit down and I obeyed.

"Now," she said. "Tea or coffee?"

"Well, actually," I began, "I didn't come to stay . . ."

"Nonsense, you can't call without some hospitality in return," she breathed. "I do like to give my policemen a drink or two. Biscuits?"

And before I could answer, she whisked away towards her pantry somewhere along the corridor and returned with a plate full of chocolate biscuits. She placed these on a low table, which she eased towards me and said, "Tea won't be a jiffy."

At that, she settled on the chair opposite and began to ask about my family. I happily obliged, occasionally trying to explain the real purpose of my visit, but it was quite plain she'd interpreted this as a purely social call, a "get-to-know-you" exercise. So I played along with this, knowing it would please her. She told me of her father, a senior army officer in India years ago, and of her brothers who were very clever and doing well in London, one a barrister and the other in exports of some kind. She spent well over forty minutes telling me all about herself and asking all about me. She was a charming lady, most articulate and well read, and I knew I was going to have difficulty getting away. Furthermore, I had to find out where Mr MacDonald had gone – perhaps he was still in the house?

I managed to include his name in the conversation as I found myself telling her the names of those people with whom I'd made contact in the short time I'd been here. When I mentioned Alex MacDonald, she said,

"Oh, nice man. Very nice man. I had him in here before you came. He came to fix my television set, it was doing funny things. He's good at fixing things, is Mr MacDonald, very good."

"I'd like to meet him," I said, thinking of the broken clock key in my pocket.

"He said he was going down to old Mr Nash's house," she said.

"I'll see him later," I said. "It wasn't important."

"Well, I mustn't keep you," she beamed. "It was so kind of you to call. Do call again, anytime you like, and we'll have tea."

And so I walked into the fresh air, rather baffled by her warm reception, but determined to call again and hear more of her fascinating life.

I knew Mr Nash. He was an old gentleman who had retired from a life in the city, something to do with accountancy, and I often chattered to him in the street, or in the shop. I knew he would welcome me, and that he was a kindred spirit of Alex MacDonald. I found his neat semi tucked well into the corner of a new estate, and walked up the path. He was gardening and observed my approach.

He raised a soil-stained hand in greeting as I strode along his path.

"Hello, Mr Nash. Still tidying up then?"

"There's always work in a garden," he said, leaning on his rake. "But it keeps me busy. My wife has gone into York, looking for a new dress, so I pretended I had this patch to get raked over urgently . . ." and he grinned wickedly at his private conspiracy.

"I'm looking for Alex MacDonald," I said. "I heard he was here."

"Yes, he was. I got him to fix the overflow in my roof. The confounded thing keeps overflowing every time we have a bath, and as he's such a good plumber, I thought he'd fix it. He hasn't been gone long."

"Where did he go?" I asked.

"Up to Joe Steel's."

That meant the village shop.

By this stage, I was most interested in Awd Alex, as Stumpy had called him. I'd been sent to him because he was a useful welder, but already this afternoon he'd fixed Miss Crowther's television set and Mr Nash's plumbing. Why had he gone to the shop – it was closed on Saturday afternoons?

"How long since?" I asked him.

"Not long – maybe an hour, no more."

I was determined to track down the elusive Alex MacDonald, and after passing the time of day with Mr Nash and admiring his garden, I walked back up the village to the shop. Although it was shut, I knew Joe Steel would respond to my knocking. He did, and seemed pleased to see me.

"Hello, Mr Rhea. Trouble?"

"No trouble," I smiled. "Sorry to bother you, Joe, but I'm looking for Alex MacDonald."

"Oh, he's gone," he told me. "I had him here not long ago – an hour ago, not much more. He does a spot of wine-tasting for me, you know. I get wine in for my customers and he tastes samples for me – he knows a bit about his wines, he's very good with German whites . . ."

"Where did he go from here?" I heard myself ask patiently.

"Mrs Widdowson," he said. "She's having trouble with her

lights. They keep going out – there's a bad connection, I think, or a short somewhere. Bulbs keep blowing or the lights keep flickering. He's gone round there to fix them for her."

"Thanks – I'll see if he's there."

"He left about forty minutes ago," he said.

I knew I was getting warmer. The time-lapse was growing less and less as I pursued the elusive Alex around the village. Joe told me how to find Mrs Widdowson and I located her in a lovely bungalow just off the main street. She was washing her windows from a short step-ladder and would be a lady in her early fifties. She wore a flowered head-square and flat shoes.

"Hello," I shouted across to her. "Mrs Widdowson?"

"Yes," she returned my smile with that inevitable look of apprehension.

"I'm looking for Mr MacDonald," I announced. "I was told he was here."

"Yes, he was, Mr Rhea," she knew my name. "He came to fix my lights – it was a bad connection, he said. He fixed it for me. He left, though, about half an hour ago. He doesn't take long, fixing things."

"He doesn't!" I said. "Thanks – sorry to have troubled you."

"He said he was going over to Partridge Hall," she offered. "You know, that farm down the Elsinby Road."

"I know," I called, deciding to complete this tour. I had to visit the Dinsdale family at Partridge Hall sometime in the near future, to interview Terry, their seventeen-year-old son. He'd been involved in a motor-cycle accident near Manchester last week, so I could conclude these two missions together. The walk to Partridge Hall took about twenty minutes. I walked towards the spacious entrance of this lovely old building which was really a large farmhouse set among sycamores. It stood on an elevated site with ranging views across the open countryside and was clearly the home of an industrious and wealthy family.

I rang the doorbell and waited. Soon, a young woman with neat blonde hair tied with a ribbon appeared from a corridor and smiled at me.

"Hello," I said. "I'm P.C. Rhea. Is Terry Dinsdale in please?"

"Terry?" she frowned. "Is he in trouble?"

"No," I assured her. "It's about his accident last week, the one near Manchester. I've got to take a statement from him – it's for the local police. I think he was more of a witness than a casualty?"

"Yes, he was overtaken by a motor cyclist who crashed into a van. Terry fell off his motor bike because of it, but wasn't hurt. I think he's out. Just a moment, I'll fetch mum."

She disappeared the way she had come and soon a mature woman with identical blonde hair and lovely smile materialised from the house. She was dressed in painting clothes – an old apron, old dress and a clear plastic hat on her head. She carried a paint brush, the handle wrapped in a rag.

"Oh, I'm sorry," I said. "I didn't want to interrupt important work!"

"It's all right, I'm decorating our lounge," she said. "Susan said it's Terry you want?"

I explained the reason and she smiled. "Yes, he told us, but he's out, Mr Rhea. He went off to York with some pals. I expect him back about half past six."

"I'll call again."

"Shall I send him up to your house?" she offered.

"If he rings first to tell me when he's coming, that would be fine," I consented.

"He won't be prosecuted, will he?" she asked, with all the worried expressions a mother can produce.

"Not from what I saw of the report from Manchester," I confirmed. "I've been asked to take a witness statement from him, nothing more, although I will have to record details of his driving licence and insurance. That's routine."

"All right, Mr Rhea, I'll get him to ring you when he comes in."

"Thanks – now, a small thing while I'm here. I'm looking for Mr MacDonald and understand he's here."

"Yes," she smiled, and I felt a great sense of relief. "Did you want to speak to him?"

"Very briefly," and I pulled my key from my pocket. "I want him to fix this, and have been chasing him all afternoon."

"Come through," she invited, and I followed her along the elegant corridors of this beautiful old house and into a room which reeked of fresh paint. The floor and furniture were covered with white sheets and there, perched high on a step ladder, was a silver-haired gentleman with a deeply tanned face. He was the picture of health and he turned to look down as I entered the room. He was clad in a white smock and put something down on the tray at the top of his ladder. Above was a highly ornate ceiling, rich in plaster work and decorated across its entirety. He was doing something to the plaster work.

"Mr MacDonald," the lady announced. "This is P.C. Rhea, he wants a quick word with you."

"Guilty as charged!" he raised his hands in the air and laughed, then descended the tall step-ladder. "Hello, I'm Alex MacDonald." His voice had a pleasing lowland lilt.

I showed him the key and he smiled. "No problem," he said. "Is it from a gramophone or a clock?"

"A grandfather clock," I said.

"I'll fix it next week. Will you be at home on Wednesday morning?"

I made a rapid mental calculation, and said, "Yes, I'll be in my office until ten o'clock, at the Hill Top. But I can call in at your place." He took my key and popped it into his pocket.

"I take a lot of catching," he smiled. "Wednesday is my day at Ashfordly – I go to the bread shop, you know and bake their fruit cakes for them. I can drop your key in as I pass the house."

"That's fine," I said. "Really fine . . ."

My business over, I left the room and Mrs Dinsdale escorted me to the front door. "He's remarkable," she was saying. "He's putting gold leaf on to my ceiling, making a marvellous job too. We only decorate that ceiling once every fifteen years or so, and it's a job finding someone who can do that gold leaf work. I was lucky getting Mr MacDonald."

"Yes, you were," I agreed. I reached the door, and as I was about to leave, I heard footsteps behind me. Alex MacDonald was hurrying after me.

"Oh, Mr Rhea," he panted. "If that grandfather clock of yours grows awkward, you know where to find me. I'll fix it for you – re-set the timing, weights, and so forth."

"Thanks," I smiled, as I left the premises. I wondered if he was any good at working night duty for bored policemen!

*　　*　　*

Ted Williamson from Keld House rang me at seven one morning and cried, "Mr Rhea, thoo'll etti come quick. Ah've had some sheep pinched during t'night."

I didn't ask any more questions, but donned my motor-cycling gear and set out across the hills to his remote farm. It lay at the end of a deep, narrow valley high on the moors, and was extremely isolated. His sheep ran across the moors with no hedges or walls to contain them and they formed a major contribution to his meagre living standards. He did, however, keep a few sheep closer to the house and these were in a small paddock adjacent to the building. These had been bred by hand by his patient wife, the lambs of mothers who had either rejected them or who had died during lambing time. Those orphans had grown into fine animals, thanks to her atten-tion.

The noise of my arrival brought him from the kitchen and he was waiting on the concrete path as I struggled to park my bike upon an irregular and stony farmyard. At last I had the machine balanced on its stand, and removed my crash helmet which I placed on the seat.

"Morning, Ted," I greeted him. "Sad affair, eh?"

"Aye, lad, it is. Now, them sheep o' mine roam across yon heights with nivver a theft from one year end to t'next; some get knocked down and killed by cars, but thoo can expect that. Sheep aren't t'brightest o' creatures, are they?"

"No, they're a bit dim," I agreed, following him to the kitchen.

"But them in that paddock, well, they've been hand-reared by our Maud and some is as tame as a cat. Some rotten sod has pinched 'em from that paddock."

"How many?" I put to him as I pulled a chair from the table. It scraped noisily upon the sandstone floor, and I sat down without being asked. It was expected that visitors did this.

"Eight," he said. "Eight gimmers, nice animals, well fed. Nice for meat, Ah'd say, plump and fleshy. Not run to bone like them awd ewes up on t'top. Some butcher'll have 'em by now, Ah reckon, cutting 'em up."

"Morning, Mr Rhea," Maud, his plump, rosy-cheeked wife came in with a large metal teapot and said. "Tea?"

"Thanks." She began to pour a huge tin mug full, a pint pot with a metal handle.

"What are they worth, Ted?" I had to ask for my crime report.

"Fifteen quid apiece, Ah reckon."

I sipped the tea and they settled before me, sitting around the table as I produced a long sheet of paper from my inside pocket. This was a crime report, and I had to enter all the relevant details upon it. I began with the standard questions about their names, ages, addresses and occupations, and eventually got down to the basic facts of the crime. From what Ted told me, he'd checked the paddock last night about ten o'clock before turning in to bed, and at quarter to seven this morning, he'd come downstairs to find the gate open. He knew he'd locked it last night – he'd checked that very fact before going to bed.

About a dozen sheep were still in the field, huddled in a corner, and he believed they'd been terrified into moving there in the dark, and had not strayed since.

"Could it be hikers?" I asked. "Maybe somebody's walked through and just left the gate open? Could your sheep have wandered off?"

He shook his head vigorously. "Nay, lad, nivver. If that had happened, they'd still be on my land somewhere. They're not – they've been takken off in a truck of some kind."

"Truck?"

"Van mebbe. Summat light, I reckon, like a pick-up or a small van."

"How do you know that?"

"There's tracks in that gateway. Drink your tea, and Ah'll show you."

Meanwhile, I wrote into my report a description of the eight missing gimmers, the name used for young female sheep not yet ewes. All were nine months old, female of course, and marked on their left flank with a splotch of blue dye. After completing those short but essential formalities, I asked Ted to take me to the scene of the crime.

"That gate," he said.

And in the soft earth were the unmistakable tracks of a vehicle of some kind. It had reversed into the gateway, a fact revealed by marks of its front wheels made during that man-oeuvre, and there was a slight indentation a few feet into the field where a long tailboard or ramp had rested. I knew how the thief had operated – in the darkness, he would park his vehicle in the open gate and simply drive the sheep towards the truck. There may have been a dog, and he must have had lights of some kind, but it was a simple manoeuvre. Once he'd got a handful of animals aboard, he would drive off.

I squatted on my haunches to examine the marks. They were the conventional tyre marks of a four-wheeled light vehicle, and I guessed it was a pick-up of some kind, possibly a Morris. Then I noticed the irregularity in one of the rear tyre marks.

From the impressions in the soft earth, it was clear that the tyre had a defect on the inside wall, and it looked like a bubble of rubber. I knew the fault – it had once happened to my car. The tyre wall was weak and the pressure of air caused the tube and the tyre to bulge like a round bubble. If it caught a sharp stone or a nail, a puncture was inevitable. Sometimes, if the blob grew very large, it would make contact with the springs of the vehicle and create a nuisance, if only because of the repetitious noise as the wheel turned. But in time, that would rub a hole in the outer casing.

I showed this to Ted.

"Now that's a capper," he said. "Ah nivver noticed yon."

"Does it ring a bell?" I asked. "Has anybody been up here lately with a vehicle like this? I reckon it's a small pick-up, four wheels, all single and with a tail-board that comes down, like a ramp."

"And with a blob on t'rear tyre, eh? On t'inside?"

"You can see the mark in the soil, Ted." I pointed to it again, and I could see he was thinking hard.

"Noo, there was a feller up here with a truck like that, seeking work."

"When was this?" I began to grow excited.

"Two days back, no more."

"What did he want?"

"He came to my kitchen door one afternoon, three o'clock or thereabouts, and asked if Ah was looking for casual labour."

"Did you take him on, Ted?"

He shook his head, "Nay, lad. Ah've a spot of ditching and hedging that mebbe needs a feller to do it, but Ah didn't want to take onnybody on. To be honest, Ah can't afford to pay for jobs like that."

"So he left?"

"Aye, he did."

"And who was it? A local?"

"Ah didn't ask his name, Mr Rhea. But he gave some name or other. Daft of me when Ah think back, but Ah didn't write it down. You don't think at the time, do you? Ah've seen him around at market days and sheep sales, mind."

"What's he look like?" I was taking notes now.

"A little feller, with a sharp face, like a jockey or even an elf! A funny little chap, really. Scruffily dressed, mind."

Immediately, I knew my suspect. I said, "And was his van a light blue one, with rust all over? A Morris pick-up, like we thought?"

He frowned and then nodded. "Aye, now you come to mention it, it was."

"Can you remember his name? Try hard."

He shrugged his shoulders. "It didn't ring a bell, I can't remember it."

"Claude Jeremiah Greengrass?" I suggested.

"Aye!" his eyes lit up. "That was what he said. A daft sooart of a name if you ask me . . . thoo knows him?"

"I know him," I agreed. "He's a petty thief who lives on my patch near Elsinby. This is just the sort of thing he'd do."

"If you catch him, will it mean court then?"

"You bet it will!" I said. "I've been after this rogue for ages, Ted, and he always manages to get away somehow."

"Well, Ah's nut one for takking folks to court, Mr Rhea, nut if I can help it. All Ah want is them sheep back, that's all."

If I knew Claude Jeremiah, he'd have disposed of the animals very rapidly, thus getting rid of the evidence. He must have had an outlet, possibly a crooked market dealer or butcher. But I would go and see him anyway, and immediately.

"Just get them sheep back, Mr Rhea, never mind about a court. Ah'd hate to get my name in t'papers for summat like that."

"All right," I heard myself saying. "If I get the sheep back, we'll punish him ourselves, eh? Alive that is – that's if we get your sheep back alive."

"Aye, that's a deal. And if he's killed 'em and you can prove it, then take him to Eltering Magistrates. Now that's what Ah calls a fair deal."

"Or if I can prove he's stolen them and got rid of them?"

"Aye, all right. But if you get 'em back alive and well, we forget yon court?"

And so the peculiar deal was struck. I knew I'd stand little chance with Claude Jeremiah; he was cute enough not to keep the animals any longer than necessary, and I knew I would have a very slender chance of proving him to be the thief. But I knew it was him – in my bones, I knew.

My priority now was to race back to Elsinby and unearth him. I had to catch him before he disposed of the animals, and because he'd stolen them during the night, they could be seventy or eighty miles away by now, or more. I told Ted I'd be in touch if there was any development, and rode off in a cloud of spray from the damp road.

Thirty-five minutes later, I was cruising down the main street of Elsinby, and turned off the tarmac highway on to the rough track which led down to Claude Jeremiah's untidy collection of buildings. As I bumped along his road, I heard his lurcher begin to bark. Alfred, the dog, had warned him of my approach, and that's how Alfred earned his meat.

I parked the motor cycle and leaned it against a tree about fifty yards from the house and walked the rest of the journey. I saw no sign of Claude Jeremiah or of his pick-up, and so I knocked on the door.

Seconds later, the man himself answered.

"Oh, Mr Rhea, this is an early visit. Something wrong?"

"Where you out last night or early this morning, Claude?" I did not waste time with useless preliminaries. He knew the score as well as I.

"Out? Me? Good heavens no, Mr Rhea. I had an early night and have just nicely got out of bed."

"You weren't out anywhere near Ted Williamson's place then? At Keld House?"

"Keld House, Mr Rhea? Why should I go to Keld House?"

"Looking for work, maybe?" I smiled.

"Ah, yes. I'd forgotten. Yes, of course. I did go to see him. I was looking for casual work, Mr Rhea, harvesting, potato picking, hedging and ditching, anything, but that was a day or two ago."

"And he didn't have a job for you?"

"No, Mr Rhea, he didn't. Why, has he one now? Is that it? You've been up there checking your livestock registers and he's changed his mind? He liked me and wants me to work for him?" There was a wicked gleam in his bright eyes.

"No, he has no job. But he has lost some sheep, Claude."

"Sheep? Lost? I've not seen sheep up there, Mr Rhea, not me. Oh no."

"Stolen, Claude. His sheep were stolen, and I know you were there."

"Stolen? Not when I was there, Mr Rhea, surely?"

"No, last night, during the night or maybe early this morning. Eight gimmers, Claude Jeremiah, in a pick-up just like yours."

"There's lots of those little Morrises about, Mr Rhea, lots of them."

"So you didn't steal his sheep, then?"

"Now you know me, Mr Rhea. I'd never steal sheep, not me. I know I'm light-fingered and a worry to you, but I'm not a sheep-stealer. Not me."

"Then you won't mind if I take a look around your place?"

"Mind? You've no right to search my place, Mr Rhea, no right . . ."

"But you don't object, surely, do you? I mean, shall I radio my control and get a search-warrant issued? Then our C.I.D. can come here, in force, lots of them, and really search your house and premises . . ."

"There's nothing here, Mr Rhea, nothing."

"Then let me see your pick-up."

"It's in that shed." He pointed to a shed with a large wooden hasp as its lock. "There are some sheep there, as well, Mr Rhea. Don't let them out, they're waiting to be collected." And his voice trailed away.

"Eight?" I asked.

"How did you know that?" he regarded me with a steady stare.

"With blue marks on their left flanks?"

"Yes," he said, wilting now. "That's very astute of you, Mr Rhea. I got them for a friend . . ."

"You stole them from Ted Williamson," and I then remembered my unusual bargain with Ted. "Show me, Claude, and no mucking about."

Resigned to his fate, he took me to the shed and inside was his little vehicle, but it was jacked up and the rear tyre was missing.

"I just got home," he said grimly, "and was coming down my lane, when I got a puncture. There was a bleb on the inside of the tyre, Mr Rhea, so I got landed with those sheep . . . look, I'm sorry . . ."

And in a wire pen at the far end of the shed were eight gimmers contentedly chewing hay, their blue rumps readily visible.

"My spare had a puncture as well," he said. "It's not my day, Mr Rhea."

"It is your lucky day, Claude Jeremiah," I said. "If you get those sheep back to Ted's this morning, he will not take you to court."

His eyes lit up. "Really? Mr Rhea? That's gen, is it?"

"It is," I said, somewhat sadly, and then a car entered the yard. I looked out and saw it was the mechanic from Elsinby Garage. He climbed out and took a pair of wheels from his boot and trundled them over to this shed.

"Oh, hello, Mr Rhea. Not a bad morning. Claude – your tyres – one new tyre fitted and one puncture mended. Two pounds three and six please."

"I haven't any money," said Claude.

"Then I take the wheels back and you'll get 'em when you pay . . ."

"Just a minute, Graham." He changed his mind and dug deep into his pocket. He found the necessary cash and paid the mechanic who drove away contented.

"Now, Claude Jeremiah," I said. "Right now you replace that wheel and you take those sheep back to Keld Head. I'll wait until you do and I'll follow you to the farm. Right now, with no more messing about."

"But, Mr Rhea . . ."

"It's that, or court, Claude Jeremiah, and for sheep-stealing hereabouts, you're risking prison, you know."

Without a word, he bent to the task of replacing the wheel and within five minutes, the truck was roadworthy. The spare was thrown into the rear, and I instructed him to herd the sheep aboard. He succeeded without a great deal of trouble, as they were already confined in the building, and within fifteen minutes, we were heading for Keld House.

Ted was delighted. His wife was overcome because some of these had been pet lambs, and I smiled as they were replaced in their paddock in exactly the same way he'd removed them. He reversed his truck into the gate, lowered the tailboard and shooed out the animals.

"Is that it, Mr Rhea?" Claude asked me, anxious to be off.

"Not quite, Claude," I smiled at him, and I saw the look of anxiety on his face. "You've a debt to pay, haven't you?"

"Debt? Here? I don't owe money, Mr Rhea, not here."

"No, but if it wasn't for Mr and Mrs Williamson's generosity, you'd be under arrest and sitting in a cell at Ashfordly Police Station. You'd be waiting for a court appearance on a serious criminal charge and even prison."

He said nothing, but lowered his head.

"Ted," I addressed the farmer. "This morning you told me you needed some hedging and ditching doing, and couldn't afford to pay anybody?"

"Aye, things are a bit tight," he confirmed.

"Claude is good at things like that, he's very handy about a farm, Ted, and can turn his hand to anything. He won't need paying, of course, and he has volunteered to help you as an act of contrition."

"I have?" asked Claude.

"You have, just now. You will work here until Ted has got caught up with his outstanding jobs. For nowt, Claude. You work for nowt, and if you go away, or pinch anything from here, or anywhere else, we'll activate the sheep-stealing charge. That'll get you several years in clink, my lad."

"I'll put the kettle on," said Mrs Williamson.

As we discussed the tasks that awaited him, I could see Claude wilting at the thought. We entered the kitchen for a celebratory cup of tea laced with a fair helping of whisky, and I recalled the old days of threshing and harvesting on these moors.

Everybody helped one another; they loaned equipment and man-power so that all could reap their harvests as quickly as possible, and I smiled to myself.

As I drank my tea, I reminded Ted and Claude of this system, which continued to operate in some areas.

"Can you remember the days when you all helped each other, Ted?" I asked, hoping he would recognise the drift of my conversation.

"By gum, aye," he smiled. "Grand days, them. Did thoo know, Claude, we needed fourteen fellers to work on a threshing day. There was t'engine driver, forkers, corn carriers, stack builders, a lad to see t'engine allus had water, and a few more besides. We all helped out, thoo sees, lending men and machinery, moving across these hills and getting all these crops in as fast as we could."

"You can still lend a man, Ted," I smiled. "I know Claude will let himself be lent out, for nothing of course. Didn't you say you were going over to High Rigg next week?"

Ted was quick-thinking and agreed with my fictitious work idea. I knew he would offer Claude to High Rigg Farm, and I knew the little man was fixed up for work for several weeks to come. All for no pay.

It would have been cheaper to have paid a fine in court.

And, of course, it would have been better not to have stolen those sheep.

But I still had not managed to win a conviction against Claude. I could wait. One day, he'd come. One day . . .

9

"I have been in love, and in debt, and in drink,
this many and many a year."

Alexander Brome 1620–1666

Sergeant Charlie Bairstow and I were sitting in his official car, discussing a spate of vandalism which had broken out in the village of Elsinby. Our talk was not so much a plan of action, but more a small symposium of ideas for the total eradication of vandalism by saturating the village with police officers. That, in reality, meant regular visits from me. The time was approaching ten o'clock one Wednesday evening in early May and the night was dark, albeit with a hint of brightness over the distant horizon.

We were not in Elsinby at this time; in fact, I was performing a late motor-cycle patrol across the whole range of Ryedale and Sergeant Bairstow had found me just outside Malton, on the minor road to Calletby.

"Evening, Nick," he'd greeted me in his usual affable way. "Take your helmet off and sit with me a few minutes."

And that is how I came to be sitting at his side in the tiny police car some distance off my own beat. We did not make any great progress in our battle against vandals but I enjoyed the opportunity to air my views about this creeping menace, and the discussion added welcome interest to my lonely patrol.

But as we sat and talked, I heard someone running towards the car. The darkness made it difficult to identify the sex or state of the runner, but soon there was a frantic tapping on Sergeant Bairstow's window.

"By, I'm glad I found you fellers." A thick-set farm youth with corduroy trousers and an old tweed jacket was addressing us, having quickly opened Sergeant Bairstow's door.

"Summat wrong?" Bairstow used the local pronunciation.

"Aye, Sergeant," the lad said. "In yon barn of ours. There's a man and I reckon he's dead. He's laid out on our straw, and I wouldn't guess how long he's been there."

"You've not touched anything?" asked Sergeant Bairstow.

"Not a thing, Sergeant, not a thing. Ah wouldn't touch yon feller for all t'gold in China."

"Come on, show us then," and Sergeant Bairstow opened the rear door. The youth climbed in smelling strongly of pigs and guided us to the barn. It was situated about four hundred yards along the village street, and down a narrow, unmade lane. The lad was called Alan Dudley and farmed for his father; he was on his way to a telephone kiosk when he spotted our conveniently parked car. He was highly excited and chattered about his discovery as he showed us the barn. There was no light, but he located a storm lantern which he'd left near the entrance, and produced matches to ignite the wick.

Sergeant Bairstow carried a powerful torch from the car and together we entered the dark recesses of the large Dutch barn. Alan Dudley guided us unerringly to the distant corners by clambering over loose bales and piles of unstacked straw.

He halted and revealed his find by holding his lantern high to flood the corpse with a dim light. Sure enough, there was the body of a man. He lay in a prone position with his head cradled in his arms and his legs curled up in what might be described as the foetal position. The fellow was dressed in a rough grey suit with black boots, and a flat cap lay on the straw a few inches from his head. His hair was filthy and had once been fair, but was now a curious shade of tarnished gold. I guessed he was in his late forties or early fifties and he appeared to be a tramp or a roadster of some kind.

"You came straight to us?" Sergeant Bairstow asked gently.

"Aye, I did," said Alan. "Fair turned me, it did, seeing that lying there."

"You've not touched him then?"

"Not me, sergeant, never. Not a thing like yon."

"I can't say I blame you," and as Alan stood aside, Sergeant Bairstow and I edged forward in the pool of light, treading carefully upon the straw. I watched as my superior squatted on his haunches at the side of the body and touched the whiskery face.

"Warm," he said with some relief in his voice, "and he's alive."

"Alive?" cried Alan Dudley. "He looks dead to me."

"He's alive all right," and Sergeant Bairstow lowered his head to listen for breathing, then swiftly sat upright, holding his nose. "Drink," he sighed. "Meths. This fellow's a meths drinker, he's paralytic. God, he stinks!"

I went closer and sniffed the atmosphere. For my trouble, I caught a terrible whiff of the powerful odour which rose from this sleeping man. Alan came too, and creased his face in disbelief. The stench was terrible.

"We're fetching some sheep in here tonight," said Alan, looking down at the visitor. "He can't stay, some of them awd rams'll half kill him."

"He's our problem, Nick," said Bairstow softly.

"It's your car, sergeant," I reminded him, for my motor cycle was parked nearby.

"Help him into the bloody car then," and with Alan lifting and sweating, and with me hoisting the limp fellow to his feet, we managed to half-carry, half-bundle the limp lump of meths-sodden humanity towards Sergeant Bairstow's car. With much puffing and panting, he squeezed him into the rear seat and laid him flat. The stench in the car was appalling, and I didn't regret being on the motor cycle tonight. I wondered what Sergeant Bairstow would do with the fellow, and realised with horror that I was the only constable on duty tonight in this section. The problem could be mine.

We thanked Alan for his help and praised him for his public-spirited action, but wondered what on earth we could do with the meths man.

"Follow me, Nick," Bairstow ordered. I obeyed. I climbed aboard my Francis Barnett and followed the car for about two miles. Then he halted.

He left his car and approached me as I sat astride my motor cycle, awaiting further instructions.

"Nick, old son," Sergeant Bairstow placed one hand on the

handlebars of my machine. "This character is yours for the night."

"Mine?" I was horrified. I knew what was coming next.

"You are the only duty constable in the section tonight, and if we take this character into the police station, he'll have to be placed in the cells because he's drunk and incapable. That means someone has to be present all the time, watching him and caring for him, making sure he doesn't snuff it or hurt himself. Someone has to feed and water him, fetch him his breakfast, and minister to his every need."

"I'm supposed to finish at one o'clock," I reminded him, wondering if I'd get paid overtime for this duty.

"Exactly, Nick. And I'm supposed to finish when I get home in a few minutes' time. So this fellow is a problem, isn't he?"

"Yes, Sergeant." I wasn't quite sure what he was driving at, but was interested to find out. I knew the routine – a prisoner in the cells at Ashfordly Police Station meant all-night duty for the constable looking after him, and the tiny station was not really equipped for such visitors. There was no provision for food, for one thing. We could take him to Malton or one of the larger places, but I could imagine the wrath of the duty inspector if we presented him with our gift. No one wanted a smelly old meths drinker in custody if they could help it – there'd be the resultant mess in the cell to clean up.

"Well, Nick?" Sergeant Bairstow asked, after a long silence from me.

"Well what, Sergeant?"

"What shall we do with him? Any practical ideas?"

"Not really," I had to admit.

"Well I have," he beamed. "Follow me."

He started the engine of his little car and with the pungent fellow wafting evil fumes about the inside of the vehicle, Sergeant Bairstow turned around and drove towards Malton. I followed at a discreet distance and wondered what solution he had found. I was amazed to see him drive through the centre of the quiet town and across the river.

This was sacrilege! We were entering foreign territory now, because we had left our native North Riding of Yorkshire and were driving into the neighbouring East Riding, then a separate county. In those days, county boundaries were sacrosanct and jealously guarded. Although boundary rules were not quite so rigidly enforced as those in the U.S.A. during Wild West days, there was a great deal of professional jealousy between adjoining police forces. It was certainly discourteous to invade another Chief Constable's county without his knowledge and we all had instructions that whenever we crossed a boundary to make any enquiry, however minor, we must inform the local police of our presence. It was similar to getting one's passport stamped.

But this did not appear to concern Sergeant Bairstow. He trundled through Norton in our police car, and turned into the countryside with me close behind, ever vigilant for the appearance of an East Riding policeman. If one caught us, we were sunk . . .

The East Riding Constabulary differed from the North Riding Constabulary in those days, because the former wore helmets, whereas we sported flat caps. In truth, we had very little contact with these strange fellows from south of the River Derwent, and had no desire to meet them now. After two miles, Sergeant Bairstow pulled up outside a barn down a very lonely lane. I eased to a halt behind him and lifted the motor cycle on to its stand, then joined him at the car.

He spoke in whispers. "Nick," he hissed. "There's an old hay barn here. We're in East Riding territory so be careful – we don't want them to find us. We'll put Meths Maurice in his barn, then belt back into the North Riding as fast as we can."

"All right," I said, for there was nothing else I could say. After ten minutes of heaving and cursing, we extricated Meths Maurice from the car and carried him into the cosy barn. I was dressed in motor cycle gear, complete with crash helmet, and Sergeant Bairstow was capless; had anyone seen us, it was doubtful if they'd recognise us as police officers as we undertook our nefarious deed, least of all the subject of our mission.

Within fifteen minutes we had our guest neatly laid out on a bed of clean new hay. He slumbered blissfully on and curled into his foetal position as we arranged the hay around him to keep him warm. Satisfied that he was slumbering peacefully, we left him to his new abode in the East Riding of Yorkshire. If anyone found him, he would no longer be our problem; his fate rested in the hands of the East Riding Constabulary.

Sergeant Bairstow congratulated himself on this piece of strategy and we returned to our own territory, hoping that no one had noticed our little convoy of trespassing police vehicles. I followed him home, but after twenty minutes, he pulled into the side of the road and signalled me to halt. I pulled up beside him and he lowered his window.

"Nick," he said with a most apologetic tone in his voice. "We've done wrong, you know. This is no way to treat our friends in the East Riding. Just imagine – they'll be lumbered with that smelly old character now, and besides, that barn might not be warm enough. If he dies, we're for it, and I'd never forgive myself."

To cut a long story short, Sergeant Bairstow changed his mind and decided to return for the meths drinker. For the second time that night, therefore, we crept into Norton and made our way towards the old barn. I parked close to the official car and together we entered the dark, cold premises. My torch picked out the slumbering form among the hay and Sergeant Bairstow said, "Right, as before. Get him into the back seat, Nick."

"We're not taking him to the cells, are we?" I was horrified at the thought of working all through the night just to look after this character.

"No," he said, "I know a nice warm shed next door to a bakery in Malton. We'll put him there for the night – somebody from Malton will find him and see to him. They've plenty of accommodation and staff. That will satisfy my conscience."

What happened next was a most unexpected and unwelcome surprise. As we stooped to lift him from his cosy bed, the fellow suddenly hurtled from the hay and savagely attacked us. He beat us with his fists, cursed us, kicked us and began a most alarming and vicious assault upon us. He fought like a wild cat, cursing vilely and using his head in an effort to break our noses and cheek bones. He was not going to be taken anywhere.

He was shouting that he wanted to be left alone, and not taken to prison or hospital. We tried to make him understand it was for his own good, but Sergeant Bairstow's efforts to console him and reassure him were unheeded and there developed one almighty tussle in that barn. But two fit policemen are more than a match for a meths drinker in the long term, and in spite of his wild lunges, kicks and butts, we managed to quieten him and take him to our car.

I visualised problems persuading him to enter the rear seat, but by now he was his previous calm self, and meekly allowed us to sit him in the back. Sergeant Bairstow was nursing a black eye and a cut lip, and I thought I'd dislodged a tooth, in addition to having a rising swelling on my shin from a well-aimed kick. But at least he was calm, and our enterprise could continue.

Thus we kidnapped him from his East Riding nest and conveyed him back across the river into the North Riding, where Sergeant Bairstow had another home in mind. We drove into the town centre and he located the bakery with its warm shed next door to the ovens. In the shed was an old arm-chair with horsehair sticking out and a hole in the cushion, but it was warm, cosy and dry. Once again, we manhandled Meths Maurice from the car and cajoled him into this new location. Fortunately, he was enjoying that happy state between consciousness and drunkenness and seemed to have forgotten all about the wild struggle of a few minutes earlier. He contentedly settled in the old arm-chair and his head flopped to one side, into the oblivion of a deep sleep.

"Doesn't he look happy?" smiled Sergeant Bairstow, wincing as his black eye bore testimony to his kidnapping.

"He's back home," I said.

"He'll be fine; he'll sleep happily there until morning and he'll go on his way."

And so we left him in his new place of abode. Sergeant Bairstow made his way back to Ashfordly, happy in the knowledge that his cells would not be polluted by this smelly fellow. I noticed he drove with the window open to rid the car of its pungent reminder of the man's presence, and his black eye would be a more permanent relic. I patrolled the section until one o'clock, but about twelve fifteen popped into the shed near the bakery before driving home. The man was still there, fast asleep in the cosy atmosphere, with his head lolling to one side in the battered old chair. But he was safe, dry, alive and no trouble to anyone.

I finished prompt at one o'clock that morning and at nine was back on duty in Ashfordly Police Station. Sergeant Bairstow came through from his house, and he sported a gorgeous black eye. I could not help laughing but he didn't seem to think it funny. He'd told his wife he'd done it as a ruffian knocked him over when rushing out of a pub, and asked me to confirm that tale, if necessary.

As I checked the Occurrence Book for the morning's messages, the telephone rang. Sergeant Bairstow answered it, and I heard him say "Sir," to someone.

"It's the inspector," he mouthed at me. "From Malton Urgent. Don't leave yet, there might be a job for us."

I waited as Sergeant Bairstow dealt with the call. There was a good many "No, sirs," and "Yes, sirs," and in the end, he replaced the receiver, smiling broadly in spite of his bruises.

"That was the inspector," he informed me. "You know that old meths man? He went into Malton Police Station this morning about six o'clock to complain about the North Riding Police. He told the inspector he'd been asleep in a cold barn full of straw, when two nice East Riding officers, one with a helmet, had removed him to a warm barn full of hay. He remembers that but then, according to him, two awful North Riding Officers kidnapped him, assaulted him and made him sleep in a rickety arm-chair near a bakery. He's allergic to yeast and now he's come out in spots. The Inspector asked if we knew anything about it – he's checked with the East Riding lads and they don't know . . ."

"You told him 'no,' sergeant?" I said.

"I said we had no knowledge of a meths drinker last night, Nick."

"And he accepted that?" I put to him.

"He has no option – either he believes a drunken old meths drinker or he believes some of his most honourable officers. The man's fine, by the way, they've taken to a place which will cure him, they hope."

"You'd better keep out of the Inspector's way for a few days, then," I suggested.

"Why?" he asked in all innocence.

"That black eye," I said. "It might take some explaining."

*   *   *

My second problem with a body occurred soon afterwards, but the story really began during the First World War.

A farm girl called Liza Stockdale lived in an isolated homestead high in Lairsdale. She was born there at the turn of the century, 1900, and lived her first sixteen uneventful years on the farm. There she assisted around the place, looking after the hens and acting as milkmaid for her father with his busy dairy herd. Being always at work, she never travelled; she had never been to York and had not even been to Malton. Twice before her sixteenth birthday, she had visited Ashfordly on Market Day to buy livestock with her father, and that was the extent of her experience beyond the ranging drystone walls of Scar End Farm.

Then she met a soldier. A tall, dark and handsome soldier of nineteen chanced this way on an exercise, and he was in charge of a mighty gun which was being towed across the moors by a small platoon of young men. They camped near Scar End Farm, Lairsdale, and bought milk and eggs from Liza. As in all good love stories, Liza fell helplessly in love with this handsome visitor and to cut a long story short, she ran away with him.

They married soon after the 1914–18 war was over and lived in North London where her husband developed a successful business from a small draper's shop. They produced four lovely children who were a credit to the happy pair and in turn they produced a clutch of grandchildren who were also a credit to the family.

Back in the remoteness of the North Yorkshire Moors, Liza's relations continued to work on the hills, farming sheep and cattle and growing acres of corn for the cereal industry. Time went by, and the farming Stockdales prospered just as Liza had prospered in London, but there was one small blot on the happy horizon.

Liza had never returned home. Having run away, she felt she had incurred the wrath of her mother and father, and the scorn of her other strait-laced relations, consequently she never ventured back to the family homestead. Furthermore, she deliberately kept her address secret, and avoided all contact with her past.

Throughout her long and happy life, however, she'd nursed a secret desire to be invited to the moorland home of her family; her parents had died long ago but she had not attended their funeral at Lairsdale's isolated Methodist chapel. She had not been to the weddings of her brothers and sisters, nor to the christenings of their children. She had missed all this, and had often wondered about the Lairsdale branch of her family. Sometimes, she wished she had the guts to make contact.

Liza's husband, however, was not the insensitive man the family considered him to be. At the time of the elopement during the First World War, he'd been an aggressive, cocksure young man and it was his cavalier attitude and his worldly manner that had captivated the young Liza. On marrying him and settling down to a hard-working life, she realised she truly loved him and he truly loved her. Their love strengthened with the passing years, and Herbert often tried to persuade her to return to the farm, if only for a visit. He said she should write and make contact, but she never did.

Something intangible restrained her. Some unknown hand or force denied Liza the thrill of returning to her homestead, and she contented herself with life in London, the business and her family. Hers was a London family, not given to visiting remote farms in the north, consequently Liza's life bore no resemblance to her childhood surroundings and upbringing, and she had distanced herself from her roots.

Herbert never forgot that she missed Scar End Farm; he knew of her love for the area and made many attempts to persuade her to make the move. But she stubbornly and steadfastly refused. She lied when she said she had no wish to return; because she'd had to run away to marry him, her father had never owned her and the family had never made contact. She'd felt she was no part of that life in the moors.

Herbert's patience was infinite. He vowed that one day he would surprise her and take her home. She would not know where she was going until she arrived; he'd book a holiday in a nice hotel at Scarborough or York, and would hire a taxi to take her into the hills of Lairsdale and to the farm which he'd discovered was still in the family.

But somehow, that trip never materialised. Business was too

demanding, the family too busy or time too short. Gradually, Herbert's intentions faded, if only a little, and that long journey from London to the heart of the North Yorkshire moors never took place. It was always something he'd do when he had the time.

And he never did have the time.

Finally, Liza died of a heart attack. One awful June day, a Mrs Liza Frankland collapsed and died in Regent Street, London. The post-mortem revealed she had suffered a massive coronary attack, and no one could have saved her.

Her caring husband, Herbert Frankland, a retired draper, loved her more in death, and as he wept alone that night he made a resolution that Liza would at last return to her native moorland dale.

He telephoned Pastor Smith at the Manse to ask whether she could be buried in his tiny churchyard at Lairsdale, and specified that it had been his wish to have Liza cremated. The burial, if permitted, would involve a small urn of Liza's ashes and Herbert alone would accompany them. All he asked was a simple chapel service to place Liza in her resting place, and he did not tell Pastor Smith of her family links with his district, save to say it was her wish to be buried there. He'd asked his own family not to attend; they'd paid their respects at the crematorium and this was to be his personal pilgrimage. He wanted to repay the wrong he'd done all those years ago.

Pastor Smith agreed without question and so the small interment was arranged for a day in late June.

Being a man without a car, Herbert Frankland left King's Cross Station in London in the early hours of that Saturday, carrying a suitcase and contents. In the suitcase were his overnight things and a dark suit for the funeral. Also in the case was a pleasant silver casket containing the ashes of Liza, his beloved wife. It bore her maiden name, Liza Stockdale, and was carefully wrapped in tissue paper, and tucked among his clothes.

The train left King's Cross on time and Herbert settled down to his long trip north, eagerly awaiting his arrival at York. A taxi was to take him across the hills into Lairsdale, where, at two

o'clock precisely, Pastor Smith would conduct the burial ceremony. Liza would be home at last, resting eternally among her
family and the moors.

At York, Herbert Frankland, sad and thoughtful due to the
day's sorrowful occurrence, took his case from the rack, left the
train and caught a taxi out of York.

At quarter past twelve, he was knocking on my door at
Aidensfield Police House.

I answered the knock to find a lightly built man there, a man
I'd never seen before. He was smartly dressed in a light grey suit
and trilby, with a white shirt and a black tie, and would be in his
sixties. He clutched a rather battered brown leather suitcase,
and I noticed a taxi waiting outside my house.

"Yes?" I was enjoying a day off and was clad in old clothes,
because I was in the middle of decorating a bedroom. I looked
more like a painter and decorator than a policeman.

"Oh, er, is the policeman in?" he asked, smiling meekly.

"I'm the policeman," I wiped my hands on my paint-stained
trousers. "P.C. Rhea."

"Oh, well, er, I'm sorry to bother you," he began, "but it is
important."

"You'd better come in," I invited him to enter my office.
"Will the taxi wait?"

"Yes, I've asked him to," and he entered the small office,
removing his hat as he did so.

"Now, sir," I made a formal greeting. "How can I help
you?"

He placed his battered suitcase on my desk and opened it.
Inside was a collection of assorted clothes and personal belongings, and I waited for some enlightenment.

"Officer," he said. "I left London this morning, from King's
Cross, and I put my suitcase on the rack. It contained my
overnight things, and a dark suit."

I looked at the contents of this case. This belonged to a
woman, for there were feminine underclothes, perfumes, slippers, blouses and so forth.

"So this isn't yours?" I guessed.

He shook his head and for the first time, I saw tears in his
eyes.

"Would you like a cup of tea?" I offered by way of some consolation.

He nodded and I made him sit on my office chair. The poor man was obviously distressed, and at this stage I had no idea of the real reason.

I called to Mary and in spite of preparing lunch and coping with four tiny offspring, she produced two steaming cups. I closed the door and watched him sip the hot tea as he composed himself.

"I must have picked up the wrong case," he said despondently. "Mine is exactly like this one, officer, and when I got off at York, I must have collected this. It's got stickers on, you see, and mine was plain, so I should have noticed, but I didn't spot them until I was almost here, in the taxi."

"So yours is still on the train?" I ventured.

He nodded, and I noticed the returning moisture in his pale grey eyes.

"Look, Mister . . ."

"Frankland," he said. "Herbert Frankland."

"Look, Mr Frankland, there's no need to get upset. I'm sure we can trace your case very soon. I'll ring the British Transport Commission Police at York and ask them to search the train at its next stop. Let's see . . ."

I made a rapid calculation, bearing in mind the time he dismounted at York and the time at present. I reckoned his train would have passed through Thirsk, Northallerton, Darlington and even Durham. With a bit of fast work, they might catch it at Newcastle, before it left for Edinburgh. During the time it remained at Newcastle, the railway police could search for Mr Frankland's missing case.

I explained to him my plan and he seemed relieved.

"Er," he said after I had explained my intended action, "There is one problem, Mr Rhea."

"Yes?"

"In my case," he faltered in his short speech, "there is a small silver casket."

"Yes?" I acknowledged, not having any idea of its contents.

"It, er, contains ashes, officer. The ashes of my dear wife, Liza . . . " and he could contain himself no longer. He burst into a flood of tears and I had no idea how to cope. I stood up and patted him on the shoulder, saying he shouldn't get upset and we'd surely trace the missing suitcase. After a short time, he dried his tears and apologised for his lapse, making a brave attempt to control himself.

I sympathised with him. "I know how you feel . . ."

I asked if he could give some indication of the location of the coach in which he travelled. Was it near the front? The middle? The rear? Before or after the restaurant car?

Gradually, I produced some idea of his whereabouts on that fateful train, and having satisfied myself on the time of his departure from King's Cross, I rang the Railway Police in York. They were marvellous; their well-tested routine would be put immediately into action, and when the train halted at its next stop, they would have it searched for the missing case. I described it and its contents, but felt there was no need to rub in the fact that it contained the ashes of Liza Frankland, *née* Stockdale. I then described the case now languishing in my office with its load of feminine apparel. Somewhere, a lady would find she had the wrong case, and I wondered if she would leave the train with Herbert's case and not realise the error until she arrived home. This could cause immense problems but I did not voice this concern to Mr Frankland.

"The casket," I said once I was sure the Railway Police were in action. "Is it recognisable for what it is?"

"It's a nice casket," he said, shaping it in the air with his hands. "The lid is firmly secured and on the side there is a panel with her name. It just says Liza Stockdale. I used her maiden name, because she's home, you see . . . or she was coming home . . ."

He told me all about his wife's links with this area, and I listened to his fascinating story.

"Is the casket a particular model? I mean, is it recognisable to someone like me?" I asked at length.

He nodded. He explained it was a standard make and gave the name of it; it was obtainable from most undertakers for cremations, and the name of the deceased engraved as part of the service. Mr Frankland explained her name was in capital letters, and it gave the date of her death, the sixth of June. His story helped to compose him and I felt it did him good to tell me all about his romance and marriage.

"Well," I said eventually. "The Transport Commission Police will search the train when it gets to Newcastle or Edinburgh. Are you staying in the area?"

"I'm at the Ashfordly Hotel, in Ashfordly," he said. "I've booked in for tonight. But you see, I had arranged for a funeral at Lairsdale at two o'clock today . . ."

"I'll ring Pastor Smith," I said. "If your suitcase turns up, they'll see that it is sent back to York and it could be back with you today; you might only have to delay matters a short while. Look, Mr Frankland, you go to your hotel now, and have lunch. Stay there until I ring you – I'll let you know the minute I hear something."

"And Pastor Smith?"

"I know him personally," I soothed him. "I'll explain the problem and I know he won't mind. He'll be only too pleased to accommodate you at a time convenient to you both."

I rang Pastor Smith and explained the situation upon which he readily agreed to wait. At this, the unhappy fellow seemed a little more hopeful and he left my office to resume his journey. I kept the case of women's clothing. I heard the taxi rumble away towards Ashfordly, and broke for lunch.

I did not know whether to laugh or cry over his dilemma. For the poor old man, it must be harrowing in the extreme, but the thought of someone's wife being lost in this way, was hilarious when viewed dispassionately. I hoped the British Transport Commission Police would locate the lost property before the lady passenger walked away with it.

I enjoyed my lunch, over which I explained to Mary the delicacy of this problem. Understandably, she sympathised with the old fellow and after lunch I enjoyed some coffee before resuming my decorating. Two o'clock came and went with no word from the Transport Commission Police.

At quarter to four, P.C. Hall from the Transport Commission Police called my office.

"Hall here, BTC Police," he said. "We've searched the entire train, but that case isn't there. It stopped at Thirsk, Northallerton, Darlington, Durham and Newcastle before we searched it, so the case must have been removed by the owner of the one you've got. She's bound to realise the mistake sooner or later and call us."

"I'd appreciate a call, it's rather urgent," I said.

"It's just a lost suitcase, isn't it?" he retorted, having dealt with thousands like this.

"No, it's more than that." I decided to explain and he listened carefully.

"The poor old codger!" he cried. "Oh, bloody hell! Look, I'll have our lads give the train another going over in Edinburgh, but I'm not too hopeful. I'll ask our Lost and Found Property people to check their records for today as well. The poor old devil . . ."

I rang Pastor Smith to explain the situation upon which he murmured his condolences, and then I rang the hotel to speak to Mr Frankland. I told him the result to date, but stressed the BTC Police were making further searches. He appeared resigned to the fact that his beloved Liza was lost for ever, but said he'd stay at the hotel for two or three days if necessary.

At five o'clock, I rang Ashfordly Police Station to acquaint Sergeant Bairstow with the story, in case the BTC Police rang him tonight while Mary and I were at the pictures. He listened with interest and launched into a bout of laughter, telling me the old story of the woman whose husband had been cremated and who retained his ashes in the house. She had them put into an egg-timer, and her logic was that he'd never worked in his life, so he was going to damned well work now! Another had placed the casket of her father's ashes on the mantelshelf and someone thought it was pepper, while another accidentally sold her husband's ashes during the sale of the house contents after his death. His fate was never known. Sergeant Bairstow had a fund of stories about ashes of deceased folks, and I had unwittingly provided him with another. I failed to view it in his light-hearted manner.

Obligingly, he took details of the affair, with names and all the necessary facts, and said he'd cope if I was away from the house. I explained the need for Pastor Smith to know fairly quickly, and for Herbert Frankland to be told at the Ashfordly Hotel.

I went out to the pictures with Mary that night and returned home about eleven o'clock. The babysitter said there were no messages, so I turned in, tired but content.

Sunday was another rest day for me, and I intended to complete the painting and decorating which had been interrupted yesterday. Before doing so, I rang Ashfordly office, but got no reply. I wondered if Liza's ashes had been found, but felt I would have known. I knew the BTC Police at York would have called me, and I felt a tinge of genuine sorrow for poor Mr Frankland. He'd be sitting alone in the hotel, just waiting and able to do nothing.

At half past ten, I was in the middle of slapping some wallpaper on the bedroom wall, when there was a loud knocking on my front door. I cursed, but was obliged to answer. Mary had gone to Mass with the two elder children, for I'd attended early in order to get my decorating done. Grudgingly, I answered the door.

A large, unkempt farmer in his early forties stood there in corduroy trousers and a dark sweater, while a Landrover waited outside. I didn't know him.

"Morning. Is thoo t'bobby?" he looked me up and down, and I laughed an answer. I noticed he had a brown suitcase in his hand.

"Yes," I said. "I'm decorating. I'm P.C. Rhea."

"Oh, well, this is important," and he held up the case. Its significance did not register at that moment. "Can Ah come in?"

"Aye," I said, stepping back and he followed me into the office.

"This is a funny sooart of a gahin on," he began in the broad dialect of the moors. "Yon case isn't our lass's," he said brusquely, "but she got it off t'London train yesterday, by accident she reckons."

"The London train?" now I was taking an interest. My heart missed a beat.

"Aye, she's at Univosity doon there and came up yisterday for a break. She's gitten a brown case just like this 'un, and somebody's switched 'em. Ah reckon somebody's got hers and they must know by now, so Ah thowt Ah'd tell you fellers.

Well, there's neeabody in at Ashfordly, so Ah thowt Ah'd better come here, cos thoo's t'nearest bobby."

"Did you look inside this case?" I asked.

"She did, and Ah did a quick peep. Nut a nosey peep, thoo knoaws, but eneeagh ti see it's a feller's suit and bits and bobs. There's summat wrapped in tissue paper but Ah didn't oppen it up. That's nut my business."

I lifted the other case from the floor and placed it on my desk, flipping open the lid. I saw the amazement on his face.

"Is this your daughter's stuff?" I asked.

"Noo that's a capper," he said. "Noo that's a real capper. Aye, Ah'd say it was her stuff, but she's in t'Landrover. Ah'll shout her."

A tall, pretty teenager ran into my office, smiling at her father as he pointed to the case on my desk. "Is yon case thine, lass?"

She blushed at the lingerie and clothing which was on display and said, "Yes, it is. Good heavens . . . how . . . ?"

I decided not to mention the contents of the article wrapped in tissue paper, but did tell them about the poor gentleman who'd picked up the wrong case when he got off at York. The girl told me she'd got off the train at Thirsk, where her father had met her in the Landrover, and she'd not realised the mistake until late last night. She'd put her case on the top of her wardrobe at home, her toiletries being carried in a shoulder bag, and had gone to get the case this morning to do her washing. Then she'd found the man's stuff inside, and had not investigated further. This was the typical action of an honest dales person – they did not snoop into things that weren't their business.

I was highly relieved. I pushed aside the tissue covers of the casket and saw the silver beneath, but did not enlighten this couple of its significance. Now there were the usual formalities to complete. The girl would have to sign for her case in my found property register, and I would have to record her as the finder of the second case. Eventually, Mr Frankland would sign for his own goods.

"Right," I said. "You are the owner of the case of lady's clothes?"

The girl nodded.

"I have to make an official record of your receipt of this case," I explained. "What's your name?"

"Stockdale," she said. "Liza Stockdale."

I had the name half-written in my book before I realised its significance.

I felt faint.

"Liza Stockdale? From Crag End Farm, Lairsdale?" I spoke faintly.

"Summat up?" asked her father.

"I, er," I didn't know how to broach this one. "Why is she called Liza?" I heard myself ask.

"Oh, it's after an aunt of mine," he said. "Ah never knew her, but she cleared off with a soldier way back in t'First World War, and never came back. My dad – that was her brother – thought the world of her and she never wrote or anything. He allus talked about her, my dad did. So Ah called my first lass after her . . . just to keep t'name going, thoo sees, for my dad."

"So the family wanted her to come back?"

"Aye, of course. Yon soldier was a nice chap, by all accounts, did the right thing by her, he did. We lost touch – she was t'only member of oor family to do a thing like that. Headstrong lass, they said, but all right, not a disgrace to us."

"Is your father still alive?" I asked gently, my nervousness causing my voice to waver.

"Is thoo all right, Mr Rhea?" he asked me. "Thoo's gone all pale and shakey. Aye, my dad's alive. He's turned seventy-five now, but he's as fit as a fiddle."

"Look," I said. "You'd better sit down, both of you," and I pulled up chairs for them.

"Nay, lad, thoo'd better sit doon!" he laughed, but he took the seat.

"I don't know how to tell you this . . ."

"Summat wrang?"

I did not know how to break this news to them. I could tell them about the old man waiting so patiently in Ashfordly, or I could show them the casket bearing this girl's name. Would the shock be too much for them, or should I tell Mr Frankland first? These were sturdy, practical folk, not given to whims and fainting sessions, so I decided to tell them the story.

"Mr Stockdale and Liza," I said. "Yesterday, a man called at this house with your suitcase. He'd come up from London and had got off at York, one stop before you, Liza. He mistakenly took your suitcase, and realised when he was on his way to Ashfordly by taxi. He called here and left it with me, and I tried to trace that other case, his case, which he'd left on the train. The railway police are still looking for it."

She smiled, "And I got off at Thirsk, taking it with me because it was the only one left and because it was just like my own . . ."

"Yes," I said. "Now, this is the sad bit. That old man was on his way to a funeral. His wife's funeral. She died last week in London, and he was bringing her ashes to be buried near her home."

"Oh!" she said. "And I had them in that case?"

I chewed my lips. She did not show horror, just sorrow for him. Her father regarded me steadily, and I knew I must now lift the casket from the case.

"Yes," I said. "This is the casket," and I lifted the tissue-wrapped casket from its resting place among the smart clothes of Mr Frankland. I removed the wrappings and revealed the name. I turned it towards them so they could read it.

"Liza Stockdale!" the girl gasped. "My name?"

Her father's gaze never left me. "Thoo means this is my Aunt Liza's ashes?"

I nodded.

"By . . ." he said. "By . . . then she came home after all? Right back to Scar End! And by t'hand of her namesake . . . noo that caps owt!"

I handed the casket over and his big, clumsy hands lovingly cradled it. "Thoo said there was gahin ti be a funeral?"

"It should have been yesterday, Mr Stockdale, and Pastor Smith was going to conduct it. He wouldn't realise the Mr Frankland who arranged it was a relation of yours."

"And that poor awd chap thowt we didn't care?"

"Yes."

"Then thoo and me and oor Liza'll have to put him right, Mr Rhea. Come on, let's find him."

"But I'm in my mess . . ."

"That dissn't matter a damn, lad. Fetch yon cases – Liza, sign up, and let's be off."

We found Mr Frankland sitting in the lounge of the Ashfordly Hotel, reading the Sunday papers. He looked pale and sickly, but smiled when he saw me. His smile turned to clear relief as he saw the young girl carrying two identical suitcases towards him. He stood up to welcome the curious party consisting of a policeman in decorating gear, a farmer and a pretty girl.

"You were on the train!" he smiled at Liza. "I'm so sorry, it was all my fault. Is that my case, officer?" The relief was evident in his voice.

"Yes," I said. "It's all there, intact, thanks to this young lady."

Liza handed the case over to him.

"It's so kind of you," he said. "It did cause me a lot of distress."

Liza was weeping openly now. She put her own case on the floor and said, "Dad, tell him please . . ."

The poor old man looked horrified. I wondered if he thought she'd thrown away the ashes, or destroyed them.

"Nay, Ah can't. Ah'm all overcome," and I saw tears of happiness and emotion in the big farmer's eyes.

Mr Frankland looked at each of us for an explanation and I knew I had to speak.

"Mr Frankland," I said. "This girl's name is Liza Stockdale and she lives at Crag End Farm, Lairsdale."

There was a long, long pause and suddenly, Mr Frankland flung his arms about the girl, crying "Liza, Liza . . ."

On the day following, Monday, there was a large hurriedly arranged family funeral at the tiny chapel of Lairsdale, and Mr Frankland stayed at Crag End Farm for a long, long time.

*   *   *

MURDER AT PLUM'S

A Victorian Whodunnit

Amy Myers

Plum's in St James's Square in London, with its worn leather armchairs and cocoon of inviting warmth providing a refuge from the world, is the very acme of respectability. In short, everything an English gentleman's club should be. With one exception: excellent cuisine provided by master chef Auguste Didier. For food is the very reason the club first came into being – its founder believing that if men can enjoy food together they can get on and rule the world together. But the late Captain Plum was an incurable optimist.

The trouble really starts the day women are allowed, for the first time, within the hallowed portals to watch the time-honoured ceremony of Plum's Passing. A series of bizarre incidents has already plagued the club – a rat left upon a dining table, newspapers wantonly mutilated, death threats made to a member, even obscene letters sent to the doorman. And Auguste, having always maintained that cooking and sleuthing go naturally hand in hand, is persuaded by his friend and rival Emma Pryde to delve once more into the realms of mystery. But murder at Plum's? Impossible!

Abruptly, inevitably, however, Auguste's investigations with his friend Inspector Egbert Rose of Scotland Yard turn into a hunt for a demonically clever and ruthless killer . . .

'Reading like a cross between Hercule Poirot and Mrs Beeton, *Murder at Plum's* provides a third outing for one of fiction's most unusual detectives . . . This feast of entertainment is packed with splendid late-Victorian detail' *Evening Standard*

MAUREEN O'BRIEN
CLOSE-UP ON DEATH

A JOHN BRIGHT WHODUNNIT

A BOOK AT BEDTIME SELECTION

CLOSE-UP ON DEATH

Everybody loved Liza. Talented, pretty, popular, she had just landed a marvellous part in a new television series and her career was going from strength to strength. Then the bright flame of her life is cruelly extinguished and her hopes for a great future end with the shocking discovery of her corpse in an empty North London house.

There aren't any obvious suspects: Liza had no enemies. But Detective Inspector John Bright concentrates his investigations on her three closest associates — Liza's mother; her lover, Paul, and her best friend, Millie. Paul and Millie are also actors and find — ironically — that Liza's tragic death brings unexpected benefits to their careers. But it looks to John Bright as though everyone is performing a role and all the principal players find it hard to separate fact from fiction as suspicion mounts . . .

'More than just a crime novel — the love interest is beautifully handled, too, making this a gripping, almost hypnotic read' *Woman's World*

'A first-rate whodunnit — gripping, tantilising and with plenty of tension' *Best Magazine*

'Maureen O'Brien . . . is a dab hand at dialogue and also at thespian jealousies. A smashing debut . . .' *Evening Standard*

FICTION/CRIME   0 7472 3171 0

More Engrossing Fiction from Headline:

CHRISTINE THOMAS

HANNAH

**The poignant new saga from the
author of BRIDIE and APRIL**

Hannah Holmes has a difficult childhood to overcome. Still
bearing the scars of her separation from her mother during the
war, and of her father's inexplicable coldness to her, she is
further emotionally damaged by her parents' disintegrating
marriage and eventual traumatic divorce.

Spending her formative years in care, shunted from foster
home to Children's Home, she finds it difficult to establish a
loving relationship with anyone, and makes the mistake of
believing that she has found love with men who show her
sexual affection.

When the result of her misplaced trust becomes apparent, she
flees to Brighton and meets Joe, a young postgraduate student
who offers her room in his flat – and a shoulder to lean on.
Friendship quickly deepens into love as the two spend an
idyllic seaside summer together. It is the calm before the storm.
When Joe announces his intention to go to America to study,
Hannah sees that she is to be abandoned yet again and gives
way to despair.

But although it is deeply buried, the spirit of her indomitable
grandmother, Bridie, lives on in Hannah, and she triumphs
over adversity to achieve independence and emotional
fulfilment at last.

HANNAH concludes the East End saga of the O'Neill family,
movingly exploring the complex emotional legacies handed
down from parent to child through three generations. It starts
with BRIDIE, set in the early years of the twentieth century,
and moves on to the hardship of the Second World War with
APRIL, both available from Headline.

FICTION/GENERAL   0 7472 3641 0

More Crime Fiction from Headline:

AN ECCLESIASTICAL WHODUNNIT

CLERICAL ERRORS

D. M. GREENWOOD

In the shadow of honey-coloured Medewich Cathedral, amidst the perfect lawns of the Cathedral Close, the diocesan office of St Manicus should have been a peaceful if not an especially exciting place for nineteen-year-old Julia Smith to start her first job. Yet she has been in its precincts for less than an hour when she stumbles on a horror of Biblical proportions - a severed head in the Cathedral font.

And she has worked for the suave Canon Wheeler for less than a day when she realises that the Dean and Chapter is as riven by rivalry, ambition and petty jealousy as the court of any Renaissance prelate. In this jungle of intrigue a young deaconess, Theodora Braithwaite, stands out as a lone pillar of common sense. Taciturn but kindly, she takes Julia under her wing, and with the assistance of Ian Caretaker - a young man who hates Canon Wheeler as much as he loves the Church - they attempt to unravel the truth behind the death of a well-meaning man, the Reverend Paul Gray, late incumbent of Markham cum Cumbermound.

FICTION/CRIME   0 7472 3582 1

A selection of bestsellers from Headline

MONSIEUR PAMPLEMOUSSE ON LOCATION	Michael Bond	£4.50 ☐
THE CAT WHO WENT INTO THE CLOSET	Lilian Jackson Braun	£4.50 ☐
MURDER WEARS A COWL	P C Doherty	£4.50 ☐
CURTAINS FOR THE CARDINAL	Elizabeth Eyre	£4.99 ☐
ROUGH RIDE	John Francome	£4.99 ☐
MURDER AMONG US	Ann Granger	£4.99 ☐
DEADLY ERRAND	Christine Green	£4.99 ☐
IDOL BONES	D M Greenwood	£4.50 ☐
THE END OF THE PIER	Martha Grimes	£4.50 ☐
COPY KAT	Karen Kijewski	£4.99 ☐
CLOSE UP ON DEATH	Maureen O'Brien	£5.99 ☐
THE LATE LADY	Staynes & Storey	£4.50 ☐
SWEET DEATH COME SOFTLY	Barbara Whitehead	£4.99 ☐

All Headline books are available at your local bookshop or newsagent, or can be ordered direct from the publisher. Just tick the titles you want and fill in the form below. Prices and availability subject to change without notice.

Headline Book Publishing PLC, Cash Sales Department, Bookpoint, 39 Milton Park, Abingdon, OXON, OX14 4TD, UK. If you have a credit card you may order by telephone – 0235 831700.

Please enclose a cheque or postal order made payable to Bookpoint Ltd to the value of the cover price and allow the following for postage and packing:
UK & BFPO: £1.00 for the first book, 50p for the second book and 30p for each additional book ordered up to a maximum charge of £3.00.
OVERSEAS & EIRE: £2.00 for the first book, £1.00 for the second book and 50p for each additional book.

Name ....

Address ....

....

....

If you would prefer to pay by credit card, please complete:
Please debit my Visa/Access/Diner's Card/American Express (delete as applicable) card no:

Signature .... Expiry Date ....